(dating the letters, identifying persons mentioned, and discussing historical problems arising out of the letters) contain material of relevance for historians in several different fields. The Appendices deal at greater length with particular problems arising from the life of Peter the Venerable (including his family, health, travels, and writings against the Saracens and heretics), with the organization of Cluny and its role in the ecclesiastical world of the twelfth century, and with individual figures such as Bishop Elias of Orléans, Hugh of Crécy, Peter of Poitiers, and St. Bernard's secretary Nicholas of Montiéramey. The detailed Indices enable the student to find easily material pertaining to his special interest.

Giles Constable is Henry Charles Lea Professor of Medieval History at Harvard University. He is co-editor of *Petrus Venerabilis, 1156–1956: Studies and Texts Commemorating the Eighth Centenary of His Death* (1956), editor of David Knowles, *The Historian and Character* (1963), and author of *Monastic Tithes from Their Origins to the Twelfth Century* (1964) as well as of numerous articles.

Harvard Historical Studies / LXXVIII

PUBLISHED UNDER THE DIRECTION OF THE DEPARTMENT OF HISTORY
FROM THE INCOME OF THE HENRY WARREN TORREY FUND

THE LETTERS

OF PETER

THE VENERABLE

EDITED, WITH AN INTRODUCTION AND NOTES, BY

GILES CONSTABLE

VOLUME II

HARVARD UNIVERSITY PRESS

CAMBRIDGE, MASSACHUSETTS

1967

© Copyright 1967 by the President and Fellows of Harvard College / All rights reserved / Distributed in Great Britain by Oxford University Press, London / Publication of this work has been aided by a grant from the American Council of Learned Societies / Library of Congress Catalog Card Number 67-10086 / Made and printed in Great Britain by William Clowes and Sons, Limited, London and Beccles

Contents

VOLUME I

TEXT OF THE LETTER COLLECTION   1

VOLUME II

INTRODUCTION

I / Medieval Letters and the Letter Collection of
Peter the Venerable   1

    1. MEDIEVAL LETTER COLLECTIONS, 1. 2. THE COLLECTION OF PETER THE VENERABLE, 12. 3. WRITING, SEALING, AND SENDING, 17. 4. STYLE, 29.

II / The Text Tradition   45

    1. PRINTED EDITIONS, 45. 2. MANUSCRIPT COLLECTIONS, 48. 3. MANUSCRIPTS OF INDIVIDUAL LETTERS, 63. 4. TEXT AND ARRANGEMENT OF THE LETTERS, 74.

III / The Present Edition   81

    1. CONTENTS, 81. 2. ORDER, 82. 3. TEXT, 83. 4. ORTHOGRAPHY, 84. 5. CAPITALIZATION AND PUNCTUATION, 91. 6. TEXTUAL APPARATUS, 92.

NOTES TO THE LETTERS   93

APPENDICES

    A. The Family of Peter the Venerable   233
    B. The Health of Peter the Venerable   247
    C. Peter the Venerable, the Lateran Council of 1139, and the Case between King Stephen and the Empress Mathilda   252

D.	Chronology and Itinerary of Peter the Venerable	257
E.	The Date and Character of Letter 28	270
F.	Letter 111 and Peter's Works against the Saracens	275
G.	The Date of the *Contra Petrobrusianos*	285
H.	The Affair of the Abbeville Prebends	289
I.	Cluniac Houses in the East	291
J.	Cluniac Cardinals during the Abbacy of Peter the Venerable, with special attention to the early life of Imar of Tusculum	293
K.	The Priors of La Charité-sur-Loire, 1122–1156	296
L.	The Priors of Sauxillanges, 1049–1156	299
M.	Dr. Bartholomew	302
N.	Bishop Elias of Orléans (1137–1145/6)	304
O.	Hugh of Crécy	311
P.	Nicholas of Montiéramey and Peter the Venerable	316
Q.	Peter of Poitiers	331
R.	Officials and Functionaries at Cluny during the Abbacy of Peter the Venerable	344

BIBLIOGRAPHY OF ABBREVIATED TITLES 349

CONCORDANCE 363

INDICES

    I. Manuscripts 369

    II. Citations 371

        1. BIBLICAL, ANCIENT, AND MEDIEVAL TEXTS, 371. 2. MODERN AUTHORS, 383

    III. General Index 392

MAP 430–431

INTRODUCTION

SIGLA MANUSCRIPTORUM ET EDITIONUM

A	Douai, Bibliothèque municipale, 381
A index	Index of Douai 381, folios 11^v–12^r
Bc	*Bibliotheca Cluniacensis* (Paris, 1614)
Bern.	*Sancti Bernardi . . . opera omnia* (Paris, 1839)
C	*Petri Venerabilis . . . opera* (Paris, 1522)
Cl	Troyes, Bibliothèque municipale, 2261
O	Clm 27129 (for Letter 150)
S	Le Puy, Cathédrale (unnumbered)
T	Turin, Biblioteca nazionale, E-V-37 (for Letter 38)
Vulg.	Vulgate (Clementine Edition)

For descriptions of these manuscripts see pp. 48–74, below. For the sigla of the manuscripts of Letters 20 and 28, see pp. 63 and 70, below.

I / *Medieval Letters and the Letter Collection of Peter the Venerable*

1. MEDIEVAL LETTER COLLECTIONS

The great age of medieval letter writing was in the eleventh and twelfth centuries. At no other time in the Middle Ages, or between antiquity and the nineteenth century, was the "gentlest art" more assiduously cultivated or were letters more carefully written and collected.[1] Two of the five volumes concerned with the period from 1060 to 1180 in the *Recueil des historiens des Gaules et de la France* are filled with letters, and these are but a fraction of the total number written at this time. Almost every well-known figure of the age left at least a few letters. The fashion for writing letters was such that among the reformed monks and canons it was condemned as a vice.[2]

Historians have long recognized the historical and literary importance of these letters. "It will be admitted without difficulty, I think,"

---

[1] "One of the striking features that distinguish the intellectual life of the eleventh and twelfth centuries from those immediately preceding and following, is its wealth of large collections of letters": Raymond Klibansky, "Peter Abailard and Bernard of Clairvaux: A Letter by Abailard," *Mediaeval and Renaissance Studies*, V (1961) 1; cf. Langlois, "Formulaires," I, 4, n. 2: "Les grands épistoliers du moyen âge sont du XIIe siècle."

[2] See the preface to Bernard of Clairvaux, *De praecepto et dispensatione* (ed. Leclercq, III, 253). The receipt of letters by monks was forbidden in the so-called Third Rule of St. Augustine, which was drawn up in western France in the late eleventh or early twelfth century: J. C. Dickinson, *The Origins of the Austin Canons and Their Introduction into England* (London, 1950) p. 277. Cf. the commentary on this passage by Robert of Bridlington, writing about 1150, in *The Bridlington Dialogue* (London, 1960) p. 145: "If you could fully know, as you do know in part, what great evils there are, and what the evils are, that have been brought about for religious churches and monasteries, or that actually occur, through secret letters being mutually given and received, you would definitely be of [the] opinion that it was not for nothing that blessed Augustine . . . so earnestly forbade his brethren to receive secret letters either from one of their own number, or from someone outside"; *The Customary of the Benedictine Abbey of Eynsham in Oxfordshire*, ed. Antonia Gransden (Corpus consuetudinum monasticarum, 2; Siegburg, 1963) p. 117; and *The Ancren Riwle*, ed. James Morton (Camden Society, 57; London, 1853) p. 423.

wrote Langlois at the beginning of his series of articles on epistolary formularies, "that the most valuable documents for the history of the Middle Ages are letters, missive letters, both official and private correspondences."[3] Not all scholars, perhaps, will admit this extreme statement, and for political and institutional historians in particular medieval letters are frequently disappointing. "The amount of sentiment, and especially of religious generalities," Stubbs remarked in one of his lectures, "seems altogether out of proportion to the amount of news."[4] For historians of ideas, however, the sentiments and religious generalities in medieval letters may be of the highest interest, and historians of literature are concerned with the form and style rather than the content of the letters. For in spite of their lack of spontaneity and their studied, not to say artificial, character, many medieval letters are excellent pieces of writing; and some of the letter collections of the Middle Ages rank among its greatest literary monuments.

The internal composition and style of formal and official letters were increasingly controlled in the later Middle Ages by the rules of *dictamen* and the *cursus*, which were laid down in epistolary handbooks and formularies, but the average writer of letters in the eleventh and twelfth centuries enjoyed considerable liberty in both content and form. "The letter to a friend," according to Cheney, "was the form commonly chosen for a light essay, a sermon, a factual account of a battle, or a philosophical treatise, or a display of literary fireworks about nothing in particular."[5] The classical distinction between the public epistle and the private letter, although embodied to some extent in the epistles of the New Testament,[6] was more or less disregarded in the Middle Ages, when the sheer physical difficulties of preparation and transmission imposed on all letters a more permanent and public character than they had either in antiquity or in more

[3] Langlois, "Formulaires," I, 1. William Stubbs, in his *Seventeen Lectures on the Study of Medieval and Modern History* (Oxford, 1887) pp. 147–148, said that "the mass of twelfth century letters is so large that . . . they furnish a large contribution to the materials for national, literary, and social history . . . These collections contain news from every part of Christendom; some of them, although only a few, are really news letters, containing all that the writers could pick up, like the news letters of later times. All, however, contain evidence by which the literary culture, as well as the political interest felt at the time, may be tested." Léopold Delisle in 1877 wrote that "dans le vaste domaine encore peu exploré des recueils épistolaires, il reste de véritables découvertes à faire pour l'histoire et la littérature du XIIIe et du XIVe siècle": cited in Giry, *Manuel*, p. 491. Cf. also Maitland, *Dark Ages*, pp. 398–399.

[4] Stubbs, *Seventeen Lectures*, p. 146. He went on to emphasize that the consciously literary character of medieval letters was a factor in their lack of serious news.

[5] C. R. Cheney, "Gervase, Abbot of Prémontré: A Medieval Letter-Writer," *Bulletin of the John Rylands Library*, XXXIII (1950–51) 28.

[6] Cf. Henri Leclercq, in *DACL*, VIII.2, 2690, and Alfred Wikenhauser, *New Testament Introduction*, trans. Joseph Cunningham (New York, 1958) p. 350.

modern times.⁷ *Litterae* was almost a synonym for *epistola*, and *epistola* was equated with *libellus*.⁸ The only distinguishing mark of many medieval letters is the opening salutation: "To his faithful friend A., the humble author B., greeting." In theory, letters were also supposed to be short. Lanfranc gave "epistolary brevity" as his reason for not citing more biblical passages in his *Liber de corpore et sanguine domini*, and Idungus of St. Emmeram (Regensburg) admitted at the end of his *Super quatuor quaestionibus* that he had perhaps written more "than Your Prudence and epistolary brevity requires."⁹ By modern standards, both of these letters are substantial treatises, and very few authors allowed themselves to be seriously hampered by this theoretical restriction on length.¹⁰ A medieval letter might be a small book, a sermon, or a poem.¹¹ The consequent variety of form and content, as

---

⁷ Jean Leclercq, in *Analecta mon.*, II, 145–147. On "epistolary preaching," see *idem*, "Recherches sur d'anciens sermons monastiques," *Revue Mabillon*, XXXVI (1946) 11–12.

⁸ Peter the Venerable, for instance, referred to his own long Letter 37 as a *tractatus* (I, 118) and to the translation of the Apology of al-Kindi as *epistolam immo libellum*: Letter 111 (I, 294) and *Bibl. Clun.*, col. 1109 B. In Letter 24 he called Ambrose's letter against Symmachus *libellum siue epistolam*. The eleventh-century monk and teacher Onulf of Speyer equated the terms *opusculum, cartam*, and *epistolam* in his *Colores rhetorici*: Wilhelm Wattenbach, "Magister Onulf von Speier," *Sitzungsberichte der... Akademie der Wissenschaften zu Berlin*, 1894, p. 380. Cf. Jean Leclercq, *Saint Pierre Damien, ermite et homme d'église* (Uomini e dottrine, 8; Rome, 1960) p. 157; Eadmer, *Vita sancti Anselmi*, VII, ed. R.W. Southern (Medieval Texts; Edinburgh, 1962) pp. 72–73 (referring to a treatise by Anselm "epistolari stilo conscriptum"); and Bernard of Clairvaux, *De praecepto et dispensatione*, XX (61) (ed. Leclercq, III, 294). The term *litterae* is occasionally ambiguous and has been interpreted here in the singular or plural depending on the context.

⁹ *PL*, CL, 430 B, and *Thesaurus anecdotorum novissimus*, ed. Bernard Pez (Augsburg-Graz, 1721–1729) II.2, 542. For further references to epistolary brevity and *modus epistolaris brevitatis*, see the works of Alcuin, cited by Luitpold Wallach, *Alcuin and Charlemagne* (Cornell Studies in Classical Philology, 32; Ithaca, 1959) pp. 54–55; Peter Damiani, op. L, 15, and LI, 14 (*PL*, CXLV, 750 and 764); Anselm, ep. 37 (I, 29), ed. F. S. Schmitt, *S. Anselmi... opera omnia* (Edinburgh, 1946–1961) III, 147; Bruno of Cologne's letter to Ralph Le Vert, in *Lettres des premiers Chartreux*, p. 80; a letter from Abbot Pontius of St. Rufus to the canons of Chaumouzey (*ca.* 1120), in Charles Dereine, "Saint-Ruf et ses coutumes aux XIᵉ et XIIᵉ siècle," *Rev. Bén.*, LIX (1949) 170; Isaac of L'Étoile, *Epistola de officio missae* (*PL*, CXCIV, 1896 A: saying that a sudden attack on his abbey has prevented his exceeding "the epistolary mode"); and two treatises by Bernard of Clairvaux: *De praecepto et dispensatione*, XX (61) (ed. Leclercq, III, 294), and *De baptismo*, III (15) (Gaume ed., I.2, 1418). On brevity as an ideal of literary style, see Curtius, *Literature*, pp. 487–494 (esp. pp. 489–490 on epistolary brevity), and Leclercq, in *Analecta mon*, II, 146: "Le genre épistolaire demeurait caractérisé par la brièveté, à la différence des livres, et c'était là sans doute une exigence de la tradition littéraire, mais aussi une nécessité d'ordre pratique."

¹⁰ On the average length of classical and biblical letters, see Wikenhauser, *New Testament Introduction*, pp. 346–347. The letters of Cicero average 295 words; those of Seneca, 995; and those of Paul, about 1300. The longest letters by these three writers were 2530, 4134, and 7101 words in length, respectively.

¹¹ See Peter the Venerable, Letter 117. Letters in poetry were also written by Osbert of Clare, epp. 32 and 38 (*Letters*, pp. 115–116 and 130–132), and by Hildebert of Le Mans, Marbod of Rennes, Baudri of Bourgueil, and Ralph Tortarius: see Francis Bar, *Les épîtres latines de Raoul le Tourtier (1065?–1114?)* (Paris, 1937) pp. 6–7, who said (p. 7): "Nous entrevoyons toute une société lettrée, où l'on fait échange de poèmes."

in a *florilegium*, was an esteemed characteristic of a good collection of letters.

The formation and character of these letter collections have received less attention from scholars than the content and style of individual letters and groups of letters, isolated from the context of the collections in which they are preserved. The papal registers and other collections of official documents have been studied in works on diplomatics, but aside from a few more general works like those of Ott on early scholastic theological letters and of Erdmann on eleventh-century German letter collections, and Oehl's anthology of German mystical letters,[12] there are only individual studies on the most important collections of personal and literary letters,[13] and many of these are concerned more with the content of the letters than with how they were chosen, copied, and collected. There is still no *Corpus epistolarum medii aevi* and no satisfactory *handbuch* of medieval epistolography and letter collections.[14] The basic requirements for such a work were outlined by Schmeidler in 1926.[15] A few years later Erdmann stressed the need for new editions of almost all the post-Carolingian letter collections and for their systematic study in what he called "ein 'Wattenbach' für die Briefsammlungen."[16] In 1939 Pivec

[12] Ludwig Ott, *Untersuchungen zur theologischen Briefliteratur der Frühscholastik* (Beiträge zur Geschichte der Philosophie und Theologie des Mittelalters, 34; Münster, 1937); Carl Erdmann, *Studien zur Briefliteratur Deutschlands im elften Jahrhundert* (Schriften des Reichsinstituts für ältere deutsche Geschichtskunde, 1; Leipzig, 1938); Wilhelm Oehl, *Deutsche Mysterikerbriefe des Mittelalters 1100-1550* (Mystiker des Abendlandes, 1; Munich, 1931).

[13] In addition to the works cited below on the collections of Peter Damiani, Henri IV, Anselm, Ivo of Chartres, Ralph Tortarius, Abelard, John of Salisbury, Arnulf of Lisieux, Hildegard of Bingen, Gilbert Foliot, and Peter of Blois, see the following works on anonymous collections: Walter Möllenberg, "Der Codex Viennensis," *Sachsen und Anhalt*, III (1927) 149–176 (cf. the review by Bernhard Schmeidler in *Neues Archiv*, XLVIII [1929–30] 296–297); Werner Ohnsorge, "Eine Ebracher Briefsammlung des XII. Jahrhunderts," *Quellen und Forschungen aus italienischen Archiven und Bibliotheken*, XX (1928–29) 1–39; Franz Martin, "Zwei Salzburger Briefsammlungen des 12. Jahrhunderts (das sogen. Briefbuch Erzb. Eberhards I.)," *MIÖG*, XLII (1927) 313–342; Heinrich Koller, "Zwei Pariser Briefsammlungen," *MIÖG*, LIX (1951) 299–327 (cf. F.-J. Schmale, in *MIÖG*, LXVI [1958] 1–28); and, on the great St. Victor collection, Luchaire, *Études*, pp. 31–79, and Gerhard Laehr, "Aus den Briefsammlungen von St. Victor," *Festschrift Albert Brackmann* (Weimar, 1931) pp. 402–421.

[14] The only general studies on medieval letter writing are Wilhelm Wattenbach, "Iter Austriacum. 1853. Anhang: Über Briefsteller des Mittelalters," *Archiv für Kunde österreichischer Geschichts-Quellen*, XIV (1855) 29–94; Noël Valois, *De arte scribendi epistolas apud Gallicos medii aevi scriptores rhetoresque* (Paris, 1880); Adolf Bütow, *Die Entwicklung der mittelalterlichen Briefsteller bis zur Mitte des 12. Jahrhunderts* (Greifswald, 1908); and two articles by Jean Leclercq, "L'amitié dans les lettres au moyen âge," *Revue du Moyen Age latin*, I (1945) 391–410, and "Le genre épistolaire au moyen âge," ibid., II (1946) 63–70.

[15] Bernhard Schmeidler, "Über Briefsammlungen des früheren Mittelalters in Deutschland und ihre kritische Verwertung," *Vetenskaps-Societeten i Lund: Årsbok 1926*, pp. 5–27.

[16] Carl Erdmann, "Die Briefe Meinhards von Bamberg," *Neues Archiv*, XLIX (1930–1932) 384–385, who concluded on p. 387: "Im ganzen kann jeder, der an die Bearbeitung der mittelalterlichen Briefe herantritt, das belebende Bewusstsein haben, dass die Forschung

wrote that medieval *Briefwissenschaft* "has already established at least the recognition of its independence among the historical *Hilfswissenschaften*, although it is less developed than its older sister-discipline of diplomatics."[17] Much work still has to be done, however, and De Ghellinck wrote in 1946, twenty years after Schmeidler, that "the deep study of these collections has scarcely begun."[18]

Such study is all the more needed because the vast majority of medieval letters are preserved in collections.[19] Very few letters indeed have survived in individual copies, and almost none in their original form. Thus the entire correspondence of Aelred of Rievaulx, who is known to have written at least three hundred letters, is lost.[20] The act of collecting was thus in many ways as important as the act of writing letters, and at various times in the Middle Ages it was a distinct form of literary activity. It flourished in the Carolingian age, which produced the famous letter collections of Boniface, Alcuin, and Lupus of Ferrières. It then almost died out, and, with the sole exception of the collection of Ratherius of Verona, no letter collections are known before those of Gerbert in France and Froumond of Tegernsee in Germany at the end of the tenth and beginning of the eleventh centuries. From then on the number of collections steadily grew, and it is clear that many writers and men of affairs in the eleventh and twelfth centuries regularly kept or gathered copies of their letters with a view to eventual publication.[21]

Bernhard Schmeidler was one of the first scholars to emphasize the

---

hier erst am Anfang steht und dass der Grossteil der Arbeit noch zu leisten ist." Cf. his *Briefliteratur*, foreword and p. 1.

[17] Karl Pivec, "Stil- und Sprachenentwicklung in mittellateinischen Briefen vom 8.-12. Jh.," MÖIG, Ergänzungsband XIV (1939) 36.

[18] De Ghellinck, *Essor*, I, 112. On classical authors and their letter collections, see J. Sykutris, "Epistolographie," *Paulys Real-Encyclopädie der classischen Altertumswissenschaft*, ed. Georg Wissowa and Wilhelm Kroll, Supplementband V (Stuttgart, 1931) 185–220, esp. pp. 198–199. Cf. also, Denys Gorce, *Les voyages, l'hospitalité et le port des lettres dans le monde chrétien des IVe et Ve siècles* (Wépion-sur-Meuse and Paris, 1925) pp. 193–247; *Private Letters: Pagan and Christian*, ed. Dorothy Brooke (London, 1929); and M. Monica Wagner, "A Chapter in Byzantine Epistolography: The Letters of Theodoret of Cyrus," *Dumbarton Oaks Papers*, IV (1948) 121, who deplored the lack of works on classical and Byzantine letters.

[19] There is no complete bibliography of medieval letter collections, but a summary list of over two hundred, from the entire Middle Ages, is given in Hermann Oesterley, *Wegweiser durch die Literatur der Urkundensammlungen* (Berlin, 1885–86) I, 19–45. Cf. also Auguste Molinier, *Les sources de l'histoire de France*, I.2: *Époque féodale: Les Capétiens jusqu'en 1180* (Paris, 1902) pp. 192–204; Manitius, *Lat. Lit.*, III, 174–175 and 286–312; Ott, *Untersuchungen*, pp. 109–125; and De Ghellinck, *Essor*, I, 110.

[20] Anselm Hoste, *Bibliotheca Aelrediana* (Instrumenta patristica, 2; The Hague-Steinbrugge, 1962) pp. 15 and 137–139.

[21] Cf. Pivec, in MÖIG, Erg.-Band XIV, 45–46, who suggested that the Investiture Controversy stimulated the stylistic development of letter writing: "Die Intensivierung der Affekte, politischer und persönlicher, fand ihre Gegenspiegelung in der Intensivierung des

organic unity and personal character of many of these letter collections. Not only the ideas and factual content but also the style and organization make a letter collection into a real *Lebensbild* of the author and collector.[22] This idea was taken up by Pivec, who called the letter collection of Gerbert "an autobiography in documents" and "the forerunner of later memoire-literature."[23] This autobiographical aspect of medieval letter collections can easily be overemphasized.[24] Many individual collections shed little or no light on the life and personality of the author. But Schmeidler's work has concentrated scholarly attention, especially in Germany, on a number of significant questions which should be asked about any collection of medieval letters.

The role of the scribe, secretary, or notary was clearly of great importance in the formation of a letter collection, and he often applied to personal letters the rules and practices learned in official correspondences. It was he, according to Schmeidler, who actually wrote the letters, often under various names acting for different people, and sometimes also wrote the replies, and who either kept a letter book into which copies (*Reinschriften*) of his letters were inserted as they were written or later gathered his finished drafts (*Konzepten*) into a collection.[25] His character thus gave the collection a personal, stylistic, and chronological unity. "Since the year 1926," Schmeidler wrote in 1949, "I have stood for the idea that any large collection of early

---

sprachlichen Ausdruckes." It may be that the distinctive form of letter writing that combined subjective and objective, private and public, elements was particularly suited to the temperament of the leaders at this time, who themselves joined a deepening personal spirituality to an expanding sphere of public activity.

[22] Schmeidler, in *Lund Årsbok 1926*, pp. 10–11 and 13–14.

[23] Karl Pivec, "Die Briefsammlung Gerberts von Aurillac," *MÖIG*, XLIX (1935) 68.

[24] Cf. Erdmann, *Briefliteratur*, p. 9, n. 2, who found Pivec's "Autobiographie in Dokumenten" "zu weitgehend." On medieval autobiography in general, see Georg Misch, *Geschichte der Autobiographie* (Frankfurt a. M., 1949 ff.) and his series of studies in the *Nachrichten* of the Göttingen Academy, beginning in 1954, on the autobiographical works of Otloh of St. Emmeram, Guigo of La Chartreuse, Suger of St. Denis, and other eleventh- and twelfth-century figures.

[25] On the distinction between the *Konzept* (finished draft) and *Reinschrift* (fair copy), see esp. Schmeidler, in *Lund Årsbok 1926*, pp. 8–9, where he stressed that as a rule the *Konzept* hardly differed from the finished letter and therefore has real historical value, and "Die Briefsammlung Froumunds von Tegernsee," *Historisches Jahrbuch*, LXII–LXIX (1949) 226–227 and 237–238. Schmeidler and his critics argued for years over this question. Erdmann maintained that the Tegernsee collection was basically a copybook into which finished letters were copied over a period of years. Schmeidler believed that it was formed at one time on the basis of drafts kept by Froumond. Schmeidler in general opposed Erdmann's view of letter collections "mit Reinschrift-Character" and doubted whether a *dictator* could have carried about a copybook for many years. Luitpold Wallach has recently shown that Alcuin kept and consulted copies of his letters, contrary to the general opinion that his letters had been kept and copied by his contemporaries: *Alcuin and Charlemagne*, pp. 266–274. On the same problem for the papal registers, see Bresslau, *Urkundenlehre*, I, 116.

medieval letters that has some unity in time of origin, unity or at least homogeneity of content, and unity of manuscript tradition also goes back to the unity of a single writer-personality and can be understood and explained only by the personal collecting activity of their writer."[26] He explained this point more explicitly in an earlier work:

> The majority of surviving medieval letters are preserved in collections which go back more or less directly to the issuer: not to the issuer who is often named in the addresses, which may vary greatly in the same collection, but to the man who drew them up, the *dictator*. For the preservation of medieval letters the *dictator* in question must have kept a regular and carefully maintained letter book, and this must have been preserved in whole or in part. It follows that many more letters were written than have been preserved.[27]

Schmeidler maintained that this personal unity in a letter collection was shown principally by stylistic consistency and chronological order, presuming that the order had not been disturbed by later copyists and editors. He applied these rules, particularly his special *innerkritisch-stilvergleichende* method of stylistic criticism, to several medieval letter collections, including those of Gerbert, Froumond of Tegernsee, Hildegard of Bingen, and Abelard.[28] In some respects he applied his rules too rigidly, and many scholars and critics have not accepted his conclusions, especially his arguments for the single authorship of the correspondence between Abelard and Heloise.[29] His works mark an important advance in the study of medieval epistolography, however, and have contributed greatly to an understanding of how and when and by whom the collections of medieval letters were formed.

---

[26] Schmeidler, in *Hist. Jahrbuch*, LXII–LXIX, 220–221.

[27] Bernhard Schmeidler, *Kaiser Heinrich IV. und seine Helfer im Investiturstreit* (Leipzig, 1927) p. 344; cf. Erdmann, in *Neues Archiv*, XLIX, 335–336.

[28] In addition to the works already cited, see "Über die Tegernseer Briefsammlung (Froumund)," *Neues Archiv*, XLVI (1925–26) 395–429, stressing the unity of authorship; "Der Briefwechsel zwischen Abälard und Heloise als eine literarische Fiktion Abälards," *Zeitschrift für Kirchengeschichte*, LIV (1935) 323–338; "Der Briefwechsel zwischen Abaelard und Heloise dennoch eine literarische Fiction Abaelards," *Rev. Bén.*, LII (1940) 85–95 (defending his views and giving references to further literature); and "Bemerkungen zum Corpus der Briefe der hl. Hildegard von Bingen," *Corona Quernea: Festgabe für Karl Strecker* (Schriften des Reichsinstituts für ältere deutsche Geschichtskunde, 6; Leipzig, 1941) pp. 335–366. Schmeidler replied to critics of his "stilkritischen Methode," particularly Hirsch and Zatschek, in "Bamberg, der *Codex Udalrici* und die deutsche Reichsverwaltung im 11. und 12. Jahrhundert," *Zeitschrift für bayerische Landesgeschichte*, II (1929) 207–274.

[29] See the works on the letter collection of Gerbert, cited nn. 32 and 48 below, and on the Tegernsee collection by Erdmann, Langosch, and Otto Meyer, "Feuchtwangen, Augsburger Eigen-, Tegernseer Filialkloster," *Zeitschrift der Savigny-Stiftung für Rechtsgeschichte*, LVIII, Kanon. Abt. XXVII (1938) 599–638, who pointed out that some of the letters in the Tegernsee collection are not in chronological order and remarked generally that "das Dogma von der chronologischen Anordnung der Briefe" was primarily based upon collections in which relatively few of the letters could be definitely dated (pp. 630–631). Schmeidler replied in the *Hist. Jahrbuch*, LXII–LXIX, 220–238 (esp. pp. 230 ff.), with a strong defense of the unified authorship and chronological order of this collection.

It is impossible to formulate rules for the collecting of letters in the twelfth century, but the available scraps of evidence suggest that the collections were all the results of conscious policy but were compiled in various ways.[30] It is clear that most letter writers, including Ivo of Chartres, Geoffrey of Vendôme, Hildebert of Le Mans, Nicholas of Montiéramey (Clairvaux), Gerhoh of Reichersberg, John of Salisbury, Gilbert Foliot, Peter of Blois, and Guy of Bazoches, kept copies of the letters they wrote and received, or had copies made by a friend or amanuensis, and that these copies formed the basis of their letter collections.[31] It is not certain, however, whether the copies were the drafts of the original letters or later copies made from the originals, nor whether they were kept in bound volumes, on quires of parchment for later binding, or on separate leaves.[32] Gerhoh of Reichersberg seems to have had a regular letter book, since in the chronicle of Reichersberg the priest Magnus referred to Gerhoh's letters, "which he wrote to various people at various times and which are nearly all still found in his register or epistolary book in two volumes."[33] Prior Peter of the Augustinian house of St. John at Sens kept his letters in an archive, since he wrote to Bishop Hato of Troyes that he had received Hato's letter and had deposited it in his archive.[34] To judge from the apparently random arrangement of the early letters of John of

[30] Cf. Carl Erdmann, "Untersuchungen zu den Briefen Heinrichs IV.," *Archiv für Urkundenforschung*, XVI (1939) 235–238. Speaking about the letter collections associated with the Investiture Controversy, Erdmann here strongly argues (against Schmeidler, Hirsch, and Zatschek) that the letters were transmitted through the recipients (the principle of *Empfänger-Brieftiberlieferung*) rather than through the sender or scribe (*Konzept*- or *Kanzlei-Brieftiberlieferung*). The results of these scholarly debates are far from conclusive.

[31] In addition to the works on individual collections cited elsewhere, see Jean Leclercq, "La collection des lettres d'Yves de Chartres," *Rev. Bén.*, LVI (1945–46) 108–125, and Ivo of Chartres, *Correspondance*, ed. Jean Leclercq, I (Les classiques de l'histoire de France au Moyen Age, 22; Paris, 1949) introd.; A. Dieudonné, *Hildebert de Lavardin* (Paris-Mamers, 1898) pp. 115–239; Morey and Brooke, *Foliot*, pp. 8–31; and, more generally, Valois, *De arte*, pp. 12–15; De Ghellinck, *Essor*, I, 111; and Leclercq, in *Rev. du Moyen Age lat.*, II, 67. On the formation of the great patristic letter collections, see Henri Leclercq, in *DACL*, VIII.2, 2757 (Cyprian), 2809 (Ambrose), 2826 (Jerome), 2850 (Augustine), all of whom collected their own letters; also, on Jerome and Augustine, D. De Bruyne, "Notes sur les lettres de saint Augustin," *Rev. hist. ecc.*, XXIII (1927) 527–530.

[32] This question has been particularly debated with regard to the letter collection of Gerbert. According to Lot and Uhlirz, the registers of Gerbert's letters consisted of "small packages of parchment, each package containing somewhat related material," which accounts for "the fact that so many letters are chronologically out of place": *The Letters of Gerbert*, trans. Harriet P. Lattin (Columbia Records of Civilization, 60; New York, 1961) introd., p. 22. Cf. Julien Havet, *Lettres de Gerbert* (Collection de textes pour servir à l'étude et à l'enseignement de l'histoire, 6; Paris, 1889) introd., p. lxxiv, who held, against most other scholars, that the letters are in chronological order and criticized the previous editor, Olleris, for rearranging them "sous prétexte d'en donner un classement chronologique" (pp. lv-lvi); Schmeidler, in *Lund Årsbok 1926*, pp. 23–25; and Erdmann, *Briefliteratur*, p. 9.

[33] *MGH, Scriptores* in fol., XVII, 494; cf. Damien van den Eynde, *L'œuvre littéraire de Géroch de Reichersberg* (Spicilegium Pontificii Athenaei Antoniani, 11; Rome, 1957) p. 181.

[34] Constable, in *Petrus Ven.*, p. 52.

Salisbury, he seems to have kept his drafts or copies on separate sheets, from which his collection was later compiled.³⁵ Sometimes this work was done by a secretary. Thus the secretary of Abbot Gervase of Prémontré explained in an introductory letter to the collection of Gervase that, in addition to letters composed by Gervase and written by himself, he had included letters written before he became Gervase's secretary and some which had been sent to Gervase.³⁶

When no copies had been kept, a collection of letters might be formed either by recovering the originals at the time they were written and sent or by later gathering letters that had been kept by the recipients. Writing was a laborious business in the twelfth century; parchment was expensive; and many writers neglected to keep copies of their letters. Among these was Herbert of Losinga, who wrote to his friend Norman: "By the assiduity of your writing, you endeavor to correct my negligence in failing to keep the letters that I have written to my friends and to collect them into a small body in the form of a register."³⁷ This occurs in the introductory letter to his collection, which was presumably formed of letters recovered from the recipients. Arnulf of Lisieux likewise explained in the introductory letter to his collection, which was addressed to Giles of La Perche, archdeacon of Rouen: "I have gathered into a little volume the letters that I have at one time or another sent to various people ... I have collected those I could with the utmost diligence, since I had no copies of them but have taken them, like amends, from those who happened to have kept them."³⁸ This passage was regarded by Barlow as "a pleasant exaggeration,"³⁹ but even if Arnulf had in fact kept copies of some letters, he may well have added others recovered from the recipients. The trouble with this system was that most medieval archives were utilitarian, not literary; and very small numbers of personal letters, as opposed to charters, were kept in their original form. The very existence of a considerable collection therefore suggests that the author had in mind their eventual publication at the time they were written.

It was not uncommon to request the return of letters of which no copies had been kept. In the capitulary archives of Sant'Ambrogio at

---

³⁵ This was the opinion of R. L. Poole, "The Early Correspondence of John of Salisbury," in his *Studies*, p. 260; cf. John of Salisbury, *Letters*, I, introd.

³⁶ Cheney, in *Bull. J. Rylands Lib.*, XXXIII, 29–30.

³⁷ Herbert of Losinga, *Epistolae*, ep. 1, ed. R. Anstruther (Caxton Society; Brussels–London, 1846) p. 1, and *Ausgewählte Briefe aus der Salierzeit*, ed. Carl Erdmann (Texte zur Kulturgeschichte des Mittelalters, 7; Rome, 1933) p. 35. This interesting passage was remarked upon by Schmeidler, in *Neues Archiv*, XLVIII, 297; Erdmann, *Briefliteratur*, pp. 10–11; De Ghellinck, *Essor*, I, 111; and Klibansky, in *Med. and Ren. Studies*, V, 2.

³⁸ Arnulf of Lisieux, *Letters*, pp. 1–2; cf. *Hist. litt.*, XIV, 309.

³⁹ Arnulf of Lisieux, *Letters*, introd., p. lxi.

Milan, for instance, there is a small (and to the best of my knowledge unique) collection of original letters that were sent to various recipients, including the pope, in the middle of thet welfth century and that were probably brought back with the replies by the messenger.[40] "Keep this letter for me," wrote Peter of Celle at the end of a letter to Abbot Bernard of St. Crispin,[41] and an anonymous monk at Bec asked his friend Richard to return a letter "when it begins to bore you."[42] St. Anselm was apparently also in the habit of recovering his own letters. He wrote to the monks of Conflans that he was waiting for his letters, "which the lord Maurice should send me"; and soon after he asked Prior Baldric of Bec to send several of his own works, including any letters not sent by Maurice.[43]

In whatever way the collection was formed, the principle of selection was extremely important. Most medieval letter collections were regarded as works of literature, and their contents were chosen with care. As Sykutris said of classical collections: "One naturally did not publish all letters ... but a selection of the stylistically most successful ... The arrangement was very carefully considered," he went on, referring in particular to the collections of Pliny and Sidonius Apollinaris, "so that, letters of similar content being scattered in various books, *varietas* was observed as the highest principle."[44] Not all medieval *epistolaria* were so carefully arranged, and the organization of many appears to be almost haphazard, without regard for date,

---

[40] See pp. 21–22 below, and Walter Wache, "Eine Sammlung von Originalbriefen des 12. Jahrhunderts im Kapitelarchiv von S. Ambrogio in Mailand," *MÖIG*, L (1936) 326–328, who stressed that these letters must have been recovered from the addressees. This and some other examples of requests to return letters are cited by Erdmann, in *Archiv f. Urk.*, XVI, 233. Cf. also Hartmut Hoffmann, "Zur mittelalterlichen Brieftechnik," *Spiegel der Geschichte: Festgabe für Max Braubach* (Münster, 1964) p. 149, and, on requests to return letters in German documents of the thirteenth and fourteenth centuries, Friedrich Hefele, "'Reddite Litteras': Ein Beitrag zur Urkundenlehre," *Aus Verfassungs- und Landesgeschichte: Festschrift ... Theodor Mayer* (Constance, 1954–55) II, 425–434.

[41] Peter of Celle, ep. 97, in *PL*, CCII, 548. Peter Damiani also sometimes asked a recipient to save the letter: see Kurt Reindel, "Studien zur Überlieferung der Werke des Petrus Damiani I," *Deutsches Archiv*, XV (1959) 62.

[42] "Cum uero te coeperit esse fastidio, ad me quaeso remitte"; ed. Leclercq, in *Analecta mon.*, II, 161. Osbert of Clare asked Prior Stephen of Thetford to return a letter if he was unable to carry out its request: "Si litterae nostrae effectu caruerint, iterum ad nos redeant: si postulata obtinuerint, apud uos mansionem accipiant" (*Letters*, p. 100). Perhaps Osbert planned to use the letter again if Stephen was unable to send help.

[43] Anselm of Canterbury, epp. 104 (II, 14) and 147 (II, 51), in his *Opera omnia*, ed. Schmitt, III, 237 and 294; cf. F. S. Schmitt, "Zur Entstehungsgeschichte der handschriftlichen Sammlungen der Briefe des hl. Anselm von Canterbury," *Rev. Bén.*, XLVIII (1936) 308, who remarked: "Zu welchem Zwecke hat Anselm seine Briefe zurückverlangt? Es ist kein Zweifel: Anselm hat seine eigenen Briefe gesammelt und zwar in zwei Etappen." On Anselm's letter collection, see also André Wilmart, "La tradition des lettres de S. Anselme," *Rev. Bén.*, XLIII (1931) 38–42, and F. S. Schmitt, "Zur Ueberlieferung der Korrespondenz Anselms von Canterbury. Neue Briefe," *ibid.*, 224–238.

[44] Pauly-Wissowa, *Real-Encyclopädie*, Suppl. V, 198–199.

subject matter, or the position of the recipient.[45] Only when the letters were preserved in a book of drafts or copies are they found in the collection in strict chronological order.[46] In most collections, however, the letters were chosen with care for both the elegance of their style and the interest of their contents, and also occasionally for the rank and importance of the writer or recipient. The secretary of Gervase of Prémontré thus admitted that he had included in the collection "some letters sent to my abbot not so much because their style was elegant as because their senders were important."[47] A collection of letters might go through several editions and be enlarged and rearranged more than once.[48] The principle of *varietas* was often observed by the inclusion of epistolary treatises, poems, and sermons. These longer works have been expunged in many modern editions, but the manuscripts show that they originally formed part of the letter collections of Ivo of Chartres,[49] Peter of Celle,[50] Geoffrey of Vendôme,[51] and Peter of Blois. "The works of Peter of Blois are found in the best manuscripts as a coherent ensemble in which doctrinal treatises are inserted among the letters," wrote Leclercq, who described Peter's collection as "the most illustrious and perhaps the most widely known model of this type of writing... The example is

[45] Cf. H. M. Schaller, "Zur Entstehung der sogennanten Briefsammlung des Petrus de Vinea," *Deutsches Archiv*, XII (1956) 114–159. Even the well-organized collection of Ivo of Chartres is not strictly chronological: see his *Correspondance*, ed. Leclercq, I, introd., xxx.

[46] In the opinion of Schmeidler and Erdmann, strict chronological order was a basic characteristic of any properly preserved letter collection. The collection of Geoffrey of Vendôme is in chronological order in the earliest manuscripts but already in the twelfth century was rearranged into five books according to the ranks of the addressees: see André Wilmart, "La collection chronologique des écrits de Geoffroi abbé de Vendôme," *Rev. Bén.*, XLIII (1931) 239–245.

[47] Cheney, in *Bull. J. Rylands Lib.*, XXXIII, 30.

[48] The exact character of the two versions of Gerbert's letter collection has been a fertile field of scholarly debate: cf. Fritz Weigle, "Studien zur Überlieferung der Briefsammlung Gerberts von Reims," *Deutsches Archiv*, X (1953–54) 19–70, XI (1954–55) 393–421, and XIV (1958) 149–220, who concluded that one collection was compiled by Gerbert himself and another after his death, and Lattin, in *Letters of Gerbert*, introd., p. 22, who cited the opinion of Lot and Uhlirz that Gerbert kept two registers, of which one was secret. On the editions, or differing versions, of the letter collections of Anselm, Ivo, Bernard, Peter of Blois, and Gervase of Prémontré, see the works of Schmitt (cited n. 43 above); Leclercq, in *Rev. Bén.*, LVI, 110–112; Leclercq, *Études*, p. 88; E. S. Cohn, "The Manuscript Evidence for the Letters of Peter of Blois," *English Historical Review*, XLI (1926) 43–60, esp. p. 50; and Cheney, in *Bull. J. Rylands Lib.*, XXXIII, 45–47.

[49] Leclercq, in *Rev. Bén.*, LVI, 116.

[50] MS. Oxford, St. John's College, 126, printed under the name of Walter of Dervy, *Epistolae*, ed. C. Messiter (Caxton Society, 10; London, 1850); cf. Heinrich Hohenleutner, "Die Briefsammlung des sogennanten Walter von Dervy (Montier-en-Der) in der Oxforder Handschrift St. John's College, Mrs. 126," *Historisches Jahrbuch*, LXXIV (1955) 673–680.

[51] Wilmart, in *Rev. Bén.*, XLIII, 241, and Erdmann, *Briefliteratur*, pp. 8–9, who stressed that the inclusion of sermons and treatises in the letter collection of Geoffrey of Vendôme gave it a strongly literary character.

characteristic in that we witness through it the constitution of real 'epistolary summas.'"[52]

2. THE COLLECTION OF PETER THE VENERABLE

The letters of Peter the Venerable have long been admired by scholars and critics for their content and style. They were considered by Joan Evans to be "the most accomplished and the most personal" of Peter's writings in prose, "finished, graceful, almost artificial in style, that already prelude Petrarch's, though set in another key. It is the phrases and diction of the Psalms that most often recur in them; but there is many a phrase modelled on Horace, Virgil, and Cicero, classical allusions are not wanting, and there is often a classical grace in the turn of the phrase and the aptness of the thought."[53] Christopher Brooke cited Peter's letters as an example of the new type of twelfth-century letter collection in which "the three streams of official, pastoral, and intimate [letters] combined in one collection."[54] Most recently Paolo Lamma has studied the place of Peter's letters in the tradition of monastic writing and Cluniac historiography:

> The themes of the *Collationes* and *Occupatio* [of St. Odo], permanent traditions of monastic culture and meditation, were taken up again here with the penetrating but confident melancholy of Peter the Venerable, who in his constant colloquies with his contemporaries was looking for a testing ground for these convictions and a source of hope, albeit in the afterlife... In this vision, faith in Providence and anxiety for the proofs of existence, the desire to go beyond time and the need to intervene in the work of the world, sought to find an equilibrium between human liberty and divine intervention, and an attitude toward the meeting of old and new had to be taken at all times. There is found in this attitude, depending on the time and circumstances, either a nostalgia for the past, a sense of continuity of human values in time, or an effort to make the traditionalists and innovators live together, without conflict, in the diversity of their tasks.[55]

These three authors emphasize the consciously literary quality of Peter's letters, and the collection as a whole shows many of the characteristic features of letter collections in the twelfth century.

---

[52] Leclercq, in *Rev. du Moyen Age lat.*, II, 67. For a good example of an early thirteenth-century mixed collection, see André Wilmart, "Les mélanges de Mathieu préchantre de Rievaulx au début du XIIIe siècle," *Rev. Bén.*, LII (1940) 15–84.

[53] Evans, *Mon. Life*, p. 109. Cf. the opinion of Schönbach, *Erzählungsliteratur*, pp. 94–95, concerning the description of mountain scenery in the *De Miraculis*, I, 8: "Ich weiss keinen Schriftsteller zwischen Augustinus und Petrarca, der so klar wie dieser die gehobene Empfindung über die gewaltigen Eindrücke der Hochgebirgslandschaft aussprache."

[54] John of Salisbury, *Letters*, I, introd., xlvi.

[55] Lamma, *Momenti*, pp. 31–32. The passage is difficult to translate literally, and the version here is somewhat simplified.

Peter clearly wrote the letters with an eye to future publication, and several of the more important letters circulated widely before they were incorporated into the collection. In Letter 161, addressed to the abbots and priors of all Cluniac houses, he referred particularly to the long letters, 28 and 111, defending Cluny against the Cistercian criticisms: "I consider it superfluous to repeat here the cause and reason [for the Cluniac customs], because I have twice carefully explained this in the two letters sent some time ago to the abbot of Clairvaux." These two letters were ostensibly private, but Peter expected the Cluniac superiors to be familiar with their contents.

These two letters were in fact epistolary treatises, and the manuscript tradition of the collection, which will be studied later, shows that it originally also included the *Contra Petrobrusianos*, *Contra Iudaeos*, and the *Contra eos qui dicunt Christum numquam se in Evangeliis aperte Deum dixisse*. These were at an early date excluded from the collection, apparently on account of their length and character; and in the earliest surviving manuscript, Letter 28 was copied at the end, with only a note to indicate its original position. The collection also includes, in addition to a hundred and sixty-six letters by Peter the Venerable, twenty-nine letters addressed to him and two hymns. In its earliest form, therefore, the collection presented a mixture of letters by various hands, of dogmatic treatises, and of poems that was in the best tradition of ancient and medieval *epistolaria*.

Peter apparently chose the letters for inclusion in the collection at the time they were written. It does not contain his entire correspondence.[56] There are references to lost letters by Peter the Venerable in Letter 110 by Bernard of Clairvaux, in Letter 153 by Nicholas of Montiéramey, and in the *History of Vézelay* by Hugh of Poitiers,[57] and Peter himself, in his letters to Ademar of Figeac, Guigo of La Chartreuse, and Basil of La Chartreuse, mentioned letters that are not preserved in the collection.[58] In Letter 158 to his old friend Hugh of Amiens, Peter expressed his regret at not having "filled some of my books with letters sent to you and adorned them with your replies as with sparkling gems."

This suggests that as a rule copies of selected letters both by and to Peter were kept in letter books or registers. Sometimes, however, the originals were recovered and preserved. Peter of Poitiers, the secretary of Peter the Venerable, asked him in Letter 128 to keep two letters for

[56] Cf. Leclercq, *Pierre le Vén.*, introd., p. xvii.
[57] *Spicilegium*, II, 531, referring to a letter from Peter to the count of Nevers in 1152. Bernard mentioned a letter that apparently reproached him for silence and coldness, and Nicholas thanked Peter for a letter supporting the bishop-elect of Beauvais, Henry of France.
[58] Letters 147, 149, and 186.

him, "since I value and preserve your letters with the utmost care." Nicholas of Montiéramey wrote to Peter the Venerable, probably late in 1149: "I am sending you your letters, and the book addressed to the pope, and the two letters which you sent this year to the abbot [of Clairvaux] and to myself."[59] There is also an interesting passage in Letter 34 to the chancellor Cardinal Haimeric from Peter the Venerable, who quoted a letter to the Pope "from the self-same parchment that I had sent."[60] Peter therefore kept an archive as well as a copybook of his letters, and he consulted them from time to time. In Letter 149, written in 1149, he quoted at length from a letter written to him by Guigo of La Chartreuse in 1136/7.

The basis of letter selection seems to have been a combination of elegance and interest, occasionally taking into account the importance of the recipient. Stylistic elegance was sometimes equated, however, with mere flowery verbiage and a profusion of pious sentiments, and some of the letters are of small intrinsic interest. The variety of subject matter is very great, but all the letters in the collection have a personal touch, whether Peter the Venerable was writing as abbot of Cluny, as a spiritual adviser, or simply as a friend. As abbot of Cluny, Peter also issued any number of purely official documents, and he frequently complained in his letters of the extent of his business and travels, which kept him from his friends and from private contemplation.[61] In the relatively early Letter 16 to his brother Pontius, Peter blamed his failure to write on "the bustle of the world, the business of affairs, the involvements of litigations, with which chains you have often seen me bound, and have lamented." "Do not impute my lateness in writing to you to my negligence," he wrote in Letter 170 to the Carthusians of Meyriat, "but attribute it to the infinite importunity of cases which always troubles me. If even a short space, not to say a moment, of time had been allowed me, your eye would have seen my letter two or three months ago." He was followed by official business even when he was away from Cluny on a retreat in the nearby woods, according to his companion Gilbert in Letter 127 to Peter of Poitiers:

How can we be called solitaries, who, after we came to this solitary hermitage, have attracted so many people that we seem to have built a town rather than a hermitage? For in addition to the great crowd that gathers in throngs from

[59] Letter 153. Cf. the relevant notes to this passage and Appendix Q on Nicholas of Montiéramey.

[60] "Scriptum huiusmodi capitulum, sicut ex eadem quam misi membrana postea collegi": cf. Constable, "Cluniac Tithes," pp. 614–615.

[61] See Letters 81 (I, 218: "importunitas negotiosi temporis" prevented his writing), 109 (I, 271-272), 119 (I, 313), 139 (I, 346: "the almost continual daily importunity of the affairs of Cluny"), 176 (I, 417), 193 (I, 450, praying not to be drowned by the floods of legal cases flowing to Cluny "from Italy, Germany, Spain, England, [and] from this our own France").

the country around in order to gain respite from legal proceedings, or settlements, or judicial actions, so many messengers come to us both from across the sea to the East and from across the Alps [Pyrenees] in the West that the greatest court of a mighty king could hardly reply [to all of them].

A few of these official documents are very like personal letters,[62] and many of Peter's letters are naturally concerned with Cluniac affairs, but the distinction between his official and personal correspondence is usually clear, and there are no charters or documents with witnesses in his letter collection. No original letter by Peter the Venerable is known, and there are isolated copies of only a very few letters, mostly those that circulated independently. The only known personal letters preserved outside the collection are four in the letter collection of Suger.[63] The other letters in the supplements to the collection in the *Bibliotheca Cluniacensis* and *Patrologia latina* are really official documents.[64] If a letter was not copied at the time it was written, therefore, or recovered soon afterwards, it was lost.

The unity of the collection, such as it is, derives from the style and personality of the author. A serious question arises at this point, however, over the part played by Peter of Poitiers in the formation of the collection. He is the very type of notary or secretary who, according to Schmeidler, drew up and copied letters in the Middle Ages and who thus inserted himself between the ostensible author, or authors, and the actual texts in a collection of letters. Peter of Poitiers was certainly responsible for the work of writing and collecting many of Peter the Venerable's letters. The chronological order of the collection seems in particular to date approximately from the time that Peter of Poitiers joined the service of Peter the Venerable.[65] It is not therefore impossible that he had a hand in composing some of the letters. He was not with Peter the Venerable all of the time, however, as during the retreat in the woods near Cluny and on the visit to England in 1155, and the collection includes a considerable number of letters addressed to Peter the Venerable and from Peter the Venerable to Peter of Poitiers, in the composition of which Peter of Poitiers could hardly have had a hand; and I am inclined to believe that Peter the Venerable himself composed most of the letters written in his name and thus gives a spirit of unity to the entire collection.

The formation and perfection of the collection covered several

---

[62] Cf. *Cluny*, V, 505 and 515, nos. 4144 and 4159; *GC*, X, *instr.*, 256: a letter to the bishop of Beauvais allowing a Cluniac monk to become abbot of St. Lucien but ending, like a personal letter, with "Valete."

[63] *Bibl. Clun.*, cols. 959–960, and *Thes. nov.*, I, 416–417; cf. Suger, *Oeuvres*, pp. 293, 300, and 306.

[64] *Bibl. Clun.*, cols. 959–966, and *PL*, CLXXXIX, 471–486.

[65] See p. 80 below.

years. The earliest references to it occur in the letters written between Peter the Venerable and Peter of Poitiers while they were separated during the retreat near Cluny, probably in 1139/41. Peter the Venerable wrote in Letter 124 that he was sending a hymn he had composed in honor of St. Benedict and asked Peter of Poitiers to "take it and add it, if it seems worthy, to the others which you are accustomed to transcribe." Peter of Poitiers replied in Letter 128, cited above, praising the hymn and other letters sent him by Peter the Venerable and his companions and asking "that this letter and the smaller one [Letter 123], which was such a comfort to me, should be kept for me, since I value and preserve your letters with the utmost care." In Letter 129 Peter the Venerable wrote to Peter of Poitiers: "In order to brighten your spare time and to keep you from being entirely idle, you may send me some work by St. Augustine to console me on my wearisome journey, and my letters, and the life of the lord bishop Matthew, since the book published against the heretics is lacking in the form that it was conceived and produced from my own heart." There existed at this time, therefore, a collection of Peter's works that included the letters, the life of Matthew of Albano, which was later incorporated into the *De miraculis*,[66] and a work against the heretics, probably the *Contra Petrobrusianos*,[67] which Peter planned to revise while he was on retreat.

These letters are found at the end of the collection as it appears in MS. Douai 381,[68] which probably contains the earliest form of the collection. It included a hundred and ten letters, all written before 1142, the *Contra Petrobrusianos* and its introduction, and two prefatory letters by Peter of Poitiers to Peter the Venerable. In the first of these Peter of Poitiers wrote: "In accordance with your orders, most dearly beloved father, I have now at last corrected and edited those verses which I composed long ago ... and have transcribed and arranged them at the beginning of your letters." This letter is followed in the manuscript by a collection of poems by both Peter the Venerable and Peter of Poitiers, and then by the second prefatory letter, praising the works of Peter the Venerable. "I have seen, most dearly beloved father, and examined with care the little book, which I scarcely once put down and which attracts the spirit of the reader the more it is read and pleases him the more sweetly, the more subtly it is studied ... You will thus indeed benefit not only me but also people in the most distant lands, not only the living but also all future Christians, if in the manner of your Fathers, and as the Holy Spirit inspires

---

[66] Cf. Constable, in *Petrus Ven.*, pp. 227–228.
[67] See Appendix G.
[68] Here called MS. A: see pp. 48–55 below.

you, you leave to posterity such monuments of genius in your sermons, letters, and various treatises." Peter of Poitiers referred to the collection here both as a *libellus* and as a *praefatus codex,* and he clearly had before him a volume of the collected works of Peter the Venerable.[69]

It is impossible to determine precisely the stages in the formation of the collection. As with the letters of St. Bernard,[70] no two manuscripts contain exactly the same collection. There were clearly at least two distinct editions, however, and the collection found in MS. Douai 381 was enlarged, probably about 1152/3, into the collection of a hundred and ninety-five letters, divided into six books. The catalogue of the library of Cluny drawn up probably during the abbacy of Hugh III (1158–61) lists a "volumen in quo continentur epistole Petri abbatis Cluniacensis."[71] Radulf, the biographer of Peter the Venerable, mentioned his works and said that "his letters to various ecclesiastics confer great benefit on their readers."[72] François de Rivo in the chronicle of Cluny, which was compiled about 1500, used the letters extensively in his account of the history of Cluny during the abbacy of Peter the Venerable and gave an elaborate description of the collection.

He wrote various letters of such importance and in so exalted a style that he appears to be another Augustine in his description of the Holy Places. The book of his letters is principally divided into six books. The first book contains thirty-six letters; the second contains fifty-one; the third contains seven; the fourth contains forty-three; the fifth contains nine; the sixth contains fifty. Among these he inserted the treatise ... against the inveterate obstinacy of the Jews ... Peter the Venerable also inserted the book which he collected and wrote against the Petrobrusian heretics.[73]

The manuscript described here was in the library at Cluny but has since disappeared. The description shows, however, that in its final form the collection of Peter the Venerable included both his letters and treatises.

3. WRITING, SEALING, AND SENDING

Peter the Venerable regarded letters as the most reliable method of transacting business at a distance and of communicating with friends

---

[69] This may be the collection mentioned by Nicholas of Montiéramey in Letter 153, cited above, telling Peter the Venerable that he was sending "your letters."
[70] Leclercq, *Études,* p. 88.
[71] Delisle, *Fonds,* p. 361, no. 388. On this catalogue, see Giles Constable, "Petri Venerabilis sermones tres," *Rev. Bén.,* LXIV (1954) 230, n. 1.
[72] *Ampl. Coll.,* VI, 1193 D.
[73] *Bibl. Clun.,* cols. 590–591.

whom he could not visit in person.[74] He made use of oral messages only in matters of extreme urgency and secrecy. In about 1137 he wrote to Bernard of Clairvaux: "I am thankful that you have shown yourself not unmindful of a friend by the greeting [you have] frequently sent through various people, but I am sorry that you have not yet given more certain signs in the form of letters. I have said 'more certain' because a sheet is unable to change the words imprinted upon it, whereas a speaker's tongue often changes by adding and subtracting the truth that has been imposed upon it."[75] In 1138 he wrote Letter 69 to his friend Hato of Troyes, excusing his delay in writing and saying: "I could have loaded oral messages onto someone, but I preferred to transfer what I had to send you out of my own heart into yours [that is, by this letter] rather than out of the mouth of someone else... Words that are conveyed to the hearts of others through foreign ears have a way of increasing, changing, or losing their true meaning, which is either misunderstood, or neglected, or distorted by the ignorance, carelessness, or assiduity of the messenger."

The writing of letters was slow work in classical and medieval times, and all writers knew the distinction between writing (*scribere*) and composing (*dictare*). Writing was the work of the hand, Peter the Venerable wrote in Letter 26, composing, of the heart; and Bernard of Clairvaux in one of his letters to the canon Oger said: "Let our wits (*ingenia*) have a rest from dictating, our lips from talking, our fingers from writing, and our messengers from running to and fro."[76] Very few men of affairs had the time, or even the necessary skill, to prepare the wax tablets, papyrus, or parchment and the pen and ink and to write and seal a letter.[77] This was the work of professional secretaries

---

[74] He suggested in Letter 3 that he transacted business by letter because he was prevented by ill-health from traveling in person.

[75] Letter 65 (I, 194).

[76] Bernard, ep. 90 (Gaume ed., I.1, 263-264).

[77] On these physical aspects of letter writing, see esp. Wilhelm Wattenbach, *Das Schriftwesen im Mittelalter*, 3rd ed. (Leipzig, 1896); Lesne, *Prop. ecc.*, IV; Leo Santifaller, *Beiträge zur Geschichte der Schreibstoffe im Mittelalter*, I (MIÖG, Ergänzungsband XVI.1; Graz-Cologne, 1953); and, more briefly, Leclercq, *Amour des lettres*, p. 171.Writing was hard work in antiquity and the Middle Ages and was considered by many to be incompatible with the intellectual effort required of an author: see Eligius Dekkers, "Les autographes des Pères latins," *Colligere Fragmenta: Festschrift Alban Dold* (Texte und Arbeiten herausgegeben durch die Erzabtei Beuron, I.2; Beuron, 1952) p. 131. Dekkers emphasized that most of the Fathers dictated their works and very rarely (except as a form of physical mortification) wrote with their own hands; and he suggested that the same was true in the Middle Ages (p. 139, n. 100: "De nombreux manuscrits, réputés autographes, ne résistent pas à un examen quelque peu approfondi."). On the ability of monks to write in the late Middle Ages, see Alfred Wendehorst, "Monachus scribere nesciens," *MIÖG*, LXXI (1963) 67-75, who pointed out that " die Beherrschung der 'ars scribendi' hatte in der Schätzung des Mittelalters offensichtlich auch wenig mit Bildung zu tun" (p. 71), and that the Cistercians in particular maintained a certain reserve with regard to writing (p. 72).

and scribes, and the terms *notare* and *scribere* included both the taking of notes and the actual writing of a letter. "To tell you the truth," wrote a monk of Bec to a friend in England, "I suffer constantly from such weakness of the head that it would be easier for me to compose (*dictare*) rather than write (*notare*) even this very page."[78] The creative work of composition might be either to oneself, if the author himself wrote as he composed, or to a secretary, and it might be in the form either of a finished version or of notes, from which the secretary drafted the actual letter.[79] Thus Bernard of Clairvaux wrote to Peter the Venerable, as an excuse for a harshly worded letter, that "the mass of my work is to blame, because when my scribes do not remember my meaning properly, they sharpen their pens beyond measure, and I am unable to see what I ordered to be written."[80] Most writers dictated in full, however, or at least read over what their secretaries had written. In the introduction to the letter collection of Gervase of Prémontré, his secretary Hugh explained that he was accustomed "to write down in his [Gervase's] presence the letters which he composed" and that he had "put together some letters composed by him and written by me."[81]

[78] Leclercq, in *Analecta mon.*, II, 164.

[79] Writing in antiquity, and to a lesser extent in the Middle Ages, was usually "aloud": see Josef Balogh, "Voces paginarum," *Philologus*, LXXXII (1926–27) 204–220, who said that "writing out loud for men of antiquity was a 'talk with oneself' or a 'conversation of the hand with the paper'" (p. 214). On the meaning of *dictare* in the Middle Ages, see Wattenbach, *Schriftwesen*, pp. 457–458; Lesne, *Prop. ecc.*, IV, 353–354; Leclercq, *Recueil*, pp. 3–25, esp. p. 24, and in *Analecta mon.*, II, 147; and Reindel, in *Deutsches Archiv*, XV, 52–53 (with further references). These scholars have pointed out that "to dictate" in the Middle Ages often meant "to compose" (but cf. Dekkers, in *Colligere Fragmenta*, p. 127, n. 3, who said that he knew no certain example of such usage in patristic Latin). Alcuin thus described holy authors as writing at the dictation of God, *dictante deo*: carmina LXVI (line 4) and LXIX (line 15), in MGH, *Poetae latini aevi carolini*, I, 285 and 288, cited by Curtius, *Literature*, p. 314. Peter Damiani dictated to scribes or notaries: "Pas plus que la plupart des auteurs de son temps," said Leclercq, *Pierre Damien* (cited n. 8 above), p. 155, "il n'écrit lui-même: il confie le geste graphique à un scribe de métier; lui-même est celui qui compose, le *dictator*." (Cf. also Reindel, in *Deutsches Archiv*, XV, 52–53.) Guibert of Nogent, *Vita*, I, 15 (*ed. cit.*, p. 54), described himself as dictating (that is, composing) in bed. Abbot William of St. Père at Chartres said in a document of *ca*. 1109: "Hoc instrumentum ipse dictando sine fuco composui": *Cartulaire de l'abbaye de Saint-Père de Chartres*, ed. Benjamin Guérard (Paris, 1840) II, 417. William of Newburgh mentioned that he had "dictated" his commentary on the Song of Songs onto wax tablets and had copied it onto parchment himself: William of Newburgh, *Explanatio sacri epithalamii in matrem sponsi*, ed. John C. Gormon (Fribourg, 1960) p. 364. Bernard said that he had dictated letters 304, 307, and 310 (Gaume ed., I.1, 587, 591, and 595). According to A. H. Bredero, *Études sur la " Vita prima" de Saint Bernard* (Rome, 1960) p. 110, n. 1, Bernard wrote these letters with his own hand as evidence either of his affection or of their authenticity. He probably meant, however, that he had dictated the entire letter, not just notes, to his scribe and that his correspondent would recognize his style. On the practice in antiquity of scribes writing letters on the basis of instructions only, see Wikenhauser, *New Testament Introduction*, p. 347.

[80] Letter 148 = Bernard, ep. 387 (Gaume ed., I.1, 694); cf. Leclercq, *Recueil*, pp. 6–7.

[81] Cheney, in *Bull. J. Rylands Lib.*, XXXIII, 29–30. Erdmann, in *Archiv f. Urk.*, XVI, 252–253,

Most of the letters of Peter the Venerable were probably drawn up in their finished form by Peter of Poitiers or another secretary, but there is evidence that occasionally he wrote with his own hand. He complained in Letter 26 to Peter of Poitiers that "worldly business has completely engrossed me and has refused to free either my heart to compose (*dictare*) or my hand to write." He likewise wrote in the prefatory letter to the *Contra Petrobrusianos* that many important occupations had kept his mind from composing (*dictando*) and his pen from writing.[82] As a rule, however, he used a scribe. In an early letter to Hato of Troyes he wrote: "Both awkwardness in composing (*dictandi*) and lack of scribes impose a new silence on the tongue and idleness on the hands; [there are] no pens in the reeds, no quills in the birds, no skins on the beasts."[83] In Letter 28 he made interesting use of the distinction between composing and writing in order to justify the Cluniac interpretation of the Benedictine rule. The Holy Spirit was the *dictator*, he said, and St. Benedict only the *notarius*. "Just as it would be illogical to say that a notary is injured if a dictator, for a reason known perhaps only to himself, has what he had previously written changed either by himself or by someone else; so likewise it does not follow that St. Benedict is injured if for some reason he changed either by himself, if he would so wish, or by another, since he wished it so, either all or some of the things that Love wrote through him."[84] An author thus wrote through a scribe, and Peter the Venerable composed through his secretary. Whether he dictated at length or in brief is not known. The complaint in Letter 129, cited above, that his work against the heretics was not "in the form that it was conceived and produced from my own heart" may suggest that the secretary had failed to express properly Peter's ideas. He certainly read through and revised his letters, however, before they were published in his letter collection.[85]

Since no original letters by Peter the Venerable are known, their form can be derived only from analogous original letters of the twelfth century. Even these are exceedingly rare, since medieval archives were strictly utilitarian and personal letters were better preserved in copies than in the original, and the few surviving examples are mostly much

---

raised the important question of whether the scribes used for writing letters also drew up official documents, and concluded, with regard to the letters of Henry IV, that they were written by regular chancery scribes and that there was no special branch of the chancery concerned with letter writing. This is probably also true of St. Bernard, but there may have been some specialization of service among the scribes of prolific authors.

[82] *Bibl. Clun.*, col. 1117 D.
[83] Letter 5 (I, 10).
[84] Letter 28 (I, 98).
[85] See pp. 41–44, below.

shorter than Peter's letters.⁸⁶ These are written on folded pieces of parchment and resemble the official documents called *litterae clausae* or *brevis* (*breve*), which were also written on oblong, folded slips of parchment.⁸⁷ An original letter of about 1188 in the Salm-Horstmar Archives at Coesfeld is on an oblong strip of parchment folded three times, first lengthwise and twice crosswise, forming a small package that was then pierced, laced with a string, and probably sealed with a pendant or impressed seal. Unfolded it looks like this:

This form resembles in its essentials that of the original letters in the capitulary archives of Sant'Ambrogio at Milan.⁸⁸ These are mostly of the middle of the twelfth century and are written on oblong pieces of parchment, of varying thickness and quality, and ranging from narrow strips to almost square.⁸⁹ The letters were folded, as a rule lengthwise first and then crosswise, into small rectangles, and about a third were punched with holes for sealing. A few, including most of the sealed letters, show signs of an address. Those without addresses also show no signs of sealing and may have been carried by confidential messengers. The full name of the recipient appears only if there is an address. Initials alone were used in the salutations at the beginnings of

⁸⁶ On the rarity of original personal letters from the Middle Ages, see Giry, *Manuel*, p. 810, and Hoffmann, in *Spiegel der Geschichte*, pp. 147 and 149–150 (citing a few examples). Cf. L. Schmitz, "Zwei Original-Briefe von c. 1188," MIÖG, XXIV (1903) 345–352, who stressed that the two original letters at Coesfeld (of which only one is certainly original) are of particular value, owing to the rarity of originals, "because our knowledge of the outer form of letters, as of the way they were closed, is in general very slight up until the thirteenth century, when their number gradually grows." Originals even of semiofficial royal missive letters are almost equally rare. Three of Emperor Henry IV and two of Henry V are known: Erdmann, in *Archiv f. Urk.*, XVI, 186–187. The oldest known original Capetian letter (Louis VII in *ca.* 1146) is discussed by C. Higounet, in *BEC*, CXIX (1961) 241–243. There is an interesting chapter on letter writing in the fifteenth century, based principally on original letters in the Paston collection, in H. S. Bennett, *The Pastons and Their England*, 2nd ed. (Cambridge, Eng., 1932) pp. 114–127.

⁸⁷ Wattenbach, *Schriftwesen*, p. 201.

⁸⁸ Portfolio "Secolo XII. 1181–1200," folder 31; cf. Wache, in MÖIG, L, 261–333, esp. pp. 322–324 on the outer form of the letters.

⁸⁹ They range from about 21.5 × 13.5 cm and 26 × 8.5 cm for the larger ones; 14.5 × 3 cm and 11.5 × 5.5 cm for the smaller ones; 18.5/19 × 13/14 cm and 13 × 17 cm for the squarer ones.

the letters. Although most of these are shorter than all but the shortest letters of Peter the Venerable, longer letters were probably drawn up in the same way on a larger scale.

The commonest method of sealing letters in the Middle Ages was either, as seen above, by a string or thong passed around or through holes in the document and closed by a pendant or impressed seal, or by the method known as *sur simple queue*, by which, according to R. L. Poole, "a strip was cut from the lower margin nearly to the left edge; the document was folded small, the strip folded round it, and the seal imposed upon this."[90] To open a letter sealed in this way, the string or strip had to be cut, and no known example of a closed sealed private letter has survived from the Middle Ages.[91] The necessity of breaking the seal was the distinguishing mark of the letter "close" as distinct from the letter "patent," which might also be sealed *sur simple queue* if the strip was not folded around the letter and the seal was left hanging. For private correspondence, however, the letter close had the advantages of being more confidential, of requiring less wax for the seal, and above all of being small and easy to carry. Most scholars are therefore of the opinion that private letters in the Middle Ages, when they were sealed at all, were as a rule sent "close."[92]

The few references to sealing in the letters of Peter the Venerable and his contemporaries tend to confirm this view, though it is not always clear that the seal closed the letter. Bernard of Clairvaux always sealed his personal letters,[93] and Peter of Celle used the term *sigilla* as

---

[90] Poole, *Studies*, p. 94. He was apparently of the opinion (pp. 109-110) that the method *sur simple queue* predominated for private letters and that the method of closing the folded document with a separate strip or string came in only in the late thirteenth century. The examples cited above show that it was in fact already common in the twelfth century. On the seals used for private letters in the Middle Ages, see E. Kittel, H. Beumann, and Carl Erdmann, "Das Briefsiegel Heinrichs von Glinde," *Deutsches Archiv*, III (1939) 413-429, esp. pp. 424-429 ("Die Briefsiegel des hohen Mittelalters"), by Erdmann, who pointed out that the inscription on Henry's seal ("Accipe frange lege claude repone tege") shows that it was intended to be broken when the letter was opened, and who discussed generally the seals used for letters as distinct from those used for charters; also Hoffmann, in *Spiegel der Geschichte*, pp. 157-160. On the sealing of letters in the fourth and fifth centuries, see Gorce, *Voyages*, pp. 235-236.

[91] Poole, *Studies*, p. 94. V. H. Galbraith, *Studies in the Public Records* (Edinburgh, 1948) p. 73, however, mentioned an unopened Elizabethan letter close.

[92] Giry, *Manuel*, p. 751; Poole, *Studies*, p. 109; and Galbraith, *Public Records*, p. 73. This view has recently been questioned by Higounet, in *BEC*, CXIX, 241-243, on the basis of an original letter of Louis VII (*ca.* 1146), which was sealed *sur simple queue* and shows no signs of having been closed. But this letter was more or less official in character. On the closed and open letters of Henry IV, see Erdmann, in *Archiv f. Urk.*, XVI, 184-195, who described in detail the three surviving originals and concluded (p. 194) that closed were much more frequent than open letters.

[93] Bernard, epp. 284 (cf. Appendix Q), 298, 304 ("Sigillum non erat ad manum; sed qui legit, agnoscat stilum, quia ipse dictaui."), and 402 ("Maneries locutionis pro sigillo sit, quia ad manum non erat, nam neque Gaufridus uester.") (Gaume ed., I.1, 569-570 ,581-582,

a synonym for *epistola*,[94] in the same way that papal documents were later named for the *bulla* with which they were sealed. The correspondence between Peter the Venerable and Heloise stresses the distinction between letters patent and close. In Letter 167 Heloise asked Peter: "Please send me another sealed document (*sigillum*) in which the absolution of the master [Abelard] will be in an open letter (*litteris apertis*), so that it may be hung on his tomb." Peter replied in Letter 168 that he was sending a "written and sealed" grant of a trental and "also the absolution of master Peter, as you requested, written in a charter and sealed in similar fashion." He had apparently sent the original absolution for Abelard in a closed letter, of which the seal was broken when it was opened, and Heloise therefore asked for an open copy which could be placed on his tomb. Peter sent this written and sealed like the charter granting the trental.

The carriage and delivery of letters presented many problems in the Middle Ages,[95] and Peter the Venerable often referred in his letters to the *latores, portitores, cursores, legati,* and *nuntii*. He seems to have used these terms almost interchangeably,[96] but in practice he used two basic types of messenger. The first, and less important, was a traveler who happened to be going in the direction of the addressee and was willing to take an oral or written message. He might be a student, merchant, pilgrim, or minstrel, all of whom abounded at Cluny, or a man of high rank, to whom an important letter could be entrusted. Such a messenger was the precentor Drogo of Nevers, who on his third visit to the Holy Land carried Peter's letters to the monks of Mt.

587, and 719). Letters to more than one person were, of course, not closed with a seal. "You are getting a closed letter," Bernard wrote to Bishop Jocelyn of Soissons in ep. 223 (Gaume ed., I.1, 455), "because you were suspicious of the previous open one. But I had nothing else in mind except that it is necessary, according to custom, not to close with wax a letter written to several people (*ad diuersos*)." Cf. Valois, *De arte*, p. 9; Hoffmann, in *Spiegel der Geschichte*, pp. 163-164 (on the interpretation of the passage in ep. 304); and, on Bernard's seal, Vacandard, *St. Bernard*, II, 543-549. On monastic seals generally, see Giacomo Bascapè, "Appunti di sfragistica benedettina," *Rassegna degli Archivi di Stato*, XXI (1961) 158-184, esp. pp. 175-179, on Cistercian, and pp. 179-181, on Cluniac seals.

[94] Peter of Celle, ep. I, 13 (former I, 15), in PL, CCII, 415 C; cf. Valois, *De arte*, p. 9.

[95] On the carrying of letters, see Gorce, *Voyages*, pp. 205-225; Marc Bloch, *La société féodale: La formation des liens de dépendance* (L'évolution de l'humanité, 34; Paris, 1949) pp. 104-105, and, for the fourteenth century, Yves Renouard, "Comment les papes d'Avignon expédiaient leur courrier," *Revue historique*, CLXXX (1937) 1-29, and E. H. Wilkins, "On the Carriage of Petrarch's Letters," *Speculum*, XXXV (1960) 214-223. A secret letter from the prior of Ste.-Barbe to Empress Mathilda was carried hidden in the thick beard of a *conversus*: ed. R.-Norbert Sauvage, "La Chronique de Sainte-Barbe-en-Auge," *Mémoires de l'Académie nationale des sciences, arts et belles-lettres de Caen: Documents*, 1906, p. 51.

[96] Generally speaking, I have translated *portitor* and *lator* as "the bearer"; *cursor*, as "courier"; and *nuntius* and *legatus*, as "messenger," which implies slightly more of the status of an envoy. Peter himself more or less equated *cursores* and *nuntii* in Letter 55, *legatus* and *nuntius* in Letter 65, and *cursor* and *portitor* in Letter 81. Letter 15 suggests that he used a *cursor* when speed was necessary.

Thabor and to the king and patriarch of Jerusalem.[97] Peter also wrote some letters *ad hoc* to be taken by chance travelers. Such carriers were often slow and unreliable, however; they might lose letters and forge oral messages, like the *referentes* of whose carelessness Peter complained in Letter 69; and he probably used them as little as possible.

Most of Peter's letters were carried by professional messengers, men whose sole duty was to deliver a letter, sometimes together with an oral message, and to bring back a reply.[98] Some of these may have been more or less public couriers, who worked for various employers, but the majority were probably used by a single writer. In Letter 5 to Hato of Troyes, Peter the Venerable described the "frequent messengers" carrying successive letters between himself and Hato and "coming and going on the public road from Troyes to Cluny."[99] He wrote to Henry of Winchester in Letter 55: "I would have sent you a monk and not a courier, had I not feared to annoy the sacristan, who was about to leave. Since you have now received my courier twice, send back your messenger at least once. For they come to Marcigny, go to Lyons, enter Provence, and wander everywhere hither and yon; they avoid only Cluny, like the dogs of Scylla and the craggy peaks."[100] Peter also had couriers of his own. Nicholas of Montiéramey on one occasion asked Peter to reply "by the bearer of the present letter," but Peter refused to send more than an acknowledgment: "I was afraid that a foreign courier, hurrying back, might not carry out his orders fully or in the way I wished. I therefore sent this one back with this brief note almost as soon as I received that letter. I shall forthwith send my own [courier], who will not dare to neglect any of his instructions and will follow you and the abbot of Clairvaux wherever you may go."[101] The names of a few of these couriers are known.[102] In Letter 69 Peter mentioned using "one of the priors who surround me" as a messenger to Rome, perhaps for important business, but they were

[97] Letters 80, 82, and 83. Bernard probably had a casual messenger of this sort in mind when he excused his delay in replying to the canon Oger because "the opportunity of a messenger was lacking": ep. 87 (Gaume ed., I.1, 252).

[98] Cf. Brooke, in John of Salisbury, *Letters*, I, introd., xlv: "There was a class of professional couriers [in the twelfth century] who must have been men of efficiency and remarkable endurance." On professional couriers used by the popes in the fourteenth century, see Renouard, in *Rev. hist.*, CLXXX, 16–28.

[99] In Letter 18 Peter mentioned how Hato's messenger had followed him from Cluny to Souvigny.

[100] The precise meaning of the first sentence is uncertain. Henry may have asked for some monk who was needed at Cluny while the sacristan was away, or perhaps the sacristan would have been offended if a monk had been sent with a message that he himself might have carried.

[101] Letters 179–180. On at least one occasion, however, Peter used the messenger who had brought him a letter to carry back the reply: "Do not blame the courier that he has delayed so long," he wrote in Letter 193, "but me, and excuse him to the others."

[102] See Appendix R on officials and functionaries at Cluny.

mostly comparatively obscure members of his household. Thus Peter referred to the messenger who brought him the news of his mother's death, while he was on his way back from the Council of Pisa in 1135, as a *domesticus*. "He gave me the funereal letter when I least expected such news," he wrote in Letter 53, "for I recognized the messenger as a *domesticus*, and I presumed that from there no evil news could come."

Peter the Venerable had on the whole a low opinion of the reliability of most messengers, and there are several references in his letters to lost letters and garbled messages.[103] "I heard that the letter was brought by someone," he wrote in Letter 22 to Hato of Troyes, "but in spite of diligent investigation I was unable either to see the letter or to find its bearer." For pressing and secret business, therefore, Peter often urged his correspondents to come in person. "Come to me quickly," he told Peter of Poitiers in Letter 26, "in order that I may entrust to the ears of a safe friend what I have not dared to put down in writing, which is often untrustworthy." And in Letter 51 he asked Hugh Catula "to come to your true friend with the bearer of this letter, so that I may tell you by word of mouth what I do not want to send in this letter."

It was a common practice in the Middle Ages to send secret messages by word of mouth. "In very many cases," wrote Stubbs, "the letters were little more than credentials. The real news was carried by the bearer of the letter, and the real force of the communication was not in the postscript, we may say, but in the postman."[104] This oral element was of great importance in ancient as well as in medieval epistolography. John Chadwick said of letters in linear B, for example: "If we may judge from contemporary letters in other languages, a letter at this date was still in form if not in practice, an instruction to the messenger. At Ugarit, for instance, the regular formula at the beginning of a letter is like this: 'To the king, my master, say . . .' "[105] The terms *nuntius* and *epistola* were more or less equated in the *Digest*, and the lawyer Azo in the thirteenth century described a *nuntius* as "he who takes the place of a letter: he is just like a magpie and the voice of the principal sending him . . . and he recites the words of the principal."[106] According to Valois in his study of medieval French epistolography, "messengers were frequently commissioned to explain orally a matter briefly

---

[103] See Gorce, *Voyages*, pp. 232–234, for the opinions of Jerome and Sidonius on the unreliability of messengers. On losses of Petrarch's letters, see Wilkins, in *Speculum*, XXXV, 220–221.

[104] Stubbs, *Seventeen Lectures* (cited n. 3 above), p. 147.

[105] John Chadwick, *The Decipherment of Linear B* (New York, [1959]) p. 131.

[106] Donald E. Queller, "Thirteenth-Century Diplomatic Envoys: *Nuncii* and *Procuratores*," *Speculum*, XXXV (1960) 199.

treated in the letter, either to save space or to conceal a secret which might be discovered by enemies."[107]

These instructions are tantalizing and baffling to the modern reader of these letters. "Since the bearer of this letter is well known to you," wrote John of Salisbury, "I have omitted from the writing many things that deserve to be told and have entrusted them to his faith to be told you more secretly."[108] Writing to King Henry II in the name of Archbishop Theobald of Canterbury, John of Salisbury said that he had told the bearer to open to the King the books of his conscience and urged Henry "not to doubt that what you receive from him has come from our own heart."[109] Injunctions of this sort occur frequently in the letters of Bernard of Clairvaux: "The bearer of this letter will explain other things to you more fully"; and "My Nicholas, who is also yours, will report better by word of mouth the other things that he saw and heard"; and others.[110] And so on throughout the Middle Ages. Petrarch often entrusted oral messages to his messengers.[111] The Pastons did likewise in the fifteenth century. "You shall give credence to the bringer of this letter," wrote the earl of Oxford; and Margaret Paston said that "Pecock shall tell you by mouth of more things than I may write to you at this time."[112] No wonder that the written letters were frequently vapid!

Peter the Venerable also sent secret messages by word of mouth of his messengers, in spite of his distrust of their memories. His letters include many references to the tongues and mouths of messengers, and his complaints show that he was often forced to rely upon them. "But I do not wish to insert that into this letter I am sending," he wrote in Letter 68 to the count of Savoy, "because you will be able to hear it better from the mouth of the messenger than from the hand of the writer." To Bernard of Clairvaux he said in Letter 73: "I recently wrote at greater length; now I send a shorter letter, which is tongueless, because it rests in the tongue of the bearer and its only cause was to send the reader to the bearer and to advise that what the letter held back should be sought from him. When you have read this, therefore, ask the bearer to tell you what is here kept silent, and hear from him what you can [hear] neither from me nor from them. He of

---

[107] Valois, *De arte*, p. 7, citing John of Salisbury and Peter of Celle. Cf. Gorce, *Voyages*, pp. 214–215, and Hoffmann, in *Spiegel der Geschichte*, pp. 145–147.

[108] John of Salisbury, ep. 261, in *PL*, CXCIX, 302; cf. his epp. 234–235, 228–229, and 273, in *PL*, CXCIX, 263–264, 256–259, and 312.

[109] John of Salisbury, *Letters*, I, 217, no. 125. John frequently used pseudonyms and cryptic salutations in order to conceal the identities of his correspondents. On special "keys" of this sort, see Hoffmann, in *Spiegel der Geschichte*, pp. 164–168.

[110] Bernard, epp. 336 and 338 (Gaume ed., I.1, 627 and 632); cf. his ep. 189 (*ibid.*, p. 414).

[111] Wilkins, in *Speculum*, XXXV, 222.

[112] Cited, with similar examples, by Bennett, *Pastons*, pp. 121–122.

whom I speak is Gebuin, who is very well known and, I believe, very dear to me and to you." In Letter 164 to Bernard, Peter wrote: "I have in part secretly told the reason for their coming [that is, the meeting of Cluniac priors in 1150] to the venerable abbot of Fontanel, who brought me your letter and from whom, if you wish, you can hear it." He wrote to Suger that he had placed in the mouth of Hugh of Crécy "a certain secret that I do not wish to put into writing ... [and] which I have sent to you so that you may also know it and act with caution as seems wise to you."[113] There are similar phrases in letters to Hato of Troyes, Henry of Winchester, and Pope Eugene III;[114] and in Letter 34 to Cardinal Haimeric, Peter gave "the absence of the tongue of a mediating messenger (*mediatoris nuntii*)" as one of his reasons for writing so long a letter.

The oral element was also very important in the delivery of written letters. It was common in the Middle Ages not only for the recipient to read the letter aloud to himself but also for the messenger to read the letter to the recipient.[115] Peter the Venerable began Letter 2 to Matthew of Albano: "Hearing your messengers (*nuntios*), reading your letters ..."; and he wrote to Nicholas of Montiéramey in Letter 151: "I am writing a letter to the abbot of Clairvaux, which I want to be presented to him through you. Read it to him earnestly and carefully and urge as strongly as you can that something should be done about what I have written purely out of love." It is not always clear in these cases whether the letter was read aloud and then given to the recipient or whether, as seems to have been the case in antiquity, the letter simply formed the basis of the messenger's speech and was never physically handed over. This practice may explain the presence in some medieval letter collections of apparently original letters brought back by the messenger. In particular it may explain the puzzling passage in Letter 34, in which Peter discussed an alleged fraud by the Cluniacs and said that he could not discover the guilty party: "I only remember that from St. Ambrose I sent a courier to the

---

[113] *Bibl. Clun.*, col. 959; cf. Appendix O.

[114] Letters 61, 81, 86, 107, and 174.

[115] In both antiquity and the Middle Ages, reading was as a rule aloud. *Legere* and *audire* were used as synonyms; *tacite legere* was used for the modern custom of reading silently to oneself. See Balogh, in *Philologus*, LXXXII, 84-109 and 202-240 (citing, among others, on pp. 92-93, Plutarch to show that private letters were read aloud even when other people were present); Leclercq, in *Analecta mon.*, II, 147-148; Francesco di Capua, *Scritti minori* (Rome, 1959) II, 1-40, esp. pp. 6-8; and Pierre Riché, *Éducation et culture dans l'Occident barbare* (Patristica Sorbonensia, 4; Paris, 1962) pp. 158 and 514. Laymen in the eleventh and twelfth centuries were rarely able to read and expected to have letters read to them: see Herbert Grundmann, "Litteratus-Illiteratus," *Archiv für Kulturgeschichte*, XL (1958) 45-46, who cited as an exception Count Palatine Frederick (d. 1088), of whom it was said that he was sufficiently educated at Fulda "ut epistolas transmissas per se legeret et intelligeret" (*MGH, Scriptores* in fol., X, 148).

lord pope and to you [Cardinal Haimeric] and that by him I sent a document (*capitulum*) written in these words, as I later discovered from the self-same parchment that I sent." After quoting from this document, he went on to ask: "Who, I ask, could have perpetrated this fraud? If the courier, it is amazing that such an insignificant man could have deceived such experienced judges."[116] This passage suggests that the courier may have delivered the *capitulum* as a speech and then brought it back. The section quoted by Peter sounds more like a series of notes for oral delivery by the messenger than a finished letter to the Pope.

Finally, the speed, or rather slowness, of travel was an important factor in the writing and delivery of letters. R. L. Poole estimated on the basis of the early letters of John of Salisbury and other English sources that the journey from Rome to Canterbury in the twelfth century usually took about seven weeks, although "it was possible that news should be brought from Rome in twenty-nine days in a matter of extreme urgency."[117] The abbot of St. Albans returned to his abbey from Rome in about five weeks in 1156;[118] the abbot of Evesham took forty days to travel from Evesham to Rome in 1204;[119] and Cheney cited an exceptionally quick journey of twenty-five days from Rome to Canterbury in 1188.[120] Both Jacob and Cheney accepted seven to eight weeks as the normal time needed for the trip.[121] It is harder to find reliable evidence for the Continent. According to Bloch, an average traveler covered between thirty and forty kilometers a day, and a courier could travel at least twice as quickly.[122] A letter from Rome to Goslar in the dead of winter in 1075 took twenty-three days.[123] Nicholas of Montiéramey allowed four days to travel from

---

[116] On this case, see Constable, "Cluniac Tithes," pp. 614–615. It may be that the tongue of a messenger, upon the absence of which Peter blamed the length of this letter, was to deliver the entire contents orally, not only the confidential sections.

[117] Poole, *Studies*, pp. 263–264.

[118] Giles Constable, "The Alleged Disgrace of John of Salisbury in 1159," *English Historical Review*, LXIX (1954) 69.

[119] Knowles, *Monastic Order*, p. 337.

[120] C. R. Cheney, *From Becket to Langton* (Ford Lectures, 1955; Manchester, 1956) p. 62. This is an average of 43 miles a day, which is very fast indeed. Christina of Markyate, fleeing at top speed from Huntingdon to Flamstead, covered 30 miles in about six hours: *The Life of Christina of Markyate*, ed. and trans. C. H. Talbot (Oxford, 1959) pp. 92–93.

[121] E. F. Jacob, "To and from the Court of Rome in the Early Fifteenth Century," *Studies . . . Presented to Professor Mildred K. Pope* (Manchester, 1939) p. 168.

[122] Bloch, *Société féodale*, I, 100. Urban T. Holmes, Jr., *Daily Living in the Twelfth Century* (Madison, 1952) pp. 19 and 222, estimated the speed of travel in the twelfth century as 35 miles a day in England and 15–20 miles a day from France to Italy. Cf. for the later Middle Ages, Renouard, in *Rev. hist.*, CLXXX, 28–29, and J. Lestocquoy, "Comment on voyageait au Moyen Age," *Le monde français*, XVII (1950) 56–57.

[123] Bloch, *Société féodale*, I, 100. A winter trip from Arras to Rome in 1093–94 took from 29 December to 19 February: Lestocquoy, in *Monde français*, XVII, 57.

Montiéramey to Rheims, which is about a hundred and fifteen kilometers as the crow flies and considerably further by road.[124]

These indications roughly agree with the indications in the letters of Peter the Venerable. Letter 34 suggests that it took an express messenger about three weeks in early winter to travel from Cluny to Italy (probably Pisa).[125] The letter with the news of the election of Pope Celestine II, which was written on 3 November 1143, reached Cluny on 30 November, a total of twenty-four days, which Peter apparently regarded as slow because he apologized in Letter 112 to the Pope for the lateness of his reply. According to Letter 69, however, a messenger was away from Cluny on a mission to Rome from 11 November 1137 until 6/12 March of the following year, making about eight weeks each way, not allowing for his stay in Rome. Solemn embassies were naturally much slower than single messengers. Letters 62 and 63 show that between 20 July 1137 and 3 April 1138 two successive embassies traveled from Cluny to Rome and back, which gives an average of nine weeks for each one-way trip, again not allowing for delays at either end.[126] The speed of travel naturally varied according to the season, local conditions, and the type of travelers; and there were often long delays in transacting business, particularly at Rome. Peter the Venerable himself, who usually traveled with a considerable retinue, doubtless went much more slowly than his couriers; but even the fastest messengers traveled very slowly by modern standards, and the letters and messages they carried were subject to innumerable hazards. This delay and uncertainty of communications is a basic factor in all medieval correspondence.

4. STYLE

The art of writing letters in the Middle Ages was governed by the rules known collectively as the *dictamen* or *ars dictandi*, the art of composing. Starting from the books of formulas drawn up principally for the convenience of notaries, these rules were first formulated in Italy in the second half of the eleventh century; and in the twelfth century numerous handbooks of epistolary style were written, usually accompanied by collections of model letters designed to illustrate the theoretical precepts of the treatise.[127] In these works the masters of

---

[124] Nicholas of Montiéramey, ep. 57, in *PL*, CXCVI, 1653.
[125] Constable, "Cluniac Tithes," p. 615.
[126] Constable, "Langres," pp. 142-143.
[127] On medieval formularies and *dictamen*, see the works of Ludwig Rockinger, in particular *Briefsteller und Formelbücher des eilften bis vierzehnten Jahrhunderts* (Quellen und Erörterungen zur bayerischen und deutschen Geschichte, IX.1-2; Munich, 1863-64); Langlois, "Formulaires" (bibliography in I, 7, n. 1); Bresslau, *Urkundenlehre*, II, 225-297 (bibliography

dictamen were generally concerned with two aspects of letter writing: the form and the language in which a well-composed letter should be written. The form usually consisted of five parts, which were described by Haskins as

the salutation, a point upon which mediaeval etiquette was very severe, the form of address being elaborately fixed for each dignity and station in society; the exordium, or *captatio benevolentie,* designed to put the reader in the right frame of mind and often consisting of a proverb or scriptural quotation; the narrative or exposition; the petition, for a request was always expected and was likely to take the form of a logical deduction from the major and minor premises already laid down in the exordium and narration; and finally the conclusion.[128]

The second, and more difficult, aspect of correct epistolary style was the proper choice of words and their arrangement in such a way as to obtain the utmost effect of dignity and beauty. This was the discipline of the *cursus*,[129] which was often considered not only a branch but also the most important, and even the sole, aspect of *dictamen*.[130] The Bolognese *dictator* Master Bernard, for instance, who lived about the middle of the twelfth century, defined *dictamen* as "the harmonious and apposite statement in words of a matter which is either kept in

---

on p. 248, n. 1); and C. H. Haskins, "The Life of Mediaeval Students as Illustrated by Their Letters," and "The Early *Artes Dictandi* in Italy," in his *Mediaeval Culture*, pp. 1–35 and 170–192 (bibliographies on pp. 2, n. 2, and 6, n. 2). There are good, brief accounts in C. H. Haskins, *The Renaissance of the Twelfth Century* (Cambridge, Mass., 1927) pp. 138–146; C. S. Baldwin, *Medieval Rhetoric and Poetic* (New York, 1928) pp. 208–227 (bibliography on pp. 206–207); De Ghellinck, *Essor*, II, 54–68 (bibliography on p. 54, n. 6); and Curtius, *Literature*, pp. 75–76 and 148 ff. There is a general bibliography in L. J. Paetow, *A Guide to the Study of Medieval History*, 2nd ed. (New York, 1931) pp. 448–452.

[128] Haskins, *Renaissance*, pp. 143–144; cf. Valois, *De arte*, pp. 52–64, and Bütow, *Briefsteller*, passim.

[129] The most lucid single account of the *cursus* is still that in the pioneering study by Noël Valois, "Étude sur le rythme des bulles pontificales," *BEC*, XLII (1881) 161–198 and 257–272. Among the many other works, see esp. Wilhelm Meyer, "Die rythmische lateinische Prosa," in his *Gesammelte Abhandlungen zur mittellateinischen Rythmik* (Berlin, 1905) II, 236–286, discussing the important book by Louis Havet on the metrical prose of Symmachus; Elphège Vacandard, "Le cursus, son origine, son histoire, son emploi dans la liturgie," *Revue des questions historiques*, LXXVIII (1905) 59–102; A. C. Clark, *Fontes prosae numerosae* (Oxford, 1909) bibliography on p. 48, and *The Cursus in Mediaeval and Vulgar Latin* (Oxford, 1910) bibliography on pp. 3–4; R. L. Poole, *Lectures on the History of the Papal Chancery down to the Time of Innocent III* (Cambridge, Eng., 1915) pp. 76–97; Bresslau, *Urkundenlehre*, II, 361–370 (bibliography on p. 361, n. 3); Di Capua, *Scritti minori*, esp. vol. I; and Gudrun Lindholm, *Studien zum mittellateinischen Prosarhythmus* (Acta Universitatis Stockholmiensis: Studia latina Stockholmiensia, 10; Stockholm, 1963). M.-G. Nicholau, *L'origine du "cursus" rythmique et les débuts de l'accent d'intensité latin* (Collection d'études latines, 5; Paris, 1930), has a final chapter on the medieval period. Karl Polheim, *Die lateinische Reimprosa* (Berlin, 1925), is concerned more with rhymed than with rhythmic prose but has sections on the *cursus* and useful bibliographies on pp. 70, 132, and 430.

[130] Valois, *De arte*, p. 70.

the mind or expressed in speech or writing."[131] Not all the early *dictatores*, it is true, laid down strict rules for the choice of words, but most of them observed such rules in their own writings; and by the late twelfth century the *cursus* had an assured place in the treatises on letter writing. At its height, there were various types of *cursus*, with differing rules, but they were all designed for the composition of elegant prose, and they applied especially to the accentual patterns and word divisions at the beginnings and ends of sentences (*clausulae*). "The *cursus* was invented," according to the famous thirteenth-century dictator Pontius of Provence, "in order that the conclusion of the period and the entire letter might be presented more suitably and handsomely."[132] The *cursus* did not apply to the middle of a sentence (except that it was considered wise to maintain a careful balance of dactyls and spondees), to quotations, to the enumeration of goods and properties, or to the formal parts of a letter, such as the address and the date, where the use of proper names might make it impossible to avoid some forbidden accentual pattern. The constant aim was to achieve a style that was sonorous and dignified without being heavy.

The work of the *dictatores*, especially at Bologna, began to control the composition of letters in Italy in the first half of the twelfth century, but their influence was hardly felt north of the Alps before 1150. "The introduction of the *ars dictaminis*" in France, said Bütow, "first occurred in the middle of the twelfth century."[133] Haskins also found that there were several Italian *artes dictandi* in France about the middle of the century.[134] It was not, however, until about 1180 that a distinct style of *dictamen* was developed in France and that the *Ars dictandi Aurelianensis* was composed.[135] This influence was centered in the schools at Orléans and Tours and, somewhat surprisingly, in the monasteries of the Cistercian order. "It is known that the abbey of Clairvaux and the monasteries which depended upon it," wrote Langlois, "together with the university towns of the Loire, were the principal schools of the *ars dictaminis* in France in the twelfth and

---

[131] Bjarne Berulfsen, "Et blad av en Summa dictaminum," *Avhandlinger utgitt av Det Norske Videnskaps-Akademi i Oslo*, Hist.-Filos. Kl., 1953, no. 3, p. 12. He goes on to say that there are two types of *dictamen*, one metrical and the other prose.

[132] Charles Thurot, "Notices et extraits de divers manuscrits latins pour servir à l'histoire des doctrines grammaticales au moyen âge," *Notices et extraits des manuscrits de la Bibliothèque impériale*, XXII.2 (1868) 481.

[133] Bütow, *Briefsteller*, pp. 9–10.

[134] Haskins, *Mediaeval Culture*, p. 190.

[135] Rockinger, *Briefsteller*, pp. 95–114; Valois, *De arte*, pp. 30–52; Bresslau, *Urkundenlehre*, II, 254–256; Haskins, *Mediaeval Culture*, pp. 190–191; Franz-Josef Schmale, "Die Bologneser Schule der Ars dictandi," *Deutsches Archiv*, XIII (1957) 16–34, who considered that the influence of the Bolognese school spread outside Italy in the later twelfth century (pp. 33–34); and Lindholm, *Prosarhythmus*, pp. 19–26, who discussed the differences between the schools of Orléans and Italy.

thirteenth centuries. St. Bernard himself knew, even if he did not follow, the skills of the *dictatores*; they were practiced in his circle."[136] The *dictamen* also reached other French monasteries before the middle of the twelfth century. In MS. Berlin Phillipps 1732 the *ars dictaminis* and formulary of Albert of Samaria, the earliest of the known Bolognese *dictatores*, appear in conjunction with a group of French letters of about 1130/50 and with the letter collection of Prior Peter of St. John at Sens, who died about 1146.[137] On the basis of this manuscript, Walther Holtzmann concluded that "a north Italian *ars dictandi*... formed the basis of the instruction in letter writing in the school of the Augustinian house of St. John at Sens."[138]

The development and spread of the *cursus*, or linguistic aspect of *dictamen*, is more difficult to trace than the influence of *dictamen* on the form of letters. This is partly owing to the obscure connections of the medieval *cursus* with the rhythmical prose of antiquity; for although it has been amply established that the former was based on accent (syllabic stress) rather than on meter (syllabic length), which governed the *clausulae* of classical authors, the exact influence of classical literary traditions on medieval prose style has not yet been fully investigated. A second source of confusion is the distinction of rhythmical from rhymed prose. Bresslau in particular stressed the difficulties of looking for rhymed prose in a language with similar case endings, where a chance similarity may appear to be an intentional rhyme.[139] In his general survey of Latin rhymed prose, however, Polheim clearly demonstrated its extensive use in the Middle Ages, and especially in the eleventh and twelfth centuries, which he called "die Hochblüte der Reimprosa."[140] Yet another difficulty is to determine the influence of the papal chancery, for the most influential rules for rhythmical prose in the Middle Ages were those of the *cursus curiae Romanae*, or

---

[136] Langlois, "Formulaires," V, 413; cf. Leclercq, in *Rev. Bén.*, LVI, 123: "Le *dictamen*, c'est-à-dire l'art d'écrire de belles lettres, était florissant à Clairvaux." There was a treatise *De scientia dictandi* in the library at Rievaulx in the twelfth century: Hoste, *Bibliotheca* (cited n. 20 above), p. 155, no. 67, and Walter Daniel referred to "the brightness of the colors of the rhetorical discipline" in his letter to Maurice justifying his *Life of Ailred of Rievaulx*, ed. F. M. Powicke (Medieval Classics; Edinburgh, 1950) p. 76.

[137] This manuscript is very fully described in *Die Handschriften-Verzeichnisse der königlichen Bibliothek zu Berlin*, XII: Valentin Rose, *Verzeichniss der lateinischen Handschriften*, I (Berlin, 1893) 409–415, and was discussed by Walther Holtzmann, "Eine oberitalienische Ars dictandi und die Briefsammlung des Priors Peter von St. Jean in Sens," *Neues Archiv*, XLVI (1925–26) 33–52; C. H. Haskins, "An Early Bolognese Formulary," *Mélanges d'histoire offerts à Henri Pirenne* (Brussels, 1926) pp. 201–210, and in *Mediaeval Culture*, pp. 174–177 and 190; and Constable, in *Petrus Ven.*, pp. 38–52. The attribution to Albert of Samaria was questioned, without specific reasons, by Erdmann, in *Neues Archiv*, XLIX (1930–1932) 386, n. 2. On Albert, see Manitius, *Lat. Lit.*, III, 305–306.

[138] Holtzmann, in *Neues Archiv*, XLVI, 48.

[139] Bresslau, *Urkundenlehre*, II, 371–372.

[140] Polheim, *Reimprosa*, p. 363; cf. pp. 88–132 and 363–435.

cursus Gregorianus, as it was later called after the dictator Albert of Morra, who became Pope Gregory VIII. It seems to have been first introduced into the papal chancery by John of Gaeta, Pope Gelasius II (1118–19),[141] who was a pupil of Alberic of Monte Cassino, the author of the earliest known treatise on *dictamen*.[142] It was increasingly used by the papal notaries during the twelfth century. Its rules were codified by Albert of Morra and his deputy Trasimund towards the end of the century, and by the time of Innocent III all papal documents were composed in accordance with its prescriptions. From this time on it can be used by scholars as a reliable indication of date and authenticity.[143] Papal scribes and documents, therefore, as well as the *dictatores*, were responsible for the spread of the *cursus*, and from an early date it influenced the style of all types of medieval literature composed both in Italy and north of the Alps.

Very little work has been done on the medieval *cursus*, on the lines, for instance, of Zielinski's fundamental statistical study of the *clausulae* in Cicero's speeches.[144] A number of doctoral theses at the Catholic University of America have examined the *clausulae* in the works of Hilary of Poitiers, Ambrose, Jerome, Augustine, Cassiodorus, and Gregory the Great, and have shown both that these authors all composed the endings of their sentences according to definite rhythmical patterns and that they spanned a period of transition from a metrical to an accentual system of Latin prose.[145] But it is impossible

---

[141] Clark, *Cursus*, p. 14; Poole, *Chancery*, pp. 83–87; and Bresslau, *Urkundenlehre*, II, 364–365; cf. also Louis Duchesne, "Note sur l'origine du 'Cursus,'" *BEC*, L (1889) 161–163, and Carl Erdmann, "Leonitas: Zur mittelalterlichen Lehre von Kursus, Rhythmus und Reim," *Corona Quernea* (cited n. 28 above), pp. 15–28.

[142] Rockinger, *Briefsteller*, pp. 1–46; Haskins, *Mediaeval Culture*, pp. 171–173; Manitius, *Lat. Lit.*, III, 300–305. On Alberic, see esp. Anselmo Lentini, "Alberico di Montecassino nel quadro della Riforma Gregoriana," *Studi Gregoriani*, IV (1952) 55–109, and "Note su Alberico Cassinese maestro di retorica," *Studi medievali*, n.s. XVIII (1952) 121–137, esp. pp. 121–127 on the *Breviarium de dictamine*, *Flores rhetorici*, and *Rationes dictandi*; and Odilo Engels, "Alberich von Montecassino und sein Schüler Johannes von Gaeta," *SMGBOZ*, LXVI (1955) 35–50, who emphasized the importance of Alberic in preparing John to introduce the *cursus* into the papal chancery.

[143] On the dangers of using the papal *cursus* as a criterion outside the field of papal diplomatics, see the review by C. de Smedt, in the *Analecta Bollandiana*, XVI (1897) 501–506, of C.-F. Bellet's *L'ancienne Vie de saint Martial et la prose rythmée* (offprint from *L'université catholique*; Paris, 1897). This is not to deny that the presence or absence of rhyme or rhythm in a particular work may not be a valuable indication of authenticity. Both Manitius and Silvestre, for instance, cited the presence of rhymed prose in the *De vita vere apostolica* as evidence that it was not written by Rupert of Deutz, who never used either rhymed prose or the *cursus*: Manitius, *Lat. Lit.*, III, 135, and Hubert Silvestre, *Le Chronicon sancti Laurentii Leodiensis dit de Rupert de Deutz* (Université de Louvain: Recueil de travaux d'histoire et de philologie, 3rd ser., 43; Louvain, 1952) p. 85.

[144] T. Zielinski, *Das Clauselgesetz in Ciceros Reden* (Leipzig, 1904); cf. the important review by A. C. Clark, in *Classical Review*, XIX (1905) 164–172.

[145] Published at Washington, D.C., since 1924 in the series Patristic Studies and Studies in Medieval and Renaissance Latin Language and Literature of the Catholic University of

to generalize about the subsequent period or to estimate exactly the influences of classical literary traditions, the works of the *dictatores*, and the practices of the papal chancery.[146] Weigle and Silvestre both stressed the use of rhythmical and rhymed prose in the letters of Ratherius of Verona, in the tenth century,[147] long before the rules of the *cursus* were observed by the papal scribes or laid down by the *dictatores*. Erdmann found that rhymed prose but not the *cursus* was used in the letters of Henry IV; and Noël Valois, to whom the credit for the rediscovery of the medieval *cursus* belongs, remarked that "already in the twelfth century, before the treatises on *dictamen* were compiled, these patterns, handed down in usage and custom, are to be found in the works of certain authors."[148] Meyer pointed out the use of the *cursus* in the early twelfth-century *Polenchronik*, of which the *clausulae* were later statistically tabulated by Polheim.[149] A. C. Clark also concluded that the *cursus*, although not "always employed strictly according to the rules laid down by the *notarii* of the Roman Curia," was none the less "unmistakably present" in such works as the *Policraticus* of John of Salisbury, the letters of Heloise, and the sermons of St. Bernard.[150] The rules of the *cursus* were also clearly observed in a little formulary from Fécamp, which included five letters written by a monk in England probably before 1150 and possibly in the late eleventh century.[151] In his famous description of the educational methods of Bernard of Chartres, who retired before 1127 and probably died before 1130,[152] John of Salisbury said that Bernard told his students to imitate the works of the ancient poets and

---

America. Cf. also Di Capua, *Scritti minori*, I, 189 ff., on the use of rhythmic prose by Augustine, Leo the Great, Boethius, and other early Christian writers.

[146] Cf. Lindholm, *Prosarhythmus*, pp. 7–13, esp. the table on p. 10 showing the use of metrical conclusions by twenty-four writers from the seventh to the eleventh centuries. In the works of Peter Damiani, for instance, almost 98 per cent of the *clausula* are regular, but only 56.5 per cent in documents from the chancery of Gregory VII.

[147] Fritz Weigle, "Die Briefe Rathers von Verona," *Deutsches Archiv*, I (1937) 187, and H. Silvestre, "Comment on rédigeait une lettre au Xe siècle: L'épitre d'Éracle de Liège à Rathier de Vérone," *Moyen Age*, LVIII (1952) 23–24.

[148] Erdmann, in *Archiv f. Urk.*, XVI, 207; Valois, *De arte*, p. 79, mentioning especially the works of John of Salisbury and Arnulf of Lisieux.

[149] Meyer, *Abhandlungen*, II, 282–284; Polheim, *Reimprosa*, pp. 70–87.

[150] Clark, *Cursus*, pp. 19–20. Baldwin, *Rhetoric*, p. 224, n. 38, analyzed the *cursus* in a passage from a letter by John of Salisbury. Cf. also John of Salisbury, *Letters*, I, introd., xlvi, n. 2. Hildebert of Le Mans used the *cursus Romanus* in his solemn letters, but was fairly free about his *clausulae*, according to Nino Scivoletto, *Spiritualità medioevale e tradizione scolastica nel secolo XII in Francia* (Biblioteca del "Giornale italiano di filologia," 2; Naples, 1954) p. 152.

[151] Jean Laporte, "Epistulae Fiscannenses," *Revue Mabillon*, XLII (1953) 5–31, esp. pp. 16–17. At least one of these letters dates from the early years of Henry II, however, according to Donald Matthew, *The Norman Monasteries and Their English Possessions* (Oxford Historical Series; Oxford, 1962) p. 51, n. 8.

[152] R. L. Poole, *Studies*, pp. 228–230.

orators, "showing the groupings of the words and the elegant endings of the speeches."[153] This shows that some instruction in rhythmical prose was part of the curriculum at Chartres at a time well before the earliest *artes dictandi* are known to have reached the north of France.

These and other works amply prove that both the *dictamen* and the *cursus* were known in France in the first half of the twelfth century, but there is no evidence that their influence was felt at Cluny or in the works of Peter the Venerable. The opportunity was there: Prior Peter of St. John at Sens, whose letters were copied in conjunction with the earliest known *ars dictandi* in France, was an admirer and probably also a friend of Peter the Venerable; and Peter's co-hermit in the woods near Cluny, Arnulf, "formerly an outstanding writer (*litterator*) in the city of Rome," certainly knew the rules of *dictamen*. Several Cluniacs were distinguished writers, but they adhered to the traditional style of composition.[154] There is no treatise on *dictamen* among the various works on grammar, metrics, and other branches of rhetoric listed in the catalogue of the library at Cluny in 1158/61.[155] Peter the Venerable himself attended none of the schools where the new epistolary styles were taught. He was the product of a purely Cluniac monastic environment, and the style of his letters owes more to his wide reading in patristic and classical literature than to any formulated rules of letter writing. It seems, however, that the *dictamen* was not entirely unknown to him, and he apparently did not like it. He especially disliked the fashion for extreme brevity, and even though he occasionally apologized for the length of his own letters,[156] he clearly esteemed a leisured and elegant style. He complained in Letter 24 to the Carthusians of "the desire for brevity to which modern men are allured by I know not what inborn laziness" and which forces a writer to state briefly a matter "for which a mass of books would hardly be sufficient." Again in Letter 34 to Cardinal Haimeric he said: "Modern men are lazy and quick to call unnecessary whatever does not suit their laziness. It was different with the ancients. If you think of their [letters], even my longest ones will appear very short." And in Letter 40 to Cardinal Gilo he wrote that "the epistolary style (*modus epistolarum*), in particular of contemporaries, puts the would-be writer in such a strait jacket that he cannot

---

[153] John of Salisbury, *Metalogicon*, I, 24: "Ostendens iuncturas dictionum et elegantes sermonum clausulas," ed. C. C. J. Webb (Oxford, 1929) p. 56.

[154] On the disputed question of Cluniac culture and intellectual activity, see most recently Jean Leclercq, "Spiritualité et culture à Cluny," *Spiritualità cluniacense* (Convegni del Centro di Studi sulla Spiritualità medievale, 2; Todi, 1960) pp. 103-151, esp. pp. 121-129 on writing and study in the twelfth century; Lamma, *Momenti*; and Jean Leclercq, "Pour une histoire de la vie à Cluny," *Rev. hist. ecc.*, LVII (1962) 385-408 and 783-812.

[155] Delisle, *Fonds*, pp. 337-373.

[156] See Letters 38, 46, and 111 (I, 131, 142, and 293, respectively).

write even on business matters."[157] These remarks were clearly directed less against the *cursus*, of which the object was to ensure an eloquent style, than against the tendency of the *dictatores* to abbreviate and formalize the writing of letters.[158]

Peter's own letters were written with a considerably greater freedom of organization and style than the *dictatores* would have permitted. He showed no regard for the division into salutation, exordium, narration, petition, and conclusion prescribed in the *artes dictandi*. Even in his salutations he neglected the most elementary rules of *dictamen*. "It should be known," said Albert of Samaria in his discussion of the salutation, "that there are three ranks of people: greater, lesser, and equal. A greater person is always put first, whether he is writing or being written to. An equal, however, may be placed either before or after."[159] Except in four letters Peter the Venerable always placed his own name after that of the addressee, even when he was writing to one of his own monks. The four exceptions, in which he placed his own name first, were a sign of his severe displeasure: his angry Letter 8 to Stephen, Letter 37 "to a heretic who will be nameless," and Letters 40 and 66 to the schismatic Cardinal-Bishop Gilo of Tusculum. He used no set pattern of salutation, even in his letters to the Pope, and his only formula seems to have been in reference to himself: "frater Petrus humilis Cluniacensium abbas." Even this, to judge from the letters for which there is an independent manuscript tradition outside the collection, may have been the result of subsequent revision. Letter 20 originally had "frater Petrus Cluniacensis abbas"; Letter 28, "frater Petrus Dei utinam gratia qualiscumque Cluniacensis abbas"; and Letter 38, "frater Petrus qualiscumque Cluniacensium abbas." At an early date, however, the "humble" was added and the "of Cluny" changed to "of the Cluniacs"; and Peter's reference to himself as "frater humilis, nosti cuius hoc cognomen sit" in Letter 151 to Nicholas of Montiéramey suggests that by then the distinctive formula was well established. Peter used the same freedom in the texts of his letters as in the salutations. He had a few conven-

---

[157] Similar references appear in Letter 35, where Peter omitted various citations "which cannot easily be included by epistolary brevity," and in the final letter in the collection, Letter 193, where he said that he would have explained a certain matter "if the zeal for brevity (*breuitatis studium*) did not force me to finish the letter."

[158] Cf. John of Salisbury's strictures on the logic-chopping and clipped style of the Cornificians at Paris: C. C. J. Webb, *John of Salisbury* (London, 1932) pp. 75 ff.

[159] "Preterea sciendum est quod sunt tres ordines personarum: Maior, minor, par. Maior persona semper preponitur, siue scribat alii, siue ab alio scribatur ei. Par uero preponi et subponi potest:" MSS. Copenhagen, Gl. kgl. S. 3543, fol. 19^v, and Berlin, Phillipps 1732, fol. 57^{r-v} (aliquo *pro* alio and three differences in word order). On the increasing rigidity of the formulas of salutation in the twelfth century, see Schmale, in *Deutsches Archiv*, XIII, 27, n. 34.

tions, such as always beginning his letters to kings with a reference to God, the king of kings, but this can hardly be considered a *captatio benevolentie* and was not in accordance with the rules of *dictamen*.

Whether or not Peter the Venerable was influenced by any system of *cursus* could be established only by a complete classification of the rhythmical patterns of the *clausulae* in his letters and by comparison with those in other twelfth-century letters. Valois maintained that "those [writers] whose minds were elevated and concerned with content rather than wording avoided these trifles; neither St. Bernard nor Peter the Venerable cared about rhythm or whether their sentences ended in spondees or dactyls."[160] Polheim, on the other hand, said that "the writings of the ninth abbot [of Cluny] Peter show an abnormal use of rhyme."[161] Neither of these conflicting opinions, however, was based upon a close study of Peter's works. A rapid survey shows no definite use of the *cursus* or of rhymed prose in Peter's letters. Of the one hundred and sixty-six letters written by himself, over half end with a *clausula* acceptable to a papal notary: forty-two with a *cursus planus*, thirty-five with a *velox*, ten with a *tardus*, and eight with a series of spondees (a polysyllabic paroxytone).[162] At least two end in quotations from Scripture, and one is written in verse. The remainder end in a fashion not in accord with the *cursus curiae Romanae*. Seven end with a trispondiac (a tetrasyllabic paroxytone, preceded by a paroxytone, rather than a proparoxytone, as required by the *cursus velox*);[163] four with the ending classified by Polheim as "a" (a trisyllabic proparoxytone preceded by a paroxytone); thirteen with a "q" ending (a trisyllabic paroxytone preceded by a proparoxytone); thirteen with "u" (a two-syllable spondee preceded by a proparoxytone); and one each with "r" and "s."[164] There remain between a sixth and a seventh of the letters with a *clausula* both unacceptable to the Roman curia and not among those described by Polheim on the basis of the *clausulae* in the *Polenchronik*. Ten letters, indeed, end with a monosyllable (half-spondee), which was strictly forbidden by the Roman notaries.[165]

The narrative sections of Peter the Venerable's letters also show no regard for any recognized system of rhythmical prose. Even in Letter 125 from the former Roman notary Arnulf to Peter of Poitiers, there

[160] Valois, *De arte*, p. 79.
[161] Polheim, *Reimprosa*, p. 420. Di Capua, *Scritti minori*, II, 232, also found the influence of the so-called Isidorian style of rhythmical prose in the works of Bernard and Peter: "Pietro il Venerabile cosparge i suoi sermoni di assonanze e di paronomasie."
[162] Valois, in *BEC*, XLII, 195, said that this was allowed only in the final words of a letter.
[163] The trispondiac ending was definitely excluded from the *cursus curiae Romanae*: see Vacandard, in *Rev. quest. hist.*, LXXVIII, 83.
[164] Polheim, *Reimprosa*, pp. 70-87.
[165] Valois, in *BEC*, XLII, 189.

is almost no regard for the rules of the *cursus*. Heloise also seems to have reserved her rhythmical prose for her letters to Abelard, since in her Letter 127 to Peter the Venerable there are any number of *clausulae* that would have been unacceptable to a papal scribe. Peter's reply (Letter 168) is filled with irregular *clausulae*. Of the dozen sentence endings, only two are *velox*, one is a *planus*, and another ("qui et suscipitur") can with difficulty pass for a *tardus*. Peter showed somewhat greater regularity at the beginnings of his letters. Only one opens with the forbidden double dactyls (Letter 2: "Audiens nuncios"). But this cannot be regarded as showing more than Peter's natural regard for a dignified beginning. Unless further research shows the presence of hitherto unknown accentual patterns, therefore, the existing evidence fully supports the conclusion that Peter the Venerable made no effort to compose his sentences according to the rules of the *cursus*.

Peter's disregard for *dictamen* and the *cursus* does not mean that he was unconcerned with the literary style of his letters. It shows rather that he adhered to the older tradition of the epistolary art, which was freer and more flowery. The sober Benedictine authors of the *Histoire littéraire* especially criticized Peter's tendency toward prolixity. "Peter the Venerable avoids being short; he declares that epistolary brevity seems to him only a sign of laziness, of dryness, or of sterility. His letters are prolix, not only because he takes no trouble to make them short, but also because he particularly tries to make them long."[166] Peter's letters may be wordy, but they are never impersonal or mechanical. His style was described by Schönbach as "a personal style in Latin prose, which contains many biblical elements, is at times rather pompous, unrolls in long periods, not always smoothly, and in which can be seen a conscious, gratifying effort towards eloquence."[167]

The strongest influence on Peter's epistolary style, after the Bible, was the work of Cicero. Peter of Poitiers in his panegyric described Peter the Venerable as "equal to the ancient seers in sharpness of mind, without equal in our own age. In prose he is another Cicero; in verse, a Virgil; he disputes like Aristotle or Socrates."[168] Again in the introductory letter to the collection of letters, Peter of Poitiers asked: "What Plato ever wrote anything more subtly; what Aristotle, more persuasively; what Cicero, more beautifully or more eloquently (*copiosius*)?"[169] Richard of Poitiers in dedicating his chronicle to Peter

[166] *Hist. litt.*, XIII, 257; cf. Maitland, *Dark Ages*, p. 440.
[167] Schönbach, *Erzählungsliteratur*, p. 94.
[168] *Bibl. Clun.*, cols. 604–605 (*recte* 607–608). On Peter of Poitiers's use here of hyperbolical panegyric, and Peter the Venerable's defense of it, see Curtius, *Literature*, p. 164.
[169] *Bibl. Clun.*, col. 619.

the Venerable also said: "You who almost resemble Cicero in epistolary style."¹⁷⁰ This comparison was not entirely idle, since Peter the Venerable seems to have consciously modeled the style of his letters on that of Cicero. Above all, through the *De amicitia*, which was the most widely read treatise on friendship in the Middle Ages,¹⁷¹ Cicero influenced the content as well as the style of Peter's letters. In Letter 81 Peter cited a passage from the *De amicitia* that was also cited by Aelred of Rievaulx and Peter of Blois in their works on friendship, both of which depended heavily on Cicero.¹⁷² In Letter 179 Nicholas of Montiéramey quoted a Ciceronian fragment on friendship found in Quintilian. The overt philosophical basis of Peter's correspondence, such as it was, was thus drawn from Cicero's ideas on friendship.

Among other classical authors, the best known to Peter the Venerable were Horace and Virgil. Letter 124 in particular, which was written in a secluded hermitage far from any library, shows a remarkable knowledge of Horace. Here and in other letters Peter cited with ease the odes, satires, epistles, and *Ars poetica*. Letter 117 is evidence of his acquaintance with Virgil, both the *Aeneid* and the *Georgics*. At various points Peter also cited Caesar, Lucan, Ovid, and Sallust. None of these authors was rare in the Middle Ages, and all except Caesar were in the library at Cluny in the twelfth century, which included at least seventeen manuscripts of Cicero, two of Horace, four of Virgil, two of Lucan, three of Ovid, and two of Sallust.¹⁷³ Peter's citations show that he took advantage of the opportunity offered by this library, and they are more than enough to redeem him from Sandys's charge of being a "strong opponent of secular learning,"¹⁷⁴ but they

---

¹⁷⁰ Berger, *Richard le Poitevin*, pp. 121–122, cf. p. 75; cf. Lamma, *Momenti*, p. 45, n. 1. There were at least two manuscripts of Cicero's letters in the library at Cluny in the twelfth century: Delisle, *Fonds*, p. 369, nos. 493–494.

¹⁷¹ Cf. David Knowles, "The Humanism of the Twelfth Century," in *The Historian and Character and Other Essays* (Cambridge, Eng., 1963) p. 27, and Remo Gelsomino, "S. Bernardo di Chiaravalle e il *De amicitia* di Cicerone," *Analecta mon.*, V, 180–186. More generally on the influence of Cicero in the Middle Ages, see Étienne Gilson, *La théologie mystique de saint Bernard* (Études de philosophie médiévale, 20; Paris, 1934) pp. 19–24, and Curtius, *Literature*, p. 523.

¹⁷² Letter 81 (to Hato of Troyes); Aelred of Rievaulx, *De spirituali amicitia*, in PL, CXCV, 662 C, 664 C, and 666 C, and ed. J. Dubois (Bibliothèque de Spiritualité médiévale; Bruges-Paris, 1948) pp. 12, 22, and 30, cf. introd., pp. xlviii–lx, on Aelred and Cicero; M.-M. Davy, *Un traité de l'amour du XII⁰ siècle: Pierre de Blois* (Paris, 1932) p. 31, remarking on the influence of Cicero on the *De amicitia christiana* of Peter of Blois; cf. Walter Daniel, *Life of Ailred of Rievaulx*, ed. Powicke (cited n. 136), p. lviii. n. 1, and Ph. Delhaye, "Deux adaptations du 'De amicitia' de Cicéron au XII⁰ siècle," *Recherches de théologie ancienne et médiévale*, XV (1948) 304–331.

¹⁷³ Cf. Delisle, *Fonds*, pp. 337–373: (Cicero) nos. 412, 443, 477, 489–499, 501, 518, 544; (Horace) nos. 532, 546; (Virgil) nos. 370, 502–504; (Ovid) nos. 487, 534, 545; (Sallust) nos. 516 and 559; cf. Max Manitius, *Handschriften Antiker Autoren in mittelalterlichen Bibliothekskatalogen* (Zentralblatt für Bibliothekswesen, Beiheft 67; Leipzig, 1935) pp. 27, 58, 51, 67, and 45.

¹⁷⁴ J. E. Sandys, *A History of Classical Scholarship* (Cambridge, Eng., 1903–1908) I, 510.

are not sufficiently numerous or diverse to entitle him to a position of distinction among the classicists of his age.

Peter had a wide acquaintance with the Fathers of the Church.[175] Letter 185 to his nieces is, indeed, almost a little patristic *florilegium* on the subject of virginity and includes long passages by or attributed to Augustine, Ambrose, Jerome, Cyprian, and Hilary of Poitiers. The four Western Fathers are all represented in Peter's letters, and he also cited works by Salvian, Sidonius Apollinaris, Paulinus of Nola, Boethius, and various saints' lives and canonical sources. Not all of these authors are known to have been in the library at Cluny, and Peter may have made use of collections of excerpts. The precise versions of the texts he used could be established only by an elaborate analysis of the variants in the passages cited. Thus the variants in the letter by Pseudo-Hilary suggest that Peter used a manuscript of the group labeled μ by Schanz and coming from southern Germany and Austria. The variants in his quotations from the Rule of St. Benedict show that his text was closely related to that in a group of manuscripts at Monte Cassino.[176]

All other influences on Peter's style are overshadowed, however, by the Bible, which is cited ten times more frequently than all other quotations put together. In the introductory letter to the collection, Peter of Poitiers wrote to Peter the Venerable: "I shall not mention sacred letters, which you always have at hand by memorizing both Testaments." It may be possible when the new critical text of the Vulgate is completed to identify the version used by Peter, but he clearly had an intimate knowledge of the text and often cited it from memory. In Letter 94, for instance, he firmly corrected an erroneous citation and application of a passage from Colossians: *omnes thesauri sapientiae et scientiae etiam corporaliter absconditi.* "This precept (*sententia*)," wrote Peter, "of which part is unknown to me [that is, the apocryphal *etiam corporaliter*], is as you know apostolic, but it was said not of the Blessed Virgin but of Her Son."

Peter was not always very careful in his own use of quotations, which he often paraphrased and adapted to his own meaning.[177] "You will find this in a letter by Augustine," he wrote to the monk Gregory

---

[175] Cf. Max Manitius, "Zu Petrus' von Cluni patristischen Kenntnissen," *Speculum*, III (1928) 582–587.

[176] Cf. Bened., *Reg.*, ed. Hanslik, introd., pp. xxxvii-xli.

[177] His relative lack of concern for strict textual accuracy in biblical citations is shown by the quotation in Letter 38 from Jeremias 48.10. The error in the original version (MS. Turin E-V-37) was corrected, however, in the revised version. A good example of Peter's mixing biblical references is in Letter 186: *diriget in uiam mandatorum suorum gressus tuos.* This derives principally from Psal. 118.35 (*Deduc me in semitam mandatorum tuorum*), but it also incorporates elements from Prov. 3.6 (*in omnibus uiis tuis cogita illum, et ipse diriget gressus tuos*), Eccli. 36.19 (*dirige nos in uiam iustitiae*), Jer. 31.21 (*dirige cor tuum in uiam rectam*), Luc. 1.79 (*ad dirigendos pedes nostros in uiam pacis*), and very probably others as well.

in Letter 94, "containing the same idea although not in the same words." In Letter 190 to the Pope he also said that he was giving "the idea and not the words in their order" of a passage by St. Augustine. He freely changed the forms and constructions of his quotations to fit his own sentence structure, and he sometimes garbled and even distorted their meaning. It is not always easy to identify his citations, therefore, particularly since he was fond of rhetorical quotations, and almost every sentence includes at least a reminiscence of a biblical word or phrase.

The result is a rich and allusive style, steeped in a mixture of biblical, patristic, and classical elements and characteristic of some of the best monastic writing of the Middle Ages.[178] There is nothing academic about Peter's letters, none of the clipped, scholastic style so hated by John of Salisbury. Peter represents an older school of monastic humanism. His long sentences often appear heavily loaded and obscure to modern readers, and his fondness for rhetorical repetition was the cause of many scribal errors by homoeoteleuton in copies of his works. To his contemporaries, however, his letters did not always appear slow and pompous. "I have received with ready hands what it pleased you to write," said Bernard of Clairvaux in Letter 110, replying to a lost letter by Peter the Venerable. "I read it eagerly; I reread it gladly; and it pleases me the more it is repeated. I confess that the joke pleases me. For it is pleasant in gaiety and serious in gravity. I do not know how amid gaiety you arrange your words so judiciously that both the joke does not savor of levity and the dignity which has been preserved does not reduce the pleasure of the cheerfulness." Peter was an able poet and an experienced writer, with a strong sense for language, and his style at its best, while lacking the clarity and brilliance of Bernard's, is both eloquent and vigorous.

The clearest evidence of Peter's concern for his literary style is his successive revision of his letters. The text-histories of Letters 20, 28, 38, and 150, of which there are manuscript traditions outside the collection, and of the various forms of the collection show that he revised the letters both before they were included in the first collection and again when the final edition was compiled.[179] Most of these changes were small and made in the interests both of euphony and of meaning, often to soften a sharp word or phrase. It is impossible to analyze fully here these textual revisions, but some examples may be given, particularly from Letters 28 and 20.

[178] See, generally, Leclercq, *Amour des lettres*, esp. pp. 40–52. On epistolary style and the creation of a new, highly personal, Latin style in the eleventh and twelfth centuries, see Pivec, in *MÖIG*, Erg.-band XIV, 33–51, esp. pp. 44–45.

[179] See pp. 63–73 below, on manuscripts of individual letters and the variants in the *apparatus* to the texts of the letters. Letter 110 was preserved in Bernard's collection.

Letter 28 shows perhaps the greatest evidence of revision. An examination of the *apparatus criticus* will reveal a great number of small changes, made either by Peter the Venerable himself or by his copyists, in order to improve the style, as when "recipi praecipit" was changed to "recipi iubet," and to clarify the meaning, as when "praecipiens" was altered to "admonens" in speaking of an injunction of St. Benedict, and when "legitime" or "sufficienter" was added to soften the original verb. Peter inserted "beatus Maurus" or "sanctus Benedictus" in order to identify clearly his authority, and "Ad haec nos" and "Ad haec nostri" to mark the beginnings of his replies to the Cistercian charges against the Cluniacs. Occasionally he searched for the right word through more than one form of the letter. "Considerantes" in Oa, for instance, was changed to "intuentes" in ObL and finally to the compromise "contuentes" in the final revised version that was included in the letter collection. Some of the variants are puzzling, such as the "imperio" found only in DSb in the passage where Peter wrote that the founders of Cluny decided that "soli Romano imperio pontifici eam in aeternum subiacere." The "imperio" does not construe and may well be a scribal interpolation; but it is a curious addition to an otherwise straightforward passage, and it is possible that in his first version Peter spoke of Cluny's subjection to the *imperium* of the Roman pontiff.

The changes are sometimes important and show a definite alteration in the writer's intention. Most of these are omissions, often designed to soften the somewhat sharp tone of the original version. In the seventh chapter of his reply, for instance, Peter left out the provocative remark: "Vix enim credere possumus tantos tanta sapientia preditos uiros, talia dicere posse"; and he omitted "Stulto laboris consumeris" from the beginning of a citation from Exodus 18.18. Likewise, he inserted "uel parum" between "praue intelligentes" in a reference to the Cistercians' understanding of the Benedictine rule, and he inserted a friendly "frater karissime" in his concluding remarks. Other changes were intended to strengthen or tighten his arguments. From the beginning of the fifth reply, Peter omitted the irrelevant sentence describing the Cluniac custom of placing the bread on the table first. The most substantial addition was a description of the costume of St. Martin, which is found in no manuscript of the original version.

The revisions of Letter 28 also throw some light on Peter's epistolary and literary practices. In the salutation, for example, he changed the formula "dei utinam gratia qualiscumque Cluniacensis abbas" to "humilis Cluniacensium abbas," which was the standard formula for the other letters in the collection. He used quotations with great freedom and altered citations even from Scripture and the Rule of St. Benedict in order to suit his own meaning and grammatical constructions. He thus excised a strongly worded phrase from a passage by St. Augustine; and one of his favorite quotations from Augustine, "Habe caritatem et fac quicquid uis," which appears several times in his letters, moved a step further away from the original "dilige et quod uis fac" when, in revising Oa, the "quod" was changed to "quicquid." Citations from less eminent authors, and even from the charges to which he was replying, were treated by Peter with equally great liberty.

The changes in Letter 20 were less extensive, but here again he changed the salutation, which in all eleven manuscripts of the separate letter differs from that in the collected version. The revisions in the text mostly affected only a few words. Thus he changed "Petri apostoli rete" to "hamo Petri apostoli," "palustribus propinquus fueris locis" to "palustria prope sunt loca," and "mundanis" to "humanis." He also omitted a few words here and there: "diuitias," "nequam," and "uelud." There is no evidence in this letter, however, of successive reworking of the text. Another good example of revision between the two collections occurs in Letter 126, in which there are many changes. It includes a quotation from Letter 123 ("Valeant coheremitae uestri et socii omnes, qui uobiscum siluas incolunt."), which in the revised manuscript was changed in Letter 126 ("Valeat domnus sociique eius et coheremitae, qui cum eo siluas incolunt.") but was left unchanged in Letter 123. Letter 101 likewise shows signs of modification, on a lesser scale, between the versions found in A and in C and S.

Revisions of this sort were a common practice among writers of antiquity and the Middle Ages. "It was customary to publish letters not as they were sent but corrected and reworked," wrote Pasquali. "Like Cicero, Symmachus, and Ennodius, Petrarch continued to work methodically on his own letters... even when the original had already been in the hands of the addressee for a long time."[180] The way in which letters were sent out, copied, and later collected and revised was particularly favorable to the formation and preservation of a writer's variants.[181] "The idea and the reality of a fixed text, established *ne varietur*," according to Leclercq, "are foreign to the literary traditions both of the Middle Ages and of antiquity."[182] Many of

---

[180] Giorgio Pasquali, *Storia della tradizione e critica del testo*, 2nd ed. (Florence, 1952) pp. 451 and 457.

[181] *Ibid.*, pp. 449–450.

[182] Leclercq, *Recueil*, p. 233; cf. Louis Havet, *Manuel de critique verbale appliquée aux textes latins* (Paris, 1911) pp. 409–410. On the revision by classical authors of their own works, see in particular Hilarius Emonds, *Zweite Auflage im Altertum*, 2nd ed. (Klassisch-Philologische

Peter's revisions have been lost with the manuscripts of his letters, and only one version of most of his letters is preserved, but the surviving evidence shows that for some twenty-five years they were a changing, living text and thus a reflection in their style as well as in their content of the personality of their author.

Studien, 14; Leipzig, 1941), and N. I. Herescu, "La tradition manuscrite des poètes latins et les variantes d'auteur," *Revue des études latines*, XXXIX (1961) 135–157. Both these writers stress that textual variants in medieval manuscripts of classical authors may go back to revisions by the author. In the Middle Ages, Anselm, Eadmer, William of St. Thierry, and Bernard are known to have revised their own works: see F. S. Schmitt, "Cinq recensions de l'*Epistola de Incarnatione Verbi* de saint Anselme de Cantorbéry," *Rev. Bén.*, LI (1939) 275–287; Eadmer, *Vita Anselmi*, ed. Southern (cited n. 8 above), pp. xi ff.; J.-M. Déchanet, "Les divers états du texte de la *Lettre aux frères de Mont-Dieu* dans Charleville 114," *Scriptorium*, XI (1957) 63–86; C. H. Talbot, "The Archetypes of Saint Bernard's Sermons *Super Cantica*," *Scriptorium*, VIII (1954) 220–235; Leclercq, *Recueil*, pp. 233–234 and 243–244 (on the two distinct versions of Bernard's *Apologia*). The versions of Bernard's Letter 110 in his own letter collection and that of Peter the Venerable show that it was revised by Bernard before it was included in his collection. This is confirmed by the quotation from Letter 110 in Letter 111. On Grosseteste's revisions of his own works, see S. H. Thomson, in *Progress of Medieval and Renaissance Studies in the United States and Canada*, XVIII (1944) 58.

II / *The Text Tradition*

1. PRINTED EDITIONS

The letters of Peter the Venerable first appeared in print in a small folio volume published at Paris in 1522 under the lengthy title:

D. Petri Vene-/rabilis, Integerrimae et vere Christianae doctrinae viri, Cluniacen/sis quondam Abbatis: opera haud vulgaria, D. Petri de monte martyrum / theologicae professionis viri doctissimi, cura et labore nunc primum / in lucem edita. / Epistolarum libri .VI. Vbi multa cum philosophico, tum theo/logico more, diserte, clare et subtiliter contra haereticos disputantur. Mul/ta de virtutibus egregie disseruntur: et tandem omnium conditioni et / statui congruentia explicantur documenta, Pluribus ad eam rem sa-/crarum scripturarum locis insigniter expositis. / Item Rithmi et versus non contemnendi. / Miraculorum praeterea libri duo. Ex quibus, quid in omni / vita sequendum, fugiendumque sit, veraciter et perfecte quisque ediscere possit. / Cum privilegio / Vaeneunt in vico Iacobaeo a Damiano Hichman Bi/bliopola, ad signum quatuor Elementorum sub gratia et privilegio a / tergo huius explicandis. Parisiis .1522.[183]

The title page is printed in red and black and is adorned with the fine device of the publisher, Damian Hichman.[184] The book has two colophons, one on B4ᵛ: "Impressum Parrisiis (sic) opera egregii Impressoris Ioannis de Prato: expensis vero Honestissimi mercatoris Damiani Hichman. Anno domini .M. cccccxxii die .xxviii. Aprilis." and another on dd6ʳ: "Impressa sunt haec Petri Venerabilis opera, amore studiorum, sumptibus Damiani Hichman Bibliopole. Parisiis. Anno 1522. Die Aprilis .26."[185] The pagination is faulty, and the

---

[183] It is mentioned in E. P. Goldschmidt, *Medieval Texts and Their First Appearance in Print* (Supplement to the Bibliographical Society's Transactions, 16; London, 1943) p. 83, n. 1.

[184] H. W. Davies, *Devices of the Early Printers* (London, 1935) pp. 414–415. On Hichman (Higman, Ichman, Hicqueman), see P. Renouard, *Imprimeurs parisiens, libraires, fondeurs de caractères et correcteurs d'imprimerie depuis l'introduction de l'imprimerie à Paris (1470) jusqu'à la fin du XVIᵉ siècle* (Paris, 1898) p. 182, 2nd ed. in the *Revue des bibliothèques*, XXXIV (1924) 201.

[185] On the printer Jean (II) du Pré, see Renouard, *Imprimeurs*, p. 113, 2nd ed. in *Revue des bibliothèques*, XXXIII (1923) 231.

collation is as follows: ā⁸, a–z⁸, &⁸, A⁸, B⁴, aa⁶, bb–cc⁸, dd⁶, +⁴. In certain copies the gathering + is found bound after the gathering ā.

The first gathering (ā) consists of eight unnumbered leaves (with the exception of ā8, which is incorrectly numbered CCXI) and contains the preliminary and miscellaneous matter. The editor's letter of introduction and dedication are on the verso of the title and ā2ʳ. These are followed on ā2ᵛ by the letter "Sicut praecipere dignatus" from Peter of Poitiers to Peter the Venerable. The following leaves contain various poems by Peter of Poitiers, the panegyric and the epitaphs on Pope Gelasius II and Bishop Alfonso of Salamanca, and the *Apologium* of Peter the Venerable, written in defense of Peter of Poitiers. The privilege, signed by L. Ruze, is on ā8ʳ; ā8ᵛ is blank. The bulk of the text is in gatherings a–B2ᵛ, the leaves of which are numbered, with several errors and omissions, from I to CCXII. On folio I are found the second introductory letter by Peter of Poitiers and a letter to the reader from Pierre de Montmartre, the editor of the collection. These are followed by the letters, including the *Contra Iudaeos* and the *Contra Petrobrusianos*, with its introductory letter, and the *Contra eos qui dicunt Christum numquam se in evangeliis aperte Deum dixisse*. On folios CCXIIᵛ–CCXIIIIᵛ (B2ᵛ–B4ᵛ) is a small collection of poems and hymns by Peter the Venerable. The gatherings aa–dd are paginated separately from I to XXVIII and contain the *De miraculis*. The final gathering +, of four unnumbered leaves, includes an index.

Little is known about the editor, Pierre de Montmartre, besides the facts, found on the title page and in the introductory letter, that he was a monk of Montmartre and a theologian. Perhaps he was the "Donnus Petrus de Montmartre, sacrae theologiae professor, Cluniacensis monachus" by whom a poem is found in a collection made for Baluze in the seventeenth century.[186] He may have been a professor of theology at the College of Cluny in Paris. The workshop of Jean du Pré, the printer, was located near the College of Cluny.[187] The introductory letter on folios ā1ᵛ–2ʳ is addressed to the grand prior of Cluny and prior of La Charité-sur-Loire, who in 1522 was Jean de la Magdelaine de Ragny.[188] In this letter, Pierre de Montmartre gave three reasons for publishing the works of Peter the Venerable. The first was their intrinsic merit, in particular of the treatises against the Jews, Petrobrusians, and Saracens. Of the *Contra Sarracenos*, however, he was unable to find a complete copy and therefore did not include it.

---

[186] MS. Paris, Bibliothèque nationale, Latin 942, fol. 76ᵛ; cf. Delisle, *Fonds*, p. 227, and *Bibliothèque nationale: Catalogue général des manuscrits latins* (Paris, 1939 ff.), I, 334–335.

[187] "In vico Olearum contra Collegium Cluniacense, ad intersignium Sancti Sebastiani": Renouard, *Imprimeurs*, p. 113, 2nd ed. in *Revue des bibliothèques*, XXXIII, 231.

[188] *GC*, IV, 1171, and XII, 411.

The second reason was his obedience to the biblical injunction to honor one's parents, since Peter the Venerable was his spiritual father. Thirdly, he emphasized the suitability of the works of one Peter of Cluny being published by another. In his secondary introductory letter, on folio 1^v, Pierre de Montmartre mentioned his work as editor. He admitted that he had rearranged the order of the letters. He probably also added the summaries, the brief notes, the identifications of quotations, and perhaps also the few alternate readings that appear in the margins. He was probably likewise responsible for much of the capitalization and punctuation. On the whole, however, he seems to have adhered closely to his manuscript.

The second edition of the letters of Peter the Venerable appeared at Paris in 1614 in the *Bibliotheca Cluniacensis*, edited by Martin Marrier with the assistance of André Duchesne.[189] Since they could find no manuscript of the letters, they had to reprint, with some changes, the text of the 1522 edition. They revised the arrangement of the letters, expunged the summaries and marginal notes,[190] expanded the abbreviations, and occasionally emended the text.[191] They grouped all the poems by Peter of Poitiers at the beginning and those by Peter the Venerable at the end of his works. They added an appendix of eight letters, three of them by Peter the Venerable, drawn from various sources, and a number of other works by Peter. To all of these Duchesne wrote a series of learned and valuable notes. The collection of letters was reprinted from the *Bibliotheca Cluniacensis* in Volume XXII of the *Maxima bibliotheca veterum patrum* published at Lyons in 1677 and in Volume CLXXXIX of the *Patrologia latina* of Migne, who

---

[189] This volume was reissued at Mâcon in 1915 in a typographical (not anastatic) facsimile, with a few corrections in such matters as pagination but no changes in the text.

[190] The omission of the headings is particularly serious, because the close resemblance of the headings in C (although expanded by Pierre de Montmartre) to those in S shows that they derived from the manuscript. They often provide information about the addressees not found in the salutations or texts of the letters and were very likely written by Peter the Venerable himself or by Peter of Poitiers. Cf., on the titles of St. Augustine's letters, De Bruyne, in *Rev. hist. ecc.*, XXIII, 529, who attributed the titles to Augustine himself and stressed their importance.

[191] The text in the *Bibliotheca Cluniacensis* is therefore considerably less accurate, though much more legible, than the text in the 1522 edition. A rough count indicates that there is an average of at least one error on each page of the *Bibliotheca*. Some of these are purely typographical, including a few repeated and reversed lines (as at the beginning of Letter 89), but many are the result of editorial activity, especially expansions of abbreviations and "corrections" of the text. Letter 47, for instance, has no salutation in A, S, or C but was provided in the *Bibliotheca* with a salutation taken from Letter 2. In the salutation of Letter 169, the letter *h*, which stands for Humbertus, was expanded by Marrier and Duchesne to *humilis*. Some of these emendations are correct, but they are misleading. "Le plus grand tort en effet que l'on puisse faire à un texte est de l'amender en le copiant": A. Dain, *Les Manuscrits* (Paris, 1949) p. 18. On the whole, Duchesne was a very accurate copyist and editor: see Luchaire, *Études*, p. 33, whose conclusions have been recently confirmed by Walter Goffart in his work on the *Actus pontificum Cenomannis*.

identified a few more quotations and expanded the appendix to a total of twenty-two letters.

There have also been many reprints of individual letters and groups of letters, which are indicated in the notes to the present edition. Duchesne included four letters by Peter in Volume IV of his *Historiae Francorum scriptores*; Brial selected thirty for Volume XV of the *Recueil des historiens des Gaules et de la France*; Canivez inserted two into Volume I of his *Statuta capitulorum generalium ordinis Cisterciensis*; and others too numerous to mention. No complete translation of the letters has appeared in any language, but about sixty were translated into French, in whole or in part, as an appendix to the *Essai historique sur l'abbaye de Cluny* by P. Lorain, and translations of individual letters have appeared in several languages.[192]

All these editions and fragmentary reprints derive ultimately from the edition of 1522, of which the accuracy has long been questioned by scholars. Schönbach, for instance, said that Mabillon's edition of the letters of Bernard was "much better" than Duchesne's edition of Peter the Venerable,[193] which is not saying much, because Mabillon's edition of Bernard is by common consent the least satisfactory work of the great Maurist.[194] More recently, such authorities as Séjourné, Wilmart, D'Alverny, and Knowles have all agreed on the need of a new edition of the works of Peter the Venerable to replace that in the *Bibliotheca Cluniacensis*.[195] These scholars in fact underestimated the merits of the edition of 1522, which was based upon an excellent manuscript and is remarkably accurate for an edition of that date. It is a rare book, however, and the text has suffered in the process of reprinting. Even the *Bibliotheca Cluniacensis*, in spite of the care and ability of its editors, has an average of at least one error a page, and these are multiplied in the *Maxima bibliotheca* and *Patrologia latina*. As a result, the current text of the letters of Peter the Venerable contains a number of errors and minor textual corruptions.

2. MANUSCRIPT COLLECTIONS

A (*Aquicinensis*). MS. Douai, Bibliothèque municipale, 381 (XII, Anchin), is a large volume consisting of twenty-five gatherings,

---

[192] No translation of any work by Peter the Venerable is listed in C. P. Farrar and A. P. Evans, *Bibliography of English Translations from Medieval Sources* (Columbia Records of Civilization, 39; New York, 1946).

[193] Schönbach, *Erzählungsliteratur*, p. 97.

[194] Cf. Watkin Williams, in *Select Treatises of S. Bernard of Clairvaux* (Cambridge Patristic Texts; Cambridge, Eng., 1926) introd., pp. xv-xix, and *Monastic Studies*, pp. 148–149; and Leclercq, *Études*, pp. 202–225.

[195] Séjourné, in *DThC*, XII.2, 2080; Wilmart, "Riposte," p. 297, n. 4, and "Le poème

numbered I to XXV, of eight leaves of vellum each. The first and last leaves are missing, making a total of 198 leaves, of which the first and last are blank and the remainder numbered, in a recent hand, from 1 to 195 (58 bis). Each leaf measures 435 by 300 millimeters and is pricked and ruled with lead for two columns, 340 millimeters in height and with forty-six lines. The manuscript contains a collection of works by Peter the Venerable.[196] The first ten folios are filled with poems and preliminary material: the letter "Sicut praecipere dignatus" and the panegyric by Peter of Poitiers; the *Apologium* of Peter the Venerable;[197] the two epitaphs by Peter of Poitiers; a small collection of poems, some with music, by Peter the Venerable;[198] and the second introductory letter by Peter of Poitiers. These are followed on folios 11^v–12^r by an elaborate table of contents, which will be discussed later. Folio 12^v is blank, and the collection of letters begins on folio 13^r. On folio 26^r, following Letter 27, is a note: "Primam epistolam ad dominum Bernardum abbatem Clareuallis quae hic scribi debuisset, require in fine epistolarum ante sermonem de laude dominici sepulchri." The collection of shorter letters continues to folio 66^r and is followed by the *Contra Petrobrusianos*, with its introduction (folios 66^r–108^r) and the misplaced Letter 28, "Pro meritis uenerabili," to Bernard of Clairvaux (folios 108^r–120^v). The remainder of the volume is filled with the sermon on the Holy Sepulchre (folios 120^v–127^v),[199] three *visiones* (folios 127^v–131^r),[200] the *Contra Iudaeos* (folios 131^r–177^r), and two books of the *Contra Sarracenos* (folios 180^v–195^r),[201] including the prologue by Peter the Venerable (folios 178^r–180^v), the introductory letter from Peter of Poitiers to Peter the Venerable (folios 177^{r-v}), and the table of chapters divided into four books (folios 177^v–178^r). On the final folio, at the end of the second book of the *Contra Sarracenos*, the scribe wrote: "Desunt duo libri quos inuenire non potui."[202]

---

apologétique de Pierre le Vénérable et les poèmes connexes," *Rev. Bén.*, LI (1939) 53; D'Alverny, "Traductions," p. 72; and David Knowles, *The Prospects of Medieval Studies* (Inaugural Lecture; Cambridge, Eng., 1947) p. 12.

[196] The description of the contents by C. Dehaisnes is not complete: *Catalogue général des manuscrits des bibliothèques publiques des départements*, 4to ser., VI (Collection de documents inédits sur l'histoire de France; Paris, 1878) pp. 214–215.

[197] In a version with sixty-two more lines than are found in the 1522 edition and the *Bibl. Clun.*: see Wilmart, in *Rev. Bén.*, LI, 54–55.

[198] Including three hymns not in the 1522 edition: cf. Wilmart, in *Rev. Bén.*, LI, 53–69, and Constable, in *Petrus Ven.*, p. 238.

[199] See Constable, in *Rev. Bén.*, LXIV, 232–254.

[200] See Giles Constable, "The Vision of Gunthelm and Other *Visiones* Attributed to Peter the Venerable," *Rev. Bén.*, LXVI (1956) 92–114.

[201] See Kritzeck, *Peter the Venerable*, pp. 215–291.

[202] This note and the table of contents have led almost all authorities on Peter the Venerable to believe that two books of the *Contra Sarracenos* are lost. In the opinion of

Douai 381 is the most important surviving manuscript of the works of Peter the Venerable. It is the only known manuscript of the *Contra Sarracenos*, of three poems, and of part of the sermon on the Holy Sepulchre, and it contains all his works except for eighty-five letters, the treatise *Contra eos qui dicunt*, three sermons, the *De miraculis*, the *Statuta*, and the preliminary material to the translations from the Arabic. It was compiled at the monastery of Anchin, from where it was moved to the municipal library at Douai in 1791. The *scriptorium* at Anchin was very active during the abbacies of Alvisus (1111-31), who was later bishop of Arras, and in particular Goswin (1131-66), under whom there was a kind of "manuscript rivalry" between Anchin and the nearby monasteries of Marchiennes, St. Vaast, and St. Bertin.[203] The manuscripts at Anchin were seen in the early eighteenth century by Martène and Durand, whose knowledge of such matters was unsurpassed and who wrote that "the greatest riches of this library consist chiefly in the manuscripts, in which there are very few provincial libraries that can compare to it ... Those that seemed to me the most beautiful were the letters of Peter the Venerable and all the works of St. Bernard written about his lifetime in three great folio volumes with very great care. I have never seen anything more beautiful of this type."[204]

The manuscript was evidently prepared with the greatest possible care. No pains were spared to secure an accurate and legible text. The vellum is of fine quality and used without economy. The script is a clear and elegant minuscule. The titles are written in red and green; many of the initials are colored, and five are illuminated with a variety of gold, silver, red, green, blue, orange, pink, brown, and white.[205] The entire text is carefully punctuated. Words broken at the ends of lines are all hyphenated. Adjacent vowels that are not diphthongs but pronounced separately are marked by two small accents. Even a few textual variants and improved readings are included. Needless to say,

---

James Kritzeck, however, based on a comparison of the table of contents with the matter in the two existing books, the work is complete as it stands and follows a plan that was revised from that in the table of contents.

[203] On the library and *scriptorium* at Anchin, see E. A. Escallier, *L'abbaye d'Anchin (1079-1792)* (Lille, 1852) pp. 95-116; J. Gessler, "Une bibliothèque scolaire du XIe siècle d'après le catalogue provenant de l'abbaye d'Anchin," *L'antiquité classique*, IV (1935) 49-116; Karl F. Werner, "Andreas von Marchiennes," *Deutsches Archiv*, IX (1952) 460, who said that the library at Anchin in the twelfth century was "eine Bibliothek von ausserordentlicher Reichhaltigkeit"; and several notes and articles by André Boutemy in *Scriptorium*, II (1947-48) 287-288 and 296, III (1948-49) 110-122, and esp. "Enluminures d'Anchin au temps de l'abbé Gossuin (1131/3 à 1165)," ibid., XI (1957) 234-248.

[204] *Voyage littéraire de deux religieux bénédictins de la congrégation de Saint Maur* (Paris, 1717-1724) II, 78-79.

[205] See the reproductions on the frontispiece in *Petrus Ven.* and in *Scriptorium*, XI, 244, pl. 19 c.

it is not perfect. "There is no copy without faults."[206] In Letters 20 and 28, of which there are other copies, it includes a number of clear errors.[207] But on the whole it presents an exceptionally accurate text, written in what Knowles described as "probably the most exact and beautiful form of writing that has ever existed as common property to be used for all purposes. The scribes throughout north-western Europe," he continued, speaking of the twelfth century, "produced work of almost incredible regularity and perfect legibility, in which contractions were few and clearly indicated and every letter was formed separately."[208]

Palaeographically speaking, this manuscript can safely be assigned to the third quarter of the twelfth century. The extensive use of the ę in particular suggests that it cannot be much later, since, according to Robert, the ę "was replaced by the simple e in France and Italy beginning in the middle or end of the twelfth century and in Germany beginning in the thirteenth."[209] This is especially true because the manuscripts from Anchin tend to be palaeographically advanced. Bethmann, who visited Douai on his travels for the *Monumenta Germaniae historica*, remarked that "these [manuscripts] show premature development in the art of writing... This was very advanced: two manuscripts dated 1153 and the Papias of 1173 show graphic characteristics of the thirteenth century."[210]

This dating is supported by two pieces of external evidence. First, and most important, is the passage from Peter the Venerable's Letter 20 that is cited in the *De nouiciis instruendis* by Abbot Goswin of Anchin.[211] This treatise is found in the relatively late MS. Douai 827,[212] and it was probably written not long before Goswin's death in 1166. The passage from Letter 20 is about four hundred words in length and agrees precisely, aside from certain intentional omissions, with the text found in Douai 381. It has in particular the variant *maturis* for *maturatis*, which is found in no other manuscript. It is of

---

[206] Dain, *Manuscrits*, p. 43.

[207] On sixteen occasions in Letter 20 and fifty-one in Letter 28, I have adopted readings not in A, although not all of these are certainly errors.

[208] Knowles, *Monastic Order*, p. 521.

[209] Ulysse Robert, "Note sur l'origine de l'Ę cédillé dans les manuscrits," *Mélanges Julien Havet* (Paris, 1895) p. 633; cf. André Wilmart, "La collection d'Ebrach," *Rev. Bén.*, XLV (1933) 329, who considered the predominance of *e* over *æ* as evidence for dating a manuscript in the late twelfth century.

[210] C. L. Bethmann, *Voyage historique dans le nord de la France*, trans. Edmond de Coussemaker (Paris, 1849) p. 77.

[211] Cf. Dehaisnes, in *Cat. gén.*, 4to ser., VI, 548–551. The watermarks in the paper show that the manuscript was written in the middle of the sixteenth century, not in the thirteenth (following Dehaisnes): Charles Briquet, *Les filigranes* (Paris-Geneva, 1907) nos. 1545–1551 and 7079–7088.

[212] Cf. Leclercq, in *Petrus Ven.*, p. 120, n. 114.

course possible that the scribe of Douai 827 corrected his text from Douai 381, but it is far more probable that Goswin himself made use of this version of Peter's letter. Douai 381 must therefore have been copied, or at least the version from which it was copied must have arrived at Anchin, before Goswin's death in 1166.

The second piece of external evidence supporting this dating is derived from the history of the sister manuscript Douai 372 and from the life of the scribe Siger, the most celebrated of the eleven known scribes and illuminators who worked at Anchin during the abbacy of Goswin.[213] Siger's masterpiece was the great manuscript of the works of St. Bernard mentioned by Martène and Durand and at present MS. Douai 372.[214] This splendid manuscript contains 1120 folios, several with handsome illuminations, and is the largest collection of the works of St. Bernard to be compiled before the edition in the *Patrologia latina*. Its date has been the subject of some dispute. Séjourné and Williams were inclined to date it about 1175–80,[215] but more recently Leclercq dated it about 1165.[216] He pointed out that the name of Siger appears on no known Anchin document after 1169. The gathering and copying of this collection was a considerable undertaking. Leclercq's estimate that it was written in about a hundred and ninety days seems very short indeed.[217] The Bible, which is not much longer than the works of St. Bernard, was considered to take a year to copy. "In 1162 it is recorded as something remarkable that a Bible at Leon was copied in six months and illuminated in the seventh. In 1220–21 a copyist of

[213] Baldwin, John, Jordan, Balderic, Gerard, Lambert, Siger, Renaldus, Ailred, Oliver, and Elias: Escallier, *Anchin*, pp. 96–116; Dehaisnes, in *Cat. gén.*, 4to ser., VI, introd., iii–iv; and Boutemy, in *Scriptorium*, XI, 237.

[214] On this MS., see P. Séjourné, "Les inédits bernardins du manuscrit d'Anchin," *Saint Bernard et son temps* (Association bourguignonne des Sociétés savantes: Congrès de 1927; Dijon, 1928–29) II, 248–282; Williams, *Monastic Studies*, pp. 146–165; Leclercq, *Études*, pp. 124–136; and Boutemy, in *Scriptorium*, XI, 244–245. These authors all mention Siger, whom Séjourné called "le scribe le plus reputé de l'abbaye" (*Bernard et son temps*, II, 247). Siger signed directly after the abbot, prior, and almoner on a document of 1161: Escallier, *Anchin*, p. 116.

[215] Séjourné, in *Bernard et son temps*, II, 250–266; Williams, *Monastic Studies*, pp. 153–154.

[216] Leclercq, *Études*, p. 132. Boutemy, in *Scriptorium*, XI, 244–245, considers it was completed before 1173.

[217] Leclercq, *Études*, p. 132, n. 3. This is based upon the estimate of Philibert Schmitz that an experienced scribe could copy six pages of two columns each in a day: *Histoire de l'ordre de Saint Benoît* (Maredsous, 1942–1956) II, 67 (2nd ed., II, 70). Cf. Maitland, *Dark Ages*, p. 222 (who estimated that it would take a contemporary [in the 1830's] legal copyist ten months to copy the Bible); Wattenbach, *Schriftwesen* (cited n. 77 above), pp. 289–293; Haskins, *Renaissance*, pp. 73–74, who said that "of the actual time required, we have few exact indications before the late, and more careless period"; Lesne, *Prop. ecc.*, IV, 375–378; and Florence Edler De Roover, in J. W. Thompson, *The Medieval Library* (Chicago, 1939) p. 607, who said that "it is impossible to get an accurate idea of the average speed of a good scribe because, in almost all instances where the length of time devoted to transcription is mentioned in a subscription, it is given because the scribe is proud of the rapid rate at which he has worked."

Novara spent a year and a quarter upon a Bible."[218] Goderan of Lobbes and an assistant took four years in the late eleventh century to copy the famous Bible of Stavelot.[219] The scribe Rainald spent ten years on the great manuscript of Papias, the present Douai 751, on 187 leaves with three columns each.[220] It seems probable, therefore, that Siger worked on Douai 372 for several years at least; and presuming that he died about 1170, it probably occupied the last years of his life.

Douai 381 is the sister manuscript of Douai 372, which it resembles in script, format, and conception. Although not signed, Douai 381 can with confidence be attributed to the scribe Siger on the basis of numerous palaeographical and decorative features.[221] Wilmart's suggestion that it was written by Peter of Poitiers himself is not probable.[222] On the basis of both internal and external evidence, Douai 381 appears to have been compiled and copied before Douai 372. Among other things, Douai 372 contains a letter from Bernard to Peter the Venerable which, in the opinion of Séjourné, was taken from the collection of letters of Peter the Venerable.[223] Douai 381, therefore, was probably completed before 1165, that is to say, less than ten years after the death of Peter the Venerable in 1156.

At Anchin, furthermore, Siger was in an excellent position to gather an authoritative *corpus* of Peter's works. Although not technically subject to Cluny, the abbey of Anchin was the first monastery in the province of Rheims to adopt the *consuetudines Cluniacenses* and was a center of Cluniac influence in the north of France and in the Lowlands, especially under Abbots Alvisus and Goswin.[224] It is not improbable that Siger was in direct touch with Cluny itself, and the archetype of his copies may have come from there. He may have been in communication with Peter of Poitiers himself, but if so it is hard to explain the

[218] Haskins, Renaissance, p. 74; cf. Wattenbach, Schriftwesen, p. 291.
[219] Lesne, Prop. ecc., IV, 273.
[220] Escallier, Anchin, pp. 111-112, and Dehaisnes, in Cat. gén., 4to ser., VI, 451. William of Newburgh in the late twelfth century said that it had taken him a year to copy onto parchment his commentary on the Song of Songs (which fills about seventy-five folios in the best manuscripts) and almost three hundred printed octavo pages): William of Newburgh, Explaratio, p. 364; but he may have had other occupations.
[221] Both Dehaisnes, in Cat. gén., 4to ser., VI, 215, and Séjourné, in Bernard et son temps, II, 249 and 254, n. 2, ascribe Douai 381 to Siger, and after a close comparison with Douai 372, I feel no doubt that the two manuscripts were written by the same hand.
[222] Wilmart, in Rev. Bén., LI, 53, n. 4.
[223] Séjourné, in Bernard et son temps, II, 254, n. 2. This letter is found in no manuscript of Bernard's letter collection.
[224] Ursmer Berlière, "Les origines de Cîteaux et l'ordre bénédictin au XIIe siècle," Rev., hist. ecc., II (1901) 259-262, and Mélanges, IV, 29; Étienne Sabbe, "Notes sur la réforme de Richard de Saint-Vannes dans les Pays-Bas," Revue belge de philologie et d'histoire, VII (1928) 558-559 and 562-563; De Moreau, Église en Belgique, II, 180-181 and 187-189. On Alvisus and Anchin during his abbacy, see Heinrich Sproemberg, Beiträge zur französisch-flandrischen Geschichte, I: Alvisus, Abt von Anchin (1111-31) (Historische Studien, ed. Ebering, 202; Berlin, 1931).

gaps in the collection and Siger's futile efforts to find the apparently missing books of the *Contra Sarracenos*. Peter of Poitiers may possibly have died before Douai 381 was compiled, and Siger had therefore to be content with the copies sent by someone less familiar with the works of Peter the Venerable.

The collection of letters found in A includes a total of a hundred and ten. The shorter letters are numbered from 1 to 106 and are followed by the unnumbered letter in verse to the monk Raymond of Toulouse, the *Contra Petrobrusianos* and its introduction, and Letter 28 to Bernard of Clairvaux, which was moved "in fine epistolarum" probably on account of its length. The collection therefore contains, in the order of the manuscript, Letters 1–27, 29–36, 38–51, 37, 52–93, 95–101, 123–129, 117, the introduction and text of the *Contra Petrobrusianos*, and Letter 28. This arrangement is probably the work partly of Siger, as may be seen from the table of contents on folios 11^v–12^r, which lists the letters in their original order. The *numbering* of the items in this table is not accurate: 76 is repeated; 102 and 103 apply to one letter, of which the title is on two lines; 105 covers all three letters to Peter of Poitiers from the companions of Peter the Venerable in the forest near Cluny, which are numbered separately 102–104 in the text; the verse letter to the monk Raymond is omitted; and the sermon on the Holy Sepulchre, the *Contra Iudaeos*, and the *Contra Sarracenos* are numbered 108–110. These figures were probably added after the table had been drawn up, and with something less than Siger's usual care. The *order* of the items, on the other hand, is of great interest: Letter 28 appears in its proper place rather than at the end of the collection, and the *Contra Petrobrusianos* and its introduction appear after Letter 87 and are numbered 87 and 88 (one too few owing to the repetition of 76). It is probable that Siger also moved these two letters to the end of the collection on account of their length but omitted to insert a note to this effect, as he had when he moved Letter 28. The table of contents, therefore, represents the order of the collection as it was received at Anchin: Letters 1–36, 38–51, 37, 52–87, the introduction and text of the *Contra Petrobrusianos*, 88–93, 95–101, 123–129, and 117 (not in the table of contents), a total of a hundred and ten. To these were added the two introductory letters by Peter of Poitiers and the collection of poems by Peter the Venerable, which apparently formed part of the original collection of letters. Letter 28, on the other hand, according to Siger, came at the end of the letters, and the following works, the sermon, *Contra Iudaeos*, and *Contra Sarracenos*, were presumably not considered part of the letter collection and were added by Siger in order to complete his *corpus* of Peter's works.

The collection in A probably represents the first collection of letters drawn up by Peter of Poitiers, to which he referred in his letter "Sicut praecipere dignatus."[225] It is, perhaps, surprising that Siger was unable to secure a more complete collection, and this fact argues against any direct connection with Peter of Poitiers, who could without question have supplied all the works of Peter the Venerable. A complete collection was certainly in existence at the time A was copied, but the librarian at Cluny may have feared to send it to Anchin and therefore supplied a copy of the original collection in reply to Siger's request. This conjecture is supported by the evidence of the text, which shows signs of revision between the versions found in A and in the complete collection. The Anchin manuscript, therefore, and the collection it contains, although incomplete, is exceptionally important on account both of the care and conscientiousness of its scribe and of its provenance and early date.

C (*Cluniacensis*) is the designation given here to the lost manuscript used by Pierre de Montmartre for the edition of 1522. The fate of this manuscript is not certain, and it may be awaiting discovery in an obscure library. More probably, however, it was destroyed, as were many manuscripts from which printed editions were prepared in the fifteenth and sixteenth centuries.[226]

Pierre de Montmartre did not describe the manuscript, except to refer to it as "antiquum exemplar," but all the evidence points to its having come from Cluny. As a monk of Montmartre and perhaps a professor at the College of Cluny, Pierre de Montmartre would have had easy access to the library of Cluny. His manuscript was certainly authoritative and exceptionally complete. It contained twenty-seven more letters than any other known collection and also the rare *Contra Sarracenos*, which is found only in the Anchin manuscript and which Pierre de Montmartre did not publish because he thought it was incomplete. The library at Cluny is known to have possessed a manuscript of the letters of Peter the Venerable, from which the collection was described by François de Rivo in the late fifteenth or early sixteenth century.[227] In 1614, however, Marrier and Duchesne were unable to find any manuscript of Peter's letters,[228] and no copy is mentioned in the catalogue of the library at Cluny compiled about 1645 by Dom Anselme le Michel.[229] This manuscript, which

---

[225] See pp. 16-17 above.
[226] See R. B. McKerrow, *An Introduction to Bibliography for Literary Students* (Oxford, 1927) p. 186, n. 1, and Dain, *Manuscrits*, p. 147: "Son peu de valeur faisait qu'on le dépeçait pour la commodité des typographes, d'où il résulte qu'on ne retrouve que très rarement les manuscrits qui ont servi aux premières éditions, et pour ainsi dire jamais quand il s'agit des éditions incunables."
[227] See p. 17 above.
[228] *Bibl. Clun., notae*, col. 104.
[229] Delisle, *Fonds*, pp. 383-393.

disappeared during the course of the sixteenth century, was almost certainly that used by Pierre de Montmartre.

The edition of 1522 is apparently a faithful copy of C, and it was probably set up in type directly from the manuscript, of which it seems to preserve many peculiarities. Pierre de Montmartre, as has been seen, slightly edited and rearranged the letters. Like the scribe Siger, he in particular moved the long letters. But on the whole he preserved the order, text, and even the abbreviations of the manuscript.[230] It contained in all a hundred and ninety-seven letters divided into six books, of which the first two contained the dogmatic treatises and the last four, the remaining one hundred and ninety-three shorter letters. This arrangement of the books is the work of Pierre de Montmartre, but the order of the letters is the same as in A, except for the positions of Letters 37 and 117. The additional letters have been inserted: one between 93 and 95, twenty between 101 and 123, and sixty-four after 129. Letter 28 is in place, but the proper positions of the dogmatic treatises is not indicated.

This is the largest known collection of Peter's letters and appears to be a direct expansion of the collection found in A. The collection was not only enlarged, however, but also to a certain extent revised. In particular, the final letters of the original collection, those written to Peter of Poitiers by Peter the Venerable and his companions in the woods near Cluny, were extensively rewritten; and several other letters were changed here and there in the interests of sense and style. The additional letters were mostly written after the formation of the first collection. The date of this enlarged collection is not known, but it was probably compiled during the lifetime of Peter the Venerable and under his personal supervision. The content of C may therefore be regarded as the definitive form of the letter collection of Peter the Venerable.

S (*Sylviniaci*). MS. Le Puy, Cathédrale, unnumbered (XV, Souvigny),[231] is a folio volume recently bound in half-vellum, of ninety-six leaves of paper: one unnumbered flyleaf and the remainder numbered 1 to 95, of which 91–95 are blank. The over-all size is 407 by 290 millimeters; the written surface, 305 by 205 millimeters. The paper is watermarked with eight vertical chainlines and a stylized

---

[230] Aside from a few typographical errors, most of which are easily recognizable (such as the reversal of the *n* and *u*), the text in C is remarkably accurate.

[231] See the brief description, on the basis of a communication from M. Mercier, a canon of Le Puy, by Henri Quentin, in *Misc. Ehrle*, I, 80, and Léon Côte, *Histoire du prieuré clunisien de Souvigny* (Moulins, 1942) p. 436. Côte refers to "une excellente et très complète notice" on this manuscript drawn up by Canon Joseph Vacher, who died about 1940. The Bishop of Le Puy has kindly attempted to find this notice for me, but without success, and Côte himself has been unable to throw any light on the matter.

THE TEXT TRADITION 57

triple-peaked mountain, upside down, as a rule enclosed in a circle.[232] The writing is in faded brown ink and rubricated throughout. The *incipit* on folio 1ʳ reads: "[I]ncipiunt epistole uiri reuerentissimi et doctissimi Petri uenerabilis Cluniacensis abbatis. Et primo premittitur epistola Petri Pictauensis ad dictum Petrum uenerabilem missa, ipsius Petri multum recommendatoria."[233] This is followed by an index on folio 1ʳ⁻ᵛ, the second introductory letter of Peter of Poitiers on folio 2ʳ⁻ᵛ, and the collection of letters. The *explicit* on folio 90ᵛ reads: "Expliciunt epistole Petri uenerabilis que sunt reuerendo patri domino Oddoni de Perreria priori Siluigniaci. Si quis eas furatus fuerit anathema sit."[234]

Odo de la Perrière was prior of Souvigny between 1417 and 1424, when he became abbot of Cluny.[235] Before 1417 he had been successively a monk, claustral prior, and grand prior at Cluny. This manuscript, made for him while he was prior of Souvigny, can therefore be dated about 1420. Beyond this, almost nothing is known of its history. It bears on the recto of the front flyleaf and on folios 90ᵛ and 95ᵛ a carefully erased round stamp, and a recent oval stamp of the "Capitulum Ecclesiae Aniciensis" on the flyleaf and folios 1ʳ, 2ʳ, 90ᵛ, and 95ᵛ; but how it came to Le Puy is not known. At the top of folio 1ʳ the pressmark No. M.C.iiiiˣˣxi is written in a flourishing script, probably of the seventeenth century. There were few libraries of this size in France, and none in Auvergne, but I have been unable to discover from which one this manuscript came. The capitular library at Le Puy was old and important, but not large; and there is no reference to this manuscript either in a fifteenth-century catalogue[236] or in a list of the more important volumes compiled by Dom Estiennot in the seventeenth century.[237] Forty-nine manuscripts were acquired by Colbert in 1681,[238] and the remainder were confiscated and destroyed in 1791 by a fire at the Capuchin monastery in Le Puy.[239] Only the celebrated Bible of Theodulf, which was kept among the relics,

---

[232] Cf. Briquet, *Filigranes*, nos. 11848 (Vicenza, 1455) and 11662 (Florence, 1432).
[233] Quentin, in *Misc. Ehrle*, I, 80: Cluniacensium, Pictaviensis.
[234] *Ibid.*: qui *pro* quis.
[235] Côte, *Souvigny*, p. 134; *Bibl. Clun.*, cols. 1675–1678; *GC*, IV, 1158 and 1168–1169; cf. De Valous, *Mon. clun.*, I, 377, and II, 37.
[236] Étienne Médicis, *Chroniques*, ed. Augustin Chassaing (Le Puy, 1869–1874) I, 129–130.
[237] MS. Paris, Bibliothèque nationale, Latin 13068, fol. 9, in Léopold Delisle, *Le cabinet des manuscrits de la Bibliothèque impériale* (Histoire générale de Paris; Paris, 1868–1881) I, 509–511.
[238] Léopold Delisle, "Recherches sur l'ancienne bibliothèque de la cathédrale du Puy," *Annales de la Société d'agriculture, sciences, arts et commerce du Puy*, XXVIII (1866–67) 439–459; cf. Delisle, *Cabinet*, I, 473–474 and 511–512.
[239] Delisle, in *Annales . . . du Puy*, XXVIII, 458–459, and *Cabinet*, I, 517–518; Augustin Chassaing, in *Catalogue général des manuscrits des bibliothèques publiques de France: Départements*, 8vo ser., XIII (Paris, 1891) 338.

survived from the old library.²⁴⁰ The manuscript of the letters of Peter the Venerable, therefore, probably came into the possession of the chapter of Le Puy at a relatively recent date, as the stamps and binding also suggest. It was not seen by Delisle when he visited Le Puy in the middle of the nineteenth century, nor was it declared at the time of the secularization of ecclesiastical property in France.²⁴¹

The departure of the manuscript from Souvigny is also a mystery. The medieval library there was large,²⁴² but probably not as large as a pressmark of 1191 or of M 191 implies. The inventory made at the time the library was transferred to Moulins lists only eighty-nine manuscripts.²⁴³ It may, however, have been salvaged from the "livres incomplets ou dégradés," the liturgical manuscripts "qui n'offrent rien d'utile ni d'agréable," and the documents and "vieux ouvrages en parchemins, déchirés, souvent illisibles" which were disposed of as waste in 1808.²⁴⁴ Its travels between Souvigny and Le Puy, however, are of small importance beside the known fact that it was copied for a prominent Cluniac who was in close touch with the abbey of Cluny itself.

S contains a total of one hundred and sixty-six letters, including the introduction to the *Contra Petrobrusianos* and two letters to Master Bartholomew that are found in no other manuscript and were printed for the first time in 1924.²⁴⁵ It also contains a brief *Summa totius sectae Sarracenorum*, appended to Letter 111, which differs from the published *Summula* and is printed here in Appendix F. It omits not only the three dogmatic treatises but also thirty letters found in C: 37, 39-40, 46, 49, 53-57, 59-61, 66, 68, 70, 81, 84-86, 88-90, 92, 108, 117, 137, 139, 141, and 144. The remaining letters are in exactly the same order as in A and C, except that Letter 94 is between 112 and 113. The two letters to Master Bartholomew follow Letter 158, and the introduction to the *Contra Petrobrusianos* appears between Letters 93 and 95. These additions, as well as that of the little *Summa*, show that S is not merely a selection from C. The omissions, furthermore, present no consistent pattern of selection. S must therefore be considered as a collection intermediate between A and C. Textually, it is very much closer to C. It contains, for instance, the revised versions of Letters 126

---

²⁴⁰ Léopold Delisle, "Les Bibles de Théodulfe," BEC, XL (1879) 5-47.

²⁴¹ This may account for my difficulties in studying the manuscript and having it photographed. In his introduction to Augustin Chassaing, *Cartulaire de Chamalières-sur-Loire* (Paris, 1895) p. ii, Antoine Jacotin remarked on "les soins jaloux et méfiants" surrounding a manuscript in the episcopal archives at Le Puy, which he was unable to study closely.

²⁴² Martène and Durand, *Voyage* (cited n. 204 above), I, 46.

²⁴³ Henri Omont, in the *Cat. gén.: Départements*, 8vo ser., III (Paris, 1885) 173.

²⁴⁴ M.-A. Chazaud, "Note sur la bibliothèque et les archives de Souvigni," *Bulletin de la Société d'émulation du département de l'Allier*, XII (1870-1872) 238-239.

²⁴⁵ Quentin, in *Misc. Ehrle*, I, 83-86.

THE TEXT TRADITION   59

and 127. This textual similarity is especially marked in the cases of Letters 20 and 28, of both of which there are several manuscripts. On the three occasions where C has a variant reading in the margin, S alone also has this reading, and twice it is given as a variant, written above the preferred reading with a "uel." On several other readings C and S also agree against all other manuscripts.[246] This strongly suggests that they derive from a common source, although S has sufficient variants to show that it was not copied directly from C. The exact genesis of S is not clear, for it is surprising that a collection copied for Odo de la Perrière should be incomplete. It is probably an independent collection drawing on the same sources, perhaps a register made by Peter of Poitiers, as C.

Cl (*Clareuallensis*). MS. Troyes, Bibliothèque municipale, 2261 (XV, Clairvaux),[247] consists of four gatherings of twelve leaves and one of eight (= 56 folios). In each gathering the outer and the inner leaves are of vellum and those in between of paper, watermarked with a bull's head.[248] The over-all size is 210 by 145 millimeters; the written surface, 150 by 100 millimeters and ruled for twenty-eight lines. The leaves are numbered from 1 to 52. The last four are blank and unnumbered, and E8 is pasted to the binding. The front flyleaf is a fragment of a thirteenth-century liturgical manuscript. The script is of the fifteenth century. At the top of folio 1^r a more recent hand has written "Anno 1140" followed by the contemporary: "Sequuntur epistole uiri clarissimi atque doctissimi donni Petri venerabilis abbatis Cluniacensis ad beatum Bernardum abbatem Clareuallensem. At eciam epistole eiusdem Bernardi doctoris egregii ad eundem Petrum venerabilem amicum suum cordialissimum et unanimem."

The text includes twenty letters, all concerned with the relations between Cluny and Cîteaux. Nine are from Peter the Venerable to St. Bernard: 73, 111 (with the little *Summa* found in S), 145, 149–150, 164, 175, 181, and 192; six are from Bernard to Peter: 74, 110, 148, 152, 163, and 177; three are from Peter to Nicholas of Montiéramey: 176, 180, and 182; and one each is from Nicholas (179) and from Henry, bishop-elect of Beauvais (146), to Peter. These letters were without doubt extracted from a collection of Peter's correspondence. They are arranged in exactly the same order as in C and S. It is difficult to explain, however, the omission of several apparently relevant letters, in particular of Letters 28, 29, and 65 from Peter to Bernard, and 87,

---

[246] Further evidence of the close relation between C and S are the headings in C, which were cut out in the *Bibliotheca Cluniacensis* and which almost always agree with S against A.

[247] Briefly described in the *Cat. gén.*, 4to ser., II (Paris, 1855) 917.

[248] Cf. Briquet, *Filigranes*, nos. 15042–15111, in particular nos. 15097 (Augsburg, 1470) and 15058 (Memmingen, 1443).

151, and 193 from Peter to Nicholas, and 153 from Nicholas to Peter. The omission of Letter 28, the most important single letter in the correspondence between Bernard and Peter the Venerable, is especially surprising. The scribe may have been working from an incomplete manuscript or have followed a principle of selection known best to himself.

Both the text and the content of Cl suggest that it is related to S. The little *Summa* appended to Letter 111 is not found in the 1522 edition, although it may have been in C and omitted by Pierre de Montmartre. Cl was certainly not copied directly from S, but it probably derived from the same source. Both Cl and S, therefore, ultimately belong to the same family as C, and all may be traced to a collection of Peter's letters probably at Cluny.

B (*Blesensis*). MS. Paris, Bibliothèque nationale, Latin 2582 (XV, royal library at Blois),[249] is a manuscript of one hundred and thirteen leaves of vellum bound in gatherings of eight. The leaves measure 315 by 205 millimeters; the first one hundred and five are ruled for two columns, each of thirty lines and 222 millimeters in height; folio 106 is blank; folios 107-113 are ruled for one column of 210 millimeters. Two blank leaves precede the text. The second introductory letter of Peter of Poitiers appears on folios 1^r–2^v and is followed by "Incipiunt epistolae uiri reuerentissimi atque doctissimi domini Petri abbatis Cluniacensis." The text is very carelessly copied, and up to folio 14^r there are marginal corrections in what appears to be a slightly later hand. The initial capitals have never been completed.

The collection of letters on folios 2^v–105^r includes a total of eighty-five letters, consisting of the first eighty-seven of Peter's collection, excluding the long Letters 20 and 28. The manuscript breaks off suddenly in the middle of Letter 87. The letters are numbered from 1 to 86, omitting 20 but not 28, as in the Anchin manuscript. They are also in the same order as A, with Letter 37 between Letters 51 and 52. These two features suggest that B is of the same family as A, although it is not a direct copy. The text is too corrupt to indicate clearly to which family it belongs; and the problem is complicated by the marginal "corrections" on folios 1-14, which may have been taken either from the same manuscript from which B was copied or from another, in which case they are really variants rather than corrections. After folio 14, however, the corrector apparently gave up the job as hopeless. Letter 5 in B, for example, has thirty textual differences from A. Of these, two agree with CS and one with S alone; the remaining twenty-seven are presumably errors. There are sixteen marginal

---

[249] See *Bibliothèque nationale: Catalogue général des manuscrits latins*, II, 530.

THE TEXT TRADITION 61

corrections. Thirteen of these change the reading in B to a form agreeing with ACS; two introduce new variants found in no other manuscript; and one, changing "caligosi" to "caliginosi," agrees with C against AS, which have "caligosi." The original form of B, therefore, seems to have been related to A, but the corrections may have been taken from a manuscript of the C group. Be this as it may, the text of B is too corrupt to be of use except when it corroborates the reading of a more reliable manuscript.

Sg (*Sancti Germani*). MS. Paris, Bibliothèque nationale, Latin 13876 (XIII, St. Germain-des-Prés),[250] contains one hundred and sixty-three leaves of vellum, bound in gatherings of eight, each measuring 200 by 135 millimeters and ruled with lead for two columns of twenty-eight lines and 130 millimeters in height. On folio 1^r is the old pressmark: "Sti Germani a Pratis olim 363 N. 1300."

The volume contains four letters from Peter the Venerable to Bernard of Clairvaux: Letter 28 on folios 1^r–34^r; 111 on folios 34^r–47^v, where it breaks off suddenly at the words "quae in propria lingua alkoran uel"; 149 on folios 48^r–50^r; and 150 on folios 50^r–53^r. The rest of the volume is filled with the letters of Bernard, a copy of the *Statuta* of Peter the Venerable,[251] Franciscan statutes, and a later sermon.[252] The letters of Peter the Venerable were certainly taken from a larger collection. Letter 28 is numbered XXVIII and Letter 111, XVI, which seems to have been changed from XVII or XVIII by a later hand, presumably in order to make it conform with the number (V, 16) of this letter in the 1522 edition. These figures show that the letters were taken from a collection that was divided into books and probably, therefore, of the family of C. A does not include Letters 149 and 150, and in S the letters are not divided into books. The text of Letter 28 in Sg, which will be discussed later, shows that Sg is definitely of the revised or "collected" group but cannot be clearly associated, on the basis of its variants, with any one of them.

MSS. Rome, Biblioteca Alessandrina, 97 and 98 (XVI–XVII),[253] are two manuscripts from the collection of Dom Costantino Gaietani, the great collector and assistant of Baronius.[254] They contain a group of

---

[250] See the brief descriptions by Léopold Delisle, *Inventaires des manuscrits latins conservés à la Bibliothèque nationale sous les numéros 8823–18613* (Paris, 1863–1871) II, 120, and *Fonds*, p. 316.

[251] To be edited in the *Corpus consuetudinum monasticarum medii aevi*, under the general editorship of Kassius Hallinger.

[252] There is a table of contents on the front flyleaf.

[253] See Enrico Narducci, *Catalogus codicum manuscriptorum . . . qui in Bibliotheca Alexandrina Romae adservantur* (Rome, 1877) pp. 61–67.

[254] On Costantino Gaietani as a scholar and patron of letters, see E.-J. Léonard, "Deux lettres de Dom Costantino Gaietani . . . à Richelieu et à Mazarin," *Revue Mabillon*, XIV

forty-three letters by Peter the Venerable which were copied in the late sixteenth or early seventeenth century in a clear and regular script and were later bound in two volumes together with a large number of other monastic, spiritual, and liturgical texts.[255] Letters 28 and 161 are found on folios 585^r–614^r of MS. 98, and Letters 114, 62, 52–53, a fragment of 56, 107, 178, 71, 98, 115, 167–168, 123–124, 63–64, 1, 39, 145–146, 125–129, 84, 185, 111, 20, 113, 116, 118–119, 122, 186–187, 112, 172, 192, 4, and 44, in that order, on folios 88^r–165^r of MS. 97, of which folios 114, 118, 122, 152, 156, 162, and 164 are blank and 105 is omitted in the foliation. There are a number of marginal notes and occasional textual corrections in a more careless hand. The bizarre order of the letters is the result both of the haphazard binding and of occasional efforts on the part of the scribe to group the letters according to length, recipient, or subject. Letters 98, 115, and 167–168, for instance, which are copied together, are all concerned with Abelard; and Letters 1 and 39 are both to Pope Innocent II. When they were bound, however, only the groups copied on a single folio were as a rule kept together.[256]

There can be little question that the text of this manuscript was taken directly from the 1522 edition. The numbering of the letters and the marginal notes are, with only a few insignificant exceptions, identical with those in the printed version. Each of the ten alternate readings given by Pierre de Montmartre is also found in this manuscript. There is nothing surprising in this. The edition of 1522 was doubtless hard to obtain in Rome in the seventeenth century, and Costantino Gaietani therefore had a selection of the letters copied. This is not the only example among his papers of a manuscript copied from a printed text. From the point of view of the text of the letters of Peter the Venerable, this manuscript is of no value.

The question of the relationship between these various manuscript collections is not easily answered. Basically, there appear to be two distinct collections: the original collection, best represented by A, and the enlarged collection, best represented by C. Of the four other manuscripts, B is closer to A, and S, Sg, and Cl are closer to C; but the

---

(1924) 32–40, and J. Ruysschaert, "Costantino Gaetano, O.S.B., chasseur de manuscrits," *Mélanges Eugène Tisserant* (Studi e Testi, 231–237; Vatican City, 1964) VII, 261–326.

[255] The watermark (a goose with a C over its back, enclosed in a circle and surmounted with a P) cannot be identified precisely but is of a type common in Italy in the sixteenth century: Briquet, *Filigranes*, nos. 12202–12232. Each signature begins with a letter, except in the few cases where a letter fills more than one signature. The numbering of signatures S^2 and T^2 (fols. 159–162) in MS. 97 shows that T^2 was misbound and that the pages were numbered before they were bound.

[256] When a letter was continued from one leaf to another, the scribe occasionally noted the number of the letter at the top of the following page.

THE TEXT TRADITION   63

exact forms of the enlarged collection from which S, Sg, and Cl derive
are far from clear. It is surprising to have so many apparently distinct
collections of a text of which so relatively few manuscripts have
survived; but practically speaking, the problem is not serious, since
the known manuscripts are sufficient to establish a reasonably reliable
and authentic text and arrangement of the letters.

3. MANUSCRIPTS OF INDIVIDUAL LETTERS

A. The most widely diffused of the letters of Peter the Venerable was
Letter 28 to Bernard of Clairvaux, which is found in seventeen known
manuscripts in addition to C and the Rome manuscript, and in three
that are now lost:[257]

A: Douai 381 (XII, Anchin), folios 108^r–120^v.
S: Le Puy, unnumbered (XV, Souvigny), folios 13^v–26^r.
Sg: Paris, Bibl. nat., Latin 13876 (XIII, St. Germain-des-Prés), folios 1^r–34^r.
M: Melk, Stiftsbibliothek, 1918 (783.0.19) (XV), folios 37^r–54^r.[258]
T: Clm 18566 (Teg. 566) (XV, Tegernsee), folios 100^r–132^r.
V: Vienna, Schottenstift, 152 (52.d.3) (XV), folios 3^r–25^v.
Ss: Dijon, Archives départmentales de la Côte-d'Or, 139 (Cart. H 165) (XII–XIII, Saint Seine), pp. 110–208.
U: Urbana, University of Illinois, 6 (XII–XIII), folios 43^r–66^v.
L: Brussels, Bibl. royale, 10827–10835 (XII–XIII, St. Laurence, Liège), folios 103^r–122^r.
St: Brussels, Bibl. royale, 19593–19596 (XV, Stavelot), folios 236^r–268^v.
Ma: Douai, Bibl. municipale, 535 (XIV, Marchiennes), folios 47^r–78^v.
Ca: Cambrai, Bibl. municipale, 277 (267) (XV, St. Sepulchre, Cambrai), folios 33^v–102^v.
Ar: Arras, Bibl. municipale, 891 (XIV, St. Vaast), folios 90^v–124^v.
An: Douai, Bibl. municipale, 211 (XII, Anchin), folios 79^v–101^r.
D: Bruges, Bibl. municipale, 131 (XII, Dunes), folios 121^r–158^v.
Sb: St.-Omer, Bibl. municipale, 261 (XII, St. Bertin), folios 174^r–205^v.
Sv: Seville, Capitular Colombina, 7-2-1 (XIII), folios 155^v–176^r.

The three lost manuscripts were at Aggsbach, A 11; Louvain, Val-St.-
Martin; and Tournai, St. Martin, A 43.[259]

The differences and similarities between the texts of Letter 28 in

[257] When not otherwise indicated, consult the relevant catalogues of the libraries listed in P. O. Kristeller, *Latin Manuscript Books before 1600*, 3rd ed. (New York, 1965).

[258] This is presumably the manuscript listed under the number F 48 in the medieval catalogue of the library at Melk: Theodor Gottlieb, *Mittelalterliche Bibliothekskataloge Österreichs*, I: *Niederösterreich* (Vienna, 1915) p. 241.

[259] *Ibid.*, pp. 532–533; A. Sander, *Bibliotheca belgica manuscripta* (Lille, 1641–1644) II, 222, and I, 93; cf. [Charles Clémencet] *Histoire littéraire de S. Bernard, Abbé de Clairvaux, et de Pierre le Vénérable, abbé de Cluni* (Paris, 1773) p. 531.

these manuscripts are the result not only of scribal errors and manuscript families but also of successive revision of the text itself. Broadly speaking, the manuscripts divide into two groups: SbDAnArCaMa-LStSvU, which contain the original version in several forms, and AMTVSSgSs, which contain the revised version. Within these two groups, as will be seen, are several subgroups, which appear to represent the text at different stages of development.

The revised version is found not only in the manuscript collections (ACSSg) but also in four individual copies (MTVSs), which were probably taken from collections. The most accurate copies are, therefore, those in the collections. Of these, Sg is the least satisfactory and contains a great number of errors and variants, of which a very few agree with the original version. In collections A and S, the letter is simply entitled: "Ad domnum Bernardum abbatem Claraeuallis." Of the four individual copies, MTV, all of the fifteenth century, belong together as a "South German" group which derived from a lost copy to which I have given the *siglum* R. Here the text is entitled: "Epistola uenerabilis Petri abbatis Cluniacensis ad sanctum Bernardum super improperatione rigoris ordinis sui non seruati [seruata T]."[260] V seems to derive directly from M. Various omissions for which the reason in M is clear can be explained in V only if it was copied from M. The omission of "esse" before "oportere," for instance, is marked by a blank space in M (the prototype was presumably unclear) but not in V; and "cotidianum," omitted in both manuscripts, falls on the turn of folio 48 in M. The reading "subreperat" for "subrepat" in V is easily explained by a comparison with M, where an abbreviation mark in the line below has cut the leg of the "p" and given an appearance of "subrepat." M and T are probably sister manuscripts and both copies of the lost R. In one important particular they resemble the original rather than the revised version. The division between the eighth and ninth sections of the second part comes at the words "Hinc ad sequens" rather than "Obicitur nobis cur." This alone is sufficient to show that R was not copied directly from any known collection. It seems that it was most closely related to C, with which MTV agree in various readings and especially in the omission of the phrase "nequaquam distortos ... semitas," although this may be simply an error of parallel homoeoteleuton and not a proof of relationship. In all important respects, MTV clearly belong to the revised group, but they contain such an astonishing number of errors, omissions, and interpolations that their evidence is of small

---

[260] The lost MS. from Aggsbach was entitled "Epistola abbatis Petri Cluniacensis ad beatum Bernhardum de rigore regule sue servando." It probably belonged, therefore, to this group.

value for the establishment of the text, and their variants have for the most part not been included in the *apparatus criticus*. Ss, the fourth individual copy of the revised version of Letter 28, also contains a very faulty text, in spite of its early date (twelfth or thirteenth century) and Burgundian provenance (St. Seine). It includes over two hundred variants, many of them clearly errors, that are found in no other manuscript. The scribe was a conscientious editor, although a careless copyist, and he frequently corrected his prototype, which was probably unclear. The reading "extimamus" (for "aestimamus"), for example, he carefully changed to "existimamus." Variants of this sort, and all additions found in Ss, have been included in the *apparatus*; most of the omissions, however, and differences in word order found only in this manuscript have been excluded. Very occasionally, Ss coincides with the original version or with an individual manuscript of the original version against the consensus; but on all points of essential divergence between the two versions, it belongs with the revised group.

The original version, O, of Letter 28 is found in ten manuscripts, which presumably derive from copies distributed at the time the letter was written. They contain four, or perhaps five, apparently distinct forms of the original letter. The group SbDAn represents the letter in the form, Oa, differing most widely from the revised version. These manuscripts come from three monasteries, St. Bertin, Dunes, and Anchin, situated within a radius of fifty kilometers, and they are all of the twelfth century with the possible exception of Sb, which may be of the thirteenth.[261] In Sb and D, the text is entitled "Incipit liber primus Petri Cluniacensis [abbatis *add*. Sb] ad domnum Bernardum Clareuallensem abbatem de quibusdam obiectis ac responsis alterutrum utriusque ordinis"; and in An, "Incipit liber domni Petri Cluniacensis abbatis de questionibus Cystellensium et responsionibus Cluniacensium." Together, SbDAn have about a hundred readings to themselves. In addition, Sb and D have twenty-two readings not in An. Sb and D are, therefore, somewhat more closely related to each other than to An and may be sister manuscripts. An is presumably a cousin. All three have not only the text but also the arrangement of the original version. In the second part, sections 5 and 7 are both divided into two, beginning, respectively, at "De pulmentariis etiam" and "Ab idibus autem," and section 9 begins at "Hinc ad sequens," as mentioned above. In An these subdivisions are not numbered, but in Sb and D they are numbered with the other sections, making a total of twenty-three chapters, beginning with

---

[261] Sb lacks more than a folio at the end and breaks off at the words "hac uiolentia nam."

number one at "Et ut eo in ordine," in place of the twenty chapters found in the revised version.

The second form, Ob, of the original version is found in Ar, Ca, and Ma, which are from the monasteries at Arras, Cambrai, and Marchiennes, each within a few miles of the others and just south of the region of group Oa. All three manuscripts are late: Ar and Ma of the fourteenth century, on vellum, and Ca on paper that can be dated from the watermark about 1475.[262] Both Ma and Ar are mutilated,[263] and Ca is therefore the only complete copy of form Ob. There it is headed: "Hoc in opusculo, quorumdam religiosorum Cistellensium obiecta, contra Cluniacensium regulam continentur. Dein eadem ad obiecta Petri abbatis Cluniacensis responsio." The text of Ob agrees with Oa on over two hundred variants, which constitute the principal differences between the original and the revised versions. In certain respects, however, Ob is closer to the revised version than Oa, which has many more distinctive readings. Section 5 is not divided, and the sections are not numbered, although otherwise it has the same arrangement as Oa.

L[iège] and St[avelot] come from the area west of the regions of Oa and Ob and constitute the third group within the O manuscripts. L is a twelfth- or thirteenth-century manuscript, with corrections in a fifteenth-century hand. St is dated in the second quarter of the fifteenth century[264] and appears to be a copy of L. The correcting hand of L may indeed be the hand of the scribe of St: the insertions in L of "excusatione" in place of the omitted "dubio," and of "sed quasi" for "et quam," and of "aduersus" for "mutans" are all found in St and in no other manuscript. Variants from St alone, therefore, have not been included in the *apparatus*, and L is the only true representative of the third form of O. It is entitled "Epistola domni Petri Cluniacensis abbatis contra Cystercienses qui sibiipsis religiosi uidebantur et arguebant Cluniacenses de nonnullis punctis regule."[265] L is, unfortunately, not a careful copy, and perhaps also taken from a bad copy, but it agrees in most of its readings with OaOb and constitutes with them the basic *siglum* O of the original version, which therefore consists of SbDAnArCaMaStL. However, L is not clearly in the form of either Oa or Ob. In some ways it seems closer to Oa, and within that group to An, with which it usually agrees in the few

---

[262] Cf. Briquet, *Filigranes*, nos. 3622 (Douai, 1480) and 8658 (Pontoise, 1471).

[263] Ar includes about four fifths of the letter, up to the words "soliditatis ac forti." Ma is not only incomplete but also very carelessly copied, and I have not included its readings in the *apparatus*.

[264] On fol. 111ᵛ it is dated 1441 and on fol. 235ʳ, 1430.

[265] In St, the title is "Epistola domni Petri Cluniacensis abbatis contra Cystercienses super quibusdam punctis regule sancti Benedicti abbatis."

places where An diverges from SbD. Elsewhere, however, it agrees with Ob, in particular with Ca, against Oa and occasionally even with the revised version against O,[266] and for this reason it occupies a place apart.

Two other possible forms of O are found in Sv and U. In Sv the letter is entitled "Altercatio Cluniacensium contra Cystercienses super regula beati Benedicti." The text is clearly of the original version and is most closely related to Ob, although it agrees in some readings, even against Ob, with Oa (particularly An) and L. But it has enough readings of its own, mostly omissions and changes in word order, to distinguish it from the other groups, and its readings in the complicated passage on monastic stability in section 15 place it somewhat nearer the revised version than the other texts of O.[267] The form in U, which is of the twelfth or thirteenth century,[268] is incomplete, going as far as the words "etiam de propriis." It is entitled "Comentum domni Petri Cluniacensis abbatis contra obiectiones alborum monachorum, aduersus nos querelas excitantium." The copy is careless, and the scribe had a propensity, for instance, to omit "inquit" (four times), but the text is definitely of the original version, although in a form considerably closer to the revised version than the other forms of O. Occasionally, like Sv and L, it agrees with the revised version against O, as in the key passage on stability, where it is the only manuscript to agree exactly with C. U, therefore, stands in somewhat the same relation to the original version that Ss stands to the revised version.

The existence of several different forms of O indicates that the text of Letter 28 was more or less fluid during the lifetime of Peter the Venerable and that the term "original version" used here does not mean the "authentic" or "first" form of a fixed text but refers rather to the forms in which it circulated as a letter, as contrasted with the revised version which was included in the collection of Peter's letters. It is, therefore, natural to find in the manuscripts a much greater

---

[266] In a few places the fifteenth-century corrector changed L from O to the revised version. He may, therefore, have compared L with another manuscript.

[267] Seven different versions of this passage are found in the manuscripts, probably owing both (a) to its intrinsic complexity and liability to errors by homoeoteleuton and, even more, (b) to the tendency of scribes to copy by heart passages drawn from the Rule of St. Benedict.

[268] See *Bibliotheca medii aevi manuscripta* (Jacques Rosenthal, Katalog 83; Munich [1925]) pp. 6–7, no. 5. It is almost certainly MS. Phillipps 10234, which was described in the *Catalogus librorum manuscriptorum in bibliotheca D. Thomae Phillipps, Bart.* (Middle Hill, 1837 ff.) p. 164, as "S. Ambrosii Episcopi de Bono mortis et Fuga Seculi. Petrus Cluniacensis contra Objectiones Alborum Monachorum. 12mo. V. s. xi–xii. (Ex Bibl. Incertis)." It is bound in eighteenth-century mottled sheep, possibly French, with end papers watermarked with a serpent (?) and the name Marot. There were several paper-makers by the name of Marot in the eighteenth century at the Couze mill in Périgord, which produced paper for the Dutch market: W. A. Churchill, *Watermarks in Paper* (Amsterdam, 1935) p. 20.

variation in the texts of the original than of the revised version. Of the manuscripts of the revised version, Ss alone has substantial variants with any possible claim to authenticity. The variants between the manuscripts of O, on the other hand, can be attributed only to continual reworking of the text. It is not, of course, always possible to distinguish between changes made by Peter the Venerable himself, scribal corrections and emendations, and errors in transcription; but it is clear that there was no fixed and authoritative form of the text.

This work of revision probably began as soon as the first copies had left the *scriptorium* at Cluny. Oa apparently represents this earliest form, as it was first written,[269] and Ob shows the first signs of reworking. The comparatively late date of the manuscripts of Ob, however, suggests that it may be a later scribal revision of Oa. Many of the differences between the forms of O, indeed, may be attributed to scribes, as in the manuscripts L and Ss. The letter was circulated widely among Cluniac monasteries, and the copyists at Cluny may have drawn up slightly different versions almost at the same time. Many of the changes, however, were certainly made by Peter the Venerable himself, above all at the time the letter was included in the collection of his correspondence. Between D, the most extreme manuscript of the original version, and A, the most characteristic manuscript of the revised version, there are about three hundred and fifty differences. Many of these disappeared in the reworkings of O, but over two hundred are found in all manuscripts of the original version and were changed only at the time of the final revision.

The manuscripts of Letter 28 must therefore be seen as related through a process of textual development rather than a process of descent from one archetypal original. There are, to be sure, family groupings among the manuscripts; but these are of less importance than the claim of each group to a certain degree of authenticity and originality. The manuscripts may consequently be arranged as a spectrum rather than as a genealogical tree:

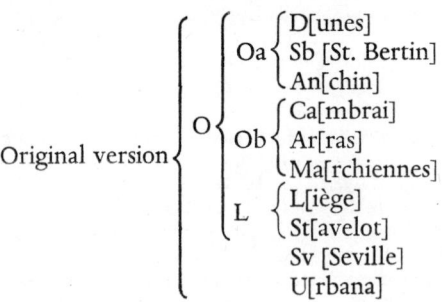

[269] See Appendix E on the date of this letter.

THE TEXT TRADITION

Revised version $\left\{ R \begin{array}{l} \text{Ss (St. Seine)} \\ \text{Sg (St. Germain)} \\ \left\{ \begin{array}{l} \text{M[elk]} \\ \text{T[egernsee]} \\ \text{V[ienna]} \end{array} \right. \\ \text{S[ouvigny]} \\ \text{C[luny]} \\ \text{A[nchin]} \end{array} \right.$

This arrangement conceals the family relationships and appears to exaggerate the degree of variation in order to show the development of the text. It suggests that there was a smooth progression from D, the "most original," to A, the "most revised," whereas there are in fact many anomalies in the relations of the manuscripts, such as the occasional similarities between An, L, and Sv. The basic distinction is between the original and revised versions. U, for instance, has more readings in common with A than any other manuscript of the O group; and Ss agrees more frequently with O than any other manuscript of the revised version; but each is firmly in its own group. On the whole, there is a solid basis of agreement between the manuscripts of each version.

This arrangement also shows that except for Sv all the manuscripts of O were from a relatively small area in the Lowlands. Two of the lost manuscripts were also in this region, though there is no way of knowing what version of the text they contained. They were in libraries not only of Cluniac houses but also of old Benedictine monasteries. One was even in a Cistercian abbey, Dunes, where it was bound with an important series of Cistercian works.[270] This concentration of manuscripts suggests that the letter was distributed and read particularly in this area, where there was an exceptional amount of monastic activity in the twelfth century. By contrast, the manuscripts of the revised version were much more widely distributed, although they show a greater textual uniformity. They come from all over France and from Germany. The titles of the letter as it appears in the manuscripts are also of interest. In Oa, it is called *liber*; in Ca, *opusculum*; in Sv, *altercatio*; in U, *comentum*.[271] L is the only manuscript of the original version in which it is entitled *epistola*, as in the revised version.

---

[270] A. de Poorter, *Catalogue des manuscrits de la Bibliothèque publique de la ville de Bruges* (Catalogue général des manuscrits des bibliothèques de Belgique, 2; Gembloux, 1934) pp. 173–175. De Poorter maintained that this collection came from Clairvaux itself; but the different parts, although bound together probably in the twelfth century, were copied separately. The signatures of Peter's Letter 28, which is the last item in the volume, are numbered I–IIII (V is unnumbered).

[271] Peter the Venerable himself called it an *opusculum* and admitted that it exceeded "epistolary brevity": I, 89 and 101.

In most of the O manuscripts, therefore, its character as a polemic treatise rather than as a pseudo-personal letter to Bernard is brought out in the title.

B. Of Letter 20 there are fifteen manuscripts in addition to C and the Rome manuscript and three that are now lost.

A: Douai 381 (XII, Anchin), folios 19^v–23^r.
S: Le Puy, unnumbered (XV, Souvigny), folios 7^v–11^r.
P1: Paris, Bibl. nat., Latin 14517 (XII, St. Victor), folios 134^v–139^r.
P2: Paris, Mazarine, 734 (XIII–XIV, Jacobins), folios 228^r–232^v.
P3: Paris, Mazarine, 741 (XIII, St. Victor), folios 162^v–169^r.
C: Cologne, Historisches Archiv, GB 4° 21 (XV, Brothers of the Holy Cross, Cologne), folios 41^v–46^v.[272]
Cr: Cracow, Jagellon Library, 2288 (AA XII 13) (XV), folios 227^v–237^r.[273]
Z: Zürich, Zentralbibliothek, Z V 322 (XV, provenance unknown), folios 17^r–22^r.
R: Clm 26818 (XV, Franciscans, Ratisbon), folios 271^v–278^v.
Al: Brussels, Bibl. royale, II.1103 (XIII, Aulne), folios 171^v–174^v.
V: Brussels, Bibl. royale, 20006–20017 (XIII, Villers), folios 98^r–105^v.
Sg: Paris, Bibl. nat., Latin 2944 (XII, St. Germer de Flay), folios 31^r–36^v.
H: Oxford, Bodleian Library, Hatton 102 (XIII–XIV, Hereford Franciscans), folios 86^r–90^v.
U: Paris, Université, 790 (1373, Whalley), folios 23^v–31^v.
Brussels, Bibl. royale, 647–650 (1560, Val-Saint-Martin, Louvain), folios 9^r–13^r.[274]

The lost manuscripts were at Aggsbach A 11, Hautmont, and Meaux.[275]

The total number of manuscripts of Letter 20 is not as great as that of Letter 28, but their geographical distribution was wider, and they occur in a remarkable variety of libraries. With the exception of the *De miraculis*, Letter 20 was probably the best known work by Peter the Venerable. In one manuscript (U), indeed, it was raised to the dignity of a monastic rule: "De institutione reclusorum"; and it was evidently widely read and studied throughout the Middle Ages.

[272] The text is incomplete, going as far as the words "magis cautus existat." There is a manuscript thesis, presented in 1957, on "Die Handschriften der Kölner Kreuzbrüder" by Erwin Gotenburg in the library of the Bibliothekar-Lehrinstitut des Landes Nordrhein-Westfalen in Cologne.

[273] "Iste est liber mgri Luce de Magna Cosmin": Wladyslaw Wislocki, *Catalogus codicum manuscriptorum bibliothecae universitatis Jagellonicae Cracoviensis* (Cracow, 1877–1881) II, 547.

[274] This manuscript, dated 31 December 1560, appears to be copied from the printed edition of 1522 and will not, therefore, be discussed further. It is mentioned in Sander, *Bibliotheca*, II, 222.

[275] Gottlieb, *Bibliothekskataloge*, I, 532–533; Jean Leclercq, "Les manuscrits de l'abbaye d'Hautmont," *Scriptorium*, VII (1953) 67; Thomas of Burton, *Chronicon monasterii de Melsa*, ed. E. A. Bond (Rolls Series, 43; London, 1866–1868) III, xci.

The most important group among the manuscripts consists of P1, P2, P3, C, Cr, Z, and R, all of which derive from P1. The group is therefore called P. P1 is a twelfth-century manuscript from St. Victor at Paris and includes several sections that were bound together before the fifteenth century. The third section (folios 82–228) was probably written by one hand, in spite of slight variations in the script and number of lines per column, and includes several interesting monastic texts: St. Bernard's *De consideratione*; Drogo's *De passione et resurrectione domini*;[276] two sermons from the *De diversis* by St. Bernard; a treatise by Hugh of St. Victor;[277] a brief excerpt from I Corinthians; the letter of Peter the Venerable; and a series of treatises and sermons by St. Bernard. The scribe of P1 was not only a copyist but also an editor, for he divided his copy of Peter's Letter 20 into fourteen sections, marked both in the text and by paragraph marks in the margins. Twice the first word of these sections was "nam," which apparently offended the stylistic sense of the scribe, who underscored the "nam" the first time and replaced it by "itaque" the second. He also corrected his copy. On one occasion, when he had written "serius" in place of "securius," he added a marginal "non" in order to have it make sense. All these and other variants, of which the genesis is apparent in P1, are found in P2, P3, C, Cr, R, and Z. They were not, apparently, copied directly from P1 but from a lost copy, X, in which several errors were made that occur in all these manuscripts except P1. P2 derives independently from X. It is a careless copy, although corrected, and has several distinctive errors. Cr, in turn, appears to derive from P2. The incomplete text in C is also most closely related to P2 and Cr, but the numerous omissions and changes in single words almost suggest that it is a later reworking of the text rather than a real copy. The three manuscripts P3, R, and Z probably derive from a lost sister or cousin of P2, Y. They were not copied from each other, but they have a sufficient number of common variants from P1 and P2 to show that they are the children of a common parent. The family grouping of these seven manuscripts may, therefore, be arranged as shown in the diagram on page 72.

A second group of manuscripts, here called B, includes Al and V, both of the thirteenth century and from Cistercian abbeys in the diocese of Liège. Al is incomplete and contains only about one half of the letter, up to the words "mammona iniquitatis, neque." After this point, the *siglum* V alone represents group B. The two manuscripts are evidently closely related, but neither is a copy of the other, since

---

[276] See Jean Leclercq, "Drogon et Saint Bernard," *Rev. Bén.*, LXIII (1953) 116–131, esp. pp. 124–128; *Recueil*, pp. 95–111, esp. pp. 103–108.

[277] *PL*, CLXXVII, 289–294.

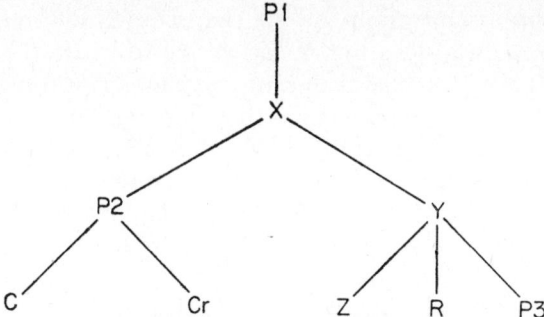

each has several distinctive errors. In V the words "G. incluso" in the salutation have been rendered "Sindulfo," but this is a scribal error and not an alternate name for the addressee.[278]

Manuscripts Sg, H, and U constitute a loose third group, called F. Sg is from the Benedictine abbey of St. Germer de Flay in the diocese of Beauvais; H is from the Franciscan house at Hereford;[279] and U was written for Thomas of Mapleton in 1373 by Richard of Hertford, a monk at the Cistercian abbey of Whalley. They are not closely related in provenance, therefore, and each manuscript, especially H and U, has many variants of its own. Sg and U as a rule agree more than Sg and H or H and U, but in spite of their differences, these manuscripts appear to agree on a core of common readings sufficient to classify them together as a group.

The three groups P, B, and F, and the individual manuscripts within these groups, present a great number of variants from the relatively uniform text found in the collections C, A, and S; but it is hard to determine whether any are the result of revision by Peter the Venerable himself. No confidence can be put in any one group of manuscripts or individual manuscript. Group P depends upon P1, of which the scribe was editor as well as copyist. Any variants found in the other manuscripts of group P are certainly errors, but a few have been included in the *apparatus* in order to guide the classification of other manuscripts. P has in all about a hundred and thirty variants from the CAS text. Of these, some fifty-five are found in P alone; twenty-five, in P and B; and fifty, in P, B, and F. Group F, in spite of considerable variation within itself, is on the whole closer to CAS. Its text, as it appears in Sg (which seems to be the most reliable manuscript of the F group) has only about twenty-five readings to itself, besides the fifty in common with P and B.

---

[278] Cf. the similar error in the title of the lost Aggsbach manuscript: "Item epistola Petri abbatis Cluniacensis ad Philibertum, seruum suum, silva inclusum," Gottlieb, *Bibliothekskataloge*, I, 532–533. There should, I think, be a period after the *silva*[*nectis*].

[279] H lacks the first folio and begins with the words "[mor]tuum non sepelire."

Any sign of revision must be sought in these fifty variants from CAS that occur in all the manuscripts of the separate copy. Those that appear in only two groups, such as the twenty-five variants found in both P and B, must in all probability be classified as related or parallel errors, mostly through homoeoteleuton or the omission of short words, the two most frequent sources of scribal mistakes. In the fifty common variants, however, may be found some real textual revisions, the nature of which has already been discussed. In the revised version found in CAS, the salutation was changed and an important heading was added, perhaps by Peter of Poitiers, "Ad seruum dei Gislebertum Siluanectis inclusum," which is the only reliable key to the identity of the addressee.[280] The revisions in the text were not as numerous or as important as those in Letter 28 and are consequently less interesting. Above all, a variant found only in one group of manuscripts cannot be considered an authentic sign of revision. Even those found in all three groups may sometimes only be scribal errors, though on the whole the manuscripts are of such varied dates and provenance that any relationship between them all is highly improbable, and most of the common variants—those marked in the *apparatus* by the *sigla* PBF—may reasonably be considered parts of the original letter which were changed when Peter prepared the letter for inclusion in his letter collection.

C. Besides the manuscripts of Letters 20 and 28, I have found only four manuscripts containing copies of isolated letters by Peter the Venerable, and of these only the first two appear to derive their texts from the letter in the form that it was first sent out.

Turin, Biblioteca nazionale, *776 (28) E-V-37 (XII-XIII, Staffarda), folios 203^r-207^v: Letter 38 to Archbishop Peter of Lyons.

Clm 27129 (X-XII, Ottobeuren), folios 120^v-121^v: Letter 150 to Bernard of Clairvaux, up to "discretione pateant / ." Owing to water stains, much of folio 121^v is almost illegible.

Lyons, Bibliothèque municipale, 949, is the first volume of an unpublished work entitled "Lugdunum sacroprofanum," written by Pierre Bullioud in 1647. On folio 22^r there are two brief extracts from Letters 38 and 54 to the archbishop of Lyons. They were without doubt taken from the printed edition.

Paris, Bibliothèque Sainte-Geneviève, 1652 (XVII), folios 26^v-27^r: two extracts from Letters 172 and 173, also taken from the printed edition.

These manuscripts are of interest not only individually for the text

---

[280] The title in the Aggsbach catalogue (cited n. 278 above), with "silva. inclusum," shows that this copy was probably taken from a collection, as was the copy of Letter 28 in the same manuscript. On the identity of G., see the biographical note to Ep. 20.

and text-history of Peter's letters but also as a group as evidence of the continued interest in his works throughout the Middle Ages. Of the thirty-six manuscripts listed above, seven are of the twelfth century, four of the twelfth/thirteenth, five of the thirteenth, two of the thirteenth/fourteenth, three of the fourteenth, eleven of the fifteenth, one of the sixteenth, and three of the seventeenth. The number of fifteenth-century manuscripts, in particular, shows that the religious revival at that time included a renewal of interest in the monastic texts of the twelfth century. The manuscripts come from all over Europe: twelve from the Lowlands, eleven from France, four from the Empire, two each from England and Italy, and one each from Spain and Poland. The provenance of two is unknown. They were in the libraries of both the secular and regular clergy and of all the more prominent orders. Of the lost manuscripts three were in the Lowlands and one each in England and the Empire.

4. TEXT AND ARRANGEMENT OF THE LETTERS

The combination of the printed edition C and of the manuscripts of the collected and individual letters provides the basis for a reliable text of the letters of Peter the Venerable. The largest collection, C, was founded on a manuscript of high authority. For the letters it contains, A also is worthy of the highest confidence. S is somewhat less reliable, but it provides a manuscript for most of the letters that are not in A, in addition to supplying two letters found in no other manuscript. There are in all only five letters, 108, 137, 139, 141, and 144, that appear in no manuscript and of which the text has to be accepted on the basis of C alone. Taken as a whole, therefore, the verification of the text presents no special problems.

The principal textual problem is to establish the nature and extent of the revisions by Peter the Venerable himself. In those cases where there is an independent manuscript tradition derived from the letters as they were first written, it is clear that they were considerably revised before they were included in the collection. Similarly, a comparison of A with CS shows that some of the letters were further revised when the original collection was enlarged into its final form, and there may even have been some revision between S and C, as in Letter 58, where an erroneous reference to Mark was corrected to Luke.[281] It is probable, therefore, that all the letters were more or less revised at one time or another. The manuscript tradition is not sufficiently complete to throw much light on this process except in

---

[281] See I, 181, variant 7, although this could be a correction by the editor Pierre de Montmartre.

Letters 20 and 28. These two examples, however, as has been seen, and the small differences between A and CS, suggest that the revision was seldom drastic. Some of the uniformity in the collection, however, as of the salutations, may be owing to revision, and the possibility of more extensive alterations cannot be excluded in the text of the collected letters.

On the whole, the arrangement of the letters is more puzzling than the text. The order of the first collection is comparatively clear from the table of contents in A, but the original arrangement of C is less easy to determine. The most valuable indication is the description of the collection in the chronicle of Cluny,[282] where François de Rivo indicated that it was divided into six books of thirty-six, fifty-one, seven, forty-three, nine, and fifty letters, respectively, making a total of a hundred and ninety-six letters, including the *Contra Iudaeos* and the *Contra Petrobrusianos*. He did not specify whether it included the *Contra eos qui dicunt*, whether the introduction to the *Contra Petrobrusianos* was numbered separately, or whether Letters 125–127 were counted as one letter (as in the 1522 edition) or as three letters (as in A and S). It has been seen, however, that the edition of 1522 probably derived from the copy described by François de Rivo. In this edition, the *Contra Iudaeos*, *Contra Petrobrusianos*, and *Contra eos qui dicunt* are in the first two books, which are followed by four books of thirty-six, fifty-nine, forty-nine, and forty-nine letters, respectively. Including the *Contra eos qui dicunt*, therefore, and counting the *Contra Petrobrusianos* and its introduction as one letter and Letters 125–127 as three letters, the 1522 edition has one hundred and ninety-six letters, as in the chronicle, but in a different arrangement.

In his letter to the reader, Pierre de Montmartre, the editor of the 1522 edition, admits that he has changed the order of the letters. "Should you compare this edition with the archetype, dear reader, do not be surprised if you find the order of the old copy reversed and altered... Principally in order that I may not be accused of publishing a work unsuitable for a theologian, I have placed in the front of the volume those works by which our Peter of Cluny may appear not least among theologians." The learned editors of the *Bibliotheca Cluniacensis*, Marrier and Duchesne, consequently attempted in their edition to restore the original order. "The author of the chronicle of Cluny alone," they wrote, "tells us in how many books they [the letters] were arranged by him [Peter the Venerable], and he records just six books and indicates how many letters each book should contain. We, therefore, have relied on his trustworthiness and evidence, on account of the lack of a manuscript, and have attempted

---

[282] See p. 17 above.

to restore the series and arrangement of these letters to their true and original order, which was changed by Pierre de Montmartre."[283] They omitted, however, the three treatises found in the first two books of the 1522 edition and therefore lacked three letters. In a note at the end they wrote:

In order to complete the number of letters in the sixth book, which is reckoned at fifty in the chronicle of Cluny, three letters seem to be needed, unless it is thought that those three to Peter of St. John [the *Contra eos qui dicunt*] and against the Petrobrusians (which are considered by many to be treatises rather than letters) should be counted with the letters. But since the chronicle shows that they should be separate and put later, we have put in their place some other letters from Suger of St. Denis, Bernard of Clairvaux, and Abbot Peter of Celle to our Peter of Cluny and a few unedited letters from Peter to Suger.[284]

Later scholars, therefore, not unnaturally assumed that the original order had been completely changed. "It is known that the editors of the letters," wrote Quentin, "completely upset the order in which they are found in the manuscripts."[285]

A comparison of the manuscripts with the printed editions, however, shows that the disorder is not as great as Quentin supposed. The only difference between the editions of 1522 and 1614 is that in the earlier edition Letter 94 is between Letters 96 and 97 and Letter 147 between Letters 143 and 144. Substantially the same order is found in all the manuscripts, even those that omit many letters. The only differences are that in A and B Letter 37 is between Letters 51 and 52, in the table of contents in A the *Contra Petrobrusianos* and its introduction are numbered 87 and 88, and in S Letter 94 is between Letters 112 and 113, 147 is between 143 and 145, and the introduction to the *Contra Petrobrusianos* is between Letters 93 and 95. It is therefore clear that Pierre de Montmartre did exactly as he said in his letter to the reader. He moved the three theological treatises to the beginning of the collection and placed Letters 37, 94, and 144, which are concerned with theological matters, at the beginnings of his fourth, fifth, and sixth books. He left the order of the other letters unchanged. The principal problem, therefore, is to determine the proper positions of the treatises and of the very few "wandering" letters found in various positions in the manuscripts. It will be remembered that the manuscripts are of assistance only for the *Contra Petrobrusianos*, which appears after Letter 87 in the index of A and of which the introduction

---

[283] *Bibl. Clun., notae,* col. 104. In a marginal note to col. 621 they again said: "Harum epistolarum seriem ac dispositionem ordini suo genuino restituimus, iuxta fidem ad testimonium Chronici Cluniacensis."
[284] *Bibl. Clun.,* cols. 957–958.
[285] Quentin, in *Misc. Ehrle,* I, 81; cf. *Hist. litt.,* XIII, 249.

is found between Letters 93 and 95 in S. Neither manuscript contains the *Contra eos qui dicunt*. The *Contra Iudaeos* is definitely outside the collection in A and is not included in S. These two works, therefore, were apparently incorporated into the collection only at the final revision.

The problem of the position of the treatises is associated with that of the division of the collection into books. In A the letters are numbered consecutively with no divisions. In S and B, a note after Letter 36 refers to the end of book one, but there are no other divisions. The arrangement into six books, therefore, was made only at the last stage when the definitive collection of a hundred and ninety-six letters was assembled. Sg is the only manuscript showing signs of this arrangement. The fact that Letter 111 in Sg is numbered XVI (changed from XVII or XVIII) is important confirmation of the statement made in the chronicle of Cluny. There the books are said to have contained, respectively, thirty-six, fifty-one, seven, forty-three, nine, and fifty letters, and Letter 111 would have been IV,17. Since there is no reason to believe that there was originally any great disparity in the length of the books, it is reasonable to assume that the treatises were found in the third and fifth books, which contained only seven and nine letters. When Pierre de Montmartre put the treatises into the first two books, he combined the remaining letters in books three and five with those in the preceding books and therefore emerged with four books containing thirty-six, fifty-nine, forty-nine, and forty-nine letters, respectively. These one hundred and ninety-three letters were then rearranged by Marrier and Duchesne into six books in accordance with the indications in the chronicle of Cluny.

The composition of the first book is reasonably certain from the notes in S and B and the evidence of the chronicle and the 1522 edition. It contained Letters 1 to 36. The second book probably consisted of Letters 37 to 87. The only variation is in the position of Letter 37, which is found between Letters 51 and 52 in A and B. Pierre de Montmartre presumably moved it in order to open his fourth book with a long and impressive theological letter, and its number in the original collection was probably II,15. The third book contained seven letters, according to the chronicle, and these almost certainly included the *Contra Petrobrusianos* and its introduction, which were probably counted together as one letter. In the index to A it comes after Letter 87, and the introduction alone comes after Letter 93 in S. It was therefore probably placed either at the beginning or at the end of the third book, which consisted of Letters 88 to 93 and the *Contra Petrobrusianos*.

The exact beginning and composition of the fourth book depend upon the position of the wandering Letter 94. It is the only letter between 1 and 101 that is not found in A, and in S it appears between Letters 112 and 113. In the chronicle of Cluny it is numbered IV,20.[286] In the 1522 edition it is the first letter in book five, between Letters 96 and 97, and in the *Bibliotheca Cluniacensis* it is the last letter in book three, between Letters 93 and 95. As in the case of Letter 37, the move in the printed editions can be plausibly explained: Pierre de Montmartre wanted to begin his fifth book with an impressive letter, and Marrier and Duchesne moved it back in order to pad out their slim third book. Thus the last two letters of the fourth book in the 1522 edition became the first two of the fourth book in the *Bibliotheca Cluniacensis*. The position of Letter 94 in the original collection is harder to ascertain. If the short treatise *Contra eos qui dicunt* was included in the first half of the original book four, however, the position of Letter 94 between Letters 112 and 113 in S would correspond exactly to its number IV,20 in the chronicle of Cluny. The fourth book may therefore have originally included Letters 95 to 112, as well as the *Contra eos qui dicunt*, Letter 94, and then Letters 113 to 135, making the total of forty-three letters mentioned in the chronicle.

The fifth book, of nine letters, would then have included Letters 136 to 143 and the *Contra Iudaeos*. Pierre de Montmartre, when he extracted the *Contra Iudaeos*, added the remaining eight letters to the original book four to make up his fifth book. He also added the following short letter, 147, and thus opened his sixth book with Letter 144, which has considerable theological interest. Marrier and Duchesne, in turn, having moved Letter 94 to the third book and 95 and 96 to the beginning of the fourth, followed the chronicle and counted forty-three letters for their fourth and nine letters for their fifth book. Had they followed the order of the 1522 edition exactly, the already short book five would have included the short Letter 147, which they therefore placed at the beginning of the more substantial book six and placed 138 to 146 in book five. The original sixth book, which had fifty letters according to the chronicle, probably contained Letters 147, 144 to 146, and 148 to 193 in that order. In the *Bibliotheca Cluniacensis*, however, as seen above, the last book lacked three letters and included only forty-seven.

This tentative reconstruction of the original six books is not as involved as it appears, but it cannot be regarded as entirely satisfactory or definite, although it answers most of the questions posed by the manuscripts and printed editions and gives a reasonably clear picture of the letter collection in its complete form, including both the letters and the theological treatises. It may be presented schematically as follows:

[286] *Bibl. Clun.*, col. 595 (*recte* 597) DE.

First Collection (A): 1–36, 38–51, 37, 52–87, *Contra Petrobrusianos*, 88–93, 95–101, 123–129, and 117.

Second Collection (C + Chronicle of Cluny)		1522		1614	
I 36	1–36	[I 1]	Contra Iudaeos	I 36	1–36
II 51	38–51, 37, 52–87	[II 2]	Contra Petro. + Contra eos qui dicunt	II 51	37–87
III 7	88–93 + *Contra Petrobrusianos*	III 36	1–36	III 7	88–94
IV 43	95–112 + *Contra eos qui dicunt*, 94, 113–135	IV 59	37–93, 95–96	IV 43	95–137
V 9	136–143 + *Contra Iudaeos*	V 49	94, 97–143, 147	V 9	138–146
VI 50	147, 144–146, 148–193	VI 49	144–146, 148–193	VI 47	147–193

This arrangement is of interest not only for the study of the letter collection as a whole, conceived of as a work of literature and as an autobiographical expression of the life and work of Peter the Venerable, but also for the general chronology of the letters. The dating of individual letters on the basis of internal evidence clearly shows that the arrangement of most of the collection, contrary to the opinion of many scholars who have used it, is chronological. This does not apply to the first fifty-seven letters, which are in no ascertainable order. But after Letter 57 almost all the letters that can be firmly dated are arranged in chronological order. Letters 58 to 101 date from early 1134 until late 1141, and Letters 102 to 193 (except for 117 and 123–129, which formed part of the first collection) run from 1143 until May 1152.[287] The last part of the collection almost has the character of a chronological register. This view is suggested, for instance, by the order of Letters 150–152, which were written at about the same time, the first two by Peter the Venerable to Bernard of Clairvaux and Nicholas of Montiéramey, the third by Bernard to Peter the Venerable. Bernard's letter seems to have crossed with Peter's and was entered in the letter book immediately after Letters 150 and 151. The only apparent exceptions to the chronological order of the later letters are Letters 102, 112, 143, 144, 145, and 158a and b, and of these the dates of 102, 145, and 158a and b are very uncertain. It is not surprising to find at least a few letters out of order, however, and especially some earlier letters among the later ones. The general order of the collection was the result not of any theoretical regard for

---

[287] Only Letter 102 in the second group seems to have been written before 1143, and its date is not certain.

chronology but of the way in which the letters were kept and copied by Peter of Poitiers, and he doubtless inserted from time to time a letter which for some reason had not been entered in its proper chronological position.

The arrangement and dating of the first fifty-seven letters is more difficult to explain. Only one, Letter 44 to King Sigurd of Norway, can with certainty be dated before 1130. Letter 49 was probably written in 1131. The remaining datable letters all fall, in haphazard order, between the summer of 1133 (Letter 39) and the autumn of 1138 (Letter 29). The possible dates of the other letters, which cannot be dated precisely, cover a wider range than 1133-8, but they may all belong in this period.

It is tempting to see the hand of Peter of Poitiers in this work of preserving and collecting the letters, and it may be no accident that the series of letters in chronological order begins with Letter 58 written by Peter the Venerable to his future secretary shortly before he joined his service.[288] From that time on he seems to have kept a selection of his master's correspondence, either those letters which were considered outstanding for their literary merit or intrinsic interest or perhaps those that he himself had helped to draw up and write, since he was probably not responsible for the entire correspondence of Peter the Venerable. When an ailment of his feet forced him to stay at Cluny while Peter the Venerable was on a retreat in the forest, probably in 1141, Peter of Poitiers busied himself, among other things, with the letters and other works of his master,[289] and it may have been at this time that he added the first fifty-seven letters, drawn from various sources, to the letters he already had. At the end of this collection he placed the letters between himself and Peter the Venerable and his companions on the retreat and so formed the first collection of Peter's letters, which was later copied at Anchin. A decade or more later, he took up the task again and added to this first collection about eighty letters and two treatises written between 1143, when he and Peter the Venerable returned from their visit to Spain, and 1152.[290] He inserted the final group of letters from the first collection into the new letters and arranged the entire collection into six books.

[288] See Appendix Q on Peter of Poitiers.
[289] Letters 123-124 and 129: see p. 16 above.
[290] On the dating of the *Contra Iudaeos*, see Constable, in *Petrus Ven.*, pp. 237-238.

III / The Present Edition

1. CONTENTS

The present edition includes all the letters found in the most complete version of the letter collection of Peter the Venerable, except for the *Contra Petrobrusianos*, the *Contra Iudaeos*, and the *Contra eos qui dicunt*, although there is little doubt that these three treatises formed part of the original collection. Peter the Venerable himself showed in Letter 129 that he regarded "the book written against the heretics" as part of the collection of his letters. The *Contra Iudaeos*, although copied separately in MS. Douai 381, was incorporated into the final version of the collection. And the inclusion of the *Contra eos qui dicunt* by Pierre de Montmartre, although it is not mentioned as part of the collection in the chronicle of Cluny, shows that it appeared in the Cluny manuscript of Peter's collected works. These treatises are not set apart from the letters either by their subject matter or by their length, since several of the letters are concerned with theological matters, and Letter 28 is considerably longer than the *Contra eos qui dicunt*.

The exclusion of the treatises is therefore a concession to tradition and to practicality. The *Contra Petrobrusianos* and the *Contra Iudaeos* are longer than the longest letter, and a new edition of the former has been independently prepared.[291] Their distinctly polemic character, furthermore, puts them into a class more with the *Contra Sarracenos*, which never formed part of the letter collection, than with the letters. Above all, they were copied separately even in the earliest surviving manuscripts of the collection. In Douai 381 the *Contra Petrobrusianos* is known to have formed part of the letter collection only from the table of contents, and in the Le Puy manuscript, S, only its introduction was included. The present edition therefore follows the example of the manuscripts, but it should be remembered that

[291] By Dr. J. V. Fearns, as a doctoral dissertation at the University of Liverpool. I am informed by Dom E. Dekkers that it will be published (together with new editions of the *Contra Iudaeos* and *Contra Sarracenos*) in the "Continuatio mediævalis" of the *CC*.

the original letter collection was more varied and comprehensive than it is here.

Aside from this omission, the character of the collection as a literary whole has been preserved as much as possible, and it makes no claims to being a complete *corpus* of the correspondence of Peter the Venerable. There is no evidence that any of the supplementary letters printed by Marrier and Duchesne or by Migne were ever part of the collection as it was formed and revised by Peter the Venerable himself, and their inclusion here would only confuse the arrangement of the whole.

2. ORDER

The order of the letters as they are found in the *Bibliotheca Cluniacensis* has been preserved for the same reasons. The order of the letters in the manuscripts has already been discussed in this Introduction. Pierre de Montmartre, the editor of the 1522 edition, was probably responsible for moving Letters 37, 94, and 144, in addition to placing the three polemic treatises in his first two books. The further moving of Letters 94 and 147 by Marrier and Duchesne was a purely conjectural emendation. These changes were so relatively small, however, and the order in the *Bibliotheca Cluniacensis* is so similar to that in the manuscripts and C, that it appears unjustified to replace its arrangement with an order that only might be closer to the original order of the final edition. Both Schmeidler and Erdmann emphasized that the order of the letters is an essential element in the text-tradition of medieval letter collections and should not be disturbed by an editor without excellent reasons.[292] No effort has therefore been made to rearrange the letters according to their dates, subject matter, or recipients.

The division into books of the *Bibliotheca Cluniacensis*, on the other hand, has not been followed in the present edition. No such divisions were made in the first edition, and the divisions into books of the final edition are now entirely lost. Even presuming that the figures in the chronicle of Cluny are accurate, as they seem to be, it would be impossible to reconstruct the six original books without knowing the exact positions of Letter 94 and of the polemic treatises. The numbering in the 1522 edition and the *Bibliotheca Cluniacensis* is inconsistent and inaccurate and has therefore been replaced here by a simple numerical sequence, as is found in the existing manuscripts. The two letters to Dr. Bartholomew, of which S is the only manuscript, are printed here in the same position in which they are found in S, but

[292] Cf. Erdmann, in *Neues Archiv* (cited n. 16 above), XLIX, 385.

they are numbered 158a and b in order to indicate that they are not part of the collection found in C.

3. TEXT

The text of the present edition is based on A whenever possible and on C for the letters not included in A. Since Peter the Venerable revised the texts of at least some of his letters, the versions found in the manuscripts have not been amalgamated here into a composite text. Manuscript A is of such exceptional accuracy and authority that it has been followed in all readings except obvious scribal errors, although the version it contains is earlier than that in C. For the letters not in A, the text of the printed edition C is better than that in the manuscript S. All the variants in S have been included in the *apparatus*, however, together with variants from Cl, O, and T and occasionally also from printed editions. Scribal slips and differences in punctuation and spelling, except of proper names, have not been included in the *apparatus*.

The only letters that present any serious textual problems, as explained previously, are Letters 20 and 28.[293] In this edition the principal text of both of these letters is that of the collected, revised version found in A, but the other versions are distinguished in the *apparatus*. Thus for Letter 20 the variants marked by the combined *sigla* PBF were probably the readings of the original version, and the other variants are those of a single manuscript or group of manuscripts. Letter 28 presents more difficulties, because it appears to have circulated in several versions during the lifetime of Peter the Venerable before it was revised for the collection. These versions are found in the groups of manuscripts labeled Oa, Ob, and L. Readings found in all three of these groups are marked O, but this is merely a convenient collective *siglum* for readings found in the manuscripts of all the so-called original versions, except U, as contrasted with the revised version, and it seems that there never was an archetypal O version from which Oa, Ob, and L descended. This is why it was impossible to present the original version as the principal text. No form of O is more authentic than the other forms, and a text based only on common readings would be an editorial composition which no contemporary could ever have seen. The text of the revised version, on the other hand, is relatively consistent and can be confidently based on A. The original versions can be found in the *apparatus*, marked O to indicate the common changes when the letter was revised for the collection and Oa, Ob, and L to distinguish the various forms found in the

[293] See pp. 63–73 above.

manuscripts. In addition to these collective *sigla*, there are several important groups of individual *sigla*. DSb indicates the most extreme form of the original version; it could also be marked Oa(-An). OaL and ObL indicate, respectively, the combinations DSbAnLSt and CaArMaLSt and could equally well be marked O(-Ob) and O(-Oa). OU shows a complete agreement of all the manuscripts of the original version. The manuscripts of the revised version, except for Ss, are in broad agreement. R marks the South German form. The most frequent combinations of *sigla* are SC, RSC, and SsR, but these show relations between manuscripts rather than textual revisions. There are, however, several more surprising combinations, which seem to cut across the classification of versions and manuscripts proposed above and which are a warning against too rigid a scheme of the versions and manuscripts of the text.

4. ORTHOGRAPHY

Manuscript A is evidence that in the middle of the twelfth century, even in a manuscript prepared and written with the greatest care, (1) there was a permissible variation in the spelling of certain words[294] and (2) a considerable number of words were normally spelled and divided in a distinctive fashion, different from the modern standards of classical orthography.[295] This manuscript was certainly not the autograph of Peter the Venerable, nor even of Peter of Poitiers, but it is sufficiently close to the original, both in date and provenance, that its spelling, accentuation, and punctuation cannot be disregarded, as with the manuscripts of most classical and medieval texts,[296] and it has served as the basis of the orthography in the present edition.

In the absence of any established rules of medieval orthography,[297]

---

[294] Orthographical inconsistency is not incompatible with a high level of creative activity in literature. Many distinguished writers have spelled the same word in several ways, and some have been attached to the peculiarities of their spelling. Boswell in the preface to his *Account of Corsica* specifically stated: "If this work should at any future period be reprinted, I hope that care will be taken of my orthography" (cited by G. B. Hill in the preface to his edition of Boswell's *Life of Johnson* [New York, 1891–1904] I, xxiii). See also the remarks on the orthography of place-names in the preface to T. E. Lawrence, *Seven Pillars of Wisdom* (New York, 1935) p. 24.

[295] The standard used here for classical orthography is the *Latin Dictionary* of Lewis and Short. On orthographical variants in the twelfth century, see among other recent works the introduction by É. M. Buytaert to his edition of Eusebius of Emesa, *Discours conservés en Latin*, I (Spicilegium sacrum Lovaniense, 26; Louvain, 1953) pp. xxi–xxiv.

[296] Cf. Dain, *Manuscrits*, p. 160, who remarked that the spelling in most manuscripts simply marks "a way of writing at a certain time and in a certain place."

[297] Some practical indications will be found in the "Report on Editing Historical Documents," *Bulletin of the Institute of Historical Research*, I (1923) 6–25, and in the "Bulletin for 1959" of the Institute of Research and Study in Medieval Canon Law, published in *Traditio*, XV (1959) 456–457.

every editor has to establish his own rules and to ask the indulgence of his readers for any peculiarities and inconsistencies.[298] Some rules are necessary in order to expand abbreviations and to harmonize the texts from different manuscripts, because not all the letters are found in manuscript A, and there is no reason to respect the orthography of S and C. These rules should not be so strict, however, or so strictly applied as to impose a rigid classical standard and artificial uniformity, which were unknown in the original text. I have therefore adopted a compromise orthography that is designed to approximate the spelling and "orthographical flavor" without confusing and annoying the reader. It is based upon three principles: (1) the preservation of all usages and spellings consistently found in A, such as the use of the small *u* and capital *V* and the avoidance of *j*;[299] (2) the preservation of a few characteristic variations, especially in the spelling of proper names and of relatively unusual words, such as *philosophus* (*phylosophus, filosophus, filosofus*, etc.), *celleraria* (*cellararia*), and *mysticus* (*misticus*);[300] and (3) the standardization of the spelling of most words to the form most frequently found in A.[301] The principal orthographical variations turn on the following points: the use of *e*, *ę*, and *ae*; interchangeable letters and diphthongs; additional letters; doubled letters; omitted letters; elisions; and divisions of words.

Use of e, ę, and ae. The manuscript presents no consistent pattern in the use of *e*, *ę*, and *ae*. During the Middle Ages, as mentioned above, there was a tendency for the *e* alone to replace the *ę* and diphthong. In A the use of the diphthong, both written out and as *ę*, is well established in a number of words, and a majority of these (about eighty out of a hundred and thirty, by a rough count) agree with accepted classical usage. About half of these are words beginning with *prae*. This is often abbreviated to *p*, but the abbreviation is written out often enough to

---

[298] On the editorial problems presented by orthographical variations in early medieval manuscripts, see Mario Esposito, "On the New Edition of the Opera Sancti Columbani," *Classica et Mediaevalia*, XXI (1960) 197, and the reply by Ludwig Bieler, "Editing Saint Columbanus: A Reply," *ibid.*, XXII (1961) 143. M. R. James, after admitting the unintentional inconsistencies in his edition of Walter Map, *De nugis curialium*, p. xvii, expressed the hope that the "confession of these shortcomings ... will be taken as sufficient to condone them."

[299] On the use of U, V, u, and v, see *Bull. Inst. Hist. Research*, I, 12: "Where the manuscript is consistent in the use of *v* and *u* its practice should be followed; where it is not consistent the modern practice—or, if preferred, the *v* form as initial, the *u* form as medial—may be adopted"; cf. H. Maxwell Lyte, "'U' and 'V': A note on Palaeography," *ibid.*, II (1925) 63–65, and *Traditio*, XV, 456.

[300] Cf. *Bull. Inst. Hist. Research*, I, 12: "Markedly peculiar spellings, such as *ewangelia*, should be retained"; and *Traditio*, XV, 457: "(e) rare words ... should be given as they appear in the manuscripts."

[301] Cf. *Traditio*, XV, 456: "(c) other typical medieval spellings ... should be retained only if used with fair consistency in the basic manuscript or manuscripts."

show that the scribe intended to use the diphthong. Among common word, *prebeo* and *presul* are the only words that are usually spelled with a diphthong in classical usage and with a simple *e* in A. There are a few words in which the diphthong and simple *e* were used interchangeably, including the common words *ceterus*, *epistola*, and *saeculum*, which are so spelled in the present edition, although in A (and in classical usage) they are often spelled *caeterus*, *aepistola*, and *seculum*. The classical *pretium* is regularly spelled *praecium* in A, but its derivative *preciosus* is spelled without the diphthong. Again as in classical usage, the terms for questioning (*quaero*, *quaeso*, *quaestio*) are normally spelled with the diphthong, but terms of complaint (*queror*, *querela*) are spelled with a simple *e*, and this distinction is preserved in the present edition, although the manuscript occasionally has both *queso* and *quaerela*. Within the space of a few lines in A are found *obedientia/obaedientia* and *tela/taela*, although these two words are usually spelled with the diphthong. *Aepula* sometimes appears as *epula*, but *cella* and *comedere* are usually spelled without the diphthong.

In addition to these words of which the spelling varied, but normally agreed with classical usage, there are a number in which *e* and *ae* were consistently used in an unclassical fashion. Among those without the diphthong are: *adheresco, amenus, eger, emulor* (and derivatives), *fex, hereo* (and compounds), *hereticus, hesitatio, ledo* (and derivatives and compounds), *mereo* (and derivatives), *pene, preter, sepe, seuus*, and *tedium*. Among the words regularly spelled with a diphthong in A are: *aecclesia, aeloquium, aequito, aeuangelista, caedo* (for *caedo* and *cedo* and most of its compounds: *excaedere, praecaedere, procaedere*, though some of these, and the important *concedere*, are often spelled without the diphthong), *caena, caenaculum, faecunditas*, and *laetalis*. Most important, perhaps, is the almost universal use of the diphthong in the past tenses of *capio* (*caepi*) and its many compounds and derivatives, as, for instance, in the very common word *praecaeptum*.

The *oe* is never spelled out in A,[302] and its use in the present edition has been restricted to a few words in which the use of *e* or *ae* might lead to ambiguity or confusion. These include *coepere, foedus, moenia*, and *poena*, which are always spelled with an ę in A and with an *oe* in classical usage.

Interchangeable letters. The principal interchangeable letters and diphthongs found in A are: *b/p, c(ch)/k, c/qu, c/t, d/t, f/ph, i/y*, and *m/n*.[303]

[302] Thus, conversely, the printed edition of 1522 (C) spells the adverb *paene* (*pene*) as *poene* and even *poenae*.

[303] Cf. the list of interchangeable letters given by Buytaert in his edition of Eusebius, cited n. 295 above. He omits *c/k* but adds *c/g, o/u,* and *s/ʒ*, which do not occur in A. *Nabugodonosor* is the only example I have noticed of an interchange between *c(ch)* and *g*.

b/p: A shows a marked preference for *p* rather than *b* in *eptomada*∗, *optempero*, *optendo*∗, *optineo*, *optuli*, *opturo*, *optutus*, *suptilis*∗, and some others. (Those marked with a star are occasionally spelled with a *b* but more often with a *p*.)

c(ch)/k: A regularly uses *c* (or *ch*, which will be discussed later) rather than *k* in *carta*, *chaos*, and *charisma*, but not in *carus* and *carissimus*, which are often spelled with a *k*. This peculiarity has been preserved in the present edition for the letters derived from A.

c/qu: A almost always uses *c* rather than *qu* before *u*, and especially in the third person plural present and past tenses of *loquor* and *sequor*, and their many compounds and derivatives, which are regularly spelled *locuntur*, *secuntur*, *locutus*, *secutus*, and others. In other words it as a rule agrees with classical usage, such as *conquasso*, *cotidie*, *liquor*, *nequitia*, and *squaleo*.

c/t: A shows little consistency in its use of *c* and *t*, and a number of words are spelled with either, including *contumacio*, *deliciae*, *hospitium*, *malitia*, *negotium* (*negotiosus*), *nequitia*, *nouicius*, *pernicies* (*perniciosus*), *segnicia*, and *tristitia*. The most usual form of these words is that given here and agrees, except for *segnicia*, with classical usage. In most other words with a possible alternative, A uses *c*, particularly in such frequent words as *auaricia*, *commercium*, *mendacium*, *ocium*, *ociositas*, *palacium*, *praecium* (*preciosus*), and *spacium*. The commonest words spelled with a *t* are *iustitia*, *nuntio* (though *pronuncio* occurs once), *nuntius*, and *tertius*.

d/t: A usually prefers *t* to *d*, as in *eptomada*.

f/ph: A uses *f* and *ph* almost interchangeably, as in the word *philosophus*. It is impossible to draw up strict rules, but *ph* is used in *blasphemus*, *cophinus*, *epitaphium* (*epytaphium*), *phantastici*, *pharetra*, *phisica*, *triumpho*, *triumphus*, and *tropheum*, all as in classical usage, and *f* is used in *gazofilatium*, *nefas*, and *omnifarius*.

i/y: *I* and *y* are also more or less interchangeable in A, and several words are spelled with both: *Cistercienses*, *cimiterium* (*cymiterium*), *epitaphium* (*epytaphium*), *hylaris*, *Hyspania*, *martyr*, *misticus* (*mysticus*), and *Sicilia* (*Sycilia*). For those of which the alternative is given in parentheses, A shows no marked preference, and both spellings have been used in the present edition. Of the words spelled regularly with *i* or *y*, *y* predominates over *i* in the approximate ratio of three to one. Among the commoner words spelled with *y* are *abyssus*, *gyganteus*, *hyems*, *hymnus* (*ymnus*), *hystoria*, *mysterium*, *paradysus*, *satyra*, *sydus*, *symbolum*, *symonia*, *synagoga*, *Syon*, *tyrannus*, *ydolatria*, *ymber*, *ypochrisis*, and *ypochrita*. Among those regularly spelled with an *i* are: *Aethiops*, *Babilon*, *diabolus*, *dialogus*, *idoneus*, *idus*, *phisica*, *presbiter*, and *stilus*.

m/n: *Nunquam*, *nunquid*, *tanquam*, and *unquam* are all regularly spelled with an *n* in A, and therefore also in the present edition. The accusative of *Sathan* is *Sathanan*, as in C and S. Among the words in which *n* is sometimes used in place of *m*, and vice versa, are *aliquandiu*, *menbrum*, *quamtalibet*, and *unaminus*. This suggests that the pronunciation of the two letters was very similar, and their use has been standardized in this edition.

Additional letters. The principal additional letters found in A, apart from doubling, are *h* and *p*.

H is used, as commonly in medieval orthography, before vowels both at the beginnings of words and in the middle and after *c* and *t*, but its use is inconsistent. *Anhelus* and *hymnus*, for instance, are spelled both with and without the *h*, and *Israel* and *Mychael* can be spelled *Israhel* and *Mychahel*. Among the words consistently spelled with an *h* are *exhaurio* (and *inexhaustus*), *exhibeo*, *harundineus*, *hortor* (and *exhortor*), *holus*, and the words listed above under *i/y*. *Iohannes* is regularly spelled with an *h*, but *abundantia*, *ortus* (a garden), and *ostium* are spelled without an *h*.

H is regularly used after *c* in several common words, including *archanus*, *brachium*, *chaos*, *inchoatus*, *michi*, *monachus*, *nichil*, *parrochia*, *pentechoste*, and *sepulchrum*. *C* alone, however, is used in *carta*, *cartula*, *coarto*, *lacrima*, and after *s* at the beginning of such words as *scedula*, *scisma*, *scismaticus*, *scola*, and *scolasticus*. *Carus* and *carissimus* are also spelled with a simple *c* when they are not spelled with a *k*. *Charisma* is on one occasion spelled with a *c* but normally with a *ch*.

H is used after *t* in *absinthium*, *cathedra*, *cathena*, *catholicus*, *rethorica*, *Sathan*, *theloneum*, and *theoria*. *Cotidie*, *cotidianus*, *pentechoste*, and *laetalis*, on the other hand, are spelled without an *h* after the *t*.

The most striking use of *h* in manuscript A is in place of *e* and *he* in proper names, such as *Ihremias*, *Ihricho*, *Ihronimus*, *Ihrusalem*, and, most important, *Ihsus*. It has been seen that *Israhel* and *Mychahel* are sometimes spelled with an *h*, which suggests that an *h* was considered to belong with an *e* and could even replace it in these names. The usage is not without exceptions. *Ihesus* is used more than once, and in Letter 24 *Ihronimus* and *Ieronimus* are found within two words of each other. Like all variations in the spelling of proper names, these have been preserved in the present edition in letters derived from A. They have all been spelled with *he* in letters derived from C.

An additional *p* is found after *m* in *alumpnus*, *calumpnia*, *contempno* (and derivatives), *dampno* (and compounds and derivatives), *sollempnis*, *sumo* (*sumptus*, and so on), *tempto*, and *uerumptamen*. *Columpna* is once spelled without the *p*. *Somnus*, however, which was often spelled with a *p* in the Middle Ages, is regularly spelled without a *p* in A.

Doubled letters. As in most medieval manuscripts, a few letters are doubled in A. The commonest is the double *i* in words like *hii* and *hiis*, in certain forms of *redeo*, and frequently (but not always) in compounds of *iacio* (*coniicio, iniicio, obiicio, proiicio*), in which the double *i* was also not unknown in classical usage. The double *p* is found in the past tense of *reperio*, the double *c* in *accidia* and in all forms of *sanccire* (*sanccivi, sanccitum*), and the double *r* in *parrochia* and *parrochialis*. These doubles have been preserved in the present edition except for *hii* and *hiis*, which have been standardized for the sake of convenience.

Omitted letters. There are relatively few omitted letters in the orthography of A, and those there are were mostly in accord with classical usage. The plural of *mille* is spelled with one *l*, *quattuor* occasionally with one *t*, the plural genitive of *sapiens*, *sapientum*, without the *i*, and *dextera* sometimes without the second *e*. *Dextra* and *dextera* occur in one letter a few lines apart. The omission of the *c* from *arctus* was also accepted in classical usage, and the spelling of *elemosina* and *elemosinarius* with a single second *e* was very common in the Middle Ages. The spelling of *absortus* without a *b* or *p* and the occasional omission of the *e* after an *h* in proper names were more unusual.

Elision. Prefixes seem to have been assimilated less frequently in A than was usual in classical spelling. It is impossible to examine this question fully here, but some examples may be given of the prefixes *ad, ex, in, ob,* and *sub*.

ad: was as a rule, though not invariably, unassimilated except before *s*, when it became *as* with a double *s*. Thus *adnuntio, adquiesco,* and *adquiro* are regularly spelled with the *d*, but *assumo, assequor, assto, asstringo, assum,* and *assumo* are spelled with *ss*, although in two cases, *astringo* and *astantibus*, the second *s* was dropped. Other exceptions to this rule are *aggaudeo, ammoneo* (though *adgaudeo* and *admoneo* are also found), *annisus,* and *annoto*.

ex: With the exception of *expectatio*, the *s* is usually preserved in A after the prefix *ex* on words beginning with *s*. There are isolated examples, however, of *expolio* and *exupero*.

in: It is impossible to formulate rules for the use of *in*. It is unassimilated in *inreparabilis* and *inreuocabilis* but assimilated in *immissio, irrefragabilis,* and *irruptio*. The style of the manuscript is followed in the present edition.

ob and *sub*: Practice with *ob* and *sub* also varies. They were not assimilated in *obfundo, subporto,* and *subpono*, although *suppono* occurs on at least one occasion. In *offero* and *succumbo*, on the other hand, they were assimilated.

Division of words. The division of words presents a special problem, since many words normally joined in classical usage are divided in A, and vice versa. As in other matters, the orthographical standard in this edition is set by the predominant usage of the manuscript, with a few concessions to custom and clarity. Thus the enclitics *ne*, *que*, and *ue* are joined in this edition, although usually separate in A, and *ipse* and its forms are separated from *me*, *te*, *michi*, *tibi*, and so forth, though in A they are often joined.

Among the words ending with *quam*, those indicating time are written as one word (*antequam, postquam, priusquam*), the rest as two (*plus quam, propter quam,* and *ultra quam*).

Among the words ending with *modo* and *modum, amodo, omnimodo, postmodum, quodammodo,* and *quomodo* are written as one word; the others, such as *nullo modo* and *tantum modo*, as two.

All terms ending in *magis* and *minus*, including *tanto magis, tanto minus, quanto magis,* and *quanto minus*, are written as two words.

The following words are joined or divided as follows:

ac si (= quasi)	non nisi
adhuc	prout
econtra, econtrario	quamdiu
econuerso	quamplures, quamplurimus
etenim	quotquotlibet
etsi	res publica
hucusque	siquidem
in quantum, in tantum	si quis, si qua, si quid
necdum	tamdiu
nedum	unus quisque
ne quis	utpote
nondum	ut quid

A also uses a number of compound words not commonly found in classical usage. Those composed of *dico* with *ante, sepe,* and *supra* have been printed separately in this edition, but some of the less usual ones, such as *extramaneo, incircumspectus, notafacio,* and *superconcupiscibilis*, have been preserved.

Special usages. Two further distinctive spellings in A, which follow no rules, are *fraglantia* for *fragrantia* and on one occasion *maglinus* for *malignus*, which may be a scribal error. *Cistersienses*, which appears once in place of *Cistercienses*, is almost certainly an error, but it is of interest for pronunciation.

Two troublesome abbreviations are $\overline{dms}$ and $sp\bar{a}lis$. It is sometimes said that in medieval usage *dominus* applied to the Deity and *domnus* to men, but in A the two spellings were used interchangeably, and *dominus* is more than once spelled out in reference to a man. In this edition, the term is normally spelled *dominus*. *Spālis* as a rule means *specialis* and is always expanded in this way in the *Bibliotheca Cluniacensis*, but it also sometimes means *spiritualis*.

Finally, two important place-names should be mentioned. The abbreviation *Clun.* can mean either *Cluniacensis* or *Cluniacensium* and has been expanded in the present edition according to the sense. *Clara Vallis* as a noun is usually written in A as two words, but as an adjective it is written as one word, *Clarauallensis*. I have noted only a few exceptions to this rule, which is followed in the present edition. In the noun, therefore, but not in the adjective, the *clara* agrees with the *uallis*.

5. CAPITALIZATION AND PUNCTUATION

Capitals have been used in the present edition at the beginnings of sentences, for proper names, and for adjectives derived from proper names. The practice of capitalization in manuscript A is not consistent, but sentences always begin with capitals and proper names in the middle of sentences sometimes begin with a modified sort of capital, something between the usual capitals and small letters in size. References to the Deity are not capitalized in A, but both *papa* and *patriarcha* are usually spelled with a capital *P*, and *regula*, when referring to the Rule of St. Benedict, is often capitalized.

The punctuation in A is exceptionally careful and complete, and the only modification in this edition has been to substitute conventional modern signs for the . and ' used in A and to introduce a very small amount of supplementary punctuation. A is inconsistent, for example, in its use of a comma before the final *et* in a series; and commas have been inserted before as well as after the names or titles of persons addressed in the text, such as *o uenerabilis pater*, which in A are followed but not preceded by a comma. Brief parenthetical remarks, such as *inquam, iuxta prophetam, quod maius est,* and *ut supra dixi*, have been left either without punctuation or occasionally simply followed by a comma, as in the manuscript.[304] The punctuation of carefully prepared manuscripts in the twelfth century was not without reason or purpose, as Southern has recently emphasized in the introduction to his edition of Eadmer's *Life* of St. Anselm. "The system paid more attention to the needs of the reader than to strict logic or grammar," he wrote. "It was therefore especially suitable for prose relatively weak in grammatical construction, and strong in rhythmical effects

---

[304] Cf. the introduction by Kassius Hallinger to the first volume of the *Corpus consuetudinum monasticarum* (Siegburg, 1963) p. lxxxix.

and other devices for easing the path of the reader and catching the attention of the listener."[305] Many, if not most, of Peter the Venerable's letters were designed to be read aloud to their recipients. The punctuation in C and S naturally deserves less respect than that in A. In letters derived from these sources, therefore, except when they agree, the punctuation has been revised *ad sensum* and in general conformity with the rules followed in A, but in no case have paragraphs been introduced where no subdivisions appear in the manuscripts.

Quotations are marked by italics, not by quotation marks. Reminiscences are indicated in the notes only. All passages clearly intended as quotations, however, have been treated as such, whether or not they agree precisely with the printed texts of the original. As seen above, Peter the Venerable often cited from memory and treated his quotations with considerable freedom, changing the word order and forms to agree with his own meaning and construction. In particular, all the divergences from the Clementine Vulgate have not been indicated.

6. TEXTUAL *APPARATUS*

The textual *apparatus*, as already explained, includes variants from the principal text, aside from obvious errors, taken from both the manuscripts and the printed editions. In view of the paucity of manuscripts for many of the letters, nearly all the variants from S (including the frequent use of *quid* in place of *quod* and of the present rather than the past tense of *contingo*) have been listed. In Letters 20 and 28, however, of which there are several manuscripts, variants from a single manuscript have not as a rule been included. A very few variants have been listed from the *Bibliotheca Cluniacensis*, although they are without manuscript authority, for their value as conjectural emendations of the text in C. Variants that agree with the Rule of St. Benedict or with the Clementine Vulgate are marked *Reg. Ben.* and *Vulg.*

Pro is used in the *apparatus* only when a single-word variant refers to several words in the text, or vice versa, or several words to several words. It is not used, except in a few cases of possible confusion, when a single-word variant refers to a single word in the text.

[305] Eadmer, *Vita Anselmi* (cited n. 8 above), p. xxxi; see pp. xxviii–xxxiv for an excellent brief account (with references to previous literature) of medieval punctuation.

Notes to the Letters

The following notes are primarily designed not to provide a running commentary on the content of the letters but to identify and date, when possible, the principal people and events concerned. They therefore supplement, but do not entirely supersede, the notes of André Duchesne in the *Bibliotheca Cluniacensis*, which in spite of their age still contain much valuable material. The notes here fall into two categories: one of general notes on the letter as a whole, the other of specific notes on individual points in the text. The three sections of the general notes should be briefly explained.

The first section is in effect a bibliography of the letter, including the sources from which the present text is derived (using the same *sigla* as in the *apparatus*), selected reprints and translations, and references to the letter in *regesta* and other works, arranged chronologically in order of their appearance. These bibliographies are far from complete—further references to various older works are given by Bréquigny and Pignot[1]—nor are the works always of scholarly value, such as the translations given by Lorain; but they give an idea of the use made of the letter by previous writers and may be useful to future scholars. I have occasionally added to this section a general comment on the nature and importance of the letter.

The second section, when necessary, deals with the recipient of the letter or, in the case of letters addressed to Peter the Venerable, with the sender. This section is omitted when no identification is necessary or when the figure has been previously discussed. Cross references to previous notes are given only when the material there is relevant to the letter in question, but the references may be located through the Index.

The third section deals with the date of the letter. When no date is

[1] In particular, references have not been included to the older biographies of Peter the Venerable, by D'Avenel, Demimuid, Duparay, Wilkens, and others, all of which depend heavily on his correspondence.

given, the chronological limits of the abbacy of Peter the Venerable may be assumed. The date is followed by a justification whenever the reasons are not obvious or supplied in later notes to the letter. No references have been given for the dates of popes, emperors, and kings that have been taken from works of generally accepted reliability, such as Grotefend's *Taschenbuch* and Cheney's *Handbook of Dates*, nor for the movements of the popes or of Peter the Venerable himself, which are derived, respectively, from Jaffé-Löwenfeld and from the itinerary in Appendix D. References are supplied, however, for all dates derived from older works, of which the accuracy is not above dispute. The dash (–) in dates is used to indicate "from ... to," inclusively; the slash (/) means "some time between," including the terminal dates. Thus the abbacy of Peter the Venerable is dated 1122–56; but a letter written at some unspecified time during his abbacy is dated 1122/56.

Considerable attention has been given to the dating, but the suggested dates are certainly far from final. Two general warnings should be made. The first is that in this sort of work the editor has frequently to rely on works of reference, such as the *Gallia christiana*, *L'art de vérifier les dates*, and the volumes of Gams and Chevalier, which are monuments of industry and learning but inevitably antiquated and inaccurate in details. Apologies must therefore be made to specialists, particularly in local history, for the dating of bishops, abbots, and other personages who appear only incidentally in these letters and upon whom some recent scholarly work has been overlooked. A second warning concerns the beginning of the year, which is often impossible to establish in letters. It is certain from Letter 158a, which was written in the week of Epiphany, that is, the first week in January, and in which Peter referred to the previous year (New Style) as "this year," that he did not use the style of the Incarnation or of January 1. He more probably used the style of the Annunciation or of Easter, which was common in Burgundy in the eleventh and twelfth centuries,[2] but the reader must be cautious whenever there are references to "this," "last," or "the coming" year.

The dates suggested here have been based on internal evidence, and no conscious weight has been given to the position of the letter in the

---

[2] In Champagne and the diocese of Langres, the year was customarily reckoned from Easter to Easter after about 1150: see Giry, *Manuel*, p. 121, and *Molesme*, I, 67–70; but there is evidence that the style of the Annunciation and the older style of the Nativity were used in Burgundy in the twelfth century: see Maurice Chaume, "Notes et documents sur le début de l'année en Bourgogne aux XIe et XIIe siècles," *Recherches d'histoire chrétienne et médiévale* (Dijon, 1947) pp. 324–328; and in the chronicle of Cluny the death of Peter the Venerable was dated Christmas 1157, "prima ipsius anni die": *Bibl. Clun.*, col. 601 A. Cf., generally, R. L. Poole, "The Beginning of the Year in the Middle Ages," in his *Studies*, pp. 20–25.

collection. It is consequently possible to see that the datable letters after Letter 57 are almost all in chronological order. The evidence of chronological order is, indeed, probably strong enough to justify a closer dating of some otherwise undatable letters on the basis of their position in the collection, and also to throw doubt on the dates assigned to the few letters that seem to be out of chronological order, especially Letters 102, 143, and 158a and b. Even for Letters 1–57, which are clearly not in chronological order, it is reasonable to regard 1133 and 1138 (or perhaps 1141) as the chronological limits except when there is strong evidence to the contrary, as in the case of Letter 44. These indications cannot be regarded as definite, but they may help in establishing more closely the dates of people and events during the lifetime of Peter the Venerable.

Notes on individual points, marked by an asterisk in the text of volume I, are identified here by a reference to the page (and, when there are two or more notes to a page, to the line) in volume I. The lines are counted from the beginning of the text of a letter, not including the title and salutation, on pages where a new letter begins, and from the top of each page when the text continues on following pages. Cross references to notes to other letters are indicated here by the number of the letter and the page (and line) in volume I to which the note refers (that is, the bold-face references on the left of the page in volume II), thus: Ep. 1, n. to p. 4, l. 6.

EPISTOLA PETRI PICTAVENSIS AD DOMINVM PETRVM ABBATEM CLVNIACENSEM

A unnumbered (fol. 10^v); S unnumbered (fol. 2^r); C unnumbered (fol. 1^r); Bc unnumbered (col. 617).

Ca. 1142(?). This letter was probably written at the time when the first collection of Peter the Venerable's letters, as found in A, was compiled: see pp. 16–17 above.

p. 1] On the importance of this reference to *libellum* and the later reference to *praefatum codicem*, see p. 17 above.

I

EPISTOLA EIVSDEM PRIMA AD PAPAM INNOCENTIVM

A 1; S 1; C III,1; Bc I,1; cf. Bréquigny, *Chartes*, III, 11 (1137); Pignot, *Cluny*, III, 168–169.

Early 1137. Peter says that the schism has gone on for seven years and that Innocent will surely be victorious in the eighth. This dating fits with the facts that the Pope was clearly not in Rome, where he returned late in 1137, and that Letter 62, dated 20 July 1137, seems to be a reply to this letter.

p. 4, l. 1] Geoffrey of Le Loroux was archbishop of Bordeaux from 1136 (see Richard, *Comtes de Poitou*, II, 43, n. 2) until his death in 1158. He first met Peter the Venerable, according to Letter 106, "iter Cartusiense," that is, on a visit to a Carthusian house, probably La Chartreuse itself, and the two men became firm friends. Bishop Bernard of Saintes referred to Geoffrey as "amicus... ecclesiae Clun." in a charter of 1149 (*Bibl. Clun.*, col. 1450; *Cluny*, V, 484, no. 4139); and while Peter was in Spain in 1142-3, Geoffrey acted as his deputy in France. He has recently been identified as the well-known preacher Geoffrey Babion by Jean-Paul Bonnes, "Un des plus grands prédicateurs du XIIe siècle: Geoffroy du Loroux, dit Geoffroy Babion," *Rev. Bén.*, LVI (1945-46) 190-198. See also J.-A. Brutails, "Geoffroi du Louroux, archévêque de Bordeaux de 1136 à 1158, et ses constructions," *BEC*, LXXXIII (1922) 54-64; W. Lampen, "De sermonibus Gaufredi Babionis, scholastici Andegavensis," *Antonianum*, XIX (1944) 145-168; and Janssen, *Legaten*, pp. 22-23 and 165.

p. 4, l. 14] On Peter's visit to the Council of Pisa (May-June 1135) and his subsequent illness, see notes to Ep. 27 and Appendices B and D.

2

AD MATHEVM ALBANENSEM EPISCOPVM

A 2; S 2; C III,2; Bc I,2; cf. Bréquigny, *Chartes*, II, 618 (1134); Berlière, *Mélanges*, IV, 43.

Matthew of Albano, former prior of St.-Martin-des-Champs at Paris and cardinal-bishop of Albano from 1127 until 1135, was throughout his life a close friend, assistant, and adviser of Peter the Venerable, who wrote his life in the *De Miraculis* (see Ep. 129, n. to p. 327): see the chronicle of Cluny (*Bibl. Clun.*, cols. 553-555 [*recte* 595-597]); *Obituaires*, I.1, 257 (St.-Germain-des-Prés) and 475 (St.-Martin-des-Champs); *Necrologium*, p. 95; Bernhardi, *Lothar*, p. 312; Berliére, *Mélanges*, IV, 1-51; Brixius, *Kardinalkollegium*, pp. 36-37 and 79; Ingeborg Schnack, *Richard von Cluny, seine Chronik und sein Kloster in den Anfängen der Kirchenspaltung von 1159* (Historische Studien, ed. Ebering, 146; Berlin, 1921) pp. 22-25; Klewitz, *Reformpapsttum*, pp. 219-220; Schmale, *Schisma*, pp. 52—53; Janssen, *Legaten*, p. 17; and Ep. 39, n. to p. 132. Berlière's study, though excellent, is now old, and Matthew would reward further study. He has been characterized as "a Cluniac die-hard" by David

Knowles, "Cistercians and Cluniacs: The Controversy between St Bernard and Peter the Venerable" (1955), in *The Historian and Character and Other Essays* (Cambridge, England, 1963) p. 52, cf. pp. 67–68; whereas Tellenbach, "Pontius," pp. 40-41 and 44—45, considered him a leader, with Peter the Venerable, of the reforming, ascetic, "spiritual" group among the Cluniacs, in contrast to the conservative traditionalists Anacletus II, Gilo of Tusculum, and Abbot Pontius.

Late 1134 (or possibly early 1135).

p. 6, l. 4] Alfonso I of Aragon died on 7 September 1134. On the troubles following his death, see *Chronica Adefonsi imperatoris*, 58–61, ed. Luis Sanchez Belda (Consejo superior de investigaciones cientificas: Escuela de estudios medievales, 14; Madrid, 1950) pp. 47–49; Ordericus Vitalis, *Hist. ecc.*, XIII, 10 (*ed. cit.*, V, 23–24); cf. Heinrich Schäfer, *Geschichte von Spanien*, III (Geschichte der europäischen Staaten; Gotha, 1861) pp. 20 ff; R. Altamira, in *CMH*, VI, 406; and H. J. Chaytor, *A History of Aragon and Catalonia* (London, 1933) pp. 55–56.

p. 6, l. 6] Two brothers named Hugo Beraldus and Peter Beraldus sold part of a forest to Cluny in 1123 (*Cluny*, V, 325–326, no. 3966; cf. IV, 708–709, no. 3574). A Hugo Berardus appeared on a charter of St. Jean d'Angély before 1131 (*Cîteaux*, p. 90, no. 84) and as chamberlain of St. Jean d'Angély, accompanying Peter the Venerable on a visit in Aquitaine, on a charter probably of 1133 (*Cluny*, V, 343, no. 3988). Cf. Duby, *Mâconnais*, pp. 447 and 636, n. 1, on the family of Béraud.

p. 6, l. 12] Bishop Hato of Troyes was a close friend of Peter the Venerable and appears frequently in his letters. He was ordained at Sens in 1095/6 and became, successively, archdeacon and dean of Sens before his elevation to the see of Troyes in about 1122: see Constable, in *Petrus Ven.*, pp. 43–44 and 49. He retired to Cluny either late in 1145 or early in 1146 (cf. Appendix N) and probably died soon afterwards. His death was commemorated on 29 August at Montiéramey and St.-Martin-des-Champs, on 30 August at Larrivour (l'Arivour) and Jully-les-Nonnains, and on 1 September at the cathedral of Troyes: *Obituaires*, I.1, 454, and IV, 260, 325, 332, and 361. Duchesne, Camuzat, and Pignot believed that as a young man he was a monk at Cluny (*Bibl. Clun.*, *notae*, col. 138; Pignot, *Cluny*, III, 263; cf. Ep. 81, n. to p. 218); but Mabillon in his note to Bernard's ep. 23 refuted this opinion on the grounds that Peter's Letters 86 and 121 show that Hato was not yet a monk (Gaume ed., I, 831–832); cf. Severt, *Chronologia*, III, 144. He was a friend of St. Bernard, who wrote several letters both to Hato himself, praising his charity and his efforts to reform the clergy, and to the Pope on Hato's behalf: Bernard, epp. 23, 152, 432–434, and 437–439 (Gaume ed., I.1, 166–168, 365, and 743–745), and ed. Kervyn de Lettenhove, "Saint Bernard: Documents inédits," *Bulletin de l'Académie royale . . . de Belgique*, 2nd ser., XI (1861) 260. He was a generous patron of Cluny, as his grants in 1130/2 and 1145 (*Cluny*, V, 371–372, no. 4017, and *Bibl. Clun.*, *notae*, cols. 104–105) show; but there appears to be no record of the grant mentioned in this letter. It was probably the prebend given to Cluny "at the request and order" of Innocent II, referred to by Peter the Venerable in Letter 69 to Hato, written in 1138. Grants of prebends were a valuable source of income at this time, when Cluny was in severe financial straits (cf. Appendix H). Duchesne in his notes in *Bibl. Clun.*, col. 106, printed a confirmation by Alexander IV of Cluniac prebends in the cathedral of Chartres.

p. 6, l. 18] This priest Constantine is otherwise unknown. The schism he promoted was doubtless that at Cluny in 1125–6, not the papal schism of 1130–8; but the subject of the case against Stephen which he took to Pisa is not known.

p. 6, l. 24] The abbot of Bonneval in question was probably Bernerius, who was abbot until 1135, according to the *GC*, VIII, 1242 (citing the list of abbots at Bonneval). His death was commemorated on 14 January at St.-Père-en-Vallée and was dated "after 1135" by Molinier, in *Obituaires*, II, 180. The death of Bernerius, and hence the succession of the well-known Abbot Arnold of Bonneval, was dated "before 1130" by A. Calendini, in *DHGE*, IX, 1063, however, although the earliest reference to Arnold as abbot in the *GC* is in 1144, and Arnold was still a monk at Marmoutier in 1138, according to A. Prévost, in *DHGE*, IV, 421 (citing *GC*, XIV, 219), though the evidence is not decisive. It is in any case unlikely that Arnold, even if abbot, would have been thinking of retiring in 1134, as mentioned in this letter. The reason for the retirement may have been associated with the burning of the town of Bonneval, all except the abbey, by Louis VI in 1132/3: see Suger, *Louis le Gros*, p. 273, and Luchaire, *Louis VI*, pp. 241–242, no. 530.

3

AD DOMINVM HAIMERICVM CANCELLARIVM

A 3; S 3; C III,3; Bc I,3; cf. Pignot, *Cluny*, III, 252.

Cardinal Haimeric was papal chancellor from 1123 until 1141 and one of the most influential members of the papal curia: see Brixius,

Kardinalkollegium, pp. 32 and 61; Klewitz, *Reformpapsttum*, pp. 223 ff.; Bloch, "Schism," p. 160; Schmale, *Schisma*, pp. 93-191 (esp. pp. 96, 168, and 188-189 on his friendship with Peter the Venerable); and Ep. 90, n. to p. 231, l. 26.

1123/41. The year 1137 is suggested by the references to Peter's poor health and the unfavorable climate of Italy, which associate this letter with Letters 1, 62, and 63.

p. 7] On later disputes between the bishop of Béziers and the monks of Aniane, see *Cartulaire d'Aniane*, ed. Léon Cassan and E. Meynial (Montpellier, 1900) pp. 112-113, 120-121, and 129, nos. 26 (1145/52), 37 (1155/9), and 48 (1154/9). These are all too late, however, to be associated with the present quarrel.

4

AD HVGONEM ARCHIEPISCOPVM ROTHOMAGENSEM

A 4; S 4; C III,4; Bc I,4.

Hugh of Amiens was a prominent Cluniac and friend of Peter the Venerable. According to his own account, he was related by blood to Matthew of Albano and was brought up at Laon (*Thes. nov.*, V, 895-897); and he was at Cluny from at least 1099 until 1113 (Peter commented on his life there in Letter 178). He then became, successively, prior of St. Martial at Limoges, prior of Lewes, abbot of Reading (in 1123), and archbishop of Rouen, where he was elected in 1129/30 and consecrated before 14 September 1130. He died on 10 November 1164 and is listed in the necrologies of St.-Martin-des-Champs and of the Paraclete, where his benefactions were mentioned and he was described as "uir magne sanctitatis ... persona modernorum excellentissima": *Obituaires*, I.1, 467, and IV, 426. In addition to the older works cited in Chevalier, *Bio-bib.*, I, 2194, see Hébert, "Hugues," pp. 325-371; Luchaire, *Études*, pp. 52-53; Osbert of Clare, *Letters*, pp. 39-48 and 183-184, who refers to him as "Hugo de Sancta Margarita" (p. 40); *Marcigny*, p. 246; Janssen, *Legaten*, pp. 32-34; Morey and Brooke, *Foliot*, p. 78; and, on Hugh as a writer and theologian, Louis Saltet, *Les réordinations* (Paris, 1907) pp. 272-276; Wilmart, "Riposte," pp. 296-344 (esp. p. 307); J. de Ghellinck, *Le mouvement théologique du XIIe siècle*, 2nd ed. (Museum Lessianum: Section historique, 10; Brussels-Paris, 1948) pp. 120-121 and 183; Schreiber, *Gemeinschaften*, pp. 347 ff.; D. Van den Eynde, "Nouvelles précisions chronologiques sur quelques oeuvres théologiques du XIIe siècle," *Franciscan Studies*, XIII (1953)

71–83; Raoul Manselli, "Per la storia dell'eresia nel secolo XII," *Bullettino dell'Istituto Storico Italiano per il Medio Evo*, LXVII (1955) 235–244; Talbot, in *Petrus Ven.*, pp. 72–80; and Francis Lecomte, "Un commentaire scripturaire du XIIe siècle: Le 'Tractatus in Hexaemeron' de Hugues d'Amiens," *Archives d'histoire doctrinale et littéraire du Moyen Age*, XXV (1958) 227–294, esp. pp. 229–232 on Hugh's life.

1130/8: between the elevations of Hugh as archbishop of Rouen and Alberic of Vézelay as cardinal-bishop of Ostia. It is impossible to date the letter more precisely within these limits from the movements either of Peter the Venerable or of Alberic, but the conjunction of 28 December and a place dedicated to St. Martin may point to 1133, when Peter is known to have spent Christmas at St.-Martin-des-Champs.

p. 8, l. 3] The identity of this William cannot be established. He may have been the prominent Cluniac who died shortly before Peter the Venerable's trip to Rome in 1145 and is mentioned in the *De miraculis*, II, 25 (*Bibl. Clun.*, col. 1324); but the fact that Peter describes him as Hugh's brother and son suggests that he was associated with either St. Martial at Limoges, Lewes, Reading, or Rouen. He died on 28 December at "the lodging-house of the poor Martin"; he invoked St. Martin on his deathbed; he was buried in the infirmary cloister in front of the chapel of Our Lady. This may point to St.-Martin-des-Champs, where there was a chapel dedicated to Our Lady of the Infirmary: Marrier, *Hist. S. Martini*, pp. 566–571; but it may have been some other house, nearer Rouen, dedicated to St. Martin.

p. 8, l. 23] This was probably Alberic, abbot of Vézelay, who became cardinal-bishop of Ostia in 1138: see Brixius, *Kardinalkollegium*, pp. 40 and 85; Constable, "Langres," p. 124; Manselli, "Alberico," pp. 23–68, who mentions Alberic's possible association with St.-Martin-des-Champs; and Janssen, *Legaten*, pp. 39–50.

5

AD ATONEM TRECENSEM EPISCOPVM

A 5; S 5; C III,5; Bc I,5; cf. Pignot, *Cluny*, III, 595.

1122/46. This letter may have been written about the same time as Letter 4 (1130/8): see note below.

p. 10] These troubles may be the same as those referred to in Letter 4.

6

AD EVNDEM

A 6; S 6; C III,6; Bc I,6.

1122/46 (after Letter 5). This letter is Peter's reply to Hato's reply to Letter 5. Hato had thought that the "silver cord" mentioned in Letter 5 referred to money, and Peter the Venerable devotes half of this letter to explaining that he meant friendship.

7

AD QVEM SVPRA

A 7; S 7; C III,7; Bc I,7; cf. Bréquigny, *Chartes*, II, 582 (1130).

1134. This letter was written after Peter's return from his second visit to Aquitaine in 1133-4.

p. 13] The priory of N.-D. at Gaye in the diocese of Troyes: De Valous, *Mon. clun.*, II, 194-195.

p. 14] On this trip to Aquitaine, see Appendices D and Q. It is not known whether or not Peter made the projected trip to Troyes.

8

AD STEPHANVM PRESBITERVM IVRISPERITVM

A 8; S 8; C III,8; Bc I,8; cf. Pignot, *Cluny*, III, 587-588, who translated this letter and associated the recipient with the Cluniac schism of 1125-6.

The priest Stephen may have been the Stephen mentioned in Letter 2, who was engaged in a legal dispute with the priest Constantine, but nothing specific is known about him or his case.

9-10

AD PETRVM QVEMDAM SCOLASTICVM

A 9-10; S 9-10; C III,9-10; Bc I,9-10.

The recipient of these letters was identified as Peter Abelard by Mabillon, *Annales*, VI, 78; Pignot, *Cluny*, III, 212, n. 1; Leclercq, *Pierre le Vén.*, pp. 256-258; and Oursel, *Dispute*, pp. 26-27; and as Peter of

Poitiers by Duchesne, in *Bibl. Clun., notae*, cols. 107–108; Lecointre-Dupont, "Pierre de Poitiers," p. 371; Maitland, *Dark Ages*, pp. 453–454; and Sandys, *Class. Scholarship* (cited p. 39, n. 174, above), I, 596. Neither of these identifications is convincing, but of the two Peter Abelard is the more satisfactory. The recipient was clearly a teacher. The headings of the letters call him "scholasticus," and Peter addressed him as "magister," which suggests that he was a master in theology (cf. Molinier, *Obituaires*, p. 98). "Why, my dear friend, do you frequent the schools?" Peter asked, "Why do you teach and try to teach?" He was clearly a successful teacher, furthermore, since Peter urged him to leave his wealth and come to Cluny. These facts suit Peter Abelard better than Peter of Poitiers, who is not known ever to have taught; but Abelard is not known to have been a friend of Peter the Venerable before the very end of his life.

11

AD INNOCENTIVM PAPAM

A 11; S 11; C III,11; Bc I,11; cf. Appendix N on Bishop Elias of Orléans, esp. n.1 for references on this letter.

1136/7.

p. 18] On Peter the Venerable's use here and in Letter 141 of the concept of the pope as *vicarius Dei* (cf. also the end of Letter 32), see Michele Maccarrone, *Vicarius Christi: Storia del titolo papale* (Lateranum, n.s. 18; Rome, 1952) pp. 94–95. According to Maccarrone, Peter's works helped "a propagare l'uso di *vicarius Christi* come titolo papale" (p. 95); but they more probably reflected a current concept of the pope's position.

12

AD WILLELMVM EBREDVNENSEM EPISCOPVM

A 12; S 12; C III,12; Bc I,12; cf. Marcellin Fornier, *Histoire générale des Alpes maritimes ou cottiènes* (Paris, 1890–1892) III, 558 (ca. 1120); Chevalier, *Régeste*, no. 3340 (1122/34).

The recipient of this letter may have been either Archbishop William I of Embrun (*ca.* 1120–1134/5), as Fornier and Chevalier assumed, or Archbishop William II (1135–1169?): see Gams, *Series*, p. 548, and Kramp, in *Misc. Ehrle*, I, 73, who examined the matter because Peter's *Contra Petrobrusianos* was addressed, among others, to Archbishop William of Embrun (see Appendix G). Without further precisions the letter cannot be dated.

13

AD ODONEM QVONDAM BELVACI ABBATEM

A 13; S 13; C III,13; Bc I,13; cf. Duchesne, in *Bibl. Clun., notae*, cols. 108–109; L.-E. Deladreue and Mathon, "Histoire de l'abbaye royale de Saint-Lucien," *Mémoires de la Société académique d'archéologie, sciences et arts du département de l'Oise*, VIII.2 (1872) 311.

The recipient of this letter, according to Deladreue and Mathon, was the former Abbot Odo of St. Symphorien at Beauvais, who retired to his previous abbey of St.-Germer-de-Fly in about 1126 and appeared on a document in 1132: *GC*, IX, 808. He was identified by Duchesne as the future Prior Odo of St.-Martin-des-Champs (see biographical note to Ep. 135) and by other scholars as an otherwise unknown Abbot Odo of St. Lucien at Beauvais; but neither of these suggestions is probable.

14

AD DOMINVM THEODARDVM

A 14; S 14; C III,14; Bc I,14.

Theodard was prior of La Charité-sur-Loire from after 1130 (?) until 1138/9: see Appendix K. Duchesne, in *Bibl. Clun., notae*, col. 109, believed that this letter was written before he became prior, but the use of the terms "dominus" and "frater" suggest that he held a position of responsibility, and I am therefore inclined to date this letter during his priorate.

1122/39 (probably 1130/9).

15

AD ADHELAM MARCINIACI MONACHAM PRIVS BLESENSEM COMITISSAM

A 15; S 15; C III,15; Bc I,15; cf. Mabillon, *Annales*, VI, 239 (1135); Bréquigny, *Chartes*, II, 626 (1135); *RHGF*, XV, 632 (1135); Pignot, *Cluny*, III, 278–279.

Adela was the daughter of William the Conqueror, the wife of Count Stephen of Blois and Chartres, and the mother of, among other children, King Stephen of England, Count Theobald of Blois, and

Bishop Henry of Winchester. The date of her entry into Marcigny is given as 1117 by Delisle in his notes to Ordericus Vitalis, *Hist. ecc.*, XI, 5 (*ed. cit.*, IV, 189–190; cf. other references to Adela in the index, V, 252); as 1122 by Johnson and Cronne, in *Regesta Regum Anglo-Norm.*, II, no. 1599a (no reference); and as after 1122 by D'Arbois de Jubainville, *Comtes de Champagne*, II, 254. She was mentioned by Peter the Venerable in the *De miraculis*, I, 26 (*Bibl. Clun.*, col. 1289 E) and died in 1137, according to the continuator of William of Jumièges: see J. H. Ramsay, *The Foundations of England* (London, 1898) II, 154.

Early 1136. Henry I died on 1 December 1135, and the time for the news to reach Cluny and the delay in writing mentioned by Peter would date this letter early the following year.

p. 22, l. 1] King Henry I of England, Adela's brother.

p. 22, l. 7] Lyons-la-Forêt, where Henry had been hunting: see C. H. Haskins, *Norman Institutions* (Harvard Historical Studies, 24; Cambridge, Mass., 1918) p. 320; William Farrer, *An Outline Itinerary of King Henry I* (Oxford, 1919) p. 154; A. L. Poole, *From Domesday Book to Magna Carta, 1087–1216*, 2nd ed. (Oxford History of England, 3; Oxford, 1955) p. 129; *Regesta Regum Anglo-Norm.*, II, xxxi. The place was identified as St.-Denis-le-Ferment by Ramsay, *Foundations*, II, 317.

p. 22, l. 8] On Archbishop Hugh of Rouen, see biographical note to Ep. 4. His messenger carrying the news of Henry's death to the Pope probably went by way of Cluny: see Hébert, "Hugues," pp. 349–350.

p. 22, l. 10] The date of Henry's death is given as 1 December by William of Malmesbury, Ordericus Vitalis (in two places), and Henry of Huntingdon, who are followed by all the authorities cited in n. to l. 7 above. Here, however, Peter the Venerable gives the date as 2 December, which is also found in a number of other contemporary sources, including, at one point, Ordericus Vitalis, *Hist. ecc.*, XI, 5 (*ed. cit.*, IV, 189); William of Jumièges, *Historia Normannorum*, VIII, 33, in *Historiae Normannorum scriptores antiqui*, ed. André Duchesne (Paris, 1619) p. 309; both Richard and John of Hexham, ed. James Raine, *The Priory of Hexham* (Surtees Society, 44 and 46; Durham, 1864–65) I, 63 and 113; a twelfth-century obituary from Lincoln Cathedral, printed in Gerald of Wales, *Opera*, ed. J. S. Brewer, J. F. Dimock, and G. F. Warner (Rolls Series, 21; London, 1861–1891) VII, 163; the account of the origins of Mortemer in MS. Paris, Bibl. nat., Latin 18369, printed by J. Bouvet, "Le récit de la fondation de Mortemer," *Collectanea ordinis Cisterciensium reformatorum*, XXII (1960) 154; the chronicle of Bec, *s.a.* 1135, ed.

AD INNOCENTIVM PAPAM

A. Porée (Société de l'histoire de Normandie; Rouen, 1883) p. 9; *Necrologium*, p. 90; and *The Chronicle of John Worcester, 1118—1140*, ed. J. R. H. Weaver (Anecdota Oxoniensia, IV, 13; Oxford, 1908) p. 39, which was followed by the annalist of Winchcombe, ed. R. R. Darlington, in *A Medieval Miscellany for Doris Mary Stenton* (Publications of the Pipe Roll Society, 76; London, 1962) p. 127. Raine explained this discrepancy of a day by pointing out that according to Ordericus, *Hist. ecc.*, XIII, 19 (ed. cit., V, 49), Henry died at nightfall; and Dimock also suggested that the evening of December 1 "by some would be reckoned as December 2." More specifically, D'Arbois de Jubainville, *Comtes de Champagne*, II, 255, n. 1, pointed out that Peter the Venerable and the monastic chroniclers, in accordance with liturgical usage, presumably started the day at sunset.

p. 22, l. 12] See Ramsay, *Foundations*, II, 317-318. On Earl Robert of Gloucester, an illegitimate son of Henry I and later the principal supporter of his half-sister Mathilda against King Stephen, see Round, *Geoffrey*, pp. 420-436.

p. 22, l. 13] See Ramsay, *Foundations*, II, 341-342, and Haskins, *Norman Institutions*, pp. 123 ff., on the confusion in Normandy following the death of Henry I.

16

AD PONTIVM RELIGIOSVM COGNATVM SVVM

A 16; S 16; C III,16; Bc I,16.

1122/38. This letter was written between the beginning of the abbacy of Peter the Venerable and the elevation of his brother Pontius to abbot of Vézelay in 1138. The date of Pontius's pilgrimage to adore "the tombs of the precious martyrs" (possibly at Rome) cannot be established.

p. 23] These ten years that Peter the Venerable spent with his brother Pontius were not necessarily at Vézelay, as was assumed by Pignot, *Cluny*, III, 60-61; Louis, *Girart*, I, 177 and 181-186; and Oursel, *Dispute*, p. 21 (cf. Appendix D).

17

AD INNOCENTIVM PAPAM

A 17; S 17; C III,17; Bc I,17; cf. Gérard Dubois, *Historia ecclesiae Parisiensis* (Paris, 1690-1710) II, 36-37; Bréquigny, *Chartes*, II, 582 (1130); *RHGF*, XV, 629 (1133); Pignot, *Cluny*, III, 233-235.

Late in 1133/4.

p. 25, l. 7] This refers to the two notorious murders of Subdean Archibald of Orléans, who was killed by the supporters of his enemy Archdeacon John probably between February and August 1133, and of the reforming prior Thomas of St. Victor at Paris, who was murdered on 20 August 1133 by the nephews of Archdeacon Theobald: see Ordericus Vitalis, *Hist. ecc.*, XIII, 12 (*ed. cit.*, V, 28); Bernard, epp. 158–163 (Gaume ed., I.1, 370–375); JL 7636, 7642, and 7666; Luchaire, *Louis VI*, introd., p. liii, and pp. 237–238, 240, 242, and 249, nos. 518–519, 526, 531, and 546; Fourier Bonnard, *St. Victor*, I, 37–40; *Bernard de Clairvaux*, pp. 317–322; Janssen, *Legaten*, pp. 20–21; and Appendix N.

p. 25, l. 15] The date of the Synod of Jouarre, upon which the date of this letter depends, is not certain. It was dated November 1134 by Luchaire, *Louis VI*, p. 249, no. 546; and this was accepted by Fourier Bonnard, *St. Victor*, I, 40 ("vers la fin de l'année 1134"); Williams, *St. Bernard*, pp. 129–130; and Grebenc, "Itinerar," pp. 52–57. Vacandard, *St. Bernard*, I, 350, n. 3, however, pointed out that this dating depended upon a misunderstanding of the position of JL 7666 (the papal bull, addressed to the archbishops of Rheims, Sens, Rouen, and Tours, confirming the sentence of the synod), which is undated and was placed by Löwenfeld at the end of 1134 (i.e., at any time during the year), not in November 1134, as Luchaire assumed. Vacandard therefore suggested that the council probably followed the papal bull of 16 November 1133 (JL 7636), calling on the archbishops of Rheims and Sens and their suffragans to punish the murderers of Thomas. The council may even have been called before the Pope's letter arrived. This earlier date was accepted by Hébert, "Hugues," p. 347, n. 4 (soon after November 1133); Hefele-Leclercq, *Conciles*, V.1, 704–705 (dating the council 1134 but citing Vacandard almost verbatim); De Warren, in *Bernard de Clairvaux*, pp. 320–321 and 587; Janssen, *Legaten*, p. 20 (early 1134); and the editor of the letter of Guigo of La Grande Chartreuse to the council, in *Lettres des premiers Chartreux*, p. 198 (end of 1133). Jean Quéguiner, in *L'abbaye royale Notre-Dame de Jouarre* (Paris, 1961) I, 91, n. 12, expressed no opinion between 1133 and 1134. I am inclined to agree with Vacandard that Luchaire's date (which is clearly based upon a misunderstanding of JL) is too late and that the council met either late in 1133 or early in 1134. This agrees with the known movements of Peter the Venerable, who was in the region of Paris late in 1133 and early in 1134 (although it is not certain from the wording of the letter that Peter himself attended the council). This letter was written soon afterward, as he says, and certainly before JL 7666 arrived in France.

p. 25, l. 25] Hébert, "Hugues," p. 347, discusses the reasons for the offense of the "royal majesty" of Henry I against Hugh of Rouen. It is possible that Hugh himself carried the decisions of the Council of Jouarre, which he attended, to Rome.

18

AD ATHONEM TRECENSEM EPISCOPVM

A 18; S 18; C III,18; Bc I,18.

1122/46. Both the visit of Peter the Venerable to the Auvergne (see note below) and the subject matter of this letter suggest a relatively late date between the limits of 1122 and 1146. Hato had clearly been crossed in some way by the Pope, who had perhaps refused him permission to resign, and Peter urged him to visit Cluny. Peter may have hoped that the visit would be permanent.

p. 26] This trip to the Auvergne and Souvigny around Easter may have been associated with his visit to Aquitaine in 1133-4, when he may have left in the spring and gone to Poitiers by way of Souvigny. I am inclined to believe that this was a later trip, however, perhaps in 1137 or 1138, during both of which years Peter visited eastern France.

19

AD DVLCIANVM MONTIS PESSVLANI IVRIS PERITVM

A 19; S 19; C III,19; Bc I,19.

Dulcianus was a lawyer in Montpellier, according to the headings in A, S, and C, and was a layman, if the sons mentioned in this letter were real sons. He is not mentioned in any history of the town or in the chartulary of the University of Montpellier, but it is interesting that the earliest reference to Montpellier as a center of learning and medical studies was in 1137, about the time this letter was written: see Hastings Rashdall, *The Universities of Europe in the Middle Ages*, ed. F. M. Powicke and A. B. Emden (Oxford, 1936) II, 119. It is not known whether Dulcianus became a monk at Cluny, as Peter the Venerable urged, or sent one of his sons as an *alter ego*.

20

AD SERVVM DEI GISLEBERTVM SILVANECTIS INCLVSVM

See pp. 70-73 above on the manuscripts of this letter; C III, 20; Bc I,20; cf. Maitland, *Dark Ages*, pp. 458-460; Pignot, *Cluny*, III,

473–476; and esp. Leclercq, in *Petrus Ven.*, pp. 99–120. I have been unable to see Benedetto Calati, "Un trattato su la vita eremitica di Pietro il Venerabile," *Vita monastica*, 1962, pp. 51–72, cited in *Bulletin d'histoire bénédictine*, VI, 272 (*Rev. Bén.*, LXXII.3–4).

The identity of the hermit Gilbert to whom this letter is addressed is not known. Internal evidence shows that he was a Cluniac monk (Peter the Venerable clearly had authority over him and asked him to pray "for all your Cluniac brethren"), that although a recluse he was associated with a Cluniac house (Peter referred to his prior and brethren), and that Peter had visited him not long before writing this letter, since he mentioned the suitability of his retreat, "which I recently saw, when you showed it, and, as was proper, I approved." The only other clue to his identity occurs in the heading found in A, S, and C: "Ad seruum dei Gislebertum Siluanectis inclusum." Leclercq suggested that this referred to La Silvacane (*Petrus Ven.*, p. 112, n. 64); but this was a Cistercian house in Provence, founded in 1147 (after the probable date of this letter), and was usually named *Silvacana* in Latin. *Silva necta* was the Latin form of Senlis (St. Liz), and Cluny had two dependencies in the diocese of Senlis: the abbey of St. Arnulf at Crépy-en-Valois and the priory of St. Nicholas at Acy, a dependency of St.-Martin-des-Champs: see *GC*, X, 1484–1493 and 1518–1522; *Cluny*, V, 48, no. 3699; *Bull. Clun.*, p. 46 (JL 7429; = *Cluny*, V, 360, no. 4005); J. Vendeuvre, "La 'libertas' royale des communautés religieuses au XIe siècle [fin]," *Nouvelle revue historique de droit français et étranger*, XXXIV (1910) 353. St. Arnulf had several small dependencies, including one near Crépy dedicated to St. Agatha (*Bibl. Clun.*, col. 1720) and another "cellam quae uocatur Moranum monasterium" (Marestmontiers), mentioned in the papal bull of 1130 (*Bull. Clun.*, p. 46). Gilbert may have inhabited one of these, or a dependency of St. Nicholas, which was nearer Senlis. Peter the Venerable is known to have been in Paris in 1133–4, and he may have passed through the diocese of Senlis on his way back to Cluny. There is no reliable indication, however, of the date of this letter.

p. 33] Cf. the passage on *accidia* in Cassian, *De institutis coenobiorum*, X (*CSEL*, XVII.1, 172 ff.), and the discussion by E. K. Rand, *The Founders of the Middle Ages* (Cambridge, Mass., 1928) pp. 235–236.

p. 34] Cf. Bernard, *Apologia*, XII (ed. Leclerq, III, 104–106).

p. 35] On this concept, see M. Bernards, "Nudus nudum Christum sequi," *Wissenschaft und Weisheit*, XIV (1951) 148–151 (citing this passage on p. 149, n. 17), to whose examples may be added those in Letter 86 and in the *Liber de diversis ordinibus et professionibus quae sunt in ecclesia*, XXIII (*PL*, CCXIII, 824 B: cf. Ep. 28, n. to p. 86).

p. 37] The following passage ("Ipse dominus ... librorum tuorum.") was cited by Goswin of Anchin in his *De nouiciis instruendis* (see pp. 51–52 above).

p. 38] Cf. C. H. Haskins, *The Renaissance of the Twelfth Century* (Cambridge, Mass., 1927) pp. 72–73. In the tenth-century antiphonary of Hartkar (St. Gall 391, fol. 11), the scribe "Hartkarius reclusus" is shown offering his book; and in a manuscript of *ca.* 1150 from Prüfening (Clm 13031, fol. 1), the scribe Swicher is seen after his death with the book he copied weighing in the scale of virtue (cf. Albert Boeckler, *Die Regensburg-Prüfeninger Buchmalerei des XII. und XIII. Jahrhunderts* [Miniaturen aus Handschriften der bayerischen Staatsbibliothek in München, 8; Munich, 1924] pl. III and p. 16, saying that this is the only illustration of this subject known to him).

p. 39, l. 1] On the idea of the apostolate of the copyist, see Cassiodorus, *Institutiones*, I, 30 (ed. R. A. B. Mynors [Oxford, 1937] pp. 75–76); cf. Louis Gougaud, "Muta praedicatio," *Rev. Bén.*, XLII (1930) 171, and Jean Leclercq, in *Analecta mon.*, II, 146, n. 2.

p. 39, l. 25] Cf. Peter the Venerable, *Statuta*, XXVII.

21

AD INNOCENTIVM PAPAM

A 21; S 21; C III,21; Bc I,21; cf. *RHGF*, XV, 633–634 (1137/8).

Early 1138. This letter was in all probability a letter of introduction to the Pope for the Archbishop of Lyons on his visit to Rome in the spring of 1138: see Constable, "Langres," pp. 125 and 132. Letter 54 was probably written at the same time.

p. 42, l. 4] Peter of Burgundy, archbishop of Lyons from 1131 until 1139, had been a Cluniac monk and was an old friend of Peter the Venerable, who sent him Letters 38 and 54: see Severt, *Chronologia*, I, 239–241 (citing Letters 38, 54, and 100); Martin, *Conciles*, pp. 143–147 (dating his pontificate from 1132); Constable, "Langres," p. 130; Janssen, *Legaten*, pp. 160–161; and Ep. 38, n. to p. 125.

p. 42, l. 10] King Louis VI died on 1 August 1137. This passage on the power of the king in Burgundy was cited by Duby, *Mâconnais*, pp. 531–535 (dated *ca.* 1140), and Marcel Pacaut, *Louis VII et son royaume* (Bibliothèque générale de l'Ecole pratique des hautes études, VIe section; Paris, 1964) pp. 11, 13, 20, and 191; but the fact it is a biblical quotation somewhat reduces its value as a factual description of prevailing conditions. Peter used the same phrase to describe conditions in Burgundy and Auvergne over a decade later in Letters 171, 172, and 173 (I, 405, 408, and 410). In Letter 173 he admitted that he was using the phrase metaphorically, in contrast to another passage which he said he was using literally.

22

AD ATTHONEM TRECASSINVM EPISCOPVM

A 22; S 22; C III,22; Bc I,22; cf. Pignot, *Cluny*, III, 453, n. 1 (1144/5).

1128/46. Pignot's date for this letter seems rather late. It can be dated only between the first appearance of Hugh of Crécy and the retirement of Hato of Troyes.

p. 43] The chamberlain Hugh of Crécy: see Appendix O.

23

AD PAPAM INNOCENTIVM

A 23; S 23; C III,23; Bc I,23; cf. Bréquigny, *Chartes*, II, 594 (1131); Pignot, *Cluny*, III, 250–251 (1136/7); De Valous, *Mon. clun.*, I, 374.

1132/6. The problems discussed in this letter and in Letter 97 (see n. to p. 258) presumably arose over the election of a successor to Abbot Hugh of Luxeuil, who last appeared on a document in 1131, when the cardinal legate John of St. Chrysogonus settled a dispute between Luxeuil and Bèze (*PU in Frankreich*, II, 21–23, no. 3; Janssen, *Legaten*, pp. 17–18), and, according to the GC, XV, 153, was still alive in 1132. The next abbot, Joceran, is mentioned in a papal confirmation for Luxeuil issued on 21 November 1136: GC, XV, *instr.*, 30–31; JL 7797. I am inclined to date the intervention of Peter the Venerable, which was preceded by a visit to the Pope, in 1133 or 1134. Cf. H. Baumont, *De Luxoviensium abbatum potestate* (Nancy, 1894) pp. 14–15, who mentioned the dispute without dating it.

p. 43, l. 1] The ancient abbey of Luxeuil, near Besançon.

p. 43, l. 8] The papal documents concerned with this case have all disappeared, but this passage shows that the monks of Luxeuil brought Peter the Venerable a letter which they had apparently procured from Innocent II.

p. 44] The monks clearly wanted to choose their abbot themselves, but Peter the Venerable knew them too well and insisted on choosing himself. Letter 97 shows that his gloomy predictions in this letter later came true. Some Cluniac monks took over Luxeuil for a short time, but matters then became worse than ever. The monks gave up almost all regular life and the abbot was such only in name.

24

AD CARTVSIENSES

A 24; S 24; C III,24; Bc I,24; cf. Mabillon, *Annales*, VI, 120 (1125); Maitland, *Dark Ages*, pp. 449-450; Lorain, *Cluny*, pp. 393 and 423-425; Pignot, *Cluny*, III, 267-269 (1132); Le Couteulx, *Ann. Carth.*, I, 356-358 (1132); Chevalier, *Régeste*, no. 3475 (1132).

Guigo of Le Chatel, the fifth prior of La Grande Chartreuse, lived from 1083/4 until 27 July 1137. He was a notable writer and legislator for his order and a friend of Peter the Venerable. André Wilmart, *Auteurs spirituels et textes dévots du moyen âge latin* (Paris, 1932) p. 222, n. 1, mentions their correspondence. This friendship, and Peter's admiration for the Carthusians, dated back to his time as prior of Domène. His biographer Radulf said that Peter loved the Carthusians dearly and visited them "semel in anno" (*Ampl. Coll.*, VI, 1200 E). He praised them highly in the *De miraculis*, II, 28 (*Bibl. Clun.*, cols. 1328-1330): cf. Letters 48 and 186, and A. de Meyer and J. M. de Smet, "Notes sur quelques sources littéraires relatives à Guigue Ier," *Rev. hist. ecc.*, XLVIII (1953) 178-180; *La Grande Chartreuse*, pp. 33, n. 2, and 66, n. 3; Lamma, *Momenti*, p. 76; and *Magna vita sancti Hugonis*, ed. Decima Douie and Hugh Farmer (Nelson's Medieval Texts; Edinburgh, 1961-62) I, xxii-xxiii. The Carthusian chapter general, in return, established liturgical commemoration for Peter the Venerable "quando eum obire contigerit" (*Thes. nov.*, IV, 1242).

1136/7. The reference in Guigo's reply (Letter 25) to Prior Arbertus of Cluny dates this letter between his first appearance (1136) and Guigo's death in 1137.

p. 47, l. 12] See the catalogue of the library of Cluny in Delisle, *Fonds*, pp. 342 and 344, nos. 83 (St. Hilary) and 118 (St. Ambrose). There is no known catalogue of the library at St. Jean d'Angély.

p. 47, l. 16] Peter the Venerable remarked in the *De miraculis*, II, 28 (*Bibl. Clun.*, col. 1330 A) that the Carthusians spent their time in silence, prayer, reading, and manual labor, "above all in writing books." This letter, together with Letters 132 and 169-170, is evidence of the literary intercourse between the Carthusians and Cluniacs in the first half of the twelfth century and of the techniques of procuring and copying books, including the delightful detail of the manuscript of the letters of St. Augustine which was partially eaten by a bear. Guigo II praised the work of copying, ornamenting, and binding books in his *Liber de exercitio cellae*, XXXVI. "Et cum hoc in omni ordine decens et congruum sit," he said, "sed magis in ordine nostro Carthusiensi, aptum utique hoc est, et pulchrum" (*PL*, CLIII, 881 D). Other contemporary evidence of Carthusian interest in books and learning is found in *Lettres des premiers Chartreux*, pp. 98-99, 104, and 214-218, and Guibert of Nogent, *Vita*, I, 11 (pp. 33-34). Cf. Petit, *Ducs de Bourgogne*, II, 53-54, and Evans, *Mon. Life*, pp. 100-101, on the passage in Peter's letter, and, more generally, M. M. Davy, "La vie solitaire cartusienne d'après le *De quadripartito exercitio cellae* d'Adam le Chartreux," *Revue d'ascétique et de mystique*, XIV (1933) 143-144; Lesne, *Prop. ecc.*, IV, 790-804; Thompson, *Medieval Library* (cited above, p. 52, n. 217) p. 618; Joseph de Ghellinck, "Les catalogues des bibliothèques médiévales chez les Chartreux et un guide de lectures spirituelles," *Mélanges Marcel Viller* (*Revue d'ascétique et de mystique*, XXV.2-4; Toulouse, 1949) pp. 284-298; Bligny, *Église*, p. 286; and Ildefonso Gómez, "Los Cartujos y los estudios," *Los monjes y los estudios* (IV Semana de Estudios monasticos; Poblet, 1963) pp. 163-207, esp. pp. 183-187 on Carthusian libraries.

p. 47, l. 19] Peter of Poitiers, Peter the Venerable's secretary: see Appendix Q.

25

RESCRIPTVM CARTVSIENSIVM AD PETRVM CLVNIACENSEM ABBATEM

A 25; S 25; C III,25; Bc I,25; cf. Le Couteulx, *Ann. Carth.*, I, 358-359 (1132); Chevalier, *Régeste*, no. 3476 (1132); *Lettres des premiers Chartreux*, pp. 206-208.

1136/7 (see dating note to Ep. 24, to which this is the reply).

p. 47, l. 2] This refers to "the second cross with an image of the Savior," which Peter the Venerable said he was sending.

AD PAPAM INNOCENTIVM LETTER 27 / 113

p. 47, l. 5] The following passage ("Vnde petimus ... dignus habetur") was quoted by Peter the Venerable in Letter 149, written many years later to Bernard of Clairvaux: cf. Bligny, *Église*, p. 275.

p. 48, l. 10] Grand Prior Arbertus appears on Cluniac documents from 1136 until at least 1142: see Appendix R. He was still sacristan in December 1135, according to the *De miraculis*, II, 17 (*Bibl. Clun.*, col. 1316 C).

p. 48, l. 12] Peter of Poitiers, Peter the Venerable's secretary, who had sent his special remembrances to Guigo in Letter 24.

p. 48, l. 14] The name of the claustral prior in 1136/7 is unknown; on the chamberlain Hugh of Crécy, see Appendix O.

26

AD PETRVM PICTAVENSEM SVVM IN CHRISTO FILIVM KARISSIMVM

A 26; S 26; C III,26; Bc I,26; see the analysis of this letter in Appendix Q on Peter of Poitiers.

1134/56. Internal evidence suggests that this letter was written after Peter of Poitiers entered the service of Peter the Venerable in about 1134; but the references are too vague to allow a more precise dating.

27

AD PAPAM INNOCENTIVM

A 27; S 27; C III,27; Bc I,27; cf. Jacques Le Vasseur, *Annales de l'église de Noyon* (Paris, 1633) II, 856–857; Mabillon, *Annales*, VI, 218 (1134); *GC*, II, 50 (1139); Bréquigny, *Chartes*, II, 619 (1134), and III, 48 (1140); *RHGF*, XV, 629–630 (1134); Lorain, *Cluny*, pp. 372–374; Pignot, *Cluny*, III, 159–161; Bernhardi, *Lothar*, pp. 636, n. 7, and 643, n. 31 (refuting the suggestion of Giesebrecht that Bernard's ep. 136 referred to the same event as this letter); Chevalier, *Régeste*, no. 3554 (1135).

June 1135.

p. 51, l. 10] The Council of Pisa, which was once dated 1134 (hence the date given to this letter by Mabillon and in the *RHGF*), is now dated from 30 May to 6 June 1135 by most scholars: see Bernhardi, *Lothar*, pp. 581 and 634–643; Ernst Bernheim, "Ein bisher unbekannter

Bericht vom Concil zu Pisa im Jahr 1135," *Zeitschrift für Kirchenrecht,* XVI (1881) 147–154; JL, I, 865–866; Hefele-Leclercq, *Conciles,* V.1, 706–710; Ramackers, in *PU in den Niederlandern,* p. 118, no. 33; Foreville, in *Histoire de l'Église,* IX.1, 64–65; De Warren, in *Bernard de Clairvaux,* p. 589; Manselli, "Alberico," p. 27; etc. The council is still dated 1134 by a few scholars, however, such as Voss, *Heinrich von Blois,* p. 112; Raoul Manselli, *Studi sulle eresie del secolo XII* (Istituto storico italiano per il Medio Evo: Studi storici, 5; Rome, 1953) p. 28 (probably through inadvertance, since he elsewhere dated the council 1135); and Grebenc, "Itinerar," pp. 49–50, whose reasons for re-establishing the date 1134 are not convincing.

p. 51, l. 30] The following prelates who attended the Council of Pisa are listed here by Peter the Venerable (those marked with an asterisk also appear in the report of the council published by Bernheim in the *Zs. f. Kirchenrecht,* XVI, 149): the archbishops and bishops of Rheims, *Périgeux, Bourges, Sens, Embrun (see Ep. 12), *Troyes (see Ep. 2, n. to p. 6, l. 12), *Limoges (cf. De Lasteyrie, *St. Martial,* p. 94), *Arras, Belley, and *Rennes, and the abbots of Limoges, *Vézelay (see Ep. 4, n. to p. 8, l. 23), La Chiusa, *St.-Germain-des-Prés, *Corbie, Noyon, Bourgeuil-en-Vallée, St. Sulpicius (Bourges) (see Appendix N), St. Remy (Rheims), *La Grasse, Moûtiers-St.-Jean (Réôme), Montierender, Melun, and Saumur. The only problem among these is "Hender," which I have taken to refer to Montierender. Yerres ("Hedera") was a nunnery, and a very recent foundation in 1135. Letter 53 shows that Peter the Venerable was also accompanied on his return from Pisa by the bishops of *Coutances and *Séez.

p. 51, l. 32] The scene of this attack was near Pontremoli, an important stage on the old *Via romea, francesca,* or *francigena,* as it was variously called, connecting Rome with the ultramontane regions: see William Heywood, *A History of Pisa: Eleventh and Twelfth Centuries* (Cambridge, Eng., 1921) p. 91, and F. P. Magoun, Jr., "The Italian Itinerary of Philip II," *Speculum,* XVII (1942) 368 and 373. It is about sixty miles northwest of Pisa on the main road across the Apennines from the modern port of La Spézia to Parma.

p. 52, l. 5] Abbot Alberic of Vézelay, later cardinal-bishop of Ostia: see Ep. 4, n. to p. 8, l. 23.

p. 52, l. 20] The perpetrators of this outrage are not known. Pignot identified them as partisans of Conrad of Hohenstaufen, presumably on the basis of a reference by Peter the Venerable to an ambush by

Duke Conrad [of Hohenstaufen] in *De miraculis*, I, 8 (*Bibl. Clun.*, col. 1259 BC); but this attack took place south of Siena, while Peter was on his way to Rome with the monk Gerard (who died in 1133), and must have occurred before 1130, when Conrad returned to Germany: see Bernhardi, *Lothar*, pp. 206-207, and A. L. Poole, in *CMH*, V, 338-339. The attackers on this occasion were more probably supporters of the antipope Anacletus or of the bishops who had been deposed at the Council of Pisa (see Hefele-Leclercq, *Conciles*, V.1, 708-709). It is clear that they were not in control of the entire neighborhood, since Peter the Venerable took refuge in a nearby villa and most of the party fled to Pontremoli; and they may have been simply brigands based in the tower where the archbishop of Rheims and the bishop of Périgeux were imprisoned.

p. 52, l. 23] The bishop of Luni at this time was apparently a schismatic: see Ughelli, *Italia sacra*, I, 844, and Gams, *Series*, p. 817; but he attended the Council of Pisa (see *Zs. f. Kirchenrecht*, XVI, 148) and traveled for a while with the French supporters of Innocent II. Peter the Venerable was in sufficiently good spirits when writing this letter, in spite of the shock of the attack, to pun on the name of Luni.

28

AD DOMINVM BERNARDVM ABBATEM CLARAEVALLIS

See pp. 63-70 above on the manuscripts of this letter, and see Appendix E on its date and character. A complete bibliography and commentary on this letter, the longest and most famous in Peter's correspondence, would amount to a history not only of the monastic crisis of the eleventh and twelfth centuries but also, almost, of the development of Benedictine monasticism in the West. The annotation here will be restricted to the elucidation of obscure points and to a few references to contemporary literature, especially to the bodies of Cluniac rules and customs known as the customaries of Farfa, of Bernard of Cluny, and of Ulric of Cluny, and to the statutes of Peter the Venerable.

1127(?): see Appendix E.

p. 53] The long schedule of Cistercian charges begins at this point ("Non inquiunt ... promisimus custodimus."): see Appendix E. Individual points in the schedule will be discussed in the notes to Peter's replies.

p. 57] This is the earliest known reference to the use of white clothing by the Cistercians. The reason for this change was probably that undyed cloth was cheaper than black, and it is now known that the Cistercians were not the first monks to use it. "Indes schon der gelehrte Mauriner E. Martène hatte es ausgesprochen, dass der Farbenwechsel der Zisterzienser gar nicht so ungewöhnlich war, wie man von kluniazensischer Seite behauptete ... Es ist deshalb nicht weiter verwunderlich, wenn die benediktinischen Abzweigungen des 11. und 12. Jhs., wie Kamaldolenser, Vallumbrosaner und Fontavellaner und Zisterzienser ohne weiteres die weisse Tunika beibehielten. Aber auch der Hauptstamm des Ordens behielt in zahlreichen Gemeinschaften noch lange Zeit die weisse Tunika bei": Hallinger, *Gorze-Kluny*, II, 700, n. 100. Only later were the various supernatural explanations of the use of white clothing by the Cistercians invented: cf. J. Othon [Ducourneau], "Les origines cisterciennes [IV]," *Revue Mabillon*, XXIII (1933) 103–110. Hallinger tended to underestimate the effects of this practice, however, even if it was not an innovation; and Peter's letters show that it shocked many members of old Benedictine houses, because black was the color of repentance and white the color of glory: see Letters 111 and 150, where Peter again referred to the matter, and *Statuta*, XVI; cf. Pignot, *Cluny*, III, 89–90; Philipp Oppenheim, *Das Mönchkleid im christlichen Altertum* (Römische Quartalschrift, Supplementheft 28; Freiburg-im-Br., 1931) pp. 69–78; De Valous, *Mon. clun.*, I, 227–249, esp. p. 241; Leclercq, *Pierre le Vén.*, p. 170, citing E. Peterson, *Pour une théologie du vêtement* (Lyons, 1943) pp. 13–15; Hallinger, *Gorze-Kluny*, II, 661–734.

p. 58] The canonically prescribed year of novitiate was frequently reduced at Cluny, and Peter defended this practice both here and in Letter 111: cf. De Valous, *Mon. clun.*, I, 31. In his *Statuta*, XXXV–XXXVIII, however, Peter established certain regulations for the novitiate. In the view of David Knowles, in *Petrus Ven.*, p. 11, "perhaps the most weighty and justified charge against the Cluniacs was their manner of dealing with novices."

p. 61, l. 17] See on these points, Gratian, *Decretum*, Dist. LVI (ed. cit., cols. 219–223), and the texts cited by Stephan Kuttner, "Cardinalis: The History of a Canonical Concept," *Traditio*, III (1945) 134 and n. 7.

p. 61, l. 21] Peter the Venerable made the same point in his introduction to the *Statuta*, justifying some of his changes and innovations.

p. 62] On the use of furs at Cluny, see *Cons. Farf.*, II, 47 (ed. Albers, p. 180); Bernard, *Cons. Clun.*, I, 5 (ed. Herrgott, pp. 145–147); and Ulric,

AD DOMINVM BERNARDVM   LETTER 28 / 117

Cons. Clun., III, 11 (*PL*, CXLIX, 752); cf. Duchesne, in *Bibl. Clun.*, *notae*, col. 116, citing many examples of the wearing of furs by monks; De Valous, *Mon. clun.*, I, 242-243. Bernard of Clairvaux particularly attacked the Cluniac use of furs in his ep. 1 (Gaume ed., I.1, 109) and *Apologia*, X (ed. Leclerq, III, 101). Peter the Venerable defended the practice in both Letter 28 and Letter 111, but in *Statuta* XVII he regulated the type of fur to be used. Both Bernard and Peter cited the examples of Adam, John the Baptist, and St. Benedict, but, "to attribute this to borrowing on the part of either party raises almost insuperable difficulties," according to Knowles, in *Petrus Ven.*, p. 8, n. 24, "it is simpler to suppose that both were drawing upon the store of Cluniac controversial commonplaces."

p. 64, l. 2] On the details of monastic dress in the eleventh and twelfth centuries, see esp. Hallinger, *Gorze-Kluny*, II, 661-734.

p. 64, l. 19] On the Cluniac use of linen trousers (*femoralia*), see *Cons. Farf.*, II, 4 (ed. Albers, p. 143); Bernard, *Cons. Clun.*, I, 5 (ed. Herrgott, pp. 145-147); and Ulric, *Cons. Clun.*, III, 11 (*PL*, CXLIX, 752); cf. De Valous, *Mon. Clun.*, I, 243-244. The Cistercian avoidance of trousers attracted the attention of some contemporaries, including Walter Map, who related the embarrassment of a Cistercian monk in *De nugis curialium*, I, 25 (ed. James, p. 49), and Nigel Wireker, who asked, "Ergo quid facerem veniens si ventus ab Austro / Nudaret subito posteriora mea?" in his *Speculum stultorum*, ed. T. Wright, *The Anglo-Latin Satirical Poets and Epigrammists of the Twelfth Century* (Rolls Series, 59; London, 1872) I, 85.

p. 65] See Duchesne, in the *Bibl. Clun.*, *notae*, col. 117, and De Valous, *Mon. clun.*, I, 243-244.

p. 68] The regulations of St. Benedict for the readmittance of monks who have left the monastery are in chap. XXIX of the Rule; cf. *Cons. Farf.*, II, 40 (ed. Albers, pp. 174-175), and Bernard, *Cons. Clun.*, I, 58 (ed. Herrgott, pp. 252-255).

p. 69] On fasting at Cluny, see *Cons. Farf.*, I, 41, 75, 80, and 115 (ed. Albers, pp. 30-32, 76-78, 80-81, and 112-113); Bernard, *Cons. Clun.*, II, 13 and 25 (ed. Herrgott, pp. 302-307 and 335-336); Ulric, *Cons. Clun.*, I, 27, 39, 45, and 53 (*PL*, CXLIX, 673-674, 685, 690-691, and 697-698); and Peter the Venerable, *Statuta*, XIII-XV; cf. De Valous, *Mon. clun.*, I, 278-280, and Knowles, in *Petrus Ven.*, pp. 7-8. Fasts and abstinence were one of the three points raised at the meeting of Benedictine abbots at Rheims in 1131: see Berlière, *Mélanges*, IV, 31.

p. 70] On manual labor at Cluny, see *Cons. Farf.*, II, 8 (ed. Albers, pp. 144-145); Bernard, *Cons. Clun.*, I, 75 (ed. Herrgott, pp. 280-283); and Ulric, *Cons. Clun.*, I, 30 (*PL*, CXLIX, 675-677); cf. De Valous, *Mon. clun.*, I, 309-311, and Knowles, in *Petrus Ven.*, pp. 12-13. Peter the Venerable discussed the matter again in Letter 111 and laid down in *Statuta* XXXIX, "ut antiquum et sanctum opus manuum, uel in claustris ipsis, aut ubi honeste, remoto conspectu secularium fieri poterit, ex parte saltem aliqua restauretur."

p. 71, l. 2] On the medieval doctrine of Mary and Martha, and their relation to the active and contemplative lives, see Cuthbert Butler, *Western Mysticism*, 2nd ed. (London, 1926) pp. 160 ff.; G. B. Ladner, *The Idea of Reform* (Cambridge, Mass., 1959) pp. 331 ff.; and D. A. Csányi, "Optima pars: Die Auslegungsgeschichte von Lk 10, 38-42 bei den Kirchenvätern der ersten vier Jahrhunderte," *Studia monastica*, II (1960) 5-78.

p. 71, l. 10] The monastery of Glanfeuil (St.-Maur-sur-Loire) was thought to have been founded by St. Maurus, the disciple of St. Benedict. Its origins are in fact obscure, and nothing is known about its history before the middle of the eighth century. The *Vita S. Mauri* of the pseudo-Faustus, attributing the foundation to St. Maurus, was composed in the ninth century, probably by Abbot Odo of Glanfeuil; but the legend was soon established and was universally accepted in the twelfth century: see Bloch, "Schism," pp. 182-190, and the bibliography in Cottineau, *Répertoire*, II, 2802-2803.

p. 71, l. 32] On the treatment of guests and the duties of the *hospitalarius* at Cluny, see Bernard, *Cons. Clun.*, I, 9 (ed. Herrgott, pp. 152-155); cf. De Valous, *Mon. clun.*, I, 166-176; on the washing of feet (the *mandatum*), see Ulric, *Cons. Clun.*, II, 37 (*PL*, CXLIX, 730); cf. Pignot, *Cluny*, II, 461-462; De Valous, *Mon. clun.*, I, 366-367; and Thomas Schäfer, *Die Fusswaschung im monastischen Brauchtum und in der lateinischen Liturgie* (Texte und Arbeiten herausgegeben durch die Erzabtei Beuron, I, 47; Beuron, 1956) p. 40 (citing this passage).

p. 72] On the *metanea* (genuflex or inclination), see Peter the Venerable, *Statuta*, LIII; cf. Duchesne, in *Bibl. Clun.*, *notae*, cols. 117-118; A. D. Nock, *Conversion* (Oxford, 1933) p. 180, who discusses its use by early writers in the sense of repentance; and Leclercq, *Amour des lettres*, p. 99.

p. 73] St. Benedict established in the Rule, chap. XXXII, that the abbot should keep a register of the possessions of the monastery: cf. Duchesne, in *Bibl. Clun.*, *notae*, col. 118.

p. 75] Section 14 of Peter's reply is concerned with both items 14 and 15 in the schedule of charges. From this point on, therefore, Peter's sections are numbered one less than the charges to which they reply. At the end, however, two sections, 19 and 20, are devoted to the last charge, and the numbers come out evenly.

p. 76] The oath of the novice, according to Ulric, *Cons. Clun.*, II, 27, was: "Ego frater promitto stabilitatem monachi, et conuersionem morum meorum, et obedientiam secundum regulam S. Benedicti, coram Deo et sanctis eius in hoc monasterio quod est constructum in honore BB. apost. Petri et Pauli; in presentia domini N. abbatis" (*PL*, CXLIX, 713); cf. Ildefons Herwegen, "Geschichte der benediktinischen Professformel," *Studien zur benediktinischen Profess* (Beiträge zur Geschichte des alten Mönchtums und des Benediktinerordens, 3; Münster in Westf., 1912) pp. 50–51, on the early Cluniac profession, and De Valous, *Mon. clun.*, I, 55–87.

p. 78] The Cistercians were not alone in bringing this charge against the Cluniacs. Geoffrey of Vendôme complained in his ep. IV,2, to Abbot Pontius of Cluny that one of his monks had transferred to Cluny and that "si ea intentione actum est, ut locum, in quo secundae regenerationis habitum suscepit, relinquat, laudare non possumus, cum hoc S. Benedicti Regula omnino contradicat, et sanctorum Romanorum pontificum auctoritas, qua patrimonium Beati Petri, monasterium videlicet nostrum, munitur, sub anathemate interdicat," in *Bibl. Clun.*, cols. 561–562, and *PL*, CLVII, 147; cf. L. Compain, *Étude sur Geoffroi de Vendôme* (Bibliothèque de l'École des hautes études, 86; Paris, 1891) pp. 60–61. This practice at Cluny was based on a number of papal privileges, beginning with that of John XI in 931 (JL 3584), renewed and extended by later popes: see *Bibl. Clun.*, notae, cols. 118–121; Besse, "Ordre," pp. 35–37; Letonnelier, *Cluny*, p. 37; and De Valous, *Mon. clun.*, I, 30–31.

p. 79, l. 26] See the foundation charter of Cluny, in *Cluny*, I, 124–128, no. 112, and the papal privileges cited in *Bibl. Clun.*, notae, cols. 121–122; cf. Letonnelier, *Cluny*, pp. 23–34.

p. 79, l. 32] See the papal privileges of Paschal II, relating to the chrism, of Urban II, relating to holy orders, and of Calixtus II and Honorius II, relating to the consecration of churches and cemetaries, cited by Duchesne, in *Bibl. Clun.*, notae, cols. 122–123; cf. Letonnelier, *Cluny*, p. 29.

p. 80] On the exemption of Cluny from the authority of the diocesan bishop, see the two studies of Letonnelier, in *Millénaire de Cluny*, I, 247–263, which was expanded in his *Cluny*; De Valous, *Mon. clun.*, II, 131–140; Williams, *Monastic Studies*, pp. 28–35; the studies by Georg Schreiber ("Cluny und die Eigenkirche," "Zur cluniazensischen Reform," and "Gregor VII., Cluny, Cîteaux, Prémontré zu Eigenkirche, Parochie, Seelsorge"), reprinted in his *Gemeinschaften*; and J.-F. Lemarignier, "L'exemption monastique et les origines de la réforme grégorienne," *À Cluny* (Dijon, 1950) pp. 288–340, esp. pp. 326–329.

p. 81] See Ep. 33 and the references there on the question of monastic tithes.

p. 83] On the problem of Cluniac possession of landed estates, cf. Adrian Morey, "The Conflict of Clairvaux and Cluny," *Downside Review*, L (1932) 98–101.

p. 86] The same point was made in the *Liber de diuersis ordinibus et professionibus quae sunt in ecclesia*, XX (*PL*, CCXIII, 822), which was written about the same time as this letter, ca. 1125/30, possibly by Raimbaud, provost of the house of St. John the Evangelist at Liège: see Charles Dereine, "Les origines de Prémontré," *Rev. hist. ecc.*, XLII (1947) 359–360.

p. 88] The "unidentified proverb" (note t) "aequum est mentiri et ueritatem abscondere," probably derived ultimately from Isidore of Seville, *Sententiae*, II, 55, 3 (*PL*, LXXXIII, 727: "Unum pene crimen habent, et qui falsitatem promit, et qui supprimit ueritatem."), and Burchard of Worms, *Decretum*, XVI, 12 (*PL*, CXL, 911: "Uterque reus est, et qui ueritatem occultat, et qui mendacium dicit;" cf. Gratian, *Decretum*, C. XI, q. 3, c. 80), where it was attributed to Augustine: see Horst Fuhrmann, in his "Schlusswort" to "Die Fälschungen im Mittelalter," *Historische Zeitschrift*, CXCVII (1963) 587–588.

p. 93] From this point up to the words "nos sequi cogamus" is a rhetorical quotation attributed to the Cistercians.

29

AD BERNARDVM ABBATEM CLARAEVALLIS

A 28; S 29; C III,29; Bc I,29; cf. Constable, "Langres," for a discussion of the disputed election at Langres in 1138.

August/September 1138 (see Constable, "Langres," pp. 135-137).

p. 102, l. 4] Archbishop Peter of Lyons: see Ep. 21, n. to p. 42, l. 4.

p. 102, l. 12] Louis VII held court at Le Puy in August 1137 (see Constable, "Langres," p. 136), not in February or February/March, as proposed, respectively, by Brial, in *RHGF*, XV, 634, n. c, and Luchaire, *Louis VII*, p. 63.

30

AD THEODARDVM

A 29; S 30; C III,30; Bc I,30; cf. Pignot, *Cluny*, III, 590-591.

1122/39. This letter can be dated with certainty only between the beginning of Peter's abbacy and the end of Theodard's priorate, although the use of "dominus" and "honorandus" suggests, as with Letter 14, that Theodard was already prior (see Appendix K). It was apparently written just before or during Lent, since Peter asked Theodard to come "on the next Sunday of Lent."

p. 105, l. 13] Peter may have made this trip to Montpellier, which is otherwise unknown, for reasons of health.

p. 105, l. 16] Lurcy-le-Bourg was a dependency of Cluny in the diocese of Nevers. According to Cottineau, *Répertoire*, I, 1679, it was a priory of La Charité, which would explain the summoning of Theodard; but there is no reference to it in the papal bull for La Charité of 1144 (*Cluny*, V, 432-435, no. 4081); and it is listed as subject directly to Cluny, before the priories of La Charité, by Marrier, in *Bibl. Clun.*, col. 1716 B (and Evans, *Rom. Arch.*, p. 157); Beaunier-Besse, *Abbayes*, VI, 118; and De Valous, *Mon. Clun.*, II, 198.

31

AD EPISCOPVM DE BETHLEEM

A 30; S 31; C III,31; Bc I,31; cf. Pignot, *Cluny*, III, 297; Paul Riant, *Études sur l'histoire de l'église de Bethléem*, I (Genoa, 1889) p. 204; Appendix I on Cluniac houses in the East.

The recipient of this letter, according to Riant, may have been either Bishop Ascetinus (1110-25), Anselmus (Ascelinus) (1128-45), or Gerald (1148-53).

After 1130(?). According to Enlart (see Appendix I), Mt. Thabor adopted Cluniac customs in 1130.

32

AD PAPAM INNOCENTIVM

A 31; S 32; C III,32; Bc I,32.

1135/43: between the first appearance of Stephen of Chandieu as archdeacon and the death of Innocent II.

p. 106] The archdeacon whose name, according to Peter, was the same as that of the protomartyr was Stephen of Chandieu, a canon of Lyons from at least 1132 and archdeacon from 5 March 1135/6 until 1144: see Beyssac, *Chanoines*, pp. 29 and 252. In 1132 he appeared with Cardinal Matthew of Albano and Abbot Ilion of Lyons (see Ep. 100) on a charter recording an agreement between Cluny and Ambronay (*Bibl. Clun.*, col. 1394; with variants in *Cluny*, V, 386, no. 4030); and he appeared as archdeacon on several charters during the pontificate of Archbishop Peter of Lyons (1131–9: Ep. 21, n. to p. 42, l. 4): Pierre Juenin, *Nouvelle histoire . . . de Tournus* (Dijon, 1733) *preuves*, p. 163 (Martin, *Conciles*, no. 540); *Cluny*, V, 382–383, no. 4026 (Martin, *Conciles*, no. 541); and *Cart. lyonnais*, I, 35–36, no. 24; see also Letters 50, 99, and 100. He was, as this letter shows, a supporter of Cluny.

p. 107] The subject of the papal mandate which Stephen was almost alone in obeying is not known. It may have been associated with the election at Langres or may refer to Innocent II's letter of 17 May 1140/1 to Archbishop Falco of Lyons instructing him not to injure Cluny (JL 8326; cf. Constable, "Langres," p. 131, and Janssen, *Legaten*, p. 35 and n. 5, who proposed the date 17 May 1139, which is certainly too early, since Archbishop Peter died on 25 May 1139). In Letter 29 Peter the Venerable commented on the hostile attitude toward Cluny of the canons of Lyons, and in Letter 38 he discussed at length the troubles of the Cluniacs in the diocese of Lyons. Peter glossed over these difficulties in Letter 100, written in 1141, however, and said that the dispute mentioned in that letter was the only quarrel between Cluny and the church of Lyons "for almost twenty years."

33

AD EVNDEM

A 32; S 33; C III,33; Bc I,33; cf. Constable, "Cluniac Tithes," esp. pp. 609–617, for a discussion of this and the three following letters.

Mid-November 1132/40 (probably 1135/7).

p. 108, l. 12] Gigny was founded by St. Berno in the late ninth century but was reduced from an abbey to a conventual priory and subjected to Cluny by Gregory VII in 1075: see Beaunier-Besse, *Abbayes*, X, 167, and Constable, "Cluniac Tithes," pp. 608-609.

p. 108, l. 25] Cf. the grants to Clairvaux of the tithes of Arconville by Abbot Pontius of Cluny, confirmed by Peter the Venerable in 1122/35, in *Clairvaux*, pp. 7-8, no. 5, and to Trois-Fontaines of the tithes it had previously paid to the Cluniacs of Baudivillard in the diocese of Châlons-sur-Marne, in 1127/31, in *GC*, X, instr., 168-169 (panchart of Bishop Geoffrey of Châlons-sur-Marne).

34

AD DOMINVM HAIMERICVM CANCELLARIVM

A 33; S 34; C III,34; Bc I,34; cf. Bréquigny, *Chartes*, II, 604 (1132); Constable, "Cluniac Tithes," pp. 609-617.

Mid-November 1132/40 (probably 1135/7): written at the same time as Letter 33.

p. 110] This *generalis capitulum* may refer either to the Cluniac chapter general (see Ep. 111, n. to p. 293) or (as the juxtaposition with *uerbis* suggests) a general privilege for Cluny. Innocent is not known, however, to have granted such a privilege, with the promises mentioned by Peter the Venerable, to Cluny.

p. 111] See Ep. 33, n. to p. 108, l. 25.

p. 112, l. 11] See *De miraculis*, II, 12-13 (*Bibl. Clun.*, cols. 1310-1313), and Honorius II's bull of 20 October 1126 (JL 7268; *PL*, CLXVI, 1265-1268). For a recent discussion and interpretation of this episode, with references to previous literature, see Tellenbach, "Pontius."

p. 112, l. 18] This may refer to Puy-St.-Ambrose, a Cluniac priory in the diocese of Clermont: Beaunier-Besse, *Abbayes*, V, 138, and Cottineau, *Répertoire*, II, 2379. Peter's visit there may have been associated with the trip to Auvergne mentioned in Letter 18.

p. 112, l. 21] Le Miroir, a daughter of Cîteaux, was founded 5 September 1131: Beaunier-Besse, *Abbayes*, X, 168.

p. 112, l. 39] Innocent II consecrated the new church at Cluny on 24/5 October 1130. The date is given as 25 October in JL, I, 844, on the basis of Innocent's bull of 2 March 1132, in which he said that he consecrated the church "eodem die" as Urban had consecrated the church (*Bull. Clun.*, p. 46; JL 7548), that is, on 25 October 1095 (*Bibl. Clun.*, col. 518; JL, I, 681). The day is also given as 25 October in the necrology of Nantua: *Obituaires*, V, 342. Peter the Venerable in a charter of 1151, however, gave the day as VIIII kal. nov. (24 October): *PL*, CLXXXIX, 483, and, better, Johannes Ramackers, "Analekten zur Geschichte der Reformpapsttums und der Cluniazencer," *Quellen und Forschungen aus italienischen Archiven und Bibliotheken*, XXIII (1931–32) 51.

p. 113] Before becoming a cardinal Anacletus had been a monk at Cluny: see Richard Zoepffel, *Die Papstwahlen* (Göttingen, 1871) pp. 292–293. In a letter dated 1 May 1130, he asked for the support of Cluny: JL 8376; cf. Bloch, "Schism," p. 163; Schmale, *Schisma*, p. 75; Janssen, *Legaten*, p. 3. Bernhardi, *Lothar*, p. 326, n. 99, cited this passage as evidence that Peter the Venerable later regretted his early support of Innocent, but it was probably the result of temporary annoyance: cf. Schmale, *Schisma*, p. 165, n. 10.

35

AD ABBATES CISTERSIENSIS ORDINIS

A 34; S 35; C III,35; Bc I,35; cf. Bréquigny, *Chartes*, II, 604 (1132); Constable, "Cluniac Tithes," esp. pp. 609–617.

August/September 1132/40. The Cistercian chapter general usually met at Cîteaux in September: see Mahn, *Ordre cist.*, p. 174.

p. 114] This privilege was granted on 10 February 1132: *PL*, CLXXIX, 123; JL 7537; cf. Constable, *Monastic Tithes*, pp. 241-242.

p. 116] "This case of tithes" was certainly the dispute between Gigny and Le Miroir, discussed in Letters 33–34.

36

AD EOSDEM

A 35; S 36; C III,36; Bc I,36; cf. Bréquigny, *Chartes*, II, 594 (1131); Constable, "Cluniac Tithes," esp. pp. 609–617.

August/September 1133/40. This letter was written a year after Letter 35.

37

ADVERSVS QVENDAM FVRIOSVM APOLLINARISTAM HERETICVM

A 50; C IV,1; Bc II,1; cf. Pignot, *Cluny*, III, 517–518; Séjourné, in *DThC*, XII. 2, 2069–2070; Leclercq, *Pierre le Vén.*, pp. 215–217; Claude Bodard, "Le mystère du corps du Seigneur: Quelques aspects de la Christologie de Pierre le Vénérable," *Collectanea Ord. Cist. Ref.*, XVIII (1956) 101–102; and see pp. 76–77 above on the position of this letter in the collection. In MSS. A and B it appears between Letters 51 and 52, and it was probably moved to its present position by Pierre de Montmartre in order to provide his fourth (the second in the *Bibl. Clun.*) book with an impressive first letter. Together with Letter 94, it is one of the two strictly theological letters in the collection.

The anonymous recipient was evidently a Cluniac monk, but nothing specific is known about him. He may possibly be the heretic against whom Peter said in Letter 94 (see n. to p. 252) that he wrote "two or three years ago."

The date of this letter is unknown. Séjourné's suggestion of 1130/2 is based purely on its position in the collection.

38

AD PETRVM LVGDVNENSEM ARCHIEPISCOPVM

A 36; S 37; Turin, Bibl. naz., E-V-37, fol. 203^r; C IV,2; Bc II,2; cf. Severt, *Chronologia*, I, 239; Pignot, *Cluny*, III, 78–80, including a translation of the passage on the decline of monasticism in the diocese of Lyons. The real reason for this letter is uncertain. Peter the Venerable says that he need not explain the matter fully since the Archbishop will understand, and he mentions rumors which the Archbishop should not believe. The purpose of the letter was not "a matter of gold and silver," according to Peter, but to protest against the "various and numerous" injuries done to the property of Cluny in the diocese of Lyons by clerics and especially by monks, whose irregular way of life Peter bitterly attacked and whom he urged the Archbishop to strike with the sword and arrow of ecclesiastical justice. These troubles may be associated with those mentioned in Letter 32.

1131/9: the pontificate of Archbishop Peter of Lyons (see Ep. 21, n. to p. 42, l. 4).

p. 125] Before becoming archbishop of Lyons, Peter of Burgundy was bishop of Viviers. Peter the Venerable implies here that their friendship dated at least from that time, since he expresses the hope that the Archbishop will not be further removed in spirit when he is closer in space. This also implies that this letter was written comparatively early in Peter of Burgundy's pontificate.

p. 128] It is hard to say whether *prouincia* in this letter refers to the region of Provence or to the Archbishop's ecclesiastical province and whether or not, therefore, it should be spelled with a capital.

39

AD PAPAM INNOCENTIVM

A 37; C IV,3; Bc II,3; cf. *RHGF*, XV, 626–628 (1132); Pignot, *Cluny*, III, 166 and 176–177; Berlière, *Mélanges*, IV, 40–41.

Summer 1133.

p. 132] The illness of Matthew of Albano and his stay at Cluny, according to Berlière, *Mélanges*, IV, 42, dated from the middle of 1132 (or somewhat later) until the end of the summer of 1133. He reappeared on papal bulls on 20 December 1133. This letter was therefore written during the summer of 1133, which fits with the fact, which Peter implies, that the Pope was in Rome from late April until June 1133. He next appears in September in Siena, and then in Pisa from November on.

40

AD GILONEM SCISMATICVM

A 38; C IV,4; Bc II,4.

On Cardinal-Bishop Aegidius (Gilo) of Tusculum, see Appendix J on Cluniac cardinals.

1130/4. This letter was presumably written before the submission of the count of Poitou to Bernard of Clairvaux at Parthenay in late 1134 or early 1135 (*Bernard de Clairvaux*, p. 587), and probably before the meeting of Peter the Venerable with Gilo at Poitiers in the spring of 1133 (see Ep. 66, n. to p. 196, l. 13).

p. 135] This refers to the fact, which Peter mentions again later, that the two centers of Anacletus's power were the strongholds of the Pierleone in Rome and the lands of the count of Poitou.

41

EPISTOLA THEODARDI PRIORIS ET FRATRVM DE CARITATE AD DOMINVM PETRVM

A 39; S 38; C IV,5; Bc II,5.

Spring/summer 1132, 1134, or 1136. The precise year of this letter and the reply, Letter 42, is not known, but Peter's travels during the presumed priorate of Theodard of La Charité (*ca.* 1130-9: see Appendix K) show that they were written in either 1132, 1134, or 1136.

p. 136] This Peter, who is also mentioned in Letter 42, may be either Peter of Poitiers, Peter the Venerable's secretary, or possibly the enigmatic "prior" Peter of La Charité mentioned by Florence of Worcester (see Appendix K). If it is Peter of Poitiers, the reference would date the letter in or after 1134, when he joined the service of Peter the Venerable, but the use of "beloved brother" and "lord" here and in Letter 42 suggests a man more elevated in rank than Peter of Poitiers.

p. 137, l. 4] Letter 42 shows that this refers to the Feast of the Assumption of the Virgin (15 August).

p. 137, l. 7] Letter 42 shows that this refers to the Feast of SS. Peter and Paul (29 June).

42

RESCRIPTVM DOMINI PETRI AD THEODARDVM PRIOREM

A 40; S 39; C IV,6; Bc II,6; cf. the notes to Ep. 41, to which this is the reply.

Spring/summer 1132, 1134, or 1136.

43

ITEM AD THEODARDVM PRIOREM DE CARITATE

A 41; S 40; C IV,7; Bc II,6 [bis]; cf. Pignot, *Cluny*, III, 584-586, translating the most important parts of this letter, which is evidence both for the austerities practiced even by prominent Cluniacs and for the attitude of Peter the Venerable toward such practices.

1130/9: during the presumed priorate of Theodard of La Charité (see Appendix K).

44

AD SIGIVARDVM NORICORVM REGEM

A 42; S 41; C IV,7 [bis]; Bc II,7; cf. Bréquigny, *Chartes*, II, 604 (1132); Lorain, *Cluny*, p. 414; Pignot, *Cluny*, III, 299–301; Paul Riant, *Expéditions et pèlerinages des Scandinaves en Terre Sainte au temps des Croisades* (Paris, 1865) p. 214 (1123).

King Sigurd of Norway, known as "the Crusader," reigned from 1122 until 1130: cf. Chevalier, *Bio-bib.*, II, 4252–4253; Laurence M. Larson, *The Earliest Norwegian Laws* (Columbia Records of Civilization, 20; New York, 1935) p. 327, n. 1; and Knut Gjerset, *History of the Norwegian People* (New York, 1915) I, 333–336.

1122/30.

p. 141] On Sigurd's crusading activities, both at home and in the Holy Land, see Riant, *Expéditions*, pp. 173–215; Gjerset, *Norwegian People*, I, 333: Steven Runciman, *A History of the Crusades* (Cambridge, Eng., 1951–1954) II, 92–93; and Berry, in *Petrus Ven.*, p. 144, who associated this letter with "the new venture which he [Sigurd] was preparing against the infidels about 1130."

45

AD FRATRES DE NORANTONA PRO THOMA NOTARIO SVO

A 43; S 42; C IV,8; Bc II,8.

The Cluniac house of St. Andrew at Northampton was a dependency of La Charité, founded in 1093/1100: see Dugdale, *Monasticon*, V, 185–196; *La Charité*, pp. vii and 423; De Valous, *Mon. clun.*, II, 261–262; and Knowles and Hadcock, *Religious Houses*, p. 99.

p. 141] On Thomas [of Northampton], who is called Peter the Venerable's notary in the heading to this letter, see Appendix R on functionaries at Cluny.

46

AD PAPAM INNOCENTIVM

A 44; C IV,9; Bc II,9; cf. *RHGF*, XV, 628–629 (1132/3); Berlière, *Mélanges*, IV, 41–42; and notes to Ep. 39.

Autumn 1133. The request to the Pope to send back Matthew of Albano, and the use of the past tense in referring to his actions, show that Matthew had already left Cluny when this letter was written and was either on his way or already back in Italy. He had refused to allow Peter the Venerable or anyone else to write to the Pope on his behalf and "is hastening" to carry out the Pope's orders.

p. 142, l. 8] On the disturbed conditions in Italy, which were associated with the visit of Lothar from September 1132 until August 1133, see Bernhardi, *Lothar*, pp. 436–497, and A. L. Poole and U. Balzani, in the *CMH*, V, 340 and 364–365.

p. 142, l. 12] The Pope's letter to Matthew of Albano is lost. According to Berlière, *Mélanges*, IV, 41–42, it was "doubtless" sent before he received Peter the Venerable's Letter 39; but it is more probable that it was a reply to Peter's letter.

p. 143] The occasion of this meeting of Matthew of Albano and the three abbots, Bernard of Clairvaux, Alberic of Vézelay, and Hugh of Pontigny, is not known. Bernard was in Italy throughout the first half of 1133, but he returned to France in June and was at Cambrai and Blois in July/August, when this meeting may have taken place. Or it may have been at the Council of Jouarre, presuming this council met in 1133 (see Ep. 17, n. to p. 25, l. 15).

47

AD MATHEVM EPISCOPVM ALBANENSEM

A 45; S 43; C IV,11; Bc II, 11 (where the address, which is lacking in the manuscripts and C, is supplied from Letter 2); cf. Mabillon, *Annales*, VI, 251 (1136); Bréquigny, *Chartes*, II, 537 (1125) and 636 (1136); *RHGF*, XV, 630–632 (1134); Pignot, *Cluny*, III, 255–257 (*ca.* 1136); Louis Clouët, *Histoire de Verdun* (Verdun, 1867–1870) II, 219–222; Vacandard, *St. Bernard*, I, 197 (1136); Berlière, *Mélanges*, IV, 38–39; *Bernard de Clairvaux*, p. 216 (with bibliography in n. 95).

1131/5 (probably 1134). The date of 1136 usually given to this letter is certainly too late, since Matthew of Albano died in 1135. The pontificates of Bishops Albero of Verdun and Geoffrey II of Châlons-sur-Marne both began in 1131: Gams, *Series*, pp. 534 and 652. The sources cited in the note below point to the year 1134, especially since Matthew of Albano was at Cluny during much of 1132 and 1133, and Peter the Venerable attended the Council of Pisa in 1135.

p. 145, l. 2] The Cluniac monks of St. Paul at Verdun were expelled and replaced by Premonstratensian canons by Bishop Albero of Verdun. A lively account of the corruption of the Cluniacs, and the failure of all efforts to reform them, is found in Laurence of Liège, *Gesta episcoporum Virdunensium*, XXXIV, s.a. 1134, in *MGH, Scriptores in fol.*, X, 510. Bernard of Clairvaux mentioned the affair in this epp. 178 and 253 (Gaume ed., I.1, 399 and 527). But there is no mention of it in the *Annales S. Pauli Virdunensis*, in *MGH, Scriptores in fol.*, XV, 501. Clouët, *Verdun*, II, 219-222, cited relevant charters of the bishop of Verdun and the archbishop of Trier, dated 28 November 1135 and 20 January 1136, and confirmations of the Premonstratensians from the Emperor and Pope dated 8 January 1136 and 15 April 1137, all printed in Charles-Louis Hugo, *Sacri et canonici ordinis Praemonstratensis annales* (Nancy, 1734-35) I, *preuves*, 326-328, which was unavailable to me.

p. 145, l. 33] On Bishop Geoffrey II of Châlons-sur-Marne, a friend of Peter the Venerable and supporter of Cluny, see notes to Epp. 78-79.

48

AD CARTVSIENSES CONSOLATORIA SVPER OBITV FRATRVM

A 46; S 44; C IV,12; Bc II,12; cf. Mabillon, *Annales*, VI, 217 (1133); Bréquigny, *Chartes*, II, 612 (1133); Pignot, *Cluny*, III, 269-272; Le Couteulx, *Ann. Carth.*, I, 352-356 (1132); Chevalier, *Régeste*, no. 3474 (1132).

1122/37. The tragedy described in this letter, which caused the death of many Carthusian monks, has often been associated with the great snows and floods at the end of 1133 and beginning of 1134 mentioned by Ordericus Vitalis, *Hist. ecc.*, VI, 10, and XIII, 16 (*ed. cit.*, III, 120, and V, 37-38). This view is supported by Peter the Venerable's reference to great snows, but it is not confirmed by any definite evidence. The only certain dates for this letter, therefore, are the beginning of Peter's abbacy and the death of Guigo in 1137.

49

AD HENRICVM WINTONIENSEM EPISCOPVM

A 47; C IV,13; Bc II,12[bis]; cf. Pignot, *Cluny*, III, 596-597.

Henry of Blois, the son of Countess Adela of Blois (see biographical note to Ep. 15), was the brother of King Stephen of England. He was brought up at Cluny and became abbot of Glastonbury in 1126 and bishop of Winchester in 1129, holding the two positions concurrently until his death in 1171. He was an important figure in the secular and ecclesiastical politics of his age, a generous patron of Cluny, and a friend and adviser of Peter the Venerable, who asked him in Letter 60 to be buried at Cluny. On his gifts to Cluny, and the commemorations made for him there, see Duchesne, in *Bibl. Clun., notae*, cols. 131–132; and, more generally, Voss, *Heinrich von Blois*, pp. 108–121; Knowles, *Episcopal Colleagues*, pp. 34–37, and *Saints and Scholars* (Cambridge, Eng., 1962) pp. 51–58.

1131. This letter can be dated from the reference to the visit of Peter the Venerable to England "last year."

p. 150] This trouble at La Charité (of which, according to Peter the Venerable, Henry should have been "the revenger, not the defender, nor surely the mediator") may have been associated with the efforts of La Charité to win independence from Cluny: cf. Voss, *Heinrich von Blois*, p. 110, n. 10.

50

AD STEPHANVM CLERICVM LVGDVNENSEM

A 48; S 45; C IV,14; Bc II,14.

According to Beyssac, *Chanoines*, pp. 26–29, there were four canons of Lyons named Stephen in the second quarter of the twelfth century: Stephen Cordier (1101–32); the dean Stephen, who is mentioned in 1128 and became archbishop of Vienne in 1129; Stephen of Chandieu (see Ep. 32, n. to p. 106); and Stephen *Pinguis* or *Grossus*, precentor or chantor from 1135 to 1140. Of these, the most probable recipient of this letter is Stephen of Chandieu, about whom Letter 32 was written and to whom Letter 100 was addressed. The fact that he is called simply "a cleric of Lyons" suggests that this letter was written before he became archdeacon in *ca.* 1135/6.

Shortly before the beginning of Lent (1132/6?).

51

AD HVGONEM CATVLAM QVENDAM MILITEM

A 49; S 46; C IV,15; Bc II,15.

The knight Hugh Catula is mentioned in the chronicle of Cluny (*Bibl. Clun.*, col. 594 D), quoting this letter and saying that as a result Hugh gave up his resolve to visit Jerusalem and became a monk at Cluny.

The date of 1146/7 assigned to this letter by Berry, in *Petrus Ven.*, p. 151, is based on the presumption that Hugh's pilgrimage was associated with the Second Crusade.

p. 152] Peter the Venerable repeated his opposition to pilgrimages, especially by monks, in Letters 80, 83, and 144, and expressed the view that men are saved by good works, not by visits to holy places. This attitude was also expressed by Bernard of Clairvaux, ep. 64 (Gaume ed., I.1, 208-210), by Guigo of La Chartreuse, Meditation 262: "Ierusalem eant alii; tu usque ad humilitatem aut patientiam. Hoc est enim, te ire extra mundum, illud intra," ed. André Wilmart, *Le recueil des pensées du b. Guigue* (Études de philosophie médiévale, 22; Paris, 1936) p. 111, and by other contemporaries; cf. Constable, in *Rev. Bén.*, LXVI, 103 (cited p. 49, n. 200, above), and Lamma, *Momenti*, pp. 139-151.

52

AD FRATRES CLVNIACENSES DEPRECATORIA PRO OBITV MATRIS SVAE

A 51; S 47; C IV,16; Bc II,16; cf. Mabillon, *Annales*, VI, 221 (1134); Bréquigny, *Chartes*, II, 619 (1134); Pignot, *Cluny*, III, 161-165; Leclercq, *Pierre le Vén.*, pp. 47-50.

July/August 1135: presumably about the same time as Letter 53 (see n. to p. 154, l. 1).

p. 153, l. 5] On Peter the Venerable's mother Raingard, see Appendix A.

p. 153, l. 7] Letters 53 (I, 170) and 56 (I, 178) confirm the reading of MS. A that Raingard died on 24 June 1135. In the necrology of Marcigny, however, Raingard is entered under VII. kal. Julii (25 June): *Necrologium*, p. 49.

p. 153, l. 13] A "tricenarius missarum" was a series of thirty commemorative masses. To the examples of trentals ordered by Peter the Venerable cited by Duchesne, in *Bibl. Clun.*, notae, col. 129 (Letters 20 and 167-168, and the necrology of St.-Martin-des-Champs), may be added *Cluny*, IV, 462, no. 3366, V, 347, no. 3995, and 532-533, no. 4183 (1155/6), ordering a double trental to be sung at Cluny to commemorate Empress Mathilda, and Talbot, in *Petrus Ven.*, p. 21, who published an association between Cluny and St. Remy at Rheims arranging a trental for Peter's friend Odo of St. Remy. On anniversary masses generally, see Molinier, *Obituaires*, pp. 115-117, and at Cluny, Willibald Jorden, *Das cluniazensische Totengedächtniswesen* (Münsterische Beiträge zur Theologie, 15; Münster in Westf., 1930) esp. pp. 108-109; Schreiber, *Gemeinschaften*, pp. 81-138; C. J. Bishko, "Liturgical Intercession at Cluny for the King-Emperors of Leon," *Studia monastica*, III (1961) 53-76; and H. E. J. Cowdrey, "Unions and Confraternity with Cluny," *Journal of Ecclesiastical History*, XVI (1965) 152-162.

53

ITEM AD GERMANOS SVOS EIVSDEM MATRIS EPITAPHIVM

A 52; C IV,17; Bc II,17; cf. Paolo Lamma, "La madre di Pietro il Venerabile," *Studium*, LIV (1958) offprint of 14 pp. (reprinted in *Bullettino dell'Istituto Storico Italiano per il Medio Evo*, LXXV [1963] 175-188), who stressed the quasi-public hagiographical character of this letter. Marcigny was still at the height of its reputation in the first half of the twelfth century: cf. *De miraculis*, I, 22 (*Bibl. Clun.*, col. 1280 D) and *The Life of Christina of Markyate*, ed. C. H. Talbot (Oxford, 1959) pp. 126-127, where Archbishop Thurstan of York in about 1123 tried to send the recluse Christina "over the sea to Marcigny or at least to Fontevrault"; Rose Graham, *English Ecclesiastical Studies* (London, 1929) pp. 18-19. Marcigny was intended to be a house of ninety-nine nuns (with the hundredth place reserved for "Our Lady, the abbess") leading a life of strict *clausura* (De Valous, *Mon. clun.*, I, 382-383, and II, 221). Raingard's charitable work for knights and laymen and among "the surrounding very poor places of nuns," however, suggests that they enjoyed a certain amount of liberty. "Being noble and delicate, fragile and infirm," wrote Peter the Venerable, "they required many things on account of their sex, location, and habit." According to F. Cucherat, "Semur-en-Brionnais ... depuis l'an 860 jusqu'à nos jours," *Mémoires de la Société Éduenne*, XVI (1888) 114, n. 1, the life of Raingard in this letter was translated by Arnaud d'Andilly, *Vie des saints pères des déserts*, II, 213-272.

Late July/August 1135.

p. 154, l. 1] This reference to the Council of Pisa (30 May-6 June 1135: Ep. 27, n. to p. 51, l. 10) establishes the dates both of Raingard's death and of Letters 52-53. If Raingard died on 24 June, and Peter the Venerable heard the news on his way back from Pisa, returned to Cluny, and then spent three days at Marcigny, these letters must have been written in late July or August.

p. 154, l. 29] The archbishops and bishops of Rheims, Rouen, Troyes, Coutances, and Séez: cf. the list of French prelates who attended the Council of Pisa in Ep. 27 (n. to p. 51, l. 30).

p. 159, l. 1] The date of this meeting between Raingard and Robert of Arbrissel, the founder of Fontevrault, is not known, but the text shows that Robert visited Raingard, perhaps on a preaching tour in the Auvergne, as Pignot, *Cluny*, III, 55, suggested, not that she fled to Fontevrault, as proposed by Leclercq, *Pierre le Vén.*, p. 49; cf. Johannes von Walter, *Die ersten Wanderprediger Frankreichs*, I: *Robert von Arbrissel* (Studien zur Geschichte der Theologie und der Kirche, 9.3; Leipzig, 1903) p. 92.

p. 159, l. 37] Cf. Appendix A, pp. 237–238 and 242 below, discussing several documents in the chartulary of Sauxillanges, of which one, no. 795, appears to have been the will of Maurice of Montboissier and was witnessed by both Raingard and the young Peter the Venerable.

p. 160] On conversion *ad succurrendum* and moniage, see Louis Gougaud, *Devotional and Ascetic Practices in the Middle Ages*, trans. G. C. Bateman (London, 1927) pp. 131–145, who said that "the *moniage* of the abbey of Cluny was particularly sought after in the eleventh and twelfth centuries" (p. 135), and G. G. Coulton, *Five Centuries of Religion* (Cambridge, Eng., 1929–1950) I, 476–481. *Sauxillanges*, no. 906, mentions two knights who took the habit *ad succurrum*.

p. 161] The death of Robert of Arbrissel on 23/5 February 1117 (Chevalier, *Bio-bib.*, II, 3982; Von Walter, *Wanderprediger*, I, 179) fixes a *terminus post quem* for Raingard's entry into Marcigny.

p. 162, l. 10] (a) Geoffrey (III) of Semur-en-Brionnais was prior of Marcigny from about 1110 until his death in 1123: *De miraculis*, I, 26 (*Bibl. Clun.*, cols. 1289–1290); chronicle of Cluny (*ibid.*, col. 599); Cucherat, *Cluny*, pp. 220 and 264–265; and *Marcigny*, introd., pp. xvii–xviii. (b) Gerald, who belonged to the well-known family of Vert or Le Vert, held various offices in Cluniac houses, besides being "procurator" or chamberlain at Marcigny, before he retired to lead a solitary life and died late in 1133: see Ep. 58; *De miraculis*, I, 8 (*Bibl. Clun.*, cols. 1258–1264); Cucherat, *Cluny*, p. 265; Leclercq, in *Petrus Ven.*, p. 110; and *Marcigny*, p. 242. On the family of Le Vert, see *St. Flour*, pp.

565–566, to whose citations may be added *Cluny*, V, 305–306, no. 3950 (*ca.* 1120), on which both *Girardus Viridis* and a monk named *Berardus Viridis* appear. (c) The reference to Gerald's death in Letter 58 and this passage establish that the first draft of the *De miraculis* was written and divided into books between 1133 and 1135. In the earliest version, only two parts of I,8 are found; in the second version the entire chapter is divided into five miracles: see Constable, in *Petrus Ven.*, pp. 221 ff.

p. 162, l. 21] Hugh was claustral prior at Marcigny, in charge of the spiritual direction of the nuns, from 1109 until 1122, when he was elected abbot of Cluny to succeed Pontius: *De miraculis*, II, 12 (*Bibl. Clun.*, col. 1311); chronicle of Cluny (*ibid.*, cols. 1646–1647); *Marcigny*, introd., p. xviii, and p. 134, n. 2. He died after three months as abbot of Cluny, on 9 July, according to the necrologies of Nantua (*Obituaires*, V, 344) and Marcigny (*Necrologium*, p. 52) and was succeeded by Peter the Venerable.

p. 162, l. 27] This is the beginning of a long speech by Raingard to her companions, going from "Diu karissimi," with two short breaks, to "uado ad deum" (p. 163, l. 28).

p. 168] The structure of Raingard's dream described here resembles the dream of Samuel in I Kings 3.

p. 170] This date of 24 June (the nativity of John the Baptist) confirms the reading "viii. kal. Jul." in Letters 52 (I, 153) and 56 (I, 178).

54

AD PETRVM LVGDVNENSEM ARCHIEPISCOPVM

A 53; C IV,18; Bc II,18; cf. Severt, *Chronologia*, I, 239.

February 1138. This letter was almost certainly written at the same time as Letter 21. It refers in almost identical terms to the condition of the region around Cluny, with no rulers and "raptoribus exposita."

p. 174, l. 21] Lent in 1138 began on 20 February. The meeting planned was probably to discuss the disputed election at Langres.

p. 174, l. 27] This may refer to some actions taken as a result of the situation described in Letter 38.

p. 175] Cf. Ep. 21, n. to p. 42, l. 10, on the situation in the Mâconnais after the death of King Louis VI.

55

AD HENRICVM WINTONIENSEM EPISCOPVM

A 54; C IV,19; Bc II,19.

1131/56. This letter was an immediate reply, according to Peter the Venerable, to a letter from Henry of Winchester which was written after (and may have been a reply to) Letter 49, written in 1131.

p. 176, l. 3] Later letters show that Peter carried out his intention to write frequently.

p. 176, l. 28] The identity of this Robert who tried to sow ill will between Henry and Peter the Venerable is not known.

p. 176, l. 35] Cf. p. 24 above on this cryptic passage. The sacristan may be either Wicardus or Gervase, who appear on documents of 1133? and 1136, respectively: see Appendix R.

p. 176, l. 36] Adela of Blois, the mother of Henry of Winchester, was a nun at Marcigny: see biographical note to Ep. 15.

56

AD EVNDEM

A 55; C IV,20; Bc II,20.

July/August 1135. This letter can be dated from the references to the Council of Pisa and the death of Peter the Venerable's mother.

p. 177] It is not known which of Peter's brothers went to England at this time: see Appendix A on his family.

p. 178, l. 25] The Council of Pisa met from 30 May until 6 June 1135 (see Ep. 27, n. to p. 51, l. 10). There is another reference, in Letter 1, to Peter's illness after the council.

p. 178, l. 31] Cf. Letter 53 and Appendix A on Peter's mother Raingard; also Jorden, *Totengedächtniswesen*, p. 116 (reprinting this passage).

57

AD EVNDEM

A 56; C IV,21; Bc II,21. This is a characteristic example of the letters of friendship written by Peter when he found a messenger. The "our brother and your monk" mentioned here was presumably an official at Glastonbury or Winchester who was passing through Cluny, perhaps on his way from Rome.

1129/56.

58

AD PETRVM PICTAVENSEM SVVM IN CHRISTO FILIVM KARVM

A 57; S 48; C IV,22; Bc II, 22; cf. *RHGF*, XV, 626 (1131); Maitland, *Dark Ages*, pp. 455–457; Lorain, *Cluny*, pp. 418–423; Pignot, *Cluny*, III, 470–492; and Appendix Q on Peter of Poitiers.

Early January 1134, at the monastery of St.-Martin-des-Champs in Paris.

p. 179] William, eighth count of Poitou and tenth duke of Aquitaine (1126–37), was the principal secular supporter of Anacletus II north of the Alps: see Richard, *Comtes de Poitou*, II, 1–53.

p. 180] The references to *campi* (fields) here and below are probably a play on the name of St.-Martin-des-Champs.

p. 183] On the concept of the monk as the abbot's serf, see De Valous, *Mon. clun.*, I, 76.

p. 188] This is Gerald Le Vert (see Ep. 53, n. to p. 162, l. 10), whose death can be dated from this reference late in 1133, perhaps on 15 November, if he is the "Giraldus pie memorię armarius Cluniacensis" recorded in *Necrologium*, p. 85. Peter the Venerable remarked both here and in the *De miraculis*, I, 8 (*Bibl. Clun.*, col. 1263 AB) on his exceptional devotion to the Holy Eucharist.

59

AD HENRICVM WINTONIENSEM EPISCOPVM

A 58; C IV,23; Bc II,23.

1134/5. The dates of this letter and of Henry of Winchester's visit to Cluny mentioned here are not certain (cf. Letter 88). Voss, *Heinrich von Blois*, pp. 9 and 112, suggested 1134, following Peter the Venerable's return from the Council of Pisa (dated by her in 1134: Ep. 27, n. to p. 51, l. 10). It was certainly after August 1133, before which time Henry was busy in England: Voss, *Heinrich von Blois*, p. 8; *Regesta Regum Anglo-Norm.*, II, s.n. "Winchester, bp. Henry" in index; and it was before the death of Henry I in December 1135, after which Henry was fully occupied in England. Peter the Venerable was away from Cluny when the news of Henry's visit came, perhaps on his long trip of 1133-4, and he heard of it so late that he could not even follow Henry's traces.

p. 189] Henry probably passed through the county of Nevers in order to visit his mother at Marcigny.

p. 190] Drogo the constable appears on a charter of 1136: see Appendix R on functionaries at Cluny.

60

AD EVNDEM

A 59; C IV,24; Bc II,24; cf. biographical note to Ep. 49, referring to this letter.

1136? King Stephen's grant to Cluny in 1136 (see note below) may have been issued as a result of this letter.

p. 190] The monk Durannus mentioned here and in Letter 61 was probably the sacristan Durannus mentioned on a charter of 1145 (see Appendix R).

p. 191] This "manor of a hundred marks" is Letcombe-Regis, which was given to Cluny by King Stephen in place of the annual gift in cash made by Henry I in 1131 of a hundred marks from the farms of London and Lincoln: Berger, *Richard le Poitevin*, p. 103; *Cluny*, V, 369-371 and 374, nos. 4015-4016 and 4019; *Regesta Regum Anglo-Norm.*, II, nos. 1691, 1713, and 1721; cf. the papal confirmation in *Bibl. Clun.*, cols. 1392-1394 (JL 7476). Stephen's grant was dated from Winchester in 1136, in the first year of his reign, and was witnessed by several notables, including Henry of Winchester: *Bibl. Clun.*, cols. 1398-1399, with corrections in *Cluny*, V, 409, no. 4055, confirmed by Innocent II in 1142 (*Bibl. Clun.*, cols. 1400-1401; JL 8232). The grant was frequently confirmed by later popes and kings; but in the fifteenth century Letcombe-Regis was taken from Cluny and granted to Westminster Abbey: Duckett, *Cluni*, I, 74-75.

61

AD EVNDEM

A 60; C IV,25; Bc II,25.

1136? The reference to Durannus shows that this letter followed Letter 60, but his business is not known, unless it was concerned with the exchange of the rent of a hundred marks for a manor (see Ep. 60, n. to p. 191).

p. 191] The mission of the cleric of Auxerre and the prior of "Mons Acutis" is not otherwise known. There were two Cluniac houses named "Mons Acutis," as Duchesne pointed out in *Bibl. Clun.*, *notae*, col. 133: Montaigut, a dependency of Sauxillanges in Puy-de-Dôme (De Valous, *Mon. clun.*, II, 184), and Montacute in England (*ibid.*, p. 261). This letter probably refers to Montacute, but the priors are named only by initials in the first half of the twelfth century in the list given in *Two Cartularies of the Augustinian Priory of Bruton and the Cluniac Priory of Montacute* (Somerset Record Society, 8; London, 1894) p. lxviii.

62

EPISTOLA DOMINI PAPAE INNOCENTII AD PETRVM ABBATEM CLVNIACENSEM

A 61; S 49; C IV,26; Bc II,26; cf. *Bull. Clun.*, p. 50; *RHGF*, XV, 392-393; Bernhardi, *Lothar*, p. 738; JL 7848; Chalandon, *Dom. normande*, II, 70, n. 6, who cited the adventures of the abbot of Monte Cassino as a warning against taking too literally some of the statements in this letter.

20 July 1137. The date and wording of this letter (in particular the references to the desire of Peter the Venerable to help the Pope and to Peter's poor health) suggest that it is the reply to Letter 1.

p. 192, l. 4] Innocent II left Pisa toward the end of February 1137 and traveled south by way of Viterbo and Benevento to Bari. At the time he wrote this letter he was on his way back to Salerno and Benevento.

p. 192, l. 18] King Roger II was the chief secular supporter of the antipope Anacletus II in Italy.

63

RESCRIPTVM PETRI ABBATIS AD PAPAM INNOCENTIVM

A 61 [bis]; S 50; C IV,27; Bc II,27.

September/October 1137. This letter is Peter the Venerable's reply to Letter 62. It gives a valuable indication of the time involved in communicating with the Pope. Innocent wrote on 20 July 1137, and Peter planned to visit him before Easter 1138 (3 April), with an exchange of messengers in between, making a total of four trips in all. This suggests that a maximum of nine weeks each way was allowed, at least in winter. This agrees with the period of slightly over eight weeks in Letter 69 (n. to p. 201, l. 15). In good weather, however, the trip was certainly much quicker. In Letter 112, for instance, Peter apologized to the Pope for the late arrival of a letter that took only twenty-four days to reach Cluny from Rome, and that in November. Cf. also the references in Constable, "Langres," p. 143.

64

AD EVNDEM

A 63; S 51; C IV,28; Bc II,28; cf. Constable, "Langres," p. 124.

1 August 1136/3 April 1138: between the death of Bishop Guilencus of Langres (1/3 August 1136/7) and the consecration of Alberic of Vézelay as cardinal-bishop of Ostia (3 April 1138: see Ep. 4, n. to p. 8, l. 23). This letter was dated early 1138 by Louis, *Girart*, I, 181.

65

AD BERNARDVM ABBATEM CLARAEVALLIS

A 64; S 52; C IV,29; Bc II,29; cf. Mabillon, note to Bernard, ep. 74 (Gaume ed., I.1, 881–882); Lorain, *Cluny*, pp. 490–491; Pignot, *Cluny*, III, 175 ("vers la fin du schisme").

Late 1137. Bernard of Clairvaux made three visits to Italy during the schism: April 1132–August [early summer?] 1133; May–September [October] 1135; and November 1136/February 1137–June 1138: see Vacandard, *St. Bernard*, II, 559–560; De Warren, in *Bernard de Clairvaux*, pp. 584–593; and Grebenc, "Itinerar," pp. 60–61. This letter was almost certainly written during the last visit, since Peter the Venerable and Bernard met at Pisa in 1135. It may be associated with Letter 62 from Innocent II to Peter (20 July 1137), and the messengers whom Peter says he is sending to the Pope may have carried Letter 63, which was written in September/October 1137. Letter 74, written in February/May 1138, was probably Bernard's reply to this letter.

66

AD GILONEM SCISMATICVM

A 65; C IV,30; Bc II,30.

April/May 1138. This letter was written after the death of Anacletus (25 January 1138) and before Pentecost, which fell on 22 May in 1138 and was close at hand ("in proximo") at the time Peter was writing.

p. 196, l. 13] (a) The meeting of Peter the Venerable and Gilo of Tusculum at Poitiers presumably took place on Peter's visit there in the spring of 1133. (b) The meeting at Grenoble "in the year just gone by" (i.e., 1137 O. S.) is otherwise unknown. It must have been early in the year, before Pentecost (30 May), since Gilo apparently fixed Pentecost "as the limit of his turning back."

p. 196, l. 27] Lothar died on 3/4 December 1137 and Anacletus, on 25 January 1138.

p. 196, l. 32] Peter interprets the term "decennium" broadly here, since the schism started in February 1130.

67

AD GVILLELMVM EPISCOPVM AVRASICENSEM

A 66; S 53; C IV,31; Bc II,31; cf. *GC*, I, 774; Bréquigny, *Chartes*, III, 11 (1137); Pignot, *Cluny*, III, 252–253; *GC nov.*, VI, 45–47 (1130?).

William II of Orange was bishop from *ca.* 1130 until *ca.* 1138, according to the *GC*, I, 773–774; from 1130 until 1137/41, according to Gams, *Series*, p. 592; and from 1130 to 1138, according to the *GC nov.*, VI, 45–49. He was skilled in both canon and secular law, according to this letter, in which Peter the Venerable cited the *Digest*.

p. 198, l. 14] There is no surviving bull of Urban II (1088–99) for the priory of Piolenc; and the identity of the church of St. Martin and the date it was granted to Piolenc are not known, except that it was at least thirty years—"the legal time"—before Peter was writing.

p. 198, l. 25] Nothing specific is known about this controversy, and the Pope's bull reserving the ultimate decision for himself and forbidding the Bishop to interdict Piolenc is lost.

68

AD COMITEM AMEDEVM

A 68; C IV,32; Bc II,32; cf. Duchesne, *Scriptores*, IV, 458; J. P. Masson, *Elogia* (Paris, 1638) I, 248–250; Samuel Guichenon, *Histoire généalogique de le royale maison de Savoye* (Lyons, 1660) II (*preuves*), 33–34; Bréquigny, *Chartes*, III, 12 (1137); *RHGF*, XV, 633 (1137); Lorain, *Cluny*, pp. 374–375; Pignot, *Cluny*, III, 236–238; Hirsch, *Ludwig VII*, p. 17; C. W. Previté-Orton, *The Early History of the House of Savoy* (Cambridge, Eng., 1912) p. 291. These historians (and those cited by them) offer various explanations of the dispute between Louis VII and his uncle Count Amadeus III of Savoy, but the precise reason and object of this letter are not known.

1137/8. Louis VII succeeded to the throne of France in August 1137, and this letter was written not long afterwards.

p. 199, l. 9] This may, as Previté-Orton suggested, refer to the acquisition of Aquitaine by Louis through his marriage to the heiress Eleanor, and he may have asked for help in securing the duchy.

p. 199, l. 19] The dispute mentioned here may have concerned the dowry of Amadeus's sister, Queen Adelaide of France.

69

AD ATONEM TRECENSEM EPISCOPVM

A 68 [bis]; S 54; C IV,33; Bc II,33; cf. Mabillon, *Annales*, VI, 305 (1140); Bréquigny, *Chartes*, II, 582 (1130), and III, 48 (1140).

Mid-March (before 13 March) 1138. The year of this and the two following letters is established by three factors: (a) the reference in Letter 70 to "the legation of men from Langres" (see n. to p. 202, l. 4); (b) the fact that the Pope was clearly in Rome, where he returned in late October 1137; and (c) the reference to the new bishop of Auxerre, the Cistercian Hugh of Vitry (Mâcon, Cluny), formerly abbot of Pontigny, who was elected in 1137 (*Bernard de Clairvaux*, pp. 629–630) and consecrated about the Feast of St. Vincent (probably 22 January), 1137, according to the *Gesta pontificum Autissiodorensium*, LV, in *Bibliothèque historique de l'Yonne*, ed. L. M. Duru (Auxerre, 1850–1863) I, 417; cf. Pignot, *Cluny*, III, 258–262; the *Vita prima* of St. Bernard, book I by William of St. Thierry, III, 13–14 (Gaume ed., II.6, 2101–2102); and Appendix N on Hugh's later activities. This dating also fits with the position of these three letters in the collection, where they are surrounded by letters of 1137 and 1138.

p. 200, l. 18] "You have inquired what you should reply to the new man speaking new things concerning the ordinations at La Charité." The new man was the new bishop Hugh of Auxerre, who had objected to Hato's performing ordinations at La Charité, which was in the diocese of Auxerre. This was apparently the principal matter about which Hato had written to Peter the Venerable.

p. 200, l. 36] The right to receive ordination from any bishop was adumbrated in the privilege of Gregory V in 998/9 (*Bull. Clun.*, p. 10; JL 3896), spelled out for the first time in the great bull of John XIX in 1024 (*Bull. Clun.*, p. 8; *Bibl. Clun., notae*, cols. 136–137; JL 4065), and frequently confirmed in later privileges: see Letonnelier, *Cluny*, pp. 26 ff.

p. 200, l. 39] This letter, if it was ever written, is lost.

p. 201, l. 15] The messenger was away from 11 November until the week of 6/12 March, which allowed him slightly over eight weeks each way (cf. Ep. 63). He was probably delayed, however, by his inability to reach Rome.

p. 201, l. 23] On conditions in southern and central Italy after the departure of Lothar (who died on 3/4 December 1137) and the reinstatement of Innocent II, see Bernhardi, *Lothar*, pp. 752–782, and U. Balzani, in *CMH*, V, 367–368.

p. 201, l. 28] The identity of this chaplain of Matthew of Albano, whom Peter the Venerable's messenger must have met in some Cluniac house "on this side of the Apennines," is not known. He may have been the Pontius mentioned in *De miraculis*, II, 21 (*Bibl. Clun.*, col. 1318).

p. 201, l. 36] This seems to be an early example of a papal provision and expectancy, since Innocent had apparently ordered Hato to grant a prebend if one was free, or the first one that fell open, to the cleric Guarinus, who seems from Letter 70 to have been the brother of Archdeacon Gebuin. The following passage shows that the Pope had already "provided" prebends for the abbey of Cluny (cf. Ep. 2, n. to p. 6, l. 12) and for the son of Oduin. "The practice of provision developed gradually from a twelfth century practice of recommendation, which was quite clearly extra-legal in character," wrote Geoffrey Barraclough, "The Executors of Papal Provisions in the Canonical Theory of the Thirteenth and Fourteenth Centuries," *Acta Congressus Iuridici Internationalis*, III (Rome, 1936) offprint, p. 18, n. 52. The theory of provisions was known in the eleventh century, Barraclough wrote in his *Papal Provisions* (Oxford, 1935) p. 132, but they "did not emerge in actual practice until half a century and more after Hildebrand's death"; and this practice became a system only in the thirteenth century, according to his "Praxis Beneficiorum," *Zeitschrift der Savigny-Stiftung für Rechtsgeschichte*, LVIII, Kan. Abt., XXVII (1938) 100. Expectancies came even later, and the earliest example cited by G. Mollat, "Les graces expectatives du XIIe au XIVe siècle," *Rev. hist. ecc.*, XLII (1947) 81–82, was granted by Hadrian IV in 1156/8.

p. 201, l. 41] The truth of Peter the Venerable's information is shown by Letter 70. When Letter 69 was written, Guarinus must have already left Troyes for Rome, since he arrived at Cluny with Archdeacon Gebuin on 13 March.

70

AD EVNDEM

A 69; C IV,34; Bc II,34; cf. Bréquigny, *Chartes*, II, 582 (1130).

Mid-March (after 13 March) 1138. This letter was written a few days after Letter 69, with which, as Peter the Venerable explains at the end, it was sent.

p. 202, l. 4] Gebuin (Gibuin) was archdeacon of Brienne-le-Château in the diocese of Troyes and appears on many charters between 1129 and 1159 as cantor, precentor (1131–5), and chancellor (1145–54, that is, after the retirement of Bishop Hato): see the indices in the *Cartulaires de Troyes*; Nicolas Camuzat, *Promptuarium sacrarum antiquitatum Tricassinae dioecesis* (Troyes, 1610) fol. 175^{r-v}; Duchesne, in *Bibl. Clun.*, *notae*, col. 137; C. N. L. Brooke, in John of Salisbury, *Letters*, I, 51, n. 7; and J. Leclercq, "Gébouin de Troyes et S. Bernard," *Revue des sciences philosophiques et théologiques*, XLI (1957) 632–640 (reprinted in *Recueil*, pp. 83–93), who showed that Gebuin knew and was deeply influenced by Bernard of Clairvaux and his works. Neither Brooke nor Leclercq cited this letter or Letter 73, in which Peter the Venerable mentioned Gebuin to Bernard as "michi et uobis notissimus, michi uobisque ut credo carissimus." He is also mentioned in letters by Hildebert of Le Mans (III,18), Bernard of Clairvaux (17), and John of Salisbury (new ed., 31). The reason for his involvement in the disputed election at Langres is not known, nor whether he took any further part in the affair, but the legation to which he referred was presumably that of Archbishop Peter of Lyons, Dean Robert of Langres, and the canon Ulric in the spring of 1138: see Constable, "Langres," pp. 125–128 and 133.

p. 202, l. 9] The forces to which Peter refers here were presumably those that later elected the Cluniac William of Sabran as bishop of Langres and included not only the archbishop of Lyons and Peter the Venerable himself, but also the bishops of Autun and Mâcon and probably the duke of Burgundy: see Constable, "Langres," p. 130.

p. 203] On the prebend for Guarinus, see Ep. 69, n. to p. 201, l. 36.

71

RESCRIPTVM ATONIS EPISCOPI AD EVNDEM

A 70; S 55; C IV,35; Bc II,35.

March/April 1138. This is Hato's reply to Letters 69–70.

p. 203, l. 12] Hato eventually resigned his see and retired to Cluny in 1145/6: see Ep. 2, n. to p. 6, l. 12.

p. 203, l. 17] These "confutations of the heretics" may refer to the *Contra Petrobrusianos* (which could thus be dated before this letter) or to some lost work. The *Contra Sarracenos* and *Contra Iudaeos* were certainly later.

p. 205, l. 3] See Ep. 69, n. to p. 200, l. 18, on the dispute between Hato and Bishop Hugh of Auxerre, the former abbot of Pontigny.

p. 205, l. 12] See Ep. 69, n. to p. 201, l. 36, on the prebend for Guarinus.

p. 205, l. 18] See Letter 70 (and n. to p. 202, l. 4) and Peter the Venerable's statement there that he has sent a messenger to keep an eye on Gebuin.

p. 205, l. 21] This seems to refer to Peter the Venerable's first messenger, the Cluniac prior mentioned in Letter 69, who entrusted his mission to the former chaplain of Matthew of Albano (see Ep. 69, n. to p. 201, l. 28).

p. 205, l. 36] Archdeacon Manasses of Rumilly appears on numerous charters from the diocese of Troyes from 1129 until 1147 (see the indices to *Cartulaires de Troyes*, I and IV–VII), although he is sometimes hard to distinguish from another Manasses, who was archdeacon of Villemaur. Two Archdeacons Manasses, for instance, appear together on a charter in 1122 and on Hato's grant to Cluny in 1145 (*Bibl. Clun., notae*, col. 105; cf. *Cluny*, V, 455, no. 4105); and an unspecified Archdeacon Manasses appears on *Cluny*, V, 365 and 372, nos. 4009 (1130) and 4017 (1130/2).

p. 205, l. 38] Archdeacon Odo, Bishop Hato's nephew, appears on a number of charters between 1140 and 1145: *Cartulaires de Troyes*, I, 24 and 29 (specifically as Hato's nephew); III, 5; V, 13 and 15; and VII, 60 and 62; and Hato's grant to Cluny in *Bibl. Clun., notae*, col. 105 (see preceding note). He also appears on *Cluny*, V, 371–372 and 373–374, nos. 4017 and 4018 (as Hato's nephew), which are dated 1130/2 but may be later. References to archdeacons named Odo, but not necessarily this Odo, also occur in *Cartulaires de Troyes*, IV, 180 (1081/1121), 196 (1120), 243 (1120), and 251 (1151); and VII, 82 (1167).

p. 206, l. 2] This is the first reference in the correspondence of Peter the Venerable to Nicholas of Montiéramey, on whom see Appendix P.

p. 206, l. 4] Prior Ascelin of Margerie-Hancourt appears on a charter in *Cartulaires de Troyes*, IV, 2 ("1146 au plus tard"). Margerie-Hancourt was a Cluniac priory in the diocese of Troyes: Duchesne, in *Bibl. Clun., notae*, col. 137; De Valous, *Mon. clun.*, II, 198. Ascelin may have been recalled to Cluny in accordance with the Cluniac policy of moving around promising priors and keeping them for a time at Cluny itself.

72

AD PAPAM INNOCENTIVM

A 71; S 56; C IV,36; Bc II,36; cf. Constable, "Langres," pp. 127 and 133.

Spring 1138.

p. 206] A son of Duke Hugh II of Burgundy, probably Robert, dean of Langres (later bishop of Autun), who accompanied Archbishop Peter of Lyons and the canon Ulric of Langres to Rome in the spring of 1138.

73

AD BERNARDVM ABBATEM CLARAEVALLIS

A 72; S 57; Cl fol. 1ʳ; C IV,37; Bc II,37; cf. Lorain, *Cluny*, p. 491.

Spring 1138. This letter was probably carried to Bernard of Clairvaux in Rome (see dating note to Ep. 65) by Archdeacon Gebuin, whose trip to Rome is discussed in Letter 70. The "recent longer letter" referred to here, therefore, is Letter 65, written late in 1137.

74

RESCRIPTVM BERNARDI ABBATIS AD PETRVM CLVNIACENSIVM ABBATEM

A 73; S 58; Cl fol. 1ʳ; C IV,38; Bc II,38; Bern. ep. 147; cf. Lorain, *Cluny*, pp. 491–492; Vacandard, *St. Bernard*, II, 23 and 565; *Letters of St. Bernard*, pp. 216–217, no. 147.

February/May 1138. This letter was written between the death of Anacletus II and the final submission of his supporters in May, probably in February/March, before the dispute over the election at Langres, to which it does not refer.

p. 207, l. 21] This "evil one" is Anacletus II, who died on 25 January 1138.

p. 207, l. 25] This may refer to any one of several prominent supporters of Anacletus, such as Gilo of Tusculum (see Epp. 40 and 66 and Appendix J) or, as Mabillon suggested, Gerald of Angoulême (see his note to Bernard's ep. 147: Gaume ed., I.1, 882). Gerald died on 1 May 1136, however: Hubert Claude, "Autour du schisme d'Anaclet: saint Bernard et Girard d'Angoulême," *Mélanges St. Bernard*, p. 93.

p. 208] On Hugh of Crécy, chamberlain of Cluny, see Appendix O.

75

AD IMPERATOREM CONSTANTINOPOLITANVM

A 74; S 59; C IV,39; Bc II,39; cf. on this letter and Letter 76, Baronius, *Annales*, XVIII, 329–332 (1119); Mabillon, *Annales*, VI, 76 (1122); Lorain, *Cluny*, pp. 405–408; Pignot, *Cluny*, III, 298–299; *Cluny*, V, 321–322, no. 3963 (*ca.* 1122); Ferdinand Chalandon, *Les Comnène*, II: *Jean II Comnène et Manuel I Comnène* (Paris, 1912) p. 162, n. 1; Jules Gay, "L'abbaye de Cluny et Byzance au début du XIIe siècle," *Echos d'Orient*, XXX (1931) 84–90; Ernst Werner, *Die gesellschaftlichen Grundlagen der Klosterreform im 11. Jahrhundert* (Berlin, 1953) p. 66; Steven Runciman, *The Eastern Schism* (Oxford, 1955) p. 114 ("about 1120"); Paolo Lamma, *Comneni e Staufer* (Istituto storico italiano per il Medio Evo: Studi storici, 14–18; 22–25; Rome, 1955–1957) I, 30–33; Berry, in *Petrus Ven.*, pp. 144–145; Lamma, *Momenti*, pp. 102–103; George Every, *The Byzantine Patriarchate, 451–1204*, 2nd ed. (London, 1962) p. 189; and Appendix I on Cluniac houses in the East. Werner argued against Gay's view that these letters were associated with papal efforts for ecclesiastical union and related them to the disciplinary and liturgical links between Cluny and the Greek church (which he discusses on pp. 36–70): "Cluny could hold out its hand to Byzantium because they had so much in common" (p. 67). The friendly remarks and apparent lack of emphasis on religious differences in these letters have been used by several scholars as evidence of good will between East and West in the early twelfth century. Lamma in particular stressed Peter the Venerable's recognition of the pre-eminence of the Eastern emperor. This may all have been epistolary "captatio benevolentiae," however, designed to secure the granting of his request; and in Letter 162 he took a very different line.

John Comnenus was emperor from 1118 until 1143. On his title "Kalojohannes," which was used by Peter the Venerable in the address, see Chalandon, *Comnène*, II, 9, and Gay, in *Échos d'Orient*, XXX, 84, who attributed it to his "high moral worth."

1122/43. Most scholars have dated this and the following letter early in John's reign and Peter's abbacy. Gay suggested an association with the papal embassies of 1122–4 or 1126, before the renewed difficulties between Byzantium and Sicily in about 1130. They cannot in fact be dated more closely than between the beginning of Peter's abbacy and the end of John's reign. Peter's reference to an outburst of anti-Latin feeling at Constantinople three years earlier, however, which may have been responsible for the expulsion of the Cluniacs, suggests that these letters followed rather than preceded the breakdown of good relations; and from their position in the collection I am inclined to agree with Lamma's date (*Comneni*, I, 31–32) of 1138/9.

p. 208] Peter the Venerable used the same opening in Letter 131 to King Roger of Sicily. He apparently regarded a reference to the King of kings as a particularly suitable beginning for a letter to an earthly king.

p. 209, l. 5] Alexius Comnenus was emperor from 1081 until 1118.

p. 209, l. 14] On the monastery of Civitot near Constantinople, see Appendix I.

76

AD CONSTANTINOPOLITANVM PATRIARCHAM

A 75; S 60; C IV,40; Bc II,40; cf. bibliography for Ep. 75.

John IX was patriarch of Constantinople from 1111 to 1134, and Leo Stypes, from 1134 to 1143: V. Grumel, *Traité d'études byzantines*, I: *La chronologie* (Paris, 1958) p. 436.

1122/43.

p. 210] On the relics taken from Constantinople during the Fourth Crusade, see Paul Riant and F. de Mély, *Exuviae sacrae Constantinopolitanae* (Geneva-Paris, 1877–1904).

77

AD ROBERTVM OLIM REGIS ANGLORVM CANCELLARIVM

A 76; S 61; C IV,41; Bc II,41. This letter is characteristic of the efforts of Peter the Venerable to attract to Cluny men of proven ability and experience in worldly affairs, such as Robert de Sigillo and Natalis of Rebais, whom he planned to use for administrative and diplomatic business.

Robert de Sigillo appears frequently on charters of King Henry I of England from 1121 on and acted as his chancellor for the last two years of his reign, from 1133 to 1135. According to most recent historians, his official position was that of *magister scriptorii*, not chancellor, and his name is bracketed in the list of chancellors in the recent *Handbook of British Chronology*, ed. by F. M. Powicke and E. B. Fryde, 2nd ed. (London, 1961) p. 82. The heading of the present letter, however, is strong evidence that he was in fact chancellor, as the chronicler John of Hexham claimed. See Osbert of Clare, *Letters*, pp. 207–208; *Early Charters of the Cathedral Church of St. Paul, London*, ed. Marion Gibbs (Camden 3rd Series, 58; London, 1939) p. xxxiii, n. 1; Saltman, *Theobald*, p. 96; *Regesta Regum Anglo-Norm.*, II, x. Robert resigned after the death of Henry I and became a monk at Reading. In 1141 he became bishop of London and was consecrated probably after Easter: see Round, *Geoffrey*, p. 67. He died (of poison, according to some sources) in 1150/1: see William Stubbs, *Registrum sacrum Anglicanum*, 2nd ed. (Oxford, 1897) p. 45; Powicke and Fryde, *Handbook of British Chronology*, p. 239.

1136/41.

p. 212, l. 15] King Henry I died on 1 December 1135 (see Ep. 15, n. to p. 22, l. 10).

p. 212, l. 19] Nothing more is known about this sister of Robert de Sigillo, but the fact that she came from England to Marcigny suggests that they were of a prominent family. The "beloved son" Thomas was probably Peter the Venerable's notary Thomas of Northampton (see Appendix R).

78

EPISTOLA GAVFREDI CATHALAVNENSIS EPISCOPI AD PETRVM CLVNIACENSEM ABBATEM

A 77; S 62; C IV,42; Bc II,42.

Geoffrey, former prior of St. Nicasius at Rheims, abbot of St. Thierry, and abbot of St. Médard at Soissons, was bishop of Châlons-sur-Marne from 1131 until 1142/3. In the first year of his pontificate he served as papal legate with Matthew of Albano: Janssen, *Legaten*, p. 17. His death was dated late May 1142 by Pacaut, *Élections*, p. 98; 27 May 1142 in Gams, *Series*, p. 534; 1143 by Mabillon in his note to Bernard's ep. 66 (Gaume ed., I.1, 850–851); and 27 May 1143 in Chevalier, *Bio-bib.*, I, 1703. The latest charter issued by him among those printed in the *PL*, CLXXIII, 1395–1400, is dated 2 March 1142 (1141 O.S.). Cf. also the charter cited in Ep. 33, n. to p. 108, l. 25, and the nn. to Epp. 47 and 79. On his sermons, see B. Hauréau, *Notices et extraits de quelques manuscrits latins de la Bibliothèque nationale* (Paris, 1890–1893) II, 300–308, and

Catalogue général des manuscrits des bibliothèques publiques de la France, XXXVIII: *Reims*, ed. Henri Loriquet (Paris, 1904) pp. 738-740.

1131/43.

p. 212] The identity of Geoffrey's "Ethiopian," whom Peter the Venerable had received with kindness and promoted to prior, is unknown. The priory was probably in the diocese of Châlons, since Letter 79 shows that Peter sent him back to Geoffrey.

p. 213] Geoffrey was going to Étampes and then planned to visit Cluny the third week after Easter (Peter replied in Letter 79 that he would be there at that time), unless he were prevented by illness or by the King. This suggests that he was meeting Louis VI or Louis VII at Étampes, but the reference is of no help in dating the letter.

79

RESCRIPTVM PETRI ABBATIS AD IPSVM

A 78; S 63; C IV,43; Bc II,43; cf. *GC*, IX, 879-880 (1140); Bréquigny, *Chartes*, III, 48 (1140); Pignot, *Cluny*, III, 145-146.

1131/43. This is Peter's reply to Letter 78.

p. 213, l. 15] On the affair of the abbey of St. Paul at Verdun, see Ep. 47 (and notes to it).

p. 213, l. 18] This may refer to the chapter general of black monks in the diocese of Rheims which was called by Geoffrey at Soissons in about 1130: see Bernard of Clairvaux, ep. 91, and Mabillon's note to it (Gaume ed., I.1, 264-265 and 865); Vacandard, *St. Bernard*, I, 180-181; *Bernard de Clairvaux*, p. 201.

p. 214, l. 3] Peter the Venerable's two principal friends in the province of Belgian Gaul were Geoffrey of Châlons-sur-Marne and Bernard of Clairvaux, according to Mabillon in his note to Bernard's ep. 66 (Gaume ed., I.1, 851) and Vacandard, *St. Bernard*, I, 180-181. There is no evidence, however, that Bernard was a close friend of Peter the Venerable in the 1130's, and Clairvaux was in the ancient province of Lyons (previously Upper Germany), not Belgian Gaul. It is more probable that the second friend whom Peter had in mind was Hato of Troyes (although Troyes also was not in Belgian Gaul).

p. 214, l. 26] The subprior Garnerius whose brother Peter here recommended to Geoffrey was probably the same Garnerius who later became a Cistercian and to whom Peter referred in Letter 151 to Nicholas of Montiéramey and in Letter 181 to Bernard of Clairvaux. Nicholas in his ep. 44, written in the name of the prior of Clairvaux, congratulated Garnerius on his conversion: "Who would have thought that you would have either wished or been able to descend from so sublime to so humble a position?" (*PL*, CXCVI, 1644). He may have been the same as Garnerius of Rochefort, who later became abbot of Auberive, abbot of Clairvaux, and bishop of Langres and who was the author of an onomastic repertory in twenty-three books entitled the *Angelus*: see Chevalier, *Bio-bib.*, I, 1656, and Wilmart, "Bibliothèque," pp. 58–66. There is no evidence that Garnerius of Rochefort was ever a Cluniac, however, and the fact that he was still alive in 1216 suggests that he was a younger man than Peter's Garnerius.

80

AD FRATRES HABITANTES IN MONTE THABOR

A 79; S 64; C IV,44; Bc II,44; cf. Pignot, *Cluny*, III, 296–297; Berlière, in *SMGBOZ*, IX, 486 (cited Appendix I); Röhricht, *Regesta*, no. 260; Berry, in *Petrus Ven.*, pp. 143 and 151; notes to Ep. 31; and Appendix I on Cluniac houses in the East.

After 1130? (see dating note to Ep. 31).

p. 216] On the attitude of Peter the Venerable toward pilgrimages and crusading by monks, see Ep. 51, n. to p. 152.

81

AD ATTHONEM EPISCOPVM TRECENSEM

A 80; C IV,45; Bc II,45.

1122/46. The "feast of the apostles" to which Peter refers here was 29 June, the Feast of SS. Peter and Paul, the patron saints of Cluny; but the year is not known.

p. 217] These letters from Hato to Peter are apparently lost.

p. 218] The reference here to "Cluniacenses uestri" has been considered by some historians to show that Hato was already a Cluniac (see Ep. 2, n. to p. 6, l. 12); but it was probably just an expression of friendly devotion, as was the following "episcopum suum."

82

AD REGEM IHRVSALEM

A 81; S 65; C IV,46; Bc II,46; cf. Bréquigny, *Chartes*, III, 79 (1143); Lorain, *Cluny*, pp. 408–409; Pignot, *Cluny*, III, 297–298; Röhricht, *Regesta*, no. 260; Berry, in *Petrus Ven.*, pp. 147–148.

The recipients and date of this and the following letter (with which Letter 80 may also be associated) are uncertain. Pignot identified the recipients as King Baldwin II (1118–31) and either Patriarch Gormond (1118–28) or Stephen (1128–30); Röhricht (who apparently confused Letter 31 with Letter 82) dated them 1150; Berry associated them with the preparations for the Second Crusade and dated them 1146/7. Their position in the collection suggests that the king in question was Fulk (1131–43) or possibly his successor, Baldwin III (1143–62).

p. 219] The mission of Drogo, precentor of Nevers, cannot be dated. He appeared on two documents in 1147–8 as cantor and as precentor and chancellor of the church of Nevers: *La Charité*, pp. 136–139, nos. 56–57. In the following letter Peter says that Drogo was now on his way to Jerusalem for the third time.

83

AD PATRIARCHAM IHRVSALEM

A 82; S 66; C IV,47; Bc II,47; cf. Bréquigny, *Chartes*, III, 79 (1143); Lorain, *Cluny*, pp. 409–410; notes to Ep. 82.

As with Letter 82, the recipient and date of this letter are unknown. Several passages suggest that the patriarch in question was a monk and a Cluniac, but this is of little help in identifying him. Patriarch William I (1130–45), unlike his immediate predecessors and successor, however, was a monk and had been prior of the Holy Sepulchre: see Chevalier, *Bio-bib.*, I, 1952, and Röhricht, *Regesta*, no. 135. But there is no evidence either in the chartulary of the Holy Sepulchre or elsewhere that he was a Cluniac.

p. 220] On the attitude of Peter the Venerable toward pilgrimages and crusading by monks, see Ep. 51, n. to p. 152.

84

AD DOMINVM ALBERICVM OSTIENSEM EPISCOPVM

A 83; C IV,48; Bc II,48.

June/July 1140. Cardinal Alberic of Ostia was away from the curia as legate in the Holy Land from May 1140 until September 1141: see Manselli, "Alberico," pp. 39-50. This letter can therefore be dated in the early summer of 1140.

p. 221, l. 8] The only other Cluniac in the Sacred College, after the death of Matthew of Albano and the deposition of Gilo of Tusculum, was the cardinal-deacon Adenulf of Sta. Maria in Scola Greca: see Appendix J.

p. 221, l. 16] These letters of Alberic are lost: see Manselli, "Alberico," p. 40.

85

EPISTOLA ATHONIS TRECENSIS EPISCOPI AD EVNDEM PETRVM

A 84; C IV,49; Bc II,49.

February/March 1141. The date of this and of the two following letters depends upon the identification of Letter 86 as the "other letter" by Peter the Venerable, expressing his desire to see Hato, which is mentioned in Letter 95, written in August 1141. Letters 85-86 were therefore written some time before Holy Week (23-29 March) 1141.

p. 222, l. 19] Archdeacon Theobald of Sens appears on a number of charters dated between 1126 and 1139 in *Yonne*, I, 250, 261, 267, 270, 273, 274, 291, and 339. Hato had himself been archdeacon and dean at Sens and maintained connections there throughout his lifetime (see Ep. 2, n. to p. 6, l. 12).

p. 222, l. 21] On Nicholas's visit to Rome at this time, see Appendix P.

86

RESCRIPTVM PETRI ABBATIS AD ATHONEM EPISCOPVM

A 85; C IV,50; Bc II,50; cf. Bréquigny, *Chartes*, III, 106 (1145); Pignot, *Cluny*, III, 264-265. This letter is the reply to Letter 85 and the "other letter" mentioned in Letter 95 as expressing Peter the Venerable's "desire, indeed hunger" to see Hato (see dating note to Ep. 85). Letter 95 suggests that Hato excused himself from coming to Cluny at that time, however, because he had to help the King prepare for his summer expedition to Languedoc and Aquitaine.

March 1141.

p. 223] Peter the Venerable was clearly afraid that Hato had given up his intention of retiring to Cluny. The first reference to this plan in Peter's correspondence is in Letter 71, written in March/April 1138, in which Hato wrote to Peter: "It is enough that I should see you, that I should be with you before I die."

p. 224, l. 5] See Ep. 20, n. to p. 35, on this idea.

p. 224, l. 19] This chapel, "much finer than the [other] churches of this our Burgundy, decorated with beautiful pictures and adorned with the more remarkable miracles of the deeds of Christ," has been identified by most historians of Cluny with the chapel of the Virgin (also known as the abbot's chapel), which was dedicated by the Archbishop of Vienne, the future Pope Calixtus II, in 1118 (*Bibl. Clun.*, cols. 564–565): cf. Duchesne, in *Bibl. Clun.*, *notae*, col. 138; Pignot, *Cluny*, III, 264 (who added "of the Virgin" in his translation of the text and thus misled future scholars); Fernand Mercier, *Les primitifs français: La peinture clunysienne en Bourgogne à l'époque romane* (Paris, 1931) pp. 29, n. 1 (citing Pignot), and 90–91 (dating this letter *ca.* 1140); Virey, *Églises*, p. 191 (citing Pignot). On this chapel, see Virey, in *Millénaire de Cluny*, II, 239–240 and 243, n. 5, where he distinguished this chapel, which was quite small and near the great church (b on the plan), from the larger chapel of Our Lady of the Infirmary, which was located off the chapter house; and K. J. Conant, "Mediaeval Academy Excavations at Cluny [VIII]," *Speculum*, XXIX (1954) 29–31 (plans IX and X), showing the abbey in 1043 and 1157. The main objection to this identification is that this chapel, as might be expected, was decorated with scenes from the life of the Virgin, so far as is known, not of Christ. Another possibility is Berzé-la-Ville, which was probably decorated with scenes from the life of Christ (see Mercier, *Primitifs*, pp. 29–30, and pls. VIII and IX) and was certainly more suited than the chapel of the Virgin for the private talk mentioned by Peter the Venerable.

p. 224, l. 27] Hato's visit to Cluny on Palm Sunday was probably in

1140, since it is mentioned in no previous letter and in 1139 Peter the Venerable was at the Lateran Council in Rome for Easter.

p. 226] Bishop Justus of Lyons fled to a solitary life in Egypt after the Council of Aquileia in 381: see Louis Duchesne, *Fastes épiscopaux de l'ancienne Gaule*, 2nd ed. (Paris, 1907–1915) II, 162. This example, together with those of more recent bishops who had become Cluniac monks, was cited by Peter of St. John in his letter to Hato of Troyes after his retirement, in *Petrus Ven.*, pp. 50–51.

p. 227, l. 3] Cluny was also compared to paradise by Geoffrey of Vendôme, ep. IV,1 (*PL*, CLVII, 147A; cf. Compain, *Geoffroi de Vendôme* [cited Ep. 28, n. to p. 78], p. 59); Peter of Celle, ep. 25 (II,1) (*PL*, CCII, 428 D); and in the *Elogium Cluniacum* attributed to Rodulfus Tortarius, ll. 88–89, in *Rodulfi Tortarii Carmina*, ed. Marbury Ogle and Dorothy Schullian (Papers and Monographs of the American Academy in Rome, 8; Rome, 1933) p. 451; see Duchesne, in *Bibl. Clun.*, *notae*, col. 138.

p. 227, l. 12] Holy Week in 1141 was from 23 to 29 March.

p. 227, l. 13] See Ep. 85, n. to p. 222, l. 19, on Archdeacon Theobald.

87

AD NICOLAVM EIVSDEM EPISCOPI CAPELLANVM

A 86; S 67; C IV,51; Bc II,51; cf. notes to Epp. 85 and 86, which this probably accompanied.

March 1141.

88

AD HENRICVM EPISCOPVM VINTONIENSEM

A 87; C IV,52; Bc III,1; cf. Voss, *Heinrich von Blois*, pp. 9 and 112–113, who associated the visit to Cluny mentioned in this letter with that mentioned in Letter 59 and the request for news here with the statement in Letter 15 that he was writing to the bishop of Winchester asking for news after the death of Henry I. She thus dated this letter early in 1136. Against this view it may be argued (a) that the two visits cannot have been the same, because Peter was away from Cluny at the time of the visit mentioned in Letter 59, whereas he mentions here seeing and conversing with Henry, and (b) that although he asks in this letter for news of the state of the realm of England, it does not sound like a letter written immediately after the death of Henry of Winchester's cousin, King Henry I. I am therefore inclined to think that it refers to a later visit.

1129/56 (probably after 1135).

89

AD ALBERONEM EPISCOPVM LEODIENSEM

A 88; C IV,53; Bc III,2 (cf. p. 47, n. 191, above); cf. chronicle of Cluny, in *Bibl. Clun.*, cols. 593–594; Pignot, *Cluny*, III, 38–40; S. Balau, *Étude critique sur les sources de l'histoire du Pays de Liège au moyen âge* (Brussels, 1903) pp. 304–307; Lesne, *Prop. ecc.*, V, 92. This letter is equally celebrated among historians of theology and architecture, owing to its references to Alger and Hezelo.

Albero II was bishop of Liège from 1136 until 1145: see Jacques Stiennon, "Cluny et Saint-Trond au XIIe siècle," *Anciens pays et assemblées d'états*, VIII (1955) 73.

1136/45: during the pontificate of Albero II of Liège, and before the beginning of the abbacy of Gerard of St. Trond.

p. 229, l. 31] Hezelo (Ezelo) was a former canon of St. Lambert at Liège who became a monk at Cluny. He wrote the earliest life of St. Hugh, which is now lost, and supervised the building of the great church at Cluny. The date of his death is not known, but it was probably after 1122, since Peter the Venerable speaks of having known him personally. See Cucherat, *Cluny*, p. 132; L'Huillier, *Saint Hugues*, p. 361, dating the start of his work at Cluny in 1088; Chevalier, *Bio-bib.*, I, 1447; Victor Mortet, *Recueil de textes relatifs à l'histoire de l'architecture . . . en France au moyen âge: XIe–XIIe siècles* (Collection de textes pour servir à l'étude et à l'enseignement de l'histoire, 44; Paris, 1911) p. 271, n. 4; Virey, *Églises*, p. 213; Wattenbach-Holtzmann, *Geschichtsquellen*, I.4, 723 and 794–795, dating his life of St. Hugh ca. 1115; Charles Dereine, *Les chanoines réguliers au diocèse de Liège avant saint Norbert* (Académie royale de Belgique: Mémoires in-8°, 47.1; Brussels, 1952) pp. 42 and 50, who mentions a canon of St. Lambert named Hezelin who was converted to the monastic life "about 1100"; and Conant, in *Speculum* (cited Ep. 86, n. to p. 224, l. 19), XXIX, 11, who said that "Gunzo (or

Gauzon), a retired abbot of Baume, worked out the scheme; Etzelo (or Hézelon), a former canon of Liége, executed the building." The role of Hezelo in designing and decorating Cluny III is further discussed in Conant's forthcoming monograph on the church of Cluny; and an article on Hezelo by Jacques Stiennon will appear in the *Mélanges offerts à René Crozet*. A Cluniac monk named Hezelo, possibly this Hezelo, appears on a twelfth-century act of association from St. Martial at Limoges, in Molinier, *Obituaires*, p. 291.

p. 229, l. 36] Tezelin, who is otherwise unknown, started life as a canon of St. Lambert at Liège (see Dereine, *Chanoines*, p. 42), came to Cluny under St. Hugh, and then went to Vézelay under Abbot Rainald, who became archbishop of Lyons in 1129.

p. 230, l. 2] Very little is known about the life of the celebrated theologian Alger of Liège. According to his modern biographer, Louis Brigué, he was born in the second half of the eleventh century, came to Cluny some time after Peter the Venerable became abbot in 1122 (after the death of Bishop Frederick of Liège in 1121, according to Manitius), and died before 1145, the *terminus ante quem* of this letter. A list of his works is given in the chronicle of Cluny (*Bibl. Clun.*, col. 594). Peter the Venerable mentioned him in the *De miraculis*, I, 17 (*Bibl. Clun.*, col. 1274), and highly praised his *De sacramento altaris* in the *Contra Petrobrusianos*, where he linked Alger to Lanfranc and Guitmund of Aversa as the three great exponents of orthodox eucharistic doctrine of their age. This opinion was long regarded by scholars as influenced by Peter's friendship and admiration for Alger; but most recent authorities, including Schnitzer, De Ghellinck, and Bodard, agree with Peter the Venerable in regarding Alger as the equal, if not the superior, of his predecessors in theological precision and subtlety. See, in addition to the older works cited in Chevalier, *Bio-bib.*, I, 153, Joseph Schnitzer, *Berengar von Tours* (Munich, 1890) pp. 370–390; Saltet, *Réordinations* (cited Ep. 4), pp. 269–272; Manitius, *Lat. Lit.*, III, 100–105; A. J. MacDonald, *Berengar and the Reform of Sacramental Doctrine* (London, 1930) pp. 379–388 (who considered Peter the Venerable's praise of Alger "too fulsome" in view of his dependence on Guitmund: p. 379). G. Le Bras, "Alger de Liége et Gratien," *Revue des sciences philosophiques et théologiques*, XX (1931) 5–26 (on Alger as a canonist); Louis Brigué, *Alger de Liége* (Paris, 1936); Wattenbach-Holtzmann, *Geschichtsquellen*, I.3, 438, n. 98, and I.4, 722; De Ghellinck, *Mouvement théologique* (cited Ep. 4), p. 77; Henri de Lubac, *Corpus Mysticum: L'eucharistie et l'église au moyen âge*, 2nd ed. (Paris, 1949) pp. 166–175; Charles Dereine, "L'école canonique liègeoise et la réforme grégorienne," *Miscellanea Tornacensia*, ed. J. Cassart (Annales du Congrès archéologique et historique de Tournai, 1949; Brussels, 1951) I, 90-91, stressing the moderate, canonist tendencies in Alger's work; Bodard, in *Coll. Ord. Cist. Ref.* (cited Ep. 37), XVIII, 120, n. 69; and N. M. Haring, "A Study in the Sacramentology of Alger of Liège," *Mediaeval Studies*, XX (1958) 41-78.

p. 230, l. 20] Nothing more is known about the troubles of the Cluniac priory of Bertrée, which were the real cause of this letter. On Bertrée generally and its prior Gerard, who belonged to the family of the counts of Looz and became abbot of St. Trond in 1145, see *Cluny*, V, 332-337 and 352-353, nos. 3974-3977 and 3999; F. Baix, in *DHGE*, VIII, 1106-1108; and esp. Stiennon, in *Anciens pays*, VIII, 72-74.

90

AD ROGERIVM SICILIAE REGEM

A 89; C IV,54; Bc III,3; cf. Lorain, *Cluny*, pp. 394-396; Pignot, *Cluny*, III, 173-174; Bernhardi, *Konrad III*, p. 347 (before 30 May 1140/1); Caspar, *Roger II*, pp. 369-370 and 537-538 (1139/40); Lamma, *Momenti*, p. 113 (1140); Eugenio Dupré Theseider, "Sugli inizi dello stanziamento cisterciense nel regno di Sicilia," *Studi medievali in onore di Antonino De Stefano* (Palermo, 1956) p. 206, n. 7 (on this letter and Letters 131 and 162); and Helene Wieruszowski, "Roger II of Sicily, *Rex-Tyrannus*, in Twelfth-Century Political Thought," *Speculum*, XXXVIII (1963) 71-73, who said that "the obsequious flatteries" in this and Peter's other letters to Roger II "must be read with due reservation."

1139/41.

p. 231, l. 5] Roger II made peace with Pope Innocent II on 25 July 1139: see Chalandon, *Dom. normande*, II, 90.

p. 231, l. 26] The Roman chancellor was certainly Haimeric, on whom see biographical note to Ep. 3. He disappears from papal documents after 20 May 1141 and died on 28 May, presumably the same year. The references to Pisa and Rome probably refer to the councils held in those cities in 1135 and 1139, respectively.

p. 232] The only Cluniac house in Sicily at this time was St. Mary de Jumariis at Sciacca, which was founded between 1100 and 1136: see Albert L'Huillier, "I priorati cluniacensi in Italia," *Brixia sacra*, III

(1912) 26, dating the grant to Cluny *ca.* 1120, and Lynn White, Jr., *Latin Monasticism in Norman Sicily* (Mediaeval Academy of America Monographs, 13; Cambridge, Mass., 1938) pp. 149-151. It was natural that Roger II chose the prior Geoffrey to carry his letter and overture of peace to the Abbot of Cluny, but there is no evidence (as White pointed out on p. 56) that he acted upon Peter the Venerable's suggestion to found another Cluniac house.

91

AD PONTIVM ABBATEM VIZELIACENSEM

A 90; S 68; C IV,55; Bc III,4; cf. Appendix A on the family of Peter the Venerable.

1138/56. Pontius succeeded Alberic as abbot of Vézelay in 1138.

p. 233, l. 13] On Peter's brothers Heraclius and Eustace, see Appendix A. The cause of their quarrel, which Peter the Venerable healed, is not known.

p. 233, l. 17] The identity of this William cannot be established. He may be the William who was prior at Cluny, then abbot of Moissac, and then chamberlain and again prior at Cluny: see Appendix R on functionaries.

92

AD PAPAM INNOCENTIVM

A 91; C IV,56; Bc III,5; cf. Mabillon, *Annales*, VI, 174 (1130); Bréquigny, *Chartes*, II, 582 (1130); Pignot, *Cluny*, III, 440 (1145).

1141/2.

p. 233] Abbot Natalis (Noël) of Rebais was a figure of considerable importance, who served as chancellor for King Louis VII. In 1140 the King sent him with Bishop Alvisus of Arras and Hugh of St. Victor to settle the disputed election at Morigny. He last appeared as chancellor late in 1140 and retired to Cluny probably in 1141/2, since in Letter 103, written in 1142, Peter the Venerable referred to him as "former abbot of Rebais" and used him on a mission to the Pope. A spiritual association between Cluny and Rebais was made at his suggestion (*PL*, CLXXXIX, 477). He died on 3 December, according to the necrology of Rebais, where he was commemorated as "pater monachorum" (*Obituaires*, IV, 157), but the year is unknown. See the chronicle of Cluny (*Bibl. Clun.*, col. 553 [recte 595] A); *GC*, VIII, 1683; Luchaire, *Louis VII*, pp. 52–54, and *Histoire des institutions monarchiques de la France sous les premiers Capétiens*, 2nd ed. (Paris, 1891) II, 103–105; and *La Chronique de Morigny*, ed. Léon Mirot, 2nd ed. (Collection de textes pour servir à l'étude et à l'enseignement de l'histoire, 41; Paris, 1912) p. 77.

93

AD PONTIVM RELIGIOSVM

A 92; S 69; C IV,57; Bc III,6.

The recipient of this letter is not known. He was probably not Peter the Venerable's brother Pontius, since the heading suggests that he was a simple monk; but the informality of the address suggests that he knew Peter the Venerable well.

94

AD GREGORIVM MONACHVM

S 88; C V,1; Bc III,7; cf. Pignot, *Cluny*, III, 457–459 and 586; Séjourné, in *DThC*, XII.2, 2070–2071 (*ca.* 1135); Leclercq, *Pierre le Vén.*, pp. 218–222; and p. 76 above on the position of this letter in the collection. In MS. S it appears between Letters 112 and 113, and in the chronicle of Cluny it is numbered IV,20 (*Bibl. Clun.*, col. 595 [recte 597] DE). If the arrangement of the letters at this point is chronological, this position suggests a date of 1143/4. At least six passages from this letter were incorporated, in a transposed and frequently scrambled form, into a late twelfth-century collection of excerpts in honor of the Virgin in Paris, Bibl. nat., N. a. l. 186, folios 8^v and 144^{r-v}: "Quantum ergo ad morum puritatem ... transcendit"; "Vnde iustum erat ... eiusdem matris dei"; "Sed plane habuit ingentem ... incomprehensibilem comprehendit"; "Hac gratia hanc singularem ... dicitur mater dei"; "quam ante concaeptum ... spiritus adimpleuit"; and "Nullo autem pacto ... uolatus fuscauerit"; cf. Constable, in *Petrus Ven.*, pp. 240–242, and references there.

Nothing more is known about the recipient Gregory than appears in this letter: that he was a Cluniac monk and the author of sermons, treatises, and letters, all of which are lost. The section on Gregory in the chronicle of Cluny (*Bibl. Clun.*, col. 595 [*recte* 597] DE) is derived from this letter.

p. 236] A long quotation by Gregory begins at this point and continues, with short breaks, up to "Aegyptiorum linguam ignorasse."

p. 244] This part which Peter did not know was presumably the words "etiam corporaliter," which are not in the Vulgate and which Peter discusses later.

p. 252] This heretic, against whom Peter the Venerable says that he wrote two or three years ago, may have been the "Apollinarist" to whom Letter 37 was addressed. The sermon of the pseudo-Jerome was cited in this letter, and the heresy, although not exactly Apollinarianism, involved the Incarnation.

p. 253] This definition of the sacraments, which derived from St. Augustine, was generally accepted in the early Middle Ages: see Damian Van den Eynde, "The Theory of the Composition of the Sacraments in Early Scholasticism (1125-1240)," *Franciscan Studies*, XI (1951) 1-20 and 117-144, and XII (1952) 1-26. This whole passage is of interest for the doctrine of the sacraments in monastic, nonscholastic circles.

95

AD ATHONEM EPISCOPVM TRECENSI

A 93; S 71; C IV,58; Bc IV,1; cf. *RHGF*, XV, 636-637 (1141).

August 1141.

p. 256, l. 1] Louis VII returned from his expedition to Languedoc and Aquitaine in the autumn of 1141: Luchaire, *Louis VII*, pp. 123-124, no. 75, and Hirsch, *Ludwig VII*, p. 28. Peter's reference in this letter to the Feast of the Nativity of the Virgin (8 September) as in the future dates the King's return (and this letter) in August.

p. 256, l. 14] This "lord Hugh" was almost certainly Hugh of Crécy, on whom see Appendix O. He apparently planned to leave Cluny on 9 September, and was prepared to meet Hato in Vézelay, Auxerre, or Troyes in order to accompany him back to Cluny.

p. 256, l. 15] This apparently refers to Letter 86.

96

RESCRIPTVM ATHONIS EPISCOPI AD EVNDEM

A 94; S 72; C IV,59; Bc IV,2; cf. Appendix P on Nicholas of Montiéramey, which includes a discussion of Nicholas's trip to Rome and its possible connection with the Council of Sens.

Early September 1141. This is Hato's reply to Letter 95.

p. 256] (a) The presence of Bernard of Clairvaux at Troyes in August/September 1141 adds an entry to his known itinerary. Later in September he was back at Clairvaux: see Vacandard, *St. Bernard*, II, 202, n. 1. (b) Bishop Geoffrey of Chartres (1115-48) was papal legate: see A. Clerval, *Les écoles de Chartres au moyen âge du Ve au XVIe siècle* (Chartres, 1895) pp. 153-155; Schmale, *Schisma*, pp. 50, 130, and 224; and Janssen, *Legaten*, pp. 18-30. (c) See Appendix P on Nicholas's trip to Rome. (d) Relations between Louis VII and Count Theobald II of Champagne, who had refused to join the King's expedition to the south, deteriorated rapidly in 1141: see D'Arbois de Jubainville, *Comtes de Champagne*, II, 346; Vacandard, *St. Bernard*, II, 180; and Cartellieri, *Suger*, pp. 39 ff. and 141.

p. 257, l. 3] See Ep. 95, n. to p. 256, l. 1, on Louis's return from Aquitaine.

p. 257, l. 12] Presuming that the feast referred to was the translation (1 October) rather than the death (13 January) of St. Remy and that "quinta die" meant the fifth day before the feast, and not the fifth day of the week (Thursday), Hato wanted Hugh to be at Troyes on 26 September, which in 1141 fell on a Friday.

97

AD PAPAM INNOCENTIVM

A 95; S 73; C V,2; Bc IV,3; cf. Duchesne, *Scriptores*, IV, 459; Mabillon, *Annales*, VI, 309 (1141); Bréquigny, *Chartes*, III, 58 (1141); *RHGF*, XV, 637-638 (1142/3); Lorain, *Cluny*, pp. 376-377; Pignot, *Cluny*, III, 241 and 250-251 (1136/7).

1141/2?

p. 257, l. 8] Innocent II crowned and annointed Louis VII at the Council of Rheims in 1131: Luchaire, *Louis VI*, p. 221, no. 476.

p. 257, l. 13] Louis VII bitterly opposed the election of Peter of La Châtre as archbishop of Bourges. Peter was elected in 1141, according to most authorities, and consecrated in either 1141 or 1142: see Duchesne, in *Bibl. Clun.*, *notae*, col. 140; Gams, *Series*, p. 523; *Chronique de Morigny* (cited Ep. 92, n. to p. 233), pp. 80–81; Imbart de la Tour, *Élections*, p. 447; Vacandard, *St. Bernard*, II, 179, n. 3; Hirsch, *Ludwig VII*, p. 28; Cartellieri, *Suger*, pp. 39–43; and Pacaut, *Élections*, pp. 64 and 94–97. It is probable that the present passage refers to this dispute, as most scholars have assumed, and the letter is dated here accordingly; but it may possibly refer to a disagreement between the King and Peter's predecessor Alberic.

p. 258] See notes to Ep. 23 on the case of the abbey of Luxeuil. The "anno praeterito" in this passage, if my dating of the two letters is correct, must mean "in a former year" rather than "last year." It suggests that the date of neither letter is certain, however, and either Letter 23 may be later or Letter 97 earlier than indicated here.

98

AD EVNDEM

A 96; S 74; C V,3; Bc IV,4; cf. Manrique, *Ann. Cist.*, I, 388 (1140); Du Boulay, *Hist. univ. Paris.*, II, 198–199 (1140); Mabillon, *Annales*, VI, 300 (1140); Bréquigny, *Chartes*, III, 48 (1140); *RHGF*, XV, 636 (1140); Pignot, *Cluny*, III, 215–217; Deutsch, *Synode von Sens*, pp. 45–46; Hefele-Leclercq, *Conciles*, V.1, 786–787; Sikes, *Abailard*, pp. 235–236.

1140/1. This letter was probably written in July 1140 if, as Hefele-Leclercq assume, the papal sentence against Abelard (issued 16 July 1140) had not yet reached France; but it may be later if, as is possible, Abelard's appeal was against the papal decision.

p. 258] On the condemnation of Abelard at the Council of Sens, see pp. 317–320 below.

p. 259, l. 6] This is the only source for the meeting and reconciliation of Abelard and Bernard of Clairvaux after the Council of Sens. The passage suggests that Peter the Venerable seconded the overtures of Abbot Rainald of Cîteaux. According to Deutsch, *Synode von Sens*, p. 44, and Vacandard, *St. Bernard*, II, 169, however, Peter the Venerable himself arranged the meeting; and J.-C. Didier, in *Mélanges St. Bernard*, p. 97, suggested that Bernard took the initiative, as he did later, through John of Salisbury, in making peace with Gilbert de la Porrée after the Council of Rheims. As suggested by De Warren, in *Bernard de Clairvaux*, p. 597, the meeting probably took place at Cîteaux.

p. 259, l. 22] Cf. Letter 168 to Heloise, showing that this request was granted.

99

ITEM AD EVNDEM

A 97; S 75; C V,4; Bc IV,5; cf. Severt, *Chronologia*, I, 246.

1139/44. The exact date of Heraclius's visit to Rome is not known, but he was still provost of Brioude in 1139, and Stephen of Chandieu last appeared as archdeacon in 1144.

p. 259] On Peter the Venerable's brother Heraclius, later archbishop of Lyons, see Appendix A (pp. 241–242 below).

p. 260] On Archdeacon Stephen of Chandieu, see Ep. 32, n. to p. 106.

100

AD CLERICOS LVGDVNENSES

A 98; S 76; C V,5; Bc IV,6; cf. Severt, *Chronologia*, I, 239; Bréquigny, *Chartes*, III, 58 (1141).

(a) Ilion of Riverie was a canon of Lyons in about 1108 and abbot of St. Just from 1132 until his death in 1150, according to Jean Beyssac, "Abbés du chapitre de Lyon et abbés de Saint-Just," *Revue d'histoire de Lyon*, XII (1913) 408–409, and *Chanoines*, p. 27. In 1129 he acted in place of Bishop Pontius of Belley, together with the archbishop of Vienne and the abbot of Ambronay, in settling a dispute between Luxeuil and St. Benignus at Dijon: E. Pérard, *Recueil de plusieurs pièces curieuses servant à l'histoire de Bourgogne* (Paris, 1664) pp. 224–225, cf. Martin, *Conciles*, no. 514 (not cited by Beyssac); and in 1132 he acted as mediator between Peter the Venerable and the abbot of Ambronay: *Bibl. Clun.*, col. 1394, cf. *Cluny*, V, 386, no. 4030, and Martin, *Conciles*, no. 523.
(b) On Archdeacon Stephen of Chandieu, see Ep. 32, n. to p. 106.

Toward the end of 1141. Archbishop Peter of Lyons, during whose pontificate, according to Peter the Venerable, there was peace between

Cluny and the church of Lyons, died on 25 May 1139 (see Ep. 21, n. to p. 42, l. 4, and Ep. 32, n. to p. 107). In the year before this letter was written, however, Peter says a quarrel broke out, and Innocent II wrote on 17 May 1140/1 instructing the new archbishop Falco not to injure Cluny. An agreement was then reached, and Peter says here that the year in which the agreement was made is not yet finished. This all points to 1141, which allows enough time for the negotiations and fits the general chronology of the dispute.

p. 260] Archbishops Humbald (1119–28), Rainald (1129–31), and Peter (1131–9) of Lyons. Peter's successor, Falco (1139–42), had as dean of Lyons been a leading opponent to the Cluniac candidate in the disputed election at Langres in 1138: Constable, "Langres," pp. 129–130.

p. 261] Villefranche-sur-Saône was a very new town at the time this letter was written. It was founded, together with the nearby towns of Belleville and Thizy, by Humbert III of Beaujeu, who succeeded his father, Guichard III, in 1137: see Letter 172 and notes to it; L. Aubret, *Mémoires pour servir à l'histoire de Dombes*, ed. M.-C. Guigue (Trévoux, 1868) I, 316 ff.; *Cartulaire municipal de la ville de Villefranche (Rhône)*, ed. Abel Besançon (Villefranche-sur-Saône, 1907) introd., pp. v–vii; Duby, *Mâconnais*, p. 458; and Mathieu Méras, *Le Beaujolais au Moyen Age* (Villefranche, 1956) pp. 30 and 205–206, dating the foundation in 1140/1. It was located near Anse, a town belonging to the archbishop of Lyons, who not unnaturally opposed the foundation of a parish church and the consecration of a cemetery at Villefranche, which would encroach on his parochial rights. The intervention of Peter the Venerable was probably on account of the close ties between Cluny and the family of Beaujeu.

101

AD PAPAM INNOCENTIVM

A 99; S 77; C V,6; Bc IV,7; cf. Mabillon, *Annales*, VI, 310 (1141); *RHGF*, XV, 637 (1142); Pignot, *Cluny*, III, 236.

1141 (probably late in the year).

p. 261, l. 7] Bishop John of Lisieux died late in May 1141 and was succeeded by his nephew Arnulf, archdeacon of Séez: see Arnulf of Lisieux, *Letters*, introd., pp. xix–xx. The exact dates of his election and consecration by Archbishop Hugh of Rouen are not known.

p. 261, l. 12] Arnulf studied law in Italy in 1133 and actively supported Innocent II against Anacletus, against whose legate in France, Gerald of Angoulême, he wrote a strongly worded *Invectiva*: MGH, *Libelli de lite*, III, 81–108. "As to vileness of language and monstrosity of charges, this pamphlet easily tops the whole rich literature of *Libelli de lite*," wrote Bloch, "Schism," p. 167. Arnulf may have attended the Council of Pisa in 1135, according to Barlow, in *Letters*, introd., pp. xv–xvii.

p. 262] Arnulf was a strong supporter of Stephen of Blois owing to both personal and family ties, and he took a leading part in the proceedings at Rome in 1139: see *Letters*, introd., pp. xiv–xv, and Appendix C on Peter the Venerable and the Lateran Council. This explains the opposition to Arnulf of Geoffrey of Anjou, who kept the temporalities of the see of Lisieux in his own hand until he was at last reconciled with Arnulf in 1143.

102

AD MILONEM EPISCOPVM TARVVANENSEM

S 78; C V,7; Bc IV,8; cf. *Hist. litt.*, XIII, 256 (1141); Pignot, *Cluny*, III, 253–255; O. Bled, *Régestes des évêques de Thérouanne*, I (Saint-Omer, 1904) p. 128, no. 575 (soon after April 1139); De Moreau, *Église en Belgique*, III, 19–20.

Bishop Milo I of Thérouanne was abbot of the Premonstratensian house of St.-Josse-au-Bois before he became bishop of Thérouanne in 1130 (consecrated 1131), according to De Moreau. He died in 1158. See GC, X, 1546–1548; *Hist. litt.*, XIII, 286–287 and 601; Chevalier, *Bio-bib.*, II, 3230; Bled, *Régestes*, pp. 119–120; De Moreau, *Église en Belgique*, III, 19–20 and 678.

Soon after June 1140 (?).

p. 263] The place and date of this synod are unknown, but it was probably a diocesan synod held at Thérouanne about 1139.

p. 264] See Appendix H on this affair of the Abbeville prebends.

p. 265, l. 1] See Appendices H and P on this council at Rheims, which was probably the same as the Council of Sens in June 1140.

p. 265, l. 5] St. Bertin, Abbeville, Le Waast, and Rumilly were among the principal Cluniac houses of this region. St. Bertin, however, was freed from official subjection to Cluny at the Lateran Council of 1139: JL 8016; John of Ypres, *Chronica monasterii S. Bertiniani*, XLIII (*Thes. nov.*, III, 638; Mansi, *Concilia*, XXI, 539–542); Simon, *Gesta abbatum S. Bertini Sithiensium*, III, 6 (*MGH, Scriptores* in fol., XIII, 662); cf. Mabillon, *Annales*, VI, 292; Hefele-Leclercq, *Conciles*, V.1, 738; Bled, *Régestes*, p. 128; Georg Schreiber, *Kurie und Kloster im 12. Jahrhundert* (Kirchenrechtliche Abhandlungen, 65–68; Stuttgart, 1910) II, 309–313; Letonnelier, *Cluny*, pp. 134–138; Raphael Molitor, *Aus der Rechtsgeschichte benediktinischer Verbände*, I: *Verbände von Kloster zu Kloster* (Münster in Westf., 1928) pp. 135–136; De Moreau, *Église en Belgique*, III, 19.

103

AD PAPAM INNOCENTIVM

S 79; C V,8; Bc IV,9.

1143 (probably soon after Peter the Venerable's return from Spain).

p. 266, l. 4] On the dispute over the election of Bishop Berengar of Salamanca as successor to Archbishop Diego Gelmírez of Compostela, see Pignot, *Cluny*, III, 293, and Bishko, in *Petrus Ven.*, pp. 170–171 (with further references). Bernard of Clairvaux wrote his ep. 212 to Innocent II in support of Berengar (Gaume ed., I.1, 439–440).

p. 266, l. 22] On Natalis of Rebais, see Ep. 92, n. to p. 233.

104

AD PAPAM INNOCENTIVM

S 80; C V,9; Bc IV,10; cf. Jean Maan, *Sancta et metropolitana ecclesia Turonensis* (Tours, 1667) p. 114; Mabillon, *Annales*, VI, 310–311 (1141); Bréquigny, *Chartes*, III, 69 (1142); Pignot, *Cluny*, III, 440 (1141); Pacaut, *Élections*, p. 46 (1147).

1133/43. This letter can be definitely dated only between the beginning of Hugh's pontificate and the death of Innocent II. Pacaut's date of 1147 is certainly too late.

p. 266, l. 1] Hugh of La Ferté was archbishop of Tours from at least 1 July 1133 until 1147: see the chronicle of Cluny (*Bibl. Clun.*, col. 553 [*recte* 595] AB); B. Hauréau, in *Nouvelle biographie générale* (Paris, 1852–1866) XXVIII, 725; Luchaire, *Louis VI*, p. 234, no. 506.

p. 266, l. 3] The date of Hugh's visit to Rome and of his illness (and retirement) at La Charité cannot be determined. There is no documentary basis for the traditional date of 1141/2, although it is consistent with the position of this letter in the collection.

p. 267] (a) I have been unable to identify the archdeacon P. (b) Hugh I Bernier was abbot of Noyers from 1132 until 1149: see *GC*, XIV, 291, and C. Chevalier, "Histoire de l'abbaye de Noyers au XIe et au XIIe siècle," *Mémoires de la Société archéologique de Touraine*, XXIII (1873) cxiii–cxxvi.

105

AD AIMARDVM NARBONENSEM ARCHIEPISCOPVM

S 81; C V,10; Bc IV,11. This is another characteristic "recruiting" letter. Peter the Venerable here urged Arnold of Narbonne to resign his see and retire to Cluny.

Arnold of Levenon (Lèvezon) was archbishop of Narbonne from 1121 until 1149: see Gams, *Series*, p. 583; Devic and Vaissete, *Languedoc* (new ed.), V, 249. He was papal legate from 1129 to 1142: Janssen, *Legaten*, pp. 157–158.

1143. The reference to Peter the Venerable's return from Spain dates this letter in 1143.

p. 268, l. 2] This council was probably the council held at Rheims in October 1131 (Hefele-Leclercq, *Conciles*, V.1, 694–699); but it may have been the council, probably in June 1140, mentioned in Letter 102 (see Appendix P). The nature of the services performed for Arnold by the Cluniacs is unknown, but they may have been associated with a charge brought against him during the papal schism.

p. 268, l. 6] The troubles referred to here and in Letter 106, which required Peter to return to Cluny without visiting Narbonne and Bordeaux, may have arisen out of Cluny's financial difficulties and the visit to Cluny of Henry of Winchester in late 1143: see Voss, *Heinrich von Blois*, p. 113.

106

AD GAVFRIDVM BVRDEGALENSI ARCHIEPISCOPVM

S 82; C V,11; Bc IV,12; cf. Mabillon, *Annales*, VI, 316–317 (1141); *GC*, II, 811; Bréquigny, *Chartes*, III, 164 (1149); Pignot, *Cluny*, III, 288.

1143. The references to Peter the Venerable's return from Spain date this letter 1143, probably about the middle of the year.

p. 269, l. 12] See Ep. 1, n. to p. 4, l. 1, on this passage. The date of the "iter Cartusiense," on which Peter first met Geoffrey of Le Loroux, is not known.

p. 269, l. 21] The precise meaning of this passage is not clear. It suggests that while Peter the Venerable was in Spain he entrusted the supervision of Cluniac houses in France to the archbishop of Bordeaux. The term "uelut" in the previous sentence implies that Peter followed the pilgrimage route *as if* he were on his way to Compostela, but he probably did not go all the way: cf. Bishko, in *Petrus Ven.*, pp. 165, n. 10, and 172.

p. 269, l. 23] See Ep. 105, n. to p. 268, l. 6, on the possible nature of these troubles.

p. 269, l. 25] The nature of the business concerning St. Jean d'Angély is unknown, but the abbey had been a source of trouble during the papal schism (see Appendix Q on Peter of Poitiers).

p. 269, l. 27] This letter seems to be lost, but it may be either Letter 103 (in which case "his own messenger" was Natalis of Rebais) or Letter 104, although neither of these mentions a letter from Geoffrey of Bordeaux.

p. 270] The permission for Geoffrey to regulate Cluniac affairs "not only as a legate but as the abbot of Cluny himself" suggests that Constantine was a Cluniac monk and "Quartam leugam" a Cluniac house in the diocese of Bordeaux, but I have been unable to identify them.

107

AD DOMINVM HEINRICVM EPISCOPVM

S 83; C V,12; Bc IV,13.

1137/56.

p. 270] Both Henry's mother Adela and Peter the Venerable's mother Raingard were nuns at Marcigny: see Epp. 15 and 53 and Appendix A on Peter the Venerable's family.

108

AD GVARINVM AMBIANENSI EPISCOPVM

C V,13; Bc IV,14.

Guarinus was bishop of Amiens from 1127 until 1144, when he retired to Cluny: *GC*, X, 1173-1175. According to the necrologies of St.-Martin-des-Champs and Longpont, he died on 9 October, but the year is unknown: *Obituaires*, I.1, 461 and 527. He was a generous patron of the Cluniacs during his pontificate: see Duchesne, in *Bibl. Clun.*, *notae*, cols. 143-144; *Bibl. Clun.*, cols. 1403-1404 (1138/9, cf. *Cluny*, V, 413, no. 4061); *St. Martin des Champs*, II, 3-4, 26-27, and 100-101, nos. 193 (1127/31), 209 (1135), and 244 (1138/9); and E. Müller, *Le prieuré de Saint-Leu d'Esserent* (Pontoise, 1901) pp. 32-33, no. 28 (1127/34). He is mentioned in Letters 102 as having been dissuaded by Bishop Milo of Thérouanne from granting to Cluny the ecclesiastical rights to a prebend at Abbeville (see Appendix H).

1127/44. This letter was written in the late spring, since Peter the Venerable urged Guarinus to visit Cluny before the coming summer was over. The year is unknown, but the position of the letter in the collection indicates 1143.

109

AD SVGERIVM SANCTI DIONYSII ABBATEM

S 84; C V,14; Bc IV,15; cf. Duchesne, *Scriptores*, IV, 459; *RHGF*, XV, 644-645 (1147/8); Bréquigny, *Chartes*, III, 48 (1140); Lorain, *Cluny*, p. 415; Pignot, *Cluny*, III, 144-145; Suger, *Oeuvres*, p. 293 (1147/8); Cartellieri, *Suger*, p. 146, no. 158 (1147/9).

1130/51. This letter was written between Suger's visit to Cluny in 1130 and his death in 1151. It was clearly written in the autumn, since Peter the Venerable urged Suger to come "before the nearby winter," and its position in the collection indicates 1143; but there seems to be no reason for the date of 1147/8 assigned to this letter by Brial and Lecoy de la Marche.

p. 272] Suger visited Cluny in 1130 in order to see Pope Innocent II: see Cartellieri, *Suger*, pp. 28 and 135-136, nos. 66-67, and Suger, *Louis le Gros*, p. 260.

110

EPISTOLA BERNARDI ABBATIS CLARAEVALLIS AD DOMINVM ABBATEM

S 85; Cl fol. 2ʳ; C V,15; Bc IV,16; Bern., ep. 228; cf. Mabillon, notes to Bernard, ep. 228 (Gaume ed., I.1, 461 and 908–909) (1143); Bréquigny, *Chartes*, III, 79 (1143); Maitland, *Dark Ages*, pp. 435–436; Lorain, *Cluny*, pp. 456–457; Vacandard, *St. Bernard*, II, 501 (1143/4); *Letters of St. Bernard*, pp. 375–376, no. 305.

Late 1143 or very early 1144. Letter 111 shows that this letter reached Cluny about the middle of January 1144.

p. 272] This letter from Peter the Venerable to Bernard of Clairvaux is lost.

p. 273] According to Mabillon's notes to Bernard's ep. 228, these injuries were the election at Langres and the dispute over tithes, but Bernard may simply have been referring to the failure to write.

111

RESCRIPTVM DOMINI ABBATIS AD EVNDEM

S 86; Cl fol. 3ᵛ; C V,16; Bc IV,17; cf. Bernard, ep. 229 (Gaume ed., I.1, 463–486) (1143); Bréquigny, *Chartes*, III, 79 (1143); Maitland, *Dark Ages*, pp. 437–439; Lorain, *Cluny*, pp. 390–392 and 457–465; P.-F. Mandonnet, "Pierre le Vénérable et son activité littéraire contre l'Islam," *Revue thomiste*, I (1893) 339; E. Vacandard, "Les origines de l'hérésie albigeoise," *Revue des questions historiques*, LV (1894) 70, n. 2; Kramp, in *Misc. Ehrle*, I, 75; Sikes, *Abailard*, p. 263; Wilmart, "Riposte," p. 302; D'Alverny, "Traductions," p. 72; Leclercq, *Pierre le Vén.*, pp. 176–177; and Appendix F on this letter and Peter the Venerable's works against the Saracens.

Late spring or early summer 1144. This letter was dated 1141 by Kramp; 1142/3 by Sikes; 1143 by Mabillon, Bréquigny, Vacandard, Leclercq, and D'Alverny; and 1144 by Mandonnet and Wilmart. Internal evidence shows that it must have been written several months after March 1144, since Peter the Venerable says that he returned to Cluny from Marcigny about the beginning of Lent (13 February) in the year following his return from Spain and that he then waited first two weeks, then a month, and then several months before writing to Bernard of Clairvaux.

p. 275] This presumably refers to Peter's Letters 65 and 73 and Bernard's reply, Letter 74.

p. 277] See Constable, "Cluniac Tithes" and "Langres," on these two disputes.

p. 280] The following quotation is probably fictional, as the use of "dicetis" implies; but the use of "dixistis" on the following page shows that it may come from a real letter.

p. 282] Several of the specific differences between the Cluniacs and Cistercians discussed in the following sections were also discussed by Peter the Venerable in Letter 28, including the length of the novitiate, clothing, treatment of fugitives, fasts, manual labor, reception of guests, feeding of guests, and the principle of mitigation of the Rule, especially in view of the Cistercian effort to restore the primitive fervor of monasticism. In this letter Peter examined each topic from two different points of view, one strict and the other charitable, and he urged that they should be seen with "a single eye," that is, without caviling. He thus studied sixteen points in all, and they are so numbered in MS. S, from which the numbering here is taken.

p. 285] See Ep. 28, n. to p. 57, on the Cistercian use of white clothing.

p. 289, l. 18] In the office that Peter the Venerable composed for the Feast of the Transfiguration, he twice referred to the clothing of Our Lord as snow-white: see Leclercq, *Pierre le Vén.*, p. 383, who suggested (p. 380) that this feast (which was introduced into the Cluniac liturgy by Peter the Venerable) may have derived from Spain. Cf. De Valous, *Mon. clun.*, I, 364, and Suitbert Bäumer, *Histoire du Bréviaire*, trans. Réginald Biron (Paris, 1905) I, 428.

p. 289, l. 37] On this passage, and on the color used for mourning in Spain, see R. P. A. Dozy, *Recherches sur l'histoire politique et littéraire de l'Espagne pendant le Moyen Age* (Leiden, 1849) I, 631, and Matthäus Bernards, *Speculum Virginum* (Cologne-Graz, 1955) pp. 162–163.

p. 293] On Cluniac chapter generals in the twelfth century, see Besse, "Ordre," pp. 97 ff.; P. Anger, "Chapitres généraux de Cluny,' *Revue Mabillon*, VIII (1912) 105–147 and 213–252 (esp. pp. 110–111); and De Valous, *Mon. clun.*, II, 72–73. None of these authors, however, refers to the meetings in 1140 and 1150: see F.-J. Le Paige, *Bibliotheca Praemonstratensis Ordinis* (Paris, 1633) pp. 321–322 (a spiritual association between the Cluniacs and Premonstratensians: "Actum Cluniaci sedente Capitulo generali Anno Dominicae Incarnationis 1140."), and Epp. 164 and 166. These references, and the present passage, suggest that Cluniac chapter generals may have been more frequent during the abbacy of Peter the Venerable than is generally thought.

p. 294, l. 23] On this section, see Appendix F.

p. 294, l. 24] On Peter of Toledo, who was responsible for the translation of the *Risāla* of al-Kindi, see D'Alverny, "Traductions," p. 71, and Kritzeck, in *Petrus Ven.*, p. 178, and *Peter the Venerable*, pp. 56–58 (which appeared after the completion of the present work).

p. 294, l. 28] See Appendix Q on Peter of Poitiers.

p. 295] On this work, see D'Alverny, "Traductions," pp. 83–85, and Kritzeck, in *Petrus Ven.*, p. 181, and *Peter the Venerable*, pp. 75–83.

p. 299, l. 9] This refers to Bernard's *De praecepto et dispensatione* (ed., Leclercq, III, 253-294).

p. 299, l. 11] See Appendix G on the date of the *Contra Petrobrusianos*.

112

AD PAPAM CELESTINVM

S 87; C V,17; Bc IV,18; cf. Mabillon, *Annales*, VI, 340 (1143); Bréquigny, *Chartes*, III, 79 (1143); Pignot, *Cluny*, III, 302.

Pope Celestine II was elected and consecrated on 26 September 1143, two days after the death of Innocent II. He was a native of Città di Castello, a student of Abelard, and a learned canon lawyer. Before his elevation to the papacy, he was successively cardinal-deacon of Sta. Maria in Via Lata and cardinal-priest of St. Mark: Brixius, *Kardinalkollegium*, pp. 34–35 and 75. He died on 8 March 1144.

Early December 1143. Celestine II wrote to Peter the Venerable and the Cluniacs, notifying them of his election, on 6 November 1143 (*Bull. Clun.*, p. 51; JL 8435). This letter arrived at Cluny, according to Peter the Venerable, on 30 November, taking twenty-four days. Mabillon remarked on the speed of delivery and was surprised that Peter apologized to the Pope for the lateness of its arrival. In good weather, however, an express messenger took no more than three weeks to travel between Rome and Cluny: see notes, on travel times, to Epp. 63 and 69. Peter's reply was presumably written soon after he received the Pope's letter.

p. 301, l. 1] On the *conversi* at Cluny, see Ursmer Berlière, *La familia dans les monastères bénédictins du Moyen Age* (Académie royale de Belgique: Mémoires in-8°, 29.2; Brussels, 1931) pp. 65 ff., who pointed out that at Cluny (unlike some of the newer orders) the *conversi* were simply illiterate monks "incapable of performing the liturgical chants"; James S. Donnelly, *The Decline of the Medieval Cistercian Laybrotherhood* (Fordham University Studies: History Series, 3; New York, 1949) pp. 5–6; Kassius Hallinger, "Woher kommen die Laienbrüder?" *Analecta sacri ordinis Cisterciensis*, XII (1956) offprint, pp. 14–20. Hallinger cited Peter the Venerable's *Statuta* XXIV as evidence that by the middle of the twelfth century Cluny had *conversi barbati* who were laybrothers working for the monks; but the present passage shows that the term *conversus* alone still designated an illiterate monk.

p. 301, l. 5] Letter 113 shows that Peter the Venerable visited Rome in 1144. Celestine's charter of 24 February 1144 (*Bibl. Clun.*, cols. 1413–1414; JL 8501), confirming Cluny's possession of the church of St. Vincent at Salamanca, suggests that Peter arrived before Celestine's death on 8 March.

p. 301, l. 12] At the end of his letter to Peter the Venerable, Celestine said that for Peter's sake he was tolerating the behavior of Bishop A[imeric] of Clermont (cf. dating note to Ep. 171), who had neither appeared on 18 October, in accordance with the instructions of Innocent II, nor presented a canonical excuse. On 10 December 1143 Celestine also wrote to Archbishop Hugh of Tours, reproaching him for not appearing on 18 October, as ordered by Innocent II, and instructing him to come on the following 1 May (JL 8456). Innocent's reason for summoning the two Bishops is not known, but the news of his illness may have reached France in time to prevent their departure for Rome.

113

AD LVCIVM PAPAM

S 89; C V,18; Bc IV,19; cf. Mabillon, *Annales*, VI, 344–345 (1143); Pignot, *Cluny*, III, 302–303.

August 1144. The Pope's reply to this letter is dated 22 September, and

Peter the Venerable was writing in time to hear from him and then to send thirteen monks to arrive in Rome by the Feast of St. Andrew (30 November). This letter was therefore probably written in August.

p. 301] Since Peter the Venerable probably arrived in Rome before the death of Celestine II (see Ep. 112, n. to p. 301, l. 5), he may have been present at the election and consecration of Lucius II, formerly the papal chancellor, on 12 March: Brixius, *Kardinalkollegium*, pp. 33 and 73–74. The new Pope issued three bulls for Cluny on 22 May, confirming its possession of Letcombe-Regis (see Ep. 60, n. to p. 191), prohibiting the unauthorized building of new churches on Cluny's lands, and confirming all its possessions (*Bull. Clun.*, pp. 52–54; JL 8620–8622). Peter probably left Rome soon after the grant of these bulls and was back at Cluny by June or July.

p. 302, l. 8] Cf. Ep. 114, n. to p. 303, l. 3, on Lucius's negotiations with the King of Sicily.

p. 302, l. 23] While Peter the Venerable was in Rome early in 1144, the Pope asked him to send twelve Cluniac monks and an abbot to found a Cluniac house at Rome. He had mentioned, according to Letter 118, two possible houses in which they might be placed. Peter the Venerable here asked for confirmation of this request, and Lucius replied in Letter 114 asking Peter to send the monks as quickly as possible. Peter did as he was ordered, though not without misgivings, and sent thirteen carefully chosen monks. With them he probably sent Letter 118, asking the Pope to protect them and to keep them together. The papal bulls of 19 and 20 January 1145 (*Bull. Clun.*, p. 55; JL 8707–8708) show that Lucius placed the monks in the ancient house of S. Saba, near the Porta S. Paolo. In Letter 119, however, Peter complained to Pope Eugene III that after Lucius's death the Cluniacs were expelled, presumably by the monks whom they had replaced. Nothing more is known about the project. In addition to these letters, see L'Huillier, in *Brixia sacra* (cited Ep. 90, n. to p. 232), III, 60–61, on this affair.

114

RESCRIPTVM PAPAE LVCII AD DOMINVM ABBATEM

S 90; C V,19; Bc IV,20; cf. *RHGF*, XV, 415; Mansi, *Concilia*, XXI, 608; JL 8653; Caspar, *Roger II*, pp. 341–342.

22 September 1144.

p. 303, l. 3] On the negotiations between Lucius and Roger II of Sicily, see Chalandon, *Dom. normande*, II, 113–115. They met at Ceprano from about 4/5–17 June but were unable to reach an agreement. Roger's armies then attacked the papal states, and Lucius concluded with Roger's son a seven-year truce, which was later ratified by Roger.

p. 303, l. 7] On the sending of Cluniac monks to S. Saba, see Ep. 113, n. to p. 302, l. 23.

115

AD ELOYSAM ABBATISSAM

S 91; C V,20; Bc IV,21; cf. Du Boulay, *Hist. univ. Paris.*, II, 208–211 (1143); Mabillon, *Annales*, VI, 327–328 (1142); Bréquigny, *Chartes*, III, 69 (1142); Lorain, *Cluny*, pp. 427–428; Pignot, *Cluny*, III, 217–219; Evans, *Mon. Life*, pp. 63–64; Oursel, *Dispute*, pp. 84–86. This, one of the most famous of all Peter the Venerable's letters, is equally celebrated for its praise of Heloise and its description of Abelard's last years. It is mentioned in countless works on Abelard and Heloise.

1143/4. Abelard died on 21 April 1142 (Vacandard, *St. Bernard*, II, 173; Sikes, *Abailard*, p. 237), and this letter has therefore usually been dated in that year. At the time Abelard died, however, Peter the Venerable was probably on his way to Spain, and he could not have written this letter before his return in 1143, since he mentions having heard an account of Abelard's last days from the monks of St. Marcellus, where he died. At the beginning of the letter, furthermore, he says that there has been some delay in writing. The position of the letter in the collection further indicates that it may not have been written before 1144.

p. 303] This Theobald also appears in Letter 123, carrying greetings from Peter the Venerable to Peter of Poitiers.

p. 306, l. 25] This reference to Abelard's spending "the last years of his life" at Cluny was used by Vacandard, *St. Bernard*, II, 145, n. 1, as evidence that the Council of Sens met in 1140 rather than 1141, since Peter the Venerable would hardly have referred to less than a year as "final years." Cf. Appendix P on the date of the Council of Sens.

p. 306, l. 31] Oursel, *Dispute*, p. 85, discussed this passage and pointed out that Peter the Venerable may either have had *Saints* Germain and Martin in mind (as I am inclined to believe) or have been using the names generically (like "Tom, Dick, and Harry") in order to indicate that no one was poorer or more abject than Abelard.

p. 306, l. 32] This "superior grade" was probably not an official position at Cluny but a rank among the monks higher than that to which his recent entrance to the abbey would have entitled him.

p. 307, l. 15] Already in Letter 98 Peter the Venerable remarked that Abelard might not have long to live. He apparently suffered from Hodgkins' disease or leukemia: see J. Jeannin, "La dernière maladie d'Abélard: une alliée imprévue de saint Bernard," *Mélanges St. Bernard*, pp. 109–115. He was sent by Peter the Venerable to "Cabilonem," which was almost certainly the Cluniac priory of St. Marcellus, near Chalon-sur-Saône (Cottineau, *Répertoire*, II, 2780), although it was identified by Virey, *Églises*, p. 161, as Chevignes (Cavanias, Cavinias, Cabiniensis: cf. *Cluny*, I, 733–734, and II, 77, nos. 780 and 980).

p. 307, l. 19] Abelard wrote his *Apologia, Monitum* to Astrolabe, *Dialogus inter philosophum, iudaeum, et christianum,* and probably his *Expositio in Hexaemeron*, during his stay at Cluny and St. Marcellus: Deutsch, *Synode von Sens*, pp. 43–46; Sikes, *Abailard*, pp. 237 and 267–268; and D. Van den Eynde, "Chronologie des écrits d'Abélard à Héloise," *Antonianum*, XXXVII (1962) 347–349. He may also have corrected his other works, especially the *Dialectic*, according to Vacandard, *St. Bernard*, II, 172–173.

p. 308] On this famous passage, see Helen Waddell, *The Wandering Scholars*, 7th ed. (London, 1934) p. 109, and C. N. L. Brooke, *The Dullness of the Past* (Inaugural Lecture; Liverpool, 1957) p. 14.

116

AD DOMINVM PAPAM LVCIVM

S 92; C V,21; Bc IV,22; cf. *GC*, VIII, 1449 (1144); Pignot, *Cluny*, III, 227–9; Appendix N on Elias of Orléans.

1144 (or early 1145).

117

VERSVS DOMINI PETRI ABBATIS AD RAIMVNDVM TOLOSANVM MONACHVM

A unnumbered (fol. 66ʳ); C V,22; Bc IV,23; Devic and Vaissete,

AD LVCIVM PAPAM

Languedoc, II, 453 and 517; Pignot, *Cluny*, III, 578-579; Manitius, *Lat. Lit.*, III, 137.

The poet Raymond of Toulouse is known only from this letter. He may have been a monk at the Cluniac house of La Daurade, which was situated (unlike most monasteries in Toulouse) on the banks of the Garonne (cf. line 7). He had evidently sent Peter the Venerable a letter in verse, asking to accompany him to Rome. In the eight additional lines found in C (which were either added later or accidentally omitted in MS. A), Peter the Venerable wrote that a certain Robert had recently brought him several poems by Raymond, asking to go with Peter to Rome and telling him to reply in verse. Peter replied that he would be glad to have Raymond as a companion if he went to Rome.

The date of this epistolary poem cannot be established with certainty. Peter the Venerable's journey to Rome, to which it refers, may have been either that in 1144, as the position of the letter in the collection suggests, or that in 1145, as proposed by Pignot, who associated the troubles mentioned in the letter with the revolution in Rome led by Arnold of Brescia.

p. 310] These references to war and disturbances at Rome and in the Latin kingdoms may be allegorical.

118

AD EVNDEM LVCIVM PAPAM

S 93; C V, 23; Bc IV, 24; cf. Ep. 113, n. to p. 302, l. 23, on the affair of the Cluniac monks sent to S. Saba.

October/November 1144. This letter probably accompanied the monks sent to Rome by Peter the Venerable at the request of Pope Lucius. According to Letter 113, they were supposed to arrive by the Feast of St. Andrew (30 November), and they therefore probably started in October or early November.

p. 311] One of these monasteries was S. Saba, where the monks were settled in January 1145. The other is not known.

p. 312] One of these two monks who were Roman by origin may have been Arnulf, "previously an outstanding scribe at Rome," who accompanied Peter the Venerable on his eremitical retreat in the woods near Cluny and who wrote Letter 125 to Peter of Poitiers.

119

AD EVGENIVM PAPAM

S 94; C V,24; Bc IV,25; cf. Pignot, *Cluny*, III, 307 and 348.

1145/53. Both the reference to the affair of S. Saba and the concluding sentence, mentioning Eugene's succession and asking him to favor Cluny, suggest that this letter was written early in Eugene's pontificate, which began in February 1145.

p. 312] On the affair of S. Saba, see Ep. 113, n. to p. 302, l. 23.

p. 313] Humbert was archbishop of Besançon from 1134 until 1162 at the latest. On this case, and Peter the Venerable's support of Humbert, see F. I. Dunod, *Histoire de l'église, ville et diocèse de Besançon* (Besançon, 1750) I, 154, and *GC*, XV, 46, dating it *ca.* 1153.

120

AD RAINARDVM ABBATEM CISTERCIENSEM

S 95; C V,25; Bc IV,26; cf. Manrique, *Ann. Cist.*, II, 13–14 (1145); Mabillon, *Annales*, VI, 356–357 (1146); Bréquigny, *Chartes*, III, 106 (1145); *Hist. litt.*, XIII, 256 (*ca.* 1145); Pignot, *Cluny*, III, 477 and 608 (1145).

Rainard of Bar was abbot of Cîteaux from the beginning of 1134, at the latest, until 16 December 1150: *Cîteaux*, p. 26.

1134/50. This letter was written soon after Pentecost, since the monks who carried it arrived at Cluny "sancti spiritus die" and stayed three days, but the year is not known.

p. 313] The abbey from which these monks came, and of which the abbot had been deposed by Rainard, cannot be identified with certainty, but the letter shows that (a) it was Cistercian and probably in the direct line from Cîteaux, (b) it was presumably southwest of Cluny, since the monks came through Cluny on their way to Cîteaux, and (c) it was especially favored by the family of Peter the Venerable, which suggests that it was in the Auvergne. The authors of the *GC*, IV, 296, proposed Le Miroir, because in Letter 193 Peter the Venerable described its abbot Eustace as "consanguineus," but this was questioned by Pignot, *Cluny*, III, 608, who suggested some Cistercian abbey in the Auvergne. The most probable candidate seems to be Montpeyroux, in the diocese of Clermont, which was founded from Bonnevaux in the diocese of Vienne (itself a daughter of Cîteaux) in 1126. The founder, Amadeus of Hauterives, had been for a time a monk at Cluny, during the abbacy of Peter the Venerable, before moving to Bonnevaux: see M.-Anselme Dimier, "Vita Venerabilis Amedaei Altae Ripae († c. 1150)," *Studia monastica*, V (1963) 287–288 and 301. Members of the family of Montboissier are known to have been among its principal benefactors, but very little is known about its early history: *GC*, II, 399, listing an Abbot John in 1139 and a second abbot, Fulcher, "ex chartis Bonarum-vallium" (although there is no reference to him in the chartulary of Bonnevaux in Vienne published by U. Chevalier) and citing this letter, in spite of its association elsewhere in the *GC* with Le Miroir; Beaunier-Besse, *Abbayes*, V, 108, dating its foundation in 1155; Janauschek, *Origines*, p. 13; and Cottineau, *Répertoire*, II, 1971.

121

AD ATONEM EPISCOPVM TRECENSEM

S 96; C V,26; Bc IV,27.

Ca. 1145. The subject matter of this letter, urging Hato to fulfill his promise of retiring to Cluny (see Ep. 86, n. to p. 223), suggests a date not long before Hato finally entered Cluny in 1145/6, and this dating is supported by its position in the collection and the fact that it is the last letter in the collection from Peter the Venerable to Hato.

122

AD EVGENIVM PAPAM

S 97; C V,27; Bc IV,28; cf. Bréquigny, *Chartes*, III, 106 (1145); *GC*, VIII, 1449–1450 (1145); *RHGF*, XV, 640–641 (1145/6); Pignot, *Cluny*, III, 228 and 347–348; Appendix N on Elias of Orléans.

1145 (probably not long after the election of Eugene III in February 1145).

123

EPISTOLA PETRI PICTAVENSIS AD PETRVM ABBATEM TVNC IN SILVA CLVNIACENSI CVM PAVCIS COMMORANTEM

A 100; S 98; C V,28; Bc IV,29; cf. on this and the six following letters, Mabillon, *Annales*, VI, 320–321 (1141); Lecointre-Dupont, "Pierre de

Poitiers," pp. 380–382; Pignot, *Cluny*, III, 466–470 (1147); Evans, *Mon. Life*, pp. 59–61; Leclercq, in *Petrus Ven.*, pp. 110–111. This group of letters sheds valuable light on eremitical life at Cluny during the abbacy of Peter the Venerable. They were written while Peter was on a retreat with a few monks in the forests near Cluny. Their "hermitage" was identified by Duby, *Mâconnais*, p. 434, n. 5, as Montmain, between Cluny and Igé (presumably the chapel of St. Radegonde at Montmain), but its exact location is uncertain, except that Peter of Poitiers described it as "tam prope" to Cluny. According to the chronicle of Cluny (*Bibl. Clun.*, col. 600 BC), some four hundred monks lived in the woods around Cluny during the abbacy of Peter the Venerable, who visited them from time to time; and it lists the chapels of Cotte, St. Romain (on the present Mont St. Romain), St. Vitalis (the modern Pré-St.-Vital), St. Radegonde (at Montmain), and St. John "de Bosco," which cannot be identified with certainty but may be the modern Bussières, Ruffey, St.-Gengoux-le-Royal, or St. Nizier: see T. Chavot, *Le Mâconnais: Géographie historique* (Paris-Mâcon, 1884) pp. 124, 251, 252–253, 253–254 and (on St. John) 85–86, 240, 243–244, and 249–250, and (on Cotte) Raffin, in *Millénaire de Cluny*, II, 173, n. 1, and 177. Surviving Cluniac chapels in the area of Cluny include Chapelle Coureau, Chevignes (cf. Ep. 115, n. to p. 307, l. 15), St. Laurence at Cotte, and St. Martin at Massy: see Virey, *Églises*, pp. 129–130, 161, 266–268, and 336–339.

On Peter of Poitiers, see Appendix Q. He was unable to accompany Peter the Venerable on this occasion owing to an ailment of his feet. In the meantime he occupied himself copying books.

The date of this letter, and of Peter the Venerable's retreat, cannot be established with certainty. Peter's greetings reached Peter of Poitiers on the Feast of St. James (25 June), which suggests that the "day of the proto-martyr" mentioned at the beginning of the letter was the invention (3 August) rather than the death (26 December) of St. Stephen: cf. De Valous, *Mon. Clun.*, I, 405, on the celebration of these feasts at Cluny. This letter was therefore probably written in August, which is confirmed by the reference in Letter 124 to the Feast of St. Benedict (21 March) as "recent." The description of the "leafy roofs" in Letter 127 also confirms that the season was not winter. The year is not known, but the fact that this and the following group of letters, together with Letter 117, are the last letters in MS.A, inclines me to believe that they were written not long before Peter the Venerable's visit to Spain, that is, in 1139/41, and very likely in 1141, as Mabillon suggested: cf. p. 16 above. But this is all conjectural.

124

RESCRIPTVM DOMINI PETRI ABBATIS AD EVNDEM

A 101; S 99; C V,29; Bc IV,30, and col. 1350; cf. *Analecta hymnica medii aevi*, ed. Clemens Blume and G. M. Dreves, XLVIII (Leipzig, 1905) pp. 240–242, printing the two poems associated with this letter and listing several MSS. (not including Douai 381); André Wilmart, "Le poème apologétique de Pierre le Vénérable et les poèmes connexes," *Rev. Bén.*, LI (1939) 58, n. 2, who compared the "false sapphics" of the poems with other hymns; Leclercq, *Pierre le Vén.*, pp. 272–273, who translated the passage relating to the hymns and pointed out that they still appear in the Benedictine Breviary of the French Congregation; and Leclercq, *Amour des lettres*, p. 228.

August 1139/41 (?): see dating note to Ep. 123. Evans, *Mon. Life*, p. 111, interpreted the phrase "iam totus mundus in arma coniurat" in this letter as a reference to the Second Crusade and dated it 1147. The context suggests, however, that the passage is allegorical in meaning.

p. 318] The relevant passages in the *Dialogues* of Gregory the Great are indicated in the textual notes.

125–127

EPISTOLAE QVORVMDAM SOCIORVM AD EVNDEM
PETRVM DE SILVA CLVNIACENSI RESCRIPTAE

A 102–104; S 100–102; C V,30 (all three under one number); Bc IV, 31–33; cf. pp. 14–15, 43, and 75 above on these three letters.

The authors of these letters are identified in the headings, which were omitted in the *Bibl. Clun.*: Arnulf was a former scribe, possibly a papal notary, in Rome (cf. Ep. 118, n. to p. 312); Robert was a learned *scholasticus* and master of medicine; Gilbert was a young and educated nobleman, who stressed that he was younger and less learned than the other two writers and was probably not the hermit Gilbert of Senlis, to whom Peter the Venerable sent Letter 20, as was suggested by Leclercq, in *Petrus Ven.*, p. 113. All three were presumably monks at Cluny, since they accompanied Peter on his retreat, but nothing more is known about them. Several doctors named Robert, including one in the chartulary of St.-Martin-des-Champs (after 1096) and another in the chartulary of Longpont (*ca.* 1120), appear in Ernest Wickersheimer, *Dictionnaire biographique des médecins en France au Moyen Age* (Paris, 1936) II, 705–706, but no one can be identified with this Robert.

August 1139/41 (?): see dating note to Ep. 123.

p. 321] Duchesne, in *Bibl. Clun.*, *notae*, cols. 148-149, has a long note on the use of the term "dominus" in reference to abbots and monks.

128

RESCRIPTVM PETRI PICTAVENSIS AD DOMINVM PETRVM ABBATEM ET SOCIOS EIVS

A 105; S 103; C V,31; Bc IV,34. This is Peter of Poitiers's reply to the four preceding letters. It is certainly not by Geoffrey of Le Loroux, as proposed by Bonnes, in *Rev. Bén.* (see Ep. 1, n. to p. 4, l. 1), LVI, 195, n. 3, who presumably used the edition in the *Bibl. Clun.* or *PL*, where the heading is lacking.

August 1139/41 (?): see the dating note to Ep. 123.

p. 325] Whether or not Peter the Venerable's two hymns were sent to the monks of St.-Benoît-sur-Loire ("those monks who keep his body"), as Peter of Poitiers suggested, is not known: cf. Leclercq, *Pierre le Vén.*, p. 273.

p. 326] This may be a reference to the plague at Cluny, which killed many monks (see Letter 133).

129

EPISTOLA DOMINI PETRI ABBATIS AD EVNDEM PETRVM

A 106; S 104; C V,32; Bc IV,35. This is another letter written to Peter of Poitiers by Peter the Venerable while he was on retreat. It is not necessarily a reply to Letter 128.

August 1139/41 (?): see dating note to Ep. 123.

p. 327] These references to Peter the Venerable's own works are of great value: see Pignot, *Cluny*, III, 580, n. 1, and, on the letters, p. 16 above; on the life of Matthew of Albano, which was later incorporated into the *De miraculis*, see Berlière, *Mélanges*, IV, 50, and Constable, in *Petrus Ven.*, pp. 226-228; and on the book against the heretics, see Ep. 71, n. to p. 203, l. 17, and Appendix G.

130

AD LVDOVICVM FRANCORVM REGEM

S 105; C V,33; Bc IV,36; cf. Duchesne, *Scriptores*, IV, 460-461; Du Boulay, *Hist. univ. Paris.*, II, 219-221 (1146); Mabillon, *Annales*, VI, 375 (1146); Bréquigny, *Chartes*, III, 106 (1145); *RHGF*, XV, 641-643 (1146); Lorain, *Cluny*, pp. 401-404; Pignot, *Cluny*, III, 329-331; Bernhardi, *Konrad III*, p. 524; Berry, in *Petrus Ven.*, pp. 148-150. This letter is cited in many works on Jewish history, together with the *Contra Iudaeos* and the *Rythmus in laude Saluatoris* (*Bibl. Clun.*, col. 1348 AB), as evidence that Peter the Venerable was anti-Jewish. This is true only in a religious, not in a racial, sense. There is no hint in any of his works, for instance, that Peter's opposition to Anacletus II was inspired by his Jewish origins (cf. Bloch, "Schism," pp. 166-167). Peter the Venerable was more conscious of religious differences than many of his contemporaries and wrote against the Saracens and heretics as well as against the Jews, all of whom he hoped to convert to his own form of religious belief: cf. Leclercq, *Pierre le Vén.*, pp. 233-252. The suggestions made in this letter, however indefensible in themselves, were the result of Peter's religious sentiments.

1146 (probably after Easter).

p. 327] The Second Crusade originated in the papal bull of 1 December 1145 and was preached by Bernard of Clairvaux at Vézelay at Easter 1146, when Louis VII and many French nobles took the cross: see the references in Constable, "Second Crusade," pp. 247-248.

p. 328] The general references to Islam here and in other works by Peter the Venerable are "accurate and self-assured," according to Kritzeck, in *Petrus Ven.*, p. 189; but they were not taken directly from the translations of the so-called Toledan Collection made for Peter.

131

AD ROGERIVM SICILIAE REGEM

S 106; C V,34; Bc IV,37; cf. Mabillon, *Annales*, VI, 288 (1139); Bréquigny, *Chartes*, III, 79 (1143); Lorain, *Cluny*, pp. 397-400; Pignot, *Cluny*, III, 312-314; Francesco Cerone, *L'opera politica e militare di Ruggiero II in Africa ed in Oriente* (Catania, 1913) pp. 37 and 49-51; Lamma, *Momenti*, pp. 116-119; Wieruszowski, in *Speculum* (cited Ep. 90), XXXVIII, 72-73.

Early 1146. It is not certain from the wording whether Peter the Venerable wrote this letter while he was still in Rome or after his return to Cluny.

p. 331, l. 5] Peter the Venerable's advocacy here of a policy so diametrically opposed to the interests (and to the traditional policy) of the papacy can be explained only by his recent experience of the disorders in central Italy. Cf. Robert Davidsohn, *Geschichte von Florenz* (Berlin, 1896–1927) I, 433, and Dupré Theseider, in *Studi . . . A. De Stefano* (cited Ep. 90) p. 206, n. 7, cited by Wieruszowski, in *Speculum*, XXXVIII, 72.

p. 331, l. 33] This sole exception was presumably Lothar, who died in December 1137.

p. 332, l. 6] Peter the Venerable visited Rome during the first year of the pontificate of Eugene III and was there from before Advent in 1145 until perhaps as late as 15 February 1146.

p. 332, l. 9] The poverty of Cluny was Peter the Venerable's second reason for desiring to see Roger, and his principal reason for writing this letter.

p. 332, l. 12] On the sacristan Ademar (Aimarus), see Appendix R on functionaries at Cluny.

132

AD CARTVSIENSES

S 107; C V,35; Bc IV,38; cf. Pignot, *Cluny*, III, 272 (1137/43).

The prior of La Chartreuse to whom this letter was addressed was probably Antelmus, who became bishop of Belley in 1151, and not his successor Basil (on whom see biographical note to Ep. 186), as suggested by Duchesne, in *Bibl. Clun., notae*, col. 149.

p. 334] This is the only evidence known to me of the system instituted by Abbot Hugh at Cluny of requiring a gage for books on loan, but the system was used in various other monasteries: see *The Observances in Use at the Augustinian Priory of Barnwell, Cambridgeshire*, ed. John W. Clark (Cambridge, Eng., 1897) p. 63; John W. Clark, *The Care of Books* (Cambridge, Eng., 1901) pp. 68–69 and 74–75; and Lesne, *Prop. ecc.*, IV, 799. On the literary intercourse between Cluny and La Chartreuse during the abbacy of Peter the Venerable, see Ep. 24, n. to p. 47, l. 16.

133

AD FRATRES CLVNIACENSIS CONSOLATORIA PRO MORTALITATE

S 108; C V,36; Bc IV,39; cf. Mabillon, *Annales*, VI, 320-321 (1141); Bréquigny, *Chartes*, III, 58 (1141); Pignot, *Cluny*, III, 310-312 (1144/5).

Early 1146 (?). The date of this letter is not certain. The epidemic and consequent deaths at Cluny to which it refers may be the same as the "funera frequentia" mentioned in Letter 128, and the letter was consequently dated 1141 by Mabillon. But at that time Peter the Venerable was on a retreat in the woods near Cluny, whereas in this letter he says that he would have returned to Cluny had he not been required to visit the pope. Which visit is not known, but it may be his first to Eugene III, in 1145-6. He was probably writing from Rome, or at least from Italy, early in 1146. This dating is supported by the position of the letter in the collection and by Letter 134, which seems to relate to the same tragedy and which was written after Theobald became bishop of Paris in 1144.

134

AD THEOBALDVM PARISIVS EPISCOPVM

S 109; C V,37; Bc IV,40; cf. Bréquigny, *Chartes*, III, 69 (1142); Pignot, *Cluny*, III, 312 (1144/5).

Theobald, the former prior of St.-Martin-des-Champs, became bishop of Paris in 1144: Gams, *Series*, p. 596; Pacaut, *Élections*, p. 151; but he continued to administer St. Martin during the first year of his pontificate, according to Depoin, in *St. Martin des Champs*, II, 142, n. 237; cf. biographical note to Ep. 135.

1146 (?). This letter was certainly written after 1144 and probably after Peter the Venerable's return to Cluny from Rome in 1146, if it relates to the same tragedy as Letter 133.

135

AD ODONEM PRIOREM ET FRATRES SANCTI MARTINI DE CAMPIS

S 110; C V,38; Bc IV,41; cf. Mabillon, *Annales*, VI, 345 (1144); Bréquigny, *Chartes*, III, 91 (1144); Pignot, *Cluny*, III, 312 and 451-454; *St. Martin des Champs*, II, 180-182, no. 299 (August 1147).

On Prior Odo of St.-Martin-des-Champs, see Duchesne, in *Bibl. Clun.*, *notae*, cols. 108–109; Marrier, *Hist. S. Martini*, pp. 176–185; and *GC*, VII, 522–523. He began life as a monk at St. Martin and appeared as subprior in 1133, when Theobald was prior (Luchaire, *Louis VI*, p. 239, no. 523), as *custos ordinis* in 1134 (*St. Martin des Champs*, II, 19–21, no. 205), and again as subprior on three charters of 1140/1, where he was associated with such important figures as Suger, Bernard of Clairvaux, and the bishops of Paris and Auxerre (see Appendix O on Hugh of Crécy, nn. 9–11). In 1141 he was apparently elected abbot of Marchiennes, since the author of the *Vita Hugonis abbatis Marchianensis* described the new abbot as "dominus Odo de S. Martino in Campis" (*Thes. nov.*, III, 1725, and *GC*, III, 396). This may be an error or refer to another Odo of St.-Martin-des-Champs, but the absence from St. Martin of the former subprior Odo is confirmed by the appearance of a subprior named Peter on a document of 1141/3 (*St. Martin des Champs*, II, 124–127, no. 264). According to the *Vita*, however, he stayed at Marchiennes "scarcely two years" and then deserted his position and returned to St. Martin, where he became prior when Theobald was elected bishop of Paris. The exact dates of Odo's priorate are uncertain. It was dated 1143–50 "environ" by De Lasteyrie, in *Paris*, p. 297, n. 1, but Depoin was of the opinion that Theobald continued to administer St. Martin for some time after he became bishop and that the earliest charters on which Odo appeared as prior should be dated from 1144: *St. Martin des Champs*, II, 142, n. 237. The first known dated charter with Odo as prior is dated 20 September 1144: *Paris*, p. 293, no. 314; *St. Martin des Champs*, II, 144–145, no. 278. He in any case proved to be an ineffective prior, and in the winter of 1150 Peter the Venerable wrote to Suger that he had been forced to replace Odo by the subprior Simon: *Bibl. Clun.*, col. 960; Duchesne, *Scriptores*, IV, 533; Marrier, *Hist. S. Martini*, p. 189; *St. Martin des Champs*, II, 211–212, no. 320; cf. Suger, *Oeuvres*, p. 300 (1148/9), and Cartellieri, *Suger*, p. 159, no. 272 (1149/50). It may be to this deposition that the author of the *Vita* referred when he cryptically remarked, after mentioning Odo's departure from Marchiennes and return to St. Martin, "nec impune ferens, quoniam nec longo tempore tenuit, et ne dominaretur demum vale fecit invitus." His death was commemorated at St.-Martin-des-Champs on 30 June: *Obituaires*, I, 444.

August/September 1147/50.

p. 340] This letter seems to refer to the death of Hugh of Crécy, who died on 31 July 1147/50: see Appendix O. His death was probably not part of the general epidemic and tragedy at Cluny mentioned in Letters 133-134, as was supposed by Pignot, *Cluny*, III, 312.

136

AD ABBATEM DE RVPIBVS CONSOLATORIA PRO MORTIS FRATRIS SVI

S 111; C V,39; Bc IV,42; cf. Mabillon, *Annales*, VI, 345 (1144); Bréquigny, *Chartes*, III, 91 (1144).

The abbot of the Cistercian abbey of Les Roches, and the brother, according to the heading of this letter, of the young man John whose death Peter the Venerable announces here, was Geoffrey, a member of the influential family of Toucy, which rose into prominence in the late eleventh and early twelfth centuries: see Eugène Jarry, *Formation territoriale de la Bourgogne* (Paris, 1948) pp. 266-267. He appears on charters from 1138 until 1152 and was probably abbot of Les Roches from its foundation in 1137: *GC*, XII, 467-468, and Janauschek, *Origines*, p. 45. Iterius of Toucy referred to him as a nephew on a charter of 1147 (*Yonne*, I, 419-420), and he witnessed many charters with members of his family. Antoine Lesire, "Notes et documents pour servir à l'histoire de Toucy," *Bulletin de la Société des sciences historiques et naturelles de l'Yonne*, LXI (1907) 358-363, lists Norgaud I (1097-1120) and Iterius IV (1120-115...) as lords of Toucy during the first half of the twelfth century, but the genealogy of the whole family is far from clear. Norgaud, his wife Ermengard, his son Iterius, his daughters Beatrice and Adeline, and "other children" appear on several charters for the abbey of Molesme in the early twelfth century: *Molesme*, II, 63-65 and 136-137, nos. 1.53-54 and 139. Iterius appears with his mother Ermengard and brother Stephen on a charter of 1134 (*Yonne*, I, 301), and Stephen, "brother of Iterius of Toucy," witnessed a charter for Les Écharlis in 1120/39 (*ibid*., p. 241). He was probably the Stephen of Toucy who became a monk at Clairvaux and later abbot of Fontemoy (see the charter of 1134 cited above) and abbot of Rigny (*GC*, XII, 460-461; *Yonne*, I, 300; Janauschek, *Origines*, p. 15). Another prominent ecclesiastic who may have belonged to the family of Toucy was Bishop Norgaud of Autun (1098-1112), who was an early benefactor of Cîteaux (*GC*, IV, 384-389, and *Cîteaux*, pp. 58-59, no. 37). Iterius and Stephen also had brothers named Hugh and Norgaud, according to Lesire; but it is impossible to establish the proper place on the family tree of Geoffrey of Les Roches and his brother John.

May/June 1137/56. This letter was written after 15 May, since Peter refers to the ides of May as recent, but the year is unknown.

p. 341] This young man, John of Toucy, was evidently the abbot or prior of a Cluniac house, since Peter the Venerable refers to him as "frater noster, filius noster," and this house was not far from Cluny, since Peter was able to visit him in spite of his own ill-health and the press of Easter business. I have been unable to identify him further, however.

137

AD GAVFREDVM CARNOTENSEM EPISCOPVM

C V,40; Bc IV,43.

Geoffrey of Chartres was bishop from 1115 until 1148: Clerval, *Écoles* (cited Ep. 96, n. to p. 256), pp. 153–155. According to Gams, *Series*, p. 536, however, he died on 24 January 1149.

1135/48.

p. 343] On the Council of Pisa in 1135, see Ep. 27, n. to p. 51, l. 10.

p. 344] The priory of the Holy Sepulchre at Châteaudun was a dependency of Nogent-le-Rotrou: see Duchesne, in *Bibl. Clun.*, *notae*, col. 149; H. de Souancé and C. Métais, *Saint-Denis de Nogent-le-Rotrou, 1031–1789: Histoire et Cartulaire* (Archives du diocèse de Chartres, 1; Vannes, 1899) pp. cviii–cxvi, dating Bishop Geoffrey's grant of independence *ca.* 1130 and translating this letter (pp. cxi–cxiii); and Beaunier-Besse, *Abbayes*, I, 265. The affair mentioned here was finally settled by Bishop William of Chartres in 1166.

138

AD PETRVM ABBATEM SANCTI AVGVSTINI LEMOVICENSIS

S 112; C V,41; Bc V,1; cf. Duchesne, in *Bibl. Clun.*, *notae*, cols. 149–150; Bréquigny, *Chartes*, III, 58 (1141); Pignot, *Cluny*, III, 434–435.

Peter of Barri was abbot of St. Augustine at Limoges from at least 1145. His predecessor Philip still appears in 1137 and may have lived until 1140. Peter became abbot of St. Martial in 1161 and held both abbeys until his death in 1174. See *GC*, II, 577–578 (citing this letter), and De Lasteyrie, *St. Martial*, pp. 100–103.

1137/56.

139

AD STEPHANVM OLIM ARCHIEPISCOPVM VIENNENSIS

C V,42; Bc V,2; cf. Chevalier, *Régeste*, no. 3806 (before 22 February 1148).

Stephen of Charolais was a canon of St. Rufus near Avignon and archbishop of Vienne from 1129 until about 1145, when he resigned or, rather, was deposed, since this letter shows that he appealed his case to Rome: see Chevalier, *Bio-bib.*, I, 1391, citing *RHGF*, XV, introd., p. x, and *Hist. litt.*, XIII, 328–331; Gams, *Series*, p. 655; Janssen, *Legaten*, pp. 43 (n. 29), 161, and 181. According to Beyssac, *Chanoines*, p. 29, he may have been the Stephen who was dean of Lyons in 1128. After his deposition, he wandered from one place to another, principally his old abbey of St. Rufus and its dependencies, and Peter the Venerable in this letter urged him to settle down at Cluny. The terms of the letter, and especially the double reference to Cluny as "your," imply that Stephen may have been a Cluniac at one time, but this is not certain.

1148 (before 21 February). The reference to the Council of Rheims dates this letter 1148, and the request to visit Cluny before Quinquagesima Sunday shows it was written before 21 February.

p. 347] This certainly refers to the Council of Rheims, which opened 21 March 1148 and which Peter the Venerable is known to have attended.

140

AD STEPHANVM NOBILEM VIRVM ARVERNIAE

S 113; C V,43; Bc V,3; cf. Pignot, *Cluny*, III, 441.

The Stephen to whom this letter was addressed came from a castle in Auvergne, but there is no place simply named "Castellum" (Châtel or Château) in the *Dictionnaire topographique de la Haute-Loire*. He had made his vow to become a monk to St. Hugh, and the reference to Peter the Venerable's father suggests that he may have been a family friend. A "Stephanus de Castello" appears with Peter's mother and father on an undated charter in *Sauxillanges*, no. 796. He also appears on *Sauxillanges*, no. 906, and he may be the same as the "Stephanus de Castello Richardo" on no. 784. A "Stephanus de Castello" also witnessed an agreement between Peter the Venerable and the count of Auvergne which was arranged at Cluny in 1145/56: *Bibl. Clun.*, cols. 1411–1412; Gomot, *Mozat*, pp. 248–249 (1147); Chaix de Lavarène, "Bullaire," pp. 581–583 (1147); *Cluny*, V, 456, no. 4108 (1145/58).

The date of this letter is uncertain, but the reference to modern men fleeing the jaws of Satan and seeking the kingdom of Heaven "either by the journey to Jerusalem or by varied and sudden conversion to God" suggests that it may have been written about the time of the Second Crusade (1146-7). This may simply mean pilgrimage in a general sense, however.

141

AD PAPAM EVGENIVM

C V,44; Bc V,4; cf. Duchesne, in *Bibl. Clun.*, *notae*, col. 151; Mabillon, *Annales*, VI, 426–427 (1149); Devic and Vaissete, *Languedoc*, II, 462–463; Pignot, *Cluny*, III, 351–353; Chaix de Lavarène, "Bullaire," pp. 573–576 (1148).

Autumn 1149. The first hearing of this case, after which Abbot Jordan of Chaise-Dieu appealed to Rome, apparently occurred at Nîmes in the autumn of 1149, and Peter the Venerable wrote this letter soon after.

p. 348, l. 4] Raymond of Montredon was archbishop of Arles from 1142 until probably 1160: *GC*, I, 560–561 (1142–55); Gams, *Series*, p. 494 (1142–56); *GC nov.*, III, 212–235 (1142–60, citing this letter).

p. 348, l. 5] Bishop William of Viviers appears from 1146 until 1154: *GC*, XVI, 556–557, and Gams, *Series*, p. 656.

p. 348, l. 5] The priory of St. Baudilus of Nîmes, which was founded before 720, was restored in 1084 and subjected to La Chaise-Dieu: see Devic and Vaissete, *Languedoc* (new ed.), V, 835–836; Cottineau, *Répertoire*, II, 2075; Gaussin, *La Chaise-Dieu*, pp. 144, 157, and 268–270.

p. 348, l. 6] Adalbert of Usèz (Posquières) was bishop of Nîmes from 1141 until at least 1180: *GC*, VI, 441–443; *Hist. litt.*, XIV, 623–624; Devic and Vaissete, *Languedoc* (new ed.), V, 277–278; Gams, *Series*, p. 587; Chevalier, *Bio-bib.*, I, 30.

p. 348, l. 6] The abbot of La Chaise-Dieu (cf. *GC*, II, 327–351; Beaunier-Besse, *Abbayes*, V, 100–103; and Gaussin, *La Chaise-Dieu*) at this time was Peter the Venerable's brother Jordan: see Appendix A.

p. 348, l. 10] The papal bulls in this case were examined by Chaix de Lavarène, "Bullaire," pp. 67-71. Eugene III issued two bulls on 12 March 1150 (dated 12 March 1149 by Chaix de Lavarène): one specifically confirming the agreement between La Chaise-Dieu and the Bishop of Nîmes (cf. Mabillon, *Annales*, VI, 427, and JL 9373), the other confirming generally the privileges and possessions of La Chaise-Dieu, including the priory of St. Baudilus at Nîmes (*PU in Frankreich*, VI, 47-50, no. 18; not in JL). Eugene's previous letters dealing with this case, including the one referred to here by Peter the Venerable, appear to be lost.

142

AD PAPAM EVGENIVM

S 114; C V,45; Bc V,5; cf. *RHGF*, XV, 646-647 (1148/9); Pignot, *Cluny*, III, 349-350. On the disputed election at Angoulême in 1148/9, for which this letter is an important source, see J. Ramackers, "Sur l'histoire de l'élection de l'évêque Hugues d'Angoulême (1149)," *Moyen Âge*, XLVI (1936) 244-248, who associated this letter with that published by André Wilmart, *Analecta reginensia* (Studi e testi, 59; Vatican City, 1933) pp. 249-251, and who dated Hugh's election shortly before the death of his predecessor Lambert on 29 May 1149; cf. also Pacaut, *Élections*, pp. 45 (n. 1), 126, and 150, who dated Hugh's pontificate from both 1148 and 1149. The new bishop was a pupil of Gilbert de la Porrée: see *Historia pontificum et comitum Engolismensium*, XXXVIII, ed. Jacques Boussard (Bibliothèque Elzévirienne; Paris, 1957) p. 44.

1149. This letter was written after the election and before the consecration of Bishop Hugh, which must have followed his predecessor Lambert's death.

p. 351] The archbishop of Bordeaux, whom Peter the Venerable here accused of trying to subjugate the church of Angoulême, as he had that of Saintes, was his old friend Geoffrey of Le Loroux, on whom see Ep. 1, n. to p. 4, l. 1. Peter clearly disagreed with Geoffrey's policy on this occasion, but his remark at the end of the letter that "I do not sufficiently love that man, as you know," presumably means that the Pope was aware that Peter loved Geoffrey too well knowingly to bring a false charge against him.

143

AD HVMBERTVM ARCHIDIACONVM EDVENSEM

S 115; C V,46; Bc V,6; cf. Samuel Guichenon, *Histoire de Bresse et de*

Bugey (Lyons, 1650) I, 48; Bréquigny, *Chartes*, III, 48 (1140); Pignot, *Cluny*, III, 439.

Humbert of Baugé, archdeacon of Autun, was elected bishop of Autun in 1140, following the short-lived Bishop Robert, and was confirmed by Pope Innocent II in a bull dated 21 January 1141 (JL 8124). He was elevated to the see of Lyons in 1148 and resigned in 1153 to become a Carthusian: cf. *GC*, IV, 120–121, and Constable, "Cluniac Tithes," pp. 620–621.

1140 (?). This letter was probably written after the death of Bishop Stephen of Autun, during the short pontificate of his successor Robert.

p. 353] Stephen of Baugé (who was probably Humbert's uncle) was bishop of Autun from 1112 until 1138/9, when he retired to Cluny and apparently died soon after: cf. Constable, "Langres," p. 139, n. 99. His death was commemorated on 24 May at Nevers and on 30/31 May at Lyons: *Obituaires*, III, 465, and V, 81, 234, and 249.

144

AD THEOBALDVM ABBATEM MONASTERII SANCTAE COLVMBAE IN SVBVRBIO SENONENSI

C VI,1; Bc V,7; cf. *GC*, XII, 150 (1147); Pignot, *Cluny*, III, 338.

Abbot Theobald of St. Columba at Sens, who subscribed to a charter of Bishop Hato of Troyes for Cluny in 1145 (*Bibl. Clun.*, notae, col. 105), took the cross at Vézelay in 1146 (*Petrus Ven.*, p. 150, citing the *Gesta Ludovici VII*, in *RHGF*, XII, 200) and died in Asia Minor on 7 April 1147/8: see *GC*, XII, 149–150; Louis Brullée, *Histoire de l'abbaye royale de Sainte-Colombe-lez-Sens* (Paris, 1852) pp. 109 and 278–279; *Obituaires*, I.1, 16 (St. Columba at Sens), 433 (St.-Martin-des-Champs), and 522 (Longpont).

1146 (after the council at Vézelay).

p. 354, l. 23] The desire of the abbey of St. Columba to adopt Cluniac customs by instruction from some monks of La Charité, without formally subjecting itself to Cluny, is further evidence of the high prestige of Cluny at Sens: cf. Constable, in *Petrus Ven.*, pp. 38–52.

p. 354, l. 26] On the theological section that follows, and on Peter the Venerable's view of the reiterability of sacraments, see Duchesne, in

Bibl. Clun., notae, col. 152; Séjourné, in *DThC,* XII.2, 2072; Leclercq, *Pierre le Vén.,* pp. 222-223; H. Rochais, "Textes anciens sur la discipline monastique," *Revue Mabillon,* XLIII (1953) 44; and Jean Lebourlier, "Un témoin dans l'élaboration de la liste des sacrements," *Recherches de théologie ancienne et médiévale,* XXI (1954) 136, n. 42.

p. 358] This passage shows that for Peter the Venerable the crusade was above all a pilgrimage. Only the later reference to possible spoils from a conquered foe show that it was also a warlike expedition. On Peter's attitude toward pilgrimages by monks, see the text and notes of Letters 51, 80, and 83.

p. 359] On the privileges granted to crusaders in Eugene III's bull *Quantum predecessores,* see Constable, "Second Crusade," pp. 247-253.

145

AD BERNARDVM CLARAEVALLIS ABBATEM

S 117; Cl fol. 28^r; C VI,2; Bc V,8; cf. Manrique, *Ann. Cist.,* II, 165 (1150); Mabillon, note to Bernard, ep. 307 (Gaume ed., I.1, 936-937); *GC,* IX, 723-724 (1149); Bréquigny, *Chartes,* III, 164 (1149); *RHGF,* XV, 647-648 (1149); Lorain, *Cluny,* pp. 485-486; Pignot, *Cluny,* III, 478-479; Vacandard, *St. Bernard,* II, 476. This was apparently the letter shown to the archbishops and bishops of France (see Ep. 153 below), which influenced them in favor of Henry of France.

Autumn 1149.

p. 360, l. 2] On the election of Henry of France as bishop of Beauvais, upon which the dating of this letter and of Letters 146-153 depends, see Duchesne, in *Bibl. Clun., notae,* 152-153; *GC,* IX, 723-724 (1149); L.-H. Labande, *Histoire de Beauvais et de ses institutions communales* (Paris, 1892) p. 63 (1149); Vacandard, *St. Bernard,* II, 476 (end of summer, 1149); Rassow, "Kanzlei," p. 281, n. 8 (the best discussion, dating the election in the autumn of 1149); and Pacaut, *Élections,* p. 137, n. 1 (1149). On Henry himself, who was the brother of King Louis VII of France, see the bibliographies in Chevalier, *Bio-bib.,* I, 2081, and Marvin Colker, "Anecdota mediaevalia," *Traditio,* XVII (1961) 479. At the time of his election as bishop of Beauvais, Henry was a monk at Clairvaux, where he had gone either in 1146, according to the traditional dating (cf. Luchaire, *Louis VII,* p. 162, no. 197, n. 1), or in 1147, according to Mahn, *Ordre cist.,* p. 143; Marcel Pacaut, *Alexandre III*

(Paris, 1956) p. 59, n. 2; and Colker, in *Traditio*, XVII, 479. Both Pacaut and Colker said that nothing was known about Henry's life before he became a Cistercian monk; but in fact he held a variety of positions for twenty years before he entered Clairvaux. As early as 1125 he was abbot of the royal monasteries of Notre-Dame at Poissy and St. Mellon at Pontoise (Luchaire, *Louis VI*, pp. 166–167 and 250, nos. 363 and 549; cf. Fourier Bonnard, *St. Victor*, I, 20–21), and he appeared as abbot of St. Denis de la Châtre in 1138 (*St. Martin des Champs*, II, 94–99, no. 242; cf. Luchaire, *Louis VII*, pp. 102–103, no. 14), of St. Spire at Corbeil in 1137/40 (*Cartulaire de Saint-Spire de Corbeil*, ed. E. Coüard-Luys [Mémoires et documents publiés par la Société archéologique de Rambouillet, 6; Rambouillet, 1882] introd., pp. xxi–xxii, and pp. 15–19, no. 10, and Luchaire, *Louis VII*, p. 121, no. 68), and of Notre-Dame at Étampes, another royal monastery, in 1142/3 (*St. Martin des Champs*, II, 131–132, no. 266; cf. Luchaire, *Louis VII*, pp. 130–131, no. 95). At the same time, he was treasurer of St. Martin at Tours (*Layettes du trésor des chartes*, ed. A. Teulet and J. de Laborde [Paris, 1863 ff.] I, 53, no. 75; cf. Luchaire, *Louis VII*, pp. 123–124 and 137, nos. 75 and 117, and Fourier Bonnard, *St. Victor*, I, 25, n. 4, citing Henry's seal in 1146 with the legend "Henricus filius regis sancti Martini archiclavis"), archdeacon of Beauce in the diocese of Orléans (A. de Foulques de Villaret, *Recherches historiques sur l'ancien chapitre de l'église d'Orléans* [Orléans, 1882] pp. 32 and 163, and Mahn, *Ordre cist.*, p. 143), and perhaps also an archdeacon of Notre-Dame at Paris (Luchaire, *Louis VII*, p. 162, no. 197). He described himself in a charter dated *ca.* 1140 by Tardif as "by the grace of God treasurer (*archiclauis*) of St. Martin at Tours and abbot of various royal churches, that is of Our Lady at Étampes, of Our Lady at Corbeil, of Our Lady at Mantes, of Our Lady at Poissy, [and] of St. Mellon at Pontoise": Jules Tardif, *Monuments historiques* (Paris, 1866) pp. 248–249, no. 450. Henry's brother Philip, in a later letter, described himself as abbot of the same five royal churches and mentioned Henry, "who was abbot of these same churches before me": *Ampl. Coll.*, VI, 228–229. In a charter of 1146 Henry called himself "abbas regalium abbatiarum" (*Saint-Spire de Corbeil*, pp. 39–40, no. 25), and the same phrase was applied to him in a charter of Louis VII in March/July 1146 (*ibid.*, pp. 40–41, no. 26; cf. Luchaire, *Louis VII*, p. 152, no. 166, and Fourier Bonnard, *St. Victor*, I, 25–26). This is the last known dated reference to Henry before he gave up his multiple benefices and entered Clairvaux. On his conversion, see the *Vita prima* of St. Bernard, book IV by Geoffrey of Auxerre, III, 15 (Gaume ed., II.6, 2223–2224) and Caesarius of Heisterbach, *Dialogus miraculorum*, I, 19, trans. H. v. E. Scott and C. C. Swinton Bland (Broadway Medieval Library; London, 1929) I, 27–28.

p. 360, l. 19] This letter from Eugene III to the archbishop of Rheims is apparently lost.

146

EPISTOLA HENRICI FRATRIS REGIS, EX MONACHO IN EPISCOPVM ELECTI

S 118; Cl fol. 29ʳ; C VI,3; Bc V,9; cf. Manrique, *Ann. Cist.*, II, 165–166 (1150); Mabillon, note to Bernard, ep. 307 (Gaume ed., I.1, 936–937); Bréquigny, *Chartes*, III, 163 (1149); GC, IX, 724–725; *RHGF*, XV, 648 (1149); Pignot, *Cluny*, III, 478–479; note to Ep. 145.

1149. This letter was clearly written after Letter 145 reached Clairvaux, probably late in 1149.

147

AD ADEMARVM

S 116; C V,48 [*pro* 47]; Bc VI,1.

Ademar II is the only abbot of Figeac between 1119 and 1180 mentioned in the GC, I, 174, where he is dated *ca.* 1140. Eugene III addressed a bull to him in January 1147 (JL 8994).

This letter was written toward the end of the year, since Peter the Venerable urged Ademar to visit Cluny at Christmas or Advent, but the year is unknown.

148

EPISTOLA BERNARDI ABBATIS CLARAEVALLIS AD DOMINVM ABBATEM

S 119; Cl fol. 30ʳ; C VI,4; Bc VI,2; Bern. ep. 387; cf. Mabillon, notes to Bernard, ep. 387 (Gaume ed., I.1, 694–695 and 948) (1150); Bréquigny, *Chartes*, III, 180 (1150); Maitland, *Dark Ages*, pp. 439–440; *Letters of St. Bernard*, pp. 378–379, no. 308.

June/July 1149. The date of this letter can be established by working backward from Letter 149 (Peter the Venerable's reply) and Letter 152 (Bernard's reply to Letter 149).

p. 363, l. 13] No surviving letter of Bernard of Clairvaux fits this description, according to Mabillon.

p. 363, l. 17] On this important passage, see the note of Mabillon; Jean Leclercq, "Saint Bernard et ses secrétaires," in *Recueil*, pp. 6–7; and p. 19 above, and Appendix P.

149
RESCRIPTVM DOMINI ABBATIS AD IPSVM

S 120; Cl fol. 30ᵛ; C VI,5; Bc VI,3; cf. Bernard, ep. 388 (Gaume ed., I.1, 695–698: "circa annum 1150"); Bréquigny, *Chartes*, III, 164 (1149); Maitland, *Dark Ages*, pp. 440–442; Lorain, *Cluny*, pp. 496–500; Pignot, *Cluny*, III, 479–482; Le Couteulx, *Ann. Carth.*, II, 88 (1149); Vacandard, *St. Bernard*, II, 490, n. 2 (1149); Chevalier, *Régeste*, no. 3836 (1150); *Cîteaux*, p. 115, no. 133 (1149). This letter is an elaborate reply, with extensive quotations, to Letter 148 from Bernard of Clairvaux.

September 1149. Bernard's reply, Letter 152, can be dated October (?) 1149 and shows that this letter was written before the meeting of the Cistercian chapter general in that year.

p. 364] On Guigo of La Chartreuse and the passage quoted here by Peter the Venerable, see Epp. 24–25.

p. 365] Nothing more is known about this affair of "a certain English abbot."

p. 366, l. 11] The earliest reference to Baro seems to be his promotion to subdeacon in 1118, during the pontificate of Gelasius II, in the *Liber pontificalis*, ed. Louis Duchesne (Paris, 1955–1957) II, 315. He subscribed to a document dated 22 April 1138 as "Baro sacri palatii subdiaconus et prior scolae Crucis ss.": *Acta pontificum Romanorum inedita*, ed. J. von Pflugk-Harttung (Tübingen-Stuttgart, 1880–1888) II, 295 (JL 7890); and he acted as datary for a number of papal documents issued from 1141–6: see JL, II, 7 and 21, and Bresslau, *Urkundenlehre*, I, 246. On his will, see Mabillon's note to Bernard, ep. 388 (Gaume ed., I.1, 927), and the works cited above.

p. 366, l. 26] Bishop Hugh II of Grenoble became archbishop of Vienne in 1148 (see biographical note to Ep. 154). He was succeeded at Grenoble by the Carthusian Othmar, whose exact dates are not known. Yet another Carthusian, Geoffrey, was bishop from at least 1151: see GC, XVI, 237–239; *La Grande Chartreuse*, pp. 56, n. 5, and 62, n. 9. Bernard of Clairvaux in his ep. 270, written early in 1151 (Vacandard, *St. Bernard*, II, 498, n. 2), said that "Carthusienses turbati sunt," and

Mabillon in his note to this letter dated the dispute at Grenoble in 1150-1 (Gaume ed., I.1, 921-922). The real causes of the trouble are not known. Only the divisions among the Carthusians themselves are mentioned by Bernard and Peter the Venerable, who gives in Letter 158 a vivid picture of the dilemma of would-be hermits who were increasingly forced to take an active part in the affairs of "this world."

p. 366, l. 34] Cf. the end of Letter 152. On the time of meeting of the Cistercian chapter general, see dating note to Ep. 35.

150

ITEM AD EVNDEM

S 121; Cl fol. 33^v; O fol. 120^v; C VI,6; Bc VI,4; cf. Manrique, *Ann. Cist.*, II, 160-162 (1150); Bréquigny, *Chartes*, III, 183 (1150); Lorain, *Cluny*, pp. 465-471; Pignot, *Cluny*, III, 482-485; Canivez, *Statuta*, I, 39 (1150).

Mid-October 1149. The association with Letter 152 dates this letter in 1149, and the need for speed in order to arrive at Clairvaux before the meeting on All Saints' Day (1 November) suggests mid-October.

p. 368] Peter the Venerable cited the same two passages in his discussion of black and white clothing in Letter 111.

p. 369] The date of this visit to Clairvaux is not known, but depending upon the interpretation of "nuper" it presumably took place in early or middle 1149.

p. 370] Cf. Peter the Venerable, *Statuta*, XXIII, excluding clerics and laymen from the cloister except when they had some work there or wished to see the buildings "as honest guests are wont to do."

p. 371] The meeting to which Peter refers here may be the Cistercian chapter general (which usually met, however, in September) or another meeting of Cistercian abbots. The fact that Bernard made no reference to Peter's request in Letter 152 (written *after* the chapter general of 1149) suggests either that Peter's letter arrived too late for consideration at the chapter general or that Peter had some other meeting in mind. No action, in any case, seems to have been taken by the Cistercians (cf. Pignot, *Cluny*, III, 485, n. 1). The statutes of 1152 and 1154/6 both included regulations concerning visitors (Canivez, *Statuta*, I, 45-49 and 56-59), but they do not correspond to Peter's requests.

151

AD NICHOLAVM MONACHVM

S 122; C VI,7; Bc VI,5; cf. Manrique, *Ann. Cist.*, II, 162 (1150); Bréquigny, *Chartes*, III, 183 (1150); Maitland, *Dark Ages*, p. 443; Pignot, *Cluny*, III, 484-485 and 490.

Mid-October 1149. The fact that Henry "the brother of the king" was still at Clairvaux dates this letter in 1149. The reference to the coming feast of All Saints (and the association with Letter 150) places it in mid-October.

p. 372, l. 14] This is certainly Letter 150, as the later reference to All Saints' Day shows.

p. 372, l. 19] See Ep. 150, n. to p. 371, and Appendix P on Nicholas of Montiéramey.

p. 372, l. 19] "The brother of the king" was Henry, bishop-elect of Beauvais, on whom see Ep. 145, n. to p. 360, l. 2.

p. 372, l. 20] Philip of Liège first appeared as prior of Clairvaux on a document of 1152, but the position of his name in this letter (after Henry of France but before the cellarer) suggests that he was already prior in 1149: see D'Arbois de Jubainville, *Études*, p. 188. He was identified by Mabillon and D'Arbois as the former Archbishop Philip of Taranto, on the basis of a list of the priors of Clairvaux printed in D'Arbois de Jubainville, *Études*, p. 357; but he was in fact the former Archdeacon Philip of Liège, to whom Nicholas of Montiéramey sent his ep. 33 (*PL*, CXCVI, 1623-1625) and who joined Bernard of Clairvaux while he was preaching the Second Crusade in Flanders in 1146: see Vacandard, *St. Bernard*, I, introd., p. xxxii, and II, 280, 347, and 381, and Rassow, "Kanzlei," p. 284. He had a hand in compiling the *Historia miraculorum in itinere Germanico patratorum*: see A. H. Bredero, *Études sur la "Vita prima" de Saint Bernard* (Rome, 1960) pp. 79-82, 84-85, 87-90. Cf. also Letters 182-183.

p. 372, l. 20] The cellarer Galcher of Clairvaux was a friend and correspondent of Nicholas of Montiéramey, who mentioned him in ep. 7, sent in 1145 to the prior and elders of Clairvaux, and sent him ep. 45: *PL*, CXCVI, 1602 and 1645-1646; *Clairvaux*, p. 52, no. 28 (charter of 1157); cf. Vacandard, *St. Bernard*, II, 385; *Bernard de Clairvaux*, p. 716; Ep. 184 below; and, on the position of cellarer at Clairvaux, D'Arbois de Jubainville, *Études*, pp. 227-231, who mentions a cellarer named Galcher on documents in 1162, 1164, 1171, and 1174 (p. 230). He should not be confused with his nephew, also named Galcher, who was first a Cluniac and then became a Cistercian. In May/June 1150 Bernard wrote to Peter the Venerable: "We furthermore recommend to Your Grace your Galcher, the nephew of our Galcher (who is indeed also yours) [and] a young man who loves you greatly just as if he were your disciple (*alumnus*)": Satabin, "Lettre," p. 323. In his ep. 267 Bernard wrote to Peter: "Your son brother Galcher has become ours as well;" and he asked Peter not to love him the less because he belonged to them both (Gaume ed., I.1, 549). Galcher the cellarer mentioned his nephew in a letter written for him by Nicholas: "My nephew Galcher is coming to you, who will represent me before you both in name and in blood" (*PL*, CXCVI, 1617 B).

p. 372, l. 21] "Our Garnerius" was probably the subprior Garnerius of Cluny, who became a Cistercian: see Ep. 79, n. to p. 214, l. 26, and Ep. 181, n. to p. 424, l. 16.

p. 372, l. 21] Fromont was the hospitaler at Clairvaux and the recipient of ep. 46 of Nicholas of Montiéramey, concerning the conversion of Nicholas to Clairvaux in 1145: *PL*, CXCVI, 1647-1648; Vacandard, *St. Bernard*, II, 385; and, on the office of hospitaler at Clairvaux, D'Arbois de Jubainville, *Études*, pp. 219-224.

152

EPISTOLA BERNARDI CLARAEVALLIS AD DOMINVM ABBATEM

S 123; Cl fol. 37^v; C VI,8; Bc VI,6; Bern. ep. 389; cf. Mabillon, note to Bernard, ep. 389 (Gaume ed., I.1, 699) (1150); Bréquigny, *Chartes*, III, 179 (1150); Maitland, *Dark Ages*, pp. 443-444; Le Couteulx, *Ann. Carth.*, II, 88 (1149); Vacandard, *St. Bernard*, II, 476, n. 1 (September 1149); Chevalier, *Régeste*, no. 3837 (1150); *Letters of St. Bernard*, pp. 379-380, no. 309.

October (?) 1149. The references to Henry of France and to the Cistercian chapter general date this letter after September 1149. The references to Baro's will, the Grenoble election, and the commemoration of Peter the Venerable in the chapter general at Cîteaux all show that this is Bernard's reply to Peter's Letter 149. The absence of any reference to Letters 150-151 suggests that it was written before these letters reached Clairvaux.

p. 373, l. 2] This may be the meeting on 1 November, presumably at Clairvaux, to which Peter the Venerable referred in Letters 150-151.

p. 373, l. 15] On Henry of France, the bishop-elect of Beauvais, see Ep. 145, n. to p. 360, l. 2.

153

EPISTOLA NICHOLAI MONACHI

S 124; C VI,9; Bc VI,7; cf. Nicholas of Montiéramey, ep. 54 (*PL*, CXCVI, 1650); Manrique, *Ann. Cist.*, II, 165 (1150); Bréquigny, *Chartes*, III, 182 (1150).

1149/50 (before 16 April). "This year" for Nicholas would have run from 3 April 1149 until 16 April 1150 by modern reckoning, since in the diocese of Langres the year was usually reckoned from Easter to Easter. This letter was written late in 1149 *vetus stilus*.

p. 373, l. 1] This shows that Nicholas was planning to visit Peter the Venerable early in 1150.

p. 373, l. 2] The later reference to two other letters suggests that "your letters" here refers to a collection of Peter's correspondence.

p. 373, l. 4] This sentence shows that the first part of *De consideratione* was completed in 1149: cf. Vacandard, *St. Bernard*, II, 436. The two letters "which you sent to the lord abbot and to me this year" were probably Letters 150-151.

p. 373, l. 8] On Henry of France, see Ep. 145, n. to p. 360, l. 2. The letter of Peter the Venerable that helped to promote Henry was probably Letter 145.

154

EPISTOLA PAPAE EVGENII AD HVGONEM

S 125; C VI,10; Bc VI,8; cf. JL 9666 (1147/53). Hugh of Vienne clearly sent this letter from the Pope to Peter the Venerable together with Letter 155.

The Carthusian Hugh was bishop of Grenoble from 1132 until 1148 and archbishop of Vienne from 1148 until 1153, when he retired to the Carthusian abbey of Portes, where he died in 1155: see Le Couteulx,

Ann. Carth., I, 344-345; Chevalier, *Bio-bib.*, I, 2205; *La Grande Chartreuse*, p. 56, n. 5.

1148/51. The date of this and the two following letters is not known. Chevalier, *Régeste*, nos. 3820-3821, placed them at the end of 1148, immediately after Hugh became archbishop of Vienne. The letters show, however, that he had been archbishop long enough for protests to accumulate from both Cluniacs and Cistercians, and the letter was probably written in 1149 or 1150. The terminal date of 1151 is established by the reference in Letter 158 to Letter 156 as "recently sent."

155

EPISTOLA HVGONIS ARCHIEPISCOPI AD DOMINVM ABBATEM

S 126; C VI,11; Bc VI,9; cf. Bréquigny, *Chartes*, III, 181 (1150). Hugh of Vienne sent this letter to Peter the Venerable together with Letter 154 which he had received from the Pope.

1148/51 (see dating note to Ep. 154).

156

EPISTOLA DOMINI ABBATIS AD PAPAM EVGENIVM

S 127; C VI,12; Bc VI,10; cf. Bréquigny, *Chartes*, III, 220 (1153); Bligny, *Église*, pp. 314 and 369. This letter defending Hugh of Vienne was sent to the Pope as a consequence of Letters 154-155.

1148/51 (see dating note to Ep. 154).

p. 375, l. 18] See Letter 154, the Pope's letter to Hugh of Vienne, which Peter the Venerable is citing here.

p. 375, l. 26] Peter the Venerable was with Eugene III at Auxerre on 23 August 1147, but the "Bar" mentioned here cannot be identified with certainty. It may be Bar-sur-Seine, Bar-sur-Aube, or Bar-le-Duc, any of which Eugene may have visited on his travels in 1147-8, especially on his way from Verdun to Troyes and back in November 1147 and February 1148 and on his way from Châlons to Clairvaux in April 1148, when he presumably passed through Bar-sur-Aube. He was also in Bar-sur-Aube on 27 July 1147: *PU in den Niederlanden*, p. 186, no. 64; Gleber, *Eugen III*, p. 197, no. 113; and I am inclined to think that Peter the Venerable was with him then, immediately before going on to Auxerre.

157

AD EVNDEM EVGENIVM PAPAM

S 128; C VI,13; Bc VI,11; cf. Mabillon, *Annales*, VI, 426–427 (1149); Bréquigny, *Chartes*, III, 140 (1147) and 221 (1153); Pignot, *Cluny*, III, 353; Chaix de Lavarène, "Bullaire," p. 576 (1148); Gaussin, *La Chaise-Dieu*, p. 158.

1150/3. This letter was probably written between the settlement of the case between La Chaise-Dieu and the Bishop of Nîmes (see n. to p. 376, l. 10, below) and the death of Pope Eugene III.

p. 376, l. 4] On Peter the Venerable's brother Jordan, abbot of La Chaise-Dieu, see Appendix A.

p. 376, l. 10] In view of this specific statement, it is improbable that this visit was associated with the dispute between La Chaise-Dieu and the Bishop of Nîmes (see Ep. 141), although the Pope's possible displeasure with Jordan, to which Peter refers later in the letter, may have arisen out of this case.

158

AD QVEM SVPRA

S 129; C VI,14; Bc VI,12; cf. Maitland, *Dark Ages*, pp. 412–415; Pignot, *Cluny*, III, 273; Le Couteulx, *Ann. Carth.*, II, 84–87 (1149); Chevalier, *Régeste*, no. 3833 (1150); Martin, *Conciles*, no. 573 (1149); and Ep. 149, n. to p. 366, l. 26, on the disputed election at Grenoble in 1149/51.

1149/51.

p. 378, l. 3] Peter the Venerable had had ample opportunity to observe the Carthusians while he was prior of Domène, before he became abbot of Cluny, and he maintained close relations with them for many years (see Ep. 24).

p. 378, l. 27] Ep. 156.

p. 378, l. 34] La Grande Chartreuse, Ecouges, Durbon, Portes, Meyriat, Silve-Bénite, and Arvières.

p. 379] On Arnold, Peter the Venerable's chaplain at this time, see Appendix R on functionaries at Cluny.

158a and b

AD BARTHOLOMEVM MEDICVM
RESCRIPTVM BARTHOLOMEI MEDICI

S 130-131; cf. Quentin, in *Misc. Ehrle*, I, 83-86, whose edition of the text was based upon a transcription sent by a friend and includes several serious mistakes, and Appendices B and M on Peter the Venerable's health and on Dr. Bartholomew.

January 1151. The chronology of Peter the Venerable's illness at this time is reconstructed in Appendix B.

p. 380] These cases and conferences were probably routine business (cf. Ep. 176, n. to p. 417, l. 6), unless they were associated with the meeting of Cluniac priors on 7 May mentioned in Letters 163-166.

p. 381] Cf. the list of drugs and herbs in Loren C. MacKinney, *Early Medieval Medicine* (Publications of the Institute of the History of Medicine, The Johns Hopkins University, 3rd Series, 3; Baltimore, 1937) pp. 168-169.

p. 383] See Appendix M on this *Liber graduum*.

159

AD FRATRES LEMOVICENSES

S 132; C VI,15; Bc VI,13; cf. Mabillon, *Annales*, VI, 330-331 (1142); Bréquigny, *Chartes*, III, 69 (1142).

On the abbey of St. Martial at Limoges, see De Lasteyrie, *St. Martial*, esp. pp. 83-86 on its subjection to Cluny in 1062.

p. 384] There is no reference to Prior Ranulf either in the GC or in De Lasteyrie, *St. Martial*.

160

AD FRATREM SVVM EVSTACHIVM

S 133; C VI,16; Bc VI,14.

Eustace was the only brother of Peter the Venerable in secular life at the time this letter was written: see Appendix A.

This letter was written early in the year, since Peter urged Eustace to visit Cluny before Easter, but the year is unknown.

p. 386] Cf. the passage on dreams in the *De miraculis*, I, 8 (*Bibl. Clun.*, col. 1264 A).

161

AD PRIORES VEL SVBPRIORES LOCORVM CLVNIACENSIVM

S 134; C VI,17; Bc VI,15; cf. Mabillon, *Annales*, VI, 331 (1142); Bréquigny, *Chartes*, III, 69 (1142); *Hist. litt.*, XIII, 254 (1141); Pignot, *Cluny*, III, 378–379 (1150); Knowles, in *Historian and Character* (cited Ep. 2), p. 66; Leclercq, *Amour des lettres*, p. 129. On *pitantia*, which were additions to the monastic menu resulting from pious legacies (and a frequent cause of dietary irregularities), see Molinier, *Obituaires*, pp. 119–120, who cites this letter. This letter may have been written as a result of ep. 25 (II,1) of Peter of Celle, who criticized the Cluniacs for eating meat (*PL*, CCII, 430–431). It shows clearly both the efforts of Peter the Venerable to reform the Cluniacs and his moderate attitude towards reasonable departures from literal observance of the Rule.

1144/56. The only evidence for dating this letter is the reference to Letter 111, which was written in 1144.

p. 390] This passage refers to Letters 28 and 111. It shows that Peter the Venerable expected these letters to have circulated and to have been read widely.

162

AD REGEM SICILIAE

S 135; C VI,18; Bc VI,16; cf. Mabillon, *Annales*, VI, 482 (1152); Bréquigny, *Chartes*, III, 152 (1148); *RHGF*, XV, 653–654 (1150); Lorain, *Cluny*, pp. 396–397; Pignot, *Cluny*, III, 344–345; Bernhardi, *Konrad III*, p. 814; Caspar, *Roger II*, pp. 407–408 and 572 (1149/50); Chalandon, *Dom. normande*, II, 148–149, and *Comnène* (cited Ep. 75), II, 336–337; Constable "Second Crusade," p. 236; Lamma, *Comneni* (cited Ep. 75), I, 104–105; Berry, in *Petrus Ven.*, pp. 156–157; Wieruszowski, in *Speculum* (cited Ep. 90), XXXVIII, 74–75.

1148/52. Most of the authorities cited above dated this letter about 1150 and associated it with the plans for a new crusade in that year (cf. Letter 163). This date is supported by the position of the letter in the collection, but not by any specific evidence. The outside limits of its date are the deaths of Roger II's son Roger in 1148 and of Conrad III in February 1152.

p. 394, l. 3] Roger's son Tancred died in 1138/40, Alphonso, in 1144, and the eldest son, Roger, in 1148: see Chalandon, *Dom. normande*, II, 105-106.

p. 394, l. 11] On the hostility between Roger II and Conrad III, see Chalandon, *Dom. normande*, II, 122 ff., who said that "la destruction de la monarchie normande sera un des objectifs principaux de la politique impériale à l'extérieur; pour atteindre ce but, la diplomatie allemande cherchera à s'appuyer sur tous les ennemis du nouveau royaume" (p. 122).

p. 395] On the common impression in the West that the Greeks were responsible for the failure of the Second Crusade, see Constable, "Second Crusade," pp. 272-273, and Berry, in *Petrus Ven.*, pp. 155-157.

163
EPISTOLA CLARAEVALLIS ABBATIS AD DOMINVM ABBATEM

S 136; Cl fol. 38ʳ; C VI,19; Bc VI,17; Bern., ep. 364; cf. Duchesne, *Scriptores*, IV, 456-457; Manrique, *Ann. Cist.*, II, 29-30 (1146); Mabillon, notes to Bernard, ep. 364 (Gaume ed., I.1, 663 and 944-945) (1146); Bréquigny, *Chartes*, III, 118 (1146); *Letters of St. Bernard*, pp. 469-470, no. 498. The abbot of "Fontanel" brought this letter to Peter the Venerable, according to his reply (Letter 164).

March/April 1150. This and the three following letters were traditionally associated with the Second Crusade and consequently dated 1146 by most early authorities. They were in fact concerned with the effort to organize a new crusade in 1150: see M.-J.-J. Brial, "Mémoire sur la véritable époque d'une assemblée tenue à Chartres relativement à la croisade de Louis le Jeune," *Histoire et mémoires de l'Institut royal de France: Classe d'histoire et de littérature ancienne*, IV (1818) 508-529; Achille Luchaire, "Sur la chronologie des documents et des faits relatifs à l'histoire de Louis VII pendant l'année 1150," *Annales de la Faculté des Lettres de Bordeaux*, IV (1882) 302-303, and *Louis VII*, pp. 178-179; Bernhardi, *Konrad III*, pp. 813 ff.; Vacandard, *St. Bernard*, II,

427–432; Cartellieri, *Suger*, pp. 65–67; E. Pfeiffer, "Die Stellung des hl. Bernhard zur Kreuzzugsbewegung nach seinen Schriften," *Cistercienser-Chronik*, XLVI (1934) 305–307, and XLVII (1935) 149; Gleber, *Eugen III*, pp. 127–136; Berry, in *Petrus Ven.*, pp. 159–161.

p. 396] This meeting called at Chartres on 7 May establishes the *terminus ante quem* for this letter.

164

RESCRIPTVM DOMINI ABBATIS AD IPSVM

S 137; Cl fol. 39ʳ; C VI,20; Bc VI,18; cf. Manrique, *Ann. Cist.*, II, 30 (1146); *RHGF*, XV, 649–650 (1150); Lorain, *Cluny*, pp. 379–381; Pignot, *Cluny*, III, 323–324 (1146); Cartellieri, *Suger*, p. 161, no. 289 (1150). This is Peter the Venerable's reply to Letter 163 from Bernard of Clairvaux.

April 1150.

p. 397, l. 1] This refers to Letter 163.

p. 397, l. 5] Suger's letter to Peter the Venerable is Letter 165.

p. 398, l. 10] This general meeting at Cluny on 7 May 1150 is not mentioned by Besse, Anger, or De Valous (cf. Ep. 111, n. to p. 293). According to Berry, in *Petrus Ven.*, p. 159, its purpose was to discuss "the very important subject of reforms at Cluny." Cf. Luchaire, in *Annales... de Bordeaux*, IV, 297–298, who suggested that Hugh of Rouen attended the meeting.

p. 398, l. 11] This was presumably the Cluniac house of Fontanella in the diocese of Bergamo, but it may refer to St. Wandrille, which was also known as Fontanelle (Cottineau, *Répertoire*, II, 2921). Les Fontanelles in the diocese of Poitiers was founded in 1210, according to the *GC*, II, 1433.

p. 398, l. 22] Bernard wrote again to Peter the Venerable saying that a second meeting had been arranged on 15 July at Compiègne: see Satabin, "Lettre," pp. 322–323; *Letters of St. Bernard*, pp. 472–473, no. 400. It is not known, however, whether Peter was able to attend.

165

EPISTOLA SVGERI ABBATIS SANCTI DIONYSII AD DOMINVM ABBATEM

S 138; C VI,21; Bc VI,19; cf. Suger, ep. 18 (*Oeuvres*, pp. 268-269); Cartellieri, *Suger*, p. 161, no. 285 (1150).

March/April 1150 (see dating note to Ep. 163).

p. 398] Nur ed-Din defeated and killed Raymond of Antioch on 29 June 1149 and then ravaged northern Syria as far as the sea before advancing on Damascus early in 1150, about the time this letter was written: see W. B. Stevenson, *The Crusaders in the East* (Cambridge, Eng., 1907) pp. 165-167, and Runciman, *Crusades* (cited Ep. 44, n. to p. 141), II, 325-330.

p. 399, l. 3] On the council held at Chartres on 7 May 1150, see Ep. 163.

p. 399, l. 15] On Archbishop Humbert of Lyons, see biographical note to Ep. 143.

166

RESCRIPTVM DOMINI ABBATIS AD EVNDEM

S 139; C VI,22; Bc VI,20; cf. Duchesne, *Scriptores*, IV, 535; Bréquigny, *Chartes*, III, 120 (1146); *RHGF*, XV, 648-649 (1150); Lorain, *Cluny*, pp. 378-379; Suger, *Oeuvres*, p. 311 (1150); Cartellieri, *Suger*, p. 161, no. 286 (1150). This is Peter the Venerable's reply to Letter 165 from Suger: see Epp. 163, 164, and 165.

April 1150.

167

EPISTOLA HELOISAE ABBATISSAE AD DOMINVM ABBATEM

S 140; C VI,23; Bc VI,21; cf. Duchesne, in *Bibl. Clun.*, *notae*, cols. 154-155; Du Boulay, *Hist. univ. Paris.*, II, 211-212; Bréquigny, *Chartes*, III, 68 (1142); Lorain, *Cluny*, p. 426; Ep. 115 above.

1144/54. This letter can be dated with certainty only between the deaths of Abelard and of Peter the Venerable (1142/56), but see note below.

p. 400, l. 1] Peter the Venerable visited the abbey of the Paraclete on 16 November of the year preceding that in which Heloise wrote this letter. He apparently brought with him the body of Abelard for burial, and he celebrated Mass and preached in the chapter. The year of his visit is unknown, but in the period after the death of Abelard it could have been in 1144, 1146-9, or 1152-4 (see Appendix D). He was in the region of the abbey of the Paraclete in 1147, seeing Pope Eugene III, but he could scarcely have been carrying Abelard's body with him. According to the second recension of the chronicle of Richard of Poitiers, Abelard's body was translated "not many days" after his death, but the authority for this statement is not known: L. A. Muratori, *Antiquitates Italicae medii aevi* (Milan, 1738-1742) IV, 1098; cf. Berger, *Richard le Poitevin*, p. 82.

p. 400, l. 15] On trentals of masses for the dead, see Ep. 52, n. to p. 153, l. 13.

p. 401, l. 4] The text of this "open" absolution is given by Duchesne, in *Bibl. Clun., notae*, col. 155, from the obituary of the Paraclete, but it does not appear in *Obituaires*, IV, 387-430. Under 25 December, however, the obituary lists "Petrus, Cluniacensis abbas, cujus concessu habet ecclesia nostra corpus magistri nostri Petri" (*ibid.*, p. 429).

p. 401, l. 6] Astrolabe, the son of Heloise and Abelard, was born about 1118 and was therefore in his mid-twenties at the time of his father's death.

168

RESCRIPTVM DOMINI ABBATIS

S 141; C VI,24; Bc VI,22; cf. Du Boulay, *Hist. univ. Paris.*, II, 212; Bréquigny, *Chartes*, III, 69 (1142); and notes to Ep. 167, to which this is Peter the Venerable's reply.

1144/54 (see dating note to Ep. 167).

169

EPISTOLA PRIORIS MAIOREVI AD DOMINVM ABBATEM

S 142; C unnumbered (after VI,24); Bc VI,23; cf. Pignot, *Cluny*, III, 272; and notes to Ep. 24 on the literary exchanges between the Carthusians and Cluniacs during the abbacy of Peter the Venerable.

The H. in the heading, which is found in both S and C, was expanded to "humilis" in the Bc, but it stands for Humbertus, who was the only prior of Meyriat during the lifetime of Peter the Venerable whose name began with an "h." He succeeded Prior Stephen in 1154, according to Le Couteulx, *Ann. Carth.*, II, 154, and *La Grande Chartreuse*, pp. 55, n. 2, and 60, n. 4. But the death of Stephen cannot be dated with certainty—he had been prior since 1132—and Humbert's priorate may have begun before 1154.

1150/1 (?): see dating note to Ep. 170.

p. 402] This Peter Vivian, who is otherwise unknown, was evidently a Cluniac monk, but he was probably not at Cluny itself, since Peter the Venerable wrote in Letter 170 that he would see him "if God permits."

170

RESCRIPTVM DOMINI ABBATIS

S 143; C VI,25; Bc VI,24; cf. Pignot, *Cluny*, III, 272; and Ep. 169, to which this is Peter the Venerable's reply.

1150/1 (?). This and the preceding letter cannot be dated with certainty, but the references to Peter's health here closely resemble those in Letters 164 and 166, which were written in April 1150:

164	166	170
... ab ipso natali domini fere continuum corporis mei incommodum.	... multiplex incommodum corporis mei, quod a natali domini usque ad hoc tempus, pene assidue passus sum.	... corporis multiplex incommodum, quo plusquam per dimidium annum natura laborat.

This resemblance suggests that this letter and Letter 169 were written in 1150, or possibly in 1151, after the illness described in Letter 158a (see Appendices B and M on Peter the Venerable's health and Dr. Bartholomew). This dating is rather early for the priorate of Humbert of Meyriat (see biographical note to Ep. 169), but it agrees with the position of the letters in the collection.

171

AD PAPAM EVGENIVM

S 144; C VI,26; Bc VI,25; cf. *RHGF*, XV, 643-644 (1146); Pignot, *Cluny*,

III, 353-357; Chaix de Lavarène, "Bullaire," pp. 577-580 (1143/51); Gaussin, *La Chaise-Dieu*, p. 168.

1146/51. This letter was written at least a year after Eugene III assumed office and before the death of Bishop Aimeric of Clermont, whose successor, Stephen, appears in 1151: see Gams, *Series*, p. 538, and *St. Flour*, p. 31, n. 8. The bishop involved can only have been Aimeric, because Stephen would scarcely have had time to imprison a man for two years before the death of Pope Eugene in 1153. Letter 112 shows that Peter the Venerable had defended Aimeric before Pope Celestine II on account of some earlier misdemeanor.

p. 405, l. 1] This bull, which is lost, evidently instructed Peter the Venerable and the Bishop of Limoges (Gerald of Cher) to meet with the Bishop of Clermont in order (a) to make him release a certain knight whom he had held captive for almost two years, (b) to settle the dispute over the castle of Auzon, and (c) to discuss, but not to settle, various matters concerning the bishop. Two canons of St. Julian at Brioude (of whom one was a brother of the knight in question) had procured this bull at Rome and presented it not to Peter the Venerable and the Bishop of Limoges but directly to the Bishop of Clermont, who kept it. Peter found out about it only by a copy shown him by the canons of Brioude, and he was therefore unable to fulfill the papal commission. The precise nature of the case is not known, but the information given in this letter suggests that the knight whom the bishop held captive and whose brother was a canon of Brioude was the lord of Auzon, a castle near Brioude: see Gaussin, *La Chaise-Dieu*, pp. 77 and 639, and Gabriel Fournier, *Le peuplement rural en basse Auvergne durant le haut moyen âge* (Publications de la Faculté des lettres et sciences humaines de Clermont-Ferrand, II.12; Paris, [1962]) p. 603. The family of Auzon was of some importance in the early twelfth century. Bompar (Bonuspar) of Auzon appears on several charters in the chartulary of Sauxillanges (nos. 300, 679, and 706); and during the priorate of Eustace (*ca.* 1103/4: see Appendix L), he granted his son Eustace to Sauxillanges as a monk, with an endowment, in charter no. 679, which was witnessed by Bompar, his wife Stephana, and his sons Bertrand, Stephen, and Eustace. According to Gaussin, *La Chaise-Dieu*, p. 266, Bernard of Auzon in 1091 gave the tithes of all his possessions to La Chaise-Dieu. At about the same time, B. of Auzon was abbot of Brioude: *GC*, II, 477, and Jacotin, *Polignac*, I, 98-99, no. 41, who expanded the B. to Bernard. These close ties of the family with Sauxillanges, Brioude, and La Chaise-Dieu fully account for the interest of Peter the Venerable in its affairs. Two interesting charters published by Chassaing, *Spicilegium*, pp. 25-27, nos. 15 and 16, show that in the early thirteenth century the lord of Auzon held the castles of Auzon and Rilhac from the count of Auvergne, to whom he owed liege homage, and two fiefs from the bishop of Clermont. Later the family allied with the family of Polignac and rose to considerable prominence: cf. Jacotin, *Polignac*, V, 23-24 (index *s.n.* Auzon). The fact that the Pope and papal judge-delegates were called upon to interfere in a strictly secular affair, involving a castle and liegeman of the count of Auvergne, is striking evidence of the count's weakness in the middle of the twelfth century.

p. 405, l. 39] Peter presumably dated the "almost twenty years" during which the people of Auvergne had been without a king, prince, law, or priest from the accession of Count Robert III of Auvergne, who succeeded his father William VI by at least 1136 and was in turn succeeded by his son William VII by at least 1145: see *Art de vérifier les dates*, II, 357-358. Neither Robert III nor William VII were effective rulers, and conditions in the Auvergne were doubtless unsettled (cf. Letter 174); but Peter's statement was certainly exaggerated, since Aimeric (though not, perhaps, a very worthy prelate) had been bishop since 1111/2. Yet it has been used by Duby and Pacaut (together with the same biblical passage used in Ep. 21, n. to p. 42, l. 10) as evidence of the political condition in Burgundy about 1140.

172

AD EBRARDVM TEMPLI DOMINI MAGISTRVM

S 145; C VI,27; Bc VI,26; cf. *Art de vérifier les dates*, II, 474; *RHGF*, XV, 650-651 (1150); Lorain, *Cluny*, pp. 410-413; Pignot, *Cluny*, III, 362-363; Aubret, *Dombes* (cited Ep. 100, n. to p. 261), I, 320-323 (*ca.* 1147-8); Röhricht, *Regesta*, no. 260 (*ca.* 1150); Sejourné, in *DThC*, XII.2, 2072 (on this and Letter 173); Berry, in *Petrus Ven.*, p. 157, n. 56; Méras, *Beaujolais*, pp. 32-33; Hartmut Hoffmann, *Gottesfriede und Treuga Dei* (Schriften der Monumenta Germaniae historica, 20; Stuttgart, 1964) pp. 137-138.

Everard of Barre was preceptor of the Templars from 1143 to 1147 and master from 1147 to 1149, according to Virginia Berry in her edition of Odo of Deuil, *De profectione Ludovici VII in orientem* (Columbia Records of Civilization, 42; New York, 1948) p. 54, n. 40. He appears on only one charter, not as master, in April/June 1147, in the *Cartulaire général de l'ordre du Temple, 1119?-1150*, ed. G. A. M. J. d'Albon (Paris, 1913) p. 281, no. 451; but in 1150 he made a grant as "militie Christi de Templo magister dictus": Tardif, *Monuments* (cited Ep. 145, n. to

p. 360, l. 2), p. 269, no. 506; cf. Cartellieri, *Suger*, p. 161, no. 291; and he was still master in 1154 (Röhricht, *Regesta*, no. 291) and appeared as "minister humilis milicie Templi" on a document dated *ca.* 1160 in Paris, p. 366, no. 420. He later resigned and became a monk at Clairvaux.

1148/53. It is impossible to date this and the following letter with precision. Everard of Barre became master of the Templars after April/June 1147. He went on the Second Crusade and returned *ca.* 1148. He was certainly in France at the time this letter was written.

p. 408, l. 23] Guichard III of Beaujeu became a monk at Cluny in 1137: cf. *De miraculis*, I, 27 (*Bibl. Clun.*, col. 1290); and he was succeeded by Humbert III: see the references in Ep. 100, n. to p. 261, esp. Méras, *Beaujolais*, pp. 23–29, who discusses Guichard's entry into Cluny and his subsequent activities, including his writings in French, on pp. 28–29. The dates of Humbert's visit to the Holy Land, joining the Templars, and return to France are not known (cf. *ibid*, pp. 31–32).

p. 408, l. 37] Cf. Duby, *Mâconnais*, p. 531 (and Ep. 21, n. to p. 42, l. 10) on this passage, which throws light on the disordered state of southern Burgundy in the middle of the twelfth century. There had in fact been no strong central power in this region since the ninth century.

173

AD PAPAM EVGENIVM

S 146; C VI,28; Bc VI,27; cf. *RHGF*, XV, 651–653 (1150); Martin, *Conciles*, no. 582 (1145/53); and all the references for Ep. 172. This letter was written at the same time, and sometimes uses the same words, as Letter 172.

1148/53.

p. 410] On Humbert III of Beaujeu, see Méras, *Beaujolais*, pp. 29–40, and Ep. 100, n. to p. 261, and Ep. 172, n. to p. 408, l. 23.

p. 411] The lands of the lords of Beaujeu lay between the Saône and Loire rivers.

174

AD EVNDEM

S 147; C VI,29; Bc VI,28; cf. Pignot, *Cluny*, III, 358–360.

1145/53.

p. 413] The abbey of Brioude was founded in the sixth century and became a college of secular canons in the ninth century: see Beaunier-Besse, *Abbayes*, V, 272–274; Cottineau, *Répertoire*, I, 505. Peter the Venerable's brother Heraclius was at one time provost there: see Appendix A.

p. 414, l. 5] A *philacterium* in classical usage meant an amulet or some sort of girdle, but in the Middle Ages it usually meant a reliquary, as it probably does here. Rupert of Deutz referred in his *Commentarium in Matthaeum*, XII, to "quaedam sanctorum phylacteria auro fabrefacta, quae uulgo dicimus feretra" (*PL*, CLXVIII, 1593 A). Cf. Duchesne, in *Bibl. Clun.*, notae, p. 156.

p. 414, l. 11] That is, they consulted a sorcerer rather than using the proper judicial procedures. On sorcery and its uses in the first half of the twelfth century, see John of Salisbury, *Policraticus*, I, 9–10, and II, 27–28, where he told the well-known episode of how as a boy he was used to foretell the future by "scrying" (*specularia*), ed. C. C. J. Webb (Oxford, 1909) I, 49–50 and 143–166; cf. H. C. Lea, *Materials Toward a History of Witchcraft*, ed. A. C. Howland (Philadelphia, 1939) I, 143–198.

p. 414, l. 19] The following description of the treatment of the accused and of the projected trial by fire is of special interest because the use of ordeals by either fire, water, or battle was regularly opposed by the Church in the twelfth century, and the Fourth Lateran Council in 1215 prohibited the participation of the clergy in such trials: see Duchesne, in *Bibl. Clun.*, notae, cols. 156–157; Yvonne Bongert, *Recherches sur les cours laïques du Xe au XIIIe siècle* (Paris, 1949) pp. 215–251, on the use of ordeals in ecclesiastical as well as secular courts and on the opposition of the Church (p. 220); *ODCC*, p. 987 (with a general bibliography on ordeals); and John W. Baldwin, "The Intellectual Preparation for the Canon of 1215 against Ordeals," *Speculum*, XXXVI (1961) 613–636.

p. 415] On this passage see Ep. 192, n. to p. 446, l. 20.

p. 416] The lists of the provosts and abbots of Brioude in the second quarter of the twelfth century are far from complete. I have been unable to consult Dantyl, *Chronologie du ci-devant chapitre de Saint-Julien-de-Brioude* (Paris, 1805), which is cited in the catalogue of the Bibliothèque nationale at Paris (XXXV, 787) and (as by Dantil and De Chavanat [Chavagnac]) by Marcellin Boudet, "Les Mercoeurs Seigneurs de Gerzat," *Revue de l'Auvergne*, XXII (1905) 186, n. 3, and by

Anne Marcel and Marcel Baudot, *Grand cartulaire du chapitre Saint-Julien de Brioude* (Mémoires de l'Académie... de Clermont-Ferrand, 35; Clermont-Ferrand, 1935) p. vii, n. 5. The *GC*, II, 477 and 482–483, and Chaix de Lavarène, "Bullaire," pp. 437–438, list as provosts only Odilo of Mercoeur in 1137 (Chassaing, *Spicilegium*, pp. 14–15, no. 6), Peter the Venerable's brother Heraclius in 1139 (see Appendix A), and William II in 1161 (Chassaing, *Spicilegium*, p. 18, no. 9) and 1175. As abbot they give only William IV in 1137 and 1139 (the same documents) between B. of Auzon (see Ep. 171, n. to p. 405, l. 1) in 1100 and B. in 1161 and 1162. Chaix de Lavarène remarked that "l'abbaye, d'abord première dignité du chapitre, eut rang après la prévôté dans les XIe, XIIe et XIIIe siècles." An "Odilo de Motgo" appears as a canon of Brioude on a charter of 1161 in Chassaing, *Spicilegium*, p. 18, no. 9, and Jacotin, *Polignac*, I, 108, no. 51, who suggested (V, 215) that Motgo = Montgon and Mongon = Montgontier (Haute-Loire, arr. Brioude), on which see Augustin Chassaing and Antoine Jacotin, *Dictionnaire topographique du départment de la Haute-Loire* (Paris, 1907) p. 188. "Cornon" probably refers to Cournon (Puy-de-Dôme, arr. Clermont-Ferrand). A certain John "Escot," lord of Cournon, was among the wealthiest lords in the diocese of Clermont in about 1170: see Marcellin Boudet, "Cournon et ses chartes de franchises," *Revue de l'Auvergne*, XXV (1908) 314–321; and a William of Cournon appeared as a canon of Brioude in 1222: Chassaing, *Spicilegium*, p. 28, no. 28.

175

AD BERNARDVM ABBATEM CLARAEVALLIS

S 148; Cl fol. 40v; C VI,30; Bc VI,29; cf. Manrique, *Ann. Cist.*, II, 138 (1149); Bernard, ep. 264 (Gaume ed., I.1, 546–547) (1149); Bréquigny, *Chartes*, III, 164 (1149); Maitland, *Dark Ages*, p. 444; Lorain, *Cluny*, pp. 493–494.

Autumn 1150. This letter is the first of a group, including Letters 175–177 and 179–184, concerning a prospective visit to Cluny by Nicholas of Montiéramey. Nicholas wrote that he would be seeing Peter the Venerable soon in Letter 153, written early in 1150 (late 1149 O.S.). Peter remarked in Letter 176 (which was sent with Letter 175) that he had put off writing and was in poor health; and the visit, which was at first scheduled to be before Christmas, was delayed on account of Peter's illness and rescheduled for Easter 1151. This group of letters was dated 1149–50 by Vacandard, *St. Bernard*, II, 492, n. 2, but Peter's movements in 1149–50 and the chronology of his illness (see Appendix C) clearly point to 1150–1.

176

AD NICHOLAVM MONACHVM

S 149; Cl fol. 41^v; C VI,31; Bc VI,30; cf. Manrique, *Ann. Cist.*, II, 138 (1149); Bréquigny, *Chartes*, III, 164 (1149); Maitland, *Dark Ages*, pp. 445; Pignot, *Cluny*, III, 486-487. This letter was evidently sent to Clairvaux with Letter 175, to which Peter refers in the last sentence.

Autumn 1150 (see dating note to Ep. 175).

p. 417, l. 6] This traveling and instability may have been associated with the cases and conferences mentioned in Letter 158a.

p. 417, l. 12] A "Volumen in quo continentur VI libri contra Julianum hereticum" and "Volumen in quo continetur Sedulius, historia Daretis Phrygii, liber Alexandri Macedonis, epigrammata Symposii alieque res" are listed in the catalogue of the library of Cluny (1158/61) in Delisle, *Fonds*, pp. 345 and 371, nos. 152 and 528. Augustine's *Contra Julianum* was also in the library at Clairvaux in the twelfth century: Wilmart, "Bibliothèque," pp. 13 and 17.

177

RESCRIPTVM BERNARDI ABBATIS

S 150; Cl fol. 41^v; C VI,32; Bc VI,31; Bern., ep. 265; cf. Mabillon, note to Bernard, ep. 265 (Gaume ed., I.1, 547) (1149); Bréquigny, *Chartes*, III, 161 (1149); Maitland, *Dark Ages*, p. 445; *Letters of St. Bernard*, pp. 377-378, no. 306. This letter is Bernard's reply to Letter 175 from Peter the Venerable.

Autumn 1150 (see dating note to Ep. 175).

p. 418] Letter 179 shows that Nicholas's business with Bishop Hugh of Auxerre (on whom see the dating note to Ep. 69) probably concerned the abbey of Vézelay and was undertaken at the request of Peter the Venerable.

178

AD HVGONEM ARCHIEPISCOPVM ROTHOMAGENSIS

S 151; C VI,33; Bc VI,32; cf. J. F. Pommeraye, *Histoire des archevesques de Rouen* (Rouen, 1667) pp. 336-338; Pignot, *Cluny*, III, 36.

1130/56 (cf. biographical note to Ep. 4 on Hugh of Amiens).

8+L.P.V. II

p. 420, l. 26] The identity of this Airaldus cannot be established. He had apparently been a monk at Cluny before accepting a benefice from Hugh.

p. 420, l. 29] There is no reference to either of these poems in U. Chevalier, *Repertorium hymnologicum* (Subsidia hagiographica, 4; Brussels, 1892–1921) or in Hans Walther, *Initia carminum ac versuum medii aevi posterioris latinorum* (Carmina Medii Aevi posterioris latina, 1; Göttingen, 1959).

179

EPISTOLA NICHOLAI MONACHI AD DOMINVM ABBATEM

S 152; Cl fol. 42ᵛ; C VI,34; Bc VI,33; cf. Nicholas of Montiéramey, ep. 55 (*PL*, CXCVI, 1650); Manrique, *Ann. Cist.*, II, 167–168 (1150); Bréquigny, *Chartes*, III, 182 (1150); Maitland, *Dark Ages*, pp. 446–447; Pignot, *Cluny*, III, 491 (1149).

Early (February?) 1151 (see dating note to Ep. 175).

p. 421, l. 16] Nicholas used the same quotation about Cicero in his ep. 43 to the abbot of St. Anastasius (*PL*, CXCVI, 1642 B). In ep. 35 he described Cicero as "oratorum rex et Romanae eloquentiae princeps" (*ibid.*, 1630 C).

p. 421, l. 24] This "case of the abbot of Vézelay," which Nicholas undertook at the request of Peter the Venerable, probably was the reason for his visit to the Bishop of Auxerre, which Bernard mentioned at the end of Letter 177. In 1146 Eugene III had appointed Hugh of Auxerre mediator between the abbot of Vézelay and the bishop of Autun: *GC*, XII, 282; Jean Lebeuf, *Mémoires concernant l'histoire civile et ecclésiastique d'Auxerre et de son ancien diocèse*, ed. A. Challe and M. Quantin (Auxerre-Paris, 1848–1855) I, 311.

p. 422, l. 1] On Nicholas's illness and business, see Ep. 177.

p. 422, l. 9] See Letters 181 and 183–184. Easter in 1151 fell on 8 April.

p. 422, l. 15] This request to send in secret copies of the letters to Bernard, Galcher, and Philip shows something of the conniving nature that later got Nicholas into trouble (see Appendix P). There is no evidence that Peter the Venerable complied with the request.

p. 422, l. 17] Cf. the request of Peter the Venerable at the end of Letter 176.

p. 422, l. 24] Bernard probably made this request at the meeting with Peter the Venerable mentioned in Letter 181. It suggests that Nicholas was still in Bernard's favor and needed by him, not (as Vacandard, *St. Bernard*, II, 492, n. 2, assumed on the basis of this letter and Letter 181) that Bernard already suspected Nicholas of treachery.

180

DOMINI ABBATIS AD NICHOLAVM

S 153; Cl. fol. 44^r; C VI,35; Bc VI,34; cf. Manrique, *Ann. Cist.*, II, 139 (1149). This is Peter the Venerable's reply to Letter 179. Since the messenger was in a hurry to return to Clairvaux and was not known personally to Peter, he sent him back immediately with this note and decided to send his own messenger later with a longer letter.

March 1151 (see dating note to Ep. 175).

181

AD ABBATEM CLAREVALLENSEM

S 154; Cl fol. 44^r; C VI,36; Bc VI,35; cf. Manrique, *Ann. Cist.*, II, 168-169 (1150); Bréquigny, *Chartes*, III, 183 (1150); Maitland, *Dark Ages*, pp. 447-448; Lorain, *Cluny*, pp. 487-490; Pignot, *Cluny*, III, 491 (1149). This is the letter that Peter the Venerable sent to Clairvaux by his own messenger (cf. Letter 180), together with Letters 182-184, asking that Nicholas be allowed to visit Cluny for the following Easter.

March 1151 (see dating note to Ep. 175).

p. 424, l. 16] Bernard's relation Peter does not appear on the genealogical tables in *Bernard de Clairvaux*, pp. 558-563. On his cousin Robert, to whom Bernard sent his famous first letter and who went from Clairvaux to Cluny and then back to Clairvaux, see Vacandard, *St. Bernard*, I, 85-90 (and *passim*), and *Bernard de Clairvaux*, pp. 193-194 and 738. On Garnerius, who had probably been subprior at Cluny before he went to Clairvaux, see Ep. 79, n. to p. 214, l. 26.

p. 424, l. 24] This "recent" visit of Bernard to Cluny is otherwise unknown (cf. Ep. 192, n. to p. 448, l. 11). It must have been in the fall or winter of 1150–1, since the matter of Nicholas's visit was discussed, not, apparently, for the first time.

182

ITEM AD NICHOLAVM

S 155; Cl fol. 46ʳ; C VI,37; Bc VI,36; cf. Manrique, *Ann. Cist.*, II, 168 (1150); Pignot, *Cluny*, III, 491 (1149). This is the longer letter to Nicholas that Peter the Venerable sent by his own messenger (cf. Ep. 180), together with Letters 181 and 183–184 to Bernard, Philip, and Galcher.

March 1151 (see dating note to Ep. 175).

183

AD PHILIPPVM PRIOREM CLARAEVALLIS

S 156; C VI,38; Bc VI,37; cf. Manrique, *Ann. Cist.*, II, 169 (1150); Bréquigny, *Chartes*, III, 183 (1150). This letter was sent to Clairvaux with Letters 181–182 and 184.

On Prior Philip of Clairvaux, see Ep. 151, first n. to p. 372, l. 20.

March 1151 (see dating note to Ep. 175).

184

AD GALCHERIVM CELLARARIVM

S 157; C VI,39; Bc VI,38; cf. Manrique, *Ann. Cist.*, II, 169 (1150); Bréquigny, *Chartes*, III, 183 (1150). This letter was sent to Clairvaux with Letters 181–183.

On Galcher, cellarer of Clairvaux, see Ep. 151, second n. to p. 372, l.20.

March 1151 (see dating note to Ep. 175).

185

AD NEPTES SVAS VIRGINES MARCINIACENSES

S 158; C VI,40; Bc VI,39; cf. Pignot, *Cluny*, III, 164. Peter the Venerable himself described this letter as a collection of flowers from the most flowery fields, and it is really a *florilegium* of excerpts concerning virginity, occasioned by Peter's mild surprise that his nieces should concern themselves with the worthy but worldly care of the body.

Margaret and Pontia were the daughters of Peter the Venerable's brother Hugh (see Appendix A). They had been taken to Marcigny by their grandmother, Peter the Venerable's mother Raingard, who died in 1135.

1135/56.

186

AD BASILIVM CARTVSIAE PRIOREM

S 159; C VI,41; Bc VI,40; cf. *GC* (ed. I), IV, 971; Mabillon, *Annales*, VI, 457 (1151); Bréquigny, *Chartes*, III, 183 (1150); Pignot, *Cluny*, III, 274–275; Le Couteulx, *Ann. Carth.*, II, 130–132 (1152); Chevalier, *Régeste*, no. 3913 (1152).

Basil was a former monk (and a great admirer) of Cluny: cf. his reply to this letter, Letter 187. He was prior of La Grande Chartreuse from 1151 until 1173/4, according to *La Grande Chartreuse*, p. 61, n. 5. According to the biographer of Hugh of Lincoln, Basil "was generally called a saint by all who knew him, because of his pre-eminent and exceptional merits and virtues": *Magna vita sancti Hugonis*, X (cited Ep. 24) I, 31.

November/December 1151. Peter the Venerable said that this letter was written "ab ipsis alpium faucibus" and referred to "hoc hiemali tempore." He was clearly on his way to Rome late in 1151.

p. 434, l. 2] I have been unable to identify this Cluniac *monasteriolum* named Herbins. It may be Eybens or Herbeys, south of Grenoble. But they are not among the Cluniac houses listed by Marrier, De Valous, and Evans.

p. 434, l. 4] This letter is lost.

p. 435, l. 2] Peter the Venerable crossed the Isère presumably on his way to the Mt. Cenis Pass, from where this letter was written.

p. 435, l. 20] On Guigo of La Chartreuse, see biographical note to Ep. 24.

p. 435, l. 36] (a) Brother Peter of Gap, whom Peter the Venerable had previously met at Tiron, may be the monk Peter who appears on documents of 1131 and 1131/45 in the *Cartulaire de l'abbaye de la Sainte-Trinité de Tiron* (Chartres, 1883) I, 175 and 184. (b) Brother Geoffrey is otherwise unknown. (c) The *conversus* Otmar of Valbonnais appears on documents in 1129 and 1140/2 and died in 1172, according to Le Couteulx, cited in *La Grande Chartreuse*, p. 37, n. 7.

187

RESCRIPTVM BASILII PRIORIS AD DOMINVM ABBATEM

S 160; C VI,42; Bc VI,41; cf. Mabillon, *Annales*, VI, 457–458 (1151); Bréquigny, *Chartes*, III, 178 (1150); Pignot, *Cluny*, III, 274–275; Le Couteulx, *Ann. Carth.*, II, 132 (1152); Chevalier, *Régeste*, no. 3902 (1151). This is Prior Basil's reply to Letter 186 from Peter the Venerable. It shows that Peter was unable to visit La Chartreuse on account of the snow.

November/December 1151.

188

AD PAPAM EVGENIVM

S 161; C VI,43; Bc VI,42; cf. Pignot, *Cluny*, III, 369–370; F. Malaspina, *Sulla patria e sull'età del cronografo novaliciense* (Tortona, 1816) p. 36, cited by L. C. Bollea, *Cartario della abazia di Breme* (Biblioteca della Società storica subalpina, 127; Turin, 1933) pp. 125–127, no. 96 (1145).

Spring (?) 1152.

p. 437, l. 2] The abbey of Breme is located near the river Po in the present diocese of Vigevano (then Pavia): Cottineau, *Répertoire*, I, 485.

p. 437, l. 5] Eugene III issued a confirmation for Breme at the request of its Abbot Rainald on 9 February 1152, while Peter the Venerable was with the Pope at Segni: *Monumenta Novaliciensia vetustiora*, ed. Carlo Cipolla (Fonti per la storia d'Italia, 31–32; Rome, 1898–1901) I, 250–257; JL 9549; *Italia pontificia*, VI.1, 236, no. 7.

p. 437, l. 8] Nothing is known about the early history of Abbot Rainald of Breme, except that he was a Cluniac. Breme itself was not a Cluniac house, but it had well-established ties with Cluny, since in 1027 it was under the young Cluniac Abbot Odilo, the nephew of St. Odilo: *Mon. Noval. vet.*, I, 154; *Cartario . . . di Breme*, pp. 69–70, no. 53.

p. 437, l. 15] Peter the Venerable clearly traveled from Cluny southeast across the Rhone and Isère rivers in November 1151 and then across the Mt. Cenis Pass and down to Breme, where he spent Christmas. Abbot Rainald may then have accompanied him to Venice and on to the Pope at Segni.

189

AD EVNDEM EVGENIVM PAPAM

S 162; C VI,44; Bc VI,43; cf. Pignot, *Cluny*, III, 365–366; Le Couteulx, *Ann. Carth.*, II, 58 (1147); Martin, *Conciles*, no. 576 (end of 1150); Chevalier, *Régeste*, no. 3885 (end of 1150); Noël Didier, "Les censiers du prieuré clunisien de Domène," *Cahiers d'histoire publiés par les Universités de Clermont, Lyon, Grenoble*, II (1957) 11, n. 27 (ca. 1150).

1152/3. This letter was written between Peter the Venerable's visit to the Pope and Eugene's death in July 1153.

p. 438, l. 6] Peter the Venerable had been prior of Domène before he became abbot of Cluny, and he was naturally acquainted with Guy of Domène, whose family patronized the priory.

p. 438, l. 6] Peter the Venerable was with Eugene III at Segni in February–March 1152.

p. 439, l. 1] On the technical issues of marriage mentioned here, see Séjourné, in *DThC*, XII.2, 2072, and, generally, Jean Dauvillier, *Le mariage dans le droit classique de l'Église* (Paris, 1933), esp. pp. 143–200 on impediments to marriage. Guy of Domène advanced as reasons for the invalidity of his first marriage the following points: (1) the opposition of the bishop of Grenoble (cf. Dauvillier, *Mariage*, pp. 195–197); (2) that his wife was under age; (3) consanguinity (cf. *ibid.*, pp. 146–152); (4) that the marriage was never consummated; (5) that the bishop had approved, and almost ordered, his second marriage; (6) that Eugene III had assigned the case to the archbishop of Vienne when Guy had met him on his way from France to Italy in May 1148 (cf. JL *post* 9260); and (7) that he had repeatedly expressed his readiness to submit to the bishop before he was excommunicated.

p. 439, l. 34] The occasion of this ride by Peter the Venerable and Guy from the priory of Vizille to Domène is unknown, but it must have been between 1148 and 1151.

190

AD IPSVM

S 163; C VI,45; Bc VI,44; cf. P. M. Campi, *Dell'historia ecclesiastica di Piacenza* (Piacenza, 1651–1672) II, 351–352.

1152. This letter was written by Peter either on his way back or soon after his return from Italy.

p. 440, l. 5] On the controversy between the town of Piacenza and the Patriarch of Ravenna over the consecration of the Bishop of Piacenza, see Campi, *Hist. ecc.*, I, 419–421, and Pignot, *Cluny*, III, 366–369. Eugene III's bulls of 29 March and 9–10 November 1148 and of 28 July 1152 (JL 9203, 9299–9301, and 9599; *Italia pontificia*, V, 61–63, nos. 205–211 and 215, and 450–451, nos. 38–43 and 47) dealt with the controversy. In the last bull, which may have been issued after the Pope received Peter's letter, Eugene urged Moses of Ravenna to assist Bishop John of Piacenza "lest he should regret having submitted himself to your obedience."

p. 440, l. 13] On Peter's visit to Eugene in November–December 1145, see Appendix D.

p. 440, l. 14] Marquis Opizone Malaspina was lord of Lunigiano from at least 1141 until his death in 1181: see Emanuelle Gerini, *Memorie storiche d'illustri scrittori e di uomini insigni dell'antica e moderna Lunigiano* (Massa, 1829) II, 13–17, and Chevalier, *Bio-bib.*, II, 2968.

191

AD QVEM SVPRA

S 164; C VI,46; Bc VI,45; cf. Bréquigny, *Chartes*, III, 183 (1150); *RHGF*, XV, 654–655 (1153); Lorain, *Cluny*, pp. 388–389; Pignot, *Cluny*, III, 396–397; Raffin, in *Millénaire de Cluny*, II, 175–176; Martin, *Conciles*, no. 2704 (1153).

1152 (summer?).

p. 442, l. 6] Hugh *Deschaux* ("the Barefoot"), lord of La Bussière, some eleven miles southwest of Cluny, was called variously "discalciatus" (as here), "de Scalciaco" (*Bibl. Clun.*, col. 592), "de Scalceo" (*Bibl. Clun., notae*, col. 158), "de Sarciaco" (*Bull. Clun.*, p. 74), all of which probably referred not to his poverty but to his extravagance, like Peter the Venerable's ancestor Hugh "the Unstitched" (see Appendix A). See Duby, *Mâconnais*, pp. 294–295 and 461, n. 1, on him, his family, and his efforts to build a castle on Mount Ajoux at Brandon (dated 1145).

p. 442, l. 12] Clermain was a village on the border of the seigneurie of Cluny, in the direction of La Bussière: see Raffin in *Millénaire de Cluny*, II, 174, n. 4; and Duby, *Mâconnais*, p. 457 (and the map on p. 687).

p. 443, l. 11] On Hugh III of Berzé, who held Berzé-le-Chatel and Berzé-la-Ville, on the road between Cluny and Mâcon, see Duby, *Mâconnais*, pp. 459–461. The families of Berzé and La Bussière, together with those of Beaujeu, Bagé, and Brancion, were the most influential feudal lords, under the count of Mâcon, in the region of Cluny in the twelfth century.

p. 443, l. 12] On Peter the Venerable's chamberlain Enguizo, see Appendix R on functionaries at Cluny.

p. 443, l. 22] This meeting has commonly been identified with the council described under the year 1153 in the chronicle of Cluny, which was held at Mâcon and was attended by the archbishop-elect of Lyons, the bishops of Autun, Mâcon, and Chalon-sur-Saône, the "count" of Burgundy [Mâcon?], the count of Chalon, Humbert of Beaujeu, Joceran *Grossus* of Brancion, Hugh of Berzé, Hugh *Deschaux* of La Bussière, and other Burgundian magnates: *Bibl. Clun.*, cols. 592–593; cf. Jean Richard, *Les ducs de Bourgogne et la formation du duché du XIe au XIVe siècle* (Publications de l'Université de Dijon, 12; Paris, 1954) pp. 183–184; Méras, *Beaujolais*, p. 33; Hoffmann, *Gottesfriede*, pp. 138–139. The present writer (Constable, "Cluniac Tithes," p. 622) and Janssen, *Legaten*, p. 57, have independently argued, however, that this council, which met under the auspices of the cardinal legate Odo, cannot have been held before 1154, whereas Letter 191 was written after Peter the Venerable's return from Italy in the spring of 1152 and certainly before the death of Eugene III in July 1153. It therefore seems that at least two councils of local notables were held, one in 1152 and another in 1154, in order to assure the security of Cluny. Hoffmann, *Gottesfriede*, p. 138, n. 27, has recently defended the identity of the two councils and suggested that the legate in question was not Cardinal Odo of S. Giorgio in Velabro, who was sent to France by Anastasius IV in 1154, but Cardinal Odo of S. Nicola in Carcere, who was apparently absent from the curia from 16 May to 8 September 1153 and could have come to France at that time. Both Hoffmann and Janssen, *Legaten*, p. 57, n. 3, overlooked, however, a bull of 13 June 1153 to which Odo of S. Nicola in Carcere subscribed: Carl Erdmann, *PU in Portugal*, p. 217. This reduces the time for his trip to less than three months and makes it almost impossible that he could have presided over a council at Mâcon before the death of Eugene III on 8 July 1153. I still therefore incline toward the view that at least two councils met. A decade later, in 1163, Alexander III addressed a bull to Humbert of Beaujeu, the counts Forez and Mâcon, Joceran *Grossus* of Brancion, Hugh of Berzé, Hugh *Deschaux* of La Bussière, "and all others who will conserve the sworn peace of the church of Cluny" (*Bull. Clun.*, p. 74; JL 10908).

192

AD BERNARDVM DOMINVM CLARAEVALLIS ABBATEM

S 165; Cl fol. 47^v; C VI,47; Bc VI,46; cf. Manrique, *Ann. Cist.*, II, 189–190 (1151); Mabillon, *Annales*, VI, 433–435 (1150); Bréquigny, *Chartes*, III, 196 (1151); Pignot, *Cluny*, III, 370–372 (1150) and 381–382; Vacandard, *St. Bernard*, II, 488, n. 2 (1151); Constable, "Cluniac Tithes," pp. 618–620 (erroneously dated 1151 and with further references on this letter and Letter 193).

May 1152. This and the associated Letter 193, which was written at the same time to Nicholas of Montiéramey, can be dated from the references to Peter the Venerable's travels in Italy and other internal evidence. They show that the trip was made in winter (Letter 192), that he was away for five months (Letter 193), and that he was writing near the time of Pentecost (Letter 193). Peter is known to have been with Pope Eugene III at Segni in February 1152; and 1152 fits with the closest estimate to the date of elevation to the cardinalate of Hugh of Ostia (see n. to p. 445, l. 31). Pentecost in 1152 fell on 18 May, and Peter therefore returned from Italy about Easter (30 March), since he remarked in both letters on the delay between the times of his return and of writing. This would date his departure from Cluny early in November 1151, probably soon after receiving the letter sent by the Italian priors on 25 October. Bernard of Clairvaux in all probability wrote his celebrated ep. 277, recommending Peter the Venerable to the Pope, at this time, although it was dated 1146 by Mabillon (Gaume ed., I.1, 562), Leclercq, *Pierre le Vén.*, p. 81, and M. J.-B. Auniord, "L'ami de saint Bernard," *Coll. Ord. Cist. Ref.*, XVIII (1956) 97. In this letter Bernard both referred to a visit to Italy by Peter and said that

Eugene had already met Peter, which shows (unless they had met before Eugene became pope) that the visit cannot have been that in 1145 but was probably this one in 1151–2 (cf. n. to p. 445, l. 27).

p. 443] This letter from Bernard to Peter the Venerable is lost, but much of its contents can be reconstructed from what Peter says here and below. It almost certainly concerned the controversy between Gigny and Le Miroir (see Constable, "Cluniac Tithes," pp. 608–624); and Bernard urged Peter to moderate his anger against his own monks (who had attacked and burned Le Miroir probably while he was away in Italy). Bernard apparently accused the subprior of being the ringleader and suggested meeting Peter the Venerable either at Dijon or at Clairvaux to talk the matter over.

p. 444, l. 2] On this trip to Rome, during which work piled up at Cluny, see the dating note above and Appendix D.

p. 444, l. 18] This reference to traveling for several days and nights on the river Po shows that Peter's visit to Venice in order to pray at the shrine of St. Mark and to visit his monks probably took place at this time (*PL*, CLXXXIX, 477). The Cluniac house at Venice was dedicated to the Holy Cross: *Italia pontificia*, VII.2, 192; Cottineau, *Répertoire*, II, 3321.

p. 445, l. 5] The patriarch of Ravenna from 1149 until 1154 was named Moses: see Gams, *Series*, p. 717, and the documents cited in Ep. 190, n. to p. 440, l. 5.

p. 445, l. 27] The places and dates of these meetings of Peter the Venerable with Pope Eugene (of which only the first was in Italy: cf. dating note above) are listed in Appendix D.

p. 445, l. 31] The date of the elevation of Abbot Hugh of Trois-Fontaines to the cardinal-bishopric of Ostia is of great importance for the dating of this letter and of Peter the Venerable's trip to Italy. Vacandard, *St. Bernard*, II, 488, n. 2, and 493, proposed 1150, but this was based on the erroneous indications in JL. Brixius, *Kardinalkollegium*, pp. 55 and 108, dated Hugh from 1151/2 and indicated his earliest subscription on 15 April 1152. Holtzmann, in *PU in England*, I, 291–293, published a bull dated 13 February 1152 with a subscription by Cardinal Hugh of Ostia and dated Hugh's cardinalate from 1151/2 both here and in *PU in England*, III, 211–214. Paul Kehr, however, in "Nachträge zu den Papsturkunden Italiens. V," *Nachrichten von der königlichen*

Gesellschaft der Wissenschaften zu Göttingen, Phil.-Hist. Kl., 1911, p. 288, dated Hugh from the beginning of 1152 and showed that Guy was bishop of Ostia until at least May 1151. This shows that Peter the Venerable's trip to Italy, when he met Hugh of Ostia and was back at Cluny before Pentecost, must have been after 1151.

p. 445, l. 35] The following words are by Bernard of Clairvaux, according to MS. S, but they sound (aside from "Tempus et opus esse") more like a paraphrase than a direct quotation.

p. 446, l. 3] Peter's reply to Bernard begins at this point, according to MS. S.

p. 446, l. 20] The following passage, dealing with the doctrine of the two swords, should be compared with Peter's more famous remark in Letter 174 ("Sed quamuis aecclesia non habeat imperatoris gladium, habet tamen super quoslibet minores, sed et super ipsos imperatores imperium."), which has been cited and somewhat variously interpreted by, among others, Jean Rivière, *Le problème de l'église et de l'état au temps de Philippe le Bel* (Spicilegium sacrum Lovaniense, 8; Louvain, 1926) p. 26, n. 3 (according to whom Peter "reconnaît à l'Église, non pas le glaive impérial, mais le pouvoir jusque sur les empereurs eux-mêmes"); Gerhart Ladner, "The Concepts of 'Ecclesia' and 'Christianitas' and their Relation to the Idea of Papal 'Plenitudo Potestatis' from Gregory VII to Boniface VIII," *Sacerdozio e Regno da Gregorio VII a Bonifacio VIII* (Miscellanea Historiae Pontificiae, XVII; Rome, 1954) pp. 66-67 ("he [Peter the Venerable] probably used *imperium* in the sense of *potestas*, and, no doubt, of spiritual *imperium* or *potestas*"); and Hartmut Hoffmann, "Die beiden Schwerter im hohen Mittelalter," *Deutsches Archiv*, XX (1964) 95-96, who suggested that Peter's view anticipated the distinction later made by the canonists between *auctoritas* and *administratio*, "d.h. der Papst verleiht dem Kaiser und den Fürsten die Gewalt, darf jedoch selber das Schwert night führen." A. M. Stickler has argued in a series of learned articles that the *gladius materialis* at this time referred not to civil power but to the use of physical force (as opposed to purely spiritual coercion) by the Church: see in particular "Il 'gladius' negli atti dei concilii e dei RR. Pontefici sino a Graziano e Bernardo di Clairvaux," *Salesianum*, XIII (1951) 414-445; cf. Brian Tierney, "Some Recent Works on the Political Theories of the Medieval Canonists," *Traditio*, X (1954) 609-611, and the opposing views of Hoffmann, in *Deutsches Archiv*, XX, 78-114, with references to Stickler's other articles. Among other relevant secondary works on the doctrine of the two swords, see H.-X. Arquillière,

"Origines de la théorie des deux glaives," *Studi Gregoriani*, I (1947) 501-521; Wilhelm Levison, "Die mittelalterliche Lehre von den beiden Schwerten," *Deutsches Archiv*, IX (1951) 14-42; and Walter Ullmann, *The Growth of Papal Government in the Middle Ages* (London, 1955) pp. 430-432. Peter the Venerable's view in these two letters seems to be opposed to that of St. Bernard, expressed in ep. 256 to Eugene III and in *De consideratione*, IV, 3 (Gaume ed., I.1, 538-540, and I.2, 1060), who held that both the spiritual and the material swords belonged to the Church: "Petri uterque est, alter suo nutu, alter sua manu, quoties necesse est, evaginandus" (*ibid.*, I.1, 539 A). Peter significantly omitted the *tuum* (which Bernard and later theorists stressed) in the biblical passage: "Converte gladium tuum in vaginam" (cf. Levison, in *Deutsches Archiv*, IX, 32-33 and 40); and he categorically asserted that the Church did not hold the imperial or royal sword and stressed the dualism of the staff and the sword, standing, respectively, for spiritual and for temporal power. A similar view was expressed by Peter's contemporary Gerhoh of Reichersberg in a chapter on the "Iniqua confusio duorum gladium" in his *De investigatione Antichristi*, I, 36, where he said that the passage from I Cor. 4.21 (which was also cited by Peter) referred "not to the lance or sword but to the pastoral staff": MGH, *Libelli de lite*, III, 344. Neither Peter nor Gerhoh, however, had any doubts about the superiority of ecclesiastical over secular power, and in Letter 174 Peter strongly maintained, as Ladner stressed, the spiritual *imperium* of the Church over the Empire.

p. 448, l. 11] On this proposed meeting at Dijon or Clairvaux, see Constable, "Cluniac Tithes," pp. 619-620. I there erroneously dated the meeting 1151, following Vacandard and other writers. The re-dating of Letters 192-193 to 1152 requires a revision of the chronology of the second phase of the controversy between Gigny and Le Miroir. The *concordia* between Bernard and Peter the Venerable to which Eugene III referred in his bull *Nequitia illorum* of 5 March 1152 must have been worked out not at the Dijon/Clairvaux meeting, as I suggested in "Cluniac Tithes," but by some earlier negotiations, possibly during Bernard's visit to Cluny in the fall or winter of 1150-1 (see Ep. 181, n. to p. 424, l. 24). The attack on Le Miroir by the monks of Gigny therefore occurred in the winter of 1152, while Peter the Venerable was away, and the lost letter from Bernard to Peter (see n. to p. 443 above) almost certainly concerned this outrage. Peter and Bernard then met at Cluny to discuss the matter, as Bernard wrote in ep. 283 to the Pope (written after 5 March 1152: see "Cluniac Tithes," p. 620, n. 1); and this was doubtless in place of the meeting planned in this letter.

p. 448, l. 15] Nothing more is known about this Germanus.

p. 448, l. 17] This was probably the subprior of Gigny, whom Bernard in his lost letter apparently considered the leader of the attack on Le Miroir. There is no reference to him in the papal bulls concerned with the affair, however, unless he was the same as the prior.

193

AD NICHOLAVM SVVM

S 166; C VI,47 [bis]; Bc VI,47; cf. the references for Ep. 192, which was written at the same time, and Appendix P on Nicholas of Montiéramey.

May 1152 (see dating note to Ep. 192).

p. 450, l. 18] This is Letter 192 to Bernard of Clairvaux.

p. 450, l. 20] On Abbot Eustace of Le Miroir, see *GC*, IV, 296–297; Pignot, *Cluny*, III, 608–609; and Constable, "Cluniac Tithes," p. 619. His exact relationship to Peter the Venerable is not known (cf. Appendix A).

p. 450, l. 27] On "the matter of Le Miroir" and the proposed meeting with Bernard at Dijon or Clairvaux on Pentecost (which fell on 9 June in 1152), see Constable, "Cluniac Tithes," pp. 618–620, and Ep. 192, n. to p. 448, l. 11.

Appendices

A. THE FAMILY OF PETER THE VENERABLE

The study of feudal families in the early Middle Ages has only recently been freed from the disrepute into which it was brought by genealogists and been recognized as an essential key to understanding the political and social history of the period. "Professional scholars have tended to neglect genealogical history," wrote Fawtier. "Yet a large-scale enquiry into the history of families, their marriage connections, and the changes in their landed property, would be as valuable as a feudal geography. Both are amongst the most urgent needs of the present generation of French scholars."[1] Recent research in particular has emphasized the importance of family relationships in the tenth and eleventh centuries and the survival of the Carolingian aristocracy, rather than simple considerations of power and wealth, in the medieval concept of nobility.[2]

Certainly no student of the life and works of Peter the Venerable can doubt the importance of his origins and family. His respect and affection for his mother, his associations with his brothers, his concern for his native region, particularly for the monastery of Sauxillanges, were all major, if not obtrusive, themes in his life. "Even if the Montboissier were not among the seven or eight great feudal families which ranked immediately below the count of Auvergne," wrote Pignot, referring to the tenth and eleventh centuries, "they none the less occupied a considerable position beside them and were later to rise to the same rank."[3] No single factor can have been more

[1] Robert Fawtier, *The Capetian Kings of France*, trans. Lionel Butler and R. J. Adam (London, 1960) p. 201.

[2] Cf. Georges Duby, "Une enquête à poursuivre: La noblesse dans la France médiévale," *Revue historique*, fasc. 459 (1961) offprint pp. 6–7, citing works by Genicot and Verriest. Working along these lines of genealogical and *besitzgeschichtliche* methods, the family of Abbot Odo of Cluny has recently been studied by Joachim Wollasch, "Königtum, Adel und Klöster im Berry während des 10. Jahrhundert," *Neue Forschungen über Cluny und die Cluniacenser*, ed. Gerd Tellenbach (Freiburg im Br., 1958) pp. 19–165, esp. pp. 120–142, where he establishes that Odo probably belonged to the family of the lords of Déols.

[3] Pignot, *Cluny*, III, 51. The principal families he mentions are those of La Tour d'Auvergne, Murat, Carlat, Thiers, Mercoeur, Polignac, and Montpensier. The families of Baffie and Nonette were comparable in position with the Montboissier in the first half of the twelfth century. Cf. Gaussin, *La Chaise-Dieu*, pp. 82–83, and Fournier, *Peuplement* (cited Ep. 171, n. to p. 405, l. 1), pp. 80 and 385.

important in this rise than the extraordinary careers of Peter and his brothers, of whom only two remained in secular life and four became, respectively, the archbishop of Lyons and the abbots of Vézelay, La Chaise-Dieu, and Manglieu. In the middle of the twelfth century they were without question the first ecclesiastical family of southern Burgundy, Lyonnais, and Auvergne and had great influence outside this region. These family connections are a constant factor in Peter's career and actions.

Historians before the seventeenth century were in doubt over the family origins of Peter the Venerable, and André Duchesne, according to his own account, was the first to establish that the *Mauricii* sometimes found after Peter's name was a patronymic referring to his father Maurice, who was mentioned both in the chronicle of Cluny and by Peter of Poitiers, and not a reference to the town of Mauriac. Duchesne was uncertain, however, whether Maurice belonged to the family of Montboissier or of St. Maurice. "Be this as it may," he wrote, "his [Peter's] father is known by his *cognomen* alone."[4] This problem was solved by the publication, in 1657 and 1729 respectively, of the chronicle of Geoffrey of Vigeois, who said that Peter and his brothers were of "the noble family of Montboissier, which is a castle in Auvergne," and that Peter descended from Hugh "cognomento Descousut," who founded the monastery of St. Michael at La Chiusa,[5] and by the publication of the life of Peter the Venerable by Radulf, who mentioned that Peter's great-grandfather (*proavus*) founded the abbey of La Chiusa, between Turin and Susa on the way to the Mt. Cenis Pass.[6] In addition to these works, and a few incidental references in narrative works like the *Historia Vizeliacensis* by Hugh of Poitiers, the principal sources for the history of the family of Montboissier are documents in chartularies, above all in the chartulary of Sauxillanges, which was especially patronized by the Montboissier. Little indeed would be known about the specific genealogy of the family without the charters of this single house, and accounts of the family written before their publication in 1861 are without exception inaccurate and incomplete, or, as is so often the case in genealogical works, overcomplete.[7] The documents of Sauxillanges were skillfully used by

---

[4] *Bibl. Clun.*, *notae*, col. 101. It is incorrect to call Peter the Venerable either Maurice or Peter Maurice, since the *Mauricii* after his name means "the son of Maurice."

[5] Labbé, *Nova bibl.*, II, 301 (RHGF, XII, 432).

[6] *Ampl. Coll.*, VI, 1200.

[7] Cf., for instance, J.-B.-P.-J. Courcelles, *Généalogie des Montboissier*, which is cited by Édouard de Dienne, "L'abbaye de Saint-Michel de Cluse et ses rapports avec la ville du Puy," *Congrès archéologique de France*, LXXI (1905) 286, n. 1. According to Fournier, *Peuplement*, p. 183, n. 37, "la fréquence des noms Hugues et Maurice dans cette famille rend difficile, sinon impossible, tout essai de généalogie."

Savio and De Dienne, however, in their works on the history of the abbey of La Chiusa,[8] and the following account of the early history of the family of Montboissier is to a great extent based upon their researches and a comparison of their conclusions.

Peter's earliest known ancestor was the great-grandfather mentioned by Geoffrey of Vigeois and Radulf. His name was Hugh of Palliers or Usson, but he was known on account of his extravagance as Hugh "the Unstitched" (*Dissutus, Descozuz, Descosun*), a name occasionally used by his descendants.[9] Almost nothing is known about Hugh except for his alleged foundation of La Chiusa on his return from a pilgrimage to Rome. His dates and background are the subject of dispute among historians of the abbey. Savio proposed on the basis of a reference to Pope Sylvester II that Hugh founded La Chiusa in 999/1003, not in about 966, as previously believed. He was of the opinion that Hugh lived from about 987 until 1043 and that his father was named Maitrannus and was the son of a certain Hugh and his wife Emma, who appeared as a widow in about 978–87.[10] De Dienne, on the other hand, returned to the traditional date of foundation, which he placed about 969, but believed that the abbey was actually built by Hugh's son Hugh Maurice in about 1000. He identified Hugh *Dissutus* with the Hugh who appeared with his wife Isengard on a

---

[8] Fedele Savio, *Sulle origini della abazia di S. Michele della Chiusa* (Turin, 1888), and De Dienne, in *Congrès arch.*, LXXI, 270–300. These are by far the best, indeed, the only serious studies on the early history of the family of Montboissier, but I have found no reference to them in any work on Peter the Venerable. I have been unable to consult the work of A. Mellana, *L'abbazia di S. Michele della Chiusa* (Rome, 1940), which is cited in *Rev. hist. ecc.*, XLII (1947) *Bibliographie*, no. 6362.

[9] On Hugh and his names, see De Dienne, in *Congrès arch.*, LXXI, 281, n. 1, and Boudet in *St. Flour*, introd., pp. cxxii–cxxiii, clxxxi, and p. 14, n. 3. He should not be called Hugh of Montboissier, as he was by early historians and, more recently, by Gerhard Schwartz and Elisabeth Abegg, "Das Kloster San Michele della Chiusa und seine Geschichtschreibung," *Neues Archiv*, XLV (1924) 236–237.

[10] On the basis of donors and witness lists in the early charters of Sauxillanges, Savio proposed the following genealogy:

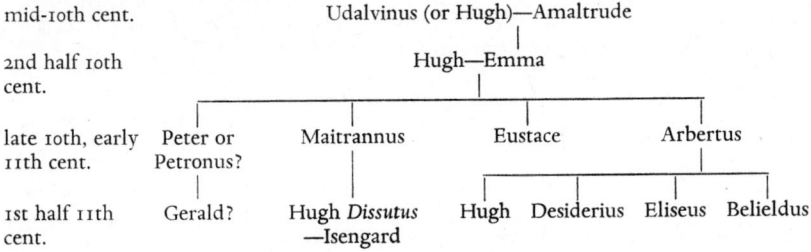

A variant of this genealogy, making Hugh *Dissutus* the son of Hugh and Emma, was apparently proposed by Antoine Lesmarie, *Saint-Étienne-sur-Usson*, cited by De Dienne, in *Congrès arch.*, LXXI, 282, n. 2.

charter of Brioude in 925/30[11] and believed that he lived from about 905 to 994 and was the son of Bego of Usson.[12] Neither of these genealogies is entirely satisfactory, but that of Savio presents fewer problems than that of De Dienne, and I am inclined to accept the later dates for the life of Hugh *Dissutus* and the foundation of La Chiusa.[13]

Hugh had at least six sons, of whom one, Maurice, was the first member of the family to be associated with the castle of Montboissier, which was probably built about the middle of the eleventh century.[14] He appeared as Maurice of Montboissier on a later confirmation of his

---

[11] *Cartulaire de Brioude*, ed. Henry Doniol, in *Mémoires de l'Académie des sciences, belles-lettres et arts de Clermont-Ferrand*, n.s. III (1861), and separately (Clermont-Ferrand and Paris, 1863), no. 73. The charter is dated in the eighth year of the reign of King Rudolf, that is, 930, but it is dated 925 by A. M. and M. Baudot, in *Mémoires . . . de Clermont-Ferrand* (cited Ep. 174, n. to p. 416), XXXV, 20. The identity of this Hugh with Hugh *Dissutus* was apparently accepted by Boudet in *St. Flour*, introd., p. cxxiii, n. 1; but the name Isengard was more frequent than De Dienne suggests (cf. *Sauxillanges*, nos. 246 and 408, and *Brioude*, nos. 147 and 228), and the identity cannot be regarded as established.

[12] De Dienne's genealogy, with the addition of some entries from the charters of Sauxillanges (the figures in parentheses), runs as follows:

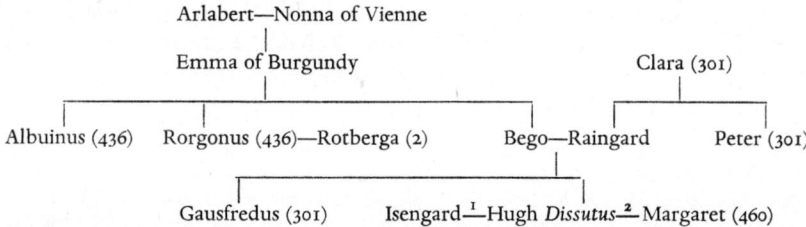

This genealogy is not impossible, but it presents several serious difficulties: (1) very long generations, ranging from 52 to 75 years; (2) Hugh's mother Raingard outlived both her husband and her son to an age of over 100; (3) Hugh's second marriage, to explain the reference by Hugh's son in charter 460 to his mother and father, Margaret and Hugh, and his grandfather Bego; and (4) the apparent conflation of Hugh's sons Hugh and Maurice into one son, Hugh Maurice, who built La Chiusa about 1000.

[13] Boudet dated the foundation in 975/85, following the chronicle of Bernard Iterus, who placed the foundation under the year 985: *Chroniques de Saint-Martial de Limoges*, ed. H. Duplès-Agier (Société de l'histoire de France; Paris, 1874) p. 44; cf. De Dienne, in *Congrès arch.*, LXXI, 279, for other dates that have been proposed. Harry Bresslau, "Erläuterungen zu den Diplomen Heinrichs II.," *Neues Archiv*, XXII (1897) 184, accepted the late date of after 999 proposed by Claretta and Savio; but from an examination of the dates of the early abbots Abegg, in *Neues Archiv*, XLV, 252–255, proposed 983/7. If this is correct, the birth date proposed for Hugh by Savio is too late. On the priories of La Chiusa in Auvergne, most of which were founded on lands given by Hugh and members of his family, see De Dienne, in *Congrès arch.*, LXXI, 289–290, and Beaunier-Besse, *Abbayes*, V, 121 (Arlanc-le-Bourg), 127 (Cunlhat), 141 (Sauviat), and 162–163 (Aurec). Two priories in the Bourbonais, Saint-Désiré and Courçais, were the subject of a long dispute in 1130–1 between La Chiusa and the abbey of St. Denis (and its dependency La Chapelle-Aude): Émile Chenon, *Histoire et coutumes du prieuré de La Chapelle-Aude* (Paris, 1915) pp. 159–162, and Fazy, *Origines*, I, 235–247 (nos. 260–262, 264–267, 272–273), and II, 103–104.

[14] The earliest reference to the castle, according to Fournier, *Peuplement*, p. 599, was in 1071/5. Gaussin, *La Chaise-Dieu*, p. 536, said that at this time it was one of only two dozen castles and strong points in all of Auvergne and Velay. It is in the modern department of Puy-de-Dôme (arr. Ambert, can. Cunlhat, cne. Brousse).

A. THE FAMILY OF PETER THE VENERABLE

gift to Sauxillanges of the monastery of St. Lupus in 1028/49.[15] Savio further attributed to him several other charters on which he appeared as Maurice alone and in one of which, dated 1043, he was described as *uir nobilissimus*.[16] De Dienne suggested that he lived from about 980 to 1066; and according to Courcelles and Jacotin he was married to Alix of Polignac, but I have found no documentary evidence for this.[17] There can be no question, however, that by this time the family enjoyed considerable power and prestige in central Auvergne.

Maurice II of Montboissier, the father of Peter the Venerable, was one of at least four brothers, the sons of Maurice I. He appears on several documents in the chartulary of Sauxillanges, of which the earliest seems to be an agreement between Prior Bertrand (1060/73) and the *vicarius* Achard.[18] Maurice was there described as *princeps*, which suggests not that he was himself a great noble but that he was among the advisers or *familiares* of the great.[19] "Mindful of the day of his death," Maurice and his wife and son (in the singular) renounced any unjust customs over the lands of Sauxillanges and renewed to Prior Letald, who probably succeeded Prior Bertrand, his promise to Bertrand to exercise no rights over the waters and forests belonging to the monks.[20] Together with his wife Raingard and his brother and sister-in-law William and Antonia, Maurice witnessed a grant during the priorate of Bernard (at least 1078–*ca.* 1090).[21] In 1096–7, according to Peter of Poitiers, he participated in the First Crusade and especially in the fighting around Antioch.[22] After his return, he appeared first among "the nobles (*proceres*) of Auvergne" who witnessed a grant in 1096/1105 and was the principal witness to a grant in 1114.[23] Finally, "for the sake of his soul and his burial, with the consent of his wife and sons," Maurice gave an estate to Sauxillanges by a charter witnessed by Raingard, his son Peter (the earliest documentary reference to Peter the Venerable), Hugh *Descosum* (probably another son), and Prior Elias, who is known to have been prior in 1119 and was replaced

---

[15] *Sauxillanges*, no. 478; cf. JL 5533.
[16] *Sauxillanges*, no. 635.
[17] De Dienne, in *Congrès arch.*, LXXI, 286–287, and the genealogical chart in vol. I of Jacotin, *Polignac*. This chart also shows marriages between Elizabeth and Richarde, the daughters of Hugh of Montboissier and his wife Margaret, to Heraclius I and Pontius II of Polignac, but again there is no documentary evidence.
[18] *Sauxillanges*, no. 790.
[19] Cf. Heinrich Koller, "Die Bedeutung des Titels 'princeps' in der Reichskanzlei unter den Saliern und Staufern," *MIÖG*, LXVIII (1960) 67, who described the *principes* of an area not as a *Stand* but as "a collection of which the membership changed from time to time."
[20] *Sauxillanges*, no. 625.
[21] *Sauxillanges*, no. 796.
[22] *Bibl. Clun.*, col. 615 A.
[23] *Sauxillanges*, nos. 958 (GC, II, *instr.*, 79–80 [1096/1100], and Jacotin, *Polignac*, I, 96, no. 38 [1096/1101]) and 634.

by 1123.[24] This charter was in fact probably his final disposition, at which Peter the Venerable himself said he was present in Letter 53 and after which Maurice took the monastic habit *ad succurrendum* at Sauxillanges. He died soon after and was buried at Sauxillanges. The necrology there recorded: "January 23 full office and penitential chant in hoods for Maurice lord of Montboissier, father of the abbot of Cluny."[25] The year of Maurice's death is unknown. Savio placed it in 1115, but since Maurice made his will during the priorate of Elias, and Rotlannus was still prior late in 1114,[26] he probably died on 23 January 1116 or 1117.[27]

Maurice II appears to have been a man of more than conventional piety and ability, who enhanced the reputation and position of his family. His wife Raingard was also a woman of superior character and talents, and her example and training were probably responsible for the ecclesiastical careers of five of her sons and for the remarkable part they played in the Church of their time.[28] It is unfortunate that nothing is known about Raingard's family. Cucherat suggested that she was a daughter of Geoffrey II of Semur-en-Brionnais, thus making her a niece (and her sons great-nephews) of St. Hugh of Cluny; and this was repeated by Graham and Evans.[29] There is no evidence for this suggestion, however, and the name Raingard, which was not uncommon in Auvergne, was almost unknown in Burgundy, and the relationship has not been accepted by specialists.[30] The principal sources for her life, besides the three charters on which she appears as the wife of Maurice of Montboissier,[31] are the life of Peter the Venerable by Radulf and above all Peter's Letter 53. These show that already before the birth of Peter the Venerable, in 1090/2, she was in touch with Hugh of Cluny, on whose advice Peter was devoted to the

---

[24] *Sauxillanges*, no. 795.

[25] Savio, *La Chiusa*, p. 30, n. 2. In *Sauxillanges*, no. 932, Peter the Venerable made provision for the liturgical commemoration of his parents and, after his own death, of himself.

[26] *Sauxillanges*, nos. 802 (22 August 1114) and 483, which is dated 31 December 1114. There was great confusion over the beginning of the year in Auvergne, however: see Giry, *Manuel*, p. 117; and if the year was dated from Christmas, the date of no. 483 would be 31 December 1113 N.S., but the numbers of the indiction (7) and the epact (12) confirm 1114.

[27] The *terminus ante quem* is Raingard's entry into Marcigny (see below).

[28] On Raingard, see the article by Lamma in *Studium* (cited Ep. 53). I have not seen the anonymous *Étude sur la be. Raingarde de Montboissier* (Clermont-Ferrand, 1888), which is cited by Chevalier, *Bio-bib.*, II, 3872. One senses that Raingard somewhat resembled in character and influence Guibert of Nogent's mother, whose life is described in Guibert of Nogent, *Vita*, I, 12–14 (pp. 36–51).

[29] Cucherat, *Cluny*, p. 91, n. 4, and in *Mém. de la Soc. Éduenne* (cited Ep. 53), XVI, 114–122; Graham, *Vézelay*, p. 49; Evans, *Mon. Life*, p. 38.

[30] Pignot, *Cluny*, III, 54–59 and 605–609; *Marcigny*, introd., p. xv, n. 1, and the genealogical chart between pp. 240–241.

[31] *Sauxillanges*, nos. 625, 795, and 796.

A. THE FAMILY OF PETER THE VENERABLE 239

monastic life, and that while her husband was still alive, before 1116/7, she met and came under the influence of St. Robert of Arbrissel, the founder of Fontevrault. After Maurice's death she refused to marry again and entered the famous Cluniac nunnery at Marcigny.[32] The exact date of her entry is uncertain. It was after the death of Robert of Arbrissel (23/5 February 1117) and while Hugh was claustral prior at Marcigny, from 1109 to 1122.[33] In Letter 53 Peter the Venerable twice said that she spent almost twenty years at Marcigny, which suggests, since she died in 1135, that she entered in 1117 or soon after.[34] Peter also said that she was cellarer and was called "mother of the monastery," which has been taken by some scholars to mean that she was prioress.[35] This was probably a metaphor, however, since in Letter 56 Peter simply said that she was a nun by profession and cellarer by office. Peter visited her frequently at Marcigny, and Letter 53 shows that she occupied an important position among the nuns there up until her death, in the odor of sanctity, on 24 June 1135.[36]

Maurice and Raingard appear to have had a family of eight sons. Peter of Poitiers described the brothers in his panegyric after mentioning the death of Maurice:

> Nec facile aduertas pulchra de coniuge natos,
> Tam sunt egregii, morumne an diuitiarum
> Fecerit haeredes senior Mauritius, atqui
> Viuere totus adhuc in fratribus otto uidetur.
> Cumque eadem pietas, uirtusque simillima patri
> In septem reliquis miro splendore nitescat.[37]

At the time Peter of Poitiers was writing, therefore, in about 1133, there were seven living brothers. One other brother had died previously, and the only puzzle in the passage is whether his name was Otto, as Duchesne, Mabillon, and Pignot assumed, or whether the *otto* should be spelled with a small letter, as I am inclined to believe,

---

[32] On Raingard's entry into Marcigny rather than Fontevrault, see Mabillon, *Annales*, VI, 9, and Lamma, in *Studium*, LIV, offprint p. 10, who suggested that she chose Marcigny on account of its *stabilitas*. The death of St. Robert and her sons' associations with Cluny may have been the decisive factors, however.

[33] See Ep. 53, n. to p. 162, l. 21.

[34] The date 1114 which is given in a list of the nuns at Marcigny printed in Cucherat, *Cluny*, p. 237, is certainly too early. Cf. *Marcigny*, introd., pp. xiv–xvi, on the reliability of this list.

[35] Lamma, *Momenti*, p. 53. The prioress at Marcigny had direct control over the nuns; the prior was in charge of running the house: Cucherat, *Cluny*, p. 220, and De Valous, *Mon. clun.*, I, 386.

[36] On the date of her death, see Ep. 52, n. to p. 153, l. 7. Peter the Venerable provided for her liturgical commemoration in *Sauxillanges*, no. 932; and in Letter 56 to Bishop Henry of Winchester he asked that a trental of masses be said for her in the abbeys and churches of the diocese of Winchester.

[37] *Bibl. Clun.*, col. 614 E.

and referred simply to the eight original brothers.³⁸ Radulf, in his life of Peter the Venerable, written after Peter's death, said that Peter had six brothers, of whom four were clerics and two were laymen.³⁹ Mabillon and Pignot added two daughters to the eight sons, but they are not mentioned in any contemporary source and may have arisen out of a confusion with Peter's two nieces Margaret and Pontia. Since there is no definite indication in the sources of the respective ages of the brothers, I shall discuss them here in alphabetical order.

Armannus (Artmannus, Hermannus)⁴⁰ was described by Radulf as abbot of Manglieu and by Geoffrey of Vigeois as "prior of Cluny and later abbot of Manglieu," which was a small and relatively unimportant house in the region of Sauxillanges and Montboissier.⁴¹ He appeared as prior of Cluny on charters of 1149 and 1151/2, and he probably became abbot of Manglieu not long after, since he was succeeded as prior of Cluny by Peter of Pithiviers.⁴² He was presumably the abbot A. of Manglieu who wrote a letter to King Louis VII.⁴³ A document of 1151/2 in the chartulary of Sauxillanges suggests that Armannus was prior of Sauxillanges before he became prior of Cluny: "De his omnibus in presentia domini Artmanni, Cluniacensis prioris, nec non Celsiniensis prioris et Hugonis ejusdem loci prioris et aliorum monachorum pacem se tenere promisit ipse [Dalmacius] et filius ejus Willemus, fuerunt que presentes multi nobiles uiri quorum nomina sunt ista: Eustachius, frater ejusdem prioris" [and others].⁴⁴ The

---

³⁸ Duchesne, in *Bibl. Clun.*, *notae*, cols. 101–102; Mabillon, *Annales*, V, 412; Pignot, *Cluny*, III, 52. The sense of the passage, and especially the reference to the piety and virtue of the father shining in the seven remaining sons, seems to indicate clearly that the *otto* means eight and not another son named Otto. The name Otto, furthermore, was very rare in Auvergne: cf. *s.n.* in the indices to the chartularies of Sauxillanges and Brioude. Cucherat, in *Mém. de la Soc. Éduenne*, XVI, 115, referred simply to eight children. Graham, *Vézelay*, p. 48, n. 1, mentioned a charter in the chartulary of La Charité, pp. 136–138 (in fact pp. 136–139, nos. 56–57), witnessed by Peter the Venerable and his brothers, but they were in fact of the family of Montenpuis, not Montboissier.

³⁹ *Ampl. Coll.*, VI, 1200.

⁴⁰ He should not be confused with the knight Armannus who became a monk at Cluny toward the end of his life and whose vision of the Devil in the form of a bear was told by Peter the Venerable in *De miraculis*, I, 18, in *Bibl. Clun.*, cols. 1275–1276; cf. chronicle of Cluny, *ibid.*, col. 596 (*recte* 598).

⁴¹ *Ampl. Coll.*, VI, 1200, and Labbé, *Nova bibl.*, II, 301 (*RHGF*, XII, 432). He is listed as abbot of Manglieu without dates in *GC*, II, 362, and Devic and Vaissete, *Languedoc* (ne wed.), V, 493.

⁴² See *s.n.* Armannus and Peter of Pithiviers in Appendix R.

⁴³ Duchesne, *Scriptores*, IV, 739–740.

⁴⁴ *Sauxillanges*, no. 961: a grant from Dalmatius of Baffie to the Cluniac house of Chaumont in the diocese of Clermont, dated the middle of Lent in 1151, which may be either 1151 or 1152, N.S., depending on the beginning of the year (cf. n. 26 above). This charter was dated 1152 by Marcellin Boudet, *Collection inédite de chartes de franchises de Basse-Auvergne*, in *Mémoires ... de Clermont-Ferrand*, n.s. XXIV (Clermont-Ferrand, 1914) p. 50. The date 1152 is slightly supported by the appearance of Stephen as bishop of Clermont: Gams, *Series*, p. 538.

A. THE FAMILY OF PETER THE VENERABLE 241

reference to "also the prior of Sauxillanges" and "the brother of the same prior" are ambiguous, but I am inclined to believe that they both refer to Armannus, since Prior Hugh of Sauxillanges appears on a document of 1135/56,[45] and Armannus is known to have had a brother named Eustace. A prior of Sauxillanges named Armannus appears on two documents, one undated and the other of 1138/51.[46]

Eustace was a knight, according to Radulf, and Peter's only living brother in secular life in about 1150, when Letter 160 was written. This letter's heading, "Dilecto germano, immo filio Eustachio," suggests that he was much younger than Peter. In Letter 91, written in about 1141, Peter mentioned a quarrel between his brothers Heraclius and Eustace. He appeared as "Eustace, the brother of the prior" on the Sauxillanges charter of 1151/2 mentioned above, presuming that the prior was Armannus of Montboissier. A few years later, however, he appears to have attacked Sauxillanges, since Peter the Venerable secured from Pope Adrian IV a bull, dated 19 April 1156, instructing the archbishops of Vienne and Lyons to keep Eustace from harming Sauxillanges.[47] According to Pignot, he was married to Heraclea of Polignac, and Lamma believed that he became a monk;[48] but there is no evidence for either of these assertions.

Heraclius (Eraclius) was the most prominent of the brothers after Peter the Venerable.[49] He spent his youth at Lyons, according to Peter's Letter 99, and then became provost of the college of secular canons of St. Julian at Brioude, according to Radulf. Provost Eraclius of Brioude witnessed a grant by the abbot W. to the monastery of Pébrac in 1139.[50] It is curious that Radulf, who was certainly writing

[45] *Sauxillanges*, no. 932: the provision made by Peter the Venerable for liturgical commemoration of his parents and himself. It can be dated with certainty after the death of Raingard in 1135 and was probably considerably later.
[46] *Sauxillanges*, nos. 944 and 949, which was dated 1141 by Boudet in *St. Flour*, introd., p. cxxxviii, n. 1, and 1145–50? by Chaix de Lavarène, "Bullaire," pp. 580–581. It can be dated with certainty between the election of Pontius as abbot of Vézelay in 1138 and the death of Bishop Aimericus of Clermont in 1151. If my identification of Prior Armannus of Sauxillanges with the later prior of Cluny and abbot of Manglieu is correct, he was the brother of the Pontius with whom he appears on this charter.
[47] *Bull. Clun.*, p. 68; cf. JL 10205 and *Cluny*, V, 536; no. 4189.
[48] Pignot, *Cluny*, III, 54, and Lamma, *Momenti*, p. 71. Gomot, *Mozat*, pp. 38–39, identified him with Abbot Eustace of Mosat (1131–47), but the date of Peter's Letter 160 excludes this possibility.
[49] The fullest account of Heraclius's early life, before he became archbishop of Lyons in 1153, are by Beyssac, in *Rev. d'hist. de Lyon* (cited bibliographical note to Ep. 100), XII, 409, and *Chanoines*, p. 30. Both he and Marcellin Boudet, "Le domaine des dauphins de Viennois et des comtes de Forez en Auvergne [suite]," *Bulletin historique et scientifique de l'Auvergne*, 1904, p. 142, overlooked the evidence that Heraclius was provost of Brioude and said that he was a canon at Lyons from 1139.
[50] *Cartularium... Piperacensis*, ed. J.-B. Payrard (Le Puy, 1875) pp. 25–26, no. 29. On the basis of this charter, misdated 1138, Heraclius was included in the lists of the provosts of Brioude in *GC*, II, 483, and Chaix de Lavarène, "Bullaire," p. 439 (cf. Ep. 174, n. to p. 416).

after the death of Peter the Venerable, described Heraclius simply as provost of Brioude rather than as archbishop of Lyons, as he later became; and it is possible that the provost Heraclius and Peter's brother Heraclius were different men.[51] The high authority of Radulf, however, and the known interest of Peter the Venerable and his family in Brioude, which was located less than twenty miles south of Montboissier,[52] both tend to confirm the accuracy of Radulf's statement. It may have been while Heraclius was at Brioude that he quarreled with his brother Eustace. He returned to Lyons before the death of Pope Innocent II in September 1143, however,[53] and soon after became archdeacon, since no other Heraclius is known to have been associated with the chapter of Lyons at this time. Heraclius appeared as archdeacon among the witnesses to two grants to Cluny in 1145/7 and on 4 November 1149.[54] In about 1150, according to Beyssac, he became abbot of St. Just at Lyons, which had become a secular collegiate church in the late eleventh or early twelfth century, and he kept this position even after his election as archbishop of Lyons in 1153. He was archbishop for ten years, until his death in 1163, and he figured prominently in the chronicles and documents of this period.[55]

Hugh was Peter's second brother in secular life and apparently died before about 1150, when Peter referred to Eustace in Letter 160 as his only [living] brother in secular life. Hugh was the father of Margaret and Pontia, Peter's two nieces who were nuns at Marcigny and to whom Letter 185 was addressed. He was in all probability the Hugh *Descosum* who appeared with Raingard and Peter the Venerable on Maurice's will in 1115/16,[56] and he thus shows the persistence in the family of the sobriquet of his great-grandfather Hugh "the Unstitched." He can thus be identified as Peter's brother Dissutus who was mentioned by Radulf and described as a knight.[57] He was prob-

---

He does not appear on the elaborate charter concerning Brioude, dated 12 March 1137, in Chassaing, *Spicilegium*, pp. 13-14, no. 6, where Odilo of Mercoeur was provost, or on any known subsequent charter.

[51] Devic and Vaissete, *Languedoc*, II, 371, said that the provost Heraclius was a son of Pontius of Polignac (and Heraclius was a known name in the family of Polignac), but he does not appear on the chart in vol. I of Jacotin, *Polignac*, which is incomplete in few respects.

[52] See Letter 174. There was a canon of Brioude named Heraclius of Montboissier in 1256: Chassaing, *Spicilegium*, pp. 86-87, no. 39.

[53] Letter 99.

[54] *Cluny*, V, 455 and 486, nos. 4106 and 4140.

[55] On Heraclius as archbishop, see Duchesne, in *Bibl. Clun., notae*, cols. 140-141; Severt, *Chronologia*, I, 244-246; Martin, *Conciles*, nos. 587-609; Constable, "Cluniac Tithes," pp. 621 ff.; and Janssen, *Legaten*, p. 162. He was listed as a benefactor in a medieval calendar from the Carthusian house of Meyriat: *Obituaires*, V, 464.

[56] *Sauxillanges*, no. 795; cf. Savio, *La Chiusa*, p. 30, n. 2; and pp. 237-238 above.

[57] *Ampl. Coll.*, VI, 1200.

ably the Hugh *princeps* of Montboissier and Hugh *princeps* who witnessed two undated grants to Sauxillanges.[58] His name and position suggest that he was the eldest son and head of the family after his father's death.

Jordan was described as abbot of La Chaise-Dieu by both Radulf and Geoffrey of Vigeois.[59] According to a later catalogue of the abbots of La Chaise-Dieu, "Lord Jordan of Montboissier... was seventh; he died on 24 November (*octavo Calendas Decembris*), concerning whom see Peter the Venerable, abbot of Cluny, the sixth book of his letters, ep. 13 [= Letter 157]."[60] He was abbot from 1146 until 1157, according to Gaussin, or 1158, according to the *Gallia christiana*,[61] and his name appears on numerous charters during this period.[62]

Pontius was the most famous of the brothers after Peter and Heraclius, and certainly the most notorious.[63] The only information concerning his early life occurs in Letter 16 of Peter the Venerable, who said that as young men he and Pontius spent about ten years together, and in the chronicle of Vézelay, according to which Pontius was "a brother of Abbot Peter of Cluny [and] was taken from the monastery of La Chiusa."[64] Most scholars have assumed that the ten years spent together by Peter and Pontius were at Vézelay, where Peter was "seniorum doctor et custos ordinis," according to Radulf, and prior during the abbacy of Pontius of Cluny, according to the chronicle of Cluny. Since Peter seems to have been at Sauxillanges until at least 1115/6, however, and became prior of Domène in 1120,

---

[58] *Sauxillanges*, nos. 907–908.

[59] *Ampl. Coll.*, VI, 1200, and Labbé, *Nova bibl.*, II, 284 and 301 (*RHGF*, XII, 432). See Gaussin, *La Chaise-Dieu*, pp. 156–159 and *s.n.* in index, who described the congregation of La Chaise-Dieu in 1146 as second in importance only to that of Cluny among Benedictine congregations (p. 220, cf. p. 369).

[60] Labbé, *Nova bibl.*, II, 660.

[61] Gaussin, *La Chaise-Dieu*, p. 159; *GC*, II, 335; cf. François Gardon, *Histoire de l'abbaye de la Chaize-Dieu*, ed. C. J. de Rosières (Le Puy, 1912) pp. 51–57.

[62] Cf. notes to Epp. 141 and 157.

[63] Hugh of Poitiers in the *Historia Vizeliacensis* twice referred to Pontius as the uterine brother of Peter the Venerable and Jordan, that is, of the same mother but a different father: D'Achery, *Spicilegium*, II, 517 and 530; and this has been followed by some historians, as in the *RHGF*, XII, 345 and 432, n. a. Peter the Venerable himself, however, and Pope Eugene III, writing to Peter, referred to Pontius respectively, as "*germanus ex carne*" and "*carnalis germanus tuus*": Letter 16 and *Spicilegium*, II, 512 (JL 9627). Hugh of Poitiers also referred to Pontius as *germanus* to Peter the Venerable at one point, a few lines after calling him uterine: *Spicilegium*, II, 530; and there can be no question that he was in fact a full brother. On Pontius, see Pignot, *Cluny*, III, 52 and 59–61; Aimé Chérest, "Étude historique sur Vézelay," *Bulletin de la Société des sciences historiques et naturelles de l'Yonne*, XVI (1862) 305–431 and 462–463, and separately, *Vézelay: Étude historique* (Auxerre, 1863–1868) I, 114–259; Graham, *Vézelay*; Louis, *Girart*, I, 181–186; and Victor Saxer, "Le statut juridique de Vézelay des origines à la fin du XII° siècle," *Revue de droit canonique*, VI (1956) 225–262, esp. pp. 247–257.

[64] Labbé, *Nova bibl.*, I, 397 (*RHGF*, XII, 345).

he probably spent less than ten years at Vézelay; and his years with Pontius may have been at Sauxillanges, when they were both boys, or later at Cluny.[65] Pontius then went to La Chiusa,[66] which had been founded by his great-grandfather, and in 1138 succeeded Alberic (who became cardinal-bishop of Ostia)[67] as abbot of Vézelay. There he became involved in a long and acrimonious controversy with the townsmen of Vézelay and the count of Nevers. He was the type of man who was made, according to De Lespinasse, "to shine at the head of an army more than in the calm of a cloister."[68] In 1152 he was exiled from Vézelay and installed as abbot of Souvigny by Peter the Venerable, at the request of Pope Eugene III. In 1154, however, Anastasius IV required Peter to withdraw this grant and several others made without the consent of the monks of Cluny.[69] Peace was re-established at Vézelay soon afterward, and Pontius died there as abbot in 1161.

It is impossible to determine exactly the respective ages of the seven brothers, but it appears that the two in secular life, Hugh and Eustace, were probably the oldest and the youngest. Peter the Venerable was probably the second oldest, since he and Hugh were the only sons to witness their father's will. Peter was probably born in 1090/2.[70] The order of the three other brothers in monastic life may be indicated in the heading to Letter 53, which was addressed "to my most dearly beloved brothers and sons Jordan, Pontius, and Armannus." Jordan also appears first in the list of Peter's brothers given by Radulf, where he is followed by Pontius, Armannus, Heraclius, and the two laymen;[71] but the position of Heraclius is uncertain.

A few other indications concerning Peter's family can be gathered from his letters and other sources. Letter 56, for instance, shows that one of his brothers visited Henry of Winchester in England in 1135; and in Letter 120 Peter referred to a Cistercian abbey patronized by his brothers and nephews. This shows that either Hugh or Eustace had sons, but nothing specific is known about them. Abbot Eustace of Le

---

[65] See Ep. 16, n. to p. 23, and Appendix D.

[66] Cf. Boudet, in *Bulletin . . . de l'Auvergne*, 1904, p. 141. According to Schnack, *Richard von Cluny* (cited Ep. 2), p. 14, n. 20, Pontius was abbot of La Chiusa.

[67] See Ep. 4, n. to p. 8, l. 23.

[68] René de Lespinasse, *Le Nivernais et les comtes de Nevers* (Paris, 1909-1914) I, 303, and 300-338 generally on the controversy.

[69] Chaix de Lavarène, "Bullaire," pp. 79-80 (*Spicilegium*, II, 512) and 82-83 (*Bull. Clun.*, p. 65); JL 9627 and 9888. On the priorate of Pontius at Souvigny, see Fazy, *Origines*, I, 282 (no. 329), 288 (no. 342), 293 (no. 350), 627-628, and II, 128, and Côte, *Souvigny*, pp. 46-47, nos. 52-54, and 129-130. According to Hugh of Poitiers in the *Hist. Viz.*, III, Peter the Venerable was angry with Pontius (*indigne tulit*) for asking the Pope to be granted Souvigny: *Spicilegium*, II, 531.

[70] See Appendix D.

[71] *Ampl. Coll.*, VI, 1200.

A. THE FAMILY OF PETER THE VENERABLE

Miroir was described in Letter 193 as "consanguineus meus." This again shows the wide ecclesiastical ramifications of the family, although the exact relationship is unknown.[72] A more tantalizing reference, which suggests connections with the upper ranks of Burgundian nobility, occurs in the *Historia Vizeliacensis* by Hugh of Poitiers, who described Pontius as a kinsman ("cognationis affinitatis") of the count of Nevers; but in spite of the guesses of historians, this riddle is also unsolved.[73]

Certain versions of the chronicle of the abbey of St. Peter at Le Puy, finally, and some of the vernacular catalogues of the bishops of Le Puy, say that Bishop Pontius II of Le Puy belonged to the family of Montboissier and died at Montboissier in about 1128. The editors of the *Gallia christiana*, following Dom Claude Estiennot, conflated the two successive bishops of Le Puy named Pontius in the early twelfth century into one who was bishop, they said, from about 1102 until 1128.[74] Devic and Vaissete, however, using the newly discovered chronicle of St. Peter, re-established that there were two bishops named Pontius: one, former abbot of La Chaise-Dieu and bishop from about 1102 to 1108/18 (probably about 1112), and the other, Pontius Mauritius of Montboissier, who was bishop from 1108/18 until 1128 and whom they call an uncle or great-uncle of Peter the Venerable. He appeared as "Pontius Mauritius abbas" together with Bishop Pontius I on a charter for Conques in Rouergue in 1105; succeeded as bishop in about 1112; went for two and a half years to Jerusalem on account of troubles in his diocese; died at Montboissier, soon after his return, on 20 April, probably in 1128; and was buried at La Chaise-Dieu.[75] The most recent edition of the chronicle omits the reference to Montboissier, however,[76] although the "cognomento Mauricius" may still suggest a relationship with the family. He was probably not an uncle or great-uncle of Peter the Venerable on his father's side, but he may have been, as Savio suggested on his genealogical chart, a cousin, perhaps a son of Peter's uncle Hugh.

---

[72] Cf. Pignot, *Cluny*, III, 608–609; Constable, "Cluniac Tithes," p. 619.
[73] Cf. Pignot, *Cluny*, III, 607–608; De Lespinasse, *Nivernais*, I, 303, n. 3.
[74] *GC*, II, 703–704.
[75] Devic and Vaissete, *Languedoc*, II, 371, 406, and 601, and *preuves*, 9–10 (chronicle of St. Peter at Le Puy) and 368–369 (charter of Conques); cf. *Cartulaire de l'abbaye de Conques en Rouergue*, ed. Gustave Desjardins (Documents historiques publiés par la Société de l'École des Chartes; Paris, 1879) p. 345, no. 475, and introd., p. xcviii. This material was reprinted verbatim in the new edition of Devic and Vaissete (III, 618, 677; IV, 147; V, 26–27 and 797), which has an additional section of the bishops of Le Puy saying that Pontius II died at Montpellier (V, 402–403).
[76] *Cartulaire de l'abbaye de St-Chaffre du Monastier*, ed. Ulysse Chevalier (Collection de cartulaires dauphinois, 8.1; Montbéliard-Paris, 1884) pp. 165–166. The version printed in Devic and Vaissete, *Languedoc*, II *preuves*, 9–10, and *RHGF*, XII, 347, includes the reference to Montboissier.

These minor references are inconclusive, therefore,[77] but they point toward both connections outside Auvergne and otherwise unsuspected ecclesiastical connections with the Cistercians and with the diocese of Le Puy. They thus add to the picture of the Montboissier as a feudal family of secondary or tertiary rank in terms of wealth and political power which was able through the Church to exercise influence of the first rank of importance.

---

[77] Cf. Pignot, *Cluny*, III, 607, who said that the references in Letter 193 and the *Historia Vizeliacensis* "teach us nothing."

B. THE HEALTH OF PETER THE VENERABLE

Peter's interest in medical matters and his concern for his health can be traced through his works for at least twenty-five years.[1] It has, indeed, been suggested that he rather prided himself on his knowledge of medicine and of its language in his letter to Heloise concerning the last illness and death of Abelard,[2] and also in the description of his own symptoms in the letter to Dr. Bartholomew. There can be no question that his sufferings were genuine, however, and that for most of his adult life he was in delicate, if not poor, health.

The earliest reference to a specific illness occurs in the *De miraculis*, II, 13, where Peter described the death of Pontius of Cluny, "tormented for some time by the Roman disease," after his trial at Rome in 1126. "The same disease also did not spare me," he continued, "and burned for more than half a year with an almost intolerable fire." His eventual recovery, which Peter compared to the recovery of Cluny from the disease of schism and disturbance, was assisted by the prayers of his monks and the medical care of a certain wise cleric.[3] Another description of this same attack of fever is found in the *De miraculis*, I, 6: "The reason that I went to Rome with many of my monks was well known to all men of that time [i.e., the schism at Cluny]. On my return I brought with me a violent Roman fever. To cure this I was advised to revisit my homeland and native climate. I therefore went to the noble Cluniac monastery of Sauxillanges and spent all of Lent there, distressed much more by the fires of the fever than by the labors of the fasts."[4] This illness can therefore be dated in the winter of 1126 and the spring of 1127.

Peter fell ill again on his visit to the Council of Pisa in June 1135, and although he recovered quickly on this occasion, as he wrote to Bishop Henry of Winchester,[5] he was convinced from this time on that the climate of Italy, and especially the heat of an Italian summer, was

---

[1] Cf. Leclercq, *Pierre le Vén.*, pp. 24–28.
[2] Jeannin, in *Mélanges St. Bernard*, p. 113.
[3] *Bibl. Clun.*, col. 1313 AB.
[4] *Bibl. Clun.*, col. 1254 B. *Sauxillanges*, no. 945 (*Cluny*, V, 378–380, no. 4023), refers to a visit of Peter to Sauxillanges before 1131.
[5] Letter 56.

fatal to his health. He wrote to Pope Innocent II early in 1137 apologizing for not coming to Italy. "The fragility of the waxen vessel [of my body] is so great, as I have often experienced, that it melts in the sun of Italy almost before it begins to appear."[6] Probably at the same time he wrote to the papal chancellor Cardinal Haimeric that "the weakness of my body and the nature of the unfavorable climate" prevented his coming.[7] Later in 1137 he again remarked on his delicate health in a letter to the Pope.[8] Innocent II wrote to Peter on 20 July 1137 mentioning "the weakness of your constitution" and Peter's inability to stand hot weather.[9] In a letter to Pope Lucius II in 1144, accompanying some Cluniac monks sent to Rome at the Pope's request, Peter commented gloomily on the death "that the Roman climate as a rule rapidly brings to our men."[10] Again in 1149 he wrote to Eugene III describing the journey to Rome as "deadly owing to the Italian diseases."[11]

Even at home in France, Peter's health was far from good during this period, and there are several references to illnesses in his letters.[12] He gave "the bad health of my body," for instance, as one of his reasons for not writing to his old friend Hato of Troyes.[13] In a general letter to the Cluniacs, written about 1146, he mentioned his illnesses while traveling.[14] And his long letter to his nieces Margaret and Pontia, which he probably wrote towards the end of his life, was occasioned by their concern for his ill-health and offer to treat him "by physical art."[15]

The most specific information about Peter's indispositions is given in the letters to and from Dr. Bartholomew.[16] These show that Bartholomew had visited Cluny for a few days during the year preceding that in which the letters were written and that Peter, therefore, sought his advice on this occasion. Each year, he wrote, he usually suffered once from "the disease that is called catarrh." This year he had had it twice, once in the late summer and early autumn and once in the winter. On account of the catarrh during the summer, he delayed his usual bloodletting, which he had as a rule every two months and had already put off owing to the press of official business,

[6] Letter 1.
[7] Letter 3.
[8] Letter 63.
[9] Letter 62; JL 7848.
[10] Letter 118.
[11] Letter 141.
[12] The visit to Montpellier mentioned in Letter 30 may have been on account of his health. On his retreat in the woods near Cluny, mentioned in Letters 123–129, he was accompanied by the learned *scholasticus* and master of medicine Robert.
[13] Letter 81.
[14] Letter 133.
[15] Letter 185.
[16] Letters 158a and b; cf., on Dr. Bartholomew, Appendix M.

B. THE HEALTH OF PETER THE VENERABLE

because he was warned that a bloodletting during an attack of catarrh might impare his voice and even kill him.[17] The bloodletting was thus delayed for almost four months until at last, fearing a fever, he had his blood let twice within three weeks. As a consequence he not only kept his catarrh but also, as predicted, lost his voice, which had been gone for three months at the time he was writing. He spat up phlegm and was constipated, and according to his doctors the phlegm that remained after his blood was let had filled his veins and vital passages and thus oppressed his chest and stomach and closed "the free and usual passage of the voice." The doctors recommended treating him with warm and wet medicines, in order to alleviate his throat and arteries, although Peter himself thought that warm and dry would be better, since the qualities of his disease were cold and wet. He went onto a special diet and took various medicines and drugs, all without effect, until after three months he decided to consult Bartholomew, whom he asked to send his assistant Bernard with medicines and instructions.

Bartholomew in his reply wrote that he was sending Bernard and advised Peter not to have his blood let until he began to recover his voice, since his nature suffered from an excess of phlegm rather than of blood. On account of the pain in his head, however, the cautery should be repeated.[18] As a medicine he prescribed myrrh, which was both dry and glutinous, "actively wet, potentially dry," and which would therefore both dry up the matter of the disease and ease the arteries and veins. "I have furthermore fully discussed with Bernard," he wrote, "concerning baths and stoves, fumigations and poultices (*fomentationes*) around the chest, and concerning pills to be held under the tongue, pills for the catarrh, a balsam potion, gargles, and similar things."

---

[17] The practice of bloodletting was all but universal in medieval monasteries: see the Carolingian monastic regulations, which laid down that bloodletting should be performed when necessary, in *Initia consuetudinis benedictinae*, ed. Kassius Hallinger (Corpus consuetudinum monasticarum, 1; Siegburg, 1963) pp. 445, 459, 518, 546. On bloodletting at Cluny, see Bernard, *Cons. Clun.*, I, 29 (ed. Herrgott, pp. 212–214), and Ulric, *Cons. Clun.*, II, 21, who also did not specify the periods for bloodletting (PL, CXLIX, 709–710); in English Benedictine monasteries, see *The Monastic Constitutions of Lanfranc*, ed. David Knowles (Medieval Classics; London, 1951) pp. 93–95 (and app. C, pp. 152–153), and *The Customary of Eynsham* (cited p. 1, n. 2, above) pp. 103–107; and in the houses of canons, see *Observances of Barnwell* (cited Ep. 132, n. to p. 334), introd., pp. lxi–lxxiii. Nicholas of Montiéramey, ep. 49 (printed among the letters of Peter of Celle, ep. 63, in PL, CCII, 491), described the bloodletting at Clairvaux and the consequent inability of the monks to work, pray, read, or even listen. Cf. Edmond Martène, *De antiquis monachorum ritibus*, II, 13, in *De antiquis ecclesiae ritibus* (Antwerp [Milan], 1736–1738) IV, 239–244; Louis Gougaud, "La pratique de la phlébotomie dans les cloîtres," *Revue Mabillon*, XIIII (1924) 1–13, esp. pp. 3–4 on Cluny; and, more generally, MacKinney, *Med. Medicine* (cited Ep. 158b, n. to p. 381), pp. 39–40.

[18] On cauterization, see MacKinney, *Med. Medicine*, pp. 41–42.

The approximate chronology of Peter's illness on this occasion can be established from his letter to Bartholomew. He had a bloodletting in either early or mid-June, after which he was busy with legal cases and conferences with the local nobility, and he therefore put off his next bloodletting "long beyond" the usual two months. Meanwhile an attack of catarrh came on "at the end of the summer and from the beginning of the autumn," that is, probably in August and September, and he delayed his bloodletting again, for a total of four months, that is, until early October. He then had two bloodlettings within three weeks, the second one being probably at the beginning of November. Three months after the first of these, in the first week of January, as Peter himself says, he wrote to Dr. Bartholomew.

The year of these events is hard to establish, but it was probably 1150. Peter wrote two letters in April 1150 to Bernard of Clairvaux and Suger, excusing his inability to attend the crusading council at Chartres and giving as one of his reasons, to Bernard, "the almost continual indisposition of my body since Christmas," and, to Suger, "the multiple indisposition of my body which I have suffered almost continually since Christmas up to this time."[19] This cannot have been the illness described in the letter to Dr. Bartholomew, which began in the late summer;[20] it may have been the winter attack of catarrh mentioned there, with which Bartholomew's short visit "in the previous year" (according to the Old Style of reckoning) may have been associated. The cases and conferences in the early summer may then refer to the aftermath of the meeting of Cluniac priors in May 1150.[21] In the autumn of 1150, according to this dating, Peter wrote to Nicholas of Montiéramey, who was planning to visit Peter, that he was forced to stay at Cluny until Christmas "by a certain misfortune of my body."[22] The letter to Dr. Bartholomew can, therefore, with some security be dated in early January 1151.[23]

---

[19] Letters 164 and 166. There is a very similar passage in Letter 170 to the Carthusians of Meyriat, in which Peter referred to "the multiple indisposition of my body, from which my constitution has suffered for more than half a year," but the date of this letter is not certain.

[20] There is no reason why Peter would have written "since Christmas" if he had in fact been ill since the previous summer.

[21] See Ep. 164, n. to p. 398, l. 10.

[22] Letter 176. This may refer to the loss of his voice.

[23] The year 1149 for the events, and January 1150 for the letter, is not impossible, however, assuming that Peter was describing the same illness in Letters 164 and 166 and in Letter 158a and for some reason said that he had been suffering since Christmas rather than since the previous summer. This fits the position of the letters in the collection, but it accords less well with Peter's known movements and activities in 1149-50 and above all with the group of letters (175-177 and 178-184) concerning Nicholas's prospective visit to Cluny. These clearly refer to an illness beginning long before Christmas and were probably written after (and almost certainly not at the same time as) the letters referring to the Council of Chartres (Letters 163-166), in which there is no mention of Nicholas's visit.

B. THE HEALTH OF PETER THE VENERABLE

Medically speaking, it is clear that Peter suffered from at least two distinct ailments: malaria and a type of chronic bronchitis.[24] The symptoms described in the *De miraculis* definitely point to malaria, which would also account for Peter's illness in 1135 and be likely to recur on any visit to Italy, particularly in summer. The troubles in 1150 and 1151 are more difficult to diagnose. Emphysema has been suggested, but Peter nowhere referred to being short of breath. It is therefore probable that he suffered from an unusually acute attack of bronchitis and laryngitis, to which he was subject, brought on, perhaps, by the hard work of the summer and aggravated, but not caused, by the loss of blood in the bloodlettings. It is not known whether or not Peter was cured by Bartholomew's prescriptions and his pupil Bernard's ministrations, but he evidently recovered during the spring and summer of 1151 and was strong and bold enough to undertake a long and strenuous trip to Italy from November 1151 until March 1152.

---

[24] I am indebted for advice on the medical aspects of Peter's health to my brother Dr. John Constable of the Massachusetts General Hospital and to Prof. Dr. Henri Isliker of the University of Lausanne.

C. PETER THE VENERABLE, THE LATERAN COUNCIL OF 1139, AND THE CASE BETWEEN KING STEPHEN AND THE EMPRESS MATHILDA

An important reference to the public life of Peter the Venerable occurs in a letter written by Gilbert Foliot to Brian Fitz-Count in 1143/4. "It is not long ago," he wrote, "that you heard that the lord pope Innocent had summoned together the Church and held a celebrated council at Rome. And I, the least of the Cluniacs, was present at that great council with my lord and father the lord abbot of Cluny. This case [between King Stephen and Empress Mathilda] was brought into the open there and discussed at some length." Gilbert then described the arguments put forward by each side in this "trial" between the rival claimants to the throne of England.[1] John of Salisbury gave a similar account, without referring to the abbot of Cluny, in his *Historia pontificalis*.[2]

This trial before the Pope was an important event in English history, and it has naturally attracted the attention of historians. One of the first scholars to study the matter with care was Round, who rejected the dates of 1152 and 1148 proposed, respectively, by Freeman and Norgate and who decided "that the council and debate at Rome belong to the early months of 1136."[3] This conclusion was accepted by Rössler, Ramsay, H. W. C. Davis, and Haskins.[4] Böhmer pointed out, however, that Innocent II was away from Rome throughout the year 1136, and he therefore proposed that John of Salisbury and Gilbert Foliot were describing different events: the former at Pisa in January

---

[1] *Gilberti... epistolae*, ed. J. A. Giles (London, 1846) I, 100, ep. 79. It was written during the pontificate of Pope Celestine II (26 September 1143—8 March 1144). On this letter, see Morey and Brooke, *Foliot*, pp. 105–123, which appeared after this appendix was written.

[2] John of Salisbury, *Hist. pont.*, XLII (ed. cit., pp. 83–86).

[3] Round, *Geoffrey*, p. 258. The entire appendix B (pp. 250–261) is entitled "The Appeal to Rome in 1136" and cites the works of Freeman and Norgate.

[4] Oskar Rössler, *Kaiserin Mathilde... und das Zeitalter der Anarchie in England* (Historische Studien, ed. Ebering, 7; Berlin, 1897) pp. 132–136; Ramsay, *Foundations* (cited Ep. 15), II, 349; H. W. C. Davis, *England under the Normans and Angevins*, 7th ed. (A History of England, ed. Charles Oman, 2; London, 1921) p. 155; Haskins, *Norman Institutions* (cited Ep. 15, n. to p. 22, l. 7), p. 125.

1136 and the latter at Rome in 1139 (the Second Lateran Council).[5] The whole matter was finally re-examined by R. L. Poole, who argued that there was only one "trial" between Stephen and Mathilda, although Stephen secured a confirmation of his position from the Pope early in 1136, and that it took place at the Lateran Council in 1139.[6] He based this conclusion on three points: Gilbert Foliot's unequivocal statement that the council was at Rome; the lack of time for a "trial" between Stephen's coronation in December 1135 and the arrival in England of the news of the papal confirmation in April 1136; and an apparent reference to the presence of Gilbert Foliot at the Lateran Council in a letter of Archbishop Theobald of Canterbury. This third point is weak, since the letter in question probably does not refer to Gilbert Foliot,[7] but Poole's arguments have been accepted by almost all subsequent authorities, who have agreed that the appeal to the papacy and the "trial" described by Gilbert Foliot and John of Salisbury took place at the Lateran Council in 1139.[8]

The fact that "the lord abbot of Cluny" was with Gilbert Foliot strongly supports the conclusion that he was referring to the Lateran Council, since Peter the Venerable is not known to have visited Italy early in 1136. His presence at the Lateran Council, however, is attested by the chronicle of St. Bertin by John of Ypres, who gave a circumstantial account of the efforts of the monks of St. Bertin to free their monastery from the control of Cluny. The representative of St. Bertin waited for Peter the Venerable at Rome, according to this account, from the winter feast of St. Martin (11 November 1138) until the middle of Lent (2 April 1139). "The time for the council came at last, and Abbot Peter of Cluny arrived safely at the council."[9] The

---

[5] Heinrich Böhmer, *Kirche und Staat in England und in der Normandie im XI. und XII. Jahrhundert* (Leipzig, 1899) p. 333, n. 1. He was followed in part by Josèphe Chartrou, *L'Anjou de 1109 à 1151* (Paris, 1928) pp. 240–243, who dated the appeal in January 1136 at Pisa.

[6] John of Salisbury, *Historia pontificalis*, ed. R. L. Poole (Oxford, 1927) pp. 107–113, esp. pp. 108–110; cf. R. L. Poole, "The English Bishops at the Lateran Council of 1139," *English Historical Review*, XXXVIII (1923) 61–63.

[7] John of Salisbury, *Letters*, I, 9, n. 1.

[8] Z. N. Brooke, *The English Church and the Papacy from the Conquest to Reign of John* (Cambridge, Eng., 1931) p. 179, n. 1; P. E. Schramm, *A History of the English Coronation*, trans. L. G. Wickham Legg (Oxford, 1937) p. 250; Arnulf of Lisieux, *Letters*, introd., p. xix; Isabel Megaw, "The Ecclesiastical Policy of Stephen, 1135–9: A Reinterpretation," *Essays in British and Irish History in Honour of James Eadie Todd* (London, 1949) pp. 31–32; Knowles, *Episcopal Colleagues*, p. 40; A. L. Poole, *Domesday Book* (cited Ep. 15, n. to p. 22, l. 7), pp. 192–193; Saltman, *Theobald*, p. 139; John of Salisbury, *Hist. pont.*, p. 83, n. 2. The only recent author whom I have found adhering to Round's date of 1136 is K. R. Potter in his edition of William of Malmesbury, *Historia novella* (Nelson's Medieval Texts; Edinburgh, 1955) introd., pp. xvi–xvii.

[9] John of Ypres, *Chronica monasterii S. Bertini*, XLIII, in *Thes. nov.*, III, 638, and Mansi, *Concilia*, XXI, 539–542; cf. Ep. 102, n. to p. 265, l. 5.

Pope issued three bulls concerning Cluniac houses on 26, 28, and 30 April, respectively.[10] Peter's statement in Letter 90 (1139/41) that he had seen the Pope at Rome may also refer to the Lateran Council, since Innocent returned to Rome in November 1137, and Peter is not known to have made any other trip to Italy before 1141.[11] The only evidence against Peter's having attended the council is a charter from La Charité-sur-Loire clearly dated 10 April 1139, in the middle of the Lateran Council, and apparently showing that Peter was at either Cluny or La Charité at that time.[12] It can also be argued that the chronicle of St. Bertin, although incorporating early materials, was composed in the fourteenth century. Finally, Christopher Brooke has pointed out to me that Gilbert's text according to the manuscripts reads *cum domino et patre nostro domino abbate Duiniacense* or *Duniacense* (rather than *Cluniacense*), although it is hard to know to whom this might refer.[13] The matter is not certain, therefore, but there is a strong probability that Peter attended the Lateran Council in 1139, and this in turn supports the accepted dating of the "trial" between Stephen and Mathilda described by Gilbert Foliot.

It is still not certain in my mind, however, that John of Salisbury and Gilbert were describing the same event. Even Round, who believed that they were referring to the same event early in 1136, admitted that "the two reports ... are not in absolute harmony."[14] This discrepancy may, of course, arise from the different points of view of the two authors, but it is not impossible that the similarity of their descriptions may be on account of the use of similar arguments by the disputants on two separate occasions, one in 1136 and the other in 1139. The points in favor of 1136 were marshaled by Round and Böhmer. Round emphasized in particular the papal letter confirming Stephen, which was in the King's hands when he issued the charter of liberties at Oxford in the spring of 1136 and which must have required a mission to the Pope. Poole and the proponents of 1139 do not deny this mission, but they argue that there was not enough time for a discussion and trial early in 1136. This point is somewhat weakened, however, by the evidence of the recently published life of Christina of

---

[10] JL 8016 (freeing St. Bertin from Cluny), 8022 (confirming a gift to Cluny by Count William of Montpellier), and 8031 (confirming the possessions of Romainmôtier); cf. *Cluny*, V, 416, nos. 4064-4066. Two of these bulls refer specifically to Peter the Venerable, but they do not prove he was present.

[11] This letter can be dated between the conclusion of peace between Innocent II and Roger of Sicily in July 1139 and the retirement of Cardinal Haimeric in May 1141.

[12] *La Charité*, pp. 184-186, no. 83. There is no reason to doubt the authenticity or dating of this charter, but it is possible that Peter was not present or that the charter was drawn up *ex post facto*.

[13] Personal letter dated 11 December 1961.

[14] Round, *Geoffrey*, p. 255, cf. p. 256 and Rössler, *Mathilde*, p. 132, n. 1.

C. THE LATERAN COUNCIL OF 1139

Markyate: "In the year when Stephen was first elected king of England, he decided on the advice of wise counsellors to send ambassadors to Pope Innocent II in order that his election might be confirmed by such an authority." It then describes the preparations of Abbot Geoffrey of St. Albans to accompany this embassy and strongly suggests that there was enough time for a discussion of the matter, if both the King and the Pope acted promptly, though it does not mention the outcome of the mission.[15] John of Salisbury further said in his description of the trial that the case of Mathilda was presented by Bishop Ulger of Angers and that of Stephen by Bishop Roger of Chester, Archdeacon Arnulf of Séez, and Lupellus, "clerk to William the late archbishop of Canterbury."[16] Böhmer made two interesting points on this basis: one that Ulger of Angers is known to have been with Innocent II at Pisa in January 1136,[17] the other that the inclusion of Lupellus in the embassy suggests that it took place before the death of his master William of Canterbury on 21 November 1136.[18] This evidence is admittedly circumstantial, but it raises the possibility that John of Salisbury was describing a "trial" early in 1136, which was then repeated at the Lateran Council three years later.

A final point is the attitude of Peter the Venerable and the Cluniacs in this controversy. Round definitely asserted, with something less than his usual caution, that Peter the Venerable supported Mathilda.

The name of Cluny leads me to break the thread for a moment for the purpose of insisting on the important fact that the sympathies of the house, under its then abbot, must have been with the Angevin cause. This is certain from the documents printed by Sir George Duckett, especially from the Mandatory Epistle of this same Abbot Peter relating to the Empress. We have here, I think, the probable explanation of the energy with which that cause was espoused by Gilbert Foliot.[19]

Ramsay went further and asserted that Mathilda actually sent Gilbert Foliot to Rome to represent her cause and that "Peter the Abbot of

---

[15] *Christina of Markyate* (cited Ep. 53), pp. 161–163. This passage, and that describing the mission to the 1139 council, are not as clear as they might be, but they confirm that Stephen planned two formal embassies to the Pope, one in the first and the other in the third year of his reign. The trips to Rome of Abbot Geoffrey of St. Albans are mentioned in the chronicle of St. Albans: cf. Böhmer, *Kirche und Staat*, p. 333, n. 1, and Knowles, *Monastic Order*, p. 409, n. 6.
[16] John of Salisbury, *Hist. pont.*, p. 83.
[17] JL 7753 and 7755.
[18] The "late" used by John of Salisbury thus referred to the time he was writing, not to the time of the embassy. Lupellus is not known to have been of any importance after his master's death, but it has been suggested that his inclusion in the embassy, if it took place in 1139, was in order to explain the late Archbishop's actions.
[19] Round, *Geoffrey*, p. 254.

Cluny also went to Rome apparently in Matilda's interest."[20] This opinion rests on the facts that Gilbert Foliot supported Mathilda in 1142/3 in the letter to Brian Fitz-Count, who was one of her most devoted supporters,[21] and that in 1145/53 Peter the Venerable visited Mathilda at Rouen and ordered liturgical commemoration of her death to be made in all Cluniac houses.[22] Against this view is the outstanding fact that the two leading Cluniacs in England and Normandy, Bishop Henry of Winchester, Stephen's brother, and Archbishop Hugh of Rouen, were both strong supporters of Stephen in the 1130's.[23] Stephen's mother Adela was a nun at Marcigny, and his grant to Cluny of the manor of Letcombe-Regis in 1136 and his confirmation of the possessions of Lewes are positive evidence of his bid for Cluniac support.[24] Peter the Venerable's later support of Arnulf of Lisieux, whose defense of Stephen and attack on Mathilda he may have witnessed, points in the same direction.[25] There is no evidence that Peter and Gilbert were participants in the trial between Stephen and Mathilda in 1139. Their sympathies may indeed have lain on different sides, but if so they represented the prudent policy of keeping a foot in both camps and of assuring that Cluny had a friend in both parties.[26]

---

[20] Ramsay, *Foundations*, II, 349.

[21] *Gesta Stephani*, ed. K. R. Potter (Nelson's Medieval Texts; Edinburgh, 1955) pp. 60 and 89; cf. H. W. C. Davis, "Henry of Blois and Brian Fitz-Count," *English Historical Review*, XXV (1910) 297-303, with an edition of Brian's letter to Henry of Winchester; A. L. Poole, *Domesday Book*, p. 139; and other works cited by Richard Southern, "The Place of Henry I in English History," *Proceedings of the British Academy*, XLVIII (1962) 142.

[22] *Cluny*, V, 532-533, no. 4183; Duckett, *Cluni*, II, 103-105; cf. Pignot, *Cluny*, III, 495-496.

[23] See the biographical notes to Epp. 4 and 49 on Hugh and Henry. According to William of Malmesbury, *Historia novella*, 470 and 475 (*ed. cit.*, pp. 28 and 32-33), Hugh was "the king's greatest champion" and even defended Stephen's arrest of the bishops of Salisbury and Ely in 1139. The *Actus pontificum Cenomannis in urbe degentium*, ed. G. Busson and A. Ledru (Archives historiques du Maine, 2; Le Mans, 1902) p. 446, commented on the activity of Hugh of Rouen and other Norman bishops "against the count [of Anjou]," that is, in support of Stephen. Cf. Rössler, *Mathilde*, p. 229; Haskins, *Norman Institutions*, pp. 125 and 129; Poole, *Domesday Book*, pp. 135 and 137; Megaw, in *Todd Essays*, p. 39. Henry of Winchester shifted his allegiance from Stephen to Mathilda in 1141, according to Ordericus Vitalis, *Hist. ecc.*, XIII, 42 (*ed. cit.*, V, 130).

[24] See Ep. 60, n. to p. 191; cf. Morey and Brooke, *Foliot*, p. 76.

[25] See Letter 101.

[26] Morey and Brooke, *Foliot*, p. 123, emphasize that Gilbert Foliot himself, in spite of his strong Angevin sympathies (cf. pp. 88 and 92), "remained in close touch with Archbishop Theobald, who was formally loyal to Stephen except during the short period of Stephen's imprisonment in 1141; and in 1148 Gilbert swore fealty to Stephen for the bishopric of Hereford, thereby incurring the wrath of the young Henry, the future Henry II."

D. CHRONOLOGY AND ITINERARY OF PETER THE VENERABLE

In the material below, doubtful dates and places are followed by a question mark. Entire entries that are in doubt are italicized.

1092 or 1094	Montboissier	The birth of Peter the Venerable. The chronicle of Cluny gives his age as 30 (alt. 28) at the time of his election as abbot of Cluny: *Bibl. Clun.*, col. 589 A.
Youth and boyhood	Sauxillanges	Radulf, *Vita*, in *Ampl. Coll.*, VI, 1189 D and 1196 E; cf. chronicle of Cluny, in *Bibl. Clun.*, col. 589 A.
Before 1109		Received monastic benediction from Hugh of Cluny "in extremum vitae suae": chronicle of Cluny, in *Bibl. Clun.*, col. 589 A.
Before 1113	Cluny	Met Hugh of Amiens at Cluny before Hugh became prior of St. Martial at Limoges: Ep. 178; cf. Ep. 4, biographical note.
1115/6–20 (?)	Vézelay	Radulf, *Vita*, in *Ampl. Coll.*, VI, 1189, says that Peter became "seniorum doctor et custos ordinis" at Vézelay while he was still "in ipsa juventutis adolescentia." According to the chronicle of Cluny, in *Bibl. Clun.*, col. 589 A, he was prior of Vézelay during the abbacy of Pontius of Cluny. Cf. Ep. 16, n. to p. 23.
1115/7	Sauxillanges or Montboissier	Witnessed his father's will: Ep. 53, n. to p. 159, l. 37; *Sauxillanges*, no. 795; cf. Appendix A.
1120–2 (?)	Domène	Peter was prior of Domène before becoming abbot of Cluny: Radulf, *Vita*, in *Ampl. Coll.*, VI, 1189; chronicle of Cluny, in *Bibl. Clun.*, col. 589 A; cf. *Cartulare*

		monasterii ... *de Domina*, ed. C. de Monteynard (Lyons, 1859) introd., p. xv; Didier, in *Cahiers d'hist.* (cited Ep. 189), II, 11–12; Bligny, *Église*, p. 239.
1122 August 22	Cluny	Election and consecration as abbot: chronicle of Cluny, in *Bibl. Clun.*, cols. 589 and 602; cf. *GC*, IV, 1137; JL 6991–6992.
1124 June 23	Spain	"*Petro testis*" on a charter in Cluny, V, 328, no. 3970.
1124	Vienne	Attended Council at Vienne: *Thes. nov.*, IV, 135; cf. Hefele-Leclercq, *Conciles*, V.1, 648, n. 1.
1125, from at least February 15 to October 1	Aquitaine	Peter's first visit to Aquitaine; met Peter of Poitiers at St. Jean d'Angély: see Appendix Q.
1125–6	Rome	Peter went directly to Rome, not to Cluny, when he heard about the *coup* of Pontius: Ordericus Vitalis, *Hist. ecc.*, XII, 30 (*ed. cit.*, IV, 426).
1126 April 24	Rome	JL 7259–7261; cf. *Cluny*, V, 344, nos. 3989–3991.
1126 late September	Rome	Pleaded against Pontius, with Matthew of St.-Martin-des-Champs: JL 7268; cf. *Hist. litt.*, XIII, 242; Berlière, *Mélanges*, IV, 10–11.
1126 October/November	Cluny	Returned from Rome about six months before Easter 1127, during which he was ill: *De miraculis*, I, 6, in *Bibl. Clun.*, col. 1254 B.
1127 at least February 20 to April 3 (Lent)	Sauxillanges	Recovering from fever caught at Rome, which lasted more than half a year: *De miraculis*, I, 6, and II, 13, in *Bibl. Clun.*, 1254 B and 1313 B.
1127 May 23	Spain	*Cluny*, V, 346–348, no. 3995.
1128 soon after 25 July	Cluny or nearby	*Cluny*, V, 356, no. 4001.
1128/9 (?)		Sat with the archbishops and bishops of Lyons, Vienne, Autun, and Belley judging a case between Luxeuil and St. Benignus at Dijon: *Cartulaire du prieuré de Saint-Étienne de Vignory*, ed. J. d'Arbaumont (Langres, 1882) p. 30 (1126); cf.

D. CHRONOLOGY AND ITINERARY OF PETER THE VENERABLE 259

		Martin, *Conciles*, nos. 513–514 (1129). Archbishop Peter of Lyons was in Rome late in 1128, when Honorius II apparently entrusted this case to him.
1129 (?)	On way to Rome, south of Siena	Ep. 27, n. to p. 52, l. 20.
1130 after Easter (March 30)	Peterborough	*The Anglo-Saxon Chronicle*, ed. Benjamin Thorpe (Rolls Series, 23; London, 1861) II, 227; *Two of the Saxon Chronicles Parallel*, ed. Charles Plummer (Oxford, 1892–1899) I, 261.
1130 ca. September 11	St. Gilles (?)	Met Innocent II coming to France: Radulf, *Vita*, in *Ampl. Coll.*, VI, 1192; JL 7423 ff.
1130 October 24/5–November 3	Cluny	Consecration of the new church by Innocent II: Ep. 34, n. to p. 112, l. 39.
1130	Nevers	*Cluny*, V, 364–365, no. 4009.
1131 May 10	Rouen	Grant of King Henry I to Cluny: Ep. 60, n. to p. 191; *Cluny*, V, 374–376, no. 4020, confirms that Peter was not at Cluny at this time, since Prior Adelelmus presided in the chapter, but it is not certain that he was in Rouen.
1131 before September 21	Sauxillanges	Baluze, *Auvergne*, II, 57–58; *Sauxillanges*, no. 945; *Cluny*, V, 378–380, no. 4023; cf. Fazy, *Origines*, I, 239–240, no. 263, and Côte, *Souvigny*, p. 43, no. 44 bis.
1131 September 21	Clermont	
1131 October	Rheims	JL 7562; cf. *Cluny*, V, 389, no. 4036; JL 7499; and Ep. 105, n. to p. 268, l. 2.
1132 February 1	Cluny	JL, I, 854.
1132 ca. February 13	Beaujeu	*Cluny*, V, 384, no. 4029.
1132 ca. February 17	Lyons	*Bibl. Clun.*, col. 1394; cf. *Cluny*, V, 386, no. 4030.
1132 March 13	Cluny	Meeting of Cluniac chapter general at Cluny: Ordericus Vitalis, *Hist. ecc.*, XIII, 13 (ed. cit., V, 29); cf. GC, IV, 1138; Vacandard, *St. Bernard*, I, 126–128; and the works cited Ep. 111, n. to p. 293.

1133 January 5	Marcigny	*Marcigny*, p. 124, no. 221.
1133 spring to autumn	Poitiers, St. Jean d'Angély, island of Aix, Anjou, Maine, Normandy, Isle-de-France	Appendix Q.
1133 after October 25 to at least 1134 January 6	Paris	Appendix Q.
Late 1133 or early 1134	Jouarre	Ep. 17 (esp. n. to p. 25, l. 15).
1135 May 30– June 6	Pisa	Epp. 1, 27 (esp. n. to p. 51, l. 10), and 56; cf. *Hist. litt.*, XIII, 244.
1135 June 24	Returning from Pisa	Heard news of his mother's death: Ep. 53.
1135 (for 3 days in July or August)	Marcigny	Ep. 53.
1136 June 2	Cluny	*Cluny*, V, 407, no. 4053, cf. V, 408–410, nos. 4054 and 4056.
1136	Cluny	*Cart. lyonnais*, I, 32–33, no. 22.
1137 (early)	Grenoble	Ep. 66.
1137 July 1	Limoges	Geoffrey of Vigeois, *Chronicon*, I, 48, in Labbé, *Nova bibl.*, II, 304–305, and *RHGF*, XII, 435; cf. Luchaire, *Louis VI*, pp. 267–268, no. 588.
1137 September/ October	Normandy	*Compendium vitae Theobaldi*, in *RHGF*, XIV, 411; cf. Saltman, *Theobald*, pp. 5 and 7.
1137	Cluny	Geoffrey of Vigeois, *Chronicon*, I, 49, in Labbé, *Nova bibl.*, II, 305; cf. De Lasteyrie, *St. Martial*, p. 95. Bishop-elect Amblard of Limoges visited Cluny at this time, but it is not certain that he saw Peter there.
1138 March– April	Cluny	Epp. 69–71.
1138 July– August	On the way to Le Puy from Poitiers	Constable, "Langres," p. 135.

1138 mid-August	Le Puy	*Ibid.*, p. 137.
1138	Cluny	*Cluny*, V, 412, no. 4059.
1139 April 3 to at least April 30	Rome	Attending the Lateran Council: Appendix C.
1140 Palm Sunday (March 31) (?)	Cluny	Ep. 86, n. to p. 224, l. 27.
1140	Cluny	*Cluny*, V, 418, no. 4068, and Ep. 111, n. to p. 293.
1141 (after May/June ?)	Pisa	This is one of the most puzzling entries in Peter's itinerary. He states in the *De miraculis*, II, 23 (*Bibl. Clun.*, col. 1322 AB) that he came to Pisa in order to make peace between Lucca and Pisa seven years after the death of Matthew of Albano. This reading ("Septem deinde annis exactis.") is confirmed by MS. Paris, Bibl. nat., Latin 17716, fol. 69^r, which is the only manuscript of this part of the *De miraculis* (see Constable, in *Petrus Ven.*, p. 228). On this basis the visit was dated 1141 by Mabillon, *Annales*, VI, 316; the authors of the *Hist. litt.*, XIII, 244-245; and Davidsohn, *Florenz* (cited Ep. 131, n. to p. 331, l. 5), I, 430-431; but it was dated 1145 by Pignot, *Cluny*, III, 307-310, and Otto Langer, *Politische Geschichte Genuas und Pisas im XII. Jahrhundert* (Historische Studien, ed. Arndt, 7; Leipzig, 1882) pp. 21-22. Heywood, *Pisa* (cited Ep. 27, n. to p. 51, l. 32), p. 89, wrote that "During the greater part of the twelfth century, Pisa was in a permanent state of war with Lucca," but he made no reference to the mission of Peter the Venerable. There is no other reference in Peter's works to this important trip, particularly not in Letters 95-96, which were written in August 1141 and referred to the trip to Rome of Nicholas of Montiéramey. It is hard to believe that there would have been no reference to Peter's trip in these letters had he just returned. Pignot and Langer may therefore be right in associating Peter's mission with a later trip to Italy. There is reason

to believe, however, that these parts of the *De miraculis* (the life of Matthew of Albano) were written before Peter's next known visit, in 1144 (cf. Ep. 129, n. to p. 327). I should therefore prefer to associate it with his visit to Rome in 1139. The statement in the *De miraculis* is categorical, however, and the argument against it is *ex silentio*, so that without further evidence the visit must be dated 1141.

1141 August–September	Cluny	Ep. 95.
1142 March 5	Cluny	*PL*, CLXXXIX, 574 (*recte* 474).
1142 Pentecost (June 7)	Spain	*De miraculis*, I, 27, in *Bibl. Clun.*, col. 1290 C.
1142 June/July (before 29 July)	Estella and Nájera, between Pamplona and Burgos	*De miraculis*, I, 28, in *Bibl. Clun.*, col. 1293; cf. Bishko, in *Petrus Ven.*, p. 166.
1142 July 29	Salamanca	*Cluny*, V, 425, no. 4072; cf. Bishko, in *Petrus Ven.*, p. 165.
1142 August	Carrión	*Cluny*, V, 426–427, no. 4073; cf. Bishko, in *Petrus Ven.*, p. 172.
1142 August	Abia de las Torres	Peter Rassow, "Urkunden Kaiser Alfons VII. von Castilien 1126–1155, III. Teil: Urkundentexte," *Archiv für Urkundenforschung*, XI (1929) 87–88; cf. Bishko, in *Petrus Ven.*, p. 172.
1142 September 7	Burgos	Rassow, in *Arch. f. Urkundenforsch.*, XI, 88–89; cf. Bishko, in *Petrus Ven.*, pp. 172–173.
1142 May 13	Le Puy	Radulf, *Vita*, in *Ampl. Coll.*, VI, 1199–1200; cf. Bishko, in *Petrus Ven.*, p. 165.
1143 November 30	Cluny	Ep. 112.
1143 Christmas–1144 February (?)	Cluny	Voss, *Heinrich von Blois*, pp. 113–114.
1144 January–*ca*. February 13	Marcigny	Ep. 111, dating note; cf. *Marcigny*, pp. 101–102, no. 171 bis.
1144 February 13	Cluny	Ep. 111, dating note.

D. CHRONOLOGY AND ITINERARY OF PETER THE VENERABLE 263

1144, at least February 24– May 22 (?)	Rome	Epp. 112–113; *La Charité*, p. 364, no. 168; cf. *Hist. litt.*, XIII, 245; Pignot, *Cluny*, III, 302–303.
1145 January 29	Cluny	*Cluny*, VI, 958–960; Leclercq, *Pierre le Vén.*, pp. 371–374.
1145 November– December	Rome	*De miraculis*, II, 25, in *Bibl. Clun.*, cols. 1324 A and 1325 C; Epp. 131, 133, 190, and 192. *Bull. Clun.*, p. 59 (JL 8844; cf. *Cluny*, V, 457, no. 4109), suggests that Peter was still in Rome on 16 January 1146; and JL 8859–8860 (cf. *Cluny*, V, 460, nos. 4113–4114) show that he may have stayed until 15 February. Cf. Mabillon, *Annales*, VI, 356–357; *Hist. litt.*, XIII, 245; Pignot, *Cluny*, III, 578–579.
1145	Marcigny	*Les chartes de Saint-Bertin*, ed. D. Haigneré and O. Bled (Société des antiquaires de la Morinie; Saint-Omer, 1886–1899) I, 84, no. 197.
1147 March 13	Frankfort	*Urkunden für die Geschichte der Stadt Bern*, ed. Karl Zeerleder (Berne, 1853–54) I, 42; cf. Bernhardi, *Konrad III*, p. 551.
1147 March 26	Cluny	Ep. 192, n. to p. 445, l. 27.
1147 before June	Souvigny	Chazaud, *Étude*, pp. 253–254; cf. GC, II, 378–379, and IV, 1138; Fazy, *Origines*, I, 273–274, no. 316; and Côte, *Souvigny*, p. 45, no. 49. In this charter Peter the Venerable came to Souvigny with "maxima pars concilii Cluniacensis" and witnessed the loan of five hundred silver marks to Archibald [VI] of Bourbon, who was "about to go to Jerusalem with King Louis of the French and many other nobles." The document is suspect because it is known only from a copy by the notorious forger Fr. André de St. Nicholas: see Chazaud, *Étude*, pp. 41–96. It was considered a forgery by Chazaud, but its authenticity was at least tentatively accepted by Fazy ("Il n'y a rien d'invraisemblable ni dans la teneur de l'acte, ni dans les témoins.") and Côte ("Ne présente rien de suspect."). The presence among the witnesses of Hugh of Crécy,

the sacristan Aimarus of Cluny, and Peter's notary Thomas tends to confirm the authenticity of the charter, or at least of the witness list, which Fr. André could hardly have made up. It may have been on this occasion, and certainly after 16 January 1146, that Dean Iterius of Périgeux found Peter the Venerable at Souvigny: *Bull. Clun.*, p. 60; cf. *Cluny*, V, 457, no. 4111. This charter was witnessed, among others, by Peter's chamberlain Enguizo, his constable Godfrey, and his chaplain Raim. It is not mentioned in either Fazy, *Origines*, or Côte, *Souvigny*, however, and the name of the prior of Souvigny, Walter (unless, as is possible, the punctuation of the charter is wrong), does not agree with that on the charter of 1147 and appears on no list of the priors of Souvigny: cf. Côte, *Souvigny*, p. 129.

1147 June 14	Cluny	*Cluny*, V, 465, no. 4122.
1147 July 27	Bar-sur-Aube	*Ep. 156, n. to p. 375, l. 26.*
1147 August 23	Auxerre	Epp. 156 and 192; *Bull. Clun.*, pp. 58 and 61; cf. JL 9122 and 9124; *Cluny*, V, 466 and 471, nos. 4124 and 4128.
1147 October 26	Châlons-sur-Marne	Ep. 192; cf. Mabillon, *Annales*, VI, 390. *Bull. Clun.*, p. 61 (JL 9156; *Cluny*, V, 471, no. 4129), suggests that Peter was with Eugene III at Châlons on 3 November.
1148 before February 21	Cluny	Ep. 139.
1148 March 21	Rheims	Epp. 139 and 192; cf. Pignot, *Cluny*, III, 339.
1149 mid-year (?)	Clairvaux	Ep. 150, n. to p. 369.
1149 August/September	Cluny	Visit of Nicholas of Montiéramey to Cluny: Appendix P.
1149 ca. November 1	Cluny	Louis VII visited Cluny on his return from the Crusade: *Bibl. Clun.*, cols. 959–960; Duchesne, *Scriptores*, IV, 529–530; cf. Suger, *Oeuvres*, pp. 306–309; Luchaire, *Louis VII*, p. 64; Cartellieri, *Suger*, p. 157, nos. 253–255.

D. CHRONOLOGY AND ITINERARY OF PETER THE VENERABLE 265

1149	Cluny	Agreement with Henry of Winchester: *Cluny*, V, 489, no. 4142; cf. Voss, *Heinrich von Blois*, p. 114.
1149	Besançon	*Cluny*, V, 486, no. 4141; cf. document cited in Ep. 34, n. to p. 112, l. 39.
1149 Christmas–1150 April	Cluny	Epp. 164 and 166; Appendix B.
1150 May 7	Cluny	Epp. 163–166 (esp. Ep. 164, n. to p. 398, l. 10).
1150 June–1151 January (?)	Cluny	Ep. 158a; Appendix B.
1150 autumn–Christmas	Cluny	Epp. 175–176.
1151 January 1	Cluny	Document cited Ep. 34, n. to p. 112, l. 39; cf. Mabillon, *Annales*, VI, 460–462.
1151 Easter (April 8)	Cluny	Requests in Letters 180–184 that Nicholas of Montiéramey visit Cluny at Easter.
1151 *ca.* October 25	Cluny	Philibert Schmitz, "Un conflit entre monastères de Clunisiennes d'après la correspondance inédite de Pierre le Vénérable," *Rev. Bén.*, XLIX (1937) 366–375.
1151 November–1152 March	Italy	Epp. 186, 188, and 192–193; cf. Mabillon, *Annales*, VI, 433–435; *Hist. litt.*, XIII, 246; Pignot, *Cluny*, III, 369–374, dating this trip in 1150.
1151 Christmas	Breme	Ep. 188.
1152 January	Pavia to Venice	Schmitz, in *Rev. Bén.*, XLIX, 372; Ep. 192, n. to p. 444, l. 18.
1152 February 20	Segni	JL 9557 (and ff.); Ep. 189. It must have been on this visit to the Pope that Peter, accompanied by the sacristan Ademar, secured a charter for Vézelay: Radulf, *Vita*, in *Ampl. Coll.*, VI, 1198; cf. Hugh of Poitiers, *Hist. Viz.*, I, in *Spicilegium*, II, 507 ff.; Graham, *Vézelay*, p. 92, who showed that Peter's brother Abbot Pontius of Vézelay was in Rome in the winter of 1151-2.
1152 March (?)	Piacenza	Ep. 190.

1152 Pentecost (May 18)	Cluny	Peter ordered Italian priors to come to Cluny at that time: Schmitz, in *Rev. Bén.*, XLIX, 373.
1152 June (?)	Cluny	Meeting with Bernard of Clairvaux and monks of Gigny: Epp. 192–193; cf. Constable, "Cluniac Tithes," p. 620.
1152 August (?)	Cluny	Meeting with Pontius of Vézelay and Cardinals John Paparo of S. Adriano and Jordan of S. Susanna: Hugh of Poitiers, *Hist. Viz.*, III, in *Spicilegium*, II, 528–530; cf. Graham, *Vézelay*, pp. 94–103, and Janssen, *Legaten*, p. 54 (pp. 51–56 on the legations of Cardinals John and Jordan). This meeting can be dated only approximately from the known movements of the two cardinals. John was still in Ireland in March: John of Salisbury, *Hist. pont.*, XXXVI (ed. cit., p. 72); cf. Saltman, *Theobald*, pp. 135–136. He was in Arras on 29 June 1152: *Cartulaire de l'abbaye de Saint-Vaast d'Arras*, ed. E. Van Drival (Documents inédits concernant l'Artois, 6; Arras, 1875) pp. 153–154. Jordan was meanwhile in Germany with Cardinal Octavian of S. Nicola in Carcere, who was back with the Curia by 26 March: Gleber, *Eugen III*, p. 145. Jordan then went to the Carthusian house of Mondaye, near Bayeux, and traveled extensively before he came to Vézelay, where he arrived after Cardinal John: John of Salisbury, *Hist. pont*, XXXIX (ed. cit., pp. 77–78); Bernard, ep. 290 (Gaume ed., I.1, 576–577); cf. Gleber, *Eugen III*, p. 145. The two cardinals were together at Vézelay for the Feast of St. Mary Magdalen (22 July), and nine days later (30 July) they went with Pontius of Vézelay to Chablis, and Pontius then went to Le-Montet-aux-Moines, near Moulins, before he rejoined the cardinals at Cluny for the meeting with Peter the Venerable, which probably took place in August. John Paparo was back with the Pope at Albano on 5 November 1152: *PU in Frankreich*, n.f. II, 138–140, no. 62.

D. CHRONOLOGY AND ITINERARY OF PETER THE VENERABLE 267

1152 end or 1153 early	Luzy (nr. Autun), Nevers, La Charité, Cluny	Meeting with the count of Nevers, Pontius of Vézelay, and the abbots of Moissac and St. Michael of La Chiusa: Hugh of Poitiers, *Hist. Viz.*, III, in *Spicilegium*, II, 531–532, and *Bull ... de l'Yonne*, XVI, 474; cf. Graham, *Vézelay*, p. 103.
1153 June 11	Worms	*Cluny*, V, 521, no. 4167. It is not certain that Peter was present at the granting of this charter by Frederick Barbarossa, but it was witnessed by Anselm of Havelberg, who in a later letter (*Cluny*, V, 527, no. 4176) mentioned that Peter had seen Frederick Barbarossa once.
1154 April 18	Rome	*Bull. Clun.*, p. 63; JL 9866; cf. *Cluny*, V, 524, no. 4170; cf. Constable, "Cluniac Tithes," p. 621. JL 9869, 9875, and 9877 (cf. *Cluny*, V, 525-526, nos. 4171-4173) suggest that Peter stayed in Rome until at least 25 April.
1154 May 3	Pavia	*PL*, CLXXXIX, 483–484; cf. Pignot, *Cluny*, III, 495, and Côte, *Souvigny*, p. 47, no. 55. If this is the visit to Pavia mentioned in Schmitz, *Rev. Bén.*, XLIX, 372, the visit of the Italian priors to Cluny should be dated 18 May 1154/5 rather than 1152 (see above). It was probably on this trip, perhaps at Brescia, that Cardinals Guido of S. Maria in Porticu and Odo of S. Nicola in Carcere arranged the agreement between Peter the Venerable and the prior of the Cluniac house of Provaglio, on one side, and the clergy of Azzano Mella, on the other, concerning the church of Pievedizio, which was confirmed by Alexander III in 1177: R. Predelli, "Bolla grande di papa Alessandro III," *Nuovo Archivio Veneto*, XII (1896) 164–166; *Italia Pontificia*, VI.1, 341, no. 3; cf. Cinzio Violante, *La Chiesa bresciana nel Medioevo* (offprint from *Storia di Brescia*, I) p. 1055.
1154 June/July (?)	Mâcon	Ep. 191, n. to p. 443, l. 22; cf. Constable, "Cluniac Tithes," p. 622.
1155 March 2	Cluny	Settlement of the controversy between Gigny and Le Miroir: *Cluny*, V, 531, no. 4180; cf. Constable, "Cluniac Tithes," p. 623 (misdated 5 March).

1155 early (March?)	Cluny	Meeting concerning Vézelay with his brothers Jordan and Heraclius: Hugh of Poitiers, *Hist. Viz.*, III, in *Bull... de l'Yonne*, XVI, 497–498 (and 378); Graham, *Vézelay*, pp. 116–117. This meeting may have taken place early in March, since Heraclius was at Cluny on 2 March (see above); it was almost certainly before the bulls of Hadrian IV dated 21 May 1155: JL 10066–10068; cf. *Cluny*, V, 532, no. 4182.
1155 June	Soissons	Meeting concerning Vézelay with King Louis VII: Hugh of Poitiers, *Hist. Viz.*, III, in *Bull... de l'Yonne*, XVI, 402 and 511; cf. Graham, *Vézelay*, p. 119. The text is damaged at this point, and the only evidence that Peter attended this meeting reads, "huic concilio intererat Clun...."
1155	England	*PL*, CLXXXIX, 661–662; Robert of Torigny, *Chronicle, s.a.* 1155, in *Chronicles of the Reigns of Stephen, Henry II, and Richard I*, ed. Richard Howlett (Rolls Series, 82; London, 1884–1889) IV, 186, who remarked that Henry of Winchester sent his treasure out of England *per* the abbot of Cluny.
1155 late or 1156 early	Reuil	According to the *De miraculis*, II, 32, in *Bibl. Clun.*, col. 1336 C, Peter stopped at the monastery of Reuil on the Marne on his return from his second visit to England: cf. Radulf, *Vita*, in *Ampl. Coll.*, VI, 1194–1195. The prior of Reuil at that time was a young Poitevin named Bernard who died soon after Peter's return to Cluny (*Bibl. Clun.*, col. 1338). The *GC*, VIII, 1672, mentions Prior Bernard of Reuil from a charter of 1156 and Prior Robert in 1158.
1156 Christmas	Cluny	Death of Peter the Venerable: chronicle of Cluny, in *Bibl. Clun.*, col. 601 A; Robert of Torigny, *Chronicle, s.a.* 1157 (*ed. cit.*, IV, 191); cf. Mabillon *Annales*, VI, 518–519; *GC*, IV, 1139; and the obituary of the abbey of the Paraclete, cited Ep. 167, n. to p. 401, l. 4.

There are also references to Peter's presence at Vézelay and Sauxillanges (Radulf, *Vita*, in *Ampl. Coll.*, VI, 1196), Nogent (Bernard of Morval, *De contemptu mundi*, ed. H. C. Hoskier [London, 1929] p. xxxviii), Rouen in 1145/53 (*Cluny*, V, 533, no. 4183; Duckett, *Cluni*, II, 103; cf. Pignot, *Cluny*, III, 495-496), in the Auvergne and at Souvigny (Letter 18), Montpellier (Letter 30), Cluny on 29 June and La Charité on 15 August in 1132, 1134, or 1136 (Letters 41-42), Cluny at Easter 1138/41 (Letter 86), a Carthusian monastery before 1136 (Letter 106), Cluny (Letters 108-109), the abbey of the Paraclete on 16 November 1142/55 (Letter 167), Tiron (Letter 186), and on his way from Vizille to Domène in 1148/51 (Letter 189).

E. THE DATE AND CHARACTER OF LETTER 28

The longest, most important, and most frequently cited letter in the letter collection of Peter the Venerable is number 28, which is the fullest contemporary statement of the controversy between the Cluniacs and the Cistercians and thus, by extension, between the old and the new monasticism in the twelfth century. It contains both a statement of the main charges, twenty in all, brought by the Cistercians against Cluny and the replies formulated by Peter the Venerable on the basis of established Cluniac theory and practice. Its interest lies therefore not only in its "horizontal" position as a contemporary defense of the old monasticism against its critics but also its "vertical" position as an explanation and justification of two centuries of Cluniac development. To appreciate its importance properly, however, it is essential to know how and when it was written. These two questions are to some extent connected and will be studied together here.

The character of Letter 28 has already been discussed in the Introduction. The manuscript tradition as well as the text show that it was not really a letter, and certainly not a personal letter, but was rather a treatise intended from the start for publication and circulation and that it was successively revised by Peter the Venerable before it was incorporated into the collection of his correspondence. Peter himself admitted in his conclusion that he had exceeded "epistolary brevity" and twice referred to it as an *opusculum* rather than a letter. Paul Giseke even went so far as to suggest that "this letter was not written by Peter himself but was an official controversial treatise of the congregation of Cluny against the Cistercians."[1] There is no evidence to support this view, or to suggest that Peter did not write Letter 28 himself; but it certainly had a public and controversial, and probably to some extent also an official, character.

A second basic characteristic of Letter 28 is that it is not an attack but a defense. It is a reply to the specific schedule of Cistercian charges incorporated into the text and going from the words *Non, inquiunt, uos regulam* to *Deo promisimus custodimus*. There is no reason to believe that

---

[1] Paul Giseke, "Uber den Gegensatz der Cluniazencer und Cisterziencer," *Jahrbuch des Pädagogiums zum Kloster Unser Lieben Frauen in Magdeburg*, 1886, p. 39, n. 25.

E. THE DATE AND CHARACTER OF LETTER 28

this schedule of charges was a literary device composed by Peter the Venerable himself, although he made use of rhetorical quotations and artificial questions later in the letter and in his other works. The passage reads like an authentic quotation. Peter called the document an "invective" and referred to "the individual chapters of this invective." At the beginning of his reply he said that he would take up the charges "in that order in which they have been placed by you." Had Peter compiled the list himself, as a basis for his defense, it is hard to believe that he would have put together such a mixture of serious and frivolous charges, one of which, he said, may even have been made in jest. The precise nature of the schedule of charges, however, is not clear. They were written, except for one isolated use of *inquam*, in the first person plural; and Peter the Venerable, addressing Bernard of Clairvaux, always referred to the authors as *uos, uestri*, or *quidam uestri* in the plural. This suggests that the authors were Cistercian monks of Clairvaux, and Peter may have believed that Bernard himself had taken part in composing the charges. They were possibly the report of an oral debate, such as Peter the Deacon held with a Cistercian monk before the emperor Lothar III at Lago Pesole in 1137.[2] Or it may have been a compilation drawn up and presented by the Cistercians. Be this as it may, Letter 28 was a reply to these charges, and Peter the Venerable cannot be considered, as some scholars have held, to have opened the written debate between the Cluniacs and Cistercians.

This raises the much-debated question of the relation between Letter 28 and Bernard's *Apologia*. Most scholars are agreed that there is no direct relation between the two works, but this point has been used, rather curiously, as evidence that Letter 28 was written before the *Apologia*. Mabillon in his *Annales* accepted that there was no correspondence between the works and said that "perhaps this letter [28] was written by Peter before the *Apologia* of Bernard came into his hand."[3] A century later Clémencet firmly insisted that "the letter of Peter is a reply to some writing of the Cistercians against the monks of Cluny but not to the *Apology* of St. Bernard. A comparison of one with the other is enough to prove the point: the articles to which Peter replies are not at all those which Bernard criticizes in his *Apology*."[4] Vacandard carried this argument a step further. "Many have believed that this letter [28] was posterior to the *Apology* of the abbot of

---

[2] *Altercatio pro cenobio Casinensi*, in Erich Caspar, *Petrus Diaconus und die Monte Cassineser Fälschungen* (Berlin, 1909) pp. 263–278.

[3] Mabillon, *Annales*, VI, 75.

[4] Charles Clémencet, *Histoire littéraire de saint Bernard et de Pierre le Vénérable* (Paris, 1773) p. 441.

Clairvaux," he wrote in his life of St. Bernard, "but the beginning and above all the end where the author asks Bernard for his opinion... prove that the abbot of Clairvaux had not yet entered into the debate. Furthermore, the complaints enumerated by Peter the Venerable correspond only imperfectly to those which are scheduled in the *Apology*."⁵ Vacandard therefore argued that Letter 28 was written before the *Apologia*, which he dated about 1124/5.⁶ This reasoning has been accepted by most recent scholars, who have dated Letter 28 in 1123/4, at the very beginning of Peter's abbacy.⁷ Even Wilmart fell into this trap, though not without some apparent misgiving. "By its composition, the *Apology* could therefore be almost contemporary with Letter 28 of Peter the Venerable, which, however, preceded it," he wrote, but he added at once that "it is not certain, for me, that it replies to it directly."⁸ More recently Knowles insisted again that "we cannot fix a certain date to Peter's letter. The inscription *Bernardo humilis Cluniaci abbas* is presumably genuine, so it must be posterior to 1122. For every other reason we should wish to put it as early as possible. Vacandard... rightly states that it precedes Bernard's *Apologia*, pointing out that the conclusion of the letter—'erit modo tuum, si aliter senseris'—shows that Bernard had not yet intervened."⁹

The fallacy of this argument can be demonstrated on two grounds. The first was formulated by Dimier: "It is difficult to follow here the opinion of Vacandard... who regards the *Apology* as provoked by a long letter of Peter the Venerable [Letter 28]... addressed to the abbot of Clairvaux, a letter generally regarded as posterior to the *Apology*. Nothing in this letter, says Vacandard, suggests that it is a reply to the *Apology*.... But it does not follow that the *Apology* is a reply to the letter of Peter the Venerable. Absolutely nothing in this work suggests it."¹⁰ Since there is no evidence that either writer had

⁵ Vacandard, *St. Bernard*, I, 101, n. 2.

⁶ *Ibid.*, 115, n. 2. This date was accepted by J.-M. Canivez, in *DHGE*, VIII, 636, and Wilmart, "Riposte," p. 301, n. 3. Mabillon was of the opinion that the *Apology* was written before Peter the Venerable became abbot of Cluny in 1122: note to Bernard, *Apologia* (Gaume ed., I.2, 1556–1557); Vacandard, in the *DThC*, II, 752, dated the *Apologia* "vers 1127."

⁷ Cf. Alice M. Cooke, "A Study in Twelfth Century Religious Revival and Reform," *Bulletin of the John Rylands Library*, IX (1925) 156; J. Othon [Ducourneau], in *Rev. Mabillon* (cited Ep. 28, n. to p. 57), XXIII, 103–104; Séjourné, in *DThC*, XII.2, 2066; Wilmart, "Riposte," p. 297; Leclercq, *Pierre le Vén.*, p. 68, n. 1; Duby, *Mâconnais*, p. 320 ("vers 1124," although he dated it "vers 1130" on p. 592). According to De Valous, *Mon. clun.*, II, 131, n. 1, Letter 28 was written in reply to Bernard's *De consideratione*, which was written in 1149–1152/3 (Vacandard, *St. Bernard*, II, 436); but this is certainly too late.

⁸ Wilmart, "Riposte," p. 298, n. 4.

⁹ David Knowles, *Cistercians and Cluniacs* (Friends of Dr. Williams's Library, Ninth Lecture; London, 1955) p. 14, n. 1 ("rightly states" changed to "argues" in the reprint in *Historian and Character* [cited Ep. 2], p. 58, n. 2).

¹⁰ M.-Anselme Dimier, *Amédée de Lausanne* (Figures monastiques; Abbaye S. Wandrille, 1949) p. 31, n. 11.

E. THE DATE AND CHARACTER OF LETTER 28

seen the work of the other at the time he was writing, it is impossible to argue on this basis that either Letter 28 or the *Apologia* was written first.[11] A second logical reason for rejecting this argument is that the date of the *Apologia* is not firmly established. "There is still room for a critical study of Bernard's *Apologia* and its satellite letters," wrote Knowles in 1940; "the *Apology*, as all careful readers must note, is a composite document, and the date and precise aim and occasion of its publication are alike uncertain."[12] This view has recently been confirmed by Leclercq's investigations into the manuscript tradition of Bernard's works.[13] It is therefore impossible to date Letter 28 by comparison with the *Apologia* or, indeed, by any other external evidence.

The evidence of the letter itself, though slim, indicates a date considerably later than 1123/4. Above all, Peter referred prominently to his long delay in writing and gave as his excuse "the great interval of lands [and] the great bitterness of the affairs and tribulations that afflict us." In the context of the early years of Peter's abbacy, these words can refer only to the invasion of Cluny by the former abbot Pontius in 1125 and the consequent trial and condemnation of Pontius in 1125 and 1126.[14] The proceedings took Peter to Rome, where he contracted malaria; and he was ill for over six months, during much of which time he was convalescent at Sauxillanges.[15] He was not therefore back at Cluny in fully restored health until the middle of 1127. These difficulties may well have been the reason for his delay in writing, mentioned in Letter 28. Certainly he had no comparable difficulties which might have prevented his writing before the affair of Pontius. The letter was probably written, therefore, after his illness in 1126-7, possibly during his period of recovery at Sauxillanges.[16]

---

[11] Had either author known the work of the other, he would presumably have mentioned it. The priority of neither Letter 28 nor the *Apologia*, therefore, can be shown by the failure to refer to the other.

[12] Knowles, *Monastic Order*, p. 224, n. 3.

[13] Jean Leclercq, "Recherches sur les sermons sur les Cantiques de Saint Bernard, IV: Les étapes de la rédaction," *Rev. Bén.*, LXV (1955) 257-258 (reprinted in *Recueil*, pp. 243-244), and "Pour l'histoire des traités de S. Bernard," *Analecta sacri ordinis Cisterciensis*, XV (1959) 72-74, where he concluded that the *Apologia* was made up of two parts, one addressed to Cistercians and the other to Cluniacs, but not of two letters. Cf. also Damien Van den Eynde, "Les débuts littéraires de Saint Bernard," *Analecta sacri ordinis Cisterciensis*, XIX (1963) 197-198, who said that the *Apologia* was written soon after Lent 1125 and put into final form before the invasion of Cluny by Pontius in Lent 1126.

[14] See Pignot, *Cluny*, III, 66-73; L. M. Smith, *Cluny in the Eleventh and Twelfth Centuries* (London, 1930) pp. 268-275; and Tellenbach, "Pontius," pp. 13-55, with references to other recent works.

[15] See Appendix D.

[16] The mention in Section XVII that the papal privileges were preserved "apud nostram matricem aecclesiam" may possibly imply that Peter was not himself at Cluny.

The fact that the letter was addressed to Bernard of Clairvaux also suggests that it was written at a later rather than an earlier date, since Bernard had evidently already emerged as the spokesman of the new monasticism from the relative obscurity of a young abbot of a new house. The *Apologia*, although it was an attack on Cluny, was addressed not to Peter the Venerable but to Bernard's friend William of St. Thierry;[17] and Bernard's passionate letter 1 was a personal appeal to his cousin Robert, who had left Clairvaux for Cluny, although it probably circulated widely. In addressing his reply to Bernard, Peter must have had some reason, even if he had never seen the *Apologia* or the letter to Robert, for associating him with the attack on Cluny and the old monasticism.[18]

Some weight may also be given to the evidence of the manuscripts and the position of the letter in the collection. As mentioned in the Introduction, the collection is arranged roughly in chronological order; and the position of Letter 28, which is well attested by the manuscripts, points to a date some time in the 1130's, especially since the collection includes only one letter that can definitely be dated in the 1120's. In itself this evidence is not worth much, since the early letters are admittedly out of order and the position of Letter 28 in any case applies only to the revised version; but it supports a relatively late date for Letter 28.

---

[17] On this "indirectness" of Bernard's attack on Cluny, and its consequences, see Bredero, in *Petrus Ven.*, p. 64.

[18] The address to Letter 28 strongly suggests that Peter already knew Bernard personally.

F. LETTER 111 AND PETER'S WORKS AGAINST THE SARACENS

The final section of Letter 111, which was written to Bernard of Clairvaux in the late spring or early summer of 1144, was concerned with the translations of the Koran and other Arabic works that were made for Peter the Venerable on his visit to Spain in 1142-3. This section very closely resembles parts of the so-called *Epistola de translatione sua*, also addressed to Bernard, and the *Summa totius haeresis Saracenorum*.[1] The relevant passages are printed below in parallel columns, where they may be compared exactly; but broadly speaking, with certain important omissions and additions, the final section of Letter 111 consists of the *Epistola* with a long passage from the *Summa* (almost half the entire work) inserted into the middle. In the manuscripts from Souvigny and Clairvaux, furthermore, Letter 111 is followed directly by a version of the beginning of the *Summa* that differs considerably from the printed version and goes almost as far as the beginning of the passage found in Letter 111.[2] Together with this supplement, therefore, Letter 111 contains almost all of the *Epistola* and the first two thirds of the *Summa*.

The question of the relation between these various texts (aside from the variant version of the beginning of the *Summa*, which has never been printed) has naturally attracted the attention of scholars interested in Peter's translations from the Arabic. The two most probable answers are either (1) that Letter 111 was written first and later used as the basis for the *Epistola* and the *Summa* or (2), vice versa, that the *Epistola* and the *Summa* were composed first and then used in part for Letter 111. Two more remote possibilities are (3) that Peter of Poitiers concocted Letter 111 out of several letters when he gathered the entire correspondence of Peter the Venerable[3] or (4) that Letter 111 and the *Epistola* were "two successive and distinct letters."[4] There

---

[1] *Bibl. Clun.*, cols. 1109-1115. These texts will be referred to here as the *Epistola* and the *Summa*.
[2] This version of the *Summa* is published below for the first time, in a parallel column with the known text.
[3] D'Alverny, "Traductions," p. 73, n. 2.
[4] *Ibid.* and Leclercq, *Pierre le Vén.*, p. 243.

is no evidence, however, that Peter of Poitiers ever took such drastic liberties with his master's letters; and the similarity between Letter 111 and the *Epistola* is too great to admit their being distinct productions. The principal question to determine, therefore, is whether Letter 111 (and its version of the beginning of the *Summa*) was written before or after the *Epistola* and the *Summa*.

D'Alverny and Kritzeck, the two scholars who have examined the subject most recently and thoroughly, were strongly of the opinion that Letter 111 was written first. The *Epistola*, according to D'Alverny, was "a somewhat modified extract" and the *Summa* "a revised and considerably expanded re-edition" of Letter 111.[5] Kritzeck likewise asserted the priority of Letter 111. For him, Letter 111 was "the archetype" and "the basis of the central portion of the *Summa*," and the *Epistola* and *Summa* were later "amplifications" of Letter 111.[6] Among previous scholars, Mandonnet also held that Letter 111 was modified in order to serve as an introduction to the collection of translations.[7] The principal evidence in support of this opinion is that toward the end of the *Summa* Peter the Venerable said that he had previously hoped that some other person would write against the Moslem heresy and had decided to do so himself only after a long wait, when no one else came forward to defend the Christian faith.[8] In Letter 111 he specifically asked Bernard "to write against so pernicious an error." This request also occurs in the *Epistola*, however, and it therefore only shows that both the *Epistola* and Letter 111 were written some time before the final section of the *Summa*. The *Epistola* and the *Summa* are not themselves a literary whole and must be broken down into their component parts for comparison with Letter 111.

Such stylistic comparisons are at best tentative and always depend to a considerable extent upon a subjective estimate of an author's manner of writing and revising a text. A careful study of the texts, however, suggests to me that Letter 111 was written after, and was to some extent based upon, the first versions of the *Epistola* and *Summa*. It is also intrinsically more probable that he constructed the final section of Letter 111 by inserting into the middle of the *Epistola* the description of Moslem doctrine taken from the *Summa* than that he put together the *Epistola* out of the beginning and end of the final section of Letter 111 and then wrote a new beginning and end for the

---

[5] D'Alverny, "Traductions," pp. 73-74.
[6] Kritzeck, in *Petrus Ven.*, pp. 179, n. 12, 185, n. 36, and 189. He expresses a similar view in *Peter the Venerable*, pp. 28-30, which appeared after this appendix was written.
[7] Mandonnet, in *Revue thomiste* (cited Ep. 111), I, 339.
[8] *Bibl. Clun.*, col. 1115; cf. Kritzeck, in *Petrus Ven.*, pp. 184-186.

Summa. It would have been much easier to have left the final section as it was. This conclusion is supported by the somewhat clumsy construction of the section from Letter 111, in which the central section, corresponding to the passage in the *Summa*, is loosely tied to the beginning and the end by two transitional sentences: "But since the matter is scattered and to a great extent hard to understand owing to the strangeness of the language, I shall briefly tell who he was and what he taught," and, at the end, "I have indicated as briefly as I could the man's life and the substance of his evil law." The *hunc* at the beginning of this central passage in Letter 111 refers to no definite person—Peter the Venerable himself is the last person mentioned—whereas in the *Summa* it clearly refers to Mohammed. A direct comparison of the texts of Letter 111 and the *Summa*, furthermore, seems to support the priority of the *Summa*. In particular the three passages found only in the *Summa*, which are almost footnotes, do not appear to be later additions.

This evidence from construction and style is not conclusive in itself, but several other factors tend to support the priority of the *Epistola* and the *Summa*. (1) The version of the *Summa* that follows Letter 111 in MSS. S and Cl seems to have been sent with the letter. It is impossible to say on purely stylistic grounds whether this version is an early draft or a revised section of the published *Summa*, and it may have been appended to the letter at a later date. If it was sent with Letter 111, however, it decisively supports the priority of the *Summa*. (2) MS. Paris, Arsenal 1162, shows that the *Epistola* and the *Summa* were copied in Spain as an introduction to the so-called Toledan Collection of translations from the Arabic, which included the *Risāla* (finished in 1142), the Koran (finished in June or July 1143), and other texts.[9] These translations are not directly quoted in the *Epistola* or *Summa*,[10] and it is therefore not certain whether they were written by Peter while he was still in Spain, that is, before the spring of 1143, or whether, as D'Alverny proposed and as appears more probable, they were written after Peter returned to Cluny and then sent back to Spain to be copied as an introduction to the entire *corpus* of translations. Be this as it may, they existed as independent works at a very early date, and their history is closely bound up with that of the translations.

Two further points are based upon internal evidence in Letter 111. (3) The section concerned with the translations from Arabic is clearly an addition to the main part of the letter, which is complete as it

---

[9] On these dates, see D'Alverny, "Traductions," pp. 77–79, 87, and 95–96.

[10] Kritzeck, in *Petrus Ven.*, p. 189, pointed out that the *Epistola* and *Summa* show a familiarity with the subject matter of the translations but include no citations proving that they were written after the translations were completed.

stands. Toward the end of this main part, indeed, Peter suggested that he was drawing to a conclusion, as he did in other letters, by remarking on the length of the letter and comparing its content with the salt that seasons everything. The final section, beginning "Misi et nouam translationem," was clearly an afterthought. (4) The use of the past tense at the beginning of this final section also suggests that it was written after the *Epistola*, which begins "Mitto uobis." This point of tenses is not decisive, however, since Peter may have changed the past to the present tense when he revised the *Epistola* to serve as an introduction to the collection of translations.[11]

I am therefore inclined to believe that Peter had before him a draft of the *Epistola* and the *Summa* at the time he was writing Letter 111 in the late spring or early summer of 1144. Having written the main part of the letter on monastic matters, he decided to mention also his translations from Arabic and if possible to enlist Bernard's help in refuting Islam, and he based this final section on the drafts he had already prepared as an introduction to the collection that was being made in Spain. The work that he sent to Bernard at this time was probably the *Risāla*, and he promised to send the rest of the *corpus*, "the book which we have not yet sent,"[12] if Bernard was interested. He apparently at the same time sent the beginning of the *Summa*, as it exists in MSS. S and Cl, going almost up to the passage he had incorporated into the final section of the letter. Later, when Peter himself undertook to write a work against the Moslems, he revised and completed the *Epistola* and *Summa* and sent them to Spain to be copied at the beginning of the entire *corpus*.

Small verbal differences (not major additions and omissions) between column A and the passages from Letter 111 in column B are indicated by italics. Omissions are indicated by suspension points. Gaps in either column show that there is an addition in the parallel text, not that there is any omission.

A (*Epistola*, from *Bibl. Clun.*, cols. 1109–1110)	B (From Letter 111)
Singulari ueneratione colendo, totis charitatis brachiis amplectendo, indiuiduo cordis *nostri* hospiti, domino Bernardo Clareuallis abbati, frater Petrus humilis *Cluniacensis* abbas, salutem ad quam suspirat, aeternam.	Singulari ueneratione colendo, totis caritatis brachiis amplectendo, indiuiduo cordis *mei* hospiti, domino Bernardo Claraeuallis abbati, frater Petrus humilis *Cluniacensium* abbas, salutem ad quam suspirat aeternam ...

[11] Similarly, the *quemadmodum misimus* ("just as I have sent") in the *Epistola* is probably a textual error for the *quem nondum misimus* ("which I have not yet sent") in Letter 111.
[12] Cf. Kritzeck, in *Petrus Ven.*, p. 185.

Mitto uobis, charissime, nouam translationem nostram, contra pessimam nequam Machumet haeresim disputantem. Quae *nuper dum* in Hispaniis morarer, meo studio de Arabica uersa est in Latinam. Feci autem eam transferri a perito utriusque linguae uiro magistro Petro Toletano. Sed quia lingua Latina non *ei adeo* familiaris, uel nota erat, ut Arabica, dedi ei coadiutorem doctum uirum dilectum filium et fratrem Petrum notarium nostrum, Reuerentiae uestrae, ut extimo, bene cognitum. Qui uerba Latina impolite uel confuse plerumque ab eo prolata poliens et ordinans, epistolam, imo libellum multis, ut credo, propter ignotarum rerum notitiam perutilem futurum perfecit. Sed et totam impiam sectam, uitamque nefarii hominis ac legem quam Alcoran, id est, Collectaneum praeceptorum, appellauit, sibique ab angelo Gabriele de coelo collatam miserrimis hominibus persuasit, nihilominus ex Arabico ad Latinitatem perduxi, interpretantibus scilicet uiris utriusque linguae peritis, Roberto Retenensi de Anglia, qui nunc Papilonensis ecclesiae archidiaconus est, Hermano quoque Dalmata acutissimi, et literati ingenii scholastico. Quos in Hispania circa Hiberum astrologicae arti studentes inueni, eosque ad haec faciendum multo precio conduxi. Fuit autem *in hoc opere intentio mea,* ut morem illum patrum sequerer, quo nullam umquam suorum temporum uel leuissimam, ut sic dicam, haeresim, silendo *praeterierunt,* quin ei totis fidei uiribus resisterent, et scriptis *atque* disputationibus esse detestandam ac damnabilem demonstrarent. *Haec* ego de hoc praecipuo errore errorum, de hac faece uniuersarum haeresum, *inquam,* omnium diabolicarum sectarum, quae ab ipso Saluatoris aduentu ortae sunt, reliquiae confluxerunt, facere uolui: Vt sicut *eius lethali* peste dimidius pene orbis infectus agnoscitur, ita quam execrandus et conculcandus detecta eius stultitia et turpitudine a nescientibus agnoscatur. Agnoscetis *ipsi* legendo, et sicut arbitror, ut dignum est, deflebitis, per tam nefarias et abiectissimas sordes tantam humani generis partem deceptam,

Misi et nouam translationem nostram contra pessimam nequam Mahumet heresim disputantem, quae *dum nuper* in Hyspaniis morarer meo studio de *lingua* Arabica uersa est in Latinam. Feci autem eam transferri a perito utriusque linguae uiro magistro Petro Toletano. Sed quia lingua Latina non *adeo ei* familiaris uel nota erat ut Arabica, dedi ei coadiutorem doctum uirum dilectum filium et fratrem Petrum notarium nostrum reuerentiae uestrae ut aestimo bene cognitum. Qui uerba Latina impolite uel confuse plerumque ab eo prolata poliens et ordinans, epistolam immo libellum multis ut credo propter ignotarum rerum notitiam perutilem futurum perfecit.

Fuit autem *in transferendo haec mea intentio* ut morem illum patrum sequerer, quo nullam unquam suorum temporum uel leuissimam ut sic dicam heresim silendo *preterirent,* quin ei totis fidei uiribus resisterent et scriptis *ac* disputationibus esse detestandam ac dampnabilem demonstrarent. *Hoc* ego de hoc praecipuo errore errorum, de hac fece uniuersarum heresum, *in quam* omnium diabolicarum sectarum quae ab ipso saluatoris aduentu ortae sunt reliquiae confluxerunt, facere uolui, ut sicut *laetali eius* peste dimidius pene orbis infectus agnoscitur, ita quam *sit* execrandus et conculcandus detecta eius stultitia et turpitudine a nescientibus agnoscatur. Agnoscetis *ipse* legendo et sicut arbitror, ut dignum est deflebitis, per tam nefarias et abiectissimas sordes tantam humani generis partem decaeptam,

eta conditore suo per spurcissimi
hominis sectam *nefariam*, etiam post
Redemptoris gratiam tam leuiter auersam.

*Specialiter autem uobis ista omnia
notificaui, ut et tanto amico studia
nostra communicarem*, et ad scribendum contra tam perniciosum errorem,
*illam uestram, quam nostris diebus
uobis Deus singulariter contulit,
doctrinae magnificentiam*, animarem.
Nam licet hoc perditis, ut extimo,
prodesse non *posset*, responsionem
tamen condignam, sicut contra alias
haereses, ita et contra hanc *pestem*
Christianum armarium habere deceret.
*Quam si superfluam esse quibusdam
uisum* fuerit, quoniam quibus resistere debeant, talibus armis *immuniti*
non assunt, *noscitur* in republica
magni regis quaedam fieri ad tutelam,
quaedam fieri ad decorem, quaedam ad
utrumque. Nam ad tutelam facta sunt
a Salomone pacifico arma, licet tempore suo minus necessaria. Praeparati
sunt a Dauid sumptus, parata et
ornamenta templi diuini constructioni
et ornatui deputata. Sed nec illa
eius tempore alicui usui profecerunt,
sed in usus diuinos post eius tempora transierunt. Manserunt itaque

et a conditore suo per spurcissimi
hominis sectam etiam post redemptoris gratiam tam leuiter auersam.
Nec ignoro equidem, quoniam scriptura
ista quae perditis illis in propria
lingua prodesse non potuit, in
Latinam uersa minus proderit. Sed
proderit fortassis aliquibus
Latinis, quos et de ignotis instruet,
et quam dampnabilis sit heresis,
quae ad aures eorum peruenerat,
impugnando et expugnando ostendet.
Et ut nichil dampnabilis sectae
nostros lateret, totam illam illorum
legem, quam in propria lingua
Alkoran uel Alkyren uocant, ex
integro et per ordinem feci transferri. Interpretatur autem Alkoran
uel Alkyren si e uerbo uerbi ex-
pressa translatio fiat collectaneus
praecaeptorum, quae sibi per partes
de caelo missa, nequam ille confinxit.
Feci insuper et quasdam eius fabulas
cum quodam Abdia Iudaeo et aliis
Iudaeis habitas transferri, quae
inauditis deliramentis et uelut
somniorum phantasiis super uniuersa
ipsius scripta nefandam sectam etiam
pecoribus ostentui faciunt. Sed
quia res diffusa est, et propter linguae
barbariem ex magna sui parte ad
intelligendum difficilis, breuiter
dico quis iste fuerit, et quid
docuerit ... [see I, 295–98] ...
*Hoc ea de causa feci, ut et rem uobis notam
facerem*, et ad scribendum contra
tam perniciosum errorem animarem.
Nam licet *ut supra dixi* hoc perditis *illis* ut aestimo prodesse non
possit, responsionem tamen condignam,
sicut contra alias, ita et contra
hanc *heresim* Christianum armarium
habere deceret. *Quae* si *superflua quilibet causatus* fuerit, quoniam quibus
resistere debeant talibus armis *muniti*
non adsunt, *nouerit* in re publica
magni regis quaedam fieri ad tutelam,
quaedam fieri ad decorem, quaedam *etiam*
ad utrumque. Nam ad tutelam facta sunt
a Salomone pacifico arma, licet tempore suo minus necessaria, praeparati
sunt a Dauid sumptus, parata et
ornamenta, templi diuini constructioni
et ornatui deputata. Sed nec illa
eius tempore alicui usui profecerunt,
sed in usus diuinos post eius tempora transierunt. Manserunt itaque

ista aliquanto tempore ociosa, sed incumbente necessitate, apparuerunt, quae diu *uacauerunt*, fructuosa. Nec tamen, ut mihi uidetur, opus istud etiam hoc tempore ociosum uocare debeo. *Quia*, iuxta Apostolum, uestrum est, et omnium doctorum uirorum, omnem scientiam extollentem se aduersus altitudinem Dei, omni studio, uerbo, et scripto impugnare, destruere, conculcare. Quod si hinc errantes conuerti non *possunt*, saltem infirmis ecclesiae, qui scandalizari, *et* occulte moueri leuibus etiam ex causis solent, consulere et prouidere doctus, uel *doctior*, si zelum habet iustitiae, non debet negligere. Propono inde uobis patres omnes, et praecipue patrem Augustinum. Qui licet Iulianum Pelagianum, licet Faustum Manichaeum uerbis et labore suo ad fidem rectam conuertere nequiuerit, non tamen *quin* de eorum errore magna contra eos uolumina *conderet*, omisit. Sic de reliquis sui temporis, et non sui temporis, haereticis, sic de Iudaeis, sic de paganis faciens, non solum contra eos sui temporis homines armauit, sed etiam ad nos, et ad posteros omnes maximae aedificationis et instructionis charisma transmisit. Si igitur reuerentiae uestrae in his laborandi Deo adspirante uoluntas *fuerit*, nam facultas per eius gratiam deesse non poterit, rescribite, et mittemus librum, *quemadmodum* misimus, ut per os uestrum ipsius laude repletum, spiritui nequitiae spiritus benignus respondeat, et *ecclesiae suae thesauros* gazis uestrae sapientiae suppleat.

(*Bibl. Clun.*, cols. 1111–1112)
Summa totius haeresis, ac diabolicae fraudis sectae Saracenorum, seu Ismahelitarum, haec est.
In primis, primus, et maximus ipsorum execrandus est error, quod trinitatem in unitate Deitatis negant. Sicque dum in una diuinitatis essentia trium personarum numerum non credunt, in unitate numerum euitantes, dum ternarium numerum, inquam, omnium formarum principium atque finem, sicque rerum formatarum causam et originem atque terminum non recipiunt,

ista aliquanto tempore ociosa, sed incumbente necessitate apparuerunt quae diu *uacauerant* fructuosa. Nec tamen, ut michi uidetur, opus istud etiam hoc tempore ociosum uocare debeo, *quoniam* iuxta apostolum: Vestrum est et omnium doctorum uirorum omnem scientiam extollentem se aduersus altitudinem Dei, omni studio, uerbo, et scripto, impugnare, destruere, conculcare. Quod si hinc errantes conuerti non *possint*, saltem infirmis aecclesiae, qui scandalizari *uel* occulte moueri leuibus etiam ex causis solent, consulere et prouidere doctus uel *doctor* si zelum habet iustitiae non debet negligere. Propono inde uobis patres omnes, et praecipue patrem Augustinum, qui licet Iulianum Pelagianum, licet Faustum Manichaeum, *et* uerbis et labore suo ad fidem rectam conuertere nequiuerit, non tamn de eorum errore magna *condere* contra eos uolumina omisit. Sic de reliquis sui temporis, et non sui temporis hereticis, sic de Iudaeis, sic de paganis faciens, non solum contra eos sui temporis homines armauit, sed etiam ad nos et ad posteros omnes maximae aedificationis et instructionis charisma transmisit. Si igitur reuerentiae uestrae in his laborandi Deo aspirante uoluntas *affuerit*, nam facultas, per eius gratiam deesse non poterit rescribite et mittemus librum *quem nondum* misimus, ut per os uestrum ipsius laude repletum, spiritui nequitiae spiritus benignus respondeat, et *thesauros aecclesiae suae* gazis uestrae sapientiae suppleat.

(S 55^v and Cl 27^v–28^r)
Cl: Summa tocius heresis Sarracenorum.
S: Summa tocius secte Sarracenorum.

In primis, primus et maximus Sarracenorum error est [S: *est om.*] notandus, qui trinitatem in unitate Deitatis negant, sicque dum in una diuinitatis essentia trium [S: trinum] personarum numerum non credunt, in unitate numerum euitantes, dum ternarium inquam omnium formarum principium atque finem, sicque rerum formatarum causam et originem atque terminum non recipiunt,

Deum licet ore confitentes, ipsum penitus nesciunt. Ipsi autem deuii, ipsi uariabiles, principium uarietatis, et alteratis [alteritatis *in marg.*] omnis, uidelicet binarium solum in unitate confitentur, scilicet ipsam diuinam essentiam, et eius animam. Vnde Deum pluraliter loquentem introducit suum Alcoran, quo nomine legem suam nuncupant. Et interpretatur Alcoran ex Arabico, collectio praeceptorum. Illi autem caeci Deum creatorem patrem esse negant, quia secundum eos nullus fit pater sine coitu. Christum itaque licet ex diuino spiritu conceptum, Dei filium esse non credunt, nec etiam Deum, sed Prophetam bonum, ueracissimum, omnis mendacii atque peccati immunem, Mariae filium, sine	Deum licet ore confitentes, ipsum penitus nesciunt. Ipsi autem [Cl: autem *om.*] uariabiles, ipsi deuii, principium uarietatis et alteritatis omnis uidelicet binarium solum in unitate confitentur, scilicet ipsam diuinam essentiam et eius animam. Vnde Deum pluraliter soquentem introducit, semper Alc[h]oran, licque dum Deum unum pluraliter dicunt, ei prorsus unitatem tollunt. Illi item [S: idem] ceci Deum creatorem dicentes, ipsum esse patrem negant, quia secundum eos nullus fit pater sine coitu. Christum itaque licet ex diuino spiritu conceptum Dei filium esse non concedunt, nec etiam Deum sed prophetam bonum, ueracissimum, omnis mendacii atque peccatorum omnium immunem, Marie filium,
patre genitum, numquam mortuum, quia morte non est dignus. Imo cum illum Iudaei interficere uellent, de manibus eorum elapsum, ascendisse ad astra, ibique nunc in carne uiuere in praesentia creatoris, usque ad aduentum Antichristi. Quem, dum uenerit, Christus idem gladio suae uirtutis interficiet, et Iudaeos residuos ad legem suam conuertet, Christianos autem, qui iam a longo tempore legem eius atque euangelium perdiderunt, tum propter eiusdem discessum, tum etiam propter apostolorum atque discipulorum mortem, legem suam perfecte docebit. In qua omnes Christiani, sicut et illi primi discipuli, saluabuntur. Cum quibus simul et omnibus creaturis, Seraphim, quem ipsi dicunt archangelum unum, sonante buccina, morietur et ipse Christus, postea resurrecturus cum caeteris, et ad iudicium suos ducturus, eisque auxiliaturus, sed nequaquam iudicaturus. Deus enim solus iudicabit: prophetae uero et legati singuli cum suis, et pro suis, intercessores aderunt, et auxiliatores. Sic enim docuit eos miserrimus atque impiissimus Machumet, qui omnia sacramenta Christianae pietatis, quibus maxime homines saluantur, abnegans, iam pene tertiam humani generis partem, nescimus quo Dei iudicio, inauditis fabularum delira-	sine patre genitum, numquam mortuum, quia morte non est dignus, ascendisse ad astra, in carne uiuentem, in presentia creatoris, usque ad aduentum Antichristi. Quem uenientem Christus gladio suo [S: suo *om.*] uirtutis sue interficiet, et Iudeos residuos ad legem suam conuertet, et Christianos qui iam fere legem Christi [S: Christi *om.*] perdiderunt, tam [S: tum] propter Christi discessum, tam [S: tum] etiam propter apostolorum atque discipulorum mortem legem suam perfecte docebit, in qua tunc sicut sui discipuli saluabuntur. Cum quibus simul et omnibus creaturis Seraphim [S: Seraphin] quem ipsi dicunt archangelum unum, non angelorum ordinem sonante buccinam, morietur, et ipse Christus, cum [S: cum *om.*] resurrecturus cum ceteris, et ad iudicium suos ducturus, eis auxiliaturus, et pro eis, oraturus sed nequaquam iudicaturus. Deus enim solus iudicabit, prophete quidem et legati singuli cum suis et pro suis intercessores aderunt et auxiliatores. [End of *Summa* in S and Cl]

mentis diabolo et morti aeternae
contradidit. De quo, quis fuerit, et
quid docuerit, propter eos qui librum
istum lecturi sunt, ut scilicet quod
legerint, melius intelligant, et
quam detestabilis tam uita quam doc-
trina ipsius extiterint, sciant,
dicendum uidetur. Putant etiam quidam
hunc Nicolaum illum, unum ex septem
diaconibus primis extitisse, et
Nicolaitarum ab eo dictorum sectam,
quae *et* in Apocalypsi *Ioannis arguitur*,
hanc modernorum Saracenorum legem
existere. Somniant et alii alios,
et sicut lectionis incuriosi, et
rerum gestarum ignari, sicut et
in aliis casibus falsa quaelibet
opinantur. Fuit autem iste, sicut
etiam Chronica ab Anastasio Romanae
Ecclesiae Bibliothecario de Graeco
in Latinum translata apertissime
narrat, tempore Imperatoris Heraclii,
paulo post tempora magni et primi
Gregorii Romani Pontificis, ante
annos quingentos *fere et* quinquaginta,
Arabs natione, uilis genere, antiquae
primum idololatriae cultor, sicut et
alii Arabes tunc adhuc erant, ineruditus
nullarum pene litterarum. Strenuus
in *singularibus*, et calliditate multa,
de ignobili et egeno in diuitem et
famosum prouectus. Hic paulatim
crescendo, et contiguos quosque *ac*
maxime sanguinis *propinquos* insidiis,
rapinis, incursionibus frequenter
insistendo, quos poterat furtim, quos
poterat publice occidendo, terrorem
sui auxit. Et saepe in congressionibus
factus superior, ad regnum suae gentis
aspirare coepit. Cumque uniuersis pari
modo resistentibus, *eiusque* ignobili-
tatem contemnentibus, uideret se
hac uia non posse consequi quod
sperabat; quia ui gladii non potuit,
religionis uelamine, et diuini
Prophetae nomine, Rex fieri attentauit.
Et quia inter barbaros barbarus,
inter idololatras et ipse idololatra
habitabat, *atque* inter illos, quos,
ut pote prae cunctis gentibus, tam
diuinae quam humanae legis *expertes*
et ignaros, faciles ad seducendum
esse nouerat, conceptae iniquitati
dare operam coepit. Et *quoniam* Pro-
phetas Dei magnos fuisse homines
audierat, Prophetam *eius se* esse
dicens, ut aliquid boni simularet,

[Letter 111, between *Quid docuerit* and *Hoc ea de causa*]
... Putant enim quidam
hunc Nicholaum illum unum ex septem
primis diaconibus fuisse, et
Nicholaitarum ab eo dictorum sectam,
quae *etiam* in apochalipsi *nominatur*,
hanc modernorum Sarracenorum legem
existere. Somniant et alii alios,
et sicut lectionis incuriosi et
rerum gestarum ignari, sicut et
in aliis casibus falsa quaelibet
opinantur. Fuit autem iste

tempore imperatoris Heraclii,
paulo post tempora magni et primi
Gregorii Romani pontificis, ante
annos *ferme* quingentos quinquaginta,
Arabs natione, uilis genere, antiquae
ydolatriae cultor,

ineruditus,
nullarum pene litterarum, strenuus
in *saecularibus*, et calliditate multa,
de ignobili et egeno in diuitem et
famosum prouectus. Hic paulatim
crescendo et contiguos quosque *et*
maxime sanguinis *proximos* insidiis,
rapinis, incursionibus frequenter
infestando, quos poterat furtim, quos
poterat publice occidendo, terrorem
sui auxit, et sepe in congressionibus
factus superior, ad regnum suae gentis
aspirare coepit. Cumque uniuersis pari
modo resistentibus, *et eius* ignobili-
tatem contempnentibus, uideret se
hac uia non posse consequi quod
sperabat, quia ui gladii non potuit,
religionis uelamine et diuini
prophetae nomine rex fieri attemptauit.
Et quia inter barbaros barbarus,
inter ydolatras et ipse ydolatra
habitabat, *et* inter illos quos
utpote prae cunctis gentibus, tam
diuinae quam humanae legis *exsortes*
et ignaros, faciles ad seducendum
esse nouerat, concaeptae iniquitati
dare operam coepit. Et *quia* pro-
phetas Dei magnos fuisse homines
audierat, prophetam *se eius* esse,
praedicare iam omnibus coepit.

ex parte illos ab idololatria, non
tamen ad Deum unum, sed ad suae, quam
parturire iam coeperat, haeresis
fallaciam, traducere conabatur. Cum
interim iudicio illius, qui terribilis   Interim iudicio illius, qui terribilis
in consiliis dicitur super filios   in consiliis dicitur super filios
hominum, et qui miseretur cui uult,   hominum, et qui miseretur cui uult,
et quem uult indurat, dedit Satan   et quem uult indurat, dedit Sathan
successum errori, et Sergium monachum   successum errori, et Sergium monachum
haeretici Nestorii sectatorem *ab*   heretici Nestorii sectatorem, *expulsum*
Ecclesia expulsum ad partes illas   *ab aecclesia*, ad partes illas
Arabiae transmisit, et monachum   Arabiae transmisit, et monachum
haereticum pseudoprophetae coniunxit.   hereticum pseudo prophetae coniunxit.
Ita*que* Sergius coniunctus Machumet,   Ita Sergius coniunctus Mahumet,
quod ei deerat, suppleuit, et   quod ei deerat suppleuit, et
scripturas sacras tam ueteris Testa-   scripturas sacras tam ueteris testa-
menti quam noui, secundum magistri   menti quam noui, secundum magistri
sui Nestorii intellectum, qui Salua-   sui Nestorii intellectum, qui Salua-
torem nostrum Deum esse negabat,   torem nostrum Deum esse negabat,
partim prout sibi uisum est, *ei*   partim prout sibi uisum est
exponens, simulque apocryphorum   *exposuit, et eum ab*
fabulis eum plenissime imbuens,   *ydolatria auertens*,
Christianum Nestorianum effecit . . .   Christianum Nestorianum effecit . . .

The two texts are sufficiently similar from this point up to the words *fecit communicant* that no comparison is necessary. There are a few differences in wording and word order, but no major additions or omissions. After *fecit communicant*, the *Summa* continues for another column and a half in the *Bibliotheca Cluniacensis*, and Letter 111 returns after a transitional sentence ("Quam breuius potui, uitam hominis summaqume nefandae legis notaui.") to the text examined above, which parallels the *Epistola*.

Additional Note

New editions of the *Epistola* and *Summa* have recently appeared in James Kritzeck, *Peter the Venerable*, pp. 204-214, printed from MS. Paris, Arsenal 1162. These versions resemble column B more closely than the versions printed here from the *Bibl. Clun*. Aside from a few readings of its own, the Arsenal MS. agrees with column B against column A in about one third of the differences marked above in the passages from Letter 111, and it agrees in ten places with the short *Summa* (from S and Cl) against the parallel passage from the long version of the *Summa*. The MS. used for the *Bibl. Clun*. was probably one of the "Cluny" as contrasted with the "Toledo" collection (cf. D'Alverny, "Traductions," pp. 108-113), and the differences between its version and that in the Arsenal MS. suggest that there may have been some revision of the text between the two collections. On all essential points, however, the two versions agree.

G. THE DATE OF THE *CONTRA PETROBRUSIANOS*

The letters of Peter the Venerable contain the only known external evidence for dating the *Contra Petrobrusianos*. The most important reference occurs in Letter 111, which was written to Bernard of Clairvaux in the late spring or early summer of 1144. Peter wrote:

I should have also sent to Your Learned Love my [letter] which I wrote four or five years ago against certain tenets of the heretics in Provence, if I had had it to hand, in order that you might read it and supplement it, if any supplement were needed, in some treatise or letter. But it was recently taken into Auvergne by one of our monks and sent by me into Provence a year ago in another volume against the same heretics, and it could not be sent to you. It will be sent, however, after I have rewritten it out of some copy.

In Letter 71, Bishop Hato of Troyes, writing in March or April of 1138, warmly praised Peter the Venerable, whom he called "another John, of our age, [you] who have imbibed the flow of doctrine from the spring of the bosom of the Lord, from which you are able to throw forth... the secrets of the heavenly mysteries, the lessons of the Scriptures, the confutations of the heretics." Finally, in Letter 129, which was written, I believe, about 1139/41, shortly before Peter's trip to Spain, he wrote from a retreat in the woods near Cluny asking his secretary Peter of Poitiers to send "some work by St. Augustine to console me on my wearisome journey, and my letters, and the life of the lord bishop Matthew, since the book published against the heretics is lacking in the form that it was conceived and produced from my own heart." These three passages therefore show, respectively, that according to his own memory Peter wrote a work against the heretics in Provence in 1139/40 (Letter 111), that he wrote some refutation of the heretics before March/April 1138 (Letter 71), and that he wished to revise his book against the heretics in 1139/41 (Letter 129). Since there is no evidence that Peter wrote more than one work against the heretics,[1] and the *liber contra hereticos* mentioned in Letter 129 was in the singular, it is justified to assume that these passages refer to the *Contra Petrobrusianos*.

---

[1] The *Contra Iudaeos* and *Contra Saracenos* were both certainly written later.

This evidence for dating the *Contra Petrobrusianos* is supported by its position in the manuscripts of Peter's letter collection discussed in the Introduction. In the index to the Anchin manuscript the *Contra Petrobrusianos* is listed between Letter 87 (March 1141) and 88 (undated); and in the Souvigny manuscript the introduction to the *Contra Petrobrusianos* appears between Letter 93 (undated) and 95 (August 1141). This shows not only that the *Contra Petrobrusianos* originally formed part of the letter collection, though it was later copied as a separate treatise, but also that its position in the collection suggests a date of about 1141. Taken together, therefore, this evidence seems to show that Peter first planned and wrote the *Contra Petrobrusianos* before 1138 and then revised it in 1141 into the final form in which it was then incorporated into the collection of his works.

This hypothesis agrees with the internal evidence in the *Contra Petrobrusianos*. At the beginning of the introductory letter, addressed to the archbishops of Arles and Embrun and the bishops of Die and Gap, Peter wrote: "I recently wrote a letter to Your Reverence arguing against the heresy of Peter of Bruys, but I have delayed sending [it] until now because numerous and important affairs have kept my spirit from dictating [and] my pen from writing."[2] This specifically confirms that Peter wrote the treatise some time before he sent it, in order, presumably, not only to revise it but also to prepare a copy for each bishop. The treatise itself was addressed to Bishops William of Embrun, Ulric of Die, and William of Gap. The omission here of the archbishop of Arles may be accidental, or his inclusion on the introductory letter may have been an afterthought, but Archbishop Bernard of Arles died on 2 March 1138, and it is possible that the treatise was first written in the interval before the election of his successor William.[3] The other three bishops are of no help in narrowing the date of the treatise. At the beginning of the text Peter said that he had noticed the incidence of the heresy in the dioceses of Embrun, Die, and Gap while he was "recently making a journey through your dioceses."[4] This may correspond either to his trip to the Council of Pisa in May–June 1135, if he was writing in 1137/8, or to his visit to Rome for the Lateran Council in 1139, if he was writing in 1139/40; but he is not known to have been in that region at any other time during the 1130's.

Two further points of internal evidence should be mentioned. The first is the reference to Alger of Liège as dead,[5] which has been used by

---

[2] *Bibl. Clun.*, col. 1117 D.
[3] Gams, *Series*, p. 494.
[4] *Bibl. Clun.*, col. 1120 D.
[5] *Bibl. Clun.*, col. 1175 DE.

G. THE DATE OF THE *CONTRA PETROBRUSIANOS*

some scholars to set a *terminus post quem* of 1131 for the *Contra Petrobrusianos*. Since the date of Alger's death is not known, however, and cannot be determined more closely than "before 1145,"[6] this reference is in fact of no value. The second and more puzzling point, which has also been noted by several scholars, is the apparent reference to a visit to Spain, since Peter described a rock-salt mountain in eastern Spain as a miracle, "which I previously scarcely believed by hearing but later could not doubt when I saw what I had heard."[7] Now it is possible that Peter visited Spain in either 1124 or 1127, but he is not known to have gone there before 1142-3. This reference is therefore of no help in dating the *Contra Petrobrusianos*, but it suggests that Peter may have inserted some finishing touches after his return from Spain in 1143.

The principal points of this argument have long been known and accepted by scholars, most of whom have relied on the reference in Letter 111 in dating the *Contra Petrobrusianos*. It was thus dated in 1137 by Sikes,[8] in 1137/8 by Döllinger,[9] in about 1138 by De Ghellinck, Séjourné, and Congar,[10] in 1139/40 by Vacandard, Didier and Maisonneuve,[11] in about 1140 by Bodard,[12] and, more generally, between 1138/9 and 1142 by Borst.[13] An important group of scholars, however, has rejected this line of reasoning altogether and dated the *Contra Petrobrusianos* before 1135, above all because Peter the Venerable made no reference in it to the condemnation of Henry of Lausanne, the follower of Peter of Bruys, at the Council of Pisa in May-June 1135. This argument was first put forward by Goldhorn in 1866 and was developed in particular by Kramp, who suggested that the letter mentioned in Letter 111 as written four or five years before was not the *Contra Petrobrusianos* but another, lost work written by Peter the Venerable against the heresy of Henry of Lausanne in 1136/7 (since he dated Letter 111 in 1141).[14] This is a farfetched hypothesis, and it is

---

[6] See Ep. 89, n. to p. 230, l. 2.
[7] *Bibl. Clun.*, col. 1190 C.
[8] Sikes, *Abailard*, p. 263.
[9] J. J. I. von Döllinger, *Beiträge zur Sektengeschichte des Mittelalters* (Munich, 1890) pp. 81-82.
[10] De Ghellinck, *Mouvement théol.* (cited Ep. 4), p. 283; Séjourné, in *DThC*, XII.2, 2073; Y. Congar, in *Saint Bernard théologien* (Analecta sacri ordinis Cisterciensis, 9.3-4; Rome, 1953) p. 180.
[11] E. Vacandard, in *Rev. quest. hist.* (cited Ep. 111), LV, 70; J. C. Didier, in *St. Bernard théologien*, p. 198; and Henri Maisonneuve, *Études sur les origines de l'Inquisition*, 2nd ed. (L'église et l'état au Moyen Age, 7; Paris, 1960) p. 122, n. 169.
[12] Bodard, in *Coll. Ord. Cist. Ref.* (cited Ep. 37), XVIII, 119.
[13] Arno Borst, *Die Katharer* (Schriften der Monumenta Germaniae historica, 12; Stuttgart, 1953) p. 3 (with an extensive bibliography of previous works on the subject); cf. also the bibliography in Chevalier, *Régeste*, no. 3583, who dated the work 1137/40.
[14] David Goldhorn, in *Zeitschrift für historische Theologie*, 1866, pp. 174-183, cited by Kramp, in *Misc. Ehrle*, I, 71-79.

based upon an argument *ex silentio*,[15] but it has been accepted by several recent scholars, including Ilarino da Milano, Manselli, and Grundmann, who dated the *Contra Petrobrusianos* "before 1134?" and said that Borst's objections to this dating "have still to be proved."[16] The burden of proof, on the contrary, rests on those who support the earlier date. The weight of both internal and external evidence supports the later date and indicates that the first draft of the *Contra Petrobrusianos* was written about 1137/8, that it was revised and published in 1140/1, and that some finishing touches were perhaps added after 1143.[17]

---

[15] Peter's failure to mention the condemnation of Henry of Lausanne at Pisa in 1135 is not so curious in view of the fact that he clearly felt the heresy was still strong.

[16] Ilarino da Milano, *L'eresia di Ugo Speroni nella confutazione del Maestro Vacario* (Studi e testi, 115; Vatican City, 1945) p. 462, n. 1; Manselli, *Studi* (cited Ep. 27, n. to p. 51, l. 10), pp. 28–29; Herbert Grundmann, "Eresie e nuovi ordini religiosi nel secolo XII," *Relazioni del X Congresso internazionale di scienze storiche*, III: *Storia del Medioevo* (Florence, 1955) p. 369.

[17] While writing this appendix, I discussed some of the points in it with Dr. James Fearns, who was preparing a new edition of the *Contra Petrobrusianos* as a Ph.D. thesis at the University of Liverpool. I have since had an opportunity of reading the thesis, which was presented in 1963. Dr. Fearns strongly supports the date 1139/40 and stresses the weakness of the arguments for an earlier date (pp. xcvi-cxii of his typescript). He suggests on pp. cxlii-cxlix that some of the variants between the manuscripts of the *Contra Petrobrusianos* are the result of revision of the text by Peter the Venerable.

H. THE AFFAIR OF THE ABBEVILLE PREBENDS

The affair of the Abbeville prebends, which Peter the Venerable discussed in Letter 102, began in 1131, when Count Guy II of Ponthieu, who administered the county of Ponthieu for his father Count William I Talevas from 1126 until 1147, established twenty prebends in the church of St. Wulfram at Abbeville.[1] The right of presentation belonged to him and his successors, and either in 1131 or later, according to Letter 102, he decided to give one of these prebends, "in so far as it pertained to the secular rights," to the Cluniac priory of SS. Peter and Paul at Abbeville, which had been richly endowed by his family in 1100.[2] This grant required the consent of the bishop of Amiens, to whom the ecclesiastical care of the prebends belonged. Bishop Guarinus of Amiens was on the whole very favorably disposed towards Cluny[3] and was willing to approve this grant, according to Peter the Venerable, but he was dissuaded from doing so by Bishop Milo of Thérouanne and a few others who were presumably enemies of Cluny.[4]

The precise date of these events is not known, except that it was between 1131 and 1144, when Bishop Guarinus retired to Cluny. The only other chronological indication is Peter's reference to the "council of bishops recently held at the city of Rheims." This cannot refer to either of the known councils at Rheims in 1131 or 1148, and both Marlot and Chevalier were of the opinion that this meeting was the

---

[1] *Recueil des actes des comtes de Pontieu*, ed. Clovis Brunel (Collection de documents inédits sur l'histoire de France; Paris, 1930) pp. 38–40, no. 21; cf. Ignace Joseph de Jesus Maria, *L'histoire ecclésiastique de la ville d'Abbeville* (Paris, 1646) pp. 85–87; F.-C. Louandre, *Histoire d'Abbeville et du comté de Ponthieu* (Abbeville, 1883–84) II, 450; and *DHGE*, I, 41. These three works also mention a further foundation of six more prebends in 1138, but this charter was shown to be a forgery by Brunel, *Recueil*, pp. 654–656, *actes faux* no. III.

[2] *Recueil*, pp. 10–20, nos. 8–9; cf. De Valous, *Mon. clun.*, II, 188.

[3] See biographical note to Ep. 108.

[4] On Milo, see biographical note to Ep. 102. In spite of his attack on Cluniac pride mentioned in this letter, Peter referred to him as a friend and said that he had attended the chapter at Cluny "two or three times." The authors of the *Gallia christiana*, X, 1547, suggested that his ill will toward Cluny on this occasion was "perhaps owing to the monks of St. Bertin," who finally won their freedom from Cluny in 1139: see Ep. 102, n. to p. 265, l. 5.

same as the Council of Sens in 1140.⁵ The four bishops mentioned by Peter, Samson of Rheims, Alvisus of Arras, Geoffrey of Châlons-sur-Marne, and Jocelin of Soissons all attended the Council of Sens, and they wrote a joint letter to the Pope concerning Abelard.⁶ It is therefore quite possible that they gathered again at Rheims after the Council of Sens. If this is so, Peter's Letter 102 can be dated soon after June 1140, and the offer of the prebend probably occurred not long before.

Although the first offer was blocked by the ill will of Milo of Thérouanne, Peter the Venerable was able to turn the tables on the enemies of Cluny a few years later when Count William of Ponthieu, after his return from the Second Crusade in 1148, visited Cluny seeking absolution for the soul of his son, who had died on the crusade, at Ephesus. Peter agreed to this, as William wrote to the countess Ida and his grandson John, on condition that the prebends be granted to the monks of SS. Peter and Paul at Abbeville.⁷ In 1152, therefore, Ida and John arranged an agreement between the Cluniacs and the canons of St. Wulfram, in accordance with which the monks, "on account of the great losses they had suffered for the previous gift" (that is, presumably, the original grant discussed in Letter 102), received two prebends in the church of St. Wulfram, in addition to the church of the Holy Sepulchre and a confirmation of their other possessions.⁸

---

⁵ Guillaume Marlot, *Histoire de la Ville, Cité et Université de Reims*, new ed. (Rheims, 1843–1846) III, 281, and Chevalier, *Topo-bib.*, II, 2523; cf. Appendix P on Nicholas of Montiéramey and the Council of Sens.

⁶ Bernard, ep. 191 (Gaume ed., I.1, 415–416); cf. Vacandard, *St. Bernard*, II, 144.

⁷ *Recueil*, pp. 72–73, no. 47; cf. S. Löwenfeld, "Documents relatifs à la croisade de Guillaume comte de Ponthieu," *Archives de l'Orient latin*, II (1884) *documents*, pp. 251–255, esp. p. 252.

⁸ *Recueil*, pp. 73–74, no. 48; cf. I. J. de Jesus Maria, *Hist. ecc.*, p. 155.

I. CLUNIAC HOUSES IN THE EAST

"The history of Cluniac monasteries in the East is little known," wrote Pignot in 1868, "and these establishments do not seem to have been numerous."[1] No new evidence has come to light in the century since Pignot was writing, and Letters 31, 75-76, and 80 of Peter the Venerable are still among the most valuable sources of information on this obscure subject.

The only house in the Holy Land that was surely Cluniac was Mt. Thabor.[2] According to the chronicle of Cluny, there was only a confraternity between Mt. Thabor and Cluny,[3] and L'Huillier said that there was no tie of subordination;[4] but Letters 31 and 80 of Peter the Venerable leave no doubt that the monks of Mt. Thabor regarded themselves as Cluniacs. Peter said in Letter 80 that they had joined the Cluniac order "moderno tempore," and according to Enlart they adopted Cluniac observances in 1130.[5] The fact that former Abbot Pontius of Cluny visited Mt. Thabor after his resignation in 1122, however,[6] suggests that there may have been ties between the two houses even before the abbacy of Peter the Venerable.

The abbey of Our Lady at Jehosaphat may also have been Cluniac,[7] although there is no reference to any dependency on Cluny in the charters published by Delaborde.[8] François de Rivo stated in the

---

[1] Pignot, *Cluny*, III, 297, n. 2. I have been unable to consult Benoît Gariador, *Les anciens monastères bénédictins en Orient* (Lille, 1912).

[2] Mt. Thabor is the only Cluniac house in the Holy Land mentioned by De Valous, *Mon. clun.*, II, 168; cf. Ursmer Berlière, "Die alten Benedictinerklöster im heiligen Lande," *SMGBOZ*, IX (1888) 486; Cottineau, *Répertoire*, II, 1909.

[3] *Bibl. Clun.*, col. 600 D.

[4] L'Huillier, *Saint Hugues*, p. 439.

[5] Camille Enlart, *Les monuments des croisés dans le royaume de Jérusalem* (Haut-Commissariat de la République française en Syrie et au Liban: Service des antiquités et des beaux-arts, Bibliothèque archéologique et historique, 7-8; Paris, 1925-1928) II, 382.

[6] Ordericus Vitalis, *Hist. ecc.*, XII, 30 (*ed. cit.*, IV, 424).

[7] It is listed as such by L'Huillier, *Saint Hugues*, p. 439; Berlière, in *SMGBOZ*, IX, 475; and Cottineau, *Répertoire*, I, 1482-1483. According to Schmitz, *Ordre de Saint Benoît* (cited p. 52, n. 217, above), I (2nd ed.), 266, "On y suivait les usages de Cluny sans toutefois appartenir à l'Ordre."

[8] *Chartes de Terre Sainte provenant de l'abbaye de N.-D. de Josaphat*, ed. H.-F. Delaborde (Bibliothèque des Écoles françaises d'Athènes et de Rome, 19; Paris, 1880).

chronicle of Cluny that Jehosaphat belonged to the order of Cluny;[9] and Gilduin, or Gelduin, who was abbot there from at least 1120 until 1130, was a Cluniac monk and a former prior of Lurcy-le-Bourg.[10] A document allegedly showing the presence of Latin monks at Jehosaphat before the First Crusade was proved to be a forgery by Lynn White, who therefore dated the foundation of the abbey after the First Crusade, but even in this forged letter the origins of Jehosaphat were associated with Cluny.[11]

In addition to Mt. Thabor and Jehosaphat, Enlart listed as Cluniac the monasteries of Bethany and the tomb of the Virgin, St. Mary the Latin, St. Anne, and St. Mary the Great at Jerusalem,[12] but none of these is certain.

Letters 75 and 76 are concerned with a Cluniac house named Civitot (Civitoth, Civinoth), a dependency of La Charité-sur-Loire, in the neighborhood of Constantinople.[13] These letters are the only evidence for the existence of this house, which was identified by Jules Gay as Civitot or Chivetot on the Gulf of Izmit. Gay also suggested that it had been founded in 1096/7, when that region was a center of Latin influence during the First Crusade.[14] There is no reference to Civitot, however, in Janin's work on the churches and monasteries in the see of Constantinople, nor in Dölger's and Grumel's editions of the *regesta* of the Byzantine emperors and patriarchs. The precise location and history of Civitot is therefore a mystery, aside from the information given in Peter's two letters. These show that the house was founded and subjected to Cluny during the reign of the emperor Alexius I, the father of John, to whom Letter 75 was addressed; and they show that under the emperor John, the Latin monks were expelled, probably during a wave of anti-Western feeling at Constantinople. Whether or not it was ever restored to Cluny is not known, but the silence of the later sources suggests that Peter's pleas to the emperor and patriarch fell on deaf ears.

---

[9] *Bibl. Clun.*, col. 600 CD.

[10] *Bibl. Clun.*, col. 565; Mabillon, *Annales*, VI, 47–48; *Chartes de Josaphat*, p. 18; Berlière, in *SMGBOZ*, IX, 475.

[11] Lynn White, Jr., "A Forged Letter Concerning the Existence of Latin Monks at St. Mary's Jehosaphat before the First Crusade," *Speculum*, IX (1934) 404–407.

[12] Enlart, *Monuments*, I, 16, and II, 230. According to George Jeffery, *A Brief Description of the Holy Sepulchre, Jerusalem* (Cambridge, Eng., 1919) pp. 180 ff., who based himself on De Vogüé, the monastery of the tomb of the Virgin was Cluniac, and its first abbot, Hugh, was appointed in 1117.

[13] Cf. *La Charité*, p. 423, and De Valous, *Mon. clun.*, II, 168. The reference in the chronicle of Cluny, in *Bibl. Clun.*, col. 600 D, to "Cuntot," described as "in suburbio Constantinopolis ciuitatis," is probably a misprint, since it is based on these letters.

[14] Gay, in *Échos d'Orient* (cited Ep. 75), XXX, 84–87.

J. CLUNIAC CARDINALS DURING THE ABBACY OF PETER THE VENERABLE, WITH SPECIAL ATTENTION TO THE EARLY LIFE OF IMAR OF TUSCULUM

There were six known Cluniac cardinals during the abbacy of Peter the Venerable. (1) The first, both in importance and in seniority, was Peter *Leonis*, the future Pope Anacletus II, who was successively a monk at Cluny, cardinal-deacon of SS. Cosmas and Damian, and cardinal-priest of Sta. Maria in Trastevere before his election to the papacy in 1130.[1] (2) The second Cluniac cardinal in terms of seniority was Aegidius, or Gilo, of Tusculum, who had also been a monk at Cluny before he was created a cardinal by Pope Calixtus II. He first subscribed to papal documents late in 1121. Nine years later he was the only French cardinal among the supports of Anacletus. He served as Anacletus's representative in France and took up residence in Poitiers, apparently after Gerald of Angoulême became archbishop of Bordeaux in 1131. After the death of Anacletus early in 1138, Gilo submitted to Innocent II and appeared on papal bulls from 21 June 1138 until 1 March 1139; but he was deposed by Innocent at the Lateran Council in April 1139.[2] (3) Prior Matthew of St.-Martin-des-Champs, who figures prominently in the letters and other works of Peter the Venerable, was cardinal-bishop of Albano from 1127 until his death in 1135.[3] (4) Pope Innocent II, early in his pontificate, created another Cluniac cardinal, Abbot Adenulf of Farfa, who became cardinal-deacon of Sta. Maria in Scola

[1] On Anacletus, see Ep. 34, n. to p. 113. On his career as a cardinal, see Brixius, *Kardinalkollegium*, pp. 38 and 80–81, and esp. Klewitz, *Reformpapsttum*, pp. 226–228, who dated his appointment as cardinal-deacon in 1113 (possibly as early as 1111/12) and as cardinal-priest in 1120, and Schmale, *Schisma*, pp. 18–22 and 66–77.

[2] There is no comprehensive account of Gilo's life, but references to him will be found in Pignot, *Cluny*, III, 170–172 and 428; Bernhardi, *Lothar*, p. 314; Petit, *Ducs de Bourgogne*, II, 57–58; Richard, *Comtes de Poitou*, II, 32–33; Brixius, *Kardinalkollegium*, pp. 31 and 71; P. David, "Le monachisme bénédictin et l'Ordre de Cluny dans la Pologne médiévale," *Revue Mabillon*, XXVII (1937) 159–160, and XXVIII (1938) 81–82, who studied Gilo's work as papal legate in Hungary and Poland in 1123–5 and attributed to him the links between Cluny and the Polish Benedictine houses; Klewitz, *Reformpapsttum*, pp. 225–226; Wattenbach-Holtzmann, *Geschichtsquellen*, I.4, 795; Bloch, "Schism," p. 171; Claude, in *Mélanges St. Bernard*, pp. 85–88; Schmale, *Schisma*, pp. 77–78; and Janssen, *Legaten*, pp. 9 ff. According to Tellenbach, "Pontius," pp. 40–41 and 44–45, Gilo was a leader, with Anacletus II and Abbot Pontius, of the conservative and traditionalist Cluniacs, in contrast to Peter the Venerable and Matthew of Albano.

[3] On Matthew, see biographical note to Ep. 2.

Greca in 1132. The three years from his elevation until the death of Matthew of Albano was the only period in the abbacy of Peter the Venerable when there were three Cluniac cardinals. Adenulf was deprived of his abbacy by Anacletus II. It was restored to him in 1137, and he lived until 1144. He was a friend of St. Bernard, and apparently an estimable man, but he seems never to have played an active role in the Sacred College.[4] (5) Innocent II created two other Cluniac cardinals: Abbot Alberic of Vézelay, cardinal-bishop of Ostia from 1138 until 1147,[5] and (6) Cardinal-Bishop Imar of Tusculum, to whose early life I shall return in a moment. Imar was created a cardinal in 1142 and subscribed to papal bulls from at least 19 April. In the schism of 1159 he supported the antipope Victor IV and died not long afterward, either in 1161 or 1162.[6] After the death of Alberic of Ostia, Imar was the only Cluniac in the Sacred College; and no other Cluniac cardinal is known before 1180: an eloquent sign of the declining influence of Cluny in the papal curia during the second half of the twelfth century.[7]

François de Rivo gave a circumstantial account of the early life of Imar of Tusculum in the chronicle of Cluny:

Bishop Imar of Tusculum lived at the time of [Abbot] Pontius [of Cluny]. At an early age he received the monastic habit at St.-Martin-des-Champs in Paris, under the lord Matthew, who was prior at that time and later venerable bishop of Albano. He was brought to Cluny by this man, his prior, and during the time of the lord abbot Pontius he was more strictly bound in the monastic sacraments by the completion of his profession and benediction. In view of his merits he was made custodian (*custos* [probably meaning prior]) of the order. He was then promoted to prior of La Charité [sur Loire] and after a time was consecrated abbot of Montierneuf at Poitiers, where he was a strict ruler and an outstanding supporter of the order and left remarkable monuments of his piety and wisdom.[8]

This account has been accepted by all subsequent writers on Imar;[9] but François de Rivo was writing more than three centuries after

---

[4] Brixius, *Kardinalkollegium*, pp. 40 and 83–85, and Klaus Ganzer, *Die Entwicklung des auswärtigen Kardinalats im hohen Mittelalter* (Bibliothek des deutschen historischen Instituts im Rom, 26; Tübingen, 1963) pp. 81–83.

[5] On Alberic, see Ep. 4, n. to p. 8, l. 23.

[6] Brixius, *Kardinalkollegium*, pp. 44 and 91–92; Janssen, *Legaten*, pp. 39–50.

[7] Cf. Janssen, *Legaten*, p. 177. It should be remembered, however, that the total number of cardinals from the monastic orders, not only the Cluniacs, was declining at this time in contrast to the first half of twelfth century: cf. Philipp Hofmeister, "Kardinäle aus dem Ordenstande," SMGBOZ, LXXII (1961) 153–170.

[8] *Bibl. Clun.*, cols. 1644–1645. This is followed by an account of Imar's elevation to the cardinalate and his later career.

[9] Mabillon, note to Bernard, ep. 219 (Gaume ed., I.1, 904); GC, II, 1267, and XII, 405; Pignot, *Cluny*, III, 428–429; Chevalier, *Bio-bib.*, I, 2247; Brixius, *Kardinalkollegium*, pp. 44 and 91–92; cf. *La Charité*, p. 427; *St. Martin des Champs*, II, 130, n. 224; *Chronique et chartes de*

Imar's death, and his sources for this passage are unfortunately lost. Only one stage in this curriculum is even tentatively confirmed by a contemporary document. An "Imarus Novi-Monasterii" witnessed the reconciliation of King Louis VII with Archdeacon Algrin of Orléans in 1140/1;[10] but there is no positive evidence that this Imar of Montierneuf was the future cardinal. The authors of the *Gallia christiana* also noticed a privilege of Pope Innocent II addressed to "Aymaro Crispei monasterii priori," that is, to the prior of the Cluniac house of St. Arnulf at Crépy in the modern diocese of Beauvais.[11] On this basis they added yet another stage to Imar's *cursus honorum* and listed him as successively a monk at St.-Martin-des-Champs, prior of Crépy, prior of La Charité, dean of Cluny, and abbot of Montierneuf at Poitiers.

Aymar was a common name in the twelfth century, however,[12] whereas Imar or Ymar was comparatively rare in that form, even though it may be the equivalent, according to Franklin, of the common name of Maurus.[13] Without further evidence, therefore, the identity of Aymar of Crépy and Imar of Tusculum must remain a matter of doubt. The identity of Imar of Montierneuf with Imar of Tusculum, however, is very much more probable, especially since it is supported by the evidence of François de Rivo, whose sources, although lost, were probably of high authority. It is possible that he was also the Imarus to whom Hugh Primas of Orléans addressed a poem, wishing him a happy sea journey. Imar of Montierneuf and Hugh Primas were active in the same region at about the same time and could easily have known each other.[14] For Imar's earlier career at St.-Martin-des-Champs, Cluny, and La Charité, however, there is only the evidence of the chronicle of Cluny.

---

l'abbaye de Saint-Mihiel, ed. André Lesort (Mettensia, 6; Paris, 1909-1912) p. 316, n. 2; and Schmitz, in *Rev. Bén.* (cited Appendix D, *s.a.* 1151), XLIX, 369, n. 2. According to the *GC*, XII, 405, Mabillon put Oldricus in place of Imar in the list of the priors of La Charité: see Appendix K.

[10] Duchesne, *Scriptores*, IV, 764 (RHGF, XVI, 6-7, and *St. Martin des Champs*, II, 116-117, no. 256); cf. C. de Chergé, "Mémoire historique su rl'abbaye de Montierneuf de Poitiers," *Mémoires de la Société des antiquaires de l'Ouest*, XI (1844) 270; and p. 309, n. 28, below, on the date.

[11] *Bull. Clun.*, p. 46; JL 7429; cf. *GC*, X, 1486.

[12] It is equated by Chevalier, *Bio-bib.*, I, 400, with Ademar; cf. Appendix R and Index s.n. Ademar.

[13] Alfred Franklin, *Dictionnaire des noms, surnoms, et pseudonymes latins de l'histoire littéraire du Moyen Age* (Paris, 1875) col. 625.

[14] Wilhelm Meyer, "Die Oxforder Gedichte des Primas, II: no 1-15 und no 23," *Nachrichten von der königlichen Gesellschaften der Wissenschaften zu Göttingen*, Phil.-hist. Kl., 1907, pp. 123-125, who stressed the rarity of the name Imar and associated the poem with some visit of Imar of Montierneuf to Rome before he became a cardinal; cf. Manitius, *Lat. Lit.*, III, 973-978, esp. p. 975, and F. J. E. Raby, *A History of Secular Latin Poetry in the Middle Ages* (Oxford, 1934) II, 171-180, who cited on p. 180 the relevant passage of the poem.

K. THE PRIORS OF LA CHARITÉ-SUR-LOIRE, 1122–1156

Five priors of La Charité are listed during the abbacy of Peter the Venerable by the authors of the *Gallia christiana* and by De Lespinasse in the chartulary of La Charité: Odo I; Imar, dated "saltem 1130"; Peter of Paul (1138–43); William or Guy (1143–50); and Theodard (1151/4).[1] According to Mabillon, who is mentioned in the *Gallia christiana*, Imar was prior in 1122 and was succeeded by Theodard, "although some people place Olricus in between."[2] The names of three of these priors, however, Imar, Olricus, and Theodard, are found on no surviving charter of La Charité, and the dates of the others are far from certain.

According to the documents, Odo was prior from at least 3 August 1119, when he appeared on a grant by King Louis VI to La Charité, until at least 1121.[3] Peter appeared as prior on documents dated 1 August 1138/22 April 1139,[4] 1143,[5] 14 April 1144,[6] and 15 May 1144,[7] and on two undated charters, one, of doubtful authenticity, dated "about 1139" by De Lespinasse,[8] the other of "about 1146."[9] He was referred to as former prior in a charter of Louis VII dated between 1 August 1146 and 2 February 1147,[10] and he was therefore prior from at least 1139 until 1147 at the latest. Prior G. appeared in a papal bull

---

[1] *GC*, XII, 405–406, and *La Charité*, p. 427. At different places De Lespinasse dated Peter "environ 1138–1143" and "1138–1147," but his list is derived from that in the *GC*, as is that in the *DHGE*, XII, 419.
[2] Mabillon, *Annales*, VI, 76.
[3] Luchaire, *Louis VI*, p. 129, no. 275, and *La Charité*, pp. 124–126, no. 49.
[4] *La Charité*, p. 128, no. 51; Luchaire, *Louis VII*, p. 108, no. 28.
[5] *GC*, XII, *instr.*, 114–115.
[6] *La Charité*, p. 364, no. 168; *Cluny*, V, 432–435, no. 4081; JL 8572.
[7] *Thes. nov.*, III, 888; JL 8609.
[8] *La Charité*, pp. 182–184, no. 82. The list of witnesses to this charter excludes the date 1139 and throws some doubt on its authenticity, although allegedly it survives in the original. Among the witnesses were G. archbishop of Bourges (the name of no known archbishop of Bourges at this time began with G.); Gui bishop of Le Mans, which may refer to Bishop William (Gui. = Guillelmus) (1145–87); R. bishop of Périgeux, which presumably refers to Bishop Raymond (1149–58: Pacaut, *Élections*, p. 126); and Cardinal-Bishop Imar of Tusculum. This would point to a date after 1149 for this charter, if it is genuine.
[9] *La Charité*, pp. 126–127, no. 50.
[10] *La Charité*, p. 130, no. 52; Luchaire, *Louis VII*, p. 159, no. 186.

dated 15 May 1153,[11] and he also wrote a letter to Suger, which was dated 1149 by Brial and Lecoy de la Marche and 1147/9 by Cartellieri,[12] and a letter to Adam fitz Swane, the founder of Monk Bretton, which has been dated by different scholars either 1153/5 or *ca.* 1154/9.[13] Finally, the charter recording the oath of the townsmen of La Charité to Peter the Venerable in 1130 should be cited, because it was witnessed by many dignitaries, including the provost Hugh of La Charité, but not by the prior.[14] This may indicate that the position of prior was vacant in 1130.

There are references to four other priors in contemporary letters and chronicles, but their dates—and even their existence—cannot be established with certainty. The least dubious is Theodard, whose name occurs several times in the letters of Peter the Venerable. He is mentioned in the *Gallia christiana*, but the dates assigned to him there and by De Lespinasse are certainly too late,[15] since the letters were in all probability written in the 1130's. Theodard therefore probably came before Peter, who was prior by 1139.[16] A second reference is a letter from a prior B. of La Charité to Archbishop Theobald of Canterbury concerning the freedom of the new abbey of Faversham, which was founded by King Stephen of England and Queen Mathilda in 1147 or 1148.[17] His full name is not known, but he must have succeeded Peter as prior. The other two are more problematical. François de Rivo, the fifteenth-century chronicler of Cluny, mentioned that Imar, the

---

[11] *La Charité*, p. 46, no. 16, also in *Epistolae Pontificum Romanorum ineditae*, ed. S. Loewenfeld (Leipzig, 1885) p. 113, no. 212; JL 9722. The name is given as "Guillelmi" by De Lespinasse and simply as "G." by Loewenfeld, who is the more reliable editor. His name may therefore be either William or Guy or some other name beginning with G.

[12] *RHGF*, XV, 510; cf. Suger, *Oeuvres*, p. 302, and Cartellieri, *Suger*, p. 146, no. 161.

[13] Dugdale, *Monasticon*, V, 136–137 (1153/5), and William Farrer, *Early Yorkshire Charters* (Edinburgh, 1914 ff.) III, 324, no. 1671 (*ca.* 1154–9). The foundation of Monk Bretton is dated 1153/5 in Knowles and Hadcock, *Religious Houses*, p. 98.

[14] *Cluny*, V, 364–365, no. 4009.

[15] De Lespinasse himself admitted in his note to the bull of 1153, referring to prior G. (n. 11 above), that William's priorate must have extended to that year and that "he was replaced by Theodard for several months, then by Raynaud."

[16] I am inclined to believe that Theodard became prior after 1130, on account both of the charter of 1130 cited above, on which he does not appear, and of the reference to "those monstrous acts committed against me" in Letter 49, written by Peter the Venerable to Henry of Winchester in 1131. These may have arisen out of the efforts of La Charité to win its independence from Cluny (cf. Ep. 49, n. to p. 150). It is hard to imagine that Theodard, who was a trusted friend and supporter of Peter the Venerable, took part in any of these activities.

[17] Dugdale, *Monasticon*, IV, 575; cf. John R. Fryar, "The Ancient and Royal Abbey of Faversham," *Downside Review*, XXX (1911) 245; Knowles and Hadcock, *Religious Houses*, p. 66 (dating the foundation of Faversham in 1148); and Saltman, *Theobald*, pp. 82–83 (dating the foundation in 1147). Dr. William Urry, keeper of manuscripts in the Cathedral Library at Canterbury has kindly verified for me from the manuscript of this letter (Ch. Ant. F 81) that the shape of the initial B. "seems to me to be quite unambiguous and the general appearance of the MS. points to an original from La Charité and not a copy into which a mistake might have crept" (letter dated 11 April 1962).

future cardinal-bishop of Tusculum, served as prior of La Charité before he became abbot of Montierneuf at Poitiers, where he appears in 1140/2.[18] This reference was the basis for the inclusion of Imar among the priors of La Charité by Mabillon and the authors of the *Gallia christiana*, but it is not confirmed by any contemporary evidence. Fourth, Florence of Worcester mentioned in his chronicle a Cluniac monk named Peter who "served for some time in the priorate of La Charité," then ruled the monastery of St. Urban in the diocese of Châlons-sur-Marne, and was finally made abbot of Malmesbury by Bishop Henry of Winchester in 1140.[19] An abbot Peter of St. Urban appears on charters of 1137, 1140, and 1146, according to the *Gallia christiana*,[20] and this Peter cannot therefore have been the same Peter who was prior of La Charité from at least 1139 until about 1146. As with Imar, there is no confirming evidence that he ever really was prior of La Charité.[21] It is possible, for instance, that both may have held some lower office, such as that of claustral prior, in the monastery, which was clearly one of the established steppingstones in the *cursus honorum* of prominent Cluniacs in the first half of the twelfth century.

On the basis of this evidence, therefore, a tentative revised list of the priors of La Charité during the abbacy of Peter the Venerable would run as follows, with their minimum certain dates: Odo (1119–21); vacant? (1130); Theodard; Peter (1139–ca. 1146); B. (1147/8); and G. (1149–53).

---

[18] See Appendix J.

[19] Florence of Worcester, *Chronicon*, s.a. 1140, ed. Benjamin Thorpe (English Historical Society; London, 1848–49) II, 129; cf. William of Malmesbury, *Historia novella*, no. 482 (*ed. cit.* p. 253, n. 8, above), p. 40, and Knowles, *Monastic Order*, p. 284.

[20] *GC*, IX, 925. The last of these references seems either to be an error or to indicate that there were two successive abbots of St. Urban named Peter, because Peter (I) definitely became abbot of Malmesbury in 1140.

[21] He may possibly have been the Peter sent to La Charité by Peter the Venerable in 1134 or 1136, during the priorate of Theodard, and warmly recommended as a personal friend in Letters 41–42.

L. THE PRIORS OF SAUXILLANGES, 1049-1156

This list of the priors of Sauxillanges during the abbacies of Hugh, Pontius, Hugh II, and Peter of Cluny was compiled in order to help date some of the charters used in Appendix A on the family of Peter the Venerable. It seems worth including here, although it makes no claims to finality,[1] because it improves on the list in the *Gallia christiana* and on account of the close ties between Sauxillanges and the family of Montboissier, and more generally between Sauxillanges and Cluny, during the second half of the eleventh and the first half of the twelfth centuries. The list in the *Gallia christiana*, II, 374-375, includes in all thirty-one priors between 1049 and 1156, but several of these appear on no surviving document in the chartulary of Sauxillanges, and the dates and order of the remainder are far from certain. The following list is based upon the charters of Sauxillanges, to which the numbers refer, and a few other sources, and it could doubtless be refined by a close study of the undated charters. I am indebted for a number of details on this list to my students Mrs. C. Bynum and Mrs. C. Lucas.

Robert[2]	at least 1031– at least 1060	347 and 672 (King Robert); 515 (Abbot Odilo); 297 (Abbot Hugh); 647 (King Philip). *GC*: Robertus I, 1069.
Gerald	1049/1109	569-570 (Abbot Hugh); 620 (mentioned as former prior). *GC*: Gerardus I, 1068.

[1] An inevitable source of weakness is that it depends in part upon the dates of the counts of Auvergne and the bishops of Clermont, which are taken (for the counts) from *L'art de vérifier les dates* and (for the bishops) from Gams, *Series*; Boudet, in *St. Flour*, introd., p. xxx; and for the bishops in the second half of the eleventh century from Alfons Becker, *Studien zum Investiturproblem in Frankreich* (Schriften der Universität des Saarlandes; Saarbrücken, 1955) pp. 56-57 and 94, and G. B. Borino, "Due vescovi di Le Puy di nome Stefano nelle lettere di Gregorio VII," *Studi Gregoriani*, V (1956) 383-389. The date of the death of Bishop William of Baffie of Clermont is especially important for dating the priors of Sauxillanges at the beginning of the twelfth century. He accompanied William of Aquitaine to the East in 1101: Albert of Aix, *Historia Hierosolymitana*, VIII, 39, in *Recueil des historiens des Croisades: Historiens occidentaux*, IV (Paris, 1879) 581; and he died on 14 January 1102/3, according to Paul Riant, "La légende du martyre en Orient de Thiemon, archevêque de Salzbourg," *Revue des questions historiques*, XXXIX (1886) 220, n. 2, citing the necrology of Clermont in MS. Paris, Bibl. nat., Lat. 9085, fol. 9.

[2] The length of time over which this prior appears suggests that there may have been two priors named Robert.

Bertrand	ca. 1060/73	486 (Bishop Stephen of Clermont and Count Robert of Auvergne). No reference in GC.
Letald	1060/1109	854 (Abbot Hugh); 625 (after Prior Bertrand). No reference in GC.
Bladinus	1073/1109	613 (Abbot Hugh; after 614, which was issued during the pontificate of Bishop William of Chamalières of Clermont). GC: Blandinus, 1121.
Bernard	at least 1078–ca. 1090	858 (dated 1078); 802;[3] 545 and 662 (Abbot Hugh). GC: Bernard I, 1078.
Hugh	at least 1096	478 (Pope Urban II and Bishop William of Clermont); 697 (First Crusade). GC: Hugo III, 1100.
Odo	1096/1103	566 (King Philip, Abbot Hugh, and Bishop William of Clermont); 689 (Abbot Hugh); 802.[3] GC: Odo II, 1071.
Stephen *Candidus*	1096/1101	613 bis and 958 (Bishop William of Clermont); 681 (Abbot Hugh); 702 (King Philip, Abbot Hugh, and Bishop William of Clermont). GC: Stephanus I, 1096.
Eustace	at least in 1103/4	299–300 (Abbot Hugh); 473 (Legate Cardinal Richard of Albano);[4] 667 (King Philip); 794 (Abbot Hugh, after Bishop William of Clermont). GC: Eustace, 1095.
Stephen	at least 1111–1112	556 and 669 (dated 1111); 700 (dated 1112). GC: Stephanus II, 1111.
Airpinus	August 1112	685 (dated August 1112). GC: Airpinus, 1112.

[3] In *Sauxillanges*, no. 802, dated 1114, a cleric named Peter confirmed both (1) a grant to Sauxillanges of himself and his paternal possessions made by his mother and uncle in the presence of Prior Odo while he himself was still a little boy (i.e., no. 633, in which Peter is called *infantulus*), and (2) the grant to Sauxillanges of himself and his property made in the presence of Prior Bernard. Since Bernard is known to have been prior in 1078 and Odo was prior during the episcopate of Bishop William of Baffie of Clermont (1095–1102/3), and Prior Hugh came in between, this charter shows that Bernard must have had a long priorate (probably into the 1090's) and Hugh a short one, because the gift of Peter and his property made in the presence of Bernard was made again in the presence of Odo *while Peter was still a small boy*. The GC shows Bernard as the only prior between 1078 and 1095.

[4] Richard of Albano was legate in France in 1102–4: Bernard Monod, *Essai sur les rapports de Pascal II avec Philippe Ier (1099–1108)* (Bibliothèque de l'École des hautes études, 164; Paris, 1907) pp. 35–43.

L. THE PRIORS OF SAUXILLANGES, 1049–1156

Rotlannus	1114	483, 634, 687, and 802 (dated 1114: cf. p. 238, n. 26, above). *GC*: Rolannus, 1114.
Elias	1119	898 (dated 1119). *GC*: Helias I, 1129.
Bernard	1123	905 (dated 1123). *GC*: Bernardus II, 1122.
Humbert	1131	945 (dated 1131). *GC*: Humbertus, 1131.
Stephen of La Tour	after Humbert	918.[5] *GC*: Stephanus III, 1123.
Armannus (of Montboissier?)	1138/51	949 and 961 (see pp. 240–241, nn. 44 and 46, above). *GC*: Armannus, 1150.
Hugh	1151/2	961 (see p. 240, n. 44, above; 932 (see p. 241, n. 45, above). *GC*: Hugo IV, 1121.
Peter	1145/56	969 (Abbot Peter of Cluny); *Bibl. Clun.*, cols. 1411–1412 (1145/56; cf. Gomot, *Mozat*, pp. 248–249 [dated 1147]; Chaix de Lavarène, "Bullaire," p. 581–583 [dated 1147]; *Cluny*, V, 456, no. 4108 [dated 1145/58]). *GC*: Petrus I, 1156.

---

[5] This charter implies, but does not state directly, that Stephen came immediately after Humbert.

M. DR. BARTHOLOMEW

The identity of Peter the Venerable's medical consultant, Dr. Bartholomew, has been a subject of disagreement among scholars ever since the letters to and from him were first published by Quentin in 1924.[1] Quentin himself proposed that he was the famous Dr. Bartholomew of Salerno, one of the earliest known medical writers and teachers in the school of Salerno; and he further suggested that the assistant Bernard whom Bartholomew sent to Peter, and whom Peter described as "our Bernard, dear to us but a disciple to you," may have been the Bernard of Provence who is known to have written a commentary on the works of Bartholomew of Salerno.[2] This conclusion was challenged by both Karl Sudhoff and Ernest Wickersheimer, who pointed out that the period of only one month allowed by Bartholomew for his assistant to reach Cluny, treat Peter the Venerable, and return was too short if he came from Salerno.[3] A return journey from Salerno to Cluny in the twelfth century, especially in winter, required much longer than a month. Jean Leclercq, who recently edited part of a medical letter to King Louis of France from a Magister Bartholomeus, also decided against Bartholomew of Salerno. "It must be a question of some French, indeed Burgundian, doctor," he concluded, "about whom we otherwise know nothing."[4] The entire text of this same letter to King Louis, however, was published by C. H. Talbot, who definitely attributed it to Bartholomew of Salerno.[5] Most recently P. O. Kristeller, in a study on medicine at Salerno in the twelfth century, argued that both the letter to King Louis and those to and from Peter the Venerable concerned Bartholomew of Salerno.[6]

[1] Letters 158a and b, which were first published from the Le Puy MS. by Quentin, in *Misc. Ehrle*, I, 80–86.
[2] Quentin, in *Misc. Ehrle*, I, 82.
[3] Karl Sudhoff, in *Mitteilungen zur Geschichte der Medizin*, XXIV (1925) 83, and Wickersheimer, *Dictionnaire des médecins*, I, 57.
[4] Jean Leclercq, "Gratien, Pierre de Troyes et la Seconde Croisade," *Studia Gratiana*, II (1954) 587–588. The king in question was probably Louis VII.
[5] C. H. Talbot, "A Letter from Bartholomew of Salerno to King Louis of France," *Bulletin of the History of Medicine*, XXX (1956) 321–328.
[6] P. O. Kristeller, "Nuove fonti per la medicina salernitana del secolo XII," *Rassegna storica Salernitana*, XVIII (1957) 63–64.

Until further evidence comes to light, therefore, the question cannot be regarded as settled. Slight support is given to Bartholomew of Salerno by the *Liber graduum* cited in the letter to Peter the Venerable. The passages seem to be more closely related to the *De gradibus simplicium* of Constantine the African than to any other known work, and Constantine may have been one of the teachers of Bartholomew of Salerno.[7] The evidence is very inconclusive, however, both because the citation is uncertain and because the works of Constantine the African were widely used. Against the identification of Peter's Dr. Bartholomew with Bartholomew of Salerno there is still the strong argument of the time needed to travel from Salerno to Cluny and back. This can be overcome only if Bartholomew of Salerno can be shown to have lived or traveled in France, since Peter said that he had visited Cluny and addressed him as a personal friend. Peter's reference to France as *noster* hardly seems to indicate, as Quentin argued, that Bartholomew lived outside France, whereas his use of *alter*, meaning any other doctor in France, may suggest the reverse.[8] Vercauteren, in his work on doctors in Belgium and the north of France from the eighth to the thirteenth century, remarked that the influence of the great southern medical centers, both at Salerno and Montpellier, hardly reached the north before the thirteenth century, but he mentioned no northern Dr. Bartholomew in the twelfth century.[9] The Cistercian Everard of Ypres in the late twelfth century cited a medical work by a Magister Bar[tholomeus],[10] who may have been the same Bartholomew who wrote to King Louis and Peter the Venerable's Doctor Bartholomew, and all three may have been the same as Bartholomew of Salerno; but it appears more probable to me that there was another doctor named Bartholomew in the north at that time.

---

[7] The possible derivation of Bartholomew's citation from the *De gradibus simplicium* of Constantine the African, printed in his *Opera* (Basel, 1536) p. 359, was pointed out by Quentin, in *Misc. Ehrle*, I, 86, n. 1, and by Loren MacKinney and Thomas Herndon of the University of North Carolina, to whom I am indebted for their help. In his description of myrrh, for instance, Constantine used the phrases *humeres putridos desiccat, asperitatem pulmonis et canalium lenit*, and *asperitatem palpebrarum lenit*, which resemble those used by Bartholomew and occur in no other known medieval *Liber graduum*. They may derive, however, either from a medical vade mecum or from notes based on Constantine's lectures.

[8] Peter assured Bartholomew in Letter 158a that he was the highest court of medical appeal, "since I should in vain seek another [doctor] in this our France if I have not taken your advice in these and similar matters."

[9] F. Vercauteren, "Les médecins dans les principautés de la Belgique et du nord de la France, du VIIIᵉ au XIIIᵉ siècle," *Moyen Age*, LVII (1951) 91.

[10] N. M. Haring, "The Cistercian Everard of Ypres and His Appraisal of the Conflict between St. Bernard and Gilbert of Poitiers," *Mediaeval Studies*, XVII (1955) 146 (*ad* n. 26).

N. BISHOP ELIAS OF ORLÉANS (1137-1145/6)

Peter the Venerable discussed the case of Bishop Elias of Orléans in three letters. In the first, Letter 11, Peter asked Pope Innocent II to confirm the election "of the lord Elias, the venerable abbot of St. Sulpicius [at Bourges], a truly religious, prudent, and lettered man." He commented on the length of the election and on the disagreements between the clergy and the people, and he therefore urged the Pope to put a speedy end to the long drawn-out troubles of the church of Orléans.

Scholars are not agreed on the date of this election, which depends to some extent upon the date of the papal bull of confirmation. Most authorities have dated the election of Elias in 1136 or 1137 and his consecration and the papal bull of confirmation on 15 April 1137.[1] Löwenfeld pointed out, however, that the papal bull was in fact issued on 15 April 1138; and Ramackers further stressed that since it was simply a confirmation, it was presumably issued after the events it described.[2] Elias still appeared as abbot of St. Sulpicius on a charter dated 1137;[3] but he also appeared as bishop, although he may have been only bishop-elect, on a charter which can be dated 1/8 August 1137.[4] On later documents Elias also dated his pontificate from 1137, although it is not known whether it was reckoned from the election or from the consecration.[5] It is therefore probable that he was elected bishop some time in 1137 before 1/8 August and that he was conse-

[1] Mabillon, *Annales*, VI, 249, and note to Bernard, ep. 245 (Gaume ed., I.1, 913); Bréquigny, *Chartes*, II, 636; *RHGF*, XV, 632–633; *GC*, VIII, 1448–1450; Pignot, *Cluny*, III, 227; Gams, *Series*, p. 593; Luchaire, *Louis VII*, p. 101, no. 11; Imbart de la Tour, *Élections*, p. 495; Bernard de Clairvaux, p. 640; Pacaut, *Élections*, pp. 84, n. 6, and 151. Severt, *Chronologia*, III, 170, dated his consecration "forte anno 1135."

[2] JL 7889; *Cartulaire de Sainte-Croix d'Orléans*, ed. Joseph Thillier and Eugène Jarry (Mémoires de la Société archéologique et historique de l'Orléanais, 30; Paris, 1906) pp. 52–53, no. 24; *PU in Frankreich*, n.f. VI, 105–106, no. 49.

[3] Louis de Kersers, "Essai de reconstitution du cartulaire A de Saint-Sulpice de Bourges," *Mémoires de la Société des antiquaires du Centre*, XXXV (1912) 144–146, no. 68. Elias is also listed as abbot of St. Sulpicius in 1137 in *GC*, II, 128.

[4] Charles de La Saussaye, *Annales ecclesiae Aurelianensis* (Paris, 1615) pp. 434–435; *GC*, VIII, *instr.*, 504; Luchaire, *Louis VII*, p. 97, no. 1.

[5] *PU in Frankreich*, n.f. VI, 105–106; cf. Constable, "Langres," pp. 145–146, on the use of pontifical years in dating documents.

crated before 15 April of the following year, when Innocent II confirmed the entire proceeding.

The opposition to Elias, however, to which Peter referred in his Letter 11, evidently continued even after the election and consecration. A few canons, seven or eight out of the total number, according to Peter the Venerable in Letter 116 to Pope Lucius II (1144-5), "pretending to seek what is God's but under this pretext, as is clear to everyone, seeking their own, just as they have mortally wounded their mother church by their revenge, so have they lifted up their heel against their father and bishop." Peter called on the Pope to support Elias, saying that he was inspired to write by "the testimony of many great and religious men, of whom some are ours [that is, Cluniacs], but many more are outsiders." Also in Elias's favor, according to Peter, was "the presence near him, for some time now, of a good, religious, and upstanding man whom we gave him as a companion at the order of Pope Celestine, not designated by name but chosen by us for his religious sense of duty." This letter shows that Innocent II's successor Celestine II (1143-4), presumably owing to criticism of Elias, had asked Peter the Venerable to give him a reliable mentor.

At about the same time Prior Peter of the Augustinian house of St. John at Sens wrote a long letter to Elias, citing several examples of bishops who had been falsely accused, in order, he said, to encourage Elias and to deter his enemies.[6] Prior Peter was a close friend of Bishop Hato of Troyes, and probably also of Peter the Venerable,[7] and he may well have been one of "the great and religious men," mentioned in Letter 116, who spoke to Peter in support of Elias.

The opposition was stronger than the defense, however, and Lucius II sent a strongly worded letter to the archbishop of Rheims and to the bishops of Beauvais and Arras, in which he criticized Elias both for his extravagance and loose-living and for breaking his oath to mend his ways. This oath had perhaps been given at the time Celestine II asked Peter the Venerable to appoint a mentor for Elias. Lucius therefore instructed the three bishops to investigate the charges and, if they were true, to depose Elias "without the obstacle of any appeal" and to arrange for a suitable successor.[8] This letter is undated, but Lucius was pope only from 12 March 1144 until 15 February 1145, and it arrived in France presumably after Peter the Venerable wrote Letter 116, which made no reference to the papal decision. The specific

---

[6] De La Saussaye, *Annales*, pp. 437-441.
[7] Cf. Constable, in *Petrus Ven.*, pp. 42-43.
[8] Wilhelm Wattenbach, "Eine Hildesheimer Briefsammlung," *Neues Archiv*, VI (1881) 171-173; JL 8696. The authenticity of this bull is not absolutely certain, but it corresponds closely to the known situation.

results of this letter are not known, but the bishops apparently found against Elias and deposed him. The death of Pope Lucius, however, and the election of the Cistercian Pope Eugene III on 15 February 1145, opened the way for a new appeal to the papacy.

Peter the Venerable again pleaded for Elias in Letter 122, which was probably his first letter to the new Pope. "The lord bishop of Orléans, a venerable man and priest of God, a son devoted to Your Paternity ... both recently took refuge and again returned to you as a peaceful port and to the safe refuge of piety, in order that the apostolic strength and mercy might be a tower of strength for him against the face of the enemy. Almost the whole Gallican church has written and entreated for him and implored as a supplicant that the pontifical dignity should not be allowed to be dishonored by infamous and most vile people and attacked by false contumelies." Peter then praised Elias both as a bishop and as a monk and asked the Pope to hear his plea and restore him to his property and men. King Louis VII also petitioned the Pope on behalf of Elias, since Bernard of Clairvaux in his letter 245 praised Eugene for considering the subject rather than the presenter of a petition: "The king was not heard on behalf of the bishop of Orléans, but he was not at all offended, since his heart is in the hand of God."[9]

This letter of Bernard shows that Eugene rejected the appeals in support of Elias. Bernard gave further details of the case in his letter 246, also addressed to the Pope:

It is time for me to write on behalf not now of a bishop, but of a poor and humble monk, and one who is the more miserable because he was reduced from wealth and dignity. This is not the place for praise but for pity. Many people wrote on his behalf, that he might remain a bishop; but this was [asking] a great deal, and I could not be brought to risk doing it. But now, if the matter be considered with greater humanity, it demands what I previously avoided. The man had hope up until now, since there was some cause for hope. He said: The state of affairs has greatly changed since the sentence of purgation was imposed upon me. And I fully accepted that grave [sentence], and what a most innocent person could fulfill with difficulty. What now, when everything has become almost impossible? There is no bishop of Nevers, nor at Troyes; the bishop of Auxerre has crossed the Alps. This is a large part of my conprovincial bishops, through whom I was to be purged. I am not lacking purgators [to clear me of the charge], but the bishops are either lacking or absent.

Bernard went on to explain that Elias had therefore approached him and "on my advice, forseeing the end and the certain blow, he put aside the bishop," that is, he resigned his see. Bernard asked the Pope to take pity on the man who remained. "He is young, he is noble by

---

[9] Bernard, ep. 245 (Gaume ed., I.1, 516); cf. Vacandard, *St. Bernard*, II, 268, n. 3, who dated this letter at the end of 1145 or the beginning of 1146.

birth, he was placed in a lofty position; and he avoids not a humble but a disgraceful one." Specifically, Bernard asked that Elias be allowed to remain a priest and to have his debts paid out of the episcopal revenues, since he was now a poor man. "It is hard to be at the same time deprived of honor and oppressed by the burden of debts."[10]

After the judgment of the three bishops, therefore, according to these letters, Elias appealed to Eugene III, with the support of Louis VII, Peter the Venerable, and other influential figures. At about the same time, however, or somewhat later, Eugene also received a letter from Archdeacon Ralph of Orléans, dated 18 November 1145, charging Elias with simony because he accepted forty shillings for the consecration of the church of St. Laurence at Orléans in March 1139 (the tenth year of the pontificate of Innocent II).[11] This serious charge, which had been carefully stored up for over six years, was presumably the trump card of the opposition. Eugene apparently refused to set aside the sentence against Elias and decreed that he must clear himself of the charges brought against him before the other bishops of his province, that is, the archbishop of Sens and the bishops of Auxerre, Chartres, Meaux, Nevers, Paris, and Troyes. Since at least two of these bishops (Paris and Troyes) were close friends of Peter the Venerable, one of Elias's most active supporters, they may as a group have been favorable to Elias; but the death of Fromond of Nevers, the resignation of Hato of Troyes, and the departure for Italy of Hugh of Auxerre made the proposed trial impossible. Fromond died on 29 November, according to the necrologies of the cathedral of Nevers and of St. Martin at Nevers.[12] The year is uncertain, and there is no charter reference after 1143 in the *Gallia christiana*,[13] but on the basis of Bernard's letter it can be dated in 1145. Hato of Troyes resigned either late in 1145 or early in 1146.[14] The date of Hugh of Auxerre's visit to Italy is uncertain, but he received two bulls from Eugene III in favor of monasteries in his diocese on 19 January 1146, and it may therefore be safely assumed that he crossed the Alps late in 1145.[15] These

---

[10] Bernard, ep. 246 (Gaume ed., I.1, 517–518), dated 1146 by Mabillon.
[11] Étienne Baluze, *Miscellanea*, ed. J. D. Mansi (Lucca, 1761–1764) IV, 18; cited in GC, VIII, 1450, and Bréquigny, *Chartes*, III, 93.
[12] *Obituaires*, III, 466–467 and 477. In the necrology of St.-Martin-des-Champs, Fromond's death was dated 30 November (ibid., I, 471).
[13] GC, XII, 638.
[14] Constable, in *Petrus Ven.*, p. 44, and Ep. 2, n. to p. 6, l. 12.
[15] GC, XII, instr., 117–118 and 118–119; JL 8846–8847. The authors of the *Gallia christiana*, XII, 292, dated this visit, for which Bernard's letter is the sole evidence, in 1146–7; but this was questioned by Lebeuf, *Mémoires* (cited Ep. 179, n. to p. 421, l. 24), I, 308, n. 2, on the basis of the number of charters witnessed in France by Hugh in 1146. This problem is solved by dating the visit in 1145–6, presuming that the bulls were issued shortly before his return. On Hugh, see the dating note to Ep. 69.

elements all fit together to date the final resignation of Elias either very late in 1145 or, more probably, early in 1146.

Nothing specific is known about Elias after his deposition and resignation. His successor Manasses of Garlande appears on a document of 20 October 1146,[16] and Elias presumably left his former episcopal city. Alberic of Trois-Fontaines recorded in his chronicle that the bishop of Orléans, presumably meaning Elias, was deposed at the Council of Rheims in 1148, and it is possible that a formal declaration of his deposition was made at the council, although Alberic may also simply have mistaken the date.[17] According to the authors of the *Gallia christiana*, Elias subscribed as former bishop of Orléans to a charter of Peter the Venerable for the monks of Balerne.[18] He may therefore have taken refuge with his old supporter and spent the remainder of his days at Cluny.

The entire case is of interest to historians not only as a minor *cause célèbre*, involving some of the most important figures of the period, but also as evidence of a serious split among the clergy of Orléans, which probably went back at least to the notorious murder of the subdean Archibald of Orléans in 1133,[19] and which may have had broader implications in both ecclesiastical and secular politics. With regard to Elias himself, there can be little doubt that he was technically in the wrong. He was evidently young and imprudent, probably extravagant, and had laid himself open to a serious charge of simony. Even his supporter Peter the Venerable realized that he needed a mentor; and Bernard of Clairvaux, while sympathizing with his youth and misfortune, clearly considered him an unsuitable bishop. Above all, he and his supporters were unable to convince three successive popes, whose impartiality in the matter can hardly be questioned, of his innocence; and he was apparently first deposed by a committee of bishops, acting on the Pope's orders, and finally acquiesced in this decision by resigning his see.

Although it thus seems certain that Elias was not above reproach, he appears at the same time to have been caught in a situation beyond his control and to have been opposed from the beginning of his pontificate by an influential group of the clergy at Orléans. The leader of this opposition was probably the archdeacon Ralph, who wrote to Eugene III against Elias in 1145. He appeared on a charter in 1136 and was a supporter of the archdeacon John, the foe of the murdered

---

[16] *GC*, VIII, *instr.*, 506–507.

[17] *MGH, Scriptores* in fol., XXIII, 840. Alberic said in the same sentence that Hato of Troyes was deposed at the same time, which is certainly wrong.

[18] *GC*, VIII, 1450. I have been unable to locate this charter.

[19] See Ep. 17, n. to p. 25, l. 7.

subdean Archibald.[20] Ralph thus belonged to the party of the powerful royal chancellor and seneschal Stephen of Garlande;[21] and it was probably no accident that Manasses, who succeeded Elias as bishop of Orléans, belonged to the family of Garlande and that Ralph was apparently at once promoted to the position of *capicerius* of the chapter at Orléans.[22] Peter the Venerable described the enemies of Elias as factional self-seekers; and it may well have been only the rash behavior of the young Bishop that lost him the support of Bernard of Clairvaux, who could hardly be described as an ally of the family of Garlande or of the opponents of the murdered subdean.

In this connection it would be interesting to know the attitude in this case of the former royal chancellor Algrin of Étampes, who was also an archdeacon of Orléans. He was an old associate of Stephen of Garlande,[23] under whom he served as vice-chancellor during the reign of Louis VI,[24] and was described by the chronicler of Morigny as "the sworn and public enemy of monks."[25] In 1132 he was among the principal supporters of the archdeacon John against the subdean Archibald.[26] He served as chancellor for Louis VII from the beginning of his reign apparently until 1140, when he fell out with the King.[27] The precise reason for their quarrel is unknown—conceivably it had something to do with Bishop Elias—but he soon after made peace with Louis through the mediation of Bernard of Clairvaux, Bishop Hugh of Auxerre, Suger of St. Denis, Imar of Montierneuf, Hugh of Crécy, Odo of St.-Martin-des-Champs, "and other religious men."[28] It

---

[20] *Cartulaire de Sainte-Croix*, p. 20, no. 9; cf. Foulques de Villaret, *Recherches* (cited Ep. 145, n. to p. 360, l. 2.), pp. 111 and 163, n. 2, who said that Ralph's archdeaconry was unknown.

[21] On Stephen and his family, see Luchaire, *Louis VI*, esp. introd., pp. xliii–liii.

[22] Ralph subscribed as *capicerius* on Manasses's first known charter (cited n. 16 above) and on several charters in *Cartulaire de Sainte-Croix*, pp. 18, 24, 142, 144, 145, and 147, nos. 8 (1155/9), 11 (1153), 72 (1153), 73 (1153), 74 (1153), and 75 (1155). There is no absolute proof of the identity of this Ralph with the archdeacon, but there was no other known member of the chapter called Ralph at that time. On the position of *capicerius* at Orléans, which corresponded to treasurer and ranked fourth among the dignities of the chapter, see Foulques de Villaret, *Recherches*, pp. 30–31 and 162, where Ralph is listed under 1146.

[23] *Morigny*, pp. 27–28; Luchaire, *Louis VI*, pp. 122 and 127, nos. 254 and 268. Algrin was associated with Henry of France and Stephen of Garlande on a document dated 1140/6 in Luchaire, *Louis VII*, p. 162, no. 197, but which may be earlier.

[24] Luchaire, *Louis VI*, pp. 305–306.

[25] *Morigny*, p. 35.

[26] Luchaire, *Louis VI*, p. 233, no. 505.

[27] Luchaire, *Louis VII*, p. 52.

[28] Duchesne, *Scriptores*, IV, 764 (also in RHGF, XVI, 6–7, and *St. Martin des Champs*, II, 116–117, no. 256); cf. Luchaire, *Louis VII*, pp. 120–121, no. 67, and Cartellieri, *Suger*, pp. 38 and 140, no. 107. Algrin was described in this document simply as archdeacon of Orléans. On Imar of Montierneuf, the future cardinal-bishop of Tusculum, see Appendix J; on Hugh of Crécy, see Appendix O; and on Odo of St.-Martin-des-Champs, see the biographical note to Ep. 135. This charter was dated *ca.* 1140 by Brial, Luchaire, and Cartellieri and 1142 by Depoin, but the appearance of Odo as subprior gives a *terminus ante quem* of 1141.

is surprising, to say the least, to find the onetime enemy of monks and accomplice of Stephen of Garlande here reconciled with the King by six of the leading monks in France, including the principal opponents of the family of Garlande, and the arrangement strongly suggests a change of heart in Algrin. It is not known, however, whether or not Algrin took part in the election of Elias, nor whether the price of his reconciliation with the King included supporting the royal and monastic candidate, but such questions again suggest that major issues may have been involved in the case of Elias of Orléans and that his deposition may have been a defeat for the monastic party and the supporters of ecclesiastical reform in France.

O. HUGH OF CRÉCY

The name Hugh of Crécy (Crécey, Cressy) is found in three groups of sources related to the history of Cluny in the first half of the twelfth century. The first was the chamberlain Hugh of Crécy of Cluny, who appeared on a charter in 1128 as "Hugh of Crécy," following the chamberlain Peter and the cellarer Bernard, in 1132 as "Hugh the chamberlain of Cluny," on a mission to the king of Spain, and on two charters in 1136 as "Hugh of Crécy, the chamberlain" and as "lord Hugh, the chamberlain of the lord abbot."[1] He also appeared in 1136 simply as "lord Hugh of Crécy," following the chamberlain Boso, on a grant by Peter the Venerable to the Carthusian house of Meyriat.[2] This shows that, unless he lost his job as chamberlain in 1136, he was only one of several chamberlains at Cluny; and he was in fact probably the chamberlain specially attached to the service and *familia* of the abbot. His last known appearance was simply as Hugh of Crécy at Souvigny in 1147, together with Peter the Venerable, his notary Thomas, and the sacristan Aimarus of Cluny.[3] Peter the Venerable used Hugh as a confidential messenger, and he became friendly with several prominent ecclesiastics. Cardinal-Bishop Matthew of Albano, on his deathbed at Pisa in 1135, sent remembrances to "the chamberlain Hugh."[4] Guigo of La Chartreuse, in a letter written in 1136/7, thanked Peter the Venerable for a visit from "lord Hugh of Crécy."[5] Bernard of Clairvaux himself sent greetings to "brother Hugh the chamberlain" in a letter to Peter the Venerable early in 1138.[6] Peter sent Hugh as a messenger to Bishop Hato of Troyes on at least two occasions: once, with some special messages to be told to Hato only by word of mouth, and again in September 1141, with instructions to meet Hato wherever he wished and to bring him back to Cluny.[7] Hugh was

---

[1] *Cluny*, V, 355, 391, and 408, nos. 4001, 4038, and 4053–4054.
[2] *Cart. lyonnais*, I, 32–33, no. 22.
[3] Chazaud, *Étude*, p. 254; on this charter, which is of dubious authenticity, see Appendix D, s.a. "1147 before June."
[4] Peter the Venerable, *De miraculis*, II, 17, in *Bibl. Clun.*, col. 1316 C.
[5] Letter 25.
[6] Letter 74; Bernard, ep. 147 (Gaume ed., I.1, 360).
[7] Letters 22 and 95. Hato replied in Letter 96 that he would expect Hugh at Troyes on 25 or 26 September.

also sent to Spain in 1132, as seen above, and on one occasion to Abbot Suger of St. Denis, with a letter from Peter the Venerable calling him "my most beloved brother and intimate friend lord Hugh of Crécy."[8]

Hugh of Crécy also occurs in a group of sources coming from St.-Martin-des-Champs, the principal Cluniac house in Paris, and from the Cluniac house of Longpont, near Paris, between about 1140 and 1147. Some time in 1140 or 1141, Luciana, "the sister of Hugh of Crécy," gave some property to Longpont with the approval of her sister and brother-in-law, Beatrice and Manasses of Tournon, and of King Louis, whose consent was witnessed by Bishop Stephen of Paris, Subprior Odo of St.-Martin-des-Champs, Hugh of Crécy, the monk Arnulf, Count Ralph (probably of Vermandois), and Manasses of Tournon.[9] "Lord Hugh of Crécy" also appeared on another charter in the chartulary of Longpont, in association with Bishop Stephen of Paris, Prior John of Longpont, and Subprior Odo of St.-Martin-des-Champs.[10] The agreement between Louis VII and the archdeacon Algrin of Orléans in 1140/1 was witnessed by Bernard of Clairvaux, Bishop Hugh of Auxerre, Suger, Imar of Montierneuf, Hugh of Crécy, Subprior Odo of St.-Martin-des-Champs, and other notables; the name of Hugh of Crécy was closely associated with that of Suger on documents of Louis VII in 1142/3 and 1147; and in 1144/5 the King granted a charter specifically "at the request of our confidant (*familiaris*) the venerable monk Hugh of Crécy."[11] He died on 31 July, according to the necrologies of St.-Martin-des-Champs, Longpont, and St. Denis.[12]

---

[8] *Bibl Clun.*, col. 959; Suger, *Oeuvres*, p. 293 (dated 1147/8, which is probably too late); Cartellieri, *Suger*, p. 146, no. 160 (1147/9).

[9] *Le cartulaire du prieuré de Notre-Dame de Longpont* (Lyons, 1879) pp. 235–236, no. 292, and (abbreviated) *St. Martin des Champs*, II, 45–46, no. 216. The charter is undated and is not listed, in spite of the confirmation by King Louis, in Luchaire, *Louis VI* or *Louis VII*. The date is given as *ca.* 1140 in the chartulary of Longpont and as 1137 by Depoin, who pointed out that Luciana's first husband, Guichard III of Beaujeu, died in 1137 and that she acted here as a single woman. This fact only establishes a *terminus a quo*. Stephen of Senlis was bishop of Paris from 1124 until 1142; Odo was subprior of St.-Martin-des-Champs from at least 1133 until 1141, when he became abbot of Marchiennes (see biographical note to Ep. 135); and Ralph of Vermandois was seneschal for both Louis VI and Louis VII, except for the years 1138 and 1139, until his death in 1152: Luchaire, *Louis VI*, p. 304, and *Louis VII*, pp. 42–46. The outside dates for this charter are therefore 1137/41 and more probably, in view of the appearance of Count Ralph, 1140/41.

[10] *Cart. de Longpont*, pp. 167–168, no. 177, also dated *ca.* 1140. The dating of Prior John depends upon this charter alone, which was probably issued about the same time as no. 292, although it cannot be dated as closely.

[11] *St. Martin des Champs*, II, 116–117 (better in Duchesne, *Scriptores*, IV, 764, and *RHGF*, XVI, 6–7: see p. 309, n. 28, above), 131–132, and 152–153, nos. 256, 266, and 284; and *Paris*, pp. 305–306, no. 331; cf. Luchaire, *Louis VII*, pp. 120–121, 130–131, 145, and 163, nos. 67, 95(1), 144, and 200; Cartellieri, *Suger*, pp. 141 and 144, nos. 109 and 136.

[12] *Obituaires*, I, 322, 449, and 525. Abbot Hugh of St.-Germain-des-Prés granted "societatem et beneficium hujus loci et ... tricesimale suum post obitum" to Hugh of Crécy and two other monks of St.-Martin-des-Champs: *ibid.*, p. 258.

Peter the Venerable's Letter 135, addressed "to the lord prior Odo and other servants of Almighty God at St.-Martin-des-Champs," probably referred to this event, since he expressed his grief "at the death of my most beloved brother and son Hugh," referred to him as "our prior," and praised his devotion to God and to Cluny "now already for twenty years." This would date Hugh's death between his last appearance in April/June 1147 and the deposition of Prior Odo in 1150.[13]

The third Hugh of Crécy was the notorious Lord Hugh of Crécy-en-Brie, who belonged to the family of the counts of Rochefort-en-Iveline and was seneschal to King Philip I in 1106 and 1107.[14] He later fell out with Philip's successor Louis VI, and after he had captured and murdered the viscount of Troyes, Milo of Bray, his own cousin and a supporter of Louis, he was defeated by the King, stripped of his lands, and entered a monastery.[15] His known connections with Cluny are not very substantial, beyond the facts that members of his family founded and patronized the Cluniac priory of Longpont, where his victim Milo of Bray was buried, and that his sister Luciana, after her betrothal to Louis VI was annulled on the grounds of consanguinity, married Guichard III of Beaujeu, who retired to Cluny in 1137.[16] It is not known which monastery Hugh entered after his disgrace. According to the chronicle of Morigny, which is the only source on this episode, he surrendered to the King at Gometz-le-Châtel, near Rambouillet, and took the monastic habit "in that place" (*illico*), which suggests either the Benedictine priory at Gometz-le-Châtel, which was a dependency of St. Florence at Saumur, or possibly Longpont itself, which was only a few miles away. The suggestions by historians that

---

[13] Ep. 135 and *St. Martin des Champs*, II, 180–182 and 211–212, nos. 299 and 320; cf. biographical note to Ep. 135. Depoin gave the date of Hugh's death definitely as 1147 (*St. Martin des Champs*, II, 45, n. 85, and 180, n. 284). He also said in his note to Peter's Letter 135 that Hugh served as prior of St.-Denis-de-la-Châtre and as sacristan of St.-Martin-des-Champs, but he gave no sources for these statements.

[14] There is considerable literature on Hugh of Crécy-en-Brie. Among the original sources, see Ordericis Vitalis, *Hist. ecc.*, XI, 36 (ed. cit., IV, 289), and Suger, *Louis le Gros*, pp. 89–97, 125–129, 149, and 163; and, among secondary works, D'Arbois de Jubainville, *Comtes de Champagne*, II, 178 ff., 239, and 272; *Cart. de Longpont*, introd., pp. 14–18; Luchaire, *Louis VI*, pp. 27, 33–34, 47, 57–58, 70–72, and 119, nos. 51, 61, 87, 107, 134, and 246, and *idem*, *Histoire des institutions monarchiques de la France sous les premiers Capétiens*, 2nd ed. (Paris, 1891) I, 182, and II, 123; *Recueil des actes de Philippe Ier, roi de France (1059–1108)*, ed. M. Prou (Chartes et diplômes relatifs à l'histoire de France; Paris, 1908) introd., p. cli; and Augustin Fliche, *Le règne de Philippe Ier, roi de France (1060–1108)* (Paris, 1912) pp. 321 (with genealogical table) and 323–325.

[15] On these events, see *Cart. de Longpont*, pp. 118–119, no. 84, and *Morigny*, pp. 22–24; cf. Luchaire, *Louis VI*, p. 119, no. 246.

[16] See Ep. 172, n. to p. 408, l. 23.

he entered either a Cluniac house,[17] or a Cistercian abbey,[18] or St. Denis[19] are all pure conjectures.

A serious problem is posed by the identities of these three Hugh's, and above all by the possibility that they were all the same man. "Identification is the crux on which a whole pedigree may turn," according to Round, "and in the case of such a name as Smith, proof of identity is vital."[20] Hugh was a very common name in the twelfth century, and there were many places named Crécy;[21] and it is therefore possible that these three were all different men named Hugh of Crécy. There are several clear indications, however, that the chamberlain Hugh and the monk Hugh of St.-Martin-des-Champs were the same man: the letter of Peter the Venerable recommending the chamberlain Hugh to Suger, with whom the monk was later closely associated, and above all Peter the Venerable's Letter 135, in which the reference to twenty years of service to God and to Cluny, in 1147/50, corresponds exactly to the first appearance of Hugh of Crécy on a Cluniac charter in 1128. The appearance of "Hugo (camer[arius])" in the necrology of Marcigny under the date 31 July, when Hugh the monk of St.-Martin-des-Champs is known to have died, strongly supports the identity of the two men.[22] An isolated reference in 1145, when a Hugh of Crécy witnessed a charter of Bishop Hato of Troyes,[23] also seems to tie the monk Hugh of St.-Martin-des-Champs to the chamberlain Hugh, who had more than once served as a messenger to Hato.

Several historians have gone further and identified this Hugh of

---

[17] *Art de vérifier les dates*, II, 660; Alexandre Huguenin, *Suger et la monarchie française au XIIe siècle* (Paris, 1857) p. 143, who said that he entered Cluny; Pignot, *Cluny*, III, 450; and D'Arbois de Jubainville, *Comtes de Champagne*, II, 239.

[18] A. Le Prévost, in Ordericus Vitalis, *Hist. ecc. (ed. cit.*, IV, 289, n. 1); cf. D'Arbois de Jubainville, *Comtes de Champagne*, II, 239, n. 1.

[19] *St. Martin des Champs*, II, 45, n. 85 (citing Luchaire, *Louis VI*, p. 119, no. 246, who did not say that Hugh entered St. Denis), and 180, n. 284.

[20] J. H. Round, *Peerage and Pedigree* (London, 1910) II, 201–202.

[21] Auguste Longnon, *Les noms de lieu de la France* (Paris, 1920–1929) p. 84; cf. André Déléage, *La vie rurale en Bourgogne* (Mâcon 1941,) p. 1403, who listed one Crécy, two Crécey, and three Cressy—six in all—in Burgundy alone. The name is spelled in various ways in the sources. The chamberlain Hugh of Cluny thus came from *Crecei, Cresciaco, Crecyaco, Creceio, Cresceio,* and *Cresseio.* There was also a Crécy in Ponthieu, and two men named Hugh of Crécy appear on charters of 1103/29 and 1158 in *Actes des comtes de Pontieu* (cited p. 289 n. 1. above), pp. 36 and 89. In the second half of the twelfth century a Hugh of Crécy was constable of Rouen and subscribed to many charters: *Recueil des actes de Henri II ... concernant les provinces françaises et les affaires de France*, ed. Léopold Delisle and Elie Berger (Chartes et diplômes relatifs à l'histoire de France; Paris, 1909–1927) III, 142 (s.n. in index), and Haskins, *Norman Institutions* (cited Ep. 15, n. 10 to p. 22, l.7), pp. 327 and 334.

[22] *Necrologium*, p. 58.

[23] *Bibl. Clun.*, notae, cols. 104–105, and (better) *Cartulaires de Troyes*, V, 15; cf. *Cluny*, V, 455, no. 4105. This could be yet another Hugh of Crécy, but it seems unlikely in view of the known association of the chamberlain Hugh with Hato of Troyes.

O. HUGH OF CRÉCY

Crécy with the former seneschal Hugh of Crécy-en-Brie.[24] It is an attractive theory that Hugh of Crécy-en-Brie spent a decade of repentance and reformation and then reappeared first as the chamberlain of Cluny, of whose antecedents nothing is otherwise known, and later as a monk at St.-Martin-des-Champs and a friend and adviser of Suger and King Louis VII. The strongest evidence in favor of this identification is the charter of Luciana, "the sister of Hugh of Crécy" (definitely Hugh of Crécy-en-Brie, who is known from other sources to have had a sister named Luciana), which was witnessed by Hugh of Crécy, the monk of St.-Martin-des-Champs and in all probability the former chamberlain of Cluny. This charter is known only from a copy, and it is curious that Luciana, who was the sister of Count Guy II of Rochefort and the widow of Guichard III of Beaujeu, was described only as the sister of a disgraced and dispossessed rebel.[25] It is also possible that two men both named Hugh of Crécy may have appeared on the same charter. Be this as it may, it seems inconceivable that Peter the Venerable could have introduced to Suger as a "beloved brother and intimate friend" a man whom Suger knew all too well and himself described in his life of Louis VI, written about 1144, as "fit for both rapine and arson and the greatest trouble-maker in the entire realm."[26] It is even harder to believe that such a man, whatever his reform, then became an associate of Suger and a *familiaris* of Louis VII. Unless further evidence comes to light, therefore, the "vital proof of identity" appears to be lacking. So far as is known, Hugh of Crécy-en-Brie disappeared permanently into a monastery after his defeat and disgrace about 1118. The career of the chamberlain Hugh of Crécy, on the other hand, can be followed at Cluny with some accuracy from 1128 until 1141, when he went to Paris and ended his life as an influential and respected monk of St.-Martin-des-Champs.

---

[24] Huguenin, *Suger*, p. 143; Pignot, *Cluny*, III, 445-454; and several of the historians cited in n. 14 above.

[25] A later scribe, believing that she was the sister of the Hugh of Crécy who appeared among the witnesses, may have interpolated the "soror Hugonis de Creciaco." The evidence of this charter cannot be altogether explained away, however. The fact that Hugh of Crécy, the monk of St.-Martin-des-Champs, appeared on the obituary of Longpont, a house patronized by the family of Hugh of Crécy-en-Brie, suggests an association between the two, although the appearance of a prominent Cluniac on the obituary roll of a nearby Cluniac house is not in itself surprising.

[26] Suger, *Louis le Gros*, XV (*ed. cit.*, p. 88); cf. introd., pp. x-xi, on the date of composition. See also the characterization of Hugh in *Morigny*, p. 22.

P. NICHOLAS OF MONTIÉRAMEY AND PETER THE VENERABLE

Several letters in the collection of Peter the Venerable help to throw light on the enigmatic character and career of Nicholas of Montiéramey while he was chaplain to Bishop Hato of Troyes and secretary to Bernard of Clairvaux, before his disgrace and expulsion from Clairvaux.[1] The earliest reference, which is also the earliest dated reference to Nicholas in any source, is in a letter written to Peter by his friend Hato in March/April 1138: "Your servant Nicholas salutes you; he places no measure on his love for you but more specially displays your memory to all men."[2] Here at the very beginning of his career, therefore, may be seen two of Nicholas's most marked characteristics: his "talent for ingratiating himself with influential patrons"[3] and his pleasure in displaying and cultivating these friendships. "From my earliest youth," he wrote many years later to Count Henry of Champagne, "I have pleased the mighty and greatest princes of this world."[4] One of the most prominent among these was Peter the Venerable, and a close, and at times emotional, friendship existed between Peter and

---

[1] This appendix makes no attempt to present a full account of Nicholas and his works: see in particular Mabillon's excellent account in his edition of the works of St. Bernard (Gaume ed., I.2, 1617–1630); M.-J.-J. Brial, in *Hist. litt.*, XIII, 553–568; D'Arbois de Jubainville, *Comtes de Champagne*, III, 124–125 and 192–199; Vacandard, *St. Bernard*, II, 384–386 and 495–498; Rassow, "Kanzlei," esp. pp. 279–289; Augustin Steiger, "Nikolaus, Mönch in Clairvaux, Sekretär des hl. Bernhard," *SMGBOZ*, XXXVIII (n.f. 7, 1917) 41–50; J. J. Ryan, "Saint Peter Damiani and the Sermons of Nicholas of Clairvaux: a Clarification," *Mediaeval Studies*, IX (1947) 151–161; Leclercq, *Études*, pp. 62–67; C. H. Talbot, "Nicholas of St. Albans and Saint Bernard," *Rev. Bén.*, LXIV (1954) 83–87; Jean Leclercq, "Les collections de sermons de Nicolas de Clairvaux," *Rev. Bén.*, LXVI (1956) 269–302; John F. Benton, "The Court of Champagne as a Literary Center," *Speculum*, XXXVI (1961) 555–557; idem, "Nicholas of Clairvaux and the Twelfth-Century Sequence," *Traditio*, XVIII (1962) 149–179; and idem, "Nicolas de Clairvaux à la recherche du vin d'Auxerre, d'après une lettre inédite du XIIe siècle," *Annales de Bourgogne*, XXXIV (1962) 252–255. Reference to earlier literature on Nicholas is given in Chevalier, *Bio-bib.*, II, 3327. In spite of this research, Nicholas remains a somewhat obscure figure. As Maitland, *Dark Ages*, p. 416, remarked: "Considering that he appears to have felt no reluctance to speak on the subject, I wish that the Secretary Nicholas had given us a fuller account of himself."

[2] Letter 71.

[3] The words are those of Benton, in *Speculum*, XXXVI, 555.

[4] Nicholas, ep. 56 (*PL*, CXCVI, 1652 A), cited by Mabillon in the works of Bernard (Gaume ed., I.2, 1629–1630).

Nicholas from at least 1138 until 1152. Their surviving correspondence is concerned principally with three episodes: Nicholas's visit to Rome in 1140–1, his visit to Cluny in 1149, and his projected visit to Cluny in 1150–1; but there is no reason to believe that all their letters to each other have been preserved.

In a letter written in February/March 1141 Hato of Troyes informed Peter the Venerable that "the affairs which your friend master Nicholas took to Rome have been handled better than we hoped."[5] Peter replied with a letter urging Hato, among other things, to visit Cluny during Holy Week, which fell on 23–29 March in 1141.[6] At the same time he wrote to Nicholas, who is referred to in the heading as "the chaplain of Bishop Hato of Troyes" and whom Peter addressed as "his most dear son," asking him to encourage Hato to visit Cluny.[7] Hato was apparently unable to come, however. He may have been occupied with the preparations for the expedition of King Louis VII to Languedoc and Aquitaine in the summer of 1141, because Peter in his next known letter to Hato said that the King had now returned from war (in August 1141) and that the lord Hugh (that is, probably, Hugh of Crécy, the chamberlain of Cluny) would meet Hato wherever he wished and bring him back to Cluny. "And since my other letter adequately expressed, I think, my desire, indeed, my hunger to see you," he concluded, doubtless referring to Letter 86, "this one will be silent, lest a mission repeated so many times without effect might seem superfluous or impertinent to someone who considered the matter carefully."[8] To this Hato replied that he would expect Hugh at Troyes on 25 or 26 September ("the fifth day before the feast of St. Remy"). At the time Peter's letter arrived, he said, he had been very busy: "The abbot of Clairvaux was here; the bishop of Chartres besieged my house. My Nicholas, who is also yours, returned from Rome; Count Theobald urgently and continually pestered me with his affairs; and behold, a friend's letter came into a friend's hand."[9]

These letters show that Nicholas was away on a visit to Rome from some time in 1140 until August or September of 1141,[10] but they do

[5] Letter 85.
[6] Letter 86.
[7] Letter 87.
[8] Letter 95.
[9] Letter 96.
[10] Since Hato had already heard by February/March 1141 that Nicholas's affairs in Rome were going well, he must have left some time before then. Peter's Letter 87 probably reached Troyes before Nicholas returned, since Hato's Letter 96 strongly implied that Nicholas had only just come back. Nicholas himself mentioned visits to Rome in two later letters. One was to Archdeacon Philip of Liège (the future prior of Clairvaux), written probably soon after Bernard's trip to Flanders in late summer 1146, in which Nicholas

not mention his business there. Bernard of Clairvaux, however, in his letters to Pope Innocent II and the papal chancellor Haimeric concerning Peter Abelard and the Council of Sens, said that they were carried by Nicholas. "My Nicholas, who is also yours," he wrote to Haimeric, "will tell you better by word of mouth about other things he saw and heard."[11] The version in MS. Berlin, Meerman 181 of Bernard's letter 330 to the Pope, dealing with the same topic, has an addition: "This man Nicholas, who is indeed mine and yours, will tell you about this matter better by word of mouth [and] can explain to you at greater length not only this but also all the other matters he has more fully learned."[12] Most scholars have assumed that this Nicholas was Nicholas of Montiéramey.[13] Martin Deutsch, indeed, used the fact that Nicholas's return from Rome was mentioned by Hato of Troyes in a letter written in September 1141 as evidence that the Council of Sens met in 1141 rather than in 1140.[14] His conclusions have not been accepted by most scholars, who have continued to date the council 2 June (the week of Pentecost) 1140.[15] Neither Deutsch nor

---

said that he had been with Philip at Rome, that they had crossed the icy mountains together and kept watch in the Tiburtine hills: ep. 33 (*PL*, CXCVI, 1623 C). In the other, to Gaucher of Clairvaux in 1145/6, Nicholas wrote: "Going to and returning from the Roman curia, full of curiosity, I made a great name for myself according to the name of the great men of this world": ep. 45 (*PL*, CXCVI, 1645 C). These passages, as Brial pointed out in *Hist. litt.*, XIII, 553, need not refer to his visit to Rome in 1140-1.

[11] Bernard, epp. 189 and 338 (Gaume ed., I.1, 414 and 632). Nicholas presumably carried these two and Bernard's other letters against Abelard to Rome and brought back the Pope's replies: cf. JL 8148-8149 and, on Bernard's letters, Rassow, "Kanzlei," pp. 86-103. The assumption that these letters were written at the same time, following Abelard's condemnation at the Council of Sens, has been questioned by L. Nicolau d'Olwer, in *Mélanges St. Bernard*, pp. 100-108, who argued that most of these letters, including ep. 338, were written *before* the council and that ep. 189 and the synodal letters (epp. 191 and 337) were written *after* the council and sent to Rome with the earlier letters and epp. 333-335. His conclusions have been accepted, with certain modifications, by Oursel, *Dispute*, pp. 89-94.

[12] Wilhelm Meyer, "Die Anklagesätze des h. Bernhard gegen Abaelard," *Nachrichten von der königl. Gesellschaft der Wissenschaften zu Göttingen*, Phil.-hist. Kl., 1898, p. 413. This addition, which was apparently overlooked by D'Olwer and Oursel (n. 11 above), argues against their point that ep. 330 was never sent, although it is odd that Bernard should have sent two letters to the Pope by the same messenger.

[13] D'Olwer, in *Mélanges St. Bernard*, p. 108, and Oursel, *Dispute*, p. 63, even call Nicholas the secretary of St. Bernard, although in 1140-1 he was certainly still chaplain to Hato of Troyes.

[14] Deutsch, *Synode von Sens*, pp. 53-54. His date of 1141 was accepted by Löwenfeld, who consequently dated the two letters of Innocent II condemning Abelard on 16 July 1141 (see n. 11 above), and by Hefele-Leclercq, *Conciles*, V.1, 754. It is still occasionally found, as in the *ODCC*, p. 4, and David Knowles, *The Evolution of Medieval Thought* (London, 1962) pp. 120 and 123.

[15] Elphège Vacandard, "Chronologie Abélardienne: La date du concile de Sens: 1140," *Revue des questions historiques*, L (1891) 235-245, and *St. Bernard*, II, 145, n. 1; Meyer, in *Göttingen Nachr.*, 1898, pp. 406 and 420-426; G. W. Greenaway, *Arnold of Brescia* (Cambridge, Eng., 1931) p. 70, n. 2; J. Rivière, "Les 'capitula' d'Abélard condamnés au concile de Sens," *Recherches de théologie ancienne et médiévale*, V (1933) 5; Raymonde Foreville, in *Histoire de*

his critics, however, noticed the reference to Nicholas's business at Rome in Hato's letter of February/March 1141, well before the date alleged by Deutsch for the Council of Sens, and the evidence of these letters therefore strongly supports the traditional dating.

There is in fact no positive proof that Bernard's messenger Nicholas was Hato's chaplain Nicholas of Montiéramey. It may be argued against their identity (a) that Bernard's use of *meus* implies that his Nicholas was a Cistercian monk, as both Mabillon and Watkin Williams assumed,[16] and (b) that the *negotia nostra* mentioned by Hato in Letter 85 does not sound like the condemnation of Abelard at the Council of Sens.[17] Although Hato attended the council and appeared on the synodal letter sent to the Pope (Bernard's letter 337), he is not known to have taken a leading part in the persecution of Abelard. His close friendship with Peter the Venerable, who later helped Abelard, suggests the reverse. Why, it may also be asked, should Bernard have chosen as his envoy for this very important business the chaplain of the Bishop of Troyes, a young and, so far as is known, inexperienced black Benedictine monk? In spite of these points, which must leave the question to some extent in doubt, I am inclined to believe that Bernard's messenger to Rome was indeed Nicholas of Montiéramey. No other Nicholas is known in the entourage of Bernard at this time,[18] and the later move of Nicholas of

---

l'Église, IX.1, 25; *Bernard de Clairvaux*, p. 597; D'Olwer, in *Mélanges St. Bernard*, p. 100; Arno Borst, "Abälard und Bernhard," *Historische Zeitschrift*, CLXXXVI (1958) 515, n. 4 (though he dated the council 2 July rather than 2 June); Klibansky, in *Med. and Ren. Studies* (cited p. 1, n. 1, above), V (1961) 8, n. 2; D. Van den Eynde, in *Antonianum* (cited Ep. 115, n. to p. 307, l. 19), XXXVII, 344–347; and Janssen, *Legaten*, p. 27. The matter was discussed by Sikes, *Abailard*, pp. 230–231, who dated the council 1140 but confused the issue by calling Hato of Troyes, "Hatto of Tours," and Nicholas, "St Bernard's secretary" (p. 235: cf. n. 13 above). He also said that "we cannot conclude that the letter [Letter 96] was sent when Nicholas was staying with Hatto on his return from Italy" and that "Nicholas might well have visited Hatto in 1141—on other business," thus overlooking the fact that at this time Nicholas was still Hato's chaplain.

[16] *Bernardi opera* (Gaume ed., I.1, 899); Williams, *St. Bernard*, p. 307, who called Nicholas a "Clairvaux monk." Nicholas of Montiéramey did not become a Cistercian until 1145 at the earliest.

[17] On 28 November 1140/2 Innocent II confirmed Hato's gift of a church to the abbey of Montierender: JL 8180; *PU in Frankreich*, n.f. I, 226, no. 38. Hato's business was probably something of this kind.

[18] The only other possibility is the "brother Nicholas" mentioned by Bernard in ep. 306 (Gaume ed., I.1, 588–589) as a possible abbot of Trois-Fontaines when Hugh became cardinal-bishop of Ostia: see Vacandard, *St. Bernard*, II, 494, and Ep. 192, n. to p. 445, l. 31. This Nicholas seems to have been a monk of Trois-Fontaines, and the support given him at this time by Bernard and Hugh suggests that he might have been a suitable messenger in 1140. The "brother" and "lord" N. in epp. 433–435 (Gaume ed., I.1, 743–744), recommending him to Pope Innocent II, was probably Nicholas of Montiéramey. If so, they were written before he joined Clairvaux and show that Bernard already regarded him as a reliable negotiator and messenger.

Montiéramey to Clairvaux suggests that he may have already known Bernard at this time. Above all, Nicholas of Montiéramey is known to have been in Rome in 1140-1, and the presence at Troyes of both Bernard and the papal legate Geoffrey of Chartres at the time Nicholas returned implies that his business there was of more than local importance. If this is so, he presumably left France shortly after the Council of Sens and stayed at Rome for the better part of a year. He thus stepped onto the larger stage of history in the somewhat unattractive role of hatchetman for Bernard in the condemnation of Abelard.[19]

Following this episode, Nicholas disappears from the correspondence of Peter the Venerable for almost a decade. During this period Bishop Hato resigned from the diocese of Troyes and retired to Cluny, probably either late in 1145 or early in 1146,[20] and Nicholas moved from Montiéramey to Clairvaux.[21] There he had a little writing room or *scriptoriolum*, as he called it, located between the cell of the novices,

---

[19] If the identity of the two Nicholas's is accepted, the Council of Sens must have been in 1140, since Nicholas of Montiéramey was in Rome in February/March 1141; but it does not establish the date of the papal bulls condemning Abelard, as some scholars have assumed: see Borst, in *Hist. Zschr.*, CLXXXVI, 522. D'Olwer and Oursel (cited n. 11 above) even argued from the alleged shortness of time between the Council of Sens (2 June 1140) and the issuing of the bulls (16 July 1140) that Bernard must have written most of his letters concerning Abelard before the council met. Nicholas's long stay in Rome and his return to Troyes in August/September 1141 in fact suggest that the bulls were not issued until 1141 and thus absolve Innocent from the possible charge of undue haste in his condemnation of Abelard.

[20] Cf. Constable, in *Petrus Ven.*, pp. 43-44, and Ep. 2, n. to p. 6., l. 12.

[21] Mabillon, in *Bernardi opera* (Gaume ed., I.2, 1617-1618), argued that Nicholas moved to Clairvaux in 1145 on the basis of his ep. 7 (*PL*, CXCVI, 1601-1603), in which he discussed his wish to leave Montiéramey for Clairvaux and which (a) referred to Pope Eugene III, who became pope in February 1145 and (b) was addressed among others to prior R. of Clairvaux, whom Mabillon identified as Rualenus, who succeeded Eugene as abbot of St. Anastasius at Rome and therefore left Clairvaux soon after Eugene's election as pope. This date was accepted by most authorities on Nicholas (see n. 1 above), including Rassow, "Kanzlei," p. 68, n. 9, who established elsewhere in his article, however, that the prior R. to whom Nicholas's ep. 7 was addressed was not Rualenus but Rainerius of Thérouanne (*ibid.*, pp. 288-289). The chronology of the priors of Clairvaux cannot be established with certainty, but Rainerius's predecessor Geoffrey of Péronne died in 1144, according to Vacandard, *St. Bernard*, I, 391 and n. 3, or on 15 January 1146, according to D'Arbois de Jubainville, *Études*, p. 187 (cf. his list of priors on p. 357), who was followed by Rassow. Nicholas's ep. 7 may not therefore have been written until 1146, and it certainly preceded his final move to Clairvaux. In ep. 45 to Gaucher of Clairvaux he described his first flight to Clairvaux, from which he was forced to return (*PL*, CXCVI, 1646). I am therefore inclined to think that Nicholas moved to Clairvaux in 1146, which fits with the fact that he probably stayed with Hato of Troyes until Hato retired to Cluny. Nicholas then presumably had to return to Montiéramey, which he may have found dull after his busy life as Hato's chaplain. By moving to Clairvaux he doubtless hoped to serve Bernard, who had already used him for important affairs. William of St. Thierry gave an account of the conversion of Nicholas (written before his disgrace) from a secular life in the world to a religious life at Clairvaux in the *Vita prima* of St. Bernard, I, XIV, 68 (Gaume ed., II.6, 2139).

the cloister, and the infirmary.[22] Nearby, presumably, was the *scriptorium* of his friend Henry of France, the brother of Louis VII, who entered Clairvaux at about the same time as Nicholas and who later became bishop of Beauvais and archbishop of Rheims.[23] Nicholas may indeed have been the librarian at Clairvaux, as some scholars have said, and the references in his letters show that he was busy copying and collating books.[24] He also served as one of Bernard's secretaries and soon became, as Rassow put it, "a sort of chancellor or *dictator*" for Bernard.[25] He helped to draw up the crusading letters of 1146-7, and he complained in his own letters of the mass of business that assailed him.[26] He found time, however, to correspond with his own friends, such as Peter of Celle, and to write letters on their behalf. "The change of order," he wrote to Abbot Odo of Pouthières, "has not changed, but rather has increased, the firmness of my friendship"; and to his friend Walter and to Henry of France, when he was away from Clairvaux, Nicholas wrote that "the absence of friends would be intolerable were it not for the remedy of letters."[27]

Peter the Venerable visited Clairvaux some time in 1149—he referred to the visit as "recent" in a letter written in October 1149[28]— and he may at that time have renewed his friendship with Nicholas. Bernard wrote to Peter about the middle of 1149 in some agitation, saying that "my Nicholas, who is also yours, has been greatly disturbed, and has disturbed me, by saying that he saw a letter from me to you in which there were some bitter words." His intention was not bitter, Bernard said: "The mass of my work is to blame, since when my scribes

---

[22] Nicholas, ep. 35 (PL, CXCVI, 1626-1627). On the *scriptoriola* at Clairvaux, see Marcel Aubert, *L'architecture cistercienne en France*, 2nd ed. (Paris, 1947) II, 30-32, esp. p. 32, n. 2. The plan of Clairvaux by Dom Milley, reproduced in Vacandard, *St. Bernard*, I, between pp. 416 and 417, and in Williams, *St. Bernard*, pp. 391-396, although inaccurate in details and showing the abbey as it was in the later Middle Ages, still shows the *cellulae scriptoriae* off the small cloister and in the same area as, though not adjacent to, the infirmary and the *novitiatus*.

[23] Nicholas, ep. 39 (PL, CXCVI, 1567 C). On Henry of France, see Ep. 145, n. to p. 360, l. 2. Henry himself took an interest in books and gave a number to Clairvaux: Wilmart, "Bibliothèque," pp. 51-58.

[24] On Nicholas's "commerce of books" at Clairvaux, see Mabillon, in *Bernardi opera* (Gaume ed., I.2, 1619-1624), who gathered all the references to books in his letters, and Steiger, in *SMGBOZ*, XXXVIII, 44.

[25] Rassow, "Kanzlei," p. 82.

[26] Nicholas, ep. 1 (PL, CXCVI, 1593 A). This, the introductory letter to the collection, is addressed to Gerard of Péronne and Henry of France.

[27] Nicholas, epp. 27, 35, and 39 (PL, CXCVI, 1620 A, 1630-1631, and 1578 A). On his correspondence with Peter of Celle, see Jean Leclercq, *La spiritualité de Pierre de Celle* (Études de théologie et d'histoire de la spiritualité, 7; Paris, 1946) pp. 21-22, and M.-D. Chenu, "Platon à Cîteaux," *Archives d'histoire doctrinale et littéraire du Moyen Age*, XXI (1954) 99-106. On his letter to Amadeus of Lausanne, see Dimier, *Amédée de Lausanne* (cited p. 272, n. 10, above), pp. 89-90 and 283-284.

[28] Letter 150.

11*

do not remember my meaning properly, they sharpen their pens beyond measure, and I am not able to see what I ordered to be written." He promised always in the future to read through his letters to Peter. Nicholas himself, whom Bernard called "this our common son," carried this letter to Cluny and was instructed by Bernard to explain certain matters to Peter fully by word of mouth.[29] Peter replied expressing his affection for Bernard and saying that he had taken no offense at the allegedly bitter words. He mentioned several matters of business, including the election at Grenoble, concerning which he placed his opinion "in the mouth of my very dear and your faithful Nicholas, so that it may be disclosed to you." At the end, he asked to be remembered at the chapter general at Cîteaux.[30] When Nicholas arrived at Clairvaux with this letter, Bernard wrote in his reply: "I tore myself away and freed myself from the petitions and disputes of everyone and shut myself up with Nicholas, whom your spirit loves." He thanked Peter for the news about the election at Grenoble: "You should know, moreover, that my heart was warmed by the words of our common son [Nicholas], which he brought me on your behalf." A commemoration of Peter had been made at the Cistercian chapter general, and at the end of the letter "the elect of Beauvais" greeted Peter, and Nicholas added a personal postscript: "I your Nicholas greet you, for ever and beyond, and the members of your household who cling to your side and spirit."[31] Since Henry of France was elected bishop of Beauvais in the late summer or autumn of 1149 and the Cistercian chapter general normally met in September, this visit of Nicholas to Cluny can be dated probably in August–September 1149.

Peter the Venerable clearly had great confidence in the ability of Nicholas and in his influence with Bernard. He had been upset on his "recent" visit to Clairvaux by certain aspects of the reception of visitors in Cistercian houses, and he sent a letter on this subject to Bernard, writing, he said, in haste in order that the subject might be discussed and appropriate measures taken by the meeting of Cistercian abbots scheduled for All Saints' Day.[32] He sent this letter not directly to Bernard, but to Nicholas, with a covering letter. "Since I love you with an unfeigned love, I cannot be unmindful of you for

---

[29] Letter 148; Bernard, ep. 387 (Gaume ed., I.1, 694). On this letter, which is important for Bernard's method of writing letters, see Leclercq, in *Recueil*, pp. 6–7.

[30] Letter 149.

[31] Letter 152; Bernard, ep. 389 (Gaume ed., I.1, 699). On the postscript by Nicholas, who may have written the entire letter, see Rassow, "Kanzlei," p. 80.

[32] Letter 150. The precise meeting of Cistercian abbots to which Peter was referring is uncertain. All Saints' Day (1 November) was very late for the meeting of the chapter general at Cîteaux, and there may have been some other meeting at Clairvaux of which Peter had heard.

long. I loved you when you were of our color [that is, a black Benedictine], and so far as I am concerned I love you none the less now that you have changed your color, but not, I think, your heart." After some more affectionate phrases, Peter went on:

> I am writing a letter to the abbot of Clairvaux, which I want to be presented to him through you. Read it to him earnestly and carefully and urge as strongly as you can that something should be done about what I have written purely out of love. Press him (since he must be pressed on account of the shortness of time) to carry out my hopes in this matter on the coming feast of All Saints and to force anyone who may disagree to come round to my view of the matter—which is, I think, also his view.

Finally, Peter asked Nicholas to greet various friends at Clairvaux, including "the brother of the king."[33] This reference to Henry, bishop-elect of Beauvais, dates the letter in 1149; and the need for speed if action were to be taken at the meeting on All Saints' Day points to the middle of October. This letter may therefore have crossed with Bernard's Letter 152 (389 in Bernard's collection) to Peter, and neither Bernard nor Nicholas referred to Peter's request in any known letter. There is also no reference to the matter in any surviving Cistercian legislation. It may be that Peter's letters arrived too late for the meeting he had in mind and were never delivered.[34]

Not long after, either late in 1149 or early in 1150, Nicholas sent a short but important letter to Peter the Venerable. "I am soon to see your face, I trust, and send you your letters together with the abbot of Clairvaux's book addressed to the lord pope and the two letters which you sent to him and me this year. Your Sublimity should furthermore know that your letter greatly assisted the promotion of brother Henry [of France], and it was heard with great pleasure by the archbishops and bishops of France; and many thanks have been given to Your Serenity, as I shall report better and more faithfully by word of mouth."[35] The reference to Henry of France again dates this letter in 1149, but "this year" by the Old Style of reckoning in the diocese of Langres (Easter to Easter) lasted until 16 April 1150 by the New Style. At the time he was writing, Nicholas evidently planned to visit Cluny soon. Whether or not he came is unknown, but it is probable that he was busy that spring with Bernard's plans for a new crusade. He added a word of greeting to the letter sent by Bernard to Peter after the

---

[33] Letter 151.

[34] The two letters may be those which Nicholas returned to Peter with his next letter, 153 (see below).

[35] Letter 153. The work by Bernard mentioned here was probably the first part of the *De consideratione*: see Vacandard, *St. Bernard*, II, 436. The two letters may have been Peter's Letters 150–151. Copies may not have been kept because they were written in haste.

Council at Chartres on 7 May, announcing another meeting at Compiègne on 15 July: "Your Nicholas greets you as yours, for he is yours."[36] But he made no reference to a visit.

Peter's letter to Bernard in the autumn of 1150, asking that Nicholas be allowed to come and stay at Cluny up until Christmas, initiated a group of letters concerned with another visit by Nicholas.[37] At the same time Peter wrote to Nicholas himself asking him to come and saying that he was forced by illness to stay at Cluny until Christmas.[38] Bernard replied that "he whom you asked to be sent to you," that is, Nicholas, was away from Clairvaux with the bishop of Auxerre, "and he is so ill that he is said to be unable yet to come even to us without serious inconvenience."[39] Nicholas himself replied to Peter, probably early in 1151, that he had been occupied with "the case of your brother, the lord abbot of Vézelay, in which at your command I had to fight with the beasts in order that man might not prevail." This case may have been Nicholas's business with the bishop of Auxerre, which Bernard mentioned. "Whose fault is it that I have so long been cheated of my desire [to see you]?" Nicholas asked. "Not mine, owing both to my illness and to the business which you imposed upon me." He then thanked Peter for his "double letter" asking him to visit Cluny and asked him to write again to Bernard, to the Prior of Clairvaux, and to Gaucher ("in all of whose affairs," he said, "I am entangled and involved"), "in order that they may send me to you for Easter." He asked Peter to send copies of these letters to him personally in secret, and he promised to return some books for which Peter had asked in Letter 176. In conclusion he wrote: "If what I asked cannot occur at Easter, at least [let it be] after Easter. I know that the lord abbot told you not to ask for me unless it was necessary, which he also said to me, but it is necessary, and very necessary to see you, although I am busy with many things. What more? Order that I come."[40]

The messenger who brought this letter to Cluny returned to

---

[36] Satabin, "Lettre," p. 323. According to Rassow, "Kanzlei," p. 290, the entire letter may have been written by Nicholas.

[37] Letter 175.

[38] Letter 176.

[39] Letter 177; Bernard, ep. 265 (Gaume ed., I.1, 547).

[40] Letter 179. Several scholars have suggested that this passage shows that Bernard already suspected Nicholas: Brial, in *Hist. litt.*, XIII, 556; Vacandard, *St. Bernard*, II, 492, n. 2; Steiger, in *SMGBOZ*, XXXVIII, 46. This is a judgment of hindsight, and it is more probable that Bernard was unwilling to let Nicholas go because he needed his services, or possibly because he felt that Peter was using Nicholas too much. The letter indeed suggests that Nicholas was overburdened by his occupations at Clairvaux, and parts of it curiously resemble Nicholas's letters in 1145/6 begging to be allowed to leave Montiéramey for Clairvaux. Cf., for instance, the passage in ep. 46 to Fromond of Clairvaux asking "ut educant me de isto carcere et inducant in locum tabernaculi admirabilis usque ad domum Dei" (*PL*, CXCVI, 1648 B).

Nicholas with a brief reply from Peter, saying that he would soon send his own messenger, "who will not dare to neglect any of his orders and will follow you and the abbot of Clairvaux wherever you may go." He said that he would do his best "neither that you will have written in vain nor that I myself will write again to the abbot in vain, as I recently did, about your long-awaited visit to us."[41] Peter then wrote four separate letters to Bernard, Nicholas, Prior Philip of Clairvaux, and the cellarer Gaucher, and presumably sent them together to Clairvaux. In the letter to Bernard, Peter expressed his love for Nicholas and asked Bernard to send Nicholas to Cluny for the coming Easter. "I love him for your sake and I love him for his own sake: for your sake, because he owes you allegiance; for his own sake, because he has deserved it by his many merits since the days of the lord bishop of Troyes." With some bitterness, Peter reminded Bernard that he had permanently given up several Cluniacs to Clairvaux and expressed his resentment that Bernard was unwilling to send Nicholas even temporarily to Cluny. "I remember that Your Sanctity asked me when you were recently at Cluny, 'Why do you want Nicholas?'" And Peter admitted that at that time he had replied one thing and thought another, since he had wanted to say, in the words of the blind man to the Pharisees (John 9.27), "I have told you already, and you have heard. Why would you hear it again?" He therefore asked Bernard to send Nicholas "not only now but also when I shall ask in the future."[42] The letter to Nicholas simply said, after much affectionate verbiage, that he had written to Bernard, the Prior, and Gaucher asking that Nicholas visit Cluny for Easter.[43] In his brief letters to Prior Philip and the cellarer Gaucher, Peter asked them to support his request for a visit from Nicholas.[44] The outcome of this barrage of letters is not known, but it is hard to believe that Bernard refused so pressing a request, and it is probable that Nicholas spent Easter (8 April) 1151 with Peter the Venerable at Cluny.

Later that year, in about November, Peter went away on a long trip to Italy, and when he returned to Cluny about March 1152, he apparently found a messenger from Nicholas with a letter asking about his trip. Shortly before Pentecost (18 May), therefore, Peter

---

[41] Letter 180.

[42] Letter 181. The reference here to Hato of Troyes is definite proof, if any is needed, of the identity of the former chaplain of the Bishop of Troyes with Nicholas of Montiéramey-Clairvaux.

[43] Letter 182. There is no suggestion that Peter sent secret copies of these letters to Nicholas, as he had asked. In his letter to Bernard, Peter told Nicholas: "I have written concerning you what you yourself will see."

[44] Letters 183–184. The reference to "before the feast" in this letter to the Prior shows that Easter was at hand.

wrote to both Bernard and Nicholas. In his letter to Nicholas he described his travels and excused his failure to write earlier. Towards the end of the letter he mentioned the dispute between the Cluniac priory of Gigny and the Cistercian abbey of Le Miroir, and he especially asked Nicholas to arrange a meeting between himself and the Abbot of Clairvaux in order to discuss the matter fully, preferably at Dijon on the third Sunday after Pentecost (8 June).[45] To Bernard, Peter wrote that he would come "wherever seems best to you or your men ... either at Dijon or at Clairvaux itself."[46] The meeting in fact probably took place at Cluny,[47] but no satisfactory solution was reached, and the dispute was not finally settled until 1153.

Peter's letter to Nicholas in May 1152 is the last in his collected correspondence and the latest reference to his friendship with Nicholas. Besides asking him to plan the meeting with Bernard, he expressed his affection for Nicholas and said that he had asked Bernard to allow him to visit Cluny very soon. "But you should not hesitate to come even sooner, for you are very necessary to me on account both of these matters and of certain others." This shows that Peter had not yet heard of Nicholas's disgrace and departure from Clairvaux, and it revises the accepted chronology that Nicholas left the service of Bernard in 1151.[48]

The first hint of trouble between Bernard and Nicholas is found in a letter from Bernard to Pope Eugene III, which was dated after 21 September 1151 by Vacandard on the basis of a reference to the bishop of Arras.[49] "I am in peril from false brethren," he wrote, citing I Cor. 11.26, "and many forged letters under my forged seal have come into the hands of many men, and it is said, what I fear more, that this falseness may even have reached you. I have therefore thrown away that [old seal] and am now using a new one, as you see, with both my image and my name."[50] Some time later Bernard wrote again to the Pope:

That man Nicholas has gone out from us because he was not of us (I John 2.19); but he has left foul traces behind him (*Aeneid*, III, 244). I had for a long time known the man [for what he was], but I waited either for God to convert him or for him to betray himself like Judas, which is what happened. For when he left there were found upon him, besides books, money, and much gold, three

---

[45] Letter 193. Cf. Constable, "Cluniac Tithes," pp. 608–624, esp. pp. 617–620, and the revisions in the notes to Ep. 192 to the chronology suggested there.
[46] Letter 192.
[47] Bernard, ep. 283 (Gaume ed., I.1, 568–569).
[48] See the authorities cited in n. 1 above.
[49] Vacandard, *St. Bernard*, II, 496, n. 4 (and II, 566, where he dated this letter 1151/2).
[50] Bernard, ep. 284 (Gaume ed., I.1, 569–570).

seals: one his own, one the Prior's, and the third one mine, and that not the old one but the new one, which I was recently forced to change on account of his deceits and secret frauds. I remember writing to you about this, naming no names but saying that I was in peril from false brethren. Who can say to how many people he has written in my name whatever he wanted, without my knowing?... It has been partly proved and partly confessed that he wrote falsely to you not just once but on several occasions. I shall not sully my lips or your ears with his base deeds, with which the earth is polluted and which have become a byword among all men. If he comes to you (for he boasted of this and relied on having friends in the curia), remember Arnold of Brescia, since here is a man worse than Arnold. No man more richly deserves perpetual imprisonment; nothing is more fitting for him than perpetual silence.[51]

The exact date of this letter is not known, but it was almost certainly after Peter's letter of May 1152. The occasion of the discovery may even have been Nicholas's departure for Cluny on the visit mentioned in Peter's letter, with books to return to the library there, money for his travels, and the three seals in order to write under the name of Bernard and the Prior while he was away; but this is a conjecture.

It is clear from both these letters that Bernard's real charge against Nicholas was breach of confidence: that he had sent out letters conceived and written by himself as if they were by Bernard. As usual when he felt strongly, Bernard chose strong words; and it is possible, as some historians have suggested, that his charges against Nicholas were exaggerated and even unjust.[52] The letter of Peter the Venerable, for instance, is evidence that Nicholas's misdeeds were not a byword among men. Bernard's pen was doubtless sharpened by his sense of outrage at having been deceived by one whom he loved and trusted and by his worry at the possible effects of Nicholas's letters, perhaps also by concern at the extent he was forced to rely upon his secretaries, as he himself confessed in his letter 387 to Peter the Venerable, and possibly by a feeling that he had been unwise in admitting to Clairvaux a man whose character and training clearly equipped him not to be a Cistercian monk but to be an amanuensis in the external business of the abbey. Even when allowance has been made for Bernard's own feelings, however, there is nothing in his

---

[51] Bernard, ep. 298 (Gaume ed., I.1, 581–582). It is translated in whole or in part in several of the works cited in n. 1 above.

[52] See in particular Barthélemy Hauréau, "Nicolas de Clairvaux," *Nouvelle biographie générale* (Paris, 1852-1866), XXXVII, 983: "Avait-il donc été mal à propos accusé par saint Bernard dont la vivacité habituelle peut bien être soupçonnée de quelque emportement, et conséquemment de quelque injustice?" and Greenaway, *Arnold*, p. 83, n. 4, who said that "the extraordinary terms in which he [Bernard] denounces his secretary" show "how far Bernard was capable of allowing his sense of proportion to be warped by personal animosity." Even Leclercq, in the *Rev. Bén.*, LXVI, 290–291, remarked that Bernard expelled Nicholas "avec une énergie dont on a pu se demander si elle n'était pas excessive."

letters to justify the extravagant charges of theft, forgery, treason, and less mentionable crimes that many historians have brought against Nicholas. Bernard did not say that Nicholas had stolen the books or money, or that he had forged the seals,[53] though the possession of these was of course improper for a monk and suspicious for a confidential secretary; nor did he say that Nicholas took flight when discovered and was arrested.[54] The comparison with Arnold of Brescia, upon which Watkin Williams put a most sinister interpretation, doubtless meant that Nicholas gave an exterior appearance of virtue but was deceitful and untrustworthy inside.[55]

The picture of Nicholas that emerges from these letters is, therefore, of an able and ingratiating, but unscrupulous and timeserving man. He clearly had considerable education, learning, and literary skill, in spite of his own description of himself, in one of his letters, as a "simple" and "rustic" man.[56] Peter the Venerable remarked to Bernard on Nicholas's knowledge of both sacred and philosophical writings and the pleasures of his conversation.[57] His own letters contain many references to the study and copying of both religious and secular books.[58] The very confusion of his own works with those of Bernard, Peter Damiani, and Nicholas of St. Albans is evidence of his

---

[53] The reference to forged letters and a forged seal in ep. 284 almost certainly meant that Nicholas had written and sealed letters fraudulently, not that he had made a replica of Bernard's seal.

[54] Cf. Vacandard, *St. Bernard*, II, 497; Rassow, "Kanzlei," p. 69; Williams, *St. Bernard*, pp. 352–353.

[55] Williams, *St. Bernard*, p. 353: "He [Bernard] is thinking, doubtless, of Arnald's fascination of Cardinal Guy of Bohemia." Williams also translated Bernard's reference to the *turpitudines* of Nicholas, in the plural, as "uncleanness." The absurdity of this suggestion, against both Arnold and Nicholas, is shown by the fact that no one of Arnold's many enemies, according to Greenaway, *Arnold*, p. 43, ever cast "the slightest reproach on his moral character." Bernard himself more than once specifically acknowledged the purity of Arnold's personal life: epp. 189 and 195 (Gaume ed., I.1, 411–414 and 421–422). In ep. 196 (Gaume ed., I.1, 423) Bernard described Arnold as a man "whose conversation is honey and whose doctrine is poison, who has the head of a dove and the tail of a scorpion." He probably felt the same way about Nicholas.

[56] Nicholas, ep. 1 (*PL*, CXCVI, 1593 BC); cf. epp. 16, 17, and 39 (*ibid.*, 1611 B, 1613 D, and 1576 B). His letters are filled with rhetorical flourishes, and his references in epp. 2 and 35 to the *captatio beneuolentiae* and *uernantes clausulae* (*ibid.*, 1594 C and 1627 C) show that he was not unfamiliar with the new *ars dictaminis*: see pp. 29–35, above. Steiger, in *SMGBOZ*, XXXVIII, 42, and Leclercq, in *Rev. Bén.*, LXVI, 291, were of the opinion that he had been a teacher at Montiéramey, but the relevant passage in his ep. 38 to Lecelinus, whom he called his "discipulus, potius autem condiscipulus, sub illo magistro cujus schola in terris est" (*PL*, CXCVI, 1633 A), suggests that they were colleagues rather than master and pupil.

[57] Letter 181.

[58] Letter 176 shows that Nicholas borrowed from Cluny both the history of Alexander the Great and the *Contra Julianum* of St. Augustine. In his ep. 40 to the abbot of Montiéramey in 1145/6 Nicholas admitted that he was "proud of his learning, although that was little or nothing" (*PL*, CXCVI, 1637 B). On his Platonic correspondence with Peter of Celle, see M.-D. Chenu, in *Archives* (cited n. 27 above), and *La théologie au douzième siècle* (Paris, 1957) p. 127.

literary skill, though not of any originality in style or content.[59] It is also clear that he was an able diplomat and secretary. Hato of Troyes referred to the successful outcome of his mission to Rome in 1140–1, and Peter the Venerable entrusted to him some business concerning his brother Abbot Pontius of Vézelay, who was at that time embroiled with the count of Nevers and the townsmen of Vézelay. Nicholas himself said that he was "entangled and involved" in the affairs of Bernard, Prior Philip, and the cellarer Gaucher; and Bernard's reluctance to let him visit Cluny was almost certainly because he needed him at Clairvaux rather than because he suspected his trustworthiness. He was in demand among his friends as a letter writer, and no less than twenty-two out of the total of fifty-five letters in his collected correspondence were written in the name of someone else.[60] To these qualities as a writer and negotiator, he must have added a high degree of personal charm, "that indescribable quality," as David Knowles recently described it, "which, like physical beauty, can dazzle the mind's eye and blind the judgement."[61] Some of the ablest men of his day, and some of the most experienced judges of men, including Peter the Venerable, Hato of Troyes, Peter of Celle, and Bernard himself at first, felt the power of his charm and lavished their praise and affection on Nicholas, "yours and mine," as they called him in their letters.

It may be that Nicholas was misled by this praise and by overconfidence in his own abilities into forgetting his subordinate position and betraying his trust to Bernard. He lacked restraint and stability. His ready discontent shows itself in his letters concerning his departure from Montiéramey and his visits to Cluny. He was "vain, inconstant, unquiet," according to Mabillon in his generally temperate judgment on Nicholas.[62] He clearly had a taste for intrigue, as his request to

---

[59] Scholars are not in agreement on the quality of Nicholas's writings, and their opinions seem in some cases to have been influenced by their unfavorable view of his character: cf. De Ghellinck, *Essor*, I, 219, who said that Nicholas, "moins préoccupé de la doctrine que du jeu de la phrase, ne parvient pas à reproduire naturellement, malgré la similitude des expressions, les élans de son maître," and Leclercq, *Amour des lettres*, p. 246. For a more favorable view of his originality, see Chenu, in *Archives*, XXI, 100, who remarked that "cette malhonnêteté morale ne doit cependant pas discréditer rétrospectivement le tonus intellectuel d'un homme," and H. Barré, "Marie et l'Église du Vénérable Bède à S. Albert le Grand," *Marie et l'Église*, I (Bulletin de la Société française d'études mariales, 9; 1951) 91 ff., who is cited by Leclercq, in *Rev. Bén.*, LXVI, 270, n. 4.

[60] Rassow, "Kanzlei," p. 82, giving the number as 21 out of 55.

[61] Knowles, *Historian and Character* (cited p. 39, n. 171, above), p. 5.

[62] Mabillon, in *Bernardi opera* (Gaume ed., I.2, 1629–1630). Maitland, *Dark Ages*, p. 450, (much of whose account of Nicholas is based on Mabillon) called him "a great rogue" and "a hypocrite, a cheat, and a thief," but he added that "how far the inconsiderate and confiding kindness of his patrons conduced to spoil a clever, conceited, ambitious young man, is more than I can pretend to say."

Peter the Venerable for secret copies of his letters shows, and he apparently enjoyed serving several masters and becoming over-involved in their affairs. The imitative quality that marked his writings seems to have extended to the realm of practical affairs and perhaps almost to an identification of himself with his masters, which is a dangerous quality when not tempered by restraint and good judgment. Nicholas may thus even have believed that he was performing his duty, or at least not exceeding it, when he wrote letters for his masters and used their seals; but if so, his lack of sense of responsibility had serious consequences for both Bernard and himself.

In the long run, however, his abilities to serve and to please the great men of this world served Nicholas in good stead, and in spite of Bernard's excoriating attack he continued to live the life of a useful and respected minor prelate for twenty-five years after his expulsion from Clairvaux.[63] Chastened, perhaps, by his experiences there, as well as by advancing age, he returned to Montiéramey, entered the service of Count Henry of Champagne, to whom he dedicated his collection of nineteen sermons, and won the good opinions of both Pope Hadrian IV and Alexander III. Whether or not he either saw or corresponded with Peter the Venerable after 1152 is not known; but Peter was not the kind of man who lightly deserted a loved and trusted friend who was in trouble, and I doubt that the débacle with Bernard brought to an end their old and close friendship.[64]

---

[63] On the later life of Nicholas of Montiéramey, up until his death in 1175/8, see the references gathered by Benton, in *Speculum*, XXXVI, 555–557. Many of these have come to light recently, and they fully disprove the statement by Vacandard, *St. Bernard*, II, 497, that Nicholas after his disgrace "disparaît à peu près de l'histoire." It is not known for certain, however, where he went immediately after leaving Clairvaux. Leclercq, in *Études*, pp. 63–64, and *Rev. Bén.*, LXVI, 290–291, suggested that he went first to Montiéramey and then to Rome.

[64] After this appendix had been written, Professor John Benton kindly sent me a copy of an unpublished letter by Nicholas in MS. Berlin, Phillipps 1719. It is without address and was perhaps written on behalf of a friend. It may have been sent to Bernard of Clairvaux in 1151 or 1152 and shows that charges had been brought against the writer (unjustly, in his opinion) by some canons of Auxerre.

Q. PETER OF POITIERS

Among the secretaries who are celebrated in the literary annals of the twelfth century, a place of honor belongs to Peter of Poitiers, the secretary or notary of Peter the Venerable, on account both of the length of his service and of the merits of his own writings.[1] His fame, however, and even his identity, have been obscured by his self-effacing devotion to his master, by the loss of most of his own works, and by confusion with other clerics and writers named Peter of Poitiers, of whom there were at least three others in the twelfth century. One was a bishop of Poitiers named Peter, who died in 1115; another was a regular canon of St. Victor at Paris; the third, and most famous, was a theologian, the successor of Peter Comestor at Paris and chancellor of Notre Dame in 1193.[2] There is even a pseudo-Peter of Poitiers, the author of a *Glossae super Sententias* which was once attributed to Peter of Poitiers the theologian.[3] It is not therefore surprising that some obscurity surrounds the secretary of Peter the Venerable, whose life is known only from his own works and those of Peter the Venerable and the historians of Cluny. "A most illustrious and learned man," he was called by François de Rivo, who compiled the chronicle of Cluny at the end of the fifteenth century, "who wrote many letters to Peter of Cluny and many other works, which are all in our library (*apud nos*)."[4] Of these only a few letters and poems, including a long panegyric in honor of Peter the Venerable, are known today; but these are enough

---

[1] On Peter of Poitiers, see in particular *Hist. litt.*, XII, 349–356; Maitland, *Dark Ages*, pp. 452–457; Lecointre-Dupont, "Pierre de Poitiers," pp. 369–391; Pignot, *Cluny*, III, 461–472; Manitius, *Lat. Lit.*, III, 900–903. On the position of secretary or notary to the abbot of Cluny, see De Valous, *Mon. clun.*, II, 40.

[2] The four Peters, though often confused, are clearly distinguished in the *index auctorum* to Du Cange, *Glossarium*, ed. Léopold Favre (Niort, 1883–1887) X, lviii; cf. Chevalier, *Bio-bib.*, II, 3737–3738, and esp. Philip Moore, *The Works of Peter of Poitiers, Master in Theology and Chancellor of Paris* (The Catholic University of America [Washington, D.C.], 1936) pp. 21–24. The chancellor Peter appears on five and the canon Peter on two obituaries in *Obituaires*, I, 174, 284, 298, 455, and 508 (on the chancellor), and 49 and 590 (on the canon).

[3] Odon Lottin, "A propos des 'Glossae super Sententias' attribuées à Pierre de Poitiers," *Psychologie et morale aux XIIᵉ et XIIIᵉ siècles*, VI (Gembloux, 1960) 119–124; cf. Van den Eynde, in *Franciscan Studies* (cited Ep. 94, n. to p. 253), XI, 118–119.

[4] *Bibl. Clun.*, col. 594.

to show that he was a man of education and culture, with a considerable knowledge of classical and patristic literature.⁵ Peter the Venerable wrote a long poem extolling him as the equal of the classical poets and of the Christian Fathers,⁶ and in Letter 58 he praised the qualities of his mind and of his conversation. "If I wanted to explore the mysteries of Holy Scripture, you were always ready. If, on the other hand, I preferred to discuss some point of secular literature, you were quick and acute. And if we were talking about contempt of the world and love of heaven... your words were so unworldly and spiritual that you seemed to speak to me already as, 'I am purposed that my mouth shall not transgress concerning the works of men.'"

Very little is known about the life of Peter of Poitiers. Even his name and place of origin are uncertain, since several historians, including his biographer Lecointre-Dupont, identified him with Peter of Pithiviers, prior of Cluny, who became abbot of St. Martial at Limoges in 1156 and died in 1160.⁷ This identification was based upon the addresses of two letters to Peter of Poitiers in the letter collection of Peter the Venerable: Letter 125 from "frater Arnulfus heremita nouicius, et coheremitarum suorum minimus... karissimo seni societatis nostrae priori Petro Pictauensi," and Letter 129 from Peter the Venerable himself "Venerabili et carissimo fratri et filio Petro." The use of *prior* by Arnulf and of the solemn formula "venerable and beloved brother and son" by Peter the Venerable has been taken to

---

⁵ His known works are all found among those of Peter the Venerable. Mabillon apparently attributed to him a chronicle of Vézelay: cf. Cottineau, *Répertoire*, II, 3356; but this may have arisen from a confusion with Hugh of Poitiers. Berger, *Richard le Poitevin*, p. 93, also attributed to him a work in verse on the Koran, which was mentioned by the chronicler Richard of Poitiers. He has also been suggested as the possible author of a sermon mentioned in a letter written about the middle of the twelfth century by an anonymous monk of Bec: "Sermonem magistri Petri Pictauensis, quem de priuilegiis beati Ioannis euangelistae in capitulo nostro solemniter edidit, sicut postulasti transmittere non possum," in Hauréau, *Notices* (cited Ep. 78), II, 240; cf. A. Porée, *Histoire de l'abbaye du Bec* (Évreux, 1901) I, 537; Leclercq, in *Analecta mon.*, II, 142 and 164. It is not likely, however, that the secretary of Peter the Venerable would have preached at Bec, or that he would have been called *magister*, a title that usually designated a master in theology (cf. Letters 9–10). This Peter of Poitiers was more probably the future chancellor of Notre Dame.

⁶ *Bibl. Clun.*, cols. 1337–1344. This poem was directed against some critics of Peter of Poitiers, in particular of his panegyric in honor of Peter the Venerable. According to Pignot, *Cluny*, III, 464, it was intended by Peter the Venerable as "un simple amusement littéraire"; cf. Petit, *Ducs de Bourgogne*, II, 59–60.

⁷ Lecointre-Dupont, "Pierre de Poitiers," p. 384; Evans, *Mon. Life*, p. 111, identified Peter of Poitiers and Peter of Pithiviers, although on p. 108, following Pignot, *Cluny*, III, 459, she distinguished them. On Peter of Pithiviers, see Geoffrey of Vigeois, *Chronicon*, I, 55, in Labbé, *Nova bibl.*, II, 309; *GC*, II, 560; and De Lasteyrie, *St. Martial*, p. 99, according to whom Peter of Pithiviers had been, successively, prior of Cluny and of St. Eutropius and provost of St. Vaury before becoming abbot of St. Martial. If this is correct, he cannot have been the secretary of Peter the Venerable.

show that Peter of Poitiers occupied an official position, but the terms need not be interpreted in this way.[8] The letters in which they appear are two of a group of four addressed to Peter of Poitiers by Peter the Venerable and his companions on a retreat in the woods near Cluny. The other two were addressed "Venerando fratri et karissimo socio Petro" (Letter 126) and "Venerando et karissimo patri domino Petro [sancti Ioannis]" (Letter 127).[9] Peter of Poitiers's reply to Peter the Venerable was headed: "Serenissimo patri et domino, Petrus licet inutilis deuotus tamen seruus et filius" (Letter 128). The style and content of these letters as a group suggest that their solemn addresses were written in a jocular spirit. Peter of Poitiers himself referred to the letters as *iocundissimi* and *ludibundi* in his Letter 128. In his other letters to Peter of Poitiers, Peter the Venerable never addressed him by his standard formula for ecclesiastical dignitaries but always used a more intimate and affectionate style of address. The salutation from "the novice hermit" Arnulf can in particular hardly have been meant seriously. The *societas* of which he called Peter of Poitiers *prior* was probably not the abbey of Cluny but the group of hermits among whom Peter the Venerable was abbot and Peter of Poitiers, though absent, prior. The tone of the letter is not that of a junior monk addressing an aged prior. Arnulf urged Peter to join the hermits. "To tell you the truth," he concluded, "we want you to visit us more than ourselves to return to you. This feeling is so universal among us that even our old cow agrees and is enraptured with the pleasant life of a hermit and chews the cud all the time, both when she is fasting and when she is full."

A more substantial objection to identifying Peter of Poitiers with Peter of Pithiviers is that Letters 125 and 129, which suggest that Peter of Poitiers may have been prior of Cluny, were almost certainly written before 1149, when the prior of Cluny was Peter the Venerable's brother Armannus, who was followed in about 1151 by Prior Peter (II), the later abbot of St. Martial.[10] Geoffrey of Vigeois, moreover, definitely stated that this Prior Peter came from "a certain camp called Pithiviers," which is in Orléanais,[11] whereas there is no reason to doubt that Peter of Poitiers came from Poitou. The position of secretary to Peter the Venerable, in addition, was not compatible with that of prior of Cluny, one of whose principal duties was to act in place of the abbot when he was away from Cluny.[12] Peter of Poitiers, on the

---

[8] Cf. *Hist. litt.*, XII, 354–355, which doubted whether the address on Arnulf's letter indicated that Peter of Poitiers was prior of Cluny.
[9] On the style "Peter of St. John," see below.
[10] *GC*, IV, 1167; Pignot, *Cluny*, III, 617; and Appendix R on functionaries at Cluny.
[11] See n. 7 above.
[12] Cf. De Valous, *Mon. clun.*, I, 114–118.

contrary, often traveled with Peter the Venerable, and it is clear from Letters 123, 124, 128, and 129 that when they were apart he was out of work. Peter of Poitiers referred to himself as useless, and Peter the Venerable called him idle. He spent his time copying books. His request in Letter 123 that Peter the Venerable order the claustral prior to supply him with parchment also shows that he cannot himself have been prior at this time.

The evidence that Peter of Poitiers was also known as Peter of St. John is very much stronger. First, there is the address on Letter 127, "domino Petro sancti Ioannis," which certainly referred to Peter of Poitiers. Mabillon and Lecointre-Dupont conjectured that he had been a monk at St. John Montierneuf in Poitiers,[13] but their evidence was not decisive, for the "sancti Ioannis" is found only in the relatively late Souvigny manuscript of the letters of Peter the Venerable, and in the first printed edition, which was based on a manuscript from Cluny. It does not appear in the Anchin manuscript, which represents the earliest text tradition. A second and more important reference, which has hitherto been overlooked, occurs in the *De miraculis*, where Peter the Venerable, after describing a miracle at the monastery of St. Jean d'Angély, said: "I learned this not from another man but from a monk of that same monastery, Peter by name, who saw and heard all of this. For he later came to Cluny, thanks to his devotion, and was my scribe and most beloved son in Christ."[14] In the printed texts of the *De miraculis* the name in this passage is given as *Lecto*, but in the only known manuscript it is clearly *Petro*.[15] This establishes with certainty that Peter of Poitiers was a monk at St. Jean d'Angély, which probably accounts for his being called Peter of St. John. Radulf, in his biography of Peter the Venerable, mentioned that a "Petrus de S. Ioanne" was with Peter the Venerable both at Sauxillanges and at Le Puy on his return from Spain in 1143.[16] Peter the Venerable also dedicated his treatise *Contra eos qui dicunt Christum numquam se in Euangeliis aperte Deum dixisse* to "Petrus de Sancto Ioanne," whom he addressed as "bono et pacifico seni, fratri et filio Petro."[17] It is not certain, however, that all of these refer to Peter of Poitiers, since Peter of St. John was not a rare name and at least one, Prior Peter of the Augustinian abbey of St. John at Sens, praised Peter the Venerable highly in a letter to Bishop Hato of Troyes in 1145/6 and may have known him person-

---

[13] Mabillon, *Annales*, VI, 321, and Lecointre-Dupont, "Pierre de Poitiers," pp. 371–372; cf. *Hist. litt.*, XII, 349, and Pignot, *Cluny*, III, 461 and 465.

[14] *De miraculis*, I, 4, in *Bibl. Clun.*, col. 1253 B.

[15] Paris, Bibl. nat., Latin 14463, fol. 124ᵛ. On this manuscript, see Constable, in *Petrus Ven.*, pp. 220–223.

[16] *Ampl. Coll.*, VI, 1197 D and 1199–1200.

[17] *Bibl. Clun.*, cols. 965–966.

ally.[18] The "good and peaceful old man" to whom the *Contra eos qui dicunt* was dedicated does not sound like Peter of Poitiers, whom Peter the Venerable described in Letter 124 as a young man. "I am already a veteran," he wrote, "and leave the fighting to you youngsters." This may be a joke, however; and the balance of probability suggests that the Peter of St. John mentioned in these sources was the same as Peter of Poitiers.

Besides the passage in the *De miraculis*, the only reliable sources for the early life of Peter of Poitiers are his panegyric in honor of Peter the Venerable and the two letters, 26 and 58, addressed to him by Peter the Venerable. Peter of Poitiers wrote in his introduction to the collection of poems and letters that he had "corrected and edited those verses which I wrote long ago, at the time when you 'brought me up out of an horrible pit, out of the miry clay' (Ps. 40.2), in honor both of the Almighty Creator, from whom you have all good things, and of yourself."[19] This shows that the panegyric was revised at least once. Its different sections, furthermore, may have been written at different times; its style is enigmatic; and its factual content is buried in a mass of flowery language, classical allusions, and figures of speech. Under this finery, however, is an account of the early meetings of Peter of Poitiers with Peter the Venerable.

The poem was apparently written on the occasion of Peter the Venerable's second visit to Aquitaine. On his first visit, in 1125,[20] he had met and probably received the monastic profession of Peter of Poitiers, who at that time was presumably a monk at St. Jean d'Angély and who described the occasion as follows:

> Oh how joyful was that day for me!
> Each year I shall celebrate that day,
> When you yourself became my Father and my Lord.[21]

Peter the Venerable promised at that time to take Peter of Poitiers away with him:

---

[18] On this Peter of St. John, see Constable, in *Petrus Ven.*, pp. 42–43, and Appendix N. There is another Peter of St. John in *Chartes et documents pour servir à l'histoire de l'abbaye de Saint-Maixent*, ed. Alfred Richard (Archives historiques du Poitou, 16 and 18; Poitiers, 1886) I, 313, no. 287 (1125/9). A "Petrus de sanicto Johanne" appears under 14 February in *Necrologium*, p. 13.

[19] *Bibl. Clun.*, 604 (recte 607) A.

[20] The date of this visit can be established from the *De miraculis*, II, 12, in *Bibl. Clun.*, col. 1311, where Peter the Venerable said that he was in Aquitaine at the time former Abbot Pontius attacked Cluny. A charter in *Cluny*, V, 339–340, no. 3983, confirms that Peter was away from Cluny and that Prior Bernard was in charge of the abbey on 11 July 1125. Cf. Richard, *Comtes de Poitou*, II, 25.

[21] *Bibl. Clun.*, col. 611 A.

> ... leaving you uttered these final words,
> Which I still cherish as a solemn pledge, as from a father:
> "Peter, I am leaving but shall soon receive you; cease to weep;
> Soon you will be mine."

The joy of Peter of Poitiers changed to grief, however, when this promise was not speedily fulfilled:

> Behold I have spent these many years in tears
> And have not seen the promised sweetness of my father.[22]

Finally Peter the Venerable returned to Aquitaine, and Peter of Poitiers apparently wrote the panegyric in order to remind him of his earlier promise. In the section entitled "How he came again to restore peace to the monasteries," Peter of Poitiers wrote:

> Rejoice, oh Poitiers, that your ramparts already shine,
> And you, oh noble hall placed near the walls.
> Although you hold schismatic and seditious men:
> If you seek peace, Peter your peace is here.
> You draw your swords in vain, oh men of Angély;
> All your efforts will be useless.[23]

These words clearly refer not, as Lecointre-Dupont supposed, to the Cluniac schism of 1125,[24] but to the papal schism of 1130-8; and the visit of Peter the Venerable therefore took place some time between 1130, when Bishop William of Poitiers, who recognized Pope Innocent II, was replaced by Peter of Châtellerault, a supporter of the antipope Anacletus II, and 1134, when in the famous meeting at Parthenay, Bernard of Clairvaux won the count of Poitou to the side of Innocent II and so ended the schism in Aquitaine.[25] Between these dates, Poitiers was a center of the antipapal party and was for a time the headquarters of Anacletus's legate, Cardinal-Bishop Gilo of Tusculum,[26] to whom Peter the Venerable sent two letters urging him to change sides. "Where is the Church," he asked in Letter 40, "in a corner of the city of Rome or in the whole world, in a little part of

---

[22] *Bibl. Clun.*, col. 611 BC.

[23] *Bibl. Clun.*, col. 609 AB. Peter the Venerable was apparently already in Poitiers at the time this was written. The monasteries mentioned are Montierneuf, near the walls of Poitiers, and St. Jean d'Angély.

[24] Lecointre-Dupont, "Pierre de Poitiers," p. 372.

[25] On the schism in Aquitaine, see Elphège Vacandard, "Saint Bernard et le schisme d'Anaclet II en France," *Revue des questions historiques*, XLIII (1888) 61-126, esp. pp. 107-121; Richard, *Comtes de Poitou*, II, 18-44; Bloch, "Schism," pp. 159-174; and Hubert Claude, "Un légat pontifical, adversaire de saint Bernard, Girard d'Angoulême," *Bulletin de la Société historique et archéologique de Langres*, XII (No. 156, 1953) 144-148, and in *Mélanges St. Bernard*, pp. 80-94; Schmale, *Schisma*, pp. 230-232; and Janssen, *Legaten*, pp. 5-14 and 19-23, who refers on p. 9 to the troubles at St. Jean d'Angély in 1131.

[26] On Gilo of Tusculum, see Appendix J.

Aquitaine or from ocean to ocean . . . ? Your side is certainly false, if its heritage and possessions are reduced to the towers of Pierleone [Anacletus] and a few miserable bastions (*paucas munitiunculas*) of the count of Poitou." The second letter to Gilo (66) was written later, after the death of Anacletus, but it included a passage mentioning "what was said at Poitiers," which may refer to Peter's visit there and his efforts to heal the schism.[27]

The final section of the panegyric is entitled "How he crossed to the island of Aix," a small island belonging to Cluny off the west coast of France, near the mouth of the Charente, between Oléron and the mainland, on which was built a priory dedicated to St. Martin.[28] Peter of Poitiers described how Peter the Venerable crossed to Aix during a miraculous calm and ended the panegyric with a prayer:

> Remember your servant, oh noble man,
> I pray; bring my hopes to fruition.
> Let me see your Cluniacs with you:
> Thus honor, virtue, and long life to you.[29]

On the basis of the panegyric, therefore, it is possible to say that Peter the Venerable made a second visit to Aquitaine some time between 1130 and 1134 and visited the Cluniac houses in Poitiers, St. Jean d'Angély, and Aix, partly in order, presumably, to win their loyalty to the cause of Innocent II. He probably met Peter of Poitiers at St. Jean d'Angély, the "horrible pit and miry clay" out of which Peter of Poitiers later said he had been rescued and which according to his own account in the panegyric—"You draw your swords in vain, oh men of Angély!"—seems to have been a center of opposition to Peter the Venerable and to Innocent II.[30] To judge from the final section of the panegyric, the two Peters may have traveled together from St. Jean d'Angély to Aix.[31]

This evidence needs to be compared with that in Letters 26 and 58

[27] On Peter's efforts to help Innocent II, see his Letter 39; cf. Berry, in *Petrus Ven.*, pp. 146–147; Schmale, *Schisma*, pp. 165, n. 10, and 222; Janssen, *Legaten*, p. 16; and Ep. 34, n. to p. 113.

[28] Beaunier-Besse, *Abbayes*, III, 162; cf. *Cluny*, IV, 522, no. 3413; Siméon Luce, "Visite par les prieurs de Barbezieux et de Saint-Sauveur de Nevers des monastères de la Congrégation de Cluny situées dans la province de Poitou. 1292," *BEC*, XX (4th ser., V, 1859) 244–245; Evans, *Rom. Arch.*, pp. 30–31; and esp. Berger, *Richard le Poitevin*, pp. 45–47 and 103. Richard had probably lived on the island and gave in the third redaction of his chronicle a description of Aix and an account of the donation of the island to Cluny by Isembert III of Châtel-Aillon. It was a house of some importance, with several dependencies.

[29] *Bibl. Clun.*, col. 615 E.

[30] According to Claude, in *Mélanges St. Bernard*, p. 81, there was greater support for Innocent II in the diocese of Saintes than in the neighboring dioceses of Limoges and Poitiers; cf. Janssen, *Legaten*, p. 9.

[31] There is no reason to agree with Lecointre-Dupont, "Pierre de Poitiers," pp. 373–374, that Peter of Poitiers had been exiled from Montierneuf to Aix.

from Peter the Venerable to Peter of Poitiers.[32] The former is too vague to be of much value. Peter the Venerable complained of his secretary's departure and contrasted his own mundane business with the peace and quiet of Peter of Poitiers.[33] His references to "the many services for which I needed you," to the fact that "I find your absence more troublesome than all my troubles," and his final request that Peter of Poitiers should hurry back "so that I may entrust to a reliable friend what I have not dared write in a letter," all suggest that this letter was written after Peter of Poitiers had entered the service of Peter the Venerable. Letter 58, on the other hand, is more specific. It opens with this statement:

After my conference with the duke of Aquitaine, who is intoxicated with the cup of Babylon and would not drink from that of Christ and who had indulged too deeply in schism to remove the taste with catholic orthodoxy, I decided for many reasons that discretion was the better part of valor and prepared to retreat. I returned not by the route I had come but through the most distant parts of Anjou and Maine [and Normandy], and when I had traveled along almost the whole coast of the Western Ocean, I arrived with my companions in [Ile de] France and celebrated Christmas at Paris.

This information helps to date Peter the Venerable's visit to Aquitaine, because he is known to have been in Paris late in 1133. In a document dated from St.-Martin-des-Champs both by the year of the Incarnation 1133 and in the twelfth year of his abbacy, Peter confirmed an agreement between the prior of St. Martin and King Louis VI, who in a charter dated after 25 October 1133 had granted St.-Denis-de-la-Châtre to St.-Martin-des-Champs in return for Montmartre. Bishop Stephen of Paris also confirmed the arrangement in a document dated after 25 October 1133.[34] Peter the Venerable wrote Letter 58 while he was still in Paris, presumably staying at St.-Martin-des-Champs. He mentioned toward the end of the letter that on the day before Epiphany he had celebrated Mass for the soul of Gerald, the news of whose death had arrived while he was writing the letter.[35] Elsewhere he remarked that he was "frozen by the northern cold."

The combined evidence of the panegyric and Letter 58 thus shows that Peter the Venerable left Cluny in the spring of 1133 and went to

---

[32] Mabillon, *Annales*, VI, 322, was of the opinion that Letter 58 was addressed not to Peter of Poitiers but to some other Peter.

[33] Peter's comparison of himself to a sailor on a stormy sea and of Peter of Poitiers to a spectator on dry land is probably allegorical.

[34] The three charters may be found in Marrier, *Hist. S. Martini*, pp. 326–328, and have been frequently reprinted. Peter's charter is also in *Bibl. Clun.*, cols. 1397–1398. Cf. Luchaire, *Louis VI*, pp. 239–240, nos. 523–524.

[35] On Gerald Le Vert, see Ep. 53, n. to p. 162, l. 10, and Ep. 58, n. to p. 188.

Poitiers, St. Jean d'Angély, and Aix.[36] He probably also visited the other Cluniac houses in the region. His complaint in Letter 58 that he had been "troubled by the attack of bandits, by the murder of my monks, by the partial depopulation of their houses" sounds like the complaint of a visitor to many monasteries. "I am tired," he said, "of litigation and legal disputes." It may have been on this trip to Aquitaine that Mascelin, the son of Godfrey, lord of the castle of Tonnay (Charente), hearing that "the abbot of Cluny, that is, the lord Peter, was coming to these parts," came before him and gave the land for the foundation of the priory of Rosne. "There were with the abbot," the charter ends, "several other monks, namely, Hugh Berardus, the chamberlain of St. Jean d'Angély, Wicardus, the sacristan of Cluny, and Bernard Morellus, the prior of Aix."[37] At Poitiers, Peter apparently met with Gilo of Tusculum, and later he had an interview with William X, count of Poitou and duke of Aquitaine, the principal secular supporter of Anacletus II in France. After the failure of this conference, Peter decided not to travel again across the heart of the region in schism but went north, along the coast, through Anjou, Maine, and Normandy, to Ile de France and Paris, where he spent Christmas, and he presumably returned to Cluny early in 1134.

Meanwhile, apparently at some time between the visit to Aix and the conference with William of Aquitaine, Peter of Poitiers left Peter the Venerable and remained behind in a wooded and mountainous retreat. Peter the Venerable in Letter 58 more than once contrasted his own position in the fields (*campis*: also a wordplay on the name of St.-Martin-des-Champs) with the position of Peter of Poitiers in the mountains, and from this he drew an allegorical contrast between his own lowly occupation with worldly affairs and Peter of Poitiers's lofty concern with spiritual matters. He envied this solitude, which he could find only within himself and not in the busy world around him. He too wanted to be a hermit, but he could only be an "inner" hermit in the middle of an active life.[38] In this spirit he upbraided Peter of Poitiers for his desertion in the hour of need. He accused him of disobedience to the will of his abbot, in spirit if not in letter, since he admitted that he had given Peter of Poitiers permission to remain. Peter of Poitiers had asked for this permission, however, knowing that he was wanted and needed, and he had thus placed his own desires above those of his abbot.

---

[36] Richard, *Comtes de Poitou*, II, 31–32, erroneously dated this visit to Aquitaine in 1131.
[37] *Cluny*, V, 342–343, no. 3988; cf. Beaunier-Besse, *Abbayes*, III, 307.
[38] On Cluniac heremitism, for which this letter is important evidence, see Leclercq, in *Petrus Ven.*, pp. 106–112.

So I obeyed your will, when I saw that you were unwilling to go on, and gave you permission to stay. You therefore changed the proper order: you made the head into the tail; you placed me, upside-down, last and yourself, first; as a son, a disciple, and a monk, you refused to follow your father, master, and abbot. Here am I laboring, while you rest; I am awake, while you sleep; I am weeping, while you are silent; I am fighting, while you relax; I am wandering over the world, while you are sitting on your mountain.

Peter the Venerable also predicted the reply Peter of Poitiers would make to these charges and other arguments designed to persuade him to leave his pleasant retreat. "As the Lord liveth and as thy soul liveth," he will say, adapting to his own uses the reply of Elisha to Elijah, "I will not follow thee." "My native land, to which I am determined never to return, forbids me to follow you," although in the revised version of this letter represented by the "Cluny" tradition, the weaker term *disposui* is found in place of *proposui*. These words imply that Peter of Poitiers had not yet definitely entered the service of Peter the Venerable. Other passages, however, such as the reference to their long and varied conversations, show that the two men had already been closely associated. Later in Letter 58 Peter again remarked: "How often when the doors were closed and no mortal soul admitted, and only He was witness Who is never absent from those thinking and speaking about Him, have we conversed about the blindness and hardness of the human heart, about the various traps set for sinners and the snares of the demons," and other, similar topics. Peter the Venerable, furthermore, definitely spoke of Peter of Poitiers as his servant, although under the circumstances this may mean no more than the natural servitude of a monk to his abbot.

These discrepancies between the panegyric and Letter 58 are hard to reconcile. It is evident that the enthusiasm for the association between the two Peters was equally great on both sides and that the delay which Peter of Poitiers lamented in the panegyric was not owing to any reluctance on the part of Peter the Venerable. Peter of Poitiers may in fact have exaggerated his own eagerness, which may well have been more to leave the region of schism than to take on the responsibilities of a new position; and when the time came he apparently hesitated to leave his life of peace and quiet in order to become the secretary of the Abbot of Cluny. It is more difficult to reconcile the strong implication in the panegyric that there was no permanent association between the two men before 1133 with the references in Letter 58 to their long conversations, to Peter of Poitiers as a servant, and to the fact that he had asked the permission of Peter the Venerable to remain behind. The trip to Aquitaine took some time, however, and the most probable explanation is that Peter of Poitiers joined

Peter the Venerable relatively early in his trip, presumably at St. Jean d'Angély, and accompanied him on his subsequent travels. Once he had left his homeland, however, to which he had sworn never to return, his resolution weakened, and he secured grudging permission to remain in some mountainous retreat while Peter the Venerable went on to his conference with William of Aquitaine and then north. There is no implication in Letter 58 that Peter of Poitiers had yet undertaken any official responsibilities as secretary to his friend and abbot.

Peter the Venerable soon overcame the reluctance of Peter of Poitiers. In Letter 58 he stressed both the duty of obedience and the merit of a life spent in the world rather than in solitary contemplation. "Our entire purpose, wherever we may be," he wrote, "at home or abroad, traveling or still, is to serve the Lord."[39] He had no patience for the unwillingness of Peter of Poitiers to revisit his homeland, where he may have feared the influence of former friends and associates, perhaps the schismatics. "I truly praise," wrote Peter the Venerable, "a careful watch against evils, but never obstinacy, even in worthy matters." He pointed out that many characters in the Bible had led good lives in their native lands and that true virtue lay in the conquest rather than in the avoidance of evil. How long it took for these and other arguments to convince Peter of Poitiers is not known, but it seems reasonable to date his permanent association with Peter the Venerable from 1134.[40]

From this time on it is almost impossible to separate the career of Peter of Poitiers from that of Peter the Venerable. His name appears on no known Cluniac charter either as a witness or as a member of the official *familia* of the abbot, such as his chaplain, chamberlain, and constable.[41] His primary concerns were literary, but he often traveled with Peter the Venerable and may also have been used for a certain amount of personal and confidential business. Prior Theodard of La Charité-sur-Loire wrote to Peter the Venerable in 1134 or 1136, thanking him for sending "the lord Peter, the pattern of your heart ... who brought your heart to our hearts and whose presence gladdened us as much as it pleases you." Peter the Venerable replied to Theodard that he had sent his "dearest brother Peter ... from my side to you" and recommended him warmly to Theodard's love and confidence.[42] This Peter may not have been Peter of Poitiers, but no

---

[39] Cf., however, the somewhat different sentiments on this topic expressed by Peter the Venerable in Letter 20 to the recluse Gilbert.

[40] As in *Hist. litt.*, XII, 350; Lecointre-Dupont, "Pierre de Poitiers," pp. 371–377; and Manitius, *Lat. Lit.*, III, 900.

[41] Cf. Appendix R on officials at Cluny.

[42] Letters 41–42 and notes to Ep. 41.

other suitable Peter is known in the entourage of Peter the Venerable. Peter of Poitiers was certainly in touch with La Chartreuse, since in a letter to Prior Guigo and the Carthusians in 1136/7 Peter the Venerable specifically included greetings from "Peter my notary," and Guigo in his reply wrote that "we also specially greet the lord Peter who is specially inserted in your letter."[43] In two letters to St. Bernard concerning the translation of the Koran and other Islamic works, Peter the Venerable mentioned the work done by "my notary Peter, a learned man [and] beloved son and brother, [who is,] I think, well known to Your Reverence."[44] Peter of Poitiers accompanied Peter the Venerable to Spain in 1142–3 and may even, according to D'Alverny, have remained there after the return of Peter the Venerable in order to supervise the project of translations from the Arabic.[45] If, however, as seems probable, he was the same as the Peter of St. John mentioned by the biographer Radulf, he returned with Peter the Venerable and was with him at Le Puy in May 1143.[46]

Most of his time, however, was spent as a secretary or notary and in writing and revising his own works.[47] Toward the end of his life, Peter of Poitiers appears to have been unable to travel on account of some trouble with his feet.[48] It was this disorder, for instance, that prevented his joining Peter the Venerable and his co-hermits on their retreat in the woods near Cluny, and during this enforced leisure he both copied books for Peter the Venerable and prepared his works for publication. The credit for the survival of several works by Peter the Venerable doubtless belongs to his faithful secretary. It was Peter of Poitiers who collected the letters, arranged the chapters and wrote the introduction to the *Contra Sarracenos*, and assisted in the translations from the Arabic. He seems never to have entirely given up, however, his desire to lead a solitary life as a hermit, a desire which was to some extent shared by Peter the Venerable and which was probably one of the strongest spiritual ties between the two men. Letter 26 may have been written in order to induce Peter of Poitiers to return from another retreat like his wooded hermitage in the hills mentioned in Letter 58. Peter the Venerable evidently felt his absence deeply. "I cannot be unsolicitous for your salvation, which I desire as my own," he wrote,

---

[43] Letters 24–25.

[44] Letter 111 and the *Epistola de translatione*, in *Bibl. Clun.*, col. 1109; cf. Appendix E.

[45] See D'Alverny, "Traductions," pp. 72 and 102–103, on Peter of Poitiers's part in these translations; cf. Kritzeck, in *Petrus Ven.*, pp. 178–179, and *Peter the Venerable*, pp. 60–61, which appeared after this appendix was written.

[46] See n. 16 above. If this identification is correct, he also accompanied Peter the Venerable on one of his visits to Sauxillanges.

[47] Cf. Lecointre-Dupont, "Pierre de Poitiers," pp. 378 ff. and 388–390.

[48] Letters 123–124 and the prefatory letter of Peter of Poitiers to the *Contra Sarracenos*, in *PL*, CLXXXIX, 662.

"and on which account I find your absence more troublesome than all my troubles." There is no reason to believe that this desertion was more than temporary, however; and although nothing specific is known about the later life of Peter of Poitiers, he presumably remained with his friend and master until the death of Peter the Venerable in 1156[49] and afterward stayed on at Cluny, still occupied with his literary activities, until his own death.

---

[49] He worked on the *Contra Sarracenos* while Peter the Venerable was in England in 1155/6.

Additional Note. The article by Angel Ferrari, "El cluniacense Pedro de Poitiers y la 'Chronica Adefonsi Imperatoris' y Poema de Almería," *Boletin de la Real Academia de la Historia*, CLIII (1963) 153–204, unfortunately appeared too late to be used in writing this appendix. Ferrari argues on the basis of content, style, and language that the *Chronica Adefonsi imperatoris* and *Poema de Almería* were written in Cluniac circles and very likely by Peter of Poitiers.

R. OFFICIALS AND FUNCTIONARIES AT CLUNY DURING THE ABBACY OF PETER THE VENERABLE

The priors (or so-called grand priors) on this list should be compared with those on the chronological list given by Maurice Chaume, "Les grands prieurs de Cluny," *Revue Mabillon*, XXVIII (1938) 147–152 (151–152 on the twelfth century).

Adelelmus (Adalelmus)	prior	*St. Martin des Champs*, II, 23, no. 207 (1126/9); *Cluny*, V, 376 and 380, nos. 4020 (1131) and 4023 (1131). He may be the same as the Adalelmus, chamberlain of Cluny, who appears on a document probably of January 1119, in *Paray-le-Monial*, pp. 105–107, no. 207 (cf. introd., p. xv, on the date). Cf. *Necrologium*, p. 32 (19 April).
Ademarus (Aimarus)	sacristan	*Cluny*, V, 367, 474, and 489, nos. 4012 (1149?), 4131 (*ca.* 1147), and 4142 (1149); Chazaud, *Étude*, p. 254 (cf. Appendix D, s.a. 1147). He was sent by Peter to Sicily in 1146 (Letter 131) and accompanied Peter to Italy in 1152, when he was sent back to Cluny with news (Radulf, *Vita*, in *Ampl. Coll.*, VI, 1198 D). Cf. *Necrologium*, p. 14 (18 February).
Arbertus (Albertus, Herbertus)	prior	*Cluny*, V, 408, 410, 427, and 474, nos. 4053 (1136), 4056 (*ca.* 1136), 4074 (1142), and 4131 (*ca.* 1147); *Cart. lyonnais*, I, 32–33, no. 22 (1136); *De miraculis*, II, 17, in *Bibl. Clun.*, col. 1316 C (1135). Cf. *Necrologium*, p. 57 (27 July).
Armannus (Artmannus, Hermannus)	prior	*Cluny*, V, 249, 367, 489, nos. 3898 (n.d.), 4012 (1149?), and 4142 (1149); *Sauxillanges*, no. 961 (1151/2). He was Peter's brother and later became prior of Manglieu: Appendix A.
Arnold	chaplain of Peter the Venerable	*Cluny*, V, 367 and 487, nos. 4012 (1149?) and 4141 (1149). He was sent by Peter on a mission to Eugene III in *ca.* 1149/50 (Letter 158).

Bernard	cellarer	*Cluny*, V, 355, no. 4001 (1128).
Bernard	*famulus* of Peter the Venerable	Radulf, *Vita*, in *Ampl. Coll.*, VI, 1197 E.
Bernard of Uxelles	prior	*Cluny*, V, 279, 283, 305–306, 326, 330, 339, 341, and 511, nos. 3926 (1117), 3929 (1117, as uncle of Bernardus *Grossus* of Uxelles), 3950 (ca. 1120, first as chamberlain, later as prior), 3966 (1123), 3972 (1124), 3983 (1125), 3984 (1125), and 4152 (n.d.); *GC*, X, instr., 168–169 (1127/31); *Clairvaux*, pp. 7–8, no. 5 (1122/31); *Paray-le-Monial*, pp. 105–107 and 108–109, nos. 207 (January 1119) and 209; Baluze, *Auvergne*, II, 53 (during the abbacy of Pontius). *Cluny*, nos. 3929 and 3950, establish that he was the same Bernard who appears as chamberlain of Cluny on *Cluny*, V, 237, 239, 247, 261, and 306, nos. 3886–3887 (1110), 3896 (1110/16), 3913 (ca. 1114, as uncle of Bernard of Uxelles), and 3950 (ca. 1120). According to Chevalier (*Paray-le-Monial*, introd., p. xv), he was previously prior of Paray; but this may be owing to a confusion with another Bernard who was prior of Cluny early in the twelfth century: *Marcigny*, pp. 83–84, no. 114 (1105).
Bonitus	preparer of parchment	Letter 123 (variant reading).
Boso	chamberlain	*Cart. lyonnais*, I, 32–33, no. 22 (1136).
Drogo	constable	*Cluny*, V, 408, no. 4054 (1136); Letter 59 (1134/5).
Durannus	sacristan	*Chartes de St. Bertin* (cited Appendix D, s.a. 1145), I, 84, no. 197. He was probably the messenger Durannus mentioned in Letters 60–61.
Enguizo	chamberlain of Peter the Venerable	*Cluny*, V, 367, 474, 487, and 489, nos. 4012 (1149?), 4131 (ca. 1147), 4141 (1149), and 4142 (1149); *Chartes de St. Bertin*, I, 84, no. 197 (1145); *Bull. Clun.*, p. 60 (1146/7); *PL*, CLXXXIX, 484 (1154); *Liber cartularis . . . monasterii Romanensis*, facsimile ed. with introduction by Albert Bruckner (Umbrae codicum occidentalium, 6; Amsterdam, 1962) fol. 29^r, l. 20 (1154) (cf. F. de

		Gingins-La-Sarra, *Cartulaire de Romainmotier* [Mémoires et documents publiés par la Société de la Suisse romande, 3; Lausanne, 1844] p. 476, who transcribed the name as "foiguironis"); *De miraculis*, II, 26, in *Bibl. Clun.*, col. 1326 B. He was responsible for the negotiations with Hugh Deschaux in 1152 (Ep. 191).
Garnerius	subprior	Ep. 79 (1131/43), n. to p. 214, l. 26.
Gervase	sacristan	*Cluny*, V, 408, no. 4054 (1136).
Gilbert Foliot	prior (?)	Foliot described himself as "Cluniaci prior quidam" in his ep. 269: *Gilberti ... epistolae* (cited p. 252, n. 1, above), I, 366 (quidem *pro* quidam); *Materials for the History of Thomas Becket*, ed. J. C. Robertson (Rolls Series, 67; London, 1875–1885) VII, 556. Since he later became prior of Abbeville, and abbot of Gloucester in 1139, it has been commonly assumed that he was previously prior at Cluny: cf. Round, *Geoffrey*, p. 253 (who suggested claustral prior); Knowles, *Episcopal Colleagues*, p. 40; *ODCC*, p. 511. There is no known reference to him, however, in any Cluniac source.
Girinus	chaplain of Peter the Venerable	*Cluny*, V, 487, no. 4141 (1149).
Godfrey	constable of Peter the Venerable	*Bull. Clun.*, p. 60 (1146/7); *PL*, CLXXXIX, 662.
Guido	*salsamentarius*	*Cluny*, V, 461, no. 4116 (1146).
Hugh	cellarer	*Cluny*, V, 367 and 463, nos. 4012 (1149?) and 4117 (1147). He should not be confused with Hugh of Bissy, who was cellarer of Cluny in 1102: *Marcigny*, p. 170, no. 288, cf. p. 246.
Hugh	claustral prior	Radulf, *Vita*, in *Ampl. Coll.*, VI, 1196 C.
Hugh	infirmarian	*Cluny*, V, 410, no. 4056 (ca. 1136).
Hugh of Crécy	chamberlain	Appendix O.
Humbert	chamberlain	*Cluny*, V, 367, no. 4012 (1149?).
Inbert	chamberlain	*Cluny*, V, 489, no. 4142 (1149), where he appears as the *socius* of the chamberlain Robert.

R. OFFICIALS AND FUNCTIONARIES AT CLUNY 347

Jarentus	almoner	*Cluny*, V, 408 and 410, nos. 4053 (1136) and 4056 (*ca.* 1136). He is probably the Jarentus who appeared as the abbot's chamberlain on *Cluny*, V, 247 and 261, nos. 3896 (1110/16) and 3913 (*ca.* 1114), and as sacristan on *Cluny*, V, 283, no. 3929 (1117), and *Necrologium*, p. 64 (22 August: "Jarento sacrista cluniacensis".) Since the name is unusual, he may be the same as the Jarenton who appeared, without description, on *Cluny*, V, 237 and 239, nos. 3886–3887 (1110); *Clairvaux*, pp. 7–8, no. 5 (1122/31); and *GC*, X, *instr.*, 168–169 (1127/31).
Leontifrid	constable of Peter the Venerable	*Cluny*, V, 487, no. 4141 (1149).
Leotaldus	chaplain of Cluny, dean of St. Hippolyte	*Cluny*, V, 282, 326, and 330, nos. 3928 (1117), 3966 (1123), and 3972 (1124).
Milo	*magister operis* at Cluny, prior of Lieu-Dieu	*Cluny*, V, 487, no. 4141 (1149).
Peter	chamberlain	*Cluny*, V, 355, no. 4001 (1128).
Peter	scribe	*Cluny*, V, 330, no. 3972 (1124).
Peter	subprior	*Cluny*, V, 489, no. 4142 (1149).
Peter of Pithiviers	prior	Appendix Q on Peter of Poitiers, with whom this Peter has been confused; cf. De Lasteyrie, *St. Martial*, p. 99; Chaume, in *Rev. Mabillon*, XXVIII, 152, dating his priorate 1151–56.
Pontius	chamberlain	*Cluny*, V, 367, no. 4012 (1149?).
Raim.	chaplain of Peter the Venerable	*Bull. Clun.*, p. 60 (1146/7).
Rainald	subprior	*Cluny*, V, 367, no. 4012 (1149?).
Robert	chamberlain	*Cluny*, V, 489, no. 4142 (1149).
Savaric	almoner	*Cluny*, V, 418 and 489, nos. 4067 (1139) and 4142 (1149).
Stephen	chamberlain	*Cluny*, V, 428, no. 4074 (1142).
Stephen	priest of Cluny	*Cluny*, V, 330 and 340, nos. 3972 (1124) and 3983 (1125), where he appears with his brother Hugh.
Theobald	messenger	*Epp.* 115 and 123.

Thomas of Northampton	notary of Peter the Venerable	Epp. 45 and 77; Chazaud, *Étude*, p. 254 "Notarius domni abbatis Cluniacensis" (1147; cf. Appendix D, *s.a.* 1147). He is probably the same as master Thomas, Peter's chaplain, who is mentioned in Radulf, *Vita*, in *Ampl. Coll.*, VI, 1197 D and 1199–1200.
Wicardus	sacristan	*Cluny*, V, 343, no. 3988 (1133?). He is probably the same as the chamberlain Wicardus who appears on *Cluny*, V, 291, 292, 293, and 300, nos. 3937–3939 (1119) and 3946 (1120); and Baluze, *Auvergne*, II, 53 (during the abbacy of Pontius). Cf. *Necrologium*, p. 79 (24 October).
Wigo	dean	*Cluny*, V, 326 and 340, nos. 3966 (1123) and 3983 (1125). He is probably the same as the chamberlain Wigo who appears on *Clairvaux*, pp. 7–8, no. 5 (1122/31), and *GC*, X, *instr.*, 168–169 (1127/31).
William	prior	According to the *De miraculis*, II, 25, in *Bibl. Clun.*, col. 1324, William was successively prior of Cluny, abbot of Moissac, and then chamberlain and again prior of Cluny. Chaume, in *Rev. Mabillon*, XXVIII, 152, dated his first priorate about 1133 and his second between 1142 (the latest certain reference to Arbertus) and 1149 (the earliest reference to Armannus). He may possibly be the G. "adjutorem Cluniacensis ordinis, pro quibusdam negotiis nostris" mentioned by Peter in a letter to Suger dated 1147/8 by Brial and Lecoy de la Marche and 1147/9 by Cartellieri: *RHGF*, XV, 645; cf. Suger, *Oeuvres*, p. 293, and Cartellieri, *Suger*, p. 146, no. 159.

Bibliography of Abbreviated Titles

This bibliography is designed to include only works that are cited at least three times in scattered places. A complete list of all authors cited in the Introduction, Notes, and Appendices may be found in the Index of Modern Authors.

AASS	*Acta sanctorum* (Antwerp, Tongerloo, and Brussels, 1643 ff.).
D'Alverny, "Traductions"	M. T. d'Alverny, "Deux traductions latines du Coran au Moyen Age," *Archives d'histoire doctrinale et littéraire du Moyen Age*, XVI (1947–48) 69–131.
Ampl. Coll.	*Veterum scriptorum et monumentorum . . . amplissima collectio*, ed. E. Martène and U. Durand (Paris, 1724–1733).
Analecta mon.	*Analecta monastica* (Studia Anselmiana; Rome, 1948 ff.).
D'Arbois de Jubainville, *Comtes de Champagne*	Henri d'Arbois de Jubainville, *Histoire des ducs et des comtes de Champagne* (Paris-Troyes, 1859–1869).
D'Arbois de Jubainville, *Études*	Henri d'Arbois de Jubainville, *Études sur l'état intérieur des abbayes cisterciennes et principalement de Clairvaux aux XIIe et au XIIIe siècle* (Paris, 1858).
Arnulf of Lisieux, *Letters*	*The Letters of Arnulf of Lisieux*, ed. Frank Barlow (Camden 3rd Series, 61; London, 1939).
Art de vérifier les dates	*L'art de vérifier les dates des faits historiques*, 3rd ed. (Paris, 1783–1787).
Augustine (Gaume ed.)	*S. Aur. Augustini . . . opera omnia* (Paris: Gaume frères, 1836–1838).
Baluze, *Auvergne*	Étienne Baluze, *Histoire généalogique de la maison d'Auvergne* (Paris, 1708).
Baronius, *Annales*	Cesare Baronius, *Annales ecclesiastici*, ed. A. Pagius (Lucca, 1738–1746).
Beaunier-Besse, *Abbayes*	(Dom) Beaunier, *Abbayes et prieurés de l'ancienne France*, ed. J.-M. Besse a.o. (Archives de la France monastique, 1, 4, 7, 10, 12, 14, 15, 17, 19, 36–37, 45; Ligugé-Paris, 1905–1941).

BEC	Bibliothèque de l'École des Chartes.
Bened., Reg.	Benedicti Regula, ed. R. Hanslik (CSEL, 75; Vienna, 1960).
Berger, Richard le Poitevin	Elie Berger, Notice sur divers manuscrits de la Bibliothèque vaticane: Richard le Poitevin (Bibliothèque des Écoles françaises d'Athènes et de Rome, 6; Paris, 1879).
Berlière, Mélanges	Ursmer Berlière, Mélanges d'histoire bénédictine (Maredsous, 1897–1902).
Bernard (Gaume ed.)	Sancti Bernardi... opera omnia (Paris: Gaume frères, 1839).
Bernard (ed. Leclercq)	Sancti Bernardi opera, ed. J. Leclercq, C. H. Talbot, and H. M. Rochais (Rome, 1957 ff.).
Bernard de Clairvaux	Bernard de Clairvaux (Commission d'histoire de l'ordre de Cîteaux, 3; Paris, 1953).
Bernard, Cons. Clun.	Bernard of Cluny, Ordo Cluniacensis, ed. Marquard Herrgott, Vetus disciplina monastica (Paris, 1726) pp. 133–364.
Bernhardi, Konrad III	Wilhelm Bernhardi, Konrad III. (Jahrbücher der deutschen Geschichte; Leipzig, 1883).
Bernhardi, Lothar	Wilhelm Bernhardi, Lothar von Supplinburg (Jahrbücher der deutschen Geschichte; Leipzig, 1879).
Besse, "Ordre"	J.-M. Besse, "L'ordre de Cluny et son gouvernement," Revue Mabillon, I (1905) 5–40, 97–138, 177–194, and II (1906) 1–22.
Beyssac, Chanoines	Jean Beyssac, Les chanoines de l'église de Lyon (Lyons, 1914).
Bibl. Clun.	Bibliotheca Cluniacensis, ed. Martin Marrier and André Duchesne (Paris, 1614). Cf. p. 47 above.
Bligny, Église	Bernard Bligny, L'église et les ordres religieux dans le royaume de Bourgogne aux XIe et XIIe siècles (Collection des cahiers d'histoire publiée par les Universités de Clermont, Lyon, Grenoble, 4; Paris, 1960).
Bloch, "Schism"	Herbert Bloch, "The Schism of Anacletus II and the Glanfeuil Forgeries of Peter the Deacon of Monte Cassino," Traditio, VIII (1952) 159–264.
Bréquigny, Chartes	L.-G. de Bréquigny, Table chronologique des diplômes, chartes, titres et actes imprimés, concernant l'histoire de France (Paris, 1769 ff.).
Bresslau, Urkundenlehre	Harry Bresslau, Handbuch der Urkundenlehre für Deutschland und Italien, 2nd ed. (Leipzig-Berlin, 1912–1960).
Brixius, Kardinalkollegium	Johannes Brixius, Die Mitglieder des Kardinalkollegiums von 1130–1181 (Inaugural-Dissertation... Strassburg; Berlin, 1912).

Bull. Clun.	Bullarium sacri ordinis Cluniacensis [ed. Pierre Symon] (Lyons, 1680).
Canivez, Statuta	Statuta capitulorum generalium ordinis Cisterciensis, ed. J.-M. Canivez (Bibliothèque de la Revue d'histoire ecclésiastique, 9–14; Louvain, 1933–1941).
Cartellieri, Suger	Otto Cartellieri, Abt Suger von Saint-Denis, 1081–1151 (Historische Studien, ed. Ebering, 11; Berlin, 1898).
Cart. lyonnais	Cartulaire lyonnais, ed. M.-C. Guigue (Collection de documents inédits pour servir à l'histoire du Lyonnais; Lyons, 1885–1893).
Cartulaires de Troyes	Collection des principaux cartulaires du diocèse de Troyes, ed. Charles Lalore (Paris-Troyes, 1875–1890).
Caspar, Roger II	Erich Caspar, Roger II. (1101–1154) und die Gründung der normannisch-sicilischen Monarchie (Innsbruck, 1904).
CC	Corpus Christianorum (Turnhout, 1954 ff.).
Chaix de Lavarène, "Bullaire"	A.-C. Chaix de Lavarène (Louis-Antoine Chaix), "Bullaire de l'Auvergne (suite)," Mémoires de l'Académie des sciences, belles-lettres et arts de Clermont-Ferrand, XVIII (1876) 391–455, XIX (1877) 23–134 and 447–615. These and the other articles in the series were published separately as Monumenta pontificia Arverniae (Clermont-Ferrand, 1886), which was not available to me.
Chalandon, Dom. normande	Ferdinand Chalandon, Histoire de la domination normande en Italie et en Sicile (Paris, 1907).
Chassaing, Spicilegium	Augustin Chassaing, Spicilegium Brivatense: Recueil de documents historiques relatifs au Brivadois et à l'Auvergne (Paris, 1886).
Chazaud, Étude	M.-A. Chazaud, Étude sur la chronologie des sires de Bourbon (X^e–XIIIe siècles), ed. Max Fazy (Moulins, 1935).
Chevalier, Bio-bib.	Ulysse Chevalier, Répertoire des sources historiques du Moyen Age: Bio-bibliographie, 2nd ed. (Paris, 1905–1907).
Chevalier, Régeste	Ulysse Chevalier, Régeste dauphinois (Valence-Vienne-Romans, 1912–1926).
Chevalier, Topo-bib.	Ulysse Chevalier, Répertoire des sources historiques du Moyen Age: Topo-bibliographie (Montbéliard, 1894–1903).
Chronicle of Cluny	The chronicle of Cluny, which is printed in the Bibl. Clun., cols. 589–602 (for the years 1122–56) and 1627–1685, was compiled by the grand prior of Cluny, François de Rivo (see Chevalier, Bio-bib., II, 3980), at the request of Jacques d'Amboise, who was abbot of Cluny from about 1481/5 until 1510 (see Bibl. Clun., cols. 1684–1686, and Chevalier, Bio-bib., I, 183). He incorporated much early material, some of which is now lost,

	and it may be used with caution as an original source. The dating of the year from Christmas, for instance, shows that he was citing an early source on the death of Peter the Venerable. Cf. pp. 17, 55, and 75 above.
Cîteaux	*Chartes et documents concernant l'abbaye de Cîteaux, 1098–1182*, ed. Jean Marilier (Bibliotheca Cisterciensis, 1; Rome, 1961).
Clairvaux	*Recueil des chartes de l'abbaye de Clairvaux*, ed. Jean Waquet, fasc. 1 (Troyes, 1950).
Cluny	*Recueil des chartes de l'abbaye de Cluny*, ed. Auguste Bernard and Alexandre Bruel (Collection de documents inédits sur l'histoire de France; Paris, 1876–1903).
CMH	*The Cambridge Medieval History* (Cambridge, Eng., 1911–1936).
Cons. Farf.	*Consuetudines Farfenses*, ed. Bruno Albers (Consuetudines monasticae, 1; Stuttgart-Vienna, 1900).
Constable, "Cluniac Tithes"	Giles Constable, "Cluniac Tithes and the Controversy between Gigny and Le Miroir," *Rev. Bén.*, LXX (1960) 591–624.
Constable, "Langres"	Giles Constable, "The Disputed Election at Langres in 1138," *Traditio*, XIII (1957) 119–152.
Constable, Monastic Tithes	Giles Constable, *Monastic Tithes from Their Origins to the Twelfth Century* (Cambridge Studies in Medieval Life and Thought, n.s. 10; Cambridge, Eng., 1964).
Constable, "Second Crusade"	Giles Constable, "The Second Crusade as Seen by Contemporaries," *Traditio*, IX (1953) 213–279.
Côte, Souvigny	Léon Côte, *Contributions à l'histoire de prieuré clunisien de Souvigny* (Moulins, 1942)—not to be confused with his larger *Histoire du prieuré clunisien de Souvigny*.
Cottineau, Répertoire	L. H. Cottineau, *Répertoire topo-bibliographique des abbayes et prieurés* (Mâcon, 1939).
CSEL	*Corpus scriptorum ecclesiasticorum latinorum* (Vienna and Prague, 1866 ff.).
Cucherat, Cluny	F. Cucherat, *Cluny au onzième siècle*, 2nd ed. (Autun, [1873]).
Curtius, Literature	Ernst Robert Curtius, *European Literature and the Latin Middle Ages*, trans. W. R. Trask (New York, 1953).
DACL	*Dictionnaire d'archéologie chrétienne et de liturgie* (Paris, 1907–1953).
Delisle, Fonds	Léopold Delisle, *Inventaire des manuscrits de la Bibliothèque nationale: Fonds de Cluni* (Paris, 1884).
Deutsch, Synode von Sens	S. Martin Deutsch, *Die Synode von Sens 1141 und die Verurteilung Abälards* (Berlin, 1880).

Devic and Vaissete, *Languedoc*	[Claude Devic and Joseph Vaissete] *Histoire générale de Languedoc* (Paris, 1730–1745), new ed. (Toulouse, 1866–1904). The new edition has been used here only for its additional material.
DHGE	*Dictionnaire d'histoire et de géographie ecclésiastiques* (Paris, 1912 ff.).
DThC	*Dictionnaire de théologie catholique* (Paris, 1903–1950).
Du Boulay, *Hist. univ. Paris.*	C. E. Du Boulay, *Historia universitatis Parisiensis* (Paris, 1665–1673).
Duby, *Mâconnais*	Georges Duby, *La société aux XIe et XIIe siècles dans la région mâconnaise* (Bibliothèque générale de l'École pratique des hautes études, VIe section; Paris, 1953).
Duchesne, *Scriptores*	*Historiae Francorum scriptores*, ed. André Duchesne (Paris, 1636–1649).
Duckett, *Cluni*	*Charters and Records among the Archives of the Ancient Abbey of Cluni, from 1077 to 1534*, ed. G. F. Duckett (Lewes, 1888).
Dugdale, *Monasticon*	William Dugdale, *Monasticon anglicanum*, ed. John Caley, Henry Ellis, and Bulkeley Bandinel (London, 1846).
Evans, *Mon. Life*	Joan Evans, *Monastic Life at Cluny, 910–1157* (Oxford, 1931).
Evans, *Rom. Arch.*	Joan Evans, *The Romanesque Architecture of the Order of Cluny* (Cambridge, Eng., 1938).
Fazy, *Origines*	Max Fazy, *Les origines du Bourbonnais* (Moulins, 1924).
Fourier Bonnard, *St. Victor*	Fourier Bonnard, *Histoire de l'Abbaye royale et de l'ordre des chanoines réguliers de St-Victor de Paris* (Paris, 1904–1908).
Gams, *Series*	P. B. Gams, *Series episcoporum ecclesiae catholicae* (Regensburg, 1873).
Gaussin, *La Chaise-Dieu*	Pierre-Roger Gaussin, *L'Abbaye de La Chaise-Dieu (1043–1518)* (Paris, 1962).
GC	*Gallia christiana* (Paris, 1656), new ed. (Paris, 1715–1865). All references are to the new edition except when stated.
GC nov.	*Gallia christiana novissima*, ed. J.-H. Albanés and U. Chevalier (Montbéliard and Valence, 1899–1920).
De Ghellinck, *Essor*	J. de Ghellinck, *L'essor de la littérature latine au XIIe siècle* (Museum Lessianum: Section historique, 4–5; Brussels-Paris, 1946).
Giry, *Manuel*	A. Giry, *Manuel de diplomatique* (Paris, 1894).
Gleber, *Eugen III*	Helmut Gleber, *Papst Eugen III. (1145–1153)* (Beiträge zur mittelalterlichen und neueren Geschichte, 6; Jena, 1936).

Gomot, *Mozat*	Hippolyte Gomot, *Histoire de l'abbaye royale de Mozat* (Paris, 1872).
Graham, *Vézelay*	Rose Graham, *An Abbot of Vézelay* (London, 1918).
La Grande-Chartreuse	*Recueil des plus anciens actes de la Grande-Chartreuse (1086–1196)*, ed. Bernard Bligny (Grenoble, 1958).
Gratian, *Decretum*	*Corpus iuris canonici*, ed. Emil Richter and Emil Friedberg, pt. I (Leipzig, 1879).
Grebenc, "Itinerar"	Maver Grebenc, "Itinerar Sv. Bernarda v Letih Anakletove Shizme: 1130–1138," *Zgodovinski Zbornik*, 1959, pp. 7–69.
Gregory, *Dial.* (ed. Moricca)	*Gregorii Magni dialogi*, ed. Umberto Moricca (Fonti per la storia d'Italia, 57; Rome, 1924).
Gregory, *ed. cit.*	*Sancti Gregorii . . . opera omnia* (Paris, 1705).
Guibert of Nogent, *Vita*	Guibert of Nogent, *De vita sua*, ed. Georges Bourgin (Collection de textes pour servir à l'étude et à l'enseignement de l'histoire, 40; Paris, 1907).
Hallinger, *Gorze-Kluny*	Kassius Hallinger, *Gorze-Kluny* (Studia Anselmiana, 22–25; Rome, 1950–51).
Haskins, *Mediaeval Culture*	Charles H. Haskins, *Studies in Mediaeval Culture* (Oxford, 1929).
Hébert, "Hugues"	P. Hébert, "Un archévêque de Rouen au XIIe siècle: Hugues III d'Amiens, 1130–1164," *Revue des questions historiques*, LXIV (1898) 325–371.
Hefele-Leclercq, *Conciles*	Charles-Joseph [Karl Josef] Hefele, *Histoire des conciles*, trans. and ed. Henri Leclercq (Paris, 1907 ff.).
Hirsch, *Ludwig VII*	Richard Hirsch, *Studien zur Geschichte König Ludwigs VII. von Frankreich (1119–1160)* (Inaugural-Dissertation . . . Leipzig; Leipzig, 1892).
Hist. litt.	*Histoire lit[t]éraire de la France* (Paris, 1733–1949).
Histoire de l'Église	*Histoire de l'Église*, ed. Augustin Fliche and Victor Martin (Paris, 1934 ff.).
Hugh of Poitiers, *Hist. Viz.*	Hugh of Poitiers, *Historia Vizeliacensis*, in *Spicilegium*, II, 498–560, and (for some missing and partly destroyed sections in MS. Auxerre 106) Aimé Chérest, "Étude historique sur Vézelay: Pièce justificative, V," *Bulletin de la Société des sciences historiques et naturelles de l'Yonne*, XVI (1862) 471–525 and, separately, *Vézelay* (Auxerre, 1863–1868) I, 307–361.
Imbart de la Tour *Élections*	Pierre Imbart de la Tour, *Les élections épiscopales dans l'église de France du IXe au XIIe siècle* (Paris, 1891).
Italia pontificia	*Italia pontificia*, ed. P. F. Kehr (Regesta pontificum Romanorum; Berlin, 1906 ff.).

Jacotin, *Polignac*	Antoine Jacotin, *Preuves de la maison de Polignac* (Paris, 1898–1906).
Janauschek, *Origines*	Leopold Janauschek, *Originum Cisterciensium tomus I* (Vienna, 1877).
Janssen, *Legaten*	Wilhelm Janssen, *Die päpstlichen Legaten in Frankreich vom Schisma Anaklets II. bis zum Tode Coelestins III. (1130–1198)* (Kölner historische Abhandlungen, 6; Cologne-Graz, 1961).
JL	Philip Jaffé, *Regesta pontificum Romanorum*, ed. S. Löwenfeld, F. Kaltenbrunner, and P. Ewald (Leipzig, 1885–1888).
John of Salisbury, *Hist. pont.*	John of Salisbury, *Historia pontificalis*, trans. and ed. Marjorie Chibnall (Nelson's Medieval Texts; Edinburgh, 1956).
John of Salisbury, *Letters*	*The Letters of John of Salisbury*, ed. W. J. Millor, H. E. Butler, and C. N. L. Brooke, I (Nelson's Medieval Texts; Edinburgh, 1955).
Klewitz, *Reformpapsttum*	Hans-Walter Klewitz, *Reformpapsttum und Kardinalkolleg* (Darmstadt, 1957). This work contains reprints of three important articles, including "Die Entstehung des Kardinalkollegiums," *Zeitschrift der Savigny-Stiftung für Rechtsgeschichte*, LVI, Kan. Abt. XXV (1936) 115–221, and "Das Ende des Reformpapsttums," *Deutsches Archiv*, III (1939) 372–412.
Knowles, *Episcopal Colleagues*	David Knowles, *The Episcopal Colleagues of Archbishop Thomas Becket* (Ford Lectures, 1949; Cambridge, Eng., 1951).
Knowles, *Monastic Order*	David Knowles, *The Monastic Order in England* (Cambridge, Eng., 1940).
Knowles and Hadcock, *Religious Houses*	David Knowles and R. Neville Hadcock, *Medieval Religious Houses: England and Wales* (London–New York–Toronto, 1953).
Kritzeck, *Peter the Venerable*	James Kritzeck, *Peter the Venerable and Islam* (Princeton Oriental Studies, 23; Princeton, 1964).
Labbé, *Nova bibl.*	Philip Labbé, *Nova bibliotheca manuscriptorum librorum* (Paris, 1657).
La Charité	*Cartulaire du prieuré de la Charité-sur-Loire*, ed. R. de Lespinasse (Nevers-Paris, 1887).
Lamma, *Momenti*	Paolo Lamma, *Momenti di storiografia cluniacense* (Istituto Storico Italiano per il Medio Evo: Studi storici, 42–44; Rome, 1961).
Langlois, "Formulaires"	Ch.-V. Langlois, "Formulaires de lettres du XIIe, du XIIIe et du XIVe siècle," *Notices et extraits des manuscrits de la Bibliothèque nationale*, XXXIV.1 (1891) 1–32 [article

	I], 305–322 [II], XXXIV.2 (1895) 1–18 [III], 19–29 [IV], XXXV.2 (1897) 409–434 [V], and 793–830 [VI].
De Lasteyrie, St. Martial	Charles de Lasteyrie, *L'abbaye de Saint-Martial de Limoges* (Paris, 1901).
Leclercq, *Amour des lettres*	Jean Leclercq, *L'Amour des lettres et le désir de Dieu* (Paris, 1957).
Leclercq, *Études*	Jean Leclercq, *Études sur saint Bernard et le texte de ses écrits* (Analecta sacri ordinis Cisterciensis, IX.1–2; Rome, 1953).
Leclercq, *Pierre le Vén.*	Jean Leclercq, *Pierre le Vénérable* (Figures monastiques; Abbaye S. Wandrille, 1946).
Leclercq, *Recueil*	Jean Leclercq, *Recueil d'études sur saint Bernard et ses écrits*, I (Storia e letteratura, 92; Rome, 1962).
Lecointre-Dupont, "Pierre de Poitiers"	Lecointre-Dupont, "Notice sur Pierre de Poitiers, grand prieur de Cluni, abbé de Saint-Martial de Limoges," *Mémoires de la Société des Antiquaires de l'Ouest*, IX (1842) 369–391.
Le Couteulx, *Ann. Carth.*	Charles Le Couteulx, *Annales ordinis Cartusiensis* (Montreuil-sur-Mer, 1887–1891).
Lesne, *Prop. ecc.*	Émile Lesne, *Histoire de la propriété ecclésiastique en France* (Mémoires et travaux publiés par des professeurs des Facultés catholiques de Lille, 6, 19, 30, 34, 44, 46, 50, 53; Lille, 1910–1943).
Letonnelier, *Cluny*	Gaston Letonnelier, *L'abbaye exempte de Cluny et le Saint-Siège* (Archives de la France monastique, 22; Ligugé-Paris, 1923).
Letters of St. Bernard	*The Letters of St. Bernard of Clairvaux*, trans. Bruno Scott James (Chicago, 1953).
Lettres des premiers Chartreux	*Lettres des premiers Chartreux*, I: *S. Bruno, Guiges, S. Anthelme* (Sources chrétiennes, 88; Paris, 1962).
L'Huillier, *Saint Hugues*	Albert L'Huillier, *Vie de Saint Hugues, abbé de Cluny, 1024–1109* (Solesmes, 1888).
Lorain, *Cluny*	Prosper Lorain, *Essai historique sur l'abbaye de Cluny* (Dijon, 1839).
Louis, *Girart*	René Louis, *Girart, comte de Vienne* (Auxerre, 1946–47).
Luchaire, *Études*	Achille Luchaire, *Études sur quelques manuscrits de Rome et de Paris* (Université de Paris: Bibliothèque de la Faculté des Lettres, 8; Paris, 1899).
Luchaire, *Louis VI*	Achille Luchaire, *Louis VI le Gros* (Paris, 1890).
Luchaire, *Louis VII*	Achille Luchaire, *Études sur les actes de Louis VII* (Paris, 1885).
Mabillon, *Annales*	Jean Mabillon, *Annales ordinis s. Benedicti* (Lucca, 1739–1745).

Mahn, *Ordre cist.*	Jean-Berthold Mahn, *L'ordre cistercien et son gouvernement des origines au milieu du XIIIe siècle (1098–1265)* (Bibliothèque des Écoles françaises d'Athènes et de Rome, 161; Paris, 1945 [reprinted 1951]).
Maitland, *Dark Ages*	S. R. Maitland, *The Dark Ages*, new ed. with introd. by Frederick Stokes (London, 1889).
Manitius, *Lat. Lit.*	Max Manitius, *Geschichte der lateinischen Literatur des Mittelalters* (Handbuch der Altertumswissenschaft, IX.2.1–3; Munich, 1911–1931).
Manrique, *Ann. Cist.*	Angel Manrique, *Cisterciensium ... annalium a condito Cistercio, tomus I* [–III] (Lyons, 1642–1649).
Manselli, "Alberico"	Raoul Manselli, "Alberico, cardinale vescovo d'Ostia e la sua attività di legato pontifico," *Archivio della Società romana di Storia patria*, LXXVIII (3rd ser., IX; 1955) 23–68.
Mansi, *Concilia*	J. D. Mansi, *Sacrorum conciliorum nova et amplissima collectio* (Florence and Venice, 1759 ff.).
Map, *De nugis curialium*	Walter Map, *De nugis curialium*, ed. M. R. James (Anecdota Oxoniensia: Mediaeval and Modern Series, 14; Oxford, 1914).
Marcigny	*Le cartulaire de Marcigny-sur-Loire (1045–1144): Essai de reconstitution d'un manuscrit disparu*, ed. Jean Richard (Analecta Burgundica; Dijon, 1957).
Marrier, *Hist. S. Martini*	Martin Marrier, *Monasterii regalis S. Martini de Campis Paris ... historia* (Paris, 1637).
Martin, *Conciles*	J.-B. Martin, *Conciles et bullaire du diocèse de Lyon* (Lyons, 1905).
Mélanges St. Bernard	*Mélanges Saint Bernard* (XXIVe Congrès de l'Association bourguignonne des sociétés savantes; Dijon, 1954).
MGH	*Monumenta Germaniae historica.*
Millénaire de Cluny	*Millénaire de Cluny* (Mâcon, 1910).
MIÖG	*Mitteilungen des Instituts für österreichische Geschichtsforschung.*
Misc. Ehrle	*Miscellanea Francesco Ehrle* (Studi e Testi, 37–42; Rome, 1924).
MÖIG	= MIÖG from 1923–1942.
Molesme	*Cartulaires de l'abbaye de Molesme*, ed. Jacques Laurent (Collection de documents publiés avec le concours de la Commission des antiquités de la Côte-d'Or, 1; Paris, 1907–1911).
Molinier, *Obituaires*	Auguste Molinier, *Les obituaires français au Moyen Age* (Paris, 1890).
De Moreau, *Église en Belgique*	Édouard de Moreau, *Histoire de l'église en Belgique*, 2nd ed. (Museum Lessianum: Section historique, 1–3, 11, 12, 15; Brussels, 1945 ff.).

Morey and Brooke, *Foliot*	Adrian Morey and C. N. L. Brooke, *Gilbert Foliot and His Letters* (Cambridge Studies in Medieval Life and Thought, n.s. 11; Cambridge, Eng., 1965).
Morigny	*La chronique de Morigny (1095–1152)*, ed. Léon Mirot, 2nd ed. (Collection de textes pour servir à l'étude et à l'enseignement de l'histoire, 41; Paris, 1912).
Necrologium	*Das Necrologium des Cluniacenser-Priorates Münchenwiler (Villars-les-Moines)*, ed. Gustav Schnürer (Collectanea Friburgensia, n.f. 10; Fribourg, 1909). This necrology in fact comes from Marcigny and is probably based on the necrology used at Cluny during the abbacy of Hugh: see J. Wollasch, "Qu'a signifié Cluny pour l'abbaye de Moissac?" *Moissac et l'Occident au XIe siècle* (Toulouse, 1964) pp. 15-21.
Obituaires	*Recueil des historiens de la France: Obituaires*, I–IV (Sens, I–IV) and V (Lyons, I) (Paris, 1902–1933).
ODCC	*The Oxford Dictionary of the Christian Church*, ed. F. L. Cross (Oxford, 1957).
Ordericus Vitalis, *Hist. ecc.*	Ordericus Vitalis, *Historia ecclesiastica*, ed. A. Le Prévost and L. Delisle (Société de l'histoire de France; Paris, 1838–1855).
Osbert of Clare, *Letters*	*The Letters of Osbert of Clare, Prior of Westminster*, ed. E. W. Williamson (Oxford, 1929).
Otto, *Sprichwörter*	August Otto, *Die Sprichwörter und sprichwörtlichen Redensarten der Römer* (Leipzig, 1890).
Oursel, *Dispute*	Raymond Oursel, *La dispute et la grace: Essai sur la rédemption d'Abélard* (Publications de l'Université de Dijon, 19; Paris, 1959).
Pacaut, *Élections*	Marcel Pacaut, *Louis VII et les élections épiscopales dans le royaume de France* (Bibliothèque de la Société d'histoire ecclésiastique de la France; Paris, 1957).
Paray-le-Monial	*Cartulaire du prieuré de Paray-le-Monial*, ed. Ulysse Chevalier (Collection de cartulaires dauphinois, 8.2; Paris, 1890).
Paris	*Cartulaire général de Paris*, ed. Robert de Lasteyrie, I (Histoire générale de Paris; Paris, 1887).
Peter the Venerable, *Statuta*	Cited from the new edition to appear in the *Corpus consuetudinum monasticarum*.
Petit, *Ducs de Bourgogne*	Ernest Petit, *Histoire des ducs de Bourgogne de la race Capétienne* (Dijon, 1885–Paris, 1905).
Petrus Ven.	*Petrus Venerabilis, 1156–1956: Studies and Texts Commemorating the Eighth Centenary of his Death*, ed. Giles Constable and James Kritzeck (Studia Anselmiana, 40; Rome, 1956).

PG	*Patrologia graeca*, ed. J.-P. Migne (Paris, 1857–1866).
Pignot, *Cluny*	J.-Henri Pignot, *Histoire de l'ordre de Cluny depuis la fondation de l'abbaye jusqu'à la mort de Pierre-le-Vénérable* (Autun-Paris, 1868).
PL	*Patrologia latina*, ed. J.-P. Migne (Paris, 1844–1864).
Poole, *Studies*	Reginald L. Poole, *Studies in Chronology and History*, ed. Austin L. Poole (Oxford, 1934).
PU	*Papsturkunden* volumes published in the *Abhandlungen der [königlichen] Gesellschaft [Akademie] der Wissenschaften zu Göttingen*, Phil.-hist. Klasse.
Rassow, "Kanzlei"	Peter Rassow, "Die Kanzlei St. Bernhards von Clairvaux," *SMGBOZ*, XXXIV (n.f. 3; 1913) 63–103 and 243–293.
Regesta Regum Anglo-Norm.	*Regesta Regum Anglo-Normannorum, 1066–1154*, I, ed. H. W. C. Davis and R. J. Whitwell, II, ed. Charles Johnson and H. A. Cronne (Oxford, 1913–1956).
Rev. Bén.	*Revue Bénédictine*.
Rev. hist. ecc.	*Revue d'histoire ecclésiastique*.
RHGF	*Recueil des historiens des Gaules et de la France* (Paris, 1738–1904).
Richard, *Comtes de Poitou*	Alfred Richard, *Histoire des comtes de Poitou, 778–1204* (Paris, 1903).
Röhricht, *Regesta*	Reinhold Röhricht, *Regesta regni Hierosolymitani (MXCVII–MCCXCI)* (Innsbruck, 1893–1904).
Round, *Geoffrey*	J. H. Round, *Geoffrey de Mandeville* (London, 1892).
St. Flour	*Cartulaire du prieuré de Saint-Flour*, ed. Marcellin Boudet (Collection de documents historiques publiés par ordre de S.A.S. le prince Albert Ier prince souverain de Monaco; Monaco, 1910).
St. Martin des Champs	*Recueil de chartes et documents de Saint-Martin-des-Champs*, ed. J. Depoin (Archives de la France monastique, 13, 16, 18, 20–1; Ligugé-Paris, 1912–1921).
Saltman, *Theobald*	Avrom Saltman, *Theobald, Archbishop of Canterbury* (University of London Historical Studies, 2; London, 1956).
Satabin, "Lettre"	J. Satabin, "Une lettre inédite de saint Bernard," *Études religieuses*, LXII (May–August, 1894) 321–327, reprinted without notes in *BEC*, LV (1894) 563–564.
Sauxillanges	*Cartulaire de Sauxillanges*, ed. Henry Doniol, in *Mémoires de l'Académie des sciences, belles-lettres et arts de Clermont-Ferrand*, n.s. III (1861) 465–1199 and separately (Clermont-Ferrand and Paris, 1864).
Schmale, *Schisma*	Franz-Josef Schmale, *Studien zum Schisma des Jahres 1130* (Forschungen zur kirchlichen Rechtsgeschichte und zum Kirchenrecht, 3; Cologne-Graz, 1961).

Schönbach, *Erzählungsliteratur*	Anton E. Schönbach, *Studien zur Erzählungsliteratur des Mittelalters* (Sitzungsberichte der kaiserlichen Akademie der Wissenschaften, Phil.-hist. Cl., CXXXIX.5; Vienna, 1898).
Schreiber, *Gemeinschaften*	Georg Schreiber, *Gesammelte Abhandlungen*, I: *Gemeinschaften des Mittelalters* (Münster in Westf., 1948).
Severt, *Chronologia*	Jacques Severt, *Chronologia historica ... archiantistitum Lugdunensis archiepiscopatus*, 2nd ed. (Lyons, 1628).
Sikes, *Abailard*	J. G. Sikes, *Peter Abailard* (Cambridge, Eng., 1932).
Singer, *Sprichwörter*	Samuel Singer, *Sprichwörter des Mittelalters* (Berne, 1944–1947).
SMGBOZ	*Studien und Mitteilungen zur Geschichte des Benediktinerordens und seiner Zweige.*
Spicilegium	*Spicilegium*, ed. Luc d'Achery, 2nd ed. (Paris, 1723).
Stevenson, *Proverbs*	Burton Stevenson, *The Home Book of Proverbs, Maxims, and Familiar Phrases* (New York, 1948).
Suger, *Louis le Gros*	Suger, *Vie de Louis VI le Gros*, trans. and ed. Henri Waquet (Les classiques de l'histoire de France au Moyen Age, 11; Paris, 1929).
Suger, *Oeuvres*	*Oeuvres complètes de Suger*, ed. A. Lecoy de la Marche (Société de l'histoire de France; Paris, 1867).
Tellenbach, "Pontius"	Gerd Tellenbach, "Der Sturz des Abtes Pontius von Cluny und seine geschichtliche Bedeutung," *Quellen und Forschungen aus italienischen Archiven und Bibliotheken*, XLII–XLIII (1963) 13–55.
Thes. nov.	*Thesaurus novus anecdotorum*, ed. E. Martène and U. Durand (Paris, 1717).
Ughelli, *Italia sacra*	Ferdinando Ughelli, *Italia sacra*, 2nd ed. (Venice, 1717–1722).
Ulric, *Cons. Clun.*	Ulric of Cluny, *Consuetudines Cluniacenses*, in PL, CXLIX, 633–778.
Vacandard, *St. Bernard*	Elphège Vacandard, *Vie de saint Bernard* (Paris, 1895). The second and later "editions" of this justly celebrated work are in reality reprints, with a few corrections but omitting many of the longer notes, five of the eight appendices, and the index.
De Valous, *Mon. clun.*	Guy de Valous, *Le monachisme clunisien des origines au XVe siècle* (Archives de la France monastique, 39–40; Ligugé-Paris, 1935).
Virey, *Églises*	Jean Virey, *Les églises romanes de l'ancien diocèse de Mâcon: Cluny et sa région* (Mâcon, 1935).
Voss, *Heinrich von Blois*	Lena Voss, *Heinrich von Blois, Bischof von Winchester (1129–71)* (Historische Studien, ed. Ebering, 210; Berlin, 1932).

Wattenbach-Holtzmann, *Geschichtsquellen*	Wilhelm Wattenbach, *Deutschlands Geschichtsquellen im Mittelalter: Deutsche Kaiserzeit*, ed. Robert Holtzmann (Tübingen, 1948).
Werner, *Sprichwörter*	Jakob Werner, *Lateinische Sprichwörter und Sinnsprüche des Mittelalters* (Sammlung mittellateinischer Texte, 3; Heidelberg, 1912).
Williams, *Monastic Studies*	Watkin Williams, *Monastic Studies* (Publications of the University of Manchester, 262: Historical Series, 76; Manchester, 1938).
Williams, *St. Bernard*	Watkin Williams, *Saint Bernard of Clairvaux* (University of Manchester Historical Series, 69; Manchester, 1935).
Wilmart, "Bibliothèque"	André Wilmart, "L'ancienne bibliothèque de Clairvaux," *Mémoires de la Société académique de l'Aube*, LXXXI (1917) 127–190 and separately paginated offprint, which is cited here.
Wilmart, "Riposte"	André Wilmart, "Une riposte de l'ancien monachisme au manifeste de S. Bernard," *Rev. Bén.*, XLVI (1934) 296–344.
Yonne	Maximilien Quantin, *Cartulaire général de l'Yonne* (Auxerre, 1854–1860).

Concordance

Errors in pagination are corrected in square brackets.

Present edition	1522 edition (number and folio)	Bibl. Clun. (number and column)	PL, CLXXXIX (number and column)
1	III.1 (85ᵛ)	I.1 (621)	I.1 (61)
2	III.2 (86)	I.2 (622)	I.2 (66)
3	III.3 (86)	I.3 (624)	I.3 (69)
4	III.4 (86ᵛ)	I.4 (624)	I.4 (70)
5	III.5 (87)	I.5 (626)	I.5 (72)
6	III.6 (87ᵛ)	I.6 (627)	I.6 (74)
7	III.7 (88)	I.7 (629)	I.7 (75)
8	III.8 (88ᵛ)	I.8 (630)	I.8 (76)
9	III.9 (88ᵛ)	I.9 (630)	I.9 (77)
10	III.10 (89)	I.10 (632)	I.10 (78)
11	III.11 (89)	I.11 (632)	I.11 (79)
12	III.12 (89ᵛ)	I.12 (633)	I.12 (80)
13	III.13 (89ᵛ)	I.13 (633)	I.13 (81)
14	III.14 (90)	I.14 (635)	I.14 (83)
15	III.15 (90)	I.15 (635)	I.15 (84)
16	III.16 (90ᵛ)	I.16 (636)	I.16 (85)
17	III.17 (91)	I.17 (637)	I.17 (87)
18	III.18 (91)	I.18 (638)	I.18 (87)
19	III.19 (91ᵛ)	I.19 (639)	I.19 (88)
20	III.20 (91ᵛ)	I.20 (640)	I.20 (89)
21	III.21 (95)	I.21 (649)	I.21 (101)
22	III.22 (95)	I.22 (650)	I.22 (101)
23	III.23 (95)	I.23 (650)	I.23 (102)
24	III.24 (95ᵛ)	I.24 (651)	I.24 (103)
25	III.25 (96ᵛ)	I.25 (653)	I.25 (106)
26	III.26 (96ᵛ)	I.26 (654)	I.26 (106)
27	III.27 (97)	I.27 (656)	I.27 (108)

Present edition	1522 edition (number and folio)	Bibl. Clun. (number and column)	PL, CLXXXIX (number and column)
28	III.28 (97^v)	I.28 (657)	I.28 (112)
29	III.29 (110^v)	I.29 (695)	I.29 (159)
30	III.30 (112[111]^v)	I.30 (697)	I.30 (161)
31	III.31 (112[111]^v)	I.31 (698)	I.31 (162)
32	III.32 (112)	I.32 (699)	I.32 (163)
33	III.33 (112^v)	I.33 (700)	I.33 (164)
34	III.34 (113)	I.34 (701)	I.34 (166)
35	III.35 (114)	I.35 (704)	I.35 (170)
36	III.36 (114^v)	I.36 (707)	I.36 (174)
37	IV.1 (115)	II.1 (707)	II.1 (175)
38	IV.2 (117)	II.2 (713)	II.2 (182)
39	IV.3 (118^v)	II.3 (718)	II.3 (189)
40	IV.4 (119^v)	II.4 (720)	II.4 (191)
41	IV.5 (120)	II.5 (721)	II.5 (193)
42	IV.6 (120)	II.6 (722)	II.6 (194)
43	IV.7 (120^v)	II.6[bis] (623[723])	II.6[bis] (194)
44	IV.7[bis] (121)	II.7 (725)	II.7 (196)
45	IV.8 (121^v)	II.8 (725)	II.8 (197)
46	IV.9 (121^v)	II.9 (726)	II.9 (198)
47	IV.11 (122)	II.11 (728)	II.11 (199)
48	IV.12 (123)	II.12 (729)	II.12 (201)
49	IV.12[bis] (123^v)	II.13 (631[731])	II.13 (204)
50	IV.14 (127[124]^v)	II.14 (733)	II.14 (206)
51	IV.15 (127[124]^v)	II.15 (733)	II.15 (206)
52	IV.16 (125)	II.16 (734)	II.16 (207)
53	IV.17 (125)	II.17 (735)	II.17 (208)
54	IV.18 (131)	II.18 (751)	II.18 (229)
55	IV.19 (131)	II.19 (753)	II.19 (230)
56	IV.20 (131^v)	II.20 (754)	II.20 (231)
57	IV.21 (132)	II.21 (755)	II.21 (233)
58	IV.22 (132)	II.22 (755)	II.22 (233)
59	IV.23 (134^v)	II.23 (763)	II.23 (242)
60	IV.24 (134^v)	II.24 (763)	II.24 (242)
61	IV.25 (134^v)	II.25 (764)	II.25 (244)
62	IV.26 (135)	II.26 (765)	II.26 (245)
63	IV.27 (135)	II.27 (765)	II.27 (245)
64	IV.28 (135)	II.28 (766)	II.28 (245)
65	IV.29 (135^v)	II.29 (766)	II.29 (247)
66	IV.30 (135^v)	II.30 (767)	II.30 (247)
67	IV.31 (136)	II.31 (769)	II.31 (249)
68	IV.32 (136^v)	II.32 (770)	II.32 (250)
69	IV.33 (136^v)	II.33 (770)	II.33 (251)
70	IV.34 (137^v)	II.34 (772)	II.34 (255)

CONCORDANCE

Present edition	1522 edition (number and folio)	Bibl. Clun. (number and column)	PL, CLXXXIX (number and column)
71	IV.35 (137^v)	II.35 (773)	II.35 (256)
72	IV.36 (138^v)	II.36 (776)	II.36 (259)
73	IV.37 (138^v)	II.37 (776)	II.37 (259)
74	IV.38 (138^v)	II.38 (776)	II.38 (259)
75	IV.39 (139)	II.39 (777)	II.39 (260)
76	IV.40 (139^v)	II.40 (778)	II.40 (262)
77	IV.41 (140)	II.41 (779)	II.41 (262)
78	IV.42 (140^v)	II.42 (780)	II.42 (264)
79	IV.43 (140^v)	II.43 (781)	II.43 (264)
80	IV.44 (141)	II.44 (782)	II.44 (266)
81	IV.45 (141^v)	II.45 (784)	II.45 (268)
82	IV.46 (142)	II.46 (785)	II.46 (269)
83	IV.47 (142^v)	II.47 (786)	II.47 (270)
84	IV.48 (142^v)	II.48 (787)	II.48 (271)
85	IV.49 (143)	II.49 (788)	II.49 (271)
86	IV.50 (143)	II.50 (788)	II.50 (272)
87	IV.51 (144^v)	II.51 (792)	II.51 (277)
88	IV.52 (145)	III.1 (793)	III.1 (277)
89	IV.53 (145)	III.2 (793)	III.2 (277)
90	IV.54 (145^v)	III.3 (795)	III.3 (280)
91	IV.55 (146)	III.4 (796)	III.4 (282)
92	IV.56 (146^v)	III.5 (797)	III.5 (282)
93	IV.57 (146^v)	III.6 (797)	III.6 (283)
94	V.1 (149 [147])	III.7 (797)	III.7 (283)
95	IV.58 (146^v)	IV.1 (813)	IV.1 (303)
96	IV.59 (146^v)	IV.2 (815)	IV.2 (303)
97	V.2 (152)	IV.3 (815)	IV.3 (304)
98	V.3 (152^v)	IV.4 (816)	IV.4 (305)
99	V.4 (152^v)	IV.5 (817)	IV.5 (306)
100	V.5 (153)	IV.6 (817)	IV.6 (307)
101	V.6 (153)	IV.7 (818)	IV.7 (309)
102	V.7 (153^v)	IV.8 (819)	IV.8 (310)
103	V.8 (154^v)	IV.9 (821)	IV.9 (313)
104	V.9 (154^v)	IV.10 (822)	IV.10 (315)
105	V.10 (155)	IV.11 (823)	IV.11 (316)
106	V.11 (155)	IV.12 (824)	IV.12 (317)
107	V.12 (155^v)	IV.13 (825)	IV.13 (318)
108	V.13 (155^v)	IV.14 (825)	IV.14 (319)
109	V.14 (156)	IV.15 (826)	IV.15 (320)
110	V.15 (156)	IV.16 (827)	IV.16 (321)
111	V.16 (156^v)	IV.17 (828)	IV.17 (321)
112	V.17 (163^v)	IV.18 (847)	IV.18 (344)
113	V.18 (164)	IV.19 (849)	IV.19 (345)

Present edition	1522 edition (number and folio)	Bibl. Clun. (number and column)	PL, CLXXXIX (number and column)
114	V.19 (164)	IV.20 (850)	IV.20 (346)
115	V.20 (164)	IV.21 (850)	IV.21 (346)
116	V.21 (165^v)	IV.22 (854)	IV.22 (353)
117	V.22 (166)	IV.23 (855)	IV.23 (354)
118	V.23 (166)	IV.24 (856)	IV.24 (355)
119	V.24 (166^v)	IV.25 (857)	IV.25 (356)
120	V.25 (166^v)	IV.26 (857)	IV.26 (356)
121	V.26 (167)	IV.27 (858)	IV.27 (357)
122	V.27 (167)	IV.28 (859)	IV.28 (358)
123	V.28 (167^v)	IV.29 (860)	IV.29 (359)
124	V.29 (167^v)	IV.30 (860)	IV.30 (360)
125		IV.31 (861)	IV.31 (360)
126	⎫V.30 (168)	IV.32 (862)	IV.32 (361)
127	⎭	IV.33 (863)	IV.33 (362)
128	V.31 (169)	IV.34 (864)	IV.34 (364)
129	V.32 (170)	IV.35 (865)	IV.35 (365)
130	V.33 (170)	IV.36 (865)	IV.36 (366)
131	V.34 (171)	IV.37 (868)	IV.37 (369)
132	V.35 (172)	IV.38 (870)	IV.38 (371)
133	V.36 (172)	IV.39 (871)	IV.39 (371[372])
134	V.37 (173^v)	IV.40 (875)	IV.40 (376)
135	V.38 (174)	IV.41 (876)	IV.41 (377)
136	V.39 (174)	IV.42 (877)	IV.42 (378)
137	V.40 (175)	IV.43 (879)	IV.43 (380)
138	V.41 (175^v)	V.1 (881)	V.1 (381)
139	V.42 (175^v)	V.2 (881)	V.2 (384)
140	V.43 (176)	V.3 (882)	V.3 (385)
141	V.44 (176)	V.4 (883)	V.4 (386)
142	V.45 (177)	V.5 (885)	V.5 (388)
143	V.46 (177)	V.6 (886)	V.6 (389)
144	VI.1 (177^v)	V.7 (887)	V.7 (391)
145	VI.2 (179^v)	V.8 (892)	V.8 (398)
146	VI.3 (179^v)	V.9 (893)	V.9 (399)
147	V.48[47] (177^v)	VI.1 (893)	VI.1 (399)
148	VI.4 (180)	VI.2 (894)	VI.2 (401)
149	VI.5 (180)	VI.3 (895)	VI.3 (401)
150	VI.6 (181)	VI.4 (897)	VI.4 (404)
151	VI.7 (182)	VI.5 (901)	VI.5 (408)
152	VI.8 (182^v)	VI.6 (901)	VI.6 (409)
153	VI.9 (182^v)	VI.7 (902)	VI.7 (409)
154	VI.10 (182^v)	VI.8 (902)	VI.8 (409)
155	VI.11 (183)	VI.9 (903)	VI.9 (409)
156	VI.12 (183)	VI.10 (903)	VI.10 (410)

CONCORDANCE 367

Present edition	1522 edition (number and folio)	Bibl. Clun. (number and column)	PL, CLXXXIX (number and column)
157	VI.13 (183ᵛ)	VI.11 (904)	VI.11 (411)
158	VI.14 (183ᵛ)	VI.12 (904)	VI.12 (411)
159	VI.15 (184)	VI.13 (906)	VI.13 (414)
160	VI.16 (184ᵛ)	VI.14 (907)	VI.14 (416)
161	VI.17 (185ᵛ)	VI.15 (909)	VI.15 (418)
162	VI.18 (187ᵛ)	VI.16 (915)	VI.16 (424)
163	VI.19 (188)	VI.17 (916)	VI.17 (425)
164	VI.20 (188)	VI.18 (916)	VI.18 (425)
165	VI.21 (188ᵛ)	VI.19 (918)	VI.19 (426)
166	VI.22 (189)	VI.20 (918)	VI.20 (426)
167	VI.23 (189)	VI.21 (919)	VI.21 (427)
168	VI.24 (189ᵛ)	VI.22 (920)	VI 22 (428)
169	unnum'd (200)	VI.23 (920)	VI.23 (429)
170	VI.25 (200)	VI.24 (921)	VI.24 (429)
171	VI.26 (200ᵛ)	VI.25 (922)	VI.25 (431)
172	VI.27 (201ᵛ)	VI.26 (924)	VI.26 (434)
173	VI.28 (202)	VI.27 (926)	VI.27 (436)
174	VI.29 (203)	VI.28 (929)	VI.28 (439)
175	VI.30 (204)	VI.29 (931)	VI.29 (443)
176	VI.31 (204)	VI.30 (932)	VI.30 (444)
177	VI.32 (204)	VI.31 (932)	VI.31 (444)
178	VI.33 (204ᵛ)	VI.32 (933)	VI.32 (444)
179	VI.34 (205)	VI.33 (934)	VI.33 (446)
180	VI.35 (205ᵛ)	VI.34 (936)	VI.34 (447)
181	VI.36 (205ᵛ)	VI.35 (936)	VI.35 (447)
182	VI.37 (206)	VI.36 (937)	VI.36 (449)
183	VI.38 (206ᵛ)	VI.37 (939)	VI.37 (450)
184	VI.39 (206ᵛ)	VI.38 (939)	VI.38 (451)
185	VI.40 (206ᵛ)	VI.39 (939)	VI.39 (451)
186	VI.41 (208ᵛ)	VI.40 (945)	VI.40 (457)
187	VI.42 (208ᵛ)	VI.41 (946)	VI.41 (458)
188	VI.43 (209)	VI.42 (946)	VI.42 (459)
189	VI.44 (209)	VI.43 (947)	VI.43 (460)
190	VI.45 (209ᵛ)	VI.44 (949)	VI.44 (462)
191	VI.46 (210)	VI.45 (951)	VI.45 (464)
192	VI.47 (210ᵛ)	VI.46 (952)	VI.46 (465)
193	VI.47bis (212)	VI.47 (956)	VI.47 (469)

I. INDEX OF MANUSCRIPTS*

(References are to volume II except when noted.)

Arras, Bibliothèque municipale, 891: 63, 66
Auxerre, Bibliothèque municipale, 106: 354

Berlin, Deutsche Staatsbibliothek, Meerman 181: 318; Phillipps 1719: 330, n. 64; Phillipps 1732: 32, 36 n. 159
Brugge (Bruges), Bibliothèque municipale, 131: 63, 65–66, 69 n. 270
Bruxelles (Brussels), Bibliothèque royale, 647–650: 70; 10827–10835: 63, 66–67, 69; 19593–19596: 63, 66–67; 20006–20017: 70, 71–72; II.1103: 70, 71–72

Cambrai, Bibliothèque municipale, 277: 63, 66, 69
Canterbury, Christ Church Archives: 297 n. 17
Coesfeld, Salm-Horstmar Archives: 21

Dijon, Archives départementales de la Côte-d'Or, 139 (Cart. H 165): 63, 64–65, 68
Douai, Bibliothèque municipale, 211: 63, 65–66; 372: 52–53; 381: 16, 17, 48–55, 63, 64, 70, 81, 83–84; 535: 63, 66; 751: 53; 827: 51–52

København (Copenhagen), Kongelige Bibliotek, Gl. kgl. S. 3543: 36 n. 159
Köln (Cologne), Historisches Archiv, GB 4° 21: 70, 71
Kraków (Cracow), Biblioteka Jagiellońska, 2288 (AA XII 13): 70, 71

Lausanne, Archives Cantonales Vaudoises: I, iv
Le Puy, Cathédrale: 56–59, 63, 64, 70, 81, 275–278
Lyon (Lyons), Bibliothèque municipale, 949: 73

Melk, Stiftsbibliothek, 1918 (783.0.19): 63, 64
Milano (Milan), Sant'Ambrogio Archives: 9–10, 21–22
München (Munich), Bayerische Staatsbibliothek, Cod. lat. 13031: 109; 18566: 63, 64; 26818: 70, 71; 27129: 73

Oxford, Bodleian Library, Hatton 102: 70, 72
———, St. John's College, 126: 11 n. 50

Paris, Bibliothèque de l'Arsenal, 1162: 277, 284
———, Bibliothèque Mazarine, 734: 70, 71; 741: 70, 71
———, Bibliothèque nationale, Latin 942: 46 n. 186; Latin 2582: 60–61; Latin 2944: 70, 72; Latin 9085: 299 n. 1; Latin 13068: 57 n. 237; Latin 13876: 61, 63, 64, 77; Latin 14463: 334; Latin 14517: 70, 71; Latin 17716: 261; Latin 18369: 104; N. a. l. 186: 161
———, Bibliothèque Sainte-Geneviève, 1652: 73
———, Bibliothèque de l'Université, 790: 70, 72

Roma (Rome), Biblioteca Alessandrina, 97–98: 61–62

* The names of places and libraries here conform to those used by Kristeller, *Manuscript Books* (cited p. 63, n. 257, above).

St.-Omer, Bibliothèque municipale, 261: 63, 65–66
Sankt Gallen (St. Gall), Stiftsbibliothek, 391: 109
Sevilla (Seville), Capitular Colombina, 7–2–1: 63, 67, 69

Torino (Turin), Biblioteca nazionale, *776 (28) E–V–37: 40 n. 177, 73
Troyes, Bibliothèque municipale, 2261: 59–60, 275–278

Urbana, University of Illinois, 6: 63, 67, 69

Wien (Vienna), Schottenstift, 152: 63, 64

Zürich, Zentralbibliothek, Z V 322: 70, 71

II. INDEX OF CITATIONS

(References are to volume I except when noted.)

1. BIBLICAL, ANCIENT, AND MEDIEVAL

BIBLICAL

Gen.
2.7: 120
3.19: 54
3.21: 62
4.11: 329
4.14: 328
8.6–7: 35
8.8–12: 9
12.1: 186
18.26: 66
19.22–23: 29
23.4: 401
24.6: 187
24.67: 156
25.33: 109
27: 394
27.27: 432
27.29: 357
27.37: 357
27.40: 358
29:21
30.32–33: 287
32.30: 246
33.3: 357
37.3: 316
37.4: 276
37.9: 354, 386
41.25–32: 386
50.1: 156
50.2: 157

Exod.
8.24: 205
12.35: 330
15.20: 241, 304
17.4: 183
18.18–22: 73
18.19: 41

19.12: 180
21.17: 308
21.24: 397
22.1–2: 118
22.4: 148
23.3: 111
23.5: 182
24.11: 240
32.11–13: 180
33.11: 246
33.20: 246, 249
33.22: 188

Levit.
2.13: 294
5.8: 139
8.7–9: 224
11.44: 215
19.15: 111
19.26: 386
20.9: 308

Num.
11.6: 392
11.10: 392
11.18–20: 392
11.33–34: 392
11.34: 393
16.48: 105
20: 183
20.16: 188
21.29: 327
23.30: 129
25.7–8: 128

Deut.
7.22: 446
15.15: 397

19.15: 224
19.21: 397
22.19: 103
23.21: 198
33.17: 309

Ios.
1.17: 316
6: 327

Iudic.
4.9: 305
5: 241
7.13 f.: 386
16: 34
17.6: 175
19.30: 413
21.6: 441
21.24: 175

Ruth
1.16–17: 185

I Reg.
2: 241
2.1: 383
2.3: 369
2.6: 336
2.7: 289
7.9: 271
15.22: 184
15.23: 139
17: 45
18.1: 13, 363
22: 51
24.7: 273

INDEX OF CITATIONS

II Reg.
1.26: 16
3.28: 57
6: 378
15.19–20: 185
15.21–22: 185
16.1–4: 351
18.33: 157
21.4: 131
24.16: 335
24.17: 335

III Reg.
13.18: 351
17.6: 394
19.4–6: 29
19.12: 300
20.41: 180
22.17: 406
22.19: 246

IV Reg.
1.3: 414
1.4: 416
1.8: 63
1.10: 128
2.2: 185
2.4: 185
2.6: 185
2.9: 242
5.13: 423
8.20: 358
19: 50
24–25: 51

II Par.
6.30: 244
14.11: 421
18.16: 406
18.18: 246
20.14: 188

I Esdr.
7–8: 177

Tob.
4.16: 418

Iudith
10.3: 224

Esther
9.22: 207

Iob
1.1: 107, 186, 384
1.5: 46

1.21: 148, 339
5.23: 331, 446
6.6: 294
10.1: 425
14.5: 367
14.14: 273
16.5: 338, 339
16.20: 331, 407
16.21: 334
19.21: 46, 334
24.20: 129
26.5: 182
26.12: 124
27.3: 333
29.17: 91, 409
29.24: 273
30.31: 207
31.4: 336
32.16: 11
33.9: 57
34.23: 416
40.10: 144
40.15: 410
40.20: 144
40.24: 20, 118, 304
41.7: 130
41.15: 196
41.21: 128
41.25: 304

Psal.
2.8: 135
2.9: 219
3.4: 207
7.5: 445
9.14: 332
9.16: 428
9.17: 19
10.14: 205
11.2: 188, 391
11.3: 11, 117, 143, 149, 263,
    331, 365, 375, 398
12.5: 437
13.3: 176, 188
15.10: 12, 123
16.4: 182, 367
16.8: 205, 300
17.38: 447
17.46: 205
18.5: 236, 239
18.7: 184
18.11: 12, 136, 175, 203
21.21: 123
21.31: 123
22.2: 163
22.5: 134
23.1: 83

23.3–4: 111
26.4: 257, 422
26.12: 375
27.7: 173
30.6: 123, 124
30.25: 17
33.11: 128
34.10: 365
34.19: 448
35.9: 171, 211
35.9–10: 104
35.10: 428
37.10: 161
37.12: 207
37.12–13: 207
37.14: 365
37.14–15: 211
37.15: 366
39.3: 435
39.8: 235
39.11: 394
40.2: 207
41.3: 421
41.6, 12: 164
42.5: 164
43.6: 309
43.22: 359
43.25: 50
44.2: 424
44.4: 128
44.8: 121, 219
47.9: 428
47.11: 415
48.15: 290
50.3: 74
50.19: 154
52.4: 188
53.8: 173
54.7–9: 46
54.8: 188, 226
54.10: 130, 226
55.3: 180
56.2: 205
57.7: 20, 27
58.12: 328
59.6: 29
59.14: 205
60.4: 23, 316
62.6: 28
62.10: 180
62.12: 369
63.4: 375
65.5: 296
65.13: 430
65.13–14: 78, 152, 393
65.15: 21
65.20: 273

INDEX OF CITATIONS

67.16–17: 193
67.36: 36, 171
68.2: 444
68.4: 196
68.5: 448
68.10: 447
68.15: 180
71.6: 205
71.8: 118, 135
73.12: 399
73.19: 337
74.11: 20
76.11: 410
77.30–31: 392, 393
77.31: 393
78.5: 128
80.7: 19
80.13: 392
83.4: 49, 172, 259
83.6: 435
83.7: 57, 377, 433
85.9: 135
87.19: 170
88.15: 415
90.3: 172, 276, 433
93.19: 300
94.6: 37, 188
95.1: 430
101.8: 324
102.5: 420, 433
103.15: 315
103.18: 172
105.14–15: 392
106.5: 28
109.3: 255
109.7: 5
111.7: 341
113.5–7: 36
113.16: 83
114.8: 172
115.5: 146
115.11: 103
118.2: 235
118.32: 17, 41
118. 35: 435
118.52–54: 207
118.60: 373
118.96: 106
118.103: 402, 426
118.120: 393
118.127: 132, 146, 229, 306, 433
119.2: 226, 377
119.7: 280, 309, 316
121.1: 174, 191, 352
121.7: 285
123.7: 20

125.2: 352
125.4: 147
126.2–3: 147
127.2: 54
128.4: 197
128.8: 137
130.1: 36
131.4: 140
131.4–5: 49
131.5: 167
131.7: 358, 399
132.2: 321, 364
132.3: 365
136.1–2, 4: 20
138.16: 361
138.21–22: 281, 328
139.4: 176, 291, 375, 377
139.6: 12
140.3: 40, 432
140.4: 78
142.2: 57
143.8: 102
143.10: 219, 230
143.11: 102
144.3: 292
144.19: 433
145.7: 350, 415
146.6: 166
147.18: 182

Prov.
3.6: 435
6.3–4: 281
6.13–14: 286
8.15: 230, 297
8.30–31: 237
9.4: 38
9.5: 38
15.17: 226
17.17: 346
18.19: 232
21.9: 226
21.25: 32
22.1: 204, 275
22.28: 198
23.2: 393
24.16: 68
25.24: 226
26.11: 128
27.1: 59, 347, 352, 367
27.6: 143
27.23: 44, 277
29.12: 176
31.10 f.: 96
31.19: 361

Eccle.
1.15: 368

2.8: 38
4.10: 232
4.12: 204
5.2: 386
5.10: 111
9.10: 367
10.1: 205
12.6: 9, 12
12.6–7: 13
12.14: 45

Cant.
1.2: 204
1.3: 106, 417
1.6: 257, 421
1.7: 135
2.3: 432
2.11–12: 207
2.12: 173, 337
2.14: 30, 188
3.4: 432
3.9: 378
4.11: 12
4.12: 432
4.16: 141
5.6: 182
5.12: 164
5.13: 12
6.8: 351
6.11: 361
6.12: 196
8.6: 21
8.7: 5, 41, 126, 204, 223, 277

Sap.
4.8–9: 75
4.11: 342
6.25: 114
7.7: 120
7.27: 120
8.1: 249
10.10: 207
14.11: 20

Eccli.
2.14: 117
5.8: 59, 347, 352
6.5: 133
6.6: 447
6.36: 176
9.15: 314, 427
10.15: 33
12.8: 195, 262, 346
14.5: 10
15.7: 388
19.2: 67

(Eccli.—cont.)
22.6: 325
22.26: 362
23.4: 361
31.6: 207
35.6: 353
36.19: 435
38.1: 428
38.16: 157, 336
38.25: 28
45.1: 340

Isai.
1.2: 394
1.5–6: 258
1.17–18: 416
1.22: 413
2.10: 29, 187
3.9: 389
3.12: 388
4.6: 183, 415
5.20: 388
5.25: 331
6.1: 246
6.5: 388
9.4: 275
9.12: 331
9.14: 271
9.17: 331
9.21: 331
10.4: 331
10.21: 329
11.2–3: 121
11.9: 118
11.10: 46, 400
13.2: 193
19.15: 271
26.1: 30
28.8: 104
28.15: 207
28.18: 334
29.1: 421
30.10: 388
30.15: 274
32.17: 274
34.11: 144
35.10: 272
36.6: 232
37.3: 50
38.14: 361
40.3: 382
40.4: 444
40.7: 342
40.12: 83
42.7: 51
42.8: 244
42.13: 393

42.14: 393
43.6: 141
48.11: 244
48.22: 290
49.2: 130
52.5: 129, 389
52.7: 174
53.5: 441
53.12: 123
56.10: 382, 388
57.21: 290
58.1: 381, 388
64.6: 57
66.14: 272

Ier.
1.10: 127, 415, 420
2.18: 74
4.22: 205
6.14: 285
7.11: 86, 330
11.16: 204
13.23: 214
17.9: 387
18.20: 123
23.25: 387
29.8: 386
36.22–23: 387
45.4: 377
48.10: 130, 132, 281, 446
51.7: 134, 179
51.40: 311
52.11: 387

Thren.
3.26: 273
3.28: 29
3.54: 450
4.1: 128
4.2: 128

Ezech.
1.14: 205, 304
3.17: 361
3.18: 127, 388
13.2–3: 387
13.5: 267, 378, 399, 409
13.17: 127, 387
18.20: 199
20.27: 394
20.33: 397
29.6: 232
31.8: 286, 304
32.2: 74
33.6: 127
33.7: 127, 361
33.8: 388

34.2: 127, 225
34.3: 74, 127
34.10: 127, 225
44.18: 64

Dan.
2 and 7: 386
10.16: 10

Ose.
3.4: 42, 405, 408, 410
7.11: 164
13.14: 421

Ioel
1.20: 133
3.18: 305, 365

Amos
5.7–8: 167
6.6: 41

Ion.
1.12: 110

Mich.
3.5: 387
6.8: 31, 211
7.6: 187

Hab.
3.18: 428

Zach.
9.3: 128
13.1: 69

I Mac.
2.58: 395
10.55: 214

Matt.
1.20: 386
2.12: 186
2.13: 243, 248
2.19–20: 386
2.20: 243
3.1: 382
4.6: 139
5.3: 15, 16, 34
5.4: 166
5.16: 385
5.23–24: 116, 262
5.33: 152
5.48: 187
6.12: 69
6.14: 68
6.20: 333

INDEX OF CITATIONS

6.21: 12
6.22: 19, 60, 66, 281, 351, 358, 378
6.22–23: 216
6.23: 359
6.24: 12
7.3: 291
7.6: 399
7.12: 55, 371, 418
7.13–14: 17
7.14: 147
8.9: 417
8.20: 34
9.9: 87
9.11: 35
9.12: 369
10.8: 241
10.16: 448
10.24: 384, 413
10.30: 336
10.36: 187
10.42: 66, 172
11.7 f.: 225
11.28: 58, 352
11.29: 15, 36, 58, 166, 307, 352, 418
11.30: 58, 211
12.37: 96
13.25: 114, 176
13.28: 437
13.43: 429
13.45: 147
14.23: 181
15.4: 308
15.6: 378
15.13: 437
15.14: 82
16.19: 79, 338
16.23: 138
16.24: 167, 360
16.27: 107
17: 216
17.2: 171
17.4: 215
17.19: 169
17.26: 35
18.6: 111, 115, 369
18.7: 108, 111, 115
18.8–9: 78
18.16: 224
18.17: 369, 389
18.18: 338
18.21–22: 68
19.6: 166, 411
19.11: 100
19.12: 100
19.19: 55, 126, 132
19.21: 58, 100
20.1–16: 348
20.2: 211
20.12: 36
20.16: 211, 385
20.28: 164, 371
21.12: 128
21.12 f.: 447
21.13: 129
21.25: 94
21.31: 225
21.33–39: 129
21.41: 129
22.14: 211, 385
22.17: 35
22.30: 431
22.39: 55, 126
22.40: 60, 90, 93, 96, 98, 237, 285
23.2: 225
23.2–3: 95
23.3: 225
23.6: 127
23.7: 127
23.14: 225
23.16: 225
23.23: 66, 73, 378
23.24: 66, 378
24.12: 133, 188
24.13: 211
24.24: 112
24.28: 173
24.31: 186
24.43: 334, 344
25.1–13: 173, 359
25.6: 345
25.8: 211
25.14–30: 2
25.18: 140
25.24: 214
25.33: 135
25.35: 55, 83
26.7: 178
26.31: 437
26.36: 181
26.38: 123, 421
26.39: 181
26.41: 37
26.52: 446
27.55: 240
28.18: 328
28.20: 299

Marc.
1.6: 63
2.16: 35
7.9: 53

7.10: 308
8.34: 167
9.4: 215
9.41: 111, 369
9.49: 294
10.8: 411
10.9: 166
10.21: 58
11.15 f.: 447
11.17: 129
11.30: 94
12.17: 25
12.42–43: 66
14.15: 426
14.34: 123, 421
14.38: 37
16.17: 241

Luc.
1.14: 170
1.28: 236, 237
1.35: 236
1.44: 241
1.47: 407, 428
1.53: 289
1.68: 192
1.79: 435
1.80: 225
2.7: 34, 106, 248
2.14: 66, 106, 114, 203
2.24: 248
2.35: 157, 248
2.48: 244
2.43–45: 243
2.52: 121
3.5: 444
4.1: 121
5.30: 35
5.31: 428, 441
6.30: 167
6.31: 371, 418
6.40: 384, 413
6.41: 291
7.8: 417
7.16: 203
8.12: 352
9.33: 215
9.58: 34
9.60: 59
9.62: 56
10.7: 56, 370
10.16: 401
10.18: 292
10.30: 151
10.39–42: 71
10.40: 165
11.4: 68, 69

INDEX OF CITATIONS

(Luc.—*cont.*)
11.8: 26
11.32: 378
11.34: 60, 66, 216, 281, 351, 358, 378
11.42: 73
11.52: 225
12.6–7: 336
12.7: 336
12.33: 232
12.39: 344
14.9: 8
14.10: 37
14.15: 389
14.22–23: 337
14.23: 386
14.24: 385
14.26: 78
14.32: 424
15.7: 16, 172
15.16: 92
15.17: 104
16.8: 448
16.9: 160
16.13: 12
16.19: 35
17.6: 169
17.10: 57
17.21: 188
17.37: 173
18.22: 58
19.22: 390
19.46: 129
20.4: 94
20.9–15: 129
20.25: 25
20.38: 255, 336
21.34: 66
22.11: 35
22.15: 422
22.26: 292
22.27: 292
22.30: 389
22.32: 4, 79
22.39: 181
22.41: 181
22.43: 181
23.46: 123, 124
24.49: 239

Ioan.
1.3–4: 255
1.7: 88
1.14: 99
1.16: 247
1.29: 181
2.17: 447
3.8: 58, 230, 240, 257, 300, 315, 352, 371, 435
3.27: 28, 352
4.9: 369
5.30: 184
6.3: 181
6.15: 225
6.27: 70
6.37: 58
6.44: 58, 352
6.45: 118
6.48: 189
6.50: 189
6.57: 189
7.50: 161
8.1–2: 181
8.18: 88
9.27: 424
10.5: 314
10.11: 124
10.12: 7, 127, 267, 351
10.12–13: 127
10.15: 123
10.17–18: 123
10.18: 123
10.24: 21
10.27: 135
10.27–28: 286, 290, 337
10.41: 242
11.25: 147, 337
12.3: 178
12.27: 123, 181
12.47: 337
13.18: 308
13.35: 114
14.12: 247
15.5: 90
15.12: 55
15.13: 123, 408
15.25: 448
15.26: 88
15.27: 88
16.20: 207
16.22: 13, 188, 293
17.11: 183
17.14: 20
18.11: 446
19.30: 124
19.38–40: 12
20.17: 57
20.18: 241
21.18: 337

Act.
1.10: 57
1.12–13: 240
1.14: 240
2.5: 373
2.27: 12, 123
2.45: 64, 67
4.32: 294
4.35: 59, 62, 64, 67–68
5.1–11: 59
6.5: 107
9: 33
9.15: 204
10.13: 315
10.38: 121

Rom.
1.4: 255
1.14: 361, 410
2.1: 20
2.3: 393
2.5: 158, 188
3.4: 103
3.12: 188
3.13: 176, 377
4.17: 255
5.5: 96, 146, 153, 183
6.3–4: 30
7.24: 257
8.3: 15, 99, 293
8.21: 168
9.5: 292
9.18: 296
10.18: 236, 239
11.26: 329
12.15: 137, 339
12.18: 260
13.3: 446
13.4: 407
13.7: 19, 87
13.8: 19
13.9: 126
13.10: 93, 96, 98, 99
13.13: 393
13.14: 62, 64
14.5: 279
14.8: 336
14.9: 336
15.4: 61

I Cor.
1.20: 16
2.9: 297
2.10: 174
2.11: 174, 377
2.14: 368
2.15: 88
3.8: 284
3.18: 16
4.4: 238

INDEX OF CITATIONS

4.8: 24
4.9–12: 367
4.20: 17
4.21: 446
5.6: 312
5.7: 378
5.8: 160
6.2: 20
6.3: 20, 88
6.4–7: 83
6.7: 197
7.7: 67, 100
7.10–11: 412
7.13: 412
7.15: 413
7.20: 24
8.13: 115
9.10: 215
9.22: 368
9.24: 151, 211, 281, 367, 368, 385
9.26: 72, 96
9.27: 361, 408
10.11: 64
10.13: 148
12.8–10: 239
12.23: 65
12.26: 16, 103
12.31: 276
13.1: 315
13.3: 101, 116, 140
13.4–5: 98, 293
13.5: 12, 126, 195, 308, 351, 377, 399
13.5–6: 92
13.7: 92, 195, 273
13.8: 126
13.12: 216, 246, 249, 422
13.13: 90, 237, 250, 276
14.34: 241
14.35: 241
15.28: 293, 430
15.32: 421
15.33: 125
15.36: 173
15.53: 173
15.54: 173
15.57: 207
16.14: 281

II Cor.
1.7: 207
1.18–19: 404
2.14–15: 419
3.6: 64
3.18: 216
5.4: 337

5.6: 188
5.10: 45
5.17: 287
6.2: 13
6.5: 367
6.6: 403
6.7: 195
6.10: 87
6.14: 216
6.15: 35
10.5: 298
10.10: 426
10.11: 426
11.2: 434
11.11: 217
11.23: 412, 441
11.26: 276
13.1: 224
13.3: 412
13.10: 143, 231
13.15: 40

Gal.
1.15: 304
2.20: 167
3.28: 287, 368
4.4: 255
4.19: 173
4.26: 428
5.2: 94
5.13: 371
5.14: 126
6.2: 278, 293
6.10: 194, 370
6.15: 287, 368

Ephes.
1.4: 254
2.14: 114, 183
2.19: 401
4.3: 339
4.5: 210
4.28: 367
5.29: 139
6.11: 187
6.12: 408
6.16: 31, 187
6.17: 130, 446

Philip.
1.21: 147, 337
1.23: 147
2.15: 384
2.21: 127
3.13: 187
3.18: 219
3.19: 389

4.1: 137
4.4: 165
4.7: 106

Col.
1.26: 254
2.3: 242, 244
2.5: 153
2.9: 120
3.2: 20
3.3: 29, 41, 173
3.4: 41, 173
3.11: 287, 368
3.13–14: 13
4.6: 166

I Thess.
2.19–20: 137
4.11: 367
4.12: 147, 156, 336, 343
4.16: 186
5.2: 334
5.5: 216
5.17–18: 37

I Tim.
1.5: 96, 237, 365
1.15: 118
2.2: 41
2.12: 241
4.2: 281
4.8: 92, 378
4.12: 139
5.8: 194
5.18: 56
5.23: 139
6.1: 389
6.8: 35

II Tim.
1.4–5: 434
2.4: 50
2.9: 25, 130
2.20: 204
2.22–24: 56
3.1: 127, 188
4.2: 61
4.7: 367, 434, 435

Tit.
2.13: 211

Philemon
1.19: 181

Hebr.
1.8: 219
3.5: 237
3.6: 237
6.6: 188
10.7: 235
10.31: 45
11.37: 36 63
12.14: 34, 260
13.4: 412

Iac.
1.12: 416, 423
1.17: 352
2.8: 126
2.10: 10
3.2: 238, 356
3.8: 176
5.14: 355
5.15: 355

I Pet.
1.16: 215
1.24: 158
2.21: 59, 430
4.8: 11
4.13: 17

II Pet
1.18: 215
2.7: 186
3.10: 334

I Ioan.
1.1: 204
1.8: 238, 239
2.16: 128
2.17: 151
2.27: 41, 348
3.2: 173, 246, 293
3.14: 277

3.18: 332, 363
4.1: 53, 282
4.8: 90, 98
5.3: 367
5.19: 188

Apoc.
2.9: 128
3.3: 334
8.1: 38
11.7: 20
12.4: 91
12.7: 45
14.4: 429, 430
17.2: 171
17.14: 135
21.4: 147
22.11: 414
22.17: 60, 353

CLASSICAL

Anthologia latina, 257, 2: 305

Caesar
  De bello gallico, VII, 4: 405
Calpurnius
  Bucolica, II, 13: 322
Cicero
  De amicitia, VI, 20, 22: 217–218
  De oratore, I: 153
  In Catalinam oratio, I: 21

Digesta, XVII, 1, 5, 1–2: 349
  XLI, 1, 9, 3: 198

Ennius
  Fragmenta incerta, XVII: 218

Horace
  Ars poetica, 1–2: 297
    1–4: 24
    138: 276
    322: 318
    364: 1
    437: 351

Carmen seculare, 59–60: 386
Carmina, I, i, 29–30: 318
  I, iii, 8: 10
  II, i, 23: 310
  III, xxiii, 9: 184
  IV, i, 3–4: 449
Epistolae, I, i, 52–54: 12
  I, ii, 27: 449
  I, vii, 44–45: 318
  I, xi, 27: 216
  II, i, 225: 310
Sat., I, i, 4–7: 425
  I, i, 27: 310
  I, vi, 67: 103

Lucan
  De bello ciuili, V, 28–29: 5

Ovid
  Heroides, IV, 49: 322
  Metamorphoses, I, 138–139: 15
    II, 846: 312
    IV, 428: 305

Persius
  Prologus, 2: 322

Sallust
  Catil., XX, 4: 183

Virgil
  Aeneid, I, 150: 25, 310
    I, 364: 159
    I, 491: 305
    I, 641: 310
    II, 560: 309
    IV, 373: 202
    VI, 126, 128–129: 151
    VI, 128: 310
    VI, 522: 310
    VI, 730–731: 223
    VIII, 303: 144
    XI, 580: 309
    XI, 662: 305
  Culex, I: 310
  Ecloga, VI, 5: 310
  Georgica, IV, 508: 310

INDEX OF CITATIONS

PATRISTIC AND MEDIEVAL

Acta S. Agathae, II, 9: 428
Ambrose
  De uirginibus, I, viii, 45–46 and 51–53: 431–432
Apophthegmata patrum: 29
Augustine
  Confessiones, VI, 2: 279
  De natura et gratia, XXXVI, 42: 239
  De sancta uirginitate, 27–28, 29–30, 53, and 54–56: 430–431
  Enarr. in Psal., CXLVII, 10: 434
  Ep. XXXVI, 32: 279
  Ep. LIV, 3: 279
  Ep. LXXXII, 3: 245
  In epist. Ioh., VII, 8: 60, 98, 281
  In euang. Ioh., VII, 3: 98
  Mor. ecc., 73: 68, 98
  Serm. LXXXIII, 8: 264
  Serm. XCIII, 4: 434

Bede
  Hist. ecc., I, 27: 61

Benedict
  Regula, Prol., 43: 13
    Prol., 49: 36, 281, 385
    Prol., 50: 17
    I, 5: 31
    II, 9: 394
    II, 37–38: 46
    VII, 34: 184
    VII, 35: 165
    VII, 51: 36, 57, 292
    XXI, 3: 73
    XXII, 2: 65
    XXIX, 1–3: 69
    XXIX, 3: 54, 282
    XXXII, 3: 55
    XXXIII: 184
    XXXIV, 1: 59, 62
    XXXIV, 1–5: 68
    XXXVI, 8–9: 390
    XXXIX, 1–2: 67
    XXXIX, 3: 54
    XXXIX, 4–5: 65
    XXXIX, 6–9: 66
    XXXIX, 11: 390
    XL, 1–7: 67
    XLI, 2–6: 54
    XLI, 5: 60, 69, 73, 281, 284
    XLI, 6: 70
    XLVII, 1: 73
    XLVIII: 54, 283
    XLVIII, 1: 70
    L, 3: 55
    LIII: 283
    LIII, 6–7: 54
    LIII, 7: 401
    LIII, 9: 370
    LIII, 12–13: 54
    LV, 57, 282
    LV, 1: 64
    LV, 1–2: 100
    LV, 1–3: 62
    LV, 4–5: 63
    LV, 7: 57, 288
    LV, 11: 62
    LV, 13: 54
    LV, 15: 54
    LVI, 1: 55, 284
    LVII, 5: 59
    LVIII, 2: 53, 282
    LVIII, 24: 84
    LXI, 2: 369
    LXI, 5: 76
    LXI, 13–14: 55
    LXIII, 15: 55
    LXIV, 8: 128
    LXIV, 19: 40, 72, 138, 284
    LXV, 11: 284
    LXVI, 1: 55
    LXVI, 3: 55

Bernard
  Super Cant., XV, 6: 204
Boethius
  Phil. cons., III, 5: 447
Burchard
  Decretum, XVI, 12: 88, n. t (see II, 120)

Council of Toledo III, cap. 4: 82
Cyprian
  De habitu uirginum, 3, 22, 23–24: 432–433

De uitis patrum, III, 109: 29

Evagrius
  Vita Anton., II, 14: 63

Faustus
  Vita S. Mauri: 284
    III, 18: 71
    VII–X: 71
    VII, 45: 71
    IX, 54: 85
    IX, 61: 85
Felix IV
  Ep. 1: 61

Gregory the Great
  Dial., II, Prol.: 352
    II, 1: 63
    II, 1–7: 319
    II, 8: 66, 93
    II, 15: 319
    II, 31: 319
    II, 33: 319, 361
    II, 35: 93, 242, 245, 319
    IV, 8(7): 93, 245
  Epist., V, 49: 80
    VIII, 17: 80, 81, 84
    XI, 56a, 5: 61
  In Cant., II, 15: 30
  In Euang., I, ix, 1: 235
    I, xiv, 2: 406
    II, xxvii, 1: 60
    II, xxx, 1: 10, 98
    II, xxxii, 1: 43
    II, xxxvi, 1: 38
    II, xxxviii, 2: 120
  In Ezech., I, vii, 10: 62
    I, xii, 30: 130
    II, iv, 3: 217
  Moralia, I, 1: 384
    V, xxxvi, 66: 29
    VI, xxvii, 58: 182
    VII, xvii, 61: 40
    X, xix, 30: 45
    XXIX, xxvii, 55: 120
    XXX, xviii, 63: 139
  Reg. past., I, 1: 368
    III, 14: 40

Ps.-Hilary
  Ep. ad Abram, 3: 432

Isidore of Seville
  Sententiae, II, 55, 3: 88, n. t (see II, 120)
Ivo of Chartres
  Decretum, Prol.: 61
    III, 61: 61
    III, 168: 82
    III, 171: 82
    VII, 11: 81, 84
    VII, 12–13: 80
    VII, 14: 80
  Panormia, Prol.: 61

Jerome
 Ep. LII, 9: 288
 Ep. LII, 17: 291
 Ep. CXXV, 11: 39, 235
 Vita S. Pauli: 234
 Contra Vigilantium, 1: 144
  15: 188
  16: 29

Ps.-Jerome
 Ep. de assump., 27: 430
  28: 120, 236
  32: 244
  61: 251, 253
  62: 252, 253, 254

 63: 253
 66: 254
John the Deacon
 Vita S. Gregorii, I, 5: 85
  I, 8: 307
Jonas
 Vita Columbani, XXX: 86

Leo I
 De quadragesima sermo, II, 4: 384

Paschasius Radbertus
 see Ps.-Jerome

Passio S. Cecilae: 166
Paul the Deacon
 Historia Theophili: 171
Paulinus of Nola
 Ep. XXVIIII, 12: 289

Sidonius Apollinaris
 Ep. V, vii, 4: 289
Sulpicius Severus
 Dial., II, 3: 57, 288
 Ep. III: 170, 268

Vita S. Odonis, III: 391–392

PROVERBS

Amarum os nunquam mel spuere possit: 28
Aquam mari [flumini] infundere: 146, 292, 345, 447
Aurea fortuna: 442
Ligna ad siluam [nemus] deferre: 146, 292, 345, 447
Mineruam docere: 204, 292, 345, 447
Pomum discordiae: 114
Primo falli incommodum est, secundo stultum, tertio turpe: 447
Primus fundationis lapis: 110
Unda cauat lapidem: 125
Urbs ... orbs: 135, 196

PARALLELS

(Authors cited in the notes but not in the text.)

Aelred of Rievaulx: 217
Alcuin
 Ep. 59: 109
 Ep. 260: 422
Ambrose
 In psalmum I, 24: 177
 In psalmum CXVIII, XIV, 34: 177
Augustine: 120
 Confessiones, VI, 16: 421
 Enarr. in Psal., CXXVII, 16: 111
Ps.-Augustine
 Regula tertia: 266

Bernard: 120
 Ep. 65: 222
 Ep. 124: 135
 De praecepto et dispensatione, III: 61
 Super Cant., XIII, 8: 151
  XXIII, 8: 40
  LXXXIII, 3: 183

Caesarius of Arles: 124
Cassian
 Conlat., II, 4: 40
  XVI, 3: 222
Cicero
 Acad. post., I, v, 18: 204
 De natura deorum, I, 19: 421

Defensor of Ligugé
 Liber scintillarum, LVIII, 35: 111

Gerbert
 Ep. 166: 109
Gervase of Canterbury
 Chronica: 447
Gratian
 Decretum, C. XII, q. 2, c. 73: 82
  C. XVIII, q. 2, c. 5: 81
  C. XVIII, q. 2, c. 6: 80
  C. XVIII, q. 2, c. 28: 80
  Dist. 73, c. 24: 135

INDEX OF CITATIONS

Gregory the Great
   Dial., II, 1: 422
Gregory IX
   Decretales, I, vi, 42: 135

Horace
   Sat., I, x, 34: 146

Jerome
   Adv. Pelag., III, 19:146
   Adv. Ruf., I, 17: 146, 204
   Comm. in Abdiam, 20–21: 177
   Ep. CXXX, 12: 183
   Ep. CXLVI, 1: 135

Nicholas of Montiéramey: 204

Osbert of Clare: 447
   Ep. 25: 292
Ovid
   Ex Ponto, IV, x, 5: 125

Peter of Blois: 217
Peter the Venerable
   Statuta, 14: 70
Polydore Virgil
   Adagia, 202: 345

Quintilian
   Inst. oratoriae, IX, ii, 41: 421

Rabanus Maurus
   Carm., 6.9–10: 109

Salvian
   De gubernatione Dei, V, 11: 177
Sidonius
   Ep. VIII, vi, 14: 177

Tertullian
   De anima: 135

Ulric
   Consuetud. Clun., II, 4: 146

Virgil
   Aeneid, VIII, 412: 431
   Vita prima S. Bernardi, 31: 183

Wibald of Corvey: 125
William of Conches: 125
William of Tyre
   Historia, XI, 19: 447

PAPAL DOCUMENTS (JAFFÉ-LÖWENFELD NUMBERS)

(References are to volume II.)

JL 3584: 119
JL 3896: 143
JL 4065: 143
JL 5533: 237 n. 15
JL 6991–6992: 258
JL 7259–7261: 258
JL 7268: 123, 258
JL 7423: 259
JL 7429: 295
JL 7476: 138
JL 7499: 259
JL 7537: 124
JL 7548: 124
JL 7562: 259
JL 7636: 106
JL 7642: 106
JL 7666: 106
JL 7753: 255 n. 17
JL 7755: 255 n. 17
JL 7797: 110
JL 7848: 139–140, 248
JL 7889: 304

JL 7890: 198
JL 8016: 254 n. 10
JL 8022: 254 n. 10
JL 8031: 254 n. 10
JL 8124: 194
JL 8148–8149: 318 n. 11
JL 8180: 319 n. 17
JL 8232: 138
JL 8326: 122
JL 8376: 124
JL 8435: 174
JL 8456: 175
JL 8501: 175
JL 8572: 296
JL 8609: 296
JL 8620–8622: 176
JL 8653: 176–177
JL 8696: 305
JL 8707–8708: 176
JL 8844: 263
JL 8846–8847: 307 n. 15

JL 8859–8860: 263
JL 8994: 197
JL 9122: 264
JL 9124: 264
JL 9156: 264
JL 9203: 224
JL 9299–9301: 224
JL 9373: 193
JL 9549: 222
JL 9557: 265
JL 9599: 224
JL 9627: 243 n. 63, 244 n. 69
JL 9666: 202–203
JL 9722: 297
JL 9866: 267
JL 9869: 267
JL 9875: 267
JL 9877: 267
JL 9888: 244 n. 69
JL 10066–10068: 268
JL 10908: 226

REFERENCES TO PETER'S LETTERS

(not including the main section of notes on each letter)

(References are to volume II.)

Ep. 1: 99, 136, 139, 248, 260
Ep. 2: 27, 38, 47 n. 191, 101
Ep. 3: 18 n. 74, 248
Ep. 4: 100
Ep. 5: 20, 24, 101
Ep. 8: 36
Ep. 11: 304–305
Ep. 14: 121
Ep. 15: 23 n. 96, 156
Ep. 16: 14, 243
Ep. 17: 260
Ep. 18: 24 n. 99, 269
Ep. 20: 36, 51, 59, 92, 132, 183, 341 n. 39; MSS., 70–73; textual revision, 41, 43, 73, 82
Ep. 21: 135, 136
Ep. 22: 25, 311
Ep. 23: 164
Ep. 24: 3 n. 8, 35, 198, 342
Ep. 25: 111, 198, 311, 342
Ep. 26: 18, 20, 25, 335, 337–338, 342
Ep. 27: 260
Ep. 28: 13, 20, 36, 51, 59–60, 61, 92, 173, 206, 270–274; date, 272–274; differing forms, 67–69; MSS., 63–70; position in collection, 49, 54; relation to Bernard's *Apologia*, 271–273; textual revision, 41–43, 82–83
Ep. 29: 80, 122
Ep. 30: 248 n. 12, 269
Ep. 31: 153, 291
Ep. 32: 102, 125, 131
Ep. 34: 14, 27–28, 29, 35
Ep. 35: 36 n. 157
Ep. 37: 3 n. 8, 36, 162; position in collection, 54, 56, 76, 77, 81
Ep. 38: 35, 36, 41, 73, 109, 122, 135
Ep. 39: 80, 129, 337 n. 27
Ep. 40: 35–36, 336–337
Ep. 41: 269, 298 n. 21, 341–342
Ep. 42: 127, 269, 298 n. 21, 341–342
Ep. 44: 80, 95
Ep. 45: 348
Ep. 46: 35, 36
Ep. 47: 47 n. 191
Ep. 48: 111
Ep. 49: 80, 136, 297 n. 16
Ep. 51: 25, 195
Ep. 52: 133, 135
Ep. 53: 25, 114, 132, 133, 136, 238, 239, 244, 260
Ep. 54: 109
Ep. 55: 23 n. 96, 24
Ep. 56: 132, 135, 239, 244, 247, 260

Ep. 58: 74, 80, 134–135, 332, 335, 337–341, 342
Ep. 59: 156, 345
Ep. 60: 131, 345
Ep. 61: 27, 345
Ep. 62: 29, 96, 99, 140, 141, 248
Ep. 63: 29, 99, 141, 248
Ep. 65: 18, 23 n. 96, 147, 173
Ep. 66: 260, 337
Ep. 68: 26
Ep. 69: 18, 24, 29, 98, 140, 146, 260
Ep. 70: 142, 144, 146, 147, 260
Ep. 71: 155, 260, 285, 316
Ep. 73: 26, 145, 173
Ep. 74: 141, 173, 311
Ep. 75: 291
Ep. 76: 291
Ep. 77: 348
Ep. 78: 151
Ep. 79: 151, 346
Ep. 80: 19, 23–24, 132, 153, 195, 291
Ep. 81: 14 n. 61, 23 n. 96, 27, 39, 248
Ep. 82: 23–24
Ep. 83: 23–24, 132, 195
Ep. 85: 317, 319
Ep. 86: 27, 97, 109, 154, 162, 269, 317
Ep. 87: 317
Ep. 89: 47 n. 191
Ep. 90: 254
Ep. 91: 241
Ep. 94: 40–41, 125; position in collection, 58, 76, 77–78, 81
Ep. 95: 154, 155, 163, 261, 262, 311, 317
Ep. 96: 261, 311 n. 7, 317
Ep. 97: 110–111
Ep. 98: 178
Ep. 99: 241, 242
Ep. 100: 122, 131
Ep. 101: 43, 256
Ep. 102: 79, 169, 171, 289–290
Ep. 103: 160, 170
Ep. 104: 170
Ep. 105: 170
Ep. 106: 96, 169, 269
Ep. 107: 27
Ep. 108: 74, 269
Ep. 109: 269
Ep. 110: 13, 41, 44 n. 182
Ep. 111: 3 n. 8, 13, 35, 44 n. 182, 58, 60, 61, 116, 118, 199, 206, 275–284, 285, 287, 342
Ep. 112: 29, 79, 140, 212, 262, 263
Ep. 113: 175, 179, 263

INDEX OF CITATIONS

Ep. 114: 176
Ep. 115: 247, 347
Ep. 116: 305
Ep. 117: 3 n. 11, 39, 182; position in collection, 54, 56
Ep. 118: 176, 248
Ep. 119: 14 n. 61, 176
Ep. 120: 244
Ep. 121: 97
Ep. 122: 306
Ep. 123: 16, 43, 80, 177, 334, 342, 345, 347
Ep. 124: 16, 39, 80, 334, 335, 342
Ep. 125: 37–38, 75, 179, 332–333
Ep. 126: 43, 58, 75, 333
Ep. 127: 14–15, 38, 59, 75, 182, 333, 334
Ep. 128: 13–14, 16, 187, 333-334
Ep. 129: 16, 20, 80, 81, 285, 332–334
Ep. 131: 149, 263, 344
Ep. 132: 112
Ep. 133: 184, 189, 248, 263
Ep. 134: 187, 189
Ep. 135: 313, 314
Ep. 137: 74
Ep. 139: 14 n. 61, 74, 264
Ep. 141: 74, 102, 248
Ep. 143: 79
Ep. 144: 74, 79, 132; position in collection, 76, 78
Ep. 145: 79, 197, 202
Ep. 147: 13; position in collection, 76, 78, 81
Ep. 148: 198, 322
Ep. 149: 13, 14, 113, 197, 201, 322
Ep. 150: 41, 73, 79, 116, 200, 201–202, 321, 322, 323 n. 35
Ep. 151: 27, 36, 79, 152, 201–202, 322–323
Ep. 152: 79, 197, 198, 199, 322, 323
Ep. 153: 13, 14, 17, 216, 323
Ep. 154: 203
Ep. 155: 202, 203
Ep. 156: 204, 264

Ep. 157: 243
Ep. 158: 13, 199, 203, 344
Ep. 158 a: 94, 211, 217, 265; and b, 58, 79, 82–83, 248–251, 302–303
Ep. 160: 241, 242
Ep. 161: 13
Ep. 162: 148
Ep. 163: 208, 265
Ep. 164: 27, 174, 207, 211, 250, 265
Ep. 165: 208, 209, 250, 265
Ep. 166: 174, 211, 265
Ep. 167: 23, 132, 269
Ep. 168: 23, 38, 132, 165
Ep. 169: 47 n. 191, 112, 211
Ep. 170: 14, 112, 211, 270
Ep. 171: 110
Ep. 172: 110
Ep. 173: 110
Ep. 174: 27, 228–229, 242
Ep. 175: 216, 217, 265, 324
Ep. 176: 14 n. 61, 216, 219, 250, 265, 324, 328 n. 58
Ep. 177: 216, 218, 324
Ep. 178: 257
Ep. 179: 24, 39, 216, 217, 219, 324
Ep. 180: 24, 216, 265, 325
Ep. 181: 152, 216, 218, 219, 220, 265, 325, 328
Ep. 182: 216, 219, 265, 325
Ep. 183: 216, 218, 219, 220, 265, 325
Ep. 184: 216, 218, 219, 220, 265, 325
Ep. 185: 40, 242, 248
Ep. 186: 13, 40 n. 177, 111, 222, 265, 269
Ep. 187: 221
Ep. 188: 265
Ep. 189: 265, 269
Ep. 190: 41, 263, 265
Ep. 191: 346
Ep. 192: 230, 263, 264, 265, 266, 326
Ep. 193: 14 n. 61, 24 n. 101, 36 n. 157, 180, 226, 229, 245, 265, 266, 326

2. MODERN AUTHORS

(References are to volume II except when noted.)

This index includes the names of all authors, editors, and translators (since 1500) who are mentioned in the text or notes, except for Bréquigny, Lorain, and Pignot when they are cited in the first section of the notes to a letter. When an author is mentioned in the text alone, or in the text and the notes, a reference only to the page is given. For references in notes that run over from one page to another, the number of the page on which the reference actually appears, together with the number of the note, is given.

Abegg, Elizabeth, 235 n. 9, 236 n. 13
Achery, Luc d', 243 n. 63
Adam, R. J., 233 n. 1

Agius, T. A., I, 120 n. h
Albers, Bruno, 117, 118
Albon, G. A. M. J. d', 213

INDEX OF CITATIONS

Altamira, R., 97
Alverny, M. T. d', 48, 49 n. 195, 172, 174, 275 n. 3, 276, 277, 284, 342 n. 45
Andilly, Arnaud d', 133
Anger, P., 173, 208
Anstruther, R., 9 n. 37
Arbaumont, J. d', 258
Arbois de Jubainville, Henri d', 104, 105, 163, 200–201, 313 n. 14, 314 nn. 17–18, 316 n. 1, 320 n. 21
Arquillière, H.-X., 228–229
Aubert, Marcel, 321 n. 22
Aubret, L., 166, 213
Auniord, M. J.-B., 226
Avenel, Joseph d', 93 n. 1

Baix, F., 159
Balau, S., 157
Baldwin, C. S., 30 n. 127, 34 n. 150
Baldwin, J. W., 215
Balogh, Josef, 19 n. 79, 27 n. 115
Baluze, Étienne, 46, 259, 307 n. 11, 345, 348
Balzani, U., 129, 143
Bar, Francis, 3 n. 11
Barlow, Frank, 9, 167
Baronius, Cesare, 61, 148
Barraclough, G., 144
Barré, H., 329 n. 59
Bascapè, Giacomo, 23 n. 93
Baudot, Anne Marcel, 216, 236 n. 11
Baudot, Marcel, 216, 236 n. 11
Bäumer, Suitbert, 173
Baumont, H., 110
Beaunier, Dom (ed. J.-M. Besse), 121, 123, 181, 190, 192, 215, 236 n. 13, 337 n. 28, 339 n. 37
Becker, Alfons, 299 n. 1
Bellet, C.-F., 33 n. 143
Bennett, H. S., 21 n. 86, 26 n. 112
Benton, John F., 316 nn. 1, 3, 330 nn. 63–64
Berger, Élie, 39 n. 170, 138, 210, 314 n. 21, 332 n. 5, 337 n. 28
Berlière, Ursmer, 53 n. 224, 96, 117, 125, 128, 129, 152, 175, 184, 258, 291 nn. 2,7, 292 n. 10
Bernards, Matthäus, 108, 173
Bernhardi, Wilhelm, 96, 113, 115, 124, 129, 139, 143, 159, 185, 206, 207, 263, 293 n. 2
Bernheim, Ernst, 113–114
Berry, Virginia, 128, 132, 148, 152, 153, 185, 206–208, 213, 337 n. 27
Berulfsen, Bjarne, 31 n. 131
Besançon, Abel, 166
Besse, J.-M., 119, 173, 208. *See also* Beaunier
Bethmann, C. L., 51

Beumann, H., 22 n. 90
Beyssac, Jean, 122, 131, 165, 191, 241 n. 49, 242
Bieler, Ludwig, 85 n. 298
Biron, Réginald, 173
Bishko, C. J., 133, 168, 170, 262
Bland, C. C. Swinton, 196
Bled, O., 167, 168, 263
Bligny, Bernard, 112, 113, 203, 258
Bloch, Herbert, I, 135 n. c; II, 99, 118, 124, 167, 185, 293 n. 2, 336 n. 25
Bloch, Marc, 23 n. 95, 28
Blume, Clemens, 183
Bodard, Claude, 125, 159, 287
Boeckler, Albert, 109
Böhmer, Heinrich, 252–255
Bollea, L. C., 222
Bond, E. A., 70 n. 275
Bongert, Yvonne, 215
Bonnard, Fourier, 106, 196
Bonnes, Jean-Paul, 96, 184
Borino, G. B., 299 n. 1
Borst, Arno, 287, 319 n. 15, 320 n. 19
Boudet, Marcellin, 215, 216, 235 n. 9, 236 nn. 11,13, 240 n. 44, 241 nn. 46,49, 244 n. 66, 299 n. 1
Boussard, Jacques, 193
Boutemy, André, 50 n. 203, 52 nn. 213–214, 216
Bouvet, J., 104
Bredero, A. H., 19 n. 79, 200, 274 n. 17
Bresslau, Harry, 6 n. 25, 29 n. 127, 30 n. 129, 31 n. 135, 32, 33 n. 141, 198, 236 n. 13
Brewer, J. S., 104
Brial, M.-J.-J., 48, 121, 171, 207, 297, 309 n. 28, 316 n. 1, 318 n. 10, 324 n. 40, 348
Brigué, Louis, 158
Briquet, Charles, 51 n. 211, 57 n. 232, 59 n. 248, 62 n. 255, 66 n. 262
Brixius, Johannes, 96, 98–99, 100, 174, 176, 227, 293 nn. 1–2, 294 nn. 4,6
Brooke, C. N. L., 8 n. 31, 12, 24 n. 98, 99, 145, 178, 252 n. 1, 254, 256 nn. 24,26
Brooke, Dorothy, 5 n. 18
Brooke, Z. N., 253 n. 8
Bruckner, Albert, 345
Brullée, Louis, 194
Brunel, Clovis, 289 n. 1
Bruns, H. T., I, 82 n. x
Brutails, J.-A., 96
Bruyne, D. de, 8 n. 31, 47 n. 190
Bullioud, Pierre, 73
Busson, G., 256 n. 23
Butler, Cuthbert, 118
Butler, Lionel, 233 n. 1
Bütow, Adolf, 4 n. 14, 30 n. 128, 31
Buytaert, É. M., 84 n. 295, 86 n. 303

INDEX OF CITATIONS 385

Calati, Benedetto, 108
Calendini, A., 98
Campi, P. M., 224
Camuzat, Nicolas, 97, 144
Canivez, J.-M., I, iii; II, 48, 199, 272 n. 6
Capelle, B., I, 30 n. q
Capua, Francesco di, 27 n. 115, 30 n. 129, 34 n. 145, 37 n. 161
Cartellieri, Otto, 163, 164, 171, 188, 208, 209, 214, 264, 297, 309 n. 28, 312 nn. 8,11, 348
Caspar, Erich, 159, 176, 206, 271 n. 2
Cassan, Léon, 99
Cassart, J., 159
Cazzaniga, E., I, 431 n. m, 432 n. n
Cerone, Francesco, 185
Chadwick, John, 25
Chaix de Lavarène, A.-C., 192, 193, 204, 212, 216, 241 nn. 46,50, 244 n. 69, 301
Chalandon, Ferdinand, 139, 148, 159, 177, 206, 207
Challe, A., 218
Chartrou, Josèphe, 253 n. 5
Chassaing, Augustin, 57 nn. 236,239, 58 n. 241, 213, 216, 242 nn. 50,52
Chaume, Maurice, 94 n. 2, 344, 347, 348
Chavot, T., 182
Chaytor, H. J., 97
Chazaud, M.-A., 58 n. 244, 263, 311 n. 3, 344, 348
Cheney, C. R., 2, 9 n. 36, 11 nn. 47–48, 19 n. 81, 28, 94
Chenon, Émile, 236 n. 13
Chenu, M.-D., 321 n. 27, 328 n. 58, 329 n. 59
Chérest, Aimé, 243 n. 63, 354
Chergé, Charles de, 295 n. 10
Chevalier, C., 169
Chevalier, Ulysse, 94, 99, 102, 111–113, 128, 130, 134, 150, 152, 153, 157, 158, 167, 181, 191, 192, 195, 198, 201, 203, 204, 218, 221, 223, 224, 238 n. 28, 245 n. 76, 287 n. 13, 289, 290 n. 5, 294 n. 9, 295 n. 12, 316 n. 1, 331 n. 2, 345
Churchill, W. A., 67 n. 268
Cipolla, Carlo, 222
Claretta, Gaudenzio, 236 n. 13
Clark, A. C., 30 n. 129, 33 nn. 141,144, 34 n. 150
Clark, John W., 186
Claude, Hubert, 147, 293 n. 2, 336 n. 25, 337 n. 30
Clémencet, Charles, 63 n. 259, 271
Clerval, A., 163, 190
Clouët, Louis, 129, 130
Cohn, E. S., 11 n. 48
Colker, Marvin, 195–196
Compain, L., 119, 156

13*

Conant, K. J., 155, 157–158
Congar, Yves-Marie, 287
Cooke, Alice M., 272 n. 7
Côte, Léon, 56 n. 231, 57 n. 235, 244 n. 69, 259, 263–264, 267
Cottineau, L. H., 118, 121, 123, 181, 192, 208, 215, 222, 227, 291 nn. 2,7, 332 n. 5
Coüard-Luys, E., 196
Coulton, G. G., 134
Courcelles, J.-B.-P.-J., 234 n. 7, 237
Coussemaker, Edmond de, 51 n. 210
Cowdrey, H. E. J., 133
Cronne, H. A., 104
Csányi, D. A., 118
Cucherat, F., 133, 134, 157, 238, 239 nn. 34–35, 240 n. 38
Cunningham, Joseph, 2 n. 6
Curtius, E. R., I, 109 n. a, 135 n. c; II, 3 n. 9, 19 n. 79, 30 n. 127, 38 n. 168, 39 n. 171

Dain, A., 47 n. 191, 51 n. 206, 55 n. 226, 84 n. 296
Dantyl (Dantil), 215
Darlington, R. R., 105
Dauvillier, Jean, 223
David, P., 293 n. 2
Davidsohn, Robert, 186, 261
Davies, H. W., 45 n. 184
Davis, H. W. C., 252, 256 n. 21
Davy, M.-M., 39 n. 172, 112
Déchanet, J.-M., 44 n. 182
Dehaisnes, C., 49 n. 196, 51 n. 211, 52 n. 213, 53 nn. 220–221
Dekkers, Eligius, 18 n. 77, 19 n. 79, 81 n. 291
Delaborde, H.-F., 291
Deladreue, L.-E., 103
Déléage, André, 314 n. 21
Delhaye, Ph., 39 n. 172
Delisle, Léopold, 2 n. 3, 17 n. 71, 35 n. 155, 39 nn. 170,173, 46 n. 186, 55 n. 229, 57 nn. 237–239, 58, 61 n. 250, 111, 217, 314 n. 21
Demimuid, M., 93 n. 1
Depoin, J., 187, 188, 309 n. 28, 312 n. 9, 313 n. 13
Dereine, Charles, 3 n. 9, 120, 157, 158–159
Desjardins, Gustave, 245 n. 75
Deutsch, S. Martin, 164, 178, 318, 319
Devic, Claude, 169, 178–179, 192, 240 n. 41, 242 n. 51, 245
Dickinson, J. C., I, 226 n. p; II, 1 n. 2
Didier, J. C., 164, 287
Didier, Noël, 223, 258
Dienne, Édouard de, 234–237 *passim*
Dieudonné, A., 8 n. 31
Dimier, M.-Anselme, 181, 272, 321 n. 27
Dimock, J. F., 104, 105
Dölger, Franz, 292
Döllinger, J. J. I. von, 287

Doniol, Henry, 236 n. 11
Donnelly, James S., 175
Douie, Decima, 111
Dozy, R. P. A., 173
Dreves, G. M., 183
Drival, E. van, 266
Dubois, Gérard, 105
Dubois, J., 39 n. 172
Du Boulay, C. E., 164, 177, 185, 209, 210
Duby, Georges, 97, 110, 166, 182, 213, 214, 225, 233 n. 2, 272 n. 7
Duchesne, André, 47, 48, 55, 75-78, 82, 93, 97, 98, 102-104, 117, 118, 131, 132, 142, 144-146, 155, 156, 163, 164, 171, 184-186, 188, 190, 192, 194-195, 207, 209, 210, 215, 234, 239, 240 nn. 38,43, 264, 295 n. 10, 309 n. 28, 312 n. 11
Duchesne, Louis, 33 n. 141, 156, 198
Duckett, George, 139, 255, 256 n. 22, 269
Ducourneau, J. Othon, 116, 272 n. 7
Dugdale, William, 128, 297 nn. 13,17
Dunod, F. I., 180
Duparay, B., 93 n. 1
Duplès-Agier, H., 236 n. 13
Dupré Theseider, Eugenio, 159, 186
Durand, Ursin, 50, 52, 58 n. 242
Duru, L. M., 143

Emden, A. B., 107
Emonds, Hilarius, 43 n. 182
Engels, Odilo, 33 n. 142
Enlart, Camille, 122, 291, 292
Erdmann, Carl, 4, 6-11 passim, 19 n. 81, 21 n. 86, 22 nn. 90,92, 32 n. 137, 33 n. 141, 34 n. 148, 82, 226
Escallier, E. A., 50 n. 203, 52 nn. 213-214, 53 n. 220
Esmein, A., I, 135 n. 1
Esposito, Mario, 85 n. 298
Estiennot, Claude, 57, 245
Evans, A. P., 48 n. 192
Evans, Joan, 12, 112, 121, 177, 182, 183, 221, 238, 332 n. 7, 337 n. 28
Every, George, 148
Eynde, Damien van den, 8 n. 33, 99, 162, 178, 273 n. 13, 319 n. 15, 331 n. 3

Farmer, Hugh, 111
Farrar, C. P., 48 n. 192
Farrer, William, 104, 297 n. 13
Favre, Léopold, 331 n. 2
Fawtier, Robert, 233
Fazy, Max, 236 n. 13, 244 n. 69, 259, 263-264
Fearns, J. V., 81 n. 291, 288 n. 17
Ferrari, Angel, 343
Fliche, Augustin, 313 n. 14
Foreville, Raymonde, 114, 318 n. 15

Fornier, Marcellin, 102
Foulques de Villaret, A. de, 196, 309 nn. 20,22
Fournier, Gabriel, 212, 233 n. 3, 234 n. 7, 236 n. 13
Franklin, Alfred, 295 n. 13
Freeman, E. A., 252
Fryar, John R., 297 n. 17
Fryde, E. B., 150
Fuhrmann, Horst, 120

Galbraith, V. H., 22 nn. 91-92
Gams, P. B., 94, 102, 115, 129, 150, 164, 169, 187, 190-192, 212, 227, 240 n. 44, 286 n. 3, 299 n. 1, 304 n. 1
Ganzer, Klaus, 294 n. 4
Gardon, François, 243 n. 61
Gariador, Benoît, 291 n. 1
Gaussin, Pierre-Roger, 192, 204, 212, 233 n. 3, 236 n. 13, 243
Gay, Jules, 148, 292
Gelsomino, Remo, 39 n. 171
Genicot, Léopold, 233 n. 2
Gerini, Emanuelle, 224
Gessler, J., 50 n. 203
Ghellinck, Joseph de, 5, 8 n. 31, 9 n. 37, 30 n. 127, 99, 112, 158, 287, 329 n. 59
Gibbs, Marion, 150
Giesebrecht, Wilhelm von, 113
Giles, J. A., 252 n. 1
Gilson, Étienne, 39 n. 171
Gingins-La-Sarra, F. de, 345-346
Giry, A., 2 n. 3, 21 n. 86, 22 n. 92, 94 n. 2, 238 n. 26
Giseke, Paul, 270
Gjerset, Knut, 128
Gleber, Helmut, 203, 208, 266
Goffart, Walter, 47 n. 191
Goldhorn, David, 287
Goldschmidt, E. P., 45 n. 183
Gómez, Ildefonso, 112
Gomot, Hippolyte, 192, 241 n. 48, 301
Gorce, Denys, 5 n. 18, 22 n. 90, 23 n. 95, 25 n. 103, 26 n. 107
Gorman, John C., 19 n. 79
Gotenburg, Erwin, 70 n. 272
Gottlieb, Theodor, 63 n. 258, 70 n. 275, 72 n. 278
Gougaud, Louis, 109, 134, 249 n. 17
Graham, Rose, 133, 238, 240 n. 38, 243 n. 63, 265-268
Gransden, Antonia, 1 n. 2
Grebenc, Maver, 106, 114, 141
Greenaway, G. W., 318 n. 15, 327 n. 52, 328 n. 55
Grotefend, H., 94
Grumel, V., 149, 292

INDEX OF CITATIONS

Grundmann, Herbert, 27 n. 115, 288
Guérard, Benjamin, 19 n. 79
Guichenon, Samuel, 142, 193-194
Guigue, M.-C., 166

Hadcock, R. Neville, 128, 297 nn. 13,17
Hahn, August, I, 124 n. e
Haigneré, D., 263
Hallinger, Kassius, 61 n. 251, 91 n. 304, 116, 117, 175, 249 n. 17
Hanslik, R., 40 n. 176
Haring, N. M., 159, 303 n. 10
Haskins, C. H., 30 nn. 127-128, 31-33, 52 n. 217, 53 n. 218, 104, 105, 109, 252, 256 n. 23, 314 n. 21
Hauréau, B., 150, 168, 327 n. 52, 332 n. 5
Havet, Julien, I, 109 n. a; II, 8 n. 32
Havet, Louis, 30 n. 129, 43 n. 182
Hébert, P., 99, 104, 106, 107
Hefele, Friedrich, 10 n. 40
Hefele, K. J. (ed. H. Leclercq), 106, 114, 115, 164, 168, 169, 258, 318 n. 14
Herescu, N. I., 44 n. 182
Herrgott, Marquard, 116-118, 249 n. 17
Herwegen, Ildefons, 119
Heywood, William, 114, 261
Higounet, C., 21 n. 86, 22 n. 92
Hill, G. B., 84 n. 294
Hirsch, Hans, 7 n. 28, 8 n. 30
Hirsch, Richard, 142, 162, 164
Hoffmann, Hartmut, 10 n. 40, 21 n. 86, 22 n. 90, 23 n. 93, 26 nn. 107,109, 213, 225, 226, 228
Hofmeister, Philipp, 294 n. 7
Hohenleutner, Heinrich, 11 n. 50
Holmes, Urban T., Jr., 28 n. 122
Holtzmann, Robert, *see* Wattenbach
Holtzmann, Walther, 32, 227
Hoskier, H. C., 269
Hoste, Anselm, 5 n. 20, 32 n. 136
Howland, A. C., 215
Howlett, Richard, 268
Hugo, Charles-Louis, 130
Huguenin, Alexandre, 314 n. 17, 315 n. 24

Ignace-Joseph de Jésus Maria, 289 n. 1, 290 n. 8
Ilarino da Milano, 288
Imbart de la Tour, Pierre, 164, 304 n. 1

Jacob, E. F., 28
Jacotin, Antoine, 58 n. 241, 212, 213, 216, 237, 242 n. 51
Jaffé, Ph., 94
James, M. R., 19, 85 n. 298, 117
Janauschek, Leopold, I, iii; II, 181, 189

Janssen, Wilhelm, 96, 99, 100, 106, 109, 110, 122, 124, 150, 163, 169, 191, 225-226, 242 n. 55, 266, 293 n. 2, 294 nn. 6-7, 319 n. 15, 336 n. 25, 337 nn. 27,30
Jarry, Eugène, 189, 304 n. 2
Jeannin, J., 178, 247 n. 2
Jeffery, George, 292 n. 12
Johnson, Charles, 104
Jorden, Willibald, 133, 136
Juenin, Pierre, 122

Kehr, Paul, 227-228
Kersers, Louis de, 304 n. 3
Kittel, E., 22 n. 90
Klewitz, Hans-Walter, 96, 99, 293 nn. 1-2
Klibansky, Raymond, 1 n. 1, 9 n. 37, 319 n. 15
Knowles, M. C. (Dom David), 28 n. 119, 39 n. 171, 48, 49 n. 195, 51, 96-97, 116-118, 128, 131, 206, 249 n. 17, 253 n. 8, 255 n. 15, 272, 273, 297 nn. 13,17, 298 n. 19, 318 n. 14, 329, 346
Koller, Heinrich, 4 n. 13, 237 n. 19
Kramp, Joseph, 102, 172, 287
Kristeller, P. O., 63 n. 257, 302, 369
Kritzeck, James, 49 n. 201, 50 n. 202, 174, 185, 276, 277 n. 10, 278 n. 12, 284, 342 n. 45
Kroll, Wilhelm, 5 n. 18
Krueger, P., I, 198 n. e
Kuttner, Stephan, 116

Labande, L.-H., 195
Labbé, Philip, 234 n. 5, 240 n. 41, 243 nn. 59-60,64, 260, 332 n. 7
Laborde, J. de, 196
Ladner, G. B., 118, 228
Laehr, Gerhard, 4 n. 13
Lambot, C., I, 120 n. h, 441 n. e
Lamma, Paolo, 12, 35 n. 154, 39 n. 170, 111, 132, 133, 148, 149, 159, 185, 206, 238 n. 28, 239 n. 32, 241
Lampen, W., 96
Langer, Otto, 261
Langlois, Ch.-V., 1 n. 1, 29 n. 127, 31-32
Langosch, Karl, 7 n. 29
Laporte, Jean, 34 n. 151
Larson, Laurence M., 128
La Saussaye, Charles de, 304 n. 4, 305 n. 6
Lasteyrie, Charles de, 114, 190, 205, 260, 332 n. 7, 347
Lasteyrie, Robert de, 188
Lattin, Harriet P., 8 n. 32, 11 n. 48
Lea, H. C., 215
Lebeuf, Jean, 218, 307 n. 15
Lebourlier, Jean, 195
Le Bras, G., 158
Leclercq, Henri, 2 n. 6, 8 n. 31. *See also* K. J. Hefele

Leclercq, Jean, I, 40 n. y, 61 n. e, 135 n. c, 151 n. d, 183 n. a, 204 n. f; II, 1–4 *passim*, 8 n. 31, 10–13, 17–19, 27 n. 115, 32 n. 136, 35 n. 154, 41 n. 178, 43, 44 n. 182, 48 n. 194, 51 n. 212, 52, 70 n. 275, 71 n. 276, 101, 107, 109, 116, 118, 125, 132, 134, 145, 161, 172–174, 182–185, 195, 198, 206, 226, 247 n. 1, 263, 272 n. 7, 273, 275 n. 4, 302, 316 n. 1, 321 n. 27, 322 n. 29, 327 n. 52, 328 n. 56, 329 n. 59, 330 n. 63, 332 n. 5, 339 n. 38
Lecointre-Dupont, G., 102, 181–182, 331 n. 1, 332, 334, 336, 337 n. 31, 341 n. 40, 342 n. 47
Lecomte, Francis, 100
Le Couteulx, Charles, 111, 112, 130, 198, 201–204, 211, 221–223
Lecoy de la Marche, A., 171, 297, 348
Ledru, A., 256 n. 23
Le Fort, Ch., I, iii
Legg, L. G. Wickham, 253 n. 8
Lemarignier, J.-F., 120
Le Michel, Anselme, 55
Lentini, Anselmo, 33 n. 142
Léonard, E.-J., 61 n. 254
Le Paige, F.-J., 173
Le Prévost, A., 314 n. 18
Lesire, Antoine, 189
Lesmarie, Antoine, 235 n. 10
Lesne, Émile, 18 n. 77, 19 n. 79, 52 n. 217, 53 n. 219, 112, 157, 186
Lesort, André, 295 n. 9
Lespinasse, René de, 244, 245 n. 73, 296, 297
Lestocquoy, J., 28 nn. 122–123
Letonnelier, Gaston, 119, 120, 143, 168
Lettenhove, Kervyn de, 98
Le Vasseur, Jacques, 113
Levison, Wilhelm, 229
L'Huillier, Albert, 157, 159–160, 176, 291
Lindholm, Gudrun, 30 n. 129, 31 n. 135, 34 n. 146
Longnon, Auguste, 314 n. 21
Loriquet, Henri, 151
Lot, F., 8 n. 32
Lottin, Odon, 331 n. 3
Louandre, F.-C., 289 n. 1
Louis, René, 105, 140, 243 n. 63
Löwenfeld (Loewenfeld), S., 94, 106, 290 n. 7, 297 n. 11, 304, 318 n. 14
Lubac, Henri de, 158
Luce, Siméon, 337 n. 28
Luchaire, Achille, 4 n. 13, 47 n. 141, 98, 99, 106, 121, 161–163, 168, 195, 196, 207, 208, 260, 264, 296 nn. 3,4,10, 304 nn. 1,4, 309 nn. 21,23,24,26–28, 312 nn. 9,11,14–15, 314 n. 19, 338 n. 34
Lullin, Paul, I, iii
Lyte, H. Maxwell, 85 n. 299

Maan, Jean, 168
Mabillon, Jean, 48, 97, 101, 103, 111, 113, 129, 130, 132, 140, 142, 147, 148, 150, 151, 160, 163, 164, 166, 168, 169, 172, 174, 175, 177, 180–182, 185, 187, 189, 192, 193, 195, 197–201, 204–207, 217, 221, 222, 226, 239, 240, 261, 263–265, 268, 271, 272 n. 6, 292 n. 10, 294 n. 9, 296, 298, 304 n. 1, 307 n. 10, 316 nn. 1,4, 319, 320 n. 21, 321 n. 24, 329, 332 n. 5, 334, 338 n. 32
Maccarone, Michele, 102
MacDonald, A. J., 158
McKerrow, R. B., 55 n. 226
MacKinney, Loren C., 205, 249 nn. 17–18, 303 n. 7
Magoun, F. P., Jr., 114
Mahn, Jean-Berthold, 124, 195, 196
Maissonneuve, Henri, 287
Maitland, S. R., 2 n. 3, 38 n. 166, 52 n. 217, 102, 107, 111, 137, 172, 197, 198, 200, 201, 204, 216–219, 316 n. 1, 329 n. 62, 331 n. 1
Malaspina, F., 222
Mandonnet, P.-F., 172, 276
Manitius, Max, I, 80 n. t; II, 5 n. 19, 32 n. 137, 33 nn. 142–143, 39 n. 173, 40 n. 175, 158, 179, 295 n. 14, 331 n. 1, 341 n. 40
Manrique, Angel, 164, 180, 195, 197, 199, 200, 202, 207, 208, 216–220, 226
Manselli, Raoul, 100, 114, 154, 288
Mansi, J. D., 168, 176, 253 n. 9, 307 n. 11
Marlot, G., 289, 290 n. 5
Marrier, Martin, 47, 55, 75–78, 82, 100, 121, 188, 221, 338 n. 34
Martène, Edmond, 50, 52, 58 n. 242, 116, 249 n. 17
Martin, Franz, 4 n. 13
Martin, J.-B., 109, 122, 165, 204, 214, 223, 224, 242 n. 55, 259
Masson, J. P., 142
Mathon, 103
Matthew, Donald, 34 n. 151
Médicis, Étienne, 57 n. 236
Megaw, Isabel, 253 n. 8, 256 n. 23
Mellana, A., 235 n. 8
Mély, F. de, 149
Méras, Matthieu, 166, 213, 214, 225
Mercier, Fernand, 155
Messiter, C., 11 n. 50
Métais, C., 190
Meyer, A. de., 111
Meyer, Otto, 7 n. 29
Meyer, Wilhelm, 30 n. 129, 34 n. 149, 295 n. 14, 318 nn. 12,15
Meynial, E., 99
Mirot, Léon, 161
Misch, Georg, 6 n. 24

INDEX OF CITATIONS

Molinier, Auguste, 5 n. 19, 98, 102, 133, 158, 206
Molitor, Raphael, 168
Mollat, G., 144
Möllenberg, Walter, 4 n. 13
Mombritius, B., I, 166 n. b
Mommsen, T., I, 198, n. e
Monod, Bernard, 300 n. 4
Monteynard, C. de, 258
Moore, Philip, 331 n. 2
Moreau, Édouard de, 53 n. 224, 167, 168
Morey, Adrian, 8 n. 31, 99, 120, 252 n. 1, 256 nn. 24,26
Moricca, U., I, 63, n. r, 66 n. 1, 93 nn. i,j, 242 n. n, 245 nn. x,y, 319 nn. a ff., 352 n. cc, 422 n. k
Mortet, Victor, 157
Morton, James, 1 n. 2
Müller, E., 171
Muratori, L. A., 210
Mynors, R. A. B., 109

Narducci, Enrico, 61 n. 253
Nicholau, M.-G., 30 n. 129
Nicolau d'Olwer, L., 318 nn. 11-13, 319 n. 15, 328 n. 19
Nock, A. D., 118
Norgate, Kate, 252

Oehl, Wilhelm, 4
Oesterley, Hermann, 5 n. 19
Ogle, Marbury, 156
Ohnsorge, Werner, 4 n. 13
Olleris, A., 8 n. 32
Omont, Henri, 58 n. 243
Oppenheim, Philipp, 116
Ott, Ludwig, 4, 5 n. 19
Otto, August, I, 125 n. b, 135 n. c, 146 n. b, 204 n. m, 305 n. g
Oursel, Raymond, 101, 105, 177, 318 nn. 11-13, 320 n. 19

Pacaut, Marcel, 110, 150, 164, 168, 187, 193, 195-196, 213, 296 n. 8, 304 n. 1
Paetow, L. J., 30 n. 127
Pasquali, Giorgio, 43
Pauly, A. (ed. G. Wissowa), I, 305 n. g; II, 10 n. 44
Payrard, J.-B., 241 n. 50
Pease, A. S., I, 421 n. e
Pérard, E., 165
Peterson, E., 116
Petit, Ernest, 112, 293 n. 2, 332 n. 6
Pez, Bernard, 3 n. 9
Pfeiffer, E., 208
Pflugk-Harttung, J. von, 198

Pierre de Montmartre, 46, 47, 55-56, 60, 62, 74 n. 281, 75-78, 81, 82, 125
Pignot, J.-Henri, 93, 97, 101, 116, 118, 134, 143, 155, 168, 180, 184, 189, 199, 224, 230, 233, 238 n. 30, 239, 240, 241, 243 n. 63, 245 nn. 72-73, 246 n. 77, 256 n. 22, 261, 263-265, 267, 269, 273 n. 14, 291, 293 n. 2, 294 n. 9, 304 n. 1, 314 n. 17, 315 n. 24, 331 n. 1, 332 nn. 6-7, 333 n. 10, 334 n. 13
Pivec, Karl, 4-6, 41 n. 178
Plummer, Charles, 259
Polheim, Karl, 30 n. 129, 32, 34 n. 149, 37
Pommeraye, J. F., 217
Poole, A. L., 104, 115, 129, 253 n. 8, 256 nn. 21,23
Poole, R. L., 9 n. 35, 22, 28, 30 n. 129, 33 n. 141, 34 n. 152, 94 n. 2, 253, 254
Poorter, A. de, 69 n. 270
Porée, A., 105, 332 n. 5
Potter, K. R., 253 n. 8, 256 n. 21
Powicke, F. M., 32 n. 136, 39 n. 172, 107, 150
Predelli, R., 267
Previté-Orton, C. W., 142
Prévost, A., 98
Prou, Maurice, 313 n. 14

Quantin, Maximilien, 218
Quasten, Johannes, I, 279 n. 5
Quéguiner, Jean, 106
Queller, Donald E., 25 n. 106
Quentin, Henri, 56 n. 231, 57 n. 233, 58 n. 245, 76, 205, 302, 303 n. 7

Raby, F. J. E., 295 n. 14
Raffin, Léonce, 182, 224, 225
Raine, James, 104, 105
Ramackers, Johannes, 114, 124, 193, 304
Ramsay, J. H., 104, 105, 252, 255-256
Rand, E. K., 108
Rashdall, Hastings, 107
Rassow, Peter, 195, 200, 262. 316 n. 1, 318 n. 11, 320 n. 21, 321, 322 n. 31, 324 n. 36, 328 n. 54, 329 n. 60
Reindel, Kurt, 10 n. 41, 19 n. 79
Renouard, P., 45 nn. 184-185, 46 n. 187
Renouard, Yves, 23 n. 95, 24 n. 98, 28 n. 122
Riant, Paul, 121, 128, 149, 299 n. 1
Richard, Alfred, 293 n. 2, 335 nn. 18,20, 336 n. 25, 339 n. 36
Richard, Jean, 96, 137, 225
Riché, Pierre, 27 n. 115
Ripberger, A., I, 120 n. h, 236 n. h, 244 n. v, 251 n. r, 252 n. s, 253 nn. t-v, 254 nn. x-y, 430 n. j
Rivière, Jean, 228, 318 n. 15
Robert, Ulysse, 51
Robertson, J. C., 346

Rochais, H., 195
Rockinger, Ludwig, 29 n. 127, 31 n. 135, 33 n. 142
Röhricht, Reinhold, 152, 153, 213, 214
Roover, F. E. de, 52 n. 217
Rose, Valentin, 32 n. 137
Rosières, C. J. de, 243 n. 61
Rössler, Oskar, 252, 254 n. 14, 256 n. 23
Round, J. H., 105, 150, 252, 254, 255, 314, 346
Runciman, Steven, 128, 148, 209
Ruysschaert, J., 62 n. 254
Ryan, J. J., 316 n. 1

Sabbe, Étienne, 53 n. 224
Saltet, Louis, 99, 158
Saltman, Avrom, 150, 253 n. 8, 260, 266, 297 n. 17
Sanchez Belda, Luis, 97
Sander, A., 63 n. 259, 70 n. 274
Sandys, J. E., 39, 102
Santifaller, Leo, 18 n. 77
Satabin, J., 201, 208, 324 n. 36
Sauvage, R.-Norbert, 23 n. 95
Savio, Fedele, 235–238, 242 n. 56, 245
Saxer, Victor, 243 n. 63
Schäfer, Heinrich, 97
Schäfer, Thomas, 118
Schaller, H. M., 11 n. 45
Schanz, M., 40
Schmale, F.-J., 4 n. 13, 31 n. 135, 36 n. 159, 96, 99, 124, 163, 293 nn. 1–2, 336 n. 25, 337 n. 27
Schmeidler, Bernhard, 4–9 *passim*, 11 n. 46, 82
Schmitt, F. S., 3 n. 9, 10 n. 43, 11 n. 48, 44 n. 182
Schmitz, L., 21 n. 86
Schmitz, Philibert, 52 n. 217, 265–267, 291 n. 7, 295 n. 9
Schnack, Ingeborg, 96, 244
Schnitzer, Joseph, 158
Schönbach, Anton E., 12 n. 53, 38, 48
Schramm, P. E., 253 n. 8
Schreiber, Georg, 99, 120, 133, 168
Schullian, Dorothy, 156
Schwartz, Gerhard, 235 n. 9
Scivoletto, Nino, 34 n. 150
Scott, H. v. E., 196
Séjourné, Paul, 48, 52, 53, 125, 161, 195, 213, 223, 272 n. 7, 287
Severt, Jacques, 97, 109, 125, 135, 165, 242 n. 55, 304 n. 1
Sikes, J. G., 164, 172, 177, 178, 287, 319 n. 15
Silvestre, Hubert, 33 n. 143, 34 n. 147
Singer, Samuel, I, 125 n. e
Smedt, C. de, 33 n. 143
Smet, J. M. de, 111
Smith, L. M., 273 n. 14

Souancé, H. de, 190
Southern, R. W., 3 n. 8, 44 n. 182, 256 n. 21
Sproemberg, Heinrich, 53 n. 224
Steiger, Augustin, 316 n. 1, 321 n. 24, 324 n. 40, 328 n. 56
Stevenson, Burton, I, 114 n. e, 345 n. a
Stevenson, W. B., 209
Stickler, A. M., 228
Stiennon, Jacques, 157–159
Stubbs, William, 2, 25, 150
Sudhoff, Karl, 302
Sykutris, J., 5 n. 18, 10

Talbot, C. H., I, 125 n. e; II, 28 n. 120, 44 n. 182, 100, 132–133, 302, 316 n. 1
Tardif, Jules, 196, 213–214
Tellenbach, Gerd, 97, 123, 233 n. 2, 273 n. 14, 293 n. 2
Teulet, A., 196
Thillier, Joseph, 304 n. 2
Thompson, J. W., 52 n. 217, 112
Thomson, S. H., 44 n. 182
Thorpe, Benjamin, 259, 298 n. 19
Thurot, Charles, 31 n. 132
Tierney, Brian, 228
Turner, C. H., I, 61 n. e

Ughelli, Ferdinando, 115
Uhlirz, Mathilde, 8 n. 32
Ullmann, Walter, 229

Vacandard, Elphège, 23 n. 93, 30 n. 129, 37 n. 163, 106, 129, 140, 147, 151, 163, 164, 172, 177, 178, 195, 198, 200–202, 207–208, 216, 219, 226, 227, 259, 271–272, 287, 290 n. 6, 306 n. 9, 316 n. 1, 318 n. 15, 319 n. 18, 320 n. 21, 321 n. 22, 323 n. 35, 324 n. 40, 326, 328 n. 54, 330 n. 63, 336 n. 25
Vacher, Joseph, 56 n. 231
Vahlen, J., I, 218 n. d
Vaissete, Jean Joseph, 169, 178–179, 192, 240 n. 41, 242 n. 51, 245
Valois, Noël, 4 n. 14, 8 n. 31, 23 nn. 93–94, 25–26, 30 nn. 128–130, 31 n. 135, 34 n. 148, 37
Valous, Guy de, 57 n. 235, 101, 110, 116–121, 128, 133, 137, 139, 146, 173, 182, 208, 221, 239 n. 35, 272 n. 7, 289 n. 2, 291 n. 2, 292 n. 13, 333 n. 12
Vendeuvre, J., 108
Verbraken, P., I, 30 n. q
Vercauteren, F., 303
Verriest, L., 233 n. 2
Violante, Cinzio, 267
Virey, Jean, 155, 157, 178, 182
Vogüé, C. J. M. de, 292 n. 12
Voss, Lena, 114, 131, 138, 156, 169, 262, 265

Wache, Walter, 10 n. 40, 21 n. 88
Waddell, Helen, 178
Wagner, M. Monica, 5 n. 18
Wallach, Luitpold, 3 n. 9, 6 n. 23
Walter, Johannes von, 134
Walther, Hans, 218
Warner, G. F., 104
Warren, H. B. de, 106, 114, 140–141, 165
Waszink, J. H., I, 135 n. c
Wattenbach, Wilhelm, 3 n. 8, 4 n. 14, 18 n. 77, 19 n. 79, 21 n. 87, 52 n. 217, 53 n. 218, 305 n. 8, (ed. Robert Holtzmann) 157, 158, 293 n. 2
Weaver, J. R. H., 105
Webb, C. C. J., 35 n. 153, 36 n. 158, 215
Weigle, Fritz, 11 n. 48, 34 n. 147
Wendehorst, Alfred, 18 n. 77
Werner, Ernst, 148
Werner, Jakob, I, 125 n. e
Werner, Karl F., 50 n. 203
White, Lynn, Jr., 160, 292

Wickersheimer, Ernest, 183, 302
Wieruszowski, Helene, 159, 185, 186, 206
Wikenhauser, Alfred, 2 n. 6, 3 n. 10, 19 n. 79
Wilkens, C. A., 93 n. 1
Wilkins, E. H., 23 n. 95, 26 n. 111
Williams, Watkin, 48 n. 194, 52, 106, 120, 319, 321 n. 22, 328
Wilmart, André, I, 60, n. z; II, 10 n. 43, 11 nn. 46, 51, 12 n. 52, 48, 49 nn. 197–198, 51 n. 209, 53, 99, 111, 132, 152, 172, 183, 193, 217, 272, 321 n. 23
Wislocki, Wladyslaw, 70 n. 273
Wissowa, Georg, I, 305 n. g; II, 5 n. 18, 10 n. 44
Wollasch, Joachim, 233 n. 2, 358
Wright, Thomas, 117

Zatschek, Heinz, 7 n. 28, 8 n. 30
Zeerleder, Karl, 263
Zielinski, T., 33
Zoepffel, Richard, 124

III. GENERAL INDEX

This index includes the names of all persons and places mentioned in the text and notes (except for some in the genealogies and lists, as in Appendices A and L). Persons of the same first name are listed, under that name, according to the office or place most prominently associated with them. Among the John's, for instance, Cardinal-Deacon John Paparo is under C, Bishop John of Lisieux under L, Pope John XIX under P, and John of Salisbury under S. The *cursus honorum* of offices held by an individual is included only when relevant.

The following abbreviations are used: abp.=archbishop; abt.=abbot; adc.=archdeacon; bp.=bishop; card.=cardinal; chron.=chronicler; ct.=count; dio.=diocese; emp.= emperor; k.=king; obit.=obituary; P.=Peter the Venerable; pr.=prior; and, for the affiliations of religious houses, Aug.=Augustinian; Ben.=Benedictine (old black); Carth.= Carthusian; Cist.=Cistercian; Cl.=Cluniac (also Cluniacs, Cluny); Prem.=Premonstratensian. Changes in affiliation are indicated by a hyphen. These indications are mostly taken from Cottineau, *Répertoire*, and cannot be relied upon absolutely.

Aaron, I, 105, 338
Abbeville, SS. Peter and Paul (Cl.), I, 264–265, II, 167, 289–290, 346; prebends in St. Wulfram granted to, I, 264–265, II, 171, 289–290; Holy Sepulchre, church of, granted to, II, 290; pr., *see* Foliot
Abbot: meals of, I, 55, 74–75, 92, 284; of lower order than abp., I, 420; power of, I, 73, 282, (over bed-coverings) I, 65, (over clothing) I, 62, 64, (over fasting) I, 69, (over food) I, 66–67, (over second professions) I, 78
Abdia the Jew, I, 295, II, 280
Abelard, II, 23, 38, 62, 174, 209, 247, 290, 318, 319, 320; Epp. 9–10 to?, I, 14–17, II, 101–102; letters of, II, 4 n. 13, 7; condemnation at Sens, II, 164; appeal to Holy See, I, 258; visit to and wish to settle at Cl., I, 258–259; peace with St. Bernard, I, 258–259, II, 164; final years at Cl., I, 306, II, 177; humility, simplicity, and poverty, I, 306–307, II, 177–178; studies, I, 307–308, II, 178; celebration of Eucharist, I, 307; sent by P. to Chalon-sur-Saône, I, 307; illness and death, I, 307, II, 178; body given to Paraclete, I, 400, II, 210; P.'s letter of absolution, I, 401–402
Abia de las Torres, II, 262
Abraham, I, 66, 186, 254
Absolution, I, 338, 342, 356, 401–402
Accidia, I, 33, 37, 39, II, 108
Achard, *vicarius*, II, 237
Active life: combined with contemplation in full Christian life, I, 21; compared to storm, *see* Storm; virtues of, I, 188–189. *See also* Martha, sister of Mary
Acy, St. Nicholas (Cl.), II, 108

Adalbert of Usèz, bp. of Nîmes, I, 348, II, 192–193, 204
Adam, use of furs, I, 62–63, II, 117
Adam fitz Swane, II, 297
Adela, countess of Blois, nun at Marcigny, I, 270, II, 103–104, 130, 136, 170, 256; Ep. 15 to, I, 22, II, 103–105
Adelaide of Savoy, queen of France, II, 142
Adelelmus, pr. of Cl., II, 259, 344
Ademar, abt. of Figeac, II, 13, 197; Ep. 147 to, I, 362, II, 197
Ademar (Aimarus), sacristan of Cl., I, 332, II, 186, 264, 265, 311, 344; mission to Roger of Sicily, I, 332
Adenulf, abt. of Farfa, card.-deacon of Sta. Maria in Scola Greca, II, 154, 293–294
Adrian, *see* Hadrian
Adriatic Sea, I, 201
Advocates, monastic, I, 344, 349; inefficiency of, I, 88
Aelred of Rievaulx, letters, II. 5, 39
Africa, conquered by Moslems, I, 298
Agatha, St., I, 428
Agde, I, 349
Age, effect on character, I, 314–315
Aggsbach (Carth.), lost MSS. from, II, 63, 64 n. 260, 70, 72 n. 278, 73 n. 280
Agnes, St., I, 428
Agricultural labor, unsuitable for hermits, I, 38; for monks, I, 84–85, 283. *See also* Manual labor
Ahab, I, 29
Ailred of Anchin, scribe, II, 52 n. 213
Aimarus, *see* Ademar, Aymar
Aimeric, bp. of Clermont, I, 405–406, II, 175, 212, 213, 241 n. 46; complaint against by canons of Brioude, I, 405; criticized by P.,

GENERAL INDEX

I, 405–406; involved in secular affairs, I, 406
Airaldus, former Cl. monk, writer of hymns, I, 420, II, 218
Aix, island of (Cl.), II, 260, 337, 339; pr., see Bernard Morellus
Alberic, abp. of Bourges, II, 164
Alberic of Monte Cassino, II, 33
Alberic, abt. of Vézelay, card.-bp. of Ostia, I, 8, 193, II, 100, 140, 154, 244, 294; Ep. 84 to, I, 221, II, 154; attacked at Pontremoli, I, 51, 52, II, 114; legate to East, I, 221, II, 154; lost letter to P., I, 221, II, 154; meeting with Matthew of Albano, I, 143, II, 129; "sole solace of our order and heart," I, 221
Alberic of Trois-Fontaines, chron., II, 308
Albero, bp. of Liège, II, 157; Ep. 89 to, I, 228–230, II, 157–159; asked by P. to help Cl. priories, I, 230; P.'s desire to see, I, 228–229
Albero, bp. of Verdun, I, 145, II, 129, 130
Albert of Morra, see Gregory VIII
Albert of Samaria, II, 32, 35
Alcuin, II, 19 n. 79; letters, II, 3 n. 9, 5, 6 n. 25
Alexander II, pope, I, 300
Alexander III, pope, II, 226, 267, 330
Alexander IV, pope, II, 98
Alexander the Great, history of, I, 417, 422, II, 217, 328 n. 58
Alexius Comnenus, emp., I, 209, 210, II, 149, 292; gifts to churches in West, I, 209, 210
Alfonso, bp. of Salamanca, II, 46
Alfonso I, k. of Aragon, II, 311; death, I, 6, II, 97
Alfonso VII, k. of Leon-Castile, I, 265–266; asks P.'s mediation with pope, I, 265; benefactor of Cl., I, 265; called emp. by P., I, 265
Alfonso, son of Roger II of Sicily, II, 207; liturgical commemoration, I, 394
Algarus, bp. of Coutances, attacked at Pontremoli, I, 154, II, 114, 134
Alger of Liège, I, 229–230, II, 158–159, 286–287; *De sacramento altaris*, I, 230
Algrin of Étampes, adc. of Orléans, royal chancellor, II, 295, 309–310, 312
Alix of Polignac, II, 237
Al-Kindi, *Risāla*, II, 3 n. 8, 174, 227, 278
Allod, foundation of Cl. upon, I, 79
Alms, given by monks, I, 116
Alps, I, 310, 434, 438, 444; crossed by P., I, 168
Altmannus, abp. of Trier, II, 130
Alvisus, abt. of Anchin, bp. of Arras, I, 264, II, 50, 53, 160, 290, 305; attacked at Pontremoli, I, 51, II, 114

Amadeus of Hauterives, II, 181
Amadeus, bp. of Lausanne, II, 321 n. 27
Amadeus III, ct. of Savoy, II, 26; Ep. 68 to, I, 199, II, 142; dispute with Louis VII, I, 199, II, 142
Amalekites, I, 142, 447
Amazons, I, 305
Ambition, I, 293
Amblard, abt. of St. Martial, Limoges, bp.-elect of Limoges, II, 260
Amboise, Jacques d', abt. of Cl., II, 351
Ambronay (Ben.), II, 122; abt., II, 165; dispute with P., II, 165
Ambrose, St., I, 2, 279, 288, 431, II, 3 n. 8, 40; letters, II, 8 n. 31; style, II, 33; works requested by Carths., I, 47, 333, II, 111
Amiens, bp., see Guarinus
Amorrhites, I, 327
Anacletus II, antipope, I, 207, II, 97, 115, 124, 137, 140, 167, 185, 293, 294, 336–337, 339; rejected by Cls., I, 113, II, 124; death, I, 196, II, 141, 147. See also Aquitaine, Pierleone, Schism (papal), William of Poitou
Ananias, I, 33, 59
Anastasius IV, pope, II, 225, 244
Anastasius Bibliothecarius, II, 283
Anathema, I, 442
Anchin (Ben.), II, 65; center of Cl. influence, II, 53; library, II, 50, 51; MSS. from, II, 50–53, 55, 63, 70; abt., see Alvisus, Goswin
Ancren Riwle, II, 1 n. 2
Angels: beatitude, I, 248–250; great number, I, 237; virginity, I, 431–433; vision of Christ, I, 249; wisdom, I, 242–243, 247–250
Angers, bp., see Ulger
Angoulême: episcopal election, I, 350–351, II, 193; bp., see Gerald, Hugh, Lambert. See also Geoffrey, abp. of Bordeaux
Aniane (Ben.), complaint against bp. of Béziers, I, 7, II, 99
Animals, lack of divine care for, I, 444
Animositas cordium, virtue of, I, 239
Anjou, I, 179, II, 260, 338, 339; ct., see Geoffrey
Anna, mother of Samuel, I, 241
Anointing, I, 354–355; of sick at Cl., I, 354, 355–356
Anse, II, 166
Anselm, bp. of Bethlehem, II, 121
Anselm, St., abp. of Canterbury, II, 3 n. 8; letters, II, 3 n. 9, 4 n. 13, 10, 11 n. 48; revised own texts, II, 44 n. 182
Anselm, bp. of Havelberg, II, 267
Antelmus, pr. of La Chartreuse, bp. of Belley, II, 186. See also La Grande Chartreuse

Anthony, St., the hermit, I, 29, 30, 234; use of furs, I, 63
Antichrist, II, 282
Antioch, II, 237; prince, *see* Raymond; siege of, I, 397, 398, 399–400, II, 209
Apennines, I, 201, II, 114; crossed by P., I, 168
Apollinarism, II, 162; antiquity of, I, 117–118; Ep. 37 concerning, I, 117–124, II, 125
Apostles: gifts received at Pentecost, I, 238–242; great number, I, 237; imitation of, I, 426; set pattern of monastic life, I, 59, 129
Apostolicus, I, 426; *numerus*, I, 313; pope, I, 316
Appeal, judicial, abuse of, I, 262
Apulia, I, 231, 330
Aquileia: council in 381, II, 156; patriarch, *see* Pellegrinus
Aquitaine, II, 107, 258; acquired by Louis VII, II, 142; duke, *see* William; support of Anacletus II, I, 135; visits of P., II, 97, 101, 335–337. *See also* Louis VII
Arabs, I, 208, 219, 327
Arbertus, pr. of Cl., I, 48, II, 111, 113, 344, 348
Archbishop, of higher order than abt., I, 420
Archibald VI of Bourbon, II, 263
Archibald, subdean of Orléans, murder of, I, 24–25, II, 106, 308–309
Archives of letters, II, 8, 14, 20
Arconville, tithes of, II, 123
Aristotle, I, 1, 15, II, 38
Arithmetic, I, 2
Arius, I, 286
Arlanc-le-Bourg, priory of La Chiusa, II, 236 n. 13
Arles, abp., *see* Bernard, Raymond of Montredon, William
Armannus, knight, II, 240 n. 40
Armannus of Montboissier, pr. of Cl., abt. of Manglieu, P.'s brother, II, 240–241, 244, 333, 344, 348; Ep. 53 to, I, 153–173, II, 133–135
Arnold, abt. of Bonneval, II, 98
Arnold of Brescia, II, 179, 327, 328
Arnold of Levenon, abp. of Narbonne, Ep. 105 to, I, 268, II, 169; P.'s plan to visit, I, 268; urged to become Cl., I, 268
Arnold, P.'s chaplain, II, 334; mission to Eugene III, I, 379, II, 204
Arnulf, Cl. monk, former Roman notary, II, 33, 37, 179, 183, 332, 333; Ep. 125 by, I, 321, II, 183–184
Arnulf, adc. of Séez, bp. of Lisieux, I, 261, II, 166–167, 255, 256; role in papal schism, I, 262, II, 167; devotion to Innocent II, I, 261–262; at Lateran Council of 1139, II, 167; support of Stephen of Blois, II, 167; Innocent II asked to approve election as bp., I, 262; learning, I, 261–262; letters, II, 4 n. 13, 9; style, II, 34 n. 148
Arnulf, monk of Longpont, II, 312
Arras, II, 266; bp., *see* Alvisus, Godescalc; St. Vaast (Ben.), II, 50, 66; MS. from, II, 63; travel from Rome, II, 28 n. 123
Arrow of ecclesiastical justice, I, 130
Ars dictandi Aurelianensis, II, 31
Arvières (Carth.), I, 378, II, 204
Ascelin, pr. of Margerie-Hancourt, I, 206, II, 146
Ascetinus, bp. of Bethlehem, II, 121
Asia, conquered by Moslems, I, 298
Astrolabe, son of Abelard, I, 401, 402, II, 210
Astrology, II, 279
Astronomy, I, 2
Auberive (Cist.), abt., *see* Garnerius
Augustine, St., I, 2, 60, 68, 98, 226, 238–239, 245, 264, 279, 281–282, 288, 321, 429, 430, 434, 441, II, 12 n. 53, 17, 40, 41, 162, 281; style, II, 33, 34 n. 145; works requested by P., I, 47, 327, 417, 422, II, 16, 217, 285; works more precious to P. than gold, I, 326–327; works against heretics, I, 298; *Contra Julianum*, I, 417, 422, II, 217, 328 n. 58; letters, I, 47, II, 8 n. 31, 47 n. 190; Rule, II, 1 n. 2
Aulne (Ben.), MS. from, II, 70
Aurec, priory of La Chiusa, II, 236 n. 13
Austerities, physical: unnecessary for hermit, I, 40; useless without Christ, I, 30; useless without love, I, 101, 140, 368. *See also* Benedict (St.), Fasts, Flagellation, Raingard, Theobald of St. Columba, Theodard of La Charité, Vigils
Austerity of Cistercian customs, I, 369
Autobiographical character of letters, II, 6
Autun, II, 267; bp., *see* Henry, Humbert of Baugé, Norgaud, Robert, Stephen of Baugé
Auvergne, I, 25, 420, II, 107; ct., II, 233 (*see also* Robert II and III, William VI and VII); weakness of ct., I, 405, II, 213; disturbed conditions, I, 405–406, II, 213; ranks of lay society, I, 406; troubles of monks, I, 406; visits of P., II, 107, 123
Auxerre, I, 256, II, 162, 264; anonymous cleric of, I, 191, II, 139; bp., *see* Hugh; meeting of Eugene III and P., I, 375, 445, II, 203
Auzon: castle, I, 405, II, 212; family of, II, 212
Avarice, I, 31, 33, 293; covered by professed desire to help poor, I, 33–34; danger to pilgrims, I, 359; overcome by reading, I, 39

GENERAL INDEX 395

Aymar, see also Ademar
Aymar, pr. of Crépy, II, 295
Aymardus, abt. of Cl., I, 3
Azo, II, 25
Azzano Mella, II, 267

B. of Auzon, abt. of Brioude, II, 212, 216
B., pr. of La Charité, II, 297, 298
Babylon: confusion of, I, 134; cup of, I, 179; merchandise of, I, 428; rivers of, I, 211
Babylonians, I, 177
Baffie, family of, II, 233 n. 3
Bagé, family of, II, 225
Baldric (Balderic) of Anchin, scribe, II, 52 n. 213
Baldric, pr. of Bec, II, 10
Baldwin of Anchin, scribe, II, 52 n. 213
Baldwin II, k. of Jerusalem, II, 153
Baldwin III, k. of Jerusalem, II, 153
Balerne (Ben.), II, 308
Baptism, anointing of, I, 354-355
Bar [-sur-Aube?], meeting of Eugene III and P., I, 375, II, 203
Bar-sur-Aube, II, 264
Barac, I, 305
Bari, I, 192, II, 139
Barnwell (Aug.), II, 186
Baro, subdeacon of Rome, will of, I, 366, 373, II, 198, 201
Bartholomew, Dr., II, 79, 82, 247, 248-251, 302-303; Ep. 158a to, I, 379-382, II, 58, 205; Ep. 158b by, I, 382-383, II, 58, 205; confraternity with Cl., I, 382; P.'s affection for, I, 379; P.'s reliance on, I, 381; visit to Cl., I, 378, 382, II, 248
Bartholomew of Salerno, II, 302-303
Basil, pr. of La Chartreuse, II, 13, 186, 221; Ep. 186 to, I, 434-435, II, 221-222; Ep. 187 by, I, 436, II, 222; admiration for Cl., I, 436; former life at Cl., I, 435
Baudivillard (Cl.), II, 123
Baudri, abt. of Bourgueil, II, 3 n. 11
Baume (Ben.-Cl.), abt., see Gunzo
Bayeux, II, 266
Bear: eaten by monks, I, 389; eats MS. in Cl. priory, I, 47, II, 112
Beatitudo, I, 15-16, 248-250. See also Life, Salvation
Beatrice of Tournon, II, 312
Beauce, adc. of, II, 196
Beaujeu, II, 259; family of, II, 225, (relations with Cl.) II, 166, 214
Beaujolais, joy at return of Humbert III, I, 408, 410
Beauvais, bp., II, 15 n. 62 (see also Henry, Odo); episcopal election, I, 360-361, II, 195; St. Lucien, abt., II, 15 n. 62 (see also Odo); St. Symphorien, abt., see Odo
Bec (Ben.), II, 10, 19, 104-105, 332 n. 5; pr., see Baldric
Bed-coverings used by monks, I, 54, 65, 91-92
Beef, eaten by monks, I, 389, 390
Behemoth, I, 196
Belleville, founded by Humbert III of Beaujeu, II, 166
Belley, bp., see Antelmus, Pontius
Benedict, St., I, 31, 46, 59, 60, 62, 66, 73, 75, 93, 97, 281-282, 284, 338, 390, 394, II, 118; *deus noster*, I, 207; austerity, I, 319; use of furs, I, 63, II, 117; knowledge, I, 245; miracles, I, 320; "notary" of God, I, 98-99, II, 20; P.'s hymns for, I, 318-320, 325, II, 16; translation, I, 320. See also *Regula Benedicti*
Benevento, II, 139
Benevolence, element in friendship, I, 217, 218
Beraldus, Cl. monk, I, 6, II, 97
Berengar, bp. of Salamanca, abp. of Compostela, II, 168; translation, I, 265-266
Bermundus, bp. of Béziers, I, 7, II, 99
Bernard Morellus, pr. of Aix, II, 339
Bernard, abp. of Arles, II, 286
Bernard, assistant to Dr. Bartholomew, I, 381, 382-383, II, 249, 251, 302
Bernard of Bologna, Master, II, 30-31
Bernard of Chartres, II, 34-35
Bernard, St., abt. of Clairvaux, I, 183, 422, 423, 426, 427, 449, 450, II, 13 n. 57, 18, 19, 24, 26, 27, 41, 113, 151, 152, 188, 218, 219, 220, 250, 266, 294, 308, 309, 311, 312, 316-330 *passim*, 336, 342; Ep. 28 to, I, 52-101, II, 115-120; Ep. 29 to, I, 101-104, II, 120-121; Ep. 35 to, I, 113-116, II, 124; Ep. 65 to, I, 194-195, II, 140-141; Ep. 73 to, I, 206, II, 147; Ep. 74 by, I, 207-208, II, 147; Ep. 110 by, I, 272-274, II, 172; Ep. 111 to, I, 274-299, II, 172-174; Ep. 145 to, I, 360-361, II, 195-197; Ep. 148 by, I, 362-363, II, 197-198; Ep. 149 to, I, 363-366, II, 198-199; Ep. 150 to, I, 367-371, II, 199; Ep. 152 by, I, 372-373, II, 201-202; Ep. 163 by, I, 395-396, II, 207-208; Ep. 164 to, I, 396-398, II, 208; Ep. 175 to, I, 416-417, II, 216; Ep. 177 by, I, 418, II, 217; Ep. 181 to, I, 423-425, II, 219-220; Ep. 192 to, I, 443-448, II, 226-230
—— (activities): busyness, I, 363, 372-373; at Cluny, I, 424, II, 219-220, 229; in Italy, II, 129, 140-141; at Rome, I, 272; at Troyes, I, 256, II, 163; witnessed grant of tithes by Cl., I, 108; asks for Cl. prayers, I, 274;

Bernard, St., abt. of Clairvaux—*continued*
fights enemies of God, I, 281; preaching of Second Crusade, II, 185, 200; submission of William of Poitou, II, 126; opposition to pilgrimage, II, 132; doctrine of two swords, II, 229. *See also* Abelard, Gebuin of Troyes, Gilbert de la Porrée, Hato of Troyes, Matthew of Albano, Nicholas of Montiéramey

—— (and Peter the Venerable): affection for P., I, 207, 363, 373; complaint at P.'s silence, I, 272–273; praise of P., I, 418; recommends P. to Eugene III, II, 226–227; P.'s affection for, I, 194–195, 364, 423, 447 ("specialissimus et sanctissimus amicus"); P.'s apology for late reply, I, 274, 275; P.'s annoyance with, I, 424, II, 325; P.'s complaint at Bernard's silence, I, 194; P.'s letters to, I, 272, 361, 372, 390, II, 79, 172; P.'s meetings with, I, 448, 450, II, 326; P.'s pleasure in Bernard's letter, I, 274–275; P.'s praise of, I, 293

—— (writings): knowledge of sacred and secular literature, I, 53; knowledge of *dictamen*, II, 32, 34, 37; revised own texts, II, 44 n. 182; chancery of, I, 363, II, 20 n. 81, 321–322; seal, II, 22, 326–327, 328; works in MS. Douai 372, II, 50–53; *Apologia*, II, 108, 247, 271–273, (date of) 272 n. 6, 273 n. 13; *De baptismo*, II, 3 n. 9; *De consideratione*, I, 373, II, 71, 202, 229, 272 n. 7, 323 n. 25; *De praecepto et dispensatione*, I, 299, II, 3 nn. 8–9, 174; letters, (collection) II, 11 n. 48, 17, 19 n. 79, 26, 59, 61, 76, (individual) I, 272, 445, II, 106, 130, 145, 168, 198–199, 201, 266, 274, 290, 306–307, (lost) I, 363, 365, 448, II, 197, 227, 229–230; urged by P. to write against Moslems, I, 298–299, II, 275–276, 278, 281; urged by P. to write against Petrobrusians, I, 299, II, 285

Bernard of Cluny, customs of, II, 115, 116, 117, 118
Bernard, cellarer of Cl., II, 311, 345
Bernard, *famulus* of P., II, 345
Bernard Iterus, chron., II, 236 n. 13
Bernard of Morval, II, 269
Bernard of Provence, II, 302
Bernard, pr. of Reuil, II, 268
Bernard, abt. of St. Crispin, Soissons, II, 10
Bernard, bp. of Saintes, II, 96
Bernard, pr. of Sauxillanges, II, 237
Bernard of Uxelles, pr. of Cl., II, 335 n. 20, 345
Bernerius, abt. of Bonneval, I, 6, II, 98
Bertrand, pr. of Sauxillanges, II, 237
Bertrée (Cl.), II, 159; pr., *see* Gerard

Berzé, family of, II, 225
Berzé-la-Ville, II, 155, 225
Berzé-le-Chatel, II, 225
Besançon, II, 265; abp., *see* Humbert
Bethany, St. Lazarus (Ben.), II, 292
Bethlehem, I, 106, 358; bp., II, 121, (Ep. 31 to) I, 105–106, II, 121–122 (*see also* Anselm, Ascetinus, Gerald); confraternity (?) with Cl., I, 106
Bèze (Ben.), II, 110
Béziers, bp., *see* Bermundus
Bible: influence on P.'s style, II, 38, 40–41; P.'s knowledge of, I, 1, II, 110. *See also* New Testament, Old Testament
Bishops: anointing of, I, 354, 355; Cluniac, I, 103–104; dispute over consecration, I, 440–442; office (dignity and dangers), I, 18, 127, 225–227, 268; who become Cluniacs, I, 225–226, 268, 353, II, 156; who become regular canons, I, 267. *See also* Elections, Exemptions, Martha, Translation of bishops
Black color: significance, I, 57, 289; use in antiquity, I, 288–289. *See also* Clothing, Mourning
Blaison, given to St. Maurus, I, 85
Blessing of younger by older monks, I, 55, 75
Blois, II, 129; ct., *see* Stephen, Theobald; countess, *see* Adela; royal library, MS. from, II, 60
Blood, ring able to staunch flow of, I, 175
Bloodletting, I, 378–379, 381, 382, II, 248–250
Boar, wild, eaten by monks, I, 389
Boethius, II, 40; style, II, 34 n. 145
Bologna, II, 31–32
Bompar of Auzon, II, 212
Boniface, St., letters, II, 5
Bonitus, preparer of parchment, II, 345
Bonneval (Ben.): abt., *see* Arnold, Bernerius; town burned by Louis VI, II, 98
Bonnevaux (Cist.), II, 181
Books: lent by Carths., I, 402; lent by Cl., I, 334, II, 186
Bordeaux: abp., *see* Geoffrey
Boso, chamberlain of Cl., II, 311, 345
Bourges: abp., *see* Alberic, G., Peter of La Châtre, Vulgrin; St. Sulpicius (Ben.), II, 304; abt., *see* Elias
Bourgueil-en-Vallée (Ben.), abt., attacked at Pontremoli, I, 51, II, 114. *See also* Baudri
Brancion, family of, II, 225
Brandon, II, 225
Bread: amount eaten by monks, I, 65; type used in Eucharist, I, 279
Breme (Ben.), I, 437, II, 222–223, 265; abt., *see* Odilo, Rainald; bad state of, I, 437

GENERAL INDEX

Brescia, II, 267
Brevis, II, 21
Brevity, epistolary, I, 44–45, 101, 115, II, 3, 35
Brian fitz Count, II, 252, 256
Bridges, built by hermits, I, 34
Brienne-le-Château, II, 144
Brioude, St. Julian, I, 405, II, 212, 215, 241–242; abt., I, 415, 416, II, 215–216 (*see also* B., William); chartulary, II, 236); contempt for pope, I, 415; corruption of, I, 413–415; exemption of, I, 413; provost, *see* Heraclius, William; theft from, I, 414
Bruno of Cologne, St., II, 3 n. 9
Building by hermits, I, 34
Burgenses: in Auvergne, I, 406; in Burgundy, I, 410; of La Charité, I, 136
Burgos, II, 262
Burgundy, I, 212, 272, 350; desire for peace, I, 410; disturbed conditions, I, 7, 42, 175, 408–411, II, 110, 136, 214; duke, *see* Hugh II; preparations for war, I, 442; nobility, I, 379, 410, 442; social groups, I, 410, 411
Burial, at Cl., I, 190–191. *See also* Death, Raingard
Bussière, La, I, 443, II, 224, 225; family of, II, 225
Bussières, II, 182

Cacus, I, 144
Caesar, I, 405, II, 39
Caesarius of Heisterbach, II, 196
Cain, I, 328
Calabria, I, 231, 330
Calixtus II, pope, I, 300, 441, II, 119, 155, 293
Camaldoli, color of clothing, II, 116
Cambrai, II, 66, 129; St. Sepulchre (Ben.), MS. from, II, 63
Canaan, I, 157
Canaanites, I, 327
Canon law, mutability of, *see* Law
Canonry, distinction of secular rights and ecclesiastical cure, II, 264
Canons, regular, tithes paid by and to, I, 110. *See also* Bishops, Premonstratensians
Canterbury: abp., *see* Anselm, Lanfranc, Theobald, William; journey to Rome from, II, 28
Carlat, family of, II, 233 n. 2
Carrión, II, 262
Carthusians, II, 35, 194, 269; Ep. 24 to, I, 44–47, II, 111–112; Ep. 48 to, I, 146–148, II, 130; Ep. 132 to, I, 333–334, II, 186; attitude in Grenoble election, I, 366, 378–379, II, 198–199; avoidance of litigation, I, 379; literary and intellectual intercourse with Cl., I, 46–47, 402, II, 112,

186, 210; liturgical commemoration for P., II, 111; monastic ideals, I, 378; order, I, 403; P.'s affection for, I, 44–45, 333, 377–378, II, 111, 204; P.'s admiration for, I, 403; P.'s visits to, II, 96, 146, 403; prayers for Cl., I, 436; superiority over other monks, I, 378, 435, 436; "vases of Christ," I, 333
Cassian, II, 108
Cassiodorus, II, 109; style, II, 33
Castellans: in Auvergne, I, 406; in Burgundy, I, 442
Castorius, bp. of Rimini, I, 80
Cecilia, St., I, 166
Celestine II, pope, I, 309, II, 29, 174–175, 212, 252 n. 1, 305; Ep. 112 to, I, 299–301, II, 174–175; letter to Cl. announcing his election, I, 300–301, II, 174; P.'s desire to visit, I, 301; death, II, 176
Cell of hermit, I, 29, 32, 33, 35, 37, 41; compared to cave, I, 37, (to prison) I, 34, (to tomb) I, 29–30, 34, 41; danger of building, I, 34; empty of money, I, 35; walls compared to Savior, I, 30
Cellarer, I, 65–66, 164. *See also* La Charité, Clairvaux, Cluny, Raingard
Cemetary at Villefranche, opposed by abp. of Lyons, I, 261, II, 166. *See also* Consecration
Census paid by serf, I, 40, 86, 87
Centaur, I, 286
Ceprano, II, 177
Cerberus, I, 144
Chablis, II, 266
Chaise-Dieu, La (Ben.), II, 192–193, 212, 234, 243, 245; abt., *see* Jordan of Montboissier; dispute over St. Baudilus, Nîmes, I, 348–349, II, 192–193, 204
Chalon-sur-Saône: bp., *see* Walter; ct., II, 225; St. Marcellus (Cl.), I, 307, II, 177, 178
Châlons-sur-Marne: bp., *see* Geoffrey, William of Champeaux; meeting of Eugene III and P., I, 445, II, 203, 204
Champagne, ct., *see* Henry, Theobald
Chancery, papal, II, 32–34. *See also* Bernard of Clairvaux
Chapelle-Aude, La (Ben.), II, 236 n. 13
Chapelle Coureau, Cl. chapel, II, 182
Chapter general, *see* Cistercians, Cluniacs
Charente River, II, 337
Charité-sur-Loire, La (Cl.), I, 150, II, 121, 131, 267, 269, 292, 294, 295, 296–297; cellarer, I, 136; chartulary, II, 240 n. 38, 254; ordinations at, I, 200, 205, II, 143; pr., II, 294 n. 9, 296–298 (*see also* Antelmus, B., G., Guy, Odo, Olricus, Peter, Ragny, Theodard, William); provost, *see* Hugh;

Charité-sur-Loire—*continued*
  reform of St. Columba, Sens, I, 354, II, 194. *See also* Civitot, Hugh of Tours, Novices, Peter of Poitiers
—, townsmen, I, 136, II, 297
Chartres: bp., *see* Geoffrey, Ivo, William; crusading council in 1150, I, 396, 398, 399, 400, II, 208, 209, 250, 324, (P.'s inability to attend) I, 398, 399-400; prebend belonging to Cl., I, 6, II, 98; St.-Père-en-Vallée, obit., II, 98, (abt.) *see* William; school, II, 34-35
Chartreuse, La Grande (Carth.), I, 269, 378, II, 96, 170, 204, 342; death of many monks, I, 146-148, II, 130; great snows, I, 146, II, 130; P.'s visits, I, 137, 138, 434-436, II, 221-222; pr. (Antelmus?), Ep. 132 to I, 333-334, II, 186 (*see also* Basil, Guigo)
Chastity: required for monks, I, 34, 89, 116, 292; one of three monastic virtues, I, 215, 433; of Mary, I, 237. *See also* Virginity
Châteaudun, Holy Sepulchre (Cl.), I, 344, II, 190
Chaumont (Cl.), II, 240 n. 44
Chaumouzey (Aug.), II, 3 n. 9
Cheese, eaten by monks, I, 389
Chester, bp., *see* Roger
Chevignes, Cl. chapel, II, 178, 182
Chézery (Cist.), I, iv
Chickens, eaten by monks, I, 389, 391
Chimera, I, 286
Chiusa, La, St. Michael (Ben.), II, 234, 235, 236, 243-244; abt., II, 267, (attacked at Pontremoli) I, 51, II, 114
Chosroes, k. of Persia, I, 400
Chrism, I, 56, 79, 354, II, 119; use in ordinations of bps. and priests, I, 355
Christ: mortal life, I, 358; birth in Bethlehem, I, 106; flight into Egypt, *see* Egypt; baptism, signified by crossing of Red Sea, I, 253; driving money-lenders from Temple, I, 128; miracles, depicted in Cl. chapel, I, 224, II, 155; prayers, I, 4, 181; dying, followed by monk, I, 360; crucified, I, 16, (contemplation of) 46 (*see also* Cross, Crucifix); burial and descent into Hell, I, 124; Transfiguration, P.'s office for, II, 173; tomb, I, 220, 359; praise of, not diminished by praising saints, I, 171; lives in Carthusians, I, 333; followed by crusaders, I, 328
—— humility, I, 34, 224, 433; knowledge, I, 244; supreme love, I, 433; poverty, I, 34-35, 224, 278, 353; virginity, I, 429, 433; signified by paschal lamb, I, 253; simultaneous priest and sacrifice, I, 220; *summus pontifex*, I, 344; divine and human natures, I, 119-124, 253, 254, (united in God's will before temporal Incarnation) 255; humanity (rational and fleshly), I, 121-122; heretical beliefs concerning, I, 118, 119, 251; divinity, I, 121-122; temporal and eternal aspects, I, 254-255; spirit, references to in Bible, I, 123; Moslem belief in, I, 296, II, 282. *See also* Imitation
Christian kings, triumphs of, compared to daily triumphs of Christ in priests over Devil, I, 219
Christina of Markyate, II, 28 n. 120, 133, 254-255
Chrysostom, life of, I, 46-47
Church: body of Christ, I, 397; fostered by Christ and St. Paul, I, 139; power over sword, I, 446
Church in East, troubles of, I, 395, 397, 398
Churches: anointing of, I, 354, 355; built by hermits, I, 34; owned by monasteries, I, 198. *See also* Cluny (constitution), Consecration, Parishes
Cicero, I, 217, 421, 426, II, 12, 38-39, 218; influence on P., II, 38-39; letters, II, 3 n. 10; revised own text, II, 43; style, II, 33
Circumcision: Moslem belief concerning, I, 297; Paul's change of opinion, I, 94
Cistercians: order, I, 370, 371, 424; abts., Ep. 35 to, I, 113-116, II, 124; Ep. 36 to, I, 116-117, II, 124; election of abt., I, 313-314; meeting of abts., I, 371, II, 199; chapter general, I, 116-117, 273, 366, 373, II, 124, 198, 199, 201, 322; clothing, (color) I, 57, 288, 290, 291, 369, II, 116, (cheapness) I, 114; food, frugality of, I, 114; interpretation of *Regula Benedicti*, I, 99-100; literary skills, II, 18 n. 77, 31; poverty, alleged, I, 111, 115; tithe privileges, I, 114; superiority, alleged, I, 291
—— (and Cluniacs): criticisms of Cls., I, 53-56, 59-60, 200-201, II, 270-271; criticisms of Cists. by Cls., I, 111, 114-115; reciprocal dislike, I, 277-278, 280, 281, 285-286, 292, 293, 368; have taken over matter and form of black monks, I, 384; called Pharisees by P., I, 57, 94; praised by P., I, 113-114; loved by Cls., I, 111; reciprocal love and unity desired by P., I, 104, 114, 424; prayers for Cls., I, 366, 373, 417, II, 201, 322; reception in Cl. monasteries, I, 370-371; alleged complaints of Cists. and Cls. against Hugh of Vienne, I, 374
Cîteaux (Cist.), II, 180, 181, 189; abt., Ep. 35 to, I, 113-116, II, 124 (*see also* Rainald); legacy from Baro, I, 366; meeting of Bernard and Abelard, II, 165; visited by

community seeking new abt., I, 313-314, II, 180-181
Città di Castello, II, 174
Civitot (Cl.): given to La Charité by Alexius Comnenus, I, 209, 210, II, 149, 292; alien monks intruded, I, 209; P. requests return, I, 209
Clairvaux (Cist.), II, 189, 195, 196, 214, 219, 220, 249 n. 17, 264, 271, 274, 316, 320, 321, 322, 324, 326-327, 329-330; name, Latin spelling of, II, 91; abt., see Bernard, Garnerius; pr., II, 152, 320 n. 21 (see also Geoffrey of Péronne, Philip, Rainerius, Rualenus); cellarer, see Galcher; hospitaler, see Fromond; legacy from Baro, I, 366; library, II, 217; MS. from, II, 59-60, 69 n. 270; P.'s generosity to, I, 366; P.'s visits, I, 369, 448, II, 199, 202, 227, 229, 230, 322, 326; tithes granted to, II, 123
Clausulae, II, 31, 32, 33, 34, 37, 38
Clement, St., I, 5
Clerics: inferior to monks, I, 267; order of, I, 24, 107; tithes paid to by Cls., I, 108, 110; visiting Cl., I, 72. See also *Cura animarum*, Priests
Clermain, I, 442, II, 225; fortified by Cls., I, 442
Clermont, II, 259; bp., power in Auvergne, I, 405 (see also Aimeric, Stephen, William of Baffie, William of Chamalières); obit., II, 299 n. 1
Cloister, see Cluny, Guests
Clothing, monastic, I, 62-64, 97, 282, II, 116-117; changes in rules concerning, I, 390; diversity, I, 279, 285-290, 368; modeled on that of Old Testament priests, I, 64; See also Abbot, Cistercians, Color, Cowl, Frock, Furs, Trousers, Tunic
Cluny (Cl.), I, 10, 274, 313, 423, 443, II, 23, 24, 53, 144, 219, 225, 242, 254; name, Latin abbreviation for, II, 91; situated in West and almost at end of world, I, 106; compared to safe valley, I, 268; "treasury of the Christian republic," I, 264, 332; foundation, I, 79, 391; church (Cluny III), I, 229, II, 157-158, (consecration) I, 112, II, 124, (relics requested for) I, 220; chapel of Virgin Mary, II, 155; cloister, I, 72, 369-371, II, 199; guest house, I, 72; library, I, 47, II, 17, 35, 39, 40, 55, 111, 217
—— (relations with outside world): confraternities, with kings, I, 209 (see also Bartholomew, Bethlehem, Henry of Rheims, Mount Thabor, Paraclete, Premonstratensians, Rebais, St. Remy [Rheims]); necrology, II, 358 (see also Marcigny [necrology]); visits, real and prospective, see Abelard, Bartholomew, Bernard of Clairvaux, Eugene III, Geoffrey of Châlons-sur-Marne, Guarinus of Amiens, Hato of Troyes, Hugh of Rouen, Milo of Thérouanne, Nicholas of Montiéramey, Pontius of Montboissier, Raingard, Suger; guests at Cluny, see Gate, Guests, Porter; enemies, I, 102-103, 346; see also Cistercians, Mâcon (viscount of), Milo of Thérouanne
—— (constitution and organization): subjection to pope, see Holy See, Pope; papal privileges, I, 79, 108, 110, 200, II, 143 (see also Exemption, Ordination); grants of monasteries customarily confirmed by papal privilege, I, 312; benefactors, see Alexius Comnenus, Baro, Henry of Winchester, Liège, kings of England, France, Germany, Hungary, Spain; financial troubles, I, 6, 111, 115, 332, II, 98, 169, 186; new churches built on lands of, I, 108, II, 176; property, see Landed estates, Property (ecclesiastical), Registers
—— (administration): abt., see Aymardus, Hugh I, II, and III, Jacques d'Amboise, Maiolus, Odilo, Odo, Odo de la Perrière, Peter the Venerable, Pontius; priors and subpriors, Ep. 161 to, I, 388-394, II, 206; responsibilities of, I, 388; meeting in 1150, I, 398, 400, II, 27, 208, 250; chapter general, I, 293, II, 173-174, 259; release of pr. from office, I, 13, 138-139; *cursus honorum* and policy of promotion, II, 146, 298; pr., see Adelelmus, Arbertus, Armannus, Bernard of Uxelles, Peter of Pithiviers, Ragny, Rivo, William; subpr., see Garnerius, Peter, Rainald; chapter, I, 263, 300; abt.'s "council," II, 263; monastic officers, I, 73, II, 344-348; almoner, I, 73 (see also Jarentus, Savaric); cellarer, I, 73 (see also Bernard, Hugh, Hugh of Bissy); chamberlain, see Boso, Hugh of Crécy, Humbert, Inbert, Peter, Pontius, Robert, Stephen, Wigo; claustral prior, I, 317, II, 334 (see also Hugh); hospitaler, I, 73, II, 118; infirmarian, I, 73 (see also Hugh); sacristan, see Ademar, Durannus, Gervase, Wicardus
—— (monks): Ep. 52 to, I, 152-153, II, 132-133; Ep. 133 to, I, 334-338, II, 187; *rei publicae nostrae senatores*, I, 419; absolved by P., I, 338; "recruiting," I, 6, 27, 151-152, 212, 233, 268, 347, 352-353, 362, II, 149, 169; bps. and abts. who have become Cls., see Bishops, Hato of Troyes, Natalis, Stephen of Autun, (papal permission for) I, 6; novices, see Novices;

Cluny—*continued*
  profession, *see* Profession; holy orders, *see* Ordination; Cls. who have become bps. and abts., I, 103–104, 345, 349; Cls. who have become Cists., I, 424
—— (life at): *clausura* of monks, I, 72, 76, 85; common *mensa* of abt. and monks, I, 75; *opus manuum*, *see* Manual labor; intercessionary prayer, I, 81–82, 228, 301, 303; liturgical commemoration, I, 153, 155, 339, 341, 394, 400, II, 132–133, 255–256; heremitical life, *see* Heremitism; intellectual and literary activity, II, 35, 68 (*see also* Carthusians, Cluny [library]); *studium scribendi* of abts., I, 3; food, *see* Fasting, Food, Meals, Meat; clothing, *see* Clothing, Color, Cowl, Frock, Fur, Trousers, Tunic; sick, treatment of, *see* Sick monks; epidemic at, I, 334–335, 338–339, 340, II, 184, 187, 188–189; *conversi*, *see* Laybrothers; *see also* Blessing, Bloodletting, Foot-washing, Hand-washing, *Metanea*, Silence, Vigils
—— (monasticism): *congregatio*, I, 220, 436; *corpus*, I, 339; *multitudo*, I, 363; *ordo*, I, 213, 389, 391, 436; *res publica*, I, 340, 346, 419; *universitas*, I, 338; discipline, (=true philosophy) I, 354, (admiration of Basil of La Chartreuse) I, 436; based on Matt. 19.21, I, 58; paradise, *see* Paradise; observance of *Regula Benedicti*, I, 57, 58, (*rectitudo regulae*) I, 53, 58, (no less observant than new monks) I, 384 (*see also Conversatio morum*, Stability); customs and traditions, I, 53, 99, 354 (*see also* Bernard of Cluny, Farfa, Ulric of Cluny)
Colbert, II, 57
Cologne, Brothers of Holy Cross, MS. from, II, 70
Color of monastic clothing, I, 57, 285–290, 291, 368, 369, 371, II, 116, 199; cause of bad feeling between Cists. and Cls., I, 285–286, 290; change of, by Nicholas of Montiéramey, I, 372; symbolic significance, I, 289; unimportance of, in P.'s opinion, I, 286–287
Colossians, I, 29
Columbanus, St., I, 85–86
Common life, apostolic, led by monks in dio. of Lyons, I, 129
Compiègne, crusading council in 1150, II, 208, 324
Compostela: abp., *see* Berenger, Diego Gelmírez; episcopal election, I, 265–266; greatness of church, I, 265; pilgrimage to, I, 269, II, 170

Confession, I, 161, 164, 342
Confessors, I, 300
Confirmation, anointing in, I, 354, 355
Conflans-Ste.-Honorine (Ben.), II, 10
Confraternity, monastic, I, 209, 394. *See also* Bartholomew, Bethlehem, Henry of Rheims, Liturgical commemoration, Mount Thabor, Paraclete, Premonstratensians, Rebais, St.-Martin-des-Champs (Paris), St. Remy (Rheims)
Conques in Rouergue (Ben.), II, 245
Conrad III (of Hohenstaufen), emp., II, 114–115, 207; dispute with Roger II of Sicily, I, 394
Consecration of churches and cemetaries, I, 56, 79, II, 119. *See also* Churches (anointing)
Consideratio of hermit, I, 36
Consilium et auxilium: given by Humbert of Beaujeu to Cl., I, 409; given by true friend, I, 222
Constantine the African, II, 303
Constantine, emp., I, 208, 210
Constantine, priest of Cl., I, 6, II, 98, 101
Constantine, monk, I, 270, II, 170
Constantinople: anti-Latin feeling at, II, 148–149, 292; church of, united in faith with West, I, 210; founded by Christ in heaven and by Constantine on earth, I, 210; patriarch, *see* John IX; P.'s desire to visit, I, 210; relics at, I, 210, II, 149
Contemplation: by hermit, I, 37; of crucified Christ, I, 46
Contemptus mundi, I, 182, 188
Contemptus temporalium, I, 352
Contrition, I, 164
Conversatio morum, among Cls., I, 55, 76, 77–78
Conversi, *see* Laybrothers
Copying of MSS., best manual labor for hermits, I, 38–39, II, 109
Corbeil, St. Spire (Ben.), II, 196
Corbie (Ben.), abt., I, 51, II, 114
Corinth, I, 403
Corporate view of Christian society, I, 397
Corruption: in dio. of Lyons, I, 127–129, II, 125; legal, I, 349–350. *See also* Dragon, Monasticism
Cotte, Cl. chapel, II, 182
Councils, of the Church, I, 94. *See also* Chartres, Compiègne, Jouarre, Laon, Mâcon, Nicaea, Pisa, Rheims, Rome, Sens, Soissons, Thérouanne, Vienne
Courçais, priory of La Chiusa, II, 236 n. 13
Coutances, bp., *see* Algarus
Cow, enjoying heremitical life, I, 321
Cowl, monastic, I, 63, 282, 287

GENERAL INDEX 401

Created beings: four kinds, I, 119–120; life and essence, I, 119; reason, I, 119–120
Crécy, name of many places, II, 314
Crépy-en-Valois, St. Arnulf (Cl.), II, 108, 295; pr., see Aymar
Cross of Christ: at Antioch, I, 397, 398, 400; carried by hermit, I, 34; carried by monk, I, 360; love of, I, 17. See also Crucifix
Crucifix: Raingard's devotion to, I, 169; sent by P. to Carths., I, 46, 47, II, 112. See also Cross of Christ
Crusade: First, II, 237, 292, 300; of Sigurd of Norway, I, 141, II, 128; Second, I, 327, 347, 354, 358–360, II, 153, 183, 185, 192, 194, 200, 214, 263, 264, 290, 321, (caelestis expeditio) I, 327, (compared to wars of Old Testament) I, 327, (exercitus dei viventis) I, 328, 395, (dangers of) I, 359, (papal privileges) I, 359, (P.'s inability to join) I, 327, (should be financed with money of Jews) I, 328–330, (treachery of Greeks) I, 395, II, 207; plans in 1150, I, 395–400, II, 206–209, 323
Crusader States, I, 208–209. See also Antioch, Jerusalem, Holy Land
Crusaders: curiositas, instabilitas, and levitas on Second Crusade, I, 359; follow Christ, I, 328
Crusades, I, 215; major role played by France, I, 215; seen as pilgrimage by P., I, 358, II, 195; success for fifty years, I, 397; way of salvation for sinners, I, 397
Cunlhat, priory of La Chiusa, II, 236 n. 13
Cupidity, I, 293
Cura animarum, I, 56, 82
Curiositas, see Crusaders
Cursus, II, 2, 30, 32–38; curiae Romanae, II, 32–34, 37
Customs, monastic, diversity of, I, 368–369, 371, (does not affect salvation) I, 280, 287, 290–291, 294, (no cause for schism) I, 278–280. See also Cluny, Bernard of Cluny, Farfa, Ulric of Cluny
Cyprian, St., I, 432, II, 40; letters, II, 8 n. 31
Cyrus, generosity of, I, 177

Dalmatius of Baffie, II, 240
Damascus, I, 187, II, 209
Daniel, I, 386
David, I, 29, 54, 69, 157, 164, 185, 298, 335, 351, 392, 426, 446, II, 280; speaking as Christ, I, 123
Day, beginning of, II, 105
De vita vere apostolica, II, 33 n. 143
Death and burial: display of grief at, I, 157, 336, 339; of Carths., consolation for, I, 146–148; of Raingard, consolation for, I, 156–157; of a monk, I, 8–9. See also Burial, La Grande Chartreuse, Gerald Le Vert, Hugh of Crécy, John of Toucy, Solitude
Deborah, I, 241, 305
Déols, family of, II, 233 n. 2
Desidia, I, 31–32
Deutz (Ben.), abt., see Rupert
Dialectic, I, 1
Dictamen, II, 2, 29–38; spread north of the Alps, II, 31–32, 35. See also Bernard of Clairvaux, Nicholas of Montiéramey
Dictation, I, 48, 49, II, 18–20
Die, bp., see Ulric
Diego Gelmírez, abp. of Compostela, II, 168
Digest, II, 25. See also Roman law
Dijon: meeting of Bernard and P. planned, I, 448, 450, II, 227, 229, 230, 326; St. Benignus (Ben.), dispute with Luxeuil, II, 165, 258
Discretion, needed by hermit in physical austerities, I, 40
Dispensation, papal, I, 441
Doctors, in France, I, 381, II, 302–303
Doeg the Edomite, I, 51
Domène (Cl.), I, 439, II, 111, 204, 223–224, 243, 257–258, 269; patronized by family of Domène, I, 438
Donatus, I, 286
Doubt, philosophical, I, 243
Dragon, I, 26, 45; = Satan, I, 292; = monastic corruption, I, 213
Dreams and visions: false, I, 387; significance, I, 386–387; of Daniel, I, 386; of Gerald Le Vert, I, 162; of Gideon, I, 386; of Joseph the patriarch, I, 354, 356–358, 386; of St. Joseph, I, 386; of Nebuchadnezzar, I, 386; of pharoh, I, 386; of Raingard, I, 168–169
Drogo, card.-bp. of Ostia, II, 71
Drogo the constable, II, 138, 345; mission to Henry of Winchester, I, 190
Drogo, precentor of Nevers, II, 23–24, 153; P.'s messenger to k. of Jerusalem, I, 219, 220–221; on third visit to Jerusalem, I, 221
Drugs and herbs used by P., I, 380, 382–383, II, 205, 249
Dulcianus, lawyer of Montpellier, Ep. 19 to, I, 27, II, 107
Dunes, Les (Cist.), II, 65, 69; MS. from, II, 63
Durannus, sacristan of Cl., II, 345; mission to Henry of Winchester, I, 190–191, II, 138, 139
Durbon (Carth.), I, 378, II, 204

Eadmer, II, 3 n. 8; revised own texts, II, 44 n. 182
Easter customs, diversity of, I, 279

Ebro River, II, 279
Écharlis, Les (Cist.), II, 189
Écouges (Carth.), I, 378, II, 204
Eggs, eaten by monks, I, 389
Egypt, I, 56, 128, 157, 164, 327;=secular world, I, 160; darkness of, I, 428; flight into, I, 236, 242, 243, 248, 386
Egyptians: wealth of, I, 53, 304, 330;= secular affairs, I, 211
Eleanor of Aquitaine, II, 142
Elections, episcopal, *see* Angoulême, Beauvais, Compostela, Grenoble, Langres, Lisieux, Orléans, Piacenza
Elections, monastic, *see* Cistercians, Montpeyroux, Morigny
Elias of Anchin, scribe, II, 52 n. 213
Elias, abt. of St. Sulpicius, Bourges, bp. of Orléans, I, 18, 308, 309, 316, II, 102, 304–310; accused of simony, II, 307; appeal to Eugene III, I, 316; attacked at Pontremoli, I, 51, II, 114; election, II, 304–305; troubles as bp., II, 305–307; resignation, II, 307
Elias, pr. of Sauxillanges, II, 237–238
Elijah, I, 29, 185–186, 242, 300, 416, 446, II, 340; crows of, I, 394; striking the proud, I, 128; use of furs, I, 63
Elisha, I, 185–186, 242, II, 340
Eloquence: of Cicero, I, 421; divine sweeter than human, I, 426
Ely, bp., *see* Nigel
Embrun, abp., *see* William
England, I, 148, 212, 450, II, 19; anonymous abt. from, I, 365; Cl. property in, I, 190–191; disturbances following death of Henry I, I, 22; gifts to Cl. from, I, 141–142, 190; ks. of, assistance to Cl., I, 178, 209, 229, 231, 332, (confraternity with Cl.) I, 209 (see also Henry I and II, Stephen, William I); MSS. from, II, 74; visits of P. to, I, 150, 168, II, 15, 131, 268
Enguizo, P.'s chamberlain, I, 443, II, 225, 264, 345–346
Ennodius, revised own text, II, 43
Envy, I, 89, 292
Ephesus, II, 290
Epistolary mode, I, 134. *See also* Brevity, Letters
Esau, I, 109; significance of subjection to Jacob, I, 357–358
Esdras, I, 177, 284
Estella, II, 262
Étampes, I, 213, II, 151; Notre Dame (Aug.), II, 196
Ethai the Gethite, I, 185
Eucharist: book of Alger of Liège on, I, 230, II, 158; devotion to, of Gerald Le Vert, I, 189, II, 137; difference between Greeks and Latins, I, 279; doctrine of, in 12th century, II, 158–159; frequent celebration, I, 189, 307
Eugene III, pope, I, 135, 360, II, 27, 176, 186, 193, 197, 204, 210, 218, 223, 227, 229, 243 n. 63, 244, 248, 264, 266, 306–307, 320 n. 21, 344; Ep. 119 to, I, 312–313, II, 180; Ep. 122 to, I, 315–316, II, 181; Ep. 141 to, I, 348–350, II, 192–193; Ep. 142 to, I, 350–351, II, 193: Ep. 154 by, I, 374, II, 202–203; Ep. 156 to, I, 375–376, II, 203; Ep. 157 to, I, 376, II, 204; Ep. 158 to, I, 377–379, II, 204; Ep. 171 to, I, 404–407, II, 211–213; Ep. 173 to, I, 410–413, II, 214; Ep. 174 to, I, 413–416, II, 214–216; Ep. 188 to, I, 437, II, 222–223; Ep. 189 to, I, 438–439, II, 223–224; Ep. 190 to, I, 440–442, II, 224; Ep. 191 to, I, 442–443, II, 224–226
—— asked to support abt. of Breme, I, 437; asked to support bp. of Orléans, I, 316; asked to support church of Piacenza, I, 441; crusading bull, II, 195; deception of, I, 375; P.'s devotion to, I, 316, 375; P.'s meetings with, I, 438, 445, II, 203, 222–223, 226; P. recommended to, by Bernard, II, 226–227; displeasure with Jordan of Montboissier, I, 376, II, 204; good health, I, 444; humility, equity, and reasonableness, I, 445; intervention on behalf of Guy of Domène, I, 438–439; kindness shown to P. and Cl., I, 444–445; lost letters, I, 360, 404–405, II, 193, 197, 212; travels, I, 439, II, 203; visit to Cl., I, 445
Eustace, abt. of Le Miroir, I, 450, II, 180, 244–245
Eustace of Montboissier, P.'s brother, I, 233, II, 160, 240–241, 242, 244; Ep. 160 to, I, 385–387, II, 205–206; dream of, I, 386–387; P.'s only brother in secular life, I, 385, 387
Eustace, abt. of Mosat, II, 241 n. 48
Eustace, pr. of Sauxillanges, II, 212
Eustorgius, bp. of Limoges, attacked at Pontremoli, I, 51, II, 114
Evander, I, 144
Everard of Barre, master of the Templars, II, 213–214; Ep. 172 to, I, 407–409, II, 213–214; asked to permit return of Humbert of Beaujeu, I, 409; P.'s hope to see him, I, 409
Everard of Ypres, II, 303
Evesham (Ben.), abt., II, 28
Excommunication of Cls. by pope, I, 79, 112
Exemption, monastic, I, 56, 79–81, 200–201, II, 120, 143; Cist. opposition to, I, 200–201; granted to many monasteries, I, 80; Gregory I on, I, 80–81. *See also* Brioude
Expectancy, papal, I, 201, II, 144

Eybens, II, 221
Eye, single, of love, I, 60, 62, 66, 281–285, 287, 351, II, 173;=pure purpose, I, 358, 359. *See also* Heart
Eynsham (Ben.), II, 1 n. 2
Ezechiel, I, 127, 207, 304

Faith, St., I, 428
Falco, abp. of Lyons, II, 122, 166
Family relationships in Middle Ages, importance of, II, 233
Famulus guards gate at Cl. when closed, I, 76. *See also* Bernard
Farfa (Ben.-Cl.), abt., *see* Adenulf; customs, II, 115, 116, 117, 118
Fasting: monastic, I, 116, 279, 282, 283, 292, 367; by Cists., I, 70; by Cls., I, 54, 69–70, 92, II, 117; by hermit, I, 30, 40, 41; by Raingard, I, 164; by Theobald of St. Columba, I, 359; by Theodard of La Charité, I, 140; useless without love, I, 140. *See also* John the Baptist, Meat
Fathers, Holy, writings of, I, 2–3, 53
Faustus the Manichaean, I, 298, II, 281
Faustus, Pseudo-, *Vita S. Mauri*, II, 118
Faversham (Ben.), II, 297
Feasts, major, fasting on, I, 282
Fécamp (Ben.), II, 34
Felix IV, pope, I, 61
Figeac (Ben.), abt., *see* Ademar
First fruits, owned by Cls., I, 56, 81–82
Fish, eaten by monks, I, 389, 391
Flagellation, by Theodard of La Charité, I, 140
Flamstead (Ben.), II, 28 n. 120
Flesh without spirit, nature of, I, 119–120
Fleury, *see* St.-Benoît-sur-Loire
Florence of Worcester, chron., II, 127, 298
Foliot, Gilbert, pr. of Abbeville, abt. of Gloucester, bp. of London, II, 252–253, 254, 255–256, 346; letters, II, 4 n.13, 8
Fontanel, abt., I, 398, II, 27, 208
Fontanella (Cl.), II, 208
Fontanelles, Les, II, 208
Fonte Avellana (Ben.), color of clothing at, II, 116
Fontemoy (Cist.), abt., *see* Stephen of Toucy
Fontevrault (Ben.), I, 159, 161, II, 133, 134, 239
Food: monastic, I, 29, 97, 388–389; heavenly, of hermits, I, 29; under control of pr., I, 67; trouble caused among monks by diversity of, I, 291. *See also* Cistercians
Foot-washing of guests, I, 54, 71–73, 92, 283–284, II, 118
Formularies, II, 2, 29, 34

Fornication, I, 89
France (*Gallia*), I, 133, 320; *nostra Gallia*, I, 130, 144, 215, 381, 444, 450; ks., I, 213, (affection and aid for Cl.) I, 209, 231, 332, (confraternity with Cl.) I, 209 (*see also* Louis VI and VII, Philip, Robert, Rudolf); queen, *see* Adelaide, Eleanor of Aquitaine; monasticism in, I, 71, 130, 145, 284; monsters in, I, 144; MSS. from, II, 74; provinces of, *see* Anjou, Aquitaine, Auvergne, Burgundy, Champagne, France (Isle-de-), Maine, Normandy, Provence. *See also* Crusades
France, Isle-de- (*Francia*), I, 213, 272, II, 260, 338, 339; abps. and bps. of, I, 373; P.'s travels in, I, 179–180
Frankfort, II, 263
Fraud, epistolary, *see* Letters
Frederick Barbarossa, emp., II, 267
Frederick, Ct. Palatine, ability to read, II, 27 n. 115
Frederick, bp. of Liège, II, 158
Friday, only day upon which Cls. fast, I, 389–390
Friendship, I, 9–10, 11–12, 18, 21, 421–422, II, 39; definitions of true friendship, I, 148–149, 183, 195, 217, 222, 364, 423; love in friendship, I, 176, 217, 218; compared to a port in storm, I, 23, 109; compared to wine, I, 427; "silver cord" of, I, 9, 12–13, II, 101; proved by actions, not words, I, 27, 177, 213, 271; "fair-weather," I, 346; bridges gap of distance, I, 174; increased by seeing friend, I, 176
Frock, monastic, I, 63
Fromond (Fromont), hospitaler of Clairvaux, I, 372, II, 201, 324 n. 40
Fromond, bp. of Nevers, II, 307
Froumond of Tegernsee, letters, II, 5, 6 n. 25, 7
Frugality, one of three monastic virtues, I, 230
Fruit, eaten by monks, I, 54
Fugitive monks, I, 54, 55, 68–69, 92, 282–283, 411, II, 117
Fulcher, abt. of Montpeyroux, II, 181
Fulda (Ben.), II, 27 n. 115
Fulk, k. of Jerusalem, II, 153
Furs, use by monks, I, 53, 62–64, 91, 99–101, 282, II, 116–117; justified by P., I, 100–101; opposed by Cists., I, 99–100; use by prophets, I, 63. *See also* Adam, Benedict, Elijah, John the Baptist

G., abp. of Bourges, II, 296 n. 8
G., pr. of La Charité, II, 296–297, 298
Gabriel, archangel, I, 237, 296, II, 279

Gaietani, Costantino, II, 61, 62
Galatians, I, 94
Galcher (Gaucher) I), cellarer of Clairvaux, I, 372, 422, 426, II, 200–201, 218, 220, 318 n. 10, 320 n. 21, 324, 325, 329; Ep. 184 to, I, 427, II, 220
Galcher (II), nephew of Galcher I, II, 201
Gap, bp., *see* William
Garlande, family of, II, 308–310
Garnerius, subpr. of Cl., I, 214, 372, 424, II, 152, 201, 219, 346
Garnerius of Rochefort, abt. of Auberive, abt. of Clairvaux, bp. of Langres, II, 152
Garonne River, I, 309, II, 179
Gates of Cl. monasteries, I, 76
Gaye (Cl.), II, 101; pr., *see* Peter
Gebuin, adc. and chancellor of Troyes, I, 202–203, 205, 206, II, 27, 144–146, 147; carries message to Bernard, I, 206; friend of Bernard, II, 145; visits Cl. on way to Rome, I, 202
Gelasius II, pope, I, 300, II, 33, 46, 198
Genuflexions, see *Metanea*
Geoffrey, ct. of Anjou, I, 262, II, 167
Geoffrey (Babion) of Le Loroux, abp. of Bordeaux, I, 4, 351, II, 96, 170, 184, 193; Ep. 106 to, I, 269–270, II, 169–170; acted for P. while in Spain, l, 269–270, II, 170; efforts to subjugate churches of Angoulême and Saintes, I, 351, II, 193; P.'s affection for, I, 269, 351, II, 193
Geoffrey, Carth. monk, I, 435, II, 222
Geoffrey, pr. of St. Nicasius, Rheims, abt. of St. Thierry, abt. of St. Médard, Soissons, bp. of Châlons-sur-Marne, I, 145, 264, II, 123, 129, 130, 150–152, 290; Ep. 78 by, I, 212–213, II, 150–151; Ep. 79 to, I, 213–214, II, 151–152; friend of, helped by P., I, 212, 214; P.'s affection for, I, 213–214; plans to visit Cl., I, 213, 214, II, 151; "principal disseminator of the Cl. order in France," I, 213; reformer of monasticism, I, 213
Geoffrey, bp. of Chartres, I, 256, II, 163, 307, 317, 320; Ep. 137 to, I, 343–345, II, 190; attended council of Pisa in 1135, I, 343; P.'s affection for, I, 343–344
Geoffrey of Péronne, pr. of Clairvaux, II, 320 n. 21
Geoffrey, bp. of Grenoble, II, 198
Geoffrey, abt. of St. Albans, II, 255
Geoffrey, pr. of St. Mary de Jumariis, Sciacca, I, 231, II, 160
Geoffrey of Semur-en-Brionnais, pr. of Marcigny, I, 162, II, 134
Geoffrey II of Semur-en-Brionnais, II, 238
Geoffrey of Toucy, abt. of Les Roches, Ep. 136 to, I, 341–343, II, 189–190

Geoffrey, abt. of Vendôme, II, 119, 156; letters, II, 11
Geoffrey, pr. of Vigeois, chron., II, 234, 235, 240, 243, 260, 332 n. 7, 333
Geometry, I, 2
Gerald, bp. of Angoulême, II, 147, 167, 293
Gerald, bp. of Bethlehem, II, 121
Gerald of Cher, bp. of Limoges, II, 212; lost letter of Eugene III to, I, 405, II, 212
Gerald Le Vert, procurator of Marcigny, I, 162, II, 134–135, 137; daily celebration of Eucharist, I, 189; death of, I, 188–189, II, 338; miracle and vision of, I, 162
Gerard of Anchin, scribe, II, 52 n. 213
Gerard, monk, with P. in Italy, II, 115
Gerard, pr. of Bertrée, abt. of St. Trond, I, 230, II, 157, 159
Gerard of Péronne, secretary of St. Bernard, II, 321 n. 26
Gerbert, *see* Sylvester II
Gerhoh, provost of Reichersberg, II, 8, 229
Germain, St., I, 306, II, 177–178
Germanus, monk, I, 448, II, 230
Germany, I, 450, II, 266; k., *see* Conrad III, Frederick Barbarossa, Henry IV and V, Lothar, (affection and aid for Cl.) I, 209, 231, 331, 332, (confraternity with Cl.) I, 209; MSS. from, II, 74
Gervase, sacristan of Cl., II, 136, 346
Gervase, abt. of Prémontré, letters, II, 9, 11, 19
Gideon, I, 386
Gigny (Cl.): dispute with Le Miroir, I, 108, 112–113, 450, II, 123, 124, 227, 229–230, 266, 267, 326; subpr., I, 448, II, 230
Gilbert, Cl. monk, II, 14, 183; Ep. 127 by, I, 323–324, II, 183–184
Gilbert de la Porrée, bp. of Poitiers, II, 165, 193
Gilbert of Senlis, hermit, II, 108, 183; Ep. 20 to, I, 27–41, II, 107–109
Gilduin, abt. of Jehosaphat, II, 292
Giles of La Perche, adc. of Rouen, II, 9
Gilo, card.-bp. of Tusculum, II, 35, 36, 97, 147, 154, 293, 336–337, 339; Ep. 40 to, I, 134–136, II, 126; Ep. 66 to, I, 195–197, II, 141; legate in Hungary and Poland, II, 293 n. 2; meetings with P., I, 196, II, 126, 141; P.'s efforts at friendship, I, 195–196; pride and obstinacy, I, 135; role in papal schism, I, 134–136; urged by P. to return to Church and Cl., I, 135–136, 196–197. *See also* Ring
Girinus, P.'s chaplain, II, 346
Glanfeuil, *see* St.-Maur-sur-Loire
Glastonbury (Ben.), II, 130, 137

Gloucester: St. Peter (Ben.), abt., *see* Gilbert Foliot; earl, *see* Robert
Goat, eaten by monks, I, 389
God: anger changed to mercy, I, 335; eternal and immutable counsel, I, 254–255; judgments hidden to men, I, 336;=love, I, 98–99, 116; speaking in Fathers, I, 2
Goderan of Lobbes, scribe, II, 53
Godescalc, bp. of Arras, II, 326
Godfrey, P.'s constable, II, 264, 346
Goliath, I, 45
Gometz-le-Châtel, II, 313
Good cheer, virtue of, see *Iocunditas, Iocundus*
Goose, eaten by monks, I, 389
Gormond, patriarch of Jerusalem, II, 153
Goslar, II, 28
Goswin, abt. of Anchin, II, 50, 51–52, 53, 109
Grace, types of, I, 247
Grammar, I, 1
Grasse, La (Ben.), abt., attacked at Pontremoli, I, 51, II, 114
Gratian, II, 116
Gravitas, I, 276
Greece, I, 209
Greek church, I, 210, II, 148; difference from Latin, I, 279; joined with Latins by love, I, 210
Greeks: attitude of P. to, I, 210; treachery on Second Crusade, I, 395
Gregory the Great, pope, I, 2, 38, 43, 45, 60, 61, 62, 80, 84, 85, 93, 130, 182, 217, 235, 245, 288, 295, 307, 312, 406, II, 283; source for P.'s hymns on St. Benedict, I, 318; style, II, 33
Gregory V, pope, II, 143
Gregory VII, pope, I, 300, II, 123, 144; chancery, II, 34 n. 146
Gregory VIII, pope, II, 33
Gregory, Cl. theologian, II, 40–41; Ep. 94 to, I, 234–255, II, 161–162; author of sermons, treatises, and letters, I, 235; philosophy of, better as Cl. monk than in academy, I, 235
Gregory of Nazianzus, life of, I, 46–47
Grenoble, I, 196, II, 141, 260; episcopal election, I, 366, 372, 378–379, II, 198–199, 201, 322; bp., forbade first marriage of Guy of Domène, I, 439, II, 223 (*see also* Geoffrey, Hugh, Otmar)
Grief: for miseries of world, I, 188; one of three monastic virtues, I, 289; signified by black color, I, 289; unfruitful, should be changed to tears, I, 339. *See also* Death, Mary (Blessed Virgin), Tears
Grosseteste, revised own works, II, 44 n. 182
Guarinus, bp. of Amiens, I, 264, II, 171, 289; Ep. 108 to, I, 271, II, 171; asked by P. to visit Cl., I, 271, II, 171; benefactor of Cl., *ibid.*
Guarinus, cleric of Troyes, I, 201, 202–203, 205, II, 144, 145; seeks prebend at Troyes, I, 202–203
Guests: reception of, I, 401, (at Marcigny) I, 166, (by Cists.) I, 369–371, II, 199, (by Cls.) I, 54, 55, 71–73, 92, 283–284, 332, 370–371, II, 118; excluded from great cloister, I, 370–371; greeted by porter, I, 75–76; great number at Cluny, I, 72, 74; meals, I, 74–75, 92; segregated from monks, I, 72, 76
Guest house, exterior, for visiting clerics and laymen, I, 370. *See also* Cluny
Guibert, abt. of Nogent, II, 19 n. 79, 112, 238 n. 28
Guichard III of Beaujeu, II, 166, 214, 312 n. 9, 313, 315
Guido, *see* Guy
Guigo I, pr. of La Chartreuse, I, 264, 333, 435, II, 6 n. 24, 13, 14, 106, 111, 198, 221, 311, 342; Ep. 24 to, I, 44–47, II, 111–112; Ep. 25 by, I, 47–48, II, 112–113; Ep. 48 to, I, 146–148, II, 130; objects to being called "father" by P., I, 48, 364; opposition to pilgrimages, II, 132
Guigo II, pr. of La Chartreuse, II, 112
Guilencus, bp. of Langres, II, 140
Guitmund of Aversa, II, 158
Gunzo, abt. of Baume, II, 157–158
Guy of Bazoches, II, 8
Guy, card.-bp. of Ostia, II, 228
Guy, card.-deacon of S. Maria in Porticu, II, 267
Guy, card.-legate to Bohemia, II, 328 n. 55
Guy (?), pr. of La Charité, II, 296
Guy of Domène, I, 438, II, 223–224; interdict of, I, 438–439; marriage of, I, 439, II, 223; meeting with Eugene III, I, 439; meeting with P., I, 439; P.'s affection and intervention with Eugene III, I, 438; visit to Rome, I, 439
Guy II, ct. of Ponthieu, II, 289; grant of canonries at Abbeville to Cl., I, 264
Guy II, ct. of Rochefort, II, 315
Guy, *salsamentarius* at Cl., II, 346

Hadrian IV, pope, II, 144, 241, 268, 330
Haimeric, card.-deacon, papal chancellor, I, 231, II, 14, 27, 28, 35, 98–99, 159, 248, 318; Ep. 3 to, I, 6–7, II, 98–99; Ep. 34 to, I, 109–113, II, 123–124; retirement, II, 254 n. 11
Hamelinus, bp. of Rennes, attacked at Pontremoli, I, 51, II, 114
Hand-washing of guests by abt., I, 71–73, 92
Hartkar, Antiphonary of, II, 109

406 GENERAL INDEX

Hato, bp. of Troyes, I, 6, 227, 423, II, 8, 20, 24, 25, 27, 97-98, 107, 142-146, 151, 152-153, 155-156, 194, 248, 285, 305, 306, 308 n. 17, 311, 314, 334; Ep. 5 to, I, 9-11, II, 100; Ep. 6 to, I, 11-13, II, 101; Ep. 7 to, I, 13-14, II, 101; Ep. 18 to, I, 25-26, II, 107; Ep. 22 to, I, 42-43, II, 110; Ep. 69 to, I, 199-201, II, 142-144; Ep. 70 to, I, 202-203, II, 144-145; Ep. 71 by, I, 203-206, II, 145-146; Ep. 81 to, I, 217-218, II, 152-153; Ep. 85 by, I, 222, II, 154; Ep. 86 to, I, 222-227, II, 154-156; Ep. 95 to, I, 256, II, 162; Ep. 96 by, I, 256-257, II, 163; Ep. 121 to, I, 314-315, II, 181; association with Nicholas of Montiéramey, II, 316-320, 325, 329; at Sens, II, 97; attacked at Pontremoli, I, 51, 154, II, 114, 134; benefactor of Cl., II, 98, 146; busyness with episcopal affairs, I, 257; dispute with Hugh of Auxerre, I, 200-201, II, 143, 145; friendship with Bernard, II, 97; friendship with P., I, 203-205, 217-218, 222-223; intention to resign and enter Cl., I, 223-227, 315, II, 155, 181; lost letters, I, 217, II, 152; ordinations at La Charité, I, 200, 205, II, 143; visits to Cl., I, 26, 218, 227, 256, II, 107, 155, 162, 163, 317; visits to Rome, I, 226
Hautmont (Ben.), lost MS. from, II, 70
Havelberg, bp., *see* Anselm
Heart: eye of, I, 216; true source of solitude, I, 188
Heir, seeking inheritance, I, 147
Heloise, abbess of Paraclete, II, 23, 165, 247; Ep. 115 to, I, 303-308, II, 177-178; Ep. 167 by, I, 400-401, II, 209-210; Ep. 168 to, I, 401-402, II, 210; learning, I, 303-306; letters, II, 7; religious studies, I, 304; style, II, 34, 38; P.'s affection for, I, 303, 401; P.'s wish she were Cl., I, 306; liturgical commemoration, I, 400, 401, II, 210
Henry, bp. of Autun, II, 225
Henry, ct. of Champagne, II, 316, 330
Henry IV, emp., letters, II, 4 n. 13, 20 n. 81, 21 n. 86, 22 n. 92, 34
Henry V, emp., letters, II, 21 n. 86
Henry I, k. of England, II, 149-150, 156-157, 259; grant to Cl., II, 138; annoyance with Hugh of Rouen, II, 107; death, I, 22, 212, II, 104-105, 138; Cl. prayers for, I, 22
Henry II, k. of England, II, 26, 256 n. 26
Henry of Glinde, seal of, II, 22 n. 90
Henry of Huntingdon, chron., II, 104
Henry of Lausanne, heretic, II, 287, 288 n. 15
Henry of France, bp. of Beauvais, abp. of Rheims, I, 360-361, 372, 373, II, 13 n. 57, 59, 195-196, 200, 201, 202, 309 n. 23, 321, 322, 323; Ep. 146 by, I, 361-362, II, 197; confraternity with Cl., I, 362
Henry, abp. of Sens, II, 106; attacked at Pontremoli, I, 51, II, 114
Henry of Blois, bp. of Winchester, I, 22, II, 24, 27, 104, 130-131, 156-157, 239 n. 36, 244, 247, 256, 265, 268, 298; Ep. 49 to, I, 148-150, II, 130-131; Ep. 55 to, I, 175-177, II, 136; Ep. 56 to, I, 177-178, II, 136; Ep. 57 to, I, 179, II, 137; Ep. 59 to, I, 189-190, II, 137-138; Ep. 60 to, I, 190-191, II, 138-139; Ep. 61 to, I, 191, II, 139; Ep. 88 to, I, 228, II, 156-157; Ep. 107 to, I, 270, II, 170; affection of Cls. for, I, 191; affection of P. for, I, 149, 177, 179; benefactor of Cl., I, 150, 177-178, 189-191, 228, II, 131; frequent communication with P., I, 175-176, 177, 190-191; involvement in secular affairs, I, 189; P.'s request that Henry be buried at Cl., I, 190; Cl. prayers for, I, 228, 301, 303; visits to Cl., I, 189, 228, II, 138, 169, 156-157
Heraclea of Polignac, II, 241
Heraclius, emp., I, 295, II, 283
Heraclius of Montboissier, provost of Brioude, abp. of Lyons, P.'s brother, I, 233, 443, II, 160, 215, 216, 225, 241-242, 244, 268; commended to Innocent II by P., I, 259-260; visit to Innocent II, II, 165
Herbert of Losinga, letters, II, 9
Herbeys, II, 221
Herbins, unidentified Cl. monastery, I, 434, II, 221
Hercules, I, 144
Hereford, Franciscans, MS. from, II, 70, 72
Heremitism and hermits, I, 29, 158, 324; Cluniac, II, 14-15, 16, 182 (*see also* Gilbert of Senlis, Peter of Poitiers, Peter the Venerable); Carth. *heremum*, I, 379, 402; hermits become prelates, I, 32; nature of, (in self) I, 188, (solitude) I, 321, 324; hermit "serf of God," I, 40; austerities, I, 39, 40; good works not to be performed, I, 36; poverty, modeled on Christ, I, 34-35, 37; prayers for others, I, 33; should allow body what nature requires, I, 40; tendency to get involved in secular affairs, I, 32-33. *See also* Solitude
Heresy and heretics, I, 4, 61, 118-119, 251-252, II, 162; Abelard called a heretic, I, 258; in antiquity, I, 286; in Provence, I, 197, 299, II, 285; refutation of, I, 203, II, 145, 279-281. *See also* Apollinarism, Henry of Lausanne, Nestorius, Nicholas, Peter of Bruys, Saracens
Herman of Dalmatia, II, 279
Herod, I, 243, 248

GENERAL INDEX

Hezelo of Liège, Cl. monk, I, 229, II, 157–158; helped build new church at Cl., I, 229
Hichman, Damian, II, 45
Hilary of Poitiers, St., I, 30, 432, II, 40; style, II, 33; work of, requested by Carths., I, 47, II, 111
Hildebert of Lavardin, bp. of Le Mans, II, 3 n. 11, 8, 145; style, II, 34 n. 150
Hildegard of Bingen, letters, II, 4 n. 13, 7
Hippocrates, I, 428
Historiography, Cl., II, 12
Holy Land, I, 327; legation of Alberic of Ostia, I, 221, II, 154; pilgrimages to, I, 344. *See also* Antioch, Crusader States, Jerusalem
Holy See: affection for Cl., I, 316; Cl. special daughter of, I, 110; devotion of Cl., I, 108; devotion of P., I, 312; judicial appeals to, I, 350, 415; rules all things, I, 193; scorned by abt. of Brioude, I, 415. *See also* Pope and names of individual popes
Holy Spirit: devotion to, *see* Raingard; dictator of *Regula Benedicti*, I, 281
Honorius II, pope, I, 300, II, 123, 259; privilege for Cl., II, 119
Horace, I, 1, 10, II, 12, 39
Hugh, bp. of Angoulême, election of, I, 351, II, 193
Hugh, abt. of Pontigny, bp. of Auxerre, I, 200–201, 205, II, 143, 188, 217, 218, 307, 309, 312, 324; dispute with Hato of Troyes, I, 200–201, II, 143, 145; meeting with Matthew of Albano, I, 143, II, 129; visit to Italy in 1145–46, II, 307
Hugh Beraldus, II, 97
Hugh Berardus, chamberlain of St. Jean d'Angély, II, 97, 339
Hugh III of Berzé, II, 225, 226; mediated dispute between Cl. and Hugh of La Bussière, I, 443
Hugh of Bissy, cellarer of Cl., II, 346
Hugh *Deschaux* of La Bussière, II, 224–225, 226, 346; castle built by, I, 442–443; dispute with Cl., *ibid.*; promise to fortify no other places, I, 443
Hugh II, duke of Burgundy, II, 145; son of (Robert?), I, 206, II, 147
Hugh, card.-bp. of Ostia, II, 226, 319 n. 18; date of elevation, II, 227–228; honor shown to P. by, I, 445
Hugh, provost of La Charité, II, 297
Hugh Catula, knight, II, 25, 131–132; Ep. 51 to, I, 151–152, II, 131–132; pilgrimage to Jerusalem, I, 152; promise to become Cl., I, 151
Hugh, cellarer of Cl., II, 346

Hugh, claustral pr. of Cl., II, 346
Hugh of Crécy, chamberlain of Cl., I, 43, 48, 208, 256, 257, 340–341, II, 27, 110, 113, 147, 162, 188–189, 263, 309, 311–313, 314–315, 317, 346; confraternity with St.-Martin-des-Champs, II, 312; mission to Spain, II, 311–312; mission to Hato of Troyes, I, 256; P.'s affection for, I, 340; service to Cl., I, 340; death, II, 313; liturgical commemoration, I, 341
Hugh of Crécy, constable of Rouen, II, 314 n. 21
Hugh of Crécy-en-Brie, II, 313–314, 315
Hugh I, abt. of Cluny, I, 3, 229, 334, 348, II, 158, 186, 191, 238–239, 257, 299, 300, 358; *Vita*, II, 157
Hugh II, claustral pr. of Marcigny, abt. of Cl., I, 3, 162, II, 135, 239, 299
Hugh III, abt. of Cl., II, 17
Hugh, infirmarian of Cl., II, 346
Hugh, St., bp. of Lincoln, II, 221
Hugh, abt. of Luxeuil, II, 110
Hugh *Dissutus* of Montboissier, P.'s brother, I, 434, II, 237, 242–243, 244
Hugh Bernier, abt. of Noyers, I, 267, II, 168
Hugh *Dissutus* of Palliers or Usson, P.'s great-grandfather, II, 225, 234, 235, 236, 242; pilgrimage to Rome, II, 235
Hugh of Poitiers, chron., II, 13, 234, 243 n. 63, 244 n. 69, 245, 265, 266, 267, 268, 332 n. 5
Hugh Primas, poet, II, 295
Hugh of Amiens, pr. of St. Martial, Limoges, pr. of Lewes, abt. of Reading, abp. of Rouen, I, 22, 25, II, 13, 99–100, 104, 106, 107, 208, 256, 257; Ep. 4 to, I, 7–9, II, 99–100; Ep. 178 to, I, 419–420, II, 217–218; attacked at Pontremoli, I, 154, II, 134; approved election of Arnulf of Lisieux, I, 261, II, 166; lost letters, I, 419; love for Cl., I, 420; loyalty, I, 419; P.'s love for, I, 419; visit to Cl., I, 420
Hugh, abt. of St.-Germain-des-Prés, II, 312 n. 12
Hugh of St. Victor, II, 71, 160
Hugh, pr. of Sauxillanges, II, 241
Hugh, secretary of Gervase of Prémontré, II, 19
Hugh of Toucy, abp. of Sens, II, 307
Hugh of La Ferté, abp. of Tours, I, 266–267, II, 106, 168–169, 175; became Cl. monk at La Charité, I, 266, II, 169
Hugh, bp. of Grenoble, abp. of Vienne, I, 438–439, II, 198, 202–203; Ep. 154 to, I, 374, II, 202–203; Ep. 155 by, I, 374, II, 203; alleged complaints against, I, 374; defended by P., I, 375–376; ordered by

Hugh bp. of Grenoble—*continued*
Eugene III to protect Cls., I, 374; ordered by Eugene III to settle case of Guy of Domène, I, 438, II, 223
Human life and sufferings of Christ, I, 122–123. *See also* Christ
Human nature, (mercy) I, 283, (kindness) I, 284
Human studies, I, 15
Humanism, monastic, II, 41
Humbald, abp. of Lyons, I, 260, II, 166
Humbert III of Beaujeu, I, 408–412, II, 214, 225, 226; desire to change religious for secular habit, I, 411; joy in Burgundy at his return, I, 408, 409, 410, 411; left wife improperly, I, 411–412; P. asks Eugene III and Master of Templars to permit him to remain, I, 409–410; towns founded by, II, 166
Humbert, abp. of Besançon, II, 180; attacks on, I, 313; P. intervenes with Eugene III on his behalf, I, 313, II, 180
Humbert, chamberlain of Cl., II, 346
Humbert of Baugé, adc. of Autun, bp. of Autun, abp. of Lyons, II, 194, 209, 218; Ep. 143 to, I, 352–353, II, 193–194; Suger's letter to, I, 399; urged by P. to become monk, I, 352–353
Humbert, pr. of Meyriat, II, 211; Ep. 169 by, I, 402, II, 210–211
Humility: monastic, I, 16, 18, 152, 224, 227, 230, 268, 305; of Virgin Mary, I, 237; of Christ, I, 34, 224, 433; of hermits, I, 37; ordered by God, I, 89; necessary to love, I, 292; one of three monastic virtues, I, 128, 215, 230, 289, 430, 433; signified by color black, I, 289
Hungary, II, 293 n. 2; ks., confraternity with Cl., I, 209
Huntingdon, II, 28 n. 120
Hus, land of, I, 384
Hydra, I, 144
Hylarion, St., I, 226
Hymns, P.'s dislike of false, I, 318. *See also* Airaldus, Benedict (St.), Peter the Venerable

Ida, countess of Ponthieu, II, 290
Idumaeans, I, 357–358
Idungus of St. Emmeram, II, 3
Igé, II, 182
Ilion of Riverie, abt. of St. Just, Lyons, II, 122, 165; Ep. 100 to, I, 260–261, II, 165–166
Imar, card.-bp. of Tusculum, II, 294–295, 296, 297–298, 309, 312
Imitation: of angels, I, 431; of apostles, fathers, and saints, I, 59, 63, 74, 230, 426, (fasts of saints) I, 283, (good works of scribes and pharisees) I, 95, (clothing of early church) I, 64; of Christ, I, 59, 184, 441, (poverty and humility) I, 34, (prayer in mountain) I, 181, (virginity) I, 429
Inbert, chamberlain of Cl., II, 346
Incarnation of Christ, I, 118–119, 251–255. *See also* Christ
Inclusio, I, 28, 29
Indian seas, I, 10
Indies, wealth of, I, 34
Inflatio, I, 293
Innocent II, pope, I, 6, 231, 269, 300, 343, II, 27–28, 62, 98, 104, 107, 115, 122, 126, 130, 138, 142–143, 159, 166, 168, 171, 175, 242, 248, 252–254, 255, 259, 290, 293, 295, 304, 318–319, 320 n. 19, 336–337; Ep. 1 to I, 4–5, II, 95–96; Ep. 11 to I, 17–18, II, 102; Ep. 17 to, I, 24–25, II, 105–107; Ep. 21 to, I, 42, II, 109–110; Ep. 23 to, I, 43–44, II, 110–111; Ep. 27 to, I, 50–52, II, 113–115; Ep. 32 to, I, 106–107, II, 122; Ep. 33 to, I, 107–109, II, 122–123; Ep. 39 to, I, 131–134, II, 126; Ep. 46 to, I, 142–144, II, 128–129; Ep. 62 by, I, 191–192, II, 139–140; Ep. 63 to, I, 192–193, II, 140; Ep. 64 to, I, 193–194, II, 140; Ep. 72 to, I, 206, II, 146–147; Ep. 92 to, I, 233–234, II, 160–161; Ep. 97 to, I, 257–258, II, 163–164; Ep. 98 to, I, 258–259, II, 164–165; Ep. 99 to, I, 259–260, II, 165; Ep. 101 to, I, 261–262, II, 166–167; Ep. 103 to, I, 265–266, II, 168; Ep. 104 to, I, 266–267, II, 168–169
—— asks for Cl. prayers, I, 192; consecrated church at Cl., I, 112, II, 124; crowned Louis VII, I, 257–258, II, 163; devotion of Cl., I, 4–5, 113; devotion of P., I, 4–5, 132, 191–192; enemies, I, 113; at Rome, I, 192, II, 126; travels, I, 192, 231, II, 139; victory over Anacletus II, I, 196. *See also* Roger II of Sicily
Innocent III, pope, II, 33
Instability: of monks in dio. of Lyons, I, 129; of P., I, 417, 425. *See also* Crusaders
Interdict: on Cls. by pope, I, 79, 108, 109, 112; on Guy of Domène, I, 438–439
Investiture Controversy, influence on letter writing, II, 5 n. 21, 8 n. 30
Iocundare in domino, I, 403, 420
Iocunditas, I, 276, 337, 419; of hermit, I, 321; of P., I, 273; supreme, unattainable in this life, I, 428
Iocundus: future life, I, 337; letters, I, 322, 325; Raingard, I, 165–166; visit to Paraclete, I, 400; weather, I, 444
Ira, overcome by holy reading, I, 39
Ireland, II, 266

GENERAL INDEX

Isaac, patriarch, I, 156, 183, 357; kids eaten by, I, 393–394
Isaac of L'Étoile, II, 3 n. 9
Isaiah, I, 29, 30, 57, 118, 123, 187, 246, 274, 388, 416
Isembert III of Châtel-Aillon, II, 337 n. 28
Isère River, I, 435, II, 221, 223
Ishmael, I, 297
Islam: beliefs of, II, 281–284; P.'s knowledge of, II, 185; P.'s translations against, I, 294–295, II, 275–279
Israelites,=religious life, I, 211
Italy, I, 226, 320, 450; climate, I, 7, 350, 444, II, 99, 247–248; disturbed conditions, I, 142–143, II, 129; lands held by Saracens, I, 330; MSS. from, II, 74; peace brought by Roger II of Sicily, I, 231; P.'s travels in, I, 168, 201, 438, 444, 449, II, 143, 223–228, 253–254, 265, 325–326; visits by Bernard, II, 140–141
Iterius, dean of Périgeux, II, 264
Iterius of Toucy, II, 189
Ivo, bp. of Chartres, letters, II, 4 n. 13, 8, 11
Izmit, Gulf of, II, 292

Jabin, k., I, 305
Jacob, patriarch, I, 109, 203, 238, 246, 287, 316, 357–358
James, St., I, 356; gifts received at Pentecost, I, 240–241
Jarentus, almoner of Cl., II, 347
Jehosaphat, Our Lady (Cl.?), II, 291–292; abt., see Gilduin
Jeremiah, I, 29, 123, 127, 128, 377, 387
Jerome, St., I, 2, 29, 39, 120, 188, 288, 291, II, 25 n. 103, 40; "greatest Christian orator," I, 144; letters, I, 47, II, 8 n. 31; style, II, 33
Jerome, Pseudo-, I, 235, 236, 244, 245, 251, 254, 430; orthodoxy of, I, 252
Jerusalem, earthly, I, 219, 220, 221, 240, 243, II, 153, 245, 263; P.'s inability to visit, I, 398; pilgrimages to, I, 152, 221, 354, 358–360, II, 132; Holy Sepulchre, I, 400, (pr.) II, 153; St. Mary the Great, II, 292; St. Mary the Latin, II, 292; Tomb of the Virgin, II, 292 (abt., see Hugh)
Jerusalem, heavenly, I, 134, 263, 280, 428; better than earthly, I, 152
Jerusalem, k., I, 208, II, 23–24; Ep. 82 to, I, 219, II, 153; besieged in Antioch, I, 397, 398; P. assists with souls and prayers, I, 219; wars against enemies of Christendom, I, 219. See also Baldwin II and III, Fulk
Jerusalem, kingdom of, I, 399. See also Crusader States, Holy Land

Jerusalem, patriarch of, II, 23–24; Ep. 83 to, I, 220–221, II, 153; honor owing to, I, 220; P.'s request for relics, I, 220; vicar of Christ, I, 220. See also Gormond, Stephen, William
Jethro, I, 73
Jews, I, 53, 177, 219, 328–330, 357–358, II, 280–282; associated with Mohammed, I, 296, 297; blasphemy of, I, 328; ecclesiastical property bought by, I, 329; make money dishonestly, I, 329; meat eaten by, I, 392–393; severity of God against, I, 328–329; should pay for Second Crusade, I, 330; should be punished not killed, I, 329, 330; works of St. Augustine against, I, 298; worse than Saracens, I, 328
Jezabel, I, 29
Job, I, 91, 118, 146, 148, 182, 186, 187, 304, 331, 334, 339, 409, 446
Jocelyn, bp. of Soissons, I, 264, II, 23 n. 93, 290
Joceran, abt. of Luxeuil, II, 110
Joceran *Grossus* of Brancion, II, 225, 226
John of Anchin, scribe, II, 52 n. 213
John the Baptist, I, 88, 94, 242, 352, 382; fasts and solitude, I, 225; use of furs, I, 63, II, 117
John Paparo, card.-deacon of S. Adriano, II, 266
John, card.-priest of St. Chrysogonus, II, 110
John IX, patriarch of Constantinople, II, 149; Ep. 76 to, I, 209–210, II, 149
John of Cournon, canon of Broude, I, 416, II, 216
John *Escot* of Cournon, II, 216
John Comnenus, emp., I, 210, II, 148, 292; Ep. 75 to, I, 208–209, II, 148–149; greatest Christian prince, I, 208; defender of Church, I, 208
John the Evangelist, I, 38, 60, 90, 98, 128, 238, 246, 247, 332, 353, 414; glossed copy of Gospel of, I, 402, 404
John of Hexham, chron., II, 104, 150
John, bp. of Lisieux, II, 166
John, pr. of Longpont, II, 312
John, abt. of Montpeyroux, II, 181
John, adc. of Orléans, II, 106, 308
John, bp. of Piacenza, I, 440, II, 224
John XI, pope, II, 119
John XIX, pope, II, 143
John of Salisbury, II, 26, 28, 34, 145, 215, 252–253, 254, 255, 266; letters, I, 4 n. 13, 8–9; style, II, 34, 36 n. 158, 41
John, bp. of Séez, I, 154, II, 114, 134
John of Toucy, Cl. monk: death and burial of, I, 341–343, II, 189–190; devotion to Virgin Mary, I, 342; piety of, I, 342

John of Worcester, chron., II, 105
John of Ypres, chron., II, 168, 253
Jordan of Anchin, scribe, II, 52 n. 213
Jordan, card.-priest of S. Susanna, II, 266
Jordan of Montboissier, abt. of La Chaise-Dieu, P.'s brother, I, 348, 376, II, 192, 204, 243, 244, 268; Ep. 53 to, I, 153-173, II, 133-135; displeasure of Eugene III with, I, 376, II, 204; visit to Eugene III, I, 376
Joseph, patriarch, I, 41, 106, 236, 243, 276, 316; dream of, I, 354, 356-358, 386
Joseph, St., I, 386-387
Joshua, I, 327
Jotcerannus, bp. of Mâcon, II, 145
Jouarre, council of, I, 25, II, 106, 107, 129, 260
Jougne, I, 439
Joy: signified by white, see White; virtue of, see *Iocunditas*
Judas, I, 242
Judicial cases at Cl., I, 6, 56, 83, 87, 324. See also Litigation
Judicial process in case of theft, I, 414, II, 215
Jugglars: abstain from meat on Sabbath, I, 388; at Cl., I, 72
Julian the Pelagian, I, 298, II, 281
Jully-les-Nonnains (Ben.), obit., II, 97
Jura mountains, I, 439
Justice: abuse of, by bp. of Clermont, I, 406; fostered by Christ, I, 139; of Virgin Mary, I, 237; perfected by love, *ibid*.
Justus, bp. of Lyons, I, 226, II, 156

Knights: in Auvergne, I, 406; in Burgundy, I, 442; name for Carths., I, 435; tithes paid to, I, 108, 110; visiting Cl., I, 72
Koran, P.'s translation of, I, 295, 296, II, 275, 277, 279-280, 282, 332 n. 5, 342

Laban, I, 287
Lambert, bp. of Angoulême, II, 193
Landed estates, monastic, I, 56, 83-88, 278, II, 120; claimed by others, I, 87-88; good management, I, 86-87; possession recognized by Gregory I, I, 81, 85; sold to satisfy desire for luxury, I, 390
Lanfranc, abp. of Canterbury, II, 3, 158
Langres: bad state of church, I, 103-104; bp., see Garnerius, Guilencus, William of Sabran; dean, see Robert; episcopal election, I, 102-104, 193-194, 202, 206, 277, II, 135, 145, 147, 166, 172, 173, (*libertas eligendi* requested from Innocent II) I, 206, (canons opposed to Cl.) I, 102-103, (Cl. bp.-elect interviewed by P.) I, 103
Languages, gift of, I, 239, 241
Laon, II, 99; meeting to plan crusade in 1150, I, 398-399

Larrivour (Cist.), obit., II, 97
Latium, disturbed conditions in, I, 201, II, 143
Laurence of Liège, II, 130
Lausanne, bp., see Amadeus
Law: ancient, I, 329; diversity of, I, 96-97; divine, I, 235; mutability of, I, 61-62, 74-75, 88-90, 92-95, 98-99, 282, 412. See also *Regula Benedicti*
Lawyer, I, 14, 349
Lay order, I, 24, 31
Laybrothers (*conversi*): at Cl., I, 300-301, II, 175; at La Grande Chartreuse, I, 435
Learning, sacred and secular, see *Sapientia*
Lecelinus, friend of Nicholas of Montiéramey, II, 328 n. 56
Legates, papal, I, 107 (to Lyons). See also Alberic of Ostia, Gilo of Tusculum, Guy, Odo
Lent, abstinence during, I, 389-390
Leo I, pope, I, 61, 384; style, II, 34 n. 145
Leon, II, 52
Leontifrid, P.'s constable, II, 347
Leotaldus, chaplain at Cl., II, 347
Letald, pr. of Sauxillanges, II, 237
Letcombe-Regis: granted to Cl., II, 138-139, 256; confirmed by Lucius II, II, 176
Letter collections, II, 4-11; editions of, II, 11; formation, II, 8-10; in antiquity, II, 5 n. 18; organization, II, 10, 95; patristic, II, 8 n. 31; role of scribes, II, 6-7
Letters: carriage of, I, 10, II, 23-29, (*see also* Messengers); forbidden to monks, II, 1; fraudulent, I, 112, II, 27-28; oral delivery, II, 25, 27-28; originals, II, 20-22, 27; value to historians, II, 1-2; variety of forms, II, 2-4; writing, I, 10, 109-110, II, 1-2, 18-20. See also Archives, Brevity, *Cursus*, *Dictamen*, Dictation, Epistolary mode, Formularies, *Litterae apertae*, *Litterae clausae*, Poems, Preaching, Registers, Scribes, Secret messages, Writing
Letters (of alphabet): additional in words, II, 88-89; capital, II, 91; interchangeable, II, 86-88; omitted, II, 89
Levi, sons of, I, 338
Levitas, avoided by P., I, 273. See also Crusaders
Lewes (Cl.), II, 99, 256; pr., see Hugh of Amiens
Lia, I, 20-21
Liber de diversis ordinibus, II, 109, 120
Liber graduum, I, 383, II, 205, 303
Liberal arts, P.'s knowledge of, I, 1-2
Libertas caelestis, awaited in monastic "prison," I, 306

GENERAL INDEX 411

Libertas eligendi, see Langres
Liège: adc., *see* Philip; bp., *see* Albero, Frederick; gifts of church to Cl., I, 229; MSS. from dio. of, II, 71; St. John the Evangelist (Aug.), provost, *see* Raimbaud; St. Lambert, II, 157, 158; St. Laurence (Ben.), MS. from, II, 63
Lieu-Dieu (Cl.), pr., *see* Milo
Life, present and eternal, compared to winter and spring, night and day, I, 173
Ligugé (Ben.), I, 288
Limoges, II, 260; bp., *see* Eustorgius, Gerald of Cher; bp.-elect, *see* Amblard; St. Augustine (Ben.), abt., *see* Peter of Barri, Philip; St. Martial (Ben.-Cl.), II, 99, 158, 257, (Ep. 159 to monks of) I, 383-385, II, 205, (abt., attacked at Pontremoli) I, 51, II, 114, *see also* Amblard, Peter of Pithiviers, (pr.) *see* Hugh of Amiens, Ranulf, (good reputation) I, 383-384, (nourished by Cl.) I, 384, (*ordo* of Fathers preserved there) I, 383, 384, (urged by P. to maintain high standard) I, 385
Limousin: attitude in papal schism, II, 337 n. 30; troubles in, I, 384
Lincoln, bp., *see* Hugh; obit., II, 104
Linear B, letters in, II, 25
Lion, I, 26
Lisieux: bp., *see* Arnulf, John; episcopal election, I, 261-262
Litigation by monks, I, 56, 83, 87-88, 278; avoided by Carths., I, 379. *See also* Judicial cases
Litterae apertae, II, 23
Litterae clausae, II, 21, 22, 23
Liturgical commemoration, I, 339, 373, 394. *See also* Confraternity, Heloise, Hugh of Crécy, Mathilda, Maurice II of Montboissier, Odo of St. Remy, Peter the Venerable, Prayer (intercessionary), Raingard, Roger II of Sicily (sons of), Trental
Liturgy, *see* Hymns, *Metanea*
Logic, study of, I, 16, 304
Loire River, I, 409, 411
London: bp., *see* Gilbert Foliot, Robert de Sigillo; Westminster Abbey (Ben.), II, 139
Longchamps, villa of, given to St. Maurus, I, 85
Longpont (Cl.), II, 312, 313; chartulary, II, 183; obit., II, 171, 194, 312, 315 n. 25; pr., *see* John
Looz, family of, II, 159
Lot, I, 186
Lothar III, emp., II, 129, 130, 143, 186, 271; death of, I, 196, II, 141

Louis VI, k. of France, II, 151, 296, 309, 312 n° 9, 313, 338; death of, II, 110, 136. *See also* Bonneval
Louis VII, k. of France, II, 151, 160, 185, 195, 196, 240, 263, 264, 268, 295, 296, 302, 303, 306-307, 309-310, 312, 315; Ep. 130 to, I, 327-330, II, 185; court held at Le Puy, I, 102, II, 121; crowned by Innocent II, I, 257-258, II, 163; dispute with Amadeus of Savoy, I, 199, II, 142; dispute with abp.-elect of Bourges, I, 257, II, 163; expedition to Languedoc and Aquitaine in 1141, I, 256, 257, II, 155, 162-163, 317; kingdom doubled in size, I, 199; original letter of, II, 21 n. 86, 22 n. 92; P. intervenes in favor of, I, 199, 257; relations with Theobald of Champagne, II, 163. *See also* Aquitaine
Louvain, Val-St.-Martin (Aug.): MS. from, II, 70; lost MS. from, II, 63
Love: of God, I, 89; of neighbor, I, 41, 42, 89, 408; office of, to seek salvation of men, I, 98; necessary to salvation, I, 239; one of three monastic virtues, I, 128, 215, 430, 433; depends upon humility, I, 292; excluded by ambition, avarice, cupidity, conceit, I, 293; harmed by disputes among monks, I, 101, 111-112, 287; essence of *Regula Benedicti*, I, 60-61, 90-93, 97-100, 284-285; justifies changing rules, I, 89-90, 92-93, 96-98, 101; brings unity and harmony, I, 93, 96-97, 126, 210, 285, 293-294, 369, 371; cause of P.'s letter to Bernard, I, 276; extends to all things, I, 68; "fountain of all virtues," I, 92; "shield," I, 92, 96; gives value to physical austerities, I, 101, 140, 368; necessary to monastic good works, I, 116; perfects justice, I, 237. *See also* Christ, Eye (single), Friendship, God
Lucan, II, 39
Lucca, II, 261
Luciana, sister of Hugh of Crécy, II, 312, 313, 315
Lucius II, pope, II, 176, 248, 305-306; Ep. 113 to, I, 301-302, II, 175-176; Ep. 114 by, I, 302-303, II, 176-177; Ep. 116 to, I, 308-309, II, 178; Ep. 118 to, I, 311-312, II, 179; P.'s affection for, I, 301-302; P.'s visit to, I, 301, II, 176; privileges for Cl., II, 176. *See also* Roger II of Sicily
Luke, St., I, 181
Luni: bp., I, 52, II, 115; dio., I, 52
Lunigniano, II, 224
Lupellus, clerk of William of Canterbury, II, 255
Lupus of Ferrières, letters, II, 5
Lurcy-le-Bourg (Cl.), I, 105, II, 121, 293

Luxeuil (Ben.), I, 43-44, 258, II, 110-111, 164; abt., *see* Hugh, Joceran; dispute with St. Benignus, Dijon, II, 165, 258; reformed by Cl., I, 43-44

Luxuria, overcome by holy reading, I, 39

Luzy, II, 267

Lying, sin of, I, 89

Lyons, I, 176, II, 24, 234, 241-242, 259; abp., *see* Falco, Heraclius, Humbald, Humbert, Justus, Peter, Rainald; dean, *see* Stephen of Charolais; precentor, *see* Stephen *Pinguis*; clergy of, I, 107, (Ep. 100 to) I, 260-261, II, 165-166; dio. of, bad times in, I, 127, 130, II, 125; obit., II, 194; relations with Cl., I, 260-261, II, 122, 165-166; superiority to other French churches, I, 130; St. Just, II, 165, 242, (abt.) *see* Ilion of Riverie

Lyons-la-Forêt, I, 22, II, 104

Maccabees, I, 284, 395, 446

Macedonia, I, 403

Macharius, St., I, 30

Mâcon: council to keep peace, I, 443, II, 225, 267; bp., *see* Jotcerannus, Pontius; ct., *see* William; viscount, hostility of to Cl., I, 409

Magi, adoring Christ, I, 186, 187

Magnus of Reichersberg, II, 8

Maine, II, 260, 338, 339; P.'s travels through, I, 179

Maiolus, abt. of Cl., I, 3

Maior et sanior pars, I, 135

Malaspina, Marquis Opizone, I, 440, II, 224

Malmesbury (Ben.), II, 298; abt., *see* Peter

Manasses, bp. of Meaux, II, 307

Manasses of Garlande, bp. of Orléans, II, 308, 309

Manasses of Rumilly, adc. of Troyes, I, 205, 206, II, 146

Manasses of Tournon, II, 312

Manasses, adc. of Villemaur, II, 146

Mandatum, see Foot-washing

Manglieu (Ben.), II, 234, 240; abt., *see* Armannus

Manichaeans, I, 286, 297

Mans, Le, bp., *see* Hildebert, William

Manual labor: by hermits, I, 38-39, 41, 54; by monks, I, 54, 70-71, 84-85, 92, 283, II, 118; changes in rules concerning, I, 290; less worthy than spiritual exercises, I, 70-71, 97; not performed by St. Maurus, I, 71; performed by abt. of La Chaise-Dieu, I, 349; replaced by holy works, I, 283

Manuscript: eaten by bear, I, 47, II, 112; length of time to write, II, 52-53

Map, Walter, II, 117

Marbod, bp. of Rennes, II, 3 n. 11

Marcellus, St., I, 5

Marchiennes (Ben.), II, 50, 66, 188, 312 n. 9; abt., *see* Odo; MS. from, II, 63

Marcigny (Cl.), I, 153-156, 161-163, 172, 176, 212, 306, 427, 433, II, 24, 133, 134, 135, 138, 150, 221, 238 n. 27, 239, 242, 256, 260, 262, 263, 358; pr., *see* Geoffrey, Hugh; procurator, *see* Gerald Le Vert; miracles at, I, 162, 170-171; obit., II, 96, 105, 132, 133, 135, 137, 314, 335, 344, 347, 348; poverty of, I, 162, 270, II, 170; reception of guests and the poor, I, 166-167; Raingard's entry, life, and burial there, I, 161-163, 172;= prison, I, 428;=tomb, I, 270; visits by P., I, 154-156, 166, 274, II, 172, 239

Marestmontiers, cell of Crépy, II, 108

Margaret of Montboissier, P.'s niece, II, 221, 240, 242, 248; Ep. 185 to, I, 427-434, II, 220-221

Margerie-Hancourt (Cl.), pr., *see* Ascelin

Mark, St., I, 181

Marmoutier (Ben.), I, 288, II, 98

Marriage: case of Guy of Domène, I, 439, II, 223; invalid between Christian and pagan, I, 413; prohibited degrees of, I, 61, 90, 93, 439; sacredness of, I, 412-413

Martha, sister of Mary, ministry of, I, 164, 167, 234, (compared to bp.'s work) I, 268. *See also* Mary, sister of Martha

Martin, St., I, 8, 57, 170, 171, 267, 268, 288, II, 100; clothing, I, 288; poverty, I, 366, II, 177-178

Martyrs, I, 300; great number, I, 237; tombs, I, 23, II, 105

Mary, Blessed Virgin, I, 106, 166, 168, 337, 338, 342; "mother of God," I, 237; *virgo virginum*, I, 428; most excellent of created beings, I, 237, 247; knowledge below that of angels but above that of men, I, 242-251; freedom from sin, I, 238, 248; sincerity, I, 237; degree of grace before and after Pentecost, I, 236-241; gift of preaching, I, 241-242; grief, I, 157; suffered death and punishment in this life, I, 248; Moslem belief concerning, II, 282; hymns in honor of, I, 420; vision of, by Raingard, I, 168-169, II, 135; chapels of, at Cl., II, 155; relics from tomb requested by P., I, 220

Mary Magdalene, St., I, 158, 164; gifts received at Pentecost, I, 240-241; lack of virginity, I, 430

Mary, prophetess, I, 304

Mary, sister of Aaron, I, 241

Mary, sister of Martha: and Martha, I, 70-71, 167, 266, 268, II, 118; occupied with

GENERAL INDEX 413

listening to Christ, I, 46; *otium* of=life of monk, I, 268
Mascelin, lord of Tonnay, II, 339
Masses: public, prohibited in monasteries by Gregory I, I, 80; for dead, *see* Liturgical commemoration, Trental
Massy, Cl. chapel, II, 182
Mathilda, empress, II, 23 n. 95; case against Stephen, II, 252-253, 254, 255; liturgical commemoration for, II, 132, 255-256
Mathilda, queen of England, II, 297
Matthew, pr. of St.-Martin-des-Champs, card.-bp. of Albano, I, 142-144, 221, II, 27, 96-98, 99, 122, 150, 154, 258, 261-262, 293-294; Ep. 2 to, I, 5-6, II, 96-98; Ep. 47 to, I, 144-145, II, 129-130; loyalty to Innocent II, I, 132-133, 142-143; role in papal schism, I, 133-134; ordered by Innocent II to return to Italy, I, 133-134, 142, II, 129; meeting with Bernard, I, 143, II, 129; illness, I, 133, 143, II, 126; death, II, 311; P.'s affection for, I, 5; *Vita* by P., I, 327, II, 16, 184, 285; chaplain of, I, 201, II, 143, 146
Matthew, precentor of Rievaulx, II, 12 n. 52
Matthew, St., I, 87; glossed copy of Gospel of, I, 402, 404
Mauriac, II, 234
Maurice I of Montboissier, P.'s grandfather, II, 236-237
Maurice II of Montboissier, P.'s father, II, 191, 237-238, 239, 242; entry to Sauxillanges *ad succurrendum*, I, 159-160; will and testament, I, 159-160, II, 134; death, I, 159-160; liturgical commemoration, II, 238 n. 25, 241 n. 45
Maurus, St., I, 325, 391, II, 118; changed *Regula Benedicti*, I, 284; property granted to, I, 85. *See also* Manual labor
Meals, at Cl., I, 54, 65-68, 92; number of dishes, I, 67
Meat: eaten by Cls., I, 388-394, II, 206; not eaten by laymen, I, 388. See also *Regula Benedicti*
Meaux, bp., *see* Manasses
Meaux (Cist.), lost MS. from, II, 70
Medicines prescribed for P., *see* Drugs
Mediocritatem vitae of Peter of Lyons, praised by P., I, 125
Meditation, I, 21, 85, 223; desire of P. for, I, 235; stimulates prayer, I, 38
Melk (Ben.), MS. from, II, 63
Melun (Ben.), abt., attacked at Pontremoli, I, 51, II, 114
Merchants, I, 231, 411; seeking profit, I, 147
Mercoeur, family of, II, 233 n. 3

Mesopotamia, I, 357
Messengers, II, 23-28; reliability of, II, 18; to Rome, I, 134, 201, II, 24
Metanea (liturgical genuflexions), I, 55, 74, II, 118; to guests, I, 71-72
Meyriat (Carth.), I, 378, II, 14, 204, 250 n. 19, 311; Ep. 170 to, I, 402-404, II, 211; pr., *see* Humbert, Stephen; P.'s inability to visit, I, 403-404; obit., II, 242 n. 55
Michael, archangel, I, 45
Micheas, I, 246
Milan, fasting at, I, 279
Milo I, bp. of Thérouanne, II, 167, 171, 289-290; Ep. 102 to, I, 262-265, II, 167-168; attack on Cl., I, 262-263; opposition to grant of canonry at Abbeville to Cl., I, 264-265; visit to Cl., I, 263
Milo of Bray, visct. of Troyes, II, 313
Milo, pr. of Lieu-Dieu, II, 347
Minerva, I, 204, 292, 345, 367, 447
Miracles, I, 58, 246-247. *See also* Benedict, Marcigny
Miroir, Le (Cist.), II, 180; abt., *see* Eustace; dispute with Gigny, *see* Gigny
Moabites, I, 414
Mohammed, I, 294, II, 277, 279, 283-284; beliefs, I, 296-297; life, I, 295-296, 297-298
Moissac (Cl.), II, 348; abt., II, 267 (*see also* William)
Molesme (Ben.), chartulary, II, 189
Moloch, I, 414
Monasteries: ceremony of entry, I, 163; compared to prison, I, 306, 428; compared to tomb, I, 270, 306, 361; easier to found new than to reform old, I, 43; new, founded near Cl. monasteries, I, 108
Monastic life: security of, I, 225, 226, 268; superiority to clerical life, I, 267; virtues of, (humility, love, poverty) I, 128, (grief, humility, penance) I, 289, (frugality, humility, poverty) I, 230, (humility, love, patience) I, 430, (chastity, humility, love) I, 215, 433. *See also* Apostles, Warfare (spiritual)
Monastic order: unity of, I, 145, 285, 293-294, 368-369; enemies of, I, 145, 263; made up of congregations, I, 293;=black Bens., I, 24, 56, 144, 145, 220, 225-226, 263, 268, 284, 313, 345, 370, 406-407, 416, 446; *antiquus ordo*=black Bens., I, 384; *ordo* of individual monastery, I, 383. *See also* Carthusians, Cistercians, Cluny, Schism
Monasticism: decline of, according to Cistercians, I, 291; at Luxeuil, I, 258; in 10th century, I, 391; in dio. of Lyons, I, 128-129, II, 125; of Cluniacs, I, 390

Monasticism, reform (renewal, revival) of, I, 284, 288; by councils of black monks, II, 151; by Geoffrey of Châlons-sur-Marne, I, 213; by Odo of Cluny, I, 391; in France in 12th century, I, 130, 145; difficulties of, I, 43, 312
Monday, abstinence from meat on, I, 388
Mondaye (Carth.), II, 266
Money-lending by Jews, I, 329
Monk Bretton (Ben.), II, 297
Monks: compared to buried men, I, 361; compared to dead men, I, 270; serf of abt., I, 183–184, II, 137; former bps. and abts., I, 225–226; seeking ecclesiastical preferment, I, 345; holy works by, useless without love, I, 116; recompense benefactors with prayers, fasts, and good works, I, 84; disputes among, I, 101, 111–112, 277–278, 287, 291; disputes with bishops, I, 7, 197–198. *See also* (among many other entries) Cistercians, Cluny, Color of clothing, Letters, Manual labor, Pilgrimages, Profession, Writing
Monsters, France free of until now, I, 144
Mont St. Romain, Cl. chapel, II, 182
Montacute? (Cl.), pr., I, 191, II, 139
Montaigut? (Cl.), pr., I, 191, II, 139
Montboissier, II, 257; castle of, II, 236, 240, 242, 245; family of, II, 181, 233–246, 299
Monte Cassino (Ben.), abt., II, 139
Montenpuis, family of, II, 240 n. 38
Montet-aux-Moines, Le, priory of La Chiusa, II, 266
Montiéramey (Ben.): II, 320 n. 21, 324 n. 40, 328 n. 56, 329, 330; obit., II, 97
Montierender (Ben.), abt., attacked at Pontremoli, I, 51, II, 114
Montmain, Cl. chapel, II, 182
Montpellier, II, 107, 245 n. 75, 269; ct., *see* William; medical center, II, 303; P.'s visit to, I, 105, II, 121
Montpensier, family of, II, 233 n. 3
Montpeyroux (Cist.), II, 180–181, 244; abt., *see* John, Fulcher; patronized by family of Montboissier, II, 181, 244
Morigny (Ben.), chron., II, 313; disputed election at, II, 160
Mortemer (Ben.-Cist.), II, 104
Mosat (Ben.-Cl.), abt., *see* Eustace
Moses, I, 73, 128, 142, 143, 183, 237, 246, 254, 296, 327, 392; injured by Christ, I, 99; spoke with God, I, 180–181
Moses, patriarch of Ravenna, I, 444, II, 227; dispute over consecration of bp. of Piacenza, I, 440–442, II, 224
Mother of God, uniqueness of title, I, 237
Moulins, II, 58, 266

Mount Cenis Pass, II, 221, 223, 234
Mount of Olives, I, 240
Mount Thabor (Cl.), I, 105, II, 23–24, 122, 291; Ep. 80 to monks of, I, 214–217, II, 152; confraternity with Cl., II, 291; monk of, at Cl., I, 215; recently joined Cl. order, I, 215; special blessing and obligations of, I, 215–216
Mountains, associated with spiritual life, I, 180–181
Mourning: color of, I, 289; customs in Spain, I, 289, II, 173
Moûtiers-St.-Jean (Réôme) (Ben.), abt., attacked at Pontremoli, I, 51, II, 114
Mule: given by P. to Theodard of La Charité, I, 136; ridden by P. in Italy, I, 444
Multiloquium, I, 31, 33, 40–41
Murat, family of, II, 233 n. 3
Music, I, 2
Mystery, definition and difference from sacrament, I, 253, 254

Nájera, II, 262
Nantua (Ben.-Cl.), obit., II, 124, 135
Naomi, I, 184
Narbonne, abp., *see* Arnold
Natalis, abt. of Rebais, I, 233–234, 266, II, 149, 160–161, 168, 170; becomes monk at Cl., I, 233
Nature: fostered by Christ, I, 139; requirements for body, I, 40
Nazareth, I, 358
Nebuchadnezzar, I, 50–51, 386
Nepotianus, letter to from St. Jerome, I, 288
Nestorius, heresy of, I, 296, 297, II, 284
Nevers, I, 189, II, 153, 259; bp., *see* Fromond; ct., II, 13 n. 57, 244, 245, 329; obit., II, 194, 307; precentor, *see* Drogo; St. Martin (Aug.), obit., II, 307
New Testament: epistles, II, 2; *veritas* of, contrasted with *umbra* of Old Testament, I, 356
Nicaea, Council of, I, 61
Nichodemus, I, 41, 161
Nicholas, advisor of Mohammed, I, 295, II, 283
Nicholas of Montiéramey, I, 205–206, 363, 366, 372, 373, 417–418, II, 14, 17 n. 69, 24, 26, 27, 28–29, 36, 39, 59, 79, 146, 152, 200–201, 202, 216, 217, 218–220, 226, 249 n. 17, 250, 264, 265, 316–330; Ep. 87 to, I, 227, II, 156; Ep. 151 to, I, 371–372, II, 200–201; Ep. 153 by, I, 373, II, 202; Ep. 176 to, I, 417, II, 217; Ep. 179 by, I, 420–422, II, 218–219; Ep. 180 to, I, 422–423, II, 219; Ep. 182 to, I, 425–426, II, 220; Ep. 193 to, I, 448–450, II, 230; affairs at Auxerre, I, 418, II, 217,

218, 324, 329, 330 n. 64; affection for P., I, 421–422; becomes Cist., II, 319–321, 322–323; disgrace, II, 219, 324 n. 40, 326–328; letters of, II, 8, 316–330 *passim*; literary activities, I, 426, II, 328–330 (knowledge of *dictamen*, II, 328 n. 56); P.'s affection for, I, 423–424, 425–426; visits to Cl., I, 417, 423–425, 427, II, 216, 250 n. 23, 317, 324–325; visits to Rome, I, 222, 256, II, 154, 163, 261, 317–320, 329
Nicholas of St. Albans, II, 328
Nicholas of Trois-Fontaines, II, 319 n. 18
Nigel, bp. of Ely, II, 256 n. 23
Nigel Wireker, II, 117
Nîmes, I, 348–349; bp., *see* Adalbert; St. Baudilus (Cl.), I, 348–350, II, 192–193, 204
Nineva, I, 164
Noah, I, 9
Nobles and nobility, II, 233; in Auvergne, I, 406; in Burgundy, I, 379, 410, 442; of the realm, I, 398–399. *See also* Castellans, Knights, *Principes*
Nogent-le-Rotrou (Ben.-Cl.), I, 344, II, 190, 269
Nogent-sous-Coucy (Ben.), abt., *see* Guibert
Nonette, family of, II, 233 n. 3
Norgaud, bp. of Autun, II, 189
Norgaud I of Toucy, II, 189
Normandy, II, 260, 338, 339; troubles following death of Henry I, I, 22, II, 105
Northampton, St. Andrew (Cl.), II, 128; Ep. 45 to monks of, I, 141–142, II, 128; P.'s special love for, I, 141
Notaries, *see* Scribes
Novara, II, 53
Novelty: annoys those used to old customs, I, 368–369; of Templars, I, 408
Novices: at Cl., I, 53, 58–62, 91, 97, 282, II, 116; changes in rules concerning, I, 390; oath of, II, 119; sent from La Charité to Cl. for profession, I, 137
Noyers (Ben.), abt., *see* Hugh
Noyon (Aug.), abt., attacked at Pontremoli, I, 51, II, 114
Nudus nudum Christum sequi, II, 108–109
Nunnery: compared to prison, I, 428; compared to tomb, I, 270
Nuns, tithes paid to, I, 110
Nur ed-Din, II, 209

Obed, I, 378
Obedience, I, 5; of hermit, I, 36; of monk, I, 55, 76, 77–78, 292, 335, 361, (=imitation of Christ) I, 184, (to will as well as word) I, 184; of Virgin Mary, I, 237. *See also* Peter (St.)
Obedientia (priory), I, 47

Oblations: given to hermits, I, 33; owned by monks, I, 81–82, 84
Obstinacy, reprehensible even in worthy cause, I, 187
Octavian, card.-deacon of S. Nicola in Carcere, II, 266
Odilo, abt. of Breme, II, 223
Odilo, abt. of Cl., II, 223, 299
Odilo of *Magone*, canon of Brioude, I, 416, II, 216
Odilo of Mercoeur, provost of Brioude, II, 216, 242 n. 50
Odo, abt. of Beauvais, II, 103; Ep. 13 to, I, 18–21, II, 103
Odo, bp. of Beauvais, II, 305
Odo, card.-deacon of S. Giorgio in Velabro, II, 225
Odo, card.-deacon of S. Nicola in Carcere, II, 225–226, 267
Odo, abt. of Cl., I, 391–392, II, 12; family, II, 233 n. 2; "first father" of Cl. order, I, 391; restorer of monasticism, I, 391; writings, I, 3
Odo de la Perrière, pr. of Souvigny, abt. of Cl., II, 57, 59
Odo, pr. of La Charité, II, 296, 298
Odo, abt. of Pouthières, II, 321
Odo, abt. of St. Lucien, Beauvais, II, 103
Odo, pr. of St.-Martin-des-Champs, Paris, abt. of Marchiennes, II, 103, 188, 309, 312, 313; Ep. 135 to, I, 339–341, II, 187–189
Odo, abt. of St.-Maur-sur-Loire, II, 118
Odo, abt. of St. Remy, Rheims, II, 133; attacked at Pontremoli, I, 51, II, 114; liturgical commemoration, II, 133
Odo, abt. of St. Symphorien, Beauvais, II, 103
Odo, adc. of Troyes, I, 205, II, 146
Odor, sweet: of Bernard, I, 52; of bp. of Bethlehem, I, 106; of Cists., I, 114; of Cl., I, 227; of hermit, I, 41; of peaceful church, I, 192
Oduin, son of, holds prebend at Troyes, I, 201, II, 144
Offices, holy: at Cl., I, 72; differences in, I, 279; of hermit, I, 39–40
Oger, canon, II, 18, 24 n. 97
Old Testament: literal and allegorical senses, I, 356–357; sets example for Church, I, 64. *See also* New Testament
Oléron, II, 337
Oliver of Anchin, scribe, II, 52 n. 213
Olricus, pr. of La Charité, II, 296
Onulf of Speyer, II, 3 n. 8
Opus manuum, *see* Manual labor
Oral messages, II, 25–28; unreliability of, I, 194–195. *See also* Letters

Orange: bp., *see* William; dio., persecution of monks in, I, 197, (schismatics and heretics in) I, 197

Ordeal: by fire, I, 414-415, II, 215; ecclesiastical opposition to, II, 215

Ordericus Vitalis, chron., II, 97, 104, 105, 106, 130, 256 n. 23, 258, 259, 291, 313 n. 14

Orders of society, should be kept separate, I, 24. *See also* Clerics, Lay order, Monastic order

Ordination of bps. and priests: nature of, I, 354, 355; of Cls., I, 56, 79, 200, II, 119, 143

Orléans, I, 17-18, 308; bp., *see* Elias, Manasses of Garlande; subdean, *see* Archibald; adc., *see* John, Ralph; Cluniac prebends, I, 6; St. Laurence, consecration of, II, 307; schools, II, 31

Orthography, II, 84-91; divisions of words, II, 89-90. *See also* Letters (of alphabet)

Osbert of Clare, II, 3 n. 11, 10 n. 42, 99, 150

Otiositas: enemy of soul, I, 283; ways to avoid, I, 70-71

Otium, blessed: monastic, I, 28, 31, 32, 41, 235, 266; *negotiosum*, I, 211, 223; not *otiosum*, I, 318, 326; of silence, I, 223; safe port in storm, I, 49; of Carths., I, 46; of Mary, sister of Martha, I, 266, 268; of Natalis of Rebais, I, 234, 266

Otloh of St. Emmeram, II, 6 n. 24

Otmar (Othmar), bp. of Grenoble, II, 198

Otmar of Valbonnais, Carth. *conversus*, I, 435, II, 222

Ottobeuren (Ben.), MS. from, II, 73

Ovid, II, 39

Oxford, II, 254

Oza, I, 378

P., adc. of Tours, I, 267, II, 169

Pagans: attacking Christian faith, I, 118; better than false Christians, I, 409, 411. *See also* Marriage, Saracens

Pamplona, II, 262, 279; adc., *see* Robert of Ketton

Papyrus, II, 18

Paraclete (Ben.), II, 269; confraternity with Cl., I, 400; obit., II, 99, 210, 268; visit by P., I, 400, 401, II, 210

Paradise:=monastic life, (at Marcigny) I, 161-162, (at Cl.) I, 227, II, 156; four rivers of,=Evangelists, I, 2; Moslem view of, I, 297

Paray-le-Monial (Cl.), II, 345

Parchment, II, 18, 20; needed by Peter of Poitiers, I, 317

Paris, I, 180, 401, II, 260, 338, 339; bp., *see* Stephen of Senlis, Theobald; adc., *see* Theobald; cath., II, 196; College of Cl., II, 46, 55; Jacobins, MS. from, II, 70; Montmartre (Ben.), II, 55, 338; St.-Denis-de-la-Châtre (Cl.), II, 196, 313 n. 13, 338; St.-Germain-des-Prés (Ben.), abt., attacked at Pontremoli, I, 51, II, 114 (*see also* Hugh), (MS. from) II, 61, 63, (obit.) II, 96; St.-Martin-des-Champs (Cl.), II, 108, 293, 294, 295, 312, 313 n. 13, 315, 338, 339, (Ep. 135 to monks of) I, 339-341, II, 187-189, (chartulary) II, 183, (confraternity) II, 312 n. 12, (obit.) II, 96, 97, 99, 132, 171, 188, 194, 307 n. 12, 312, (pr.) *see* Matthew, Odo, Simon, Theobald, (visit of P.) I, 180, II, 100, 137, 338-339; St. Victor (Aug.), letter collection of, II, 4 n. 13, (MS. from) II, 70, 71, (pr.) *see* Thomas

Parishes: held by Cl., I, 56, 81-82, 108; rights of, invaded by new churches, II, 166

Parma, II, 114

Parnassus, I, 322, 323

Parthenay, II, 126, 336

Partridges, eaten by monks, I, 389

Paschal II, pope, I, 300; privilege for Cl., II, 119

Paschal lamb, significance, I, 253-254

Paston letters, II, 21 n. 86, 26

Pater (title): applied to Guigo of La Chartreuse by P., I, 44, 48; applied to P. by Bernard, I, 362, 364

Patientia of hermit, I, 36; one of three monastic virtues, I, 430

Patria, desertion of, by Peter of Poitiers, I, 186-187

Paul, St., I, 33, 181, 300, 337, 367; changed his mind, I, 94; fostered Church, I, 139; imitation of, I, 426; letters, II, 3 n. 10; travels, I, 403-404. *See also* Peter (St.)

Paul of Thebes, St., I, 29, 234

Paulinus of Nola, St., I, 288, II, 40

Pauperes: in Auvergne, I, 159-160; in Burgundy, I, 410; *Christi*, I, 106; rights of, I, 115. *See also* Poor (care of), Poverty

Pavia, II, 222, 265, 267

Peace: desire for, in Burgundy, I, 410; councils to keep, I, 443, II, 225-226

Peasants: in Auvergne, I, 406; in Burgundy, I, 410, 411; seeking gain, I, 147; visiting Cl., I, 72

Pébrac (Aug.), II, 241

Pelagius, I, 286

Pellegrinus, patriarch of Aquileia, I, 440

Penance, I, 336-337; change in rules concerning, I, 89-90; one of three monastic virtues, I, 289; signified by color black, I, 289

Penitents, in Italy, I, 331
Pens, I, 10, II, 18, 20
Pentecost, gifts bestowed upon Apostles at, I, 238–241
Penthesilea, queen of the Amazons, I, 305
Peregrinus (foreign, strange), I, 252, 343, 389, 438, 449. See also Pilgrims
Perfection, striving for, I, 447
Périgeux: bp., see Raymond, William; dean, see Iterius
Persians, I, 219, 327
Peter of Barri, abt. of St. Augustine and of St. Martial, Limoges, II, 190; Ep. 138 to, I, 345–346, II, 190; former Cl., I, 345; thanked by P. for aid to Cls., I, 346
Peter (Beraldus?), Cl. monk, I, 6, II, 97
Peter of Blois, II, 39; letters, II, 4 n. 13, 8, 11–12
Peter of Bruys, heretic, II, 287
Peter of Celle, I, 204, II, 10, 11, 22–23, 26 n. 107, 156, 206, 249 n. 17, 321, 328 n. 58, 329; letters, II, 76
Peter, chamberlain of Cl., II, 311, 347
Peter, pr. of La Charité, II, 296, 297, 298
Peter of Châtellerault, antibp. of Poitiers, II, 336
Peter of La Châtre, abp. of Bourges, I, 257, II, 164
Peter Comestor, II, 331
Peter Damiani, St., II, 19 n. 79, 328; letters, II, 3 n. 9, 4 n. 13, 10 n. 41; style, II, 34 n. 146
Peter the Deacon, II, 271
Peter of Gap, Carth. monk, I, 435, II, 222
Peter, pr. of Gaye, I, 13
Peter, bp. of Viviers, abp. of Lyons, I, 42, 102, 260, II, 109, 121, 122, 125, 145, 147, 165–166, 258–259; Ep. 38 to, I, 125–131, II, 125–126; Ep. 54 to, I, 174–175, II, 135–136; loyalty to Innocent II, I, 42; P.'s affection for, I, 125–126, 174; P.'s gift of a ring to, I, 175; power and wealth, I, 125; second only to pope, I, 126–127; visit to Rome, II, 109
Peter, pr. of La Charité, abt. of Malmesbury, II, 298
Peter of Pithiviers, pr. of Cl., abt. of St. Martial, Limoges, II, 240, 332, 333, 347
Peter of Poitiers, P.'s secretary, I, 47, 48, 294, II, 13–14, 20, 25, 38, 40, 46, 47, 53–55, 56, 57, 59, 73, 80, 84, 112, 113, 174, 184, 234, 237, 239, 258, 275–276, 279, 331–343; introductory letter by, I, 1–3, II, 95; Epp. 9–10 to ?, I, 14–17, II, 101–102; Ep. 26 to, I, 48–50, II, 113; Ep. 58 to, I, 179–189, II, 137; Ep. 123 by, I, 317, II, 181–182; Ep. 124 to, I, 317–318, II, 182; Ep. 125 to, I, 321, II, 183–184; Ep. 126 to, I, 322–323, II, 183–184; Ep. 127 to, I, 323–324, II, 183–184; Ep. 128 by, I, 325–326, II, 184; Ep. 129 to, I, 326–327, II, 184
—— name and identity of, II, 332–335; early life, II, 335–339; resolution to leave homeland, I, 186; desertion of P., I, 183–185; heremitical retreat, I, 180–181, II, 339–340; P.'s need of him, I, 48–50, 180; possible mission to La Charité, I, 136, 137–138, II, 127, 298 n. 21, 341–342; swollen feet, I, 317, 318, 324, 325, 326, II, 182; culture and religious conversation, I, 181–183; works by, II, 16, 49, 331–332; role in collecting P.'s letters, I, 326, II, 15–16, 80, 184; panegyric, II, 335–337; translations, II, 342; possible author of Chronica Adefonsi imperatoris, II, 343
Peter, bp. of Poitiers, II, 331
Peter of Poitiers, chancellor of Paris, II, 331, 332 n. 5
Peter of Poitiers, canon of St. Victor, II, 331
Peter, relation of St. Bernard, sent from Cl. to Clairvaux, I, 424, II, 219
Peter, St., I, 4, 35, 59, 87, 121, 186, 215, 242, 300, 315, 337, 384, 446; and Paul, "special fathers" of Cl., I, 337–338; forgiven by Christ, I, 68; obedience of, I, 5; power over keys, I, 338
Peter of St. John, II, 334–335, 342. See also Peter of Poitiers, Peter (pr. of St. John, Sens)
Peter, pr. of St. John, Sens, II, 8, 32, 35, 156, 305, 334–335
Peter, abt. of St. Urban, II, 298
Peter, scribe at Cl., II, 347
Peter, subpr. of Cl., II, 347
Peter of Toledo, I, 294, II, 174, 279
Peter, unidentified, sent to La Charité by P., I, 136, 137–138, II, 127, 298 n. 21, 341–342
Peter the Venerable, abt. of Cl.: praise of, I, 1, 418; good reputation, I, 204; alter nostri saeculi Iohannes, I, 203; imperialis ac piissimus vultus, I, 326; compares himself to David, I, 45; compares himself to a warrior, I, 45–46; love and obedience of Cls., I, 325–326, 335, 449; busyness, I, 45–46, 49, 53, 131, 148, 218, 235, 340, 341, 346, (negotia infinita) 403, (infinita importunitas causarum) 404, 443, 450, II, 14–15; involvement in secular affairs, I, 19–20, 23, 28, 180, 183, 184, 233, 271–272, 275, 324; advocate for Piacenza in dispute with patriarch of Ravenna, I, 440; attends council of Rheims in 1148, I, 347, II, 191; attends Lateran Council at Rome, II, 252–256; brings treasure of Henry of

Peter the Venerable—*continued*
Winchester out of England, II, 268; colloquia with Burgundian nobles, I, 379, II, 205; efforts to heal papal schism, I, 132, II, 336-339 (*see also* Gilo of Tusculum); mediator between Innocent II and Alfonso VII, I, 265; mediator between Abelard and Bernard, I, 258-259, II, 164; mediator between Pisa and Lucca, II, 261-262; offer to mediate between Roger II of Sicily and Conrad III, I, 395; offer to help reform dio. of Lyons, I, 130-131; instability of, I, 417, 425; travels, I, 14, 25-26, 168, 335, 449, 450, II, 14-15, 106, 108 (*see also* individual places); attacked at Pontremoli, I, 52; visits to Rome, I, 168, 302, 311, 332, 335, 434, 440, 443-444, 445, II, 115, 175, 176, 179, 186, 187, 221, 227, 252-256, 273; visits to pope, I, 338 (*see also* Celestine II, Eugene III, Innocent II, Lucius II); honor shown to in Rome, I, 444; friends, I, 214 (*see also* Friendship and individual names); desire to escape secular cares, I, 425, 448; desire for peace and solitude, I, 180, II, 339; retreat in woods near Cluny, I, 317, 318, 321-327, II, 80, 179, 187, 248 n. 12, 285, 333, 342; appreciation of natural beauty, II, 12 n. 53; love of country, I, 317; love of Cl. monks, I, 335; alleged anti-Semitism, II, 185; interest in medical matters, II, 247; growing old, I, 344-345; liturgical commemoration, II, 238 n. 25, 241 n. 45; *see also* Carthusians, Cistercians, Prayer (intercessionary)

—— works of, I, 2; *Contra eos qui dicunt*, II, 13, 46, 50, 75, 76, 77, 78, 81, 334-335; *Contra Iudaeos*, II, 13, 17, 46, 49, 54, 75, 77, 78, 80 n. 290, 81, 145, 185, 285 n. 1; *Contra Petrobrusianos*, I, 299, 327, II, 13, 16, 17, 46, 49, 54, 58, 75, 76, 77, 81, 102-103, 145, 158, 174, 184, 185, 285, (date of) II, 285-288, (position in MSS. of P.'s letters) II, 286; *Contra Sarracenos*, II, 46, 49, 54, 55, 75, 81, 145, 185, 285 n. 1, 342, 343 n. 49; *De miraculis*, I, 162, II, 16, 46, 50, 70, 96, 135, (references to) II, 104, 111, 112, 113, 115, 123, 133, 134, 137, 143, 158, 184, 206, 214, 240 n. 40, 247, 251, 258, 261-262, 263, 268, 311, 334, 335, 344, 346, 348; hymns, I, 318-320, 325, 420, II, 16, 184, 218 (*see also* Hymns); letters, individual, public character of, II, 13, 270, (epistolary treatises) II, 13, (preservation of) II, 15, (lost) I, 43, 272, II, 13, 25, 172, (headings of in MSS.) II, 47 n. 190, (sealing) II, 22-23, (carriage) II, 28-29; letter collection, I, 1, 2, 7, 327, 373, (formation of) II, 15-17, 95, (unity) II, 15, (basis of selection) II, 14, (text) II, 74-75, (arrangement) II, 75-80, (division into books) II, 77-79, (chronology) II, 79-80 (*see also* Peter of Poitiers); letters, style of, II, 12, 14, 35-43, (prolixity) II, 38, (classical influences) II, 38-40, (Patristic influences) II, 40, (salutations) II, 36 (*see also* Bible, Revision); Office for the Transfiguration, II, 173; poems, II, 16, 49, 54, 183; sermons, I, 2, II, 49, 50, 54; *Statuta*, II, 50, 61, (references to) II, 109, 116, 117, 118, 175, 199; *Visiones*, II, 49. *See also* Matthew of Albano

Peter Vivian, Cl. monk, I, 402, 404, II, 211
Peterborough, II, 259
Petrarch, II, 25 n. 103, 26; letters, II, 12; revised own text, II, 43
Pharisees, I, 94, 424. *See also* Cistercians
Pheasants, eaten by monks, I, 389
Philemon, I, 181
Philip of France, Louis VII's brother, II, 196
Philip I, k. of France, II, 299, 300, 313
Philip, adc. of Liège, pr. of Clairvaux, I, 372, 422, 426, II, 200, 218, 220, 317 n. 10, 324, 325, 326, 329; Ep. 183 to, I, 427, II, 220
Philip, abt. of St. Augustine, Limoges, II, 190
Philip, abp. of Taranto, II, 200
Philistines, I, 34
Philosophers, P.'s companions on retreat so-called, I, 325, 326
Philosophy, I, 15-16; philosophical disputation contrasted with devout investigation, I, 250; philosophical terms used by P., I, 321; true,=Christian, I, 235, 304, 354
Phineas, I, 128, 446
Phisica, study of, I, 16, 304, 428
Piacenza, II, 265; bp., *see* John; dispute with patriarch of Ravenna over consecration of bp., I, 440-442, II, 224; importance, I, 441; subject to Rome only, I, 440, 442
Pierleone, support Anacletus II in Rome, I, 135, II, 126
Piety,=kingdom of God for Carths., I, 378
Pievedizio, II, 267
Pilgrimages: of Hugh of Palliers, II, 235; of Pontius of Montboissier, I, 23-24, II, 105; of Raingard, I, 159; dangers of, I, 359; opposition to, I, 152, 216, II, 132, 152, 153, 195; prohibited for monks, I, 220; useless without Christ, I, 30. *See also* Compostela, Holy Land, Jerusalem, Rome
Pilgrims, I, 313, 331; costume, I, 105, 215; pilgrim monks, I, 76-78, 215. *See also* Crusaders
Piolenc (Cl.), I, 198, II, 142

GENERAL INDEX

Pisa, I, 6, II, 98, 114, 126, 139, 252–253, 255, 260, 261–262, 311; council in 1135, I, 4, 51, 153–154, 178, 231, 343, II, 96, 113–114, 115, 129, 133–134, 135, 141, 159, 167, 190, 247, 286, 288 n. 15, (attack on prelates returning from) I, 51–52, II, 114–115, (P.'s return from) I, 52, 115, 153–154, II, 133–134, 138

Pitantia, II, 206

Plato, I, 1, 15, 304, II, 38

Plenitudo potestatis, I, 388

Pliny, letters, II, 10

Plutarch, II, 27 n. 115

Po River, I, 444, II, 227

Poems in epistolary form, II, 3

Poetry, I, 16

Poissy, N.-D. (Ben.-Aug.), II, 196

Poitiers, II, 126, 141, 260, 293, 336, 337, 339; bp., *see* Gilbert, Peter, William; antibp., *see* Peter of Châtellerault; meeting of P. and Gilo of Tusculum, I, 196; Montierneuf (Cl.), II, 294–295, 298, 334, 336–337, (abt.) *see* Imar

Poitou, I, 102; ct., *see* William

Poland, II, 293 n. 2; MS. from, II, 74

Polenchronik, II, 34, 37

Polignac, family of, II, 213, 233 n. 3, 237 n. 17, 242 n. 51

Pontarlier, I, 439

Ponthieu: ct., *see* Guy, William; countess, *see* Ida

Pontia of Montboissier, P.'s niece, II, 221, 240, 242, 248; Ep. 185 to, I, 427–434, II, 220–221

Pontigny, abt., Ep. 35 to, I, 113–116, II, 124. See also Hugh

Pontius, bp. of Belley, II, 165, 258; attacked at Pontremoli, I, 51, II, 114

Pontius, chamberlain of Cl., II, 347

Pontius,? chaplain of Matthew of Albano, II, 143

Pontius, abt. of Cl., II, 97, 119, 123, 135, 243, 247, 257, 258, 273, 291, 293 n. 2, 294, 299, 335 n. 20; schism of, I, 112, 446, II, 98, 101, 247, 273

Pontius, bp. of Mâcon, II, 225

Pontius of Montboissier, abt. of Vézelay, P.'s brother, II, 14, 105, 161, 241 n. 46, 243–244, 265, 266, 267, 329; Ep. 16 to, I, 22–24, II, 105; Ep. 53 to, I, 153–173, II, 133–135; Ep. 91 to, I, 232–233, II, 160; asked to visit Cl., I, 233; and Nicholas of Montiéramey, I, 421, II, 217, 218. *See also* Pilgrimages

Pontius of Provence, II, 31

Pontius I, bp. of Le Puy, II, 245

Pontius II, bp. of Le Puy, II, 245

Pontius, abt. of St. Rufus, II, 3 n. 9

Pontius, unidentified, Ep. 93 to, I, 234, II, 161

Pontoise, St. Mellon (Aug.), II, 196

Pontremoli, attack on prelates returning from council of Pisa, I, 51–52, II, 114

Pontus, I, 10

Poor, care of, I, 167; not proper work for hermits, I, 33–34. See also *Pauperes*, Poverty, Raingard

Pope: above human judgment, I, 79–80; affection for Cl., I, 110, 313, 316, 445; "bishop" of Cl., I, 79, 194; jurisdiction of, I, 94–95, 377; "truly apostolic men in life and office," I, 316; vicar of Christ, I, 441, II, 102; vicar of God, I, 18, 107. *See also* Holy See and individual popes

Pork, eaten by Cls., I, 389, 390

Portents, I, 144

Porter in Cl. monasteries, I, 55, 75–76

Portes (Carth.), I, 378, II, 202, 204

Potenza, I, 192

Pouthières (Ben.), abt., *see* Odo

Poverty: of hermits, I, 33–35, 37; of monks, I, 128, 152, 230; fear of, I, 31;=humility (poverty of spirit), I, 16, 34–36; depends upon expenses, I, 111, 115. *See also* Christ, Martin (St.), *Pauperes*, Poor

Prayer: of hermit, I, 37–38, (stimulated by meditation and reading) I, 38, (intercessionary) I, 41; of monks, I, 28, 85, (averts *otiositas*) I, 70–71, (worthier than cutting trees) I, 92, (intercessionary) I, 21, 81–82, 84. *See also* Carthusians, Cistercians, Henry of Winchester, Innocent II, Liturgical commemoration

Pré, Jean du, II, 45, 46

Pré-St.-Vital, Cl. chapel, II, 182

Preaching, I, 2, 139, 239, 241; by hermit, I, 40–41; by P., I, 114, 381; epistolary, II, 3 n. 7; forbidden for women, I, 241; silent, by copyist, I, 38–39, II, 109

Prebends, I, 202–203, 402, II, 144; held by Cl., *see* Abbeville, Chartres, Orléans, Troyes

Premonstratensians: confraternity with Cl., II, 173–174; intruded at Verdun, I, 144–145, II, 130

Prémontré (Prem.), abt., *see* Gervase

Pride, I, 31, 33, 39, 40, 89, 230, 263, 292; alleged of Cls., I, 263–264; danger to pilgrims, I, 359; opposite of love, I, 93

Priesthood, of "old law" and "new grace," I, 220

Priests: anointing of, I, 354, 355; daily triumphs over Satan, I, 219; dignity of, inferior to that of monks, I, 224, 227; sons

Priests—*continued*
of, change in law concerning, I, 61, 90; suspension and deposition, I, 355. *See also* Clerics, *Cura animarum*
Primitive church: effort to revive, I, 284, 327; ideal of, I, 59
Principes: attend council of Chartres, I, 396; in Burgundy, I, 410; meaning of term, II, 237
Profession: heremitical, I, 31, 39; monastic, I, 55, 77–78, 277, II, 119. *See also* Novices
Profit motive, I, 147
Property: ecclesiastical, held by monks, *see* Churches, First fruits, Oblations, Parishes, Prebends, Revenues (ecclesiastical), Tithes; owned by God, I, 84
Property, private, forbidden to clerics and monks, I, 84
Property, secular, of monks, *see* Landed estates, Serfs, Tolls
Prophecy, gift of, I, 239
Prophets, great number, I, 237; notaries of God, I, 99
Proprietary right of monks over a church, distinguished from bodily possession, I, 198
Prosper of Aquitaine, *Contra Cassianum*, I, 47
Prostitutes, abstain from meat on Sabbath, I, 388
Provaglio (Cl.), II, 267
Provence, I, 176, 349, II, 24, 126. *See also* Heretics
Provisions, papal, I, 201, 203, II, 144
Prudentius, I, 47
Prüfening (Ben.), MS. from, II, 109
Psalmody, averts *otiositas*, I, 71
Pseudonyms, II, 26 n. 109
Punctuation of MSS., II, 50, 91–92
Puy, Le, I, 102, II, 57–58, 121, 260–261, 262, 334, 342; bp., *see* Pontius I and II
Puy-St.-Ambrose? (Cl.), I, 112, II, 123
Pyrenees Mountains, I, 384

Quartam Leugam, unidentified monastery, I, 270, II, 170
Quintilian, II, 39

Rachel, I, 20–21, 358
Radulf, P.'s biographer, II, 17, 111, 234, 235, 238, 240, 241, 242, 243, 244, 257, 259, 262, 265, 268, 334, 342, 344, 345, 346, 348
Ragny, Jean de la Magdelaine de, pr. of Cl., pr. of La Charité, II, 46
Raim., P.'s chaplain, II, 264, 347
Raimbaud, provost of St. John, Liège, II, 120
Rainald of Anchin, scribe, II, 52 n. 213, 53
Rainald, abt. of Breme, I, 437, II, 222–223; placed in charge of various Cl. priories, I, 437; youth at Cl., I, 437
Rainald, abt. of Cîteaux: Ep. 120 to, I, 313–314, II, 180–181; mediated between Abelard and St. Bernard, I, 258–259, II, 164
Rainald, abt. of Vézelay, abp. of Lyons, I, 229, 260, II, 158, 166
Rainald II, abp. of Rheims, II, 106; attacked at Pontremoli, I, 51, 154, II, 114, 115, 134
Rainald, subpr. of Cl., II, 347
Rainard, *see* Rainald
Rainerius of Thérouanne, pr. of Clairvaux, II, 320 n. 21
Raingard, P.'s mother, I, 153–173 *passim*, 178, 270, 433–434, II, 25, 132–135, 136, 170, 191, 221, 237, 238–239, 242; decision to become a nun, I, 158–159, 160–161; visit to Cl., I, 161; entry to Marcigny, I, 161–163; life at Marcigny, I, 163–164; cellarer, I, 164, 178; charitable work, I, 155, 158, 159, 164–165, 166–167, 178; good cheer in ministry and in public, I, 165–166; austerity, I, 164, 167, 168; grave and holy speech, I, 166; prayers, I, 168, 170; frequent references to Holy Spirit and Virgin Mary, I, 166; devotion to crucifix, I, 169; dream, I, 168–169, II, 135; death, I, 153, 154, 168–170, 178; P.'s grief at death, I, 153, 154–156; burial, I, 156, 172; signs of sanctity, I, 170–171; prayers for, I, 155–156; liturgical commemoration, I, 153, 155, 176, II, 238 n. 25, 239 n. 36, 241 n. 45
Ralph, adc. of Orléans, II, 307, 308–309
Ralph Tortarius, II, 156; letters, II, 3 n. 11, 4 n. 13
Ralph, ct. of Vermandois, royal seneschal, II, 312
Ralph Le Vert, II, 3 n. 9
Rambouillet, II, 313
Ranulf, pr. of St. Martial, Limoges, I, 384, II, 205
Ratherius of Verona, letters, II, 5, 34
Raymond, prince of Antioch, I, 208, II, 209
Raymond of Montredon, abp. of Arles, I, 348–349, II, 192
Raymond, bp. of Périgeux, II, 296 n. 8
Raymond, monk of Toulouse, II, 179; Ep. 117 to, I, 309–311, II, 178–179; desire to see Roman ruins, I, 309, 311
Reading (Ben.), I, 22, 212, II, 99, 150; pr., *see* Hugh of Amiens
Reading: aloud of letters, II, 91–92; monastic, I, 21, 28, 38, 70–71, 85; use of voice in, I, 381
Rebais (Ben.), I, 233–234; abt., *see* Natalis; confraternity with Cl., II, 160; obit., II, 160–161
Reclusio, I, 30; useless without Christ, I, 31, 38

GENERAL INDEX 421

Red Sea, significance, I, 253
Regalia, granted by Louis VII to bp.-elect of Langres, I, 102
Regensburg (Ratisbon), Franciscans, MS. from, II, 70
Registers: epistolary, II, 8, 11, 13–14; of monastic possessions, I, 54–55, 73–74, 92, II, 118; papal, II, 4, 6 n. 25
Regula Benedicti, II, 118, 119; *rectitudo regulae*, I, 53, 58, 90, (=love) 99; dictated by love, I, 98; dictated by Holy Spirit, I, 281; common observance by monks and nuns, I, 277, 280, 281, 401; Cl. interpretation, I, 53–60, II, 20; Cist. interpretation, I, 99–100; subject to law of love, I, 90–93, 97–100; can be changed and adapted, I, 67–68, 284–285, 390; distinguishes command from advice, I, 100; permits what is necessary, I, 101; orders total abstinence from meat, I, 390; text used P., II, 40
Reichersberg (Aug.): chronicle, II, 8; provost, *see* Gerhoh
Relics: at Constantinople, I, 210, II, 149; of St. Benedict, I, 320; of tombs of Christ and Virgin Mary, I, 220; given by P. to La Charité, I, 136, 137
Reliquary, stolen at Brioude, I, 414, II, 215
Rennes, bp., *see* Hamelinus, Marbod
Requies of Carths., praised by P., I, 46
Resurrection of body, compared to growth of plants in spring, I, 173
Reuil (Cl.), II, 268; pr., *see* Bernard, Robert
Revenues, ecclesiastical: division of, I, 82; owned by monks, I, 81–82
Revision, textual: by medieval writers, II, 43–44; by P., II, 41–43, 68, 73, 74–75, 83
Rheims, II, 29, 259, 264; abp., *see* Henry, Rainald, Samson; council in 1131, I, 268, II, 117, 163, 169; council in 1140?, I, 264, II, 167, 169, 289–290; council in 1148, I, 347, II, 165, 191, 308; meeting of Eugene III and P., I, 445; St. Nicasius (Ben.), pr., *see* Geoffrey of Châlons-sur-Marne; St. Remy (Ben.), confraternity with Cluny, II, 133, (abt.) *see* Odo; St. Thierry (Ben.), abt., *see* Geoffrey of Châlons-sur-Marne, William
Rhetoric, I, 1, 14
Rhone River, I, 415, 447, II, 223
Rhymed prose, II, 30 n. 129, 32, 33 n. 143, 34
Richard, card.-bp. of Albano, II, 300
Richard of Hertford, scribe of Whalley, II, 72
Richard of Hexham, chron., II, 104
Richard of Poitiers, chron., II, 38–39, 210, 332 n. 5, 337 n. 28
Rigny (Cist.), abt., *see* Stephen of Toucy
Rilhac, castle, II, 213
Rimini, bp., *see* Castorius

Ring: able to staunch flow of blood, I, 175; given to P. by Gilo of Tusculum, I, 196
Riphaean mountains, I, 10
Rivo, François de, pr. of Cl., chron., II, 17, 55, 75, 291–292, 294, 295, 297, 331, 351
Roads, public, I, 10
Robert of Arbrissel, St., I, 158–159, 161, II, 134, 239
Robert, dean of Langres, bp. of Autun (probably son of duke of Burgundy), II, 145, 147, 194
Robert II, ct. of Auvergne, II, 300
Robert III, ct. of Auvergne, II, 213
Robert of Bridlington, II, 1 n. 2
Robert, chamberlain of Cl., II, 346, 347
Robert, Cl. monk, former scholasticus, II, 183; Ep. 126 by, I, 322–323, II, 183–184
Robert, cousin of St. Bernard, I, 424, II, 219, 274
Robert, doctor, II, 183, 248 n. 12
Robert, k. of France, II, 299
Robert, earl of Gloucester, I, 22, II, 105
Robert of Ketton, adc. of Pamplona, II, 279
Robert, pr. of Reuil, II, 268
Robert of Torigny, chron., II, 268
Robert, unidentified, brought poems by Raymond of Toulouse to P., I, 311, II, 179
Robert, unidentified, tried to sow ill will between Henry of Winchester and P., I, 176, II, 136
Rochefort-en-Iveline: family of, II, 313, 315 n. 25; ct., *see* Guy II
Roches, Les (Cist.), II, 189; abt., *see* Geoffrey of Toucy
Rodulfus, *see* Ralph
Roger, bp. of Chester, II, 255
Roger, bp. of Salisbury, II, 256 n. 23
Roger II, k. of Sicily, I, 302, II, 140, 149, 176, 177, 206–207; Ep. 90 to, I, 230–232, II, 159–160; Ep. 131 to, I, 330–333, II, 185–186; Ep. 162 to, I, 394–395, II, 206–207; asked to found another Cl. monastery in Sicily, I, 232, II, 160; asked to assist Cl., I, 332, II, 186; called tyrant by Innocent II, I, 192; hostility to Conrad III, I, 394; letter to P., I, 231; meeting with Lucius II, I, 302–303, II, 176, 177; peace brought by, to south Italy, I, 231, 330–331; peace with Innocent II, II, 159, 254 n. 11; P.'s affection and support, I, 230–231, 331; P.'s desire to visit, I, 302, II, 176; sons, death of, I, 394, II, 207
Roger, son of Roger II of Sicily, II, 207; liturgical commemoration, I, 394
Romainmôtier (Ben.-Cl.), II, 254 n. 10, 345–346
Roman emperors, confraternity with Cl., I, 209. *See also* Alexius Comnenus, John Comnenus

Roman Empire, I, 208
Roman kings, I, 231, 331. *See also* Germany
Roman law, I, 349
Roman senate, I, 445
Rome, I, 135, 192, 201, 221, 272, 310, II, 24, 107, 126, 179, 247, 258, 259, 262, 263, 265, 267; fasting at, I, 279; Lateran Council of 1139, I, 231, II, 156, 159, 167, 252-256, 261, 286, 293; Lateran Council of 1215, II, 215; named for Romulus, I, 208; ruins of, desire of monk Raymond of Toulouse to see, I, 309, 311; St. Anastasius (Cist.), abt., *see* Rualenus; St. Saba, Cl. monks at, I, 302, 303, 311-313, II, 176, 177, 179, 180, 248; speed of travel to and from, II, 28-29; unhealthiness of climate, I, 311; visits to, *see* Bernard of Clairvaux, Gebuin of Troyes, Hato of Troyes, Hugh of Palliers, Nicholas of Montiéramey, Peter the Venerable
Romulus, I, 208
Rosne (Cl.), II, 339
Rotlannus, pr. of Sauxillanges, II, 238
Rouen, I, 22, II, 259, 269; abp., *see* Hugh of Amiens; adc., *see* Giles
Rualenus, pr. of Clairvaux, abt. of St. Anastasius, Rome, II, 320 n. 21
Rudolf, k. of France, II, 236 n. 11
Ruffey, II, 182
Rumilly (Cl.), I, 265, II, 167
Rupert, abt. of Deutz, II, 33 n. 143, 215
Rush mats of hermits, I, 39
Ruth, I, 184-185

Sabbath, fasting on, I, 388
Sabellius, heretic, I, 297
Sacraments: definition of and difference from mysteries, I, 253, 254, II, 162; not to be administered by monks, I, 82; reiterability, I, 354, II, 194-195
St. Albans (Ben.), abt., II, 28. *See also* Geoffrey
Ste.-Barbe-en-Auge (Aug.), pr., II, 23 n. 95
St.-Benoît-sur-Loire (Fleury) (Ben.), I, 325, 391, II, 184
St. Bertin (Ben.-Cl.-Ben.), I, 265, II, 50, 65, 167-168, 253-254, 289 n. 4; MS. from, II, 63
St. Denis (Ben.), I, 272, II, 236 n. 13, 314; abt., *see* Suger; obit., II, 312
St.-Denis-le-Ferment, II, 104
St.-Désiré, priory of La Chiusa, II, 236 n. 13
St.-Gengoux-le-Royal, II, 182
St.-Germer-de-Flay (Ben.), II, 103; MS. from, II, 70, 72
St. Gilles (Ben.-Cl.), II, 259
St. Jean d'Angély (Cl.), I, 269, II, 97, 170, 258, 260, 334, 335, 336-337, 339, 341; chamberlain, *see* Hugh Berardus; library, I, 47, II, 111
St.-Josse-au-Bois (Prem.), II, 167
St. Lupus, priory of Sauxillanges, II, 237
St. Martin near Milan (Ben.), I, 288
St.-Maur-sur-Loire (Glanfeuil) (Ben.), I, 71, II, 118; abt., *see* Odo
St. Maurice, family of, II, 234
St. Nizier, II, 182
St. Rufus near Avignon (Aug.), I, 346, II, 191; abt., *see* Pontius
St. Seine (Ben.), MS. from, II, 63, 65
St. Trond (Ben.), abt., *see* Gerard
St. Urban, dio. Châlons-sur-Marne (Ben.), abt., *see* Peter
St. Vaury (Cl.), II, 332 n. 7
St. Wandrille? (Ben.), abt., I, 398, II, 208
Saintes: bp., *see* Bernard; dio., attitude during papal schism, II, 337 n. 30. *See also* Geoffrey of Bordeaux
Saints: lives of attest to virtue of life at Cl., I, 58; praise of does not diminish praise of Christ, I, 171; tombs, *see* Pilgrimage
Salamanca, II, 262; bp., *see* Alfonso, Berengar; St. Vincent, Cl. church, II, 175
Salerno, II, 139, 302-303
Salisbury, bp., *see* Roger
Sallust, II, 39
Salome, gifts received at Pentecost, I, 240-241
Salt: spiritual meaning, I, 294; mountain of, in Spain, II, 287
Salvation: achieved by holy works not holy places, I, 216 (*see also* Pilgrimages [opposition to]); denied by heretics, I, 119; impossible unless Christ fully human, I, 121; impossible without love, I, 239; desire for, justifies variety of and changes in monastic rules, I, 282; narrow way to, I, 17; sole office of love, I, 98. *See also* Beatitude, Life
Salvian, II, 40
Samson, I, 34
Samson, abp. of Rheims, I, 264, 360, II, 197, 290, 305
Samuel, I, 241, 446
Saône River, I, 307, 411
Sapientia: contrasted with *scientia*, I, 250, 428; true,=beatitude, I, 248-249
Sapphira, I, 59
Saracens, I, 219, 295, 327, 330, 395, 397; better than false Christians, I, 411; better than Jews, I, 328; lands in Italy, I, 330; opposed by Templars, I, 408, 411; pagans rather than heretics, I, 298; share many Christian beliefs, I, 328; victories in East, I, 297-298

Sarah, I, 167
Satan, I, 91; causes disputes among monks, I, 278. *See also* Dragon
Saul, I, 45; disobedience of, I, 184
Saumur, St. Florence (Ben.), II, 313; abt., attacked at Pontremoli, I, 51, II, 114
Sauviat, priory of La Chiusa, II, 236 n. 13
Sauxillanges (Cl.), II, 139, 191, 233, 237–238, 240, 241, 243, 244, 257, 258, 259, 269, 334, 342 n. 46; pr., II, 299–301 (*see also* Bernard, Bertrand, Elias, Eustace, Hugh, Letald, Rotlannus); chartulary, II, 134, 212, 234, 235, 236; entry of Maurice II of Montboissier, I, 160; obit., II, 238; P.'s convalescence in 1127, II, 247, 258, 273
Savaric, almoner of Cl., II, 347
Savoy, ct., *see* Amadeus
Scandal, I, 115, 129, 369
Schism, monastic, I, 279, 290–291, 370; caused by differences in color of clothing, I, 287, 290
Schism, papal, of 1130–1138, I, 4–5, 112, 133–134, 142–144, 179, 192, 195–197, 207, II, 336–339. *See also* Anacletus II, Arnulf of Lisieux, Gilo of Tusculum, Matthew of Albano, Peter the Venerable
Schismatics, in dio. of Orange, I, 197
Schools of secular studies, I, 15–16
Sciacca, St. Mary de Jumariis (Cl.), I, 231, II, 159–160; pr., *see* Geoffrey
Scientia, knowledge of created things only, I, 250. See also *Sapientia*
Scribes: role in forming letter collections, II, 6–7, 9, 15; used by Bernard, I, 363; work of writing letters, II, 18–20
Scythia, I, 10
Seals and sealing, I, iv, II, 18, 21, 22–23, 326–327, 328
Secret messages, II, 25–26
Secretaries, *see* Scribes
Secular affairs: compared to mud, I, 180; compared to war, I, 318. *See also* Egyptians, Storm
Secular literature, I, 15; Peter of Poitiers's knowledge, I, 181; St. Bernard's knowledge, I, 53
Secular studies: contrasted with religious studies, I, 304; schools of, I, 15
Séez, II, 166; bp., *see* John; adc., *see* Arnulf
Segni, II, 265; visit of P., I, 438, II, 222–223, 226
Seneca, letters, II, 3 n. 10
Senlis, II, 108
Sennacherib, I, 50
Sens, II, 97, 154; abp., *see* Henry, Hugh of Toucy; adc., *see* Theobald; council in 1140, II, 163, 164, 167, 177, 290, 318–319,

320; St. Columba (Ben.), I, 354, II, 194, (obit.) II, 194, (abt.) *see* Theobald; St. John (Aug.), pr., *see* Peter
Senses, of created beings, I, 119
Serfs: better off on monastic than secular estates, I, 86–87; forced by hardship to flee from secular lords, I, 86; owned by Cls., I, 56, 83–84, 86; refuse all but customary duties, I, 96–97;=hermit in relation to God, I, 40;=monk in relation to abt., I, 183–184, II, 137. See also *Census*
Sergius the monk, associate of Mohammed, I, 296, II, 284
Sermons, II, 2, 3. *See also* Preaching
Sicily, I, 231, 330, II, 148; k., *see* Roger II
Sick monks: anointing of, I, 354–356; care at Cl., I, 65–68, 92, 282
Sidonius Apollinaris, I, 289, II, 40; letters, II, 10
Siena, II, 115, 126, 259
Siger of Anchin, scribe, II, 52–55, 56
Sigurd, k. of Norway, II, 128; Ep. 44 to, I, 140–141, II, 128; crusade, I, 141; devotion, I, 141
Silence: of hermits, I, 40–41; of monks, I, 75, 85, 211
Silvacane, La (Cist.), II, 108
Silve-Bénite (Carth.), I, 378, II, 204
Simeon of Luke 2, I, 248
Simon, pr. of St.-Martin-des-Champs, Paris, II, 188
Simon of St. Bertin, chron., II, 168
Simony, charged against Elias of Orléans, II, 307
Simplicitas: Carth., I, 379; heremitical, I, 326
Sin, human tendency to, I, 355–356
Singing, task of women, I, 241
Singularitas, I, 31; of Cists., I, 57
Sisera, I, 241, 305
Socrates, II, 38
Sodom, I, 29, 56, 186
Sodomites, I, 66
Soissons, II, 268; bp., *see* Jocelyn; meeting of monks in 1130, II, 151; St. Crispin (Ben.), abt., *see* Bernard; St. Médard (Ben.), abt., *see* Geoffrey
Solitude and solitary life, I, 28–32, 324; compared to burial, I, 30; compared to death, I, 30; compared to warfare, I, 31; chosen by John the Baptist, I, 225; inside self, I, 188. *See also* Heremitism, Peter the Venerable
Solomon, I, 45, 59, 111, 133, 176, 195, 262, 286, 314–315, 331, 362, 378, 393, 427, 446–447, II, 280; temple, I, 254, 298; wealth, I, 34
Sorcery, I, 414, II, 215

Souvigny (Cl.), II, 244, 263-264, 269, 311; pr., see Odo de la Perrière, Walter; library, II, 58; MS. from, II, 56-59, 63, 70; P.'s visit, I, 26, II, 107

Spain, I, 310, 450, II, 258, 262; Cl. monasteries in, I, 6; ks., benefactors of Cl., I, 209, 229, 231, 332, (confraternity with Cl.) I, 209 (see also Alfonso I of Aragon, Alfonso VII of Leon-Castile); MS. from, II, 74; part conquered by Moslems, I, 298; P.'s visit, I, 269-270, 273, 289, 294, II, 80, 96, 170, 182, 275, 277, 279, 287, 334, 342; troubles after death of Alfonso I, I, 6, II, 97; use of black for mourning, I, 289, II, 173; visited by monk from Mt. Thabor, I, 215

Spézia, La, II, 114

Spirit: irrational, nature of, I, 123-124; qualities of, I, 119-120; rational, assumed by Christ, I, 119, 123-124

Spiritual gifts, minor, I, 239

Spiritualis homo, I, 28

Squirrel, eaten by monks, I, 389

Stability, monastic, I, 55, 76-79. *See also* Instability

Staffarda (Cist.), MS. from, II, 73

Stavelot (Ben.), II, 66; Bible of, II, 53; MS. from, II, 63

Stealing, sin of, I, 89

Stephen of Baugé, bp. of Autun, I, 353, II, 145, 194, 258

Stephen, ct. of Blois and Chartres, II, 103

Stephen, bp. of Clermont, II, 212, 240 n. 44, 300

Stephen *de Castello*, II, 191-192; Ep. 140 to, I, 347-348, II, 191-192; promise to become monk, I, 348

Stephen, chamberlain of Cl., II, 347

Stephen of Chandieu, canon of Lyons, I, 106-107, 259, II, 122, 131, 165; Ep. 50 to, I, 150-151, II, 131; Ep. 100 to, I, 260-261, II, 165-166; devotion to Holy See and to Cl., I, 107

Stephen of Charolais, dean of Lyons?, abp. of Vienne, II, 131, 165, 191; Ep. 139 to, I, 346-347, II, 191; misfortune, I, 346; urged by P. to come to Cl., I, 347, II, 191

Stephen Cordier, canon of Lyons, II, 131

Stephen, k. of England, II, 103, 130, 167, 255, 297; case against Empress Mathilda, II, 252-256; grants to Cl., II, 138, 256

Stephen of Garlande, royal chancellor, II, 309, 310

Stephen, patriarch of Jerusalem, II, 153

Stephen *Pinguis*, precentor of Lyons, II, 131

Stephen, pr. of Meyriat, II, 211

Stephen, priest, Ep. 8 to, I, 14, II, 101

Stephen, priest of Cl., II, 347

Stephen, St., I, 107

Stephen of Senlis, bp. of Paris, II, 188, 312, 338

Stephen of Toucy, abt. of Fontemoy and Rigny, II, 189

Stephen, pr. of Thetford, II, 10 n. 42

Stephen II, abp. of Vienne, II, 241

Stephen, unidentified, engaged in dispute with priest Constantine, I, 6, II, 101

Storm: allegory for secular life, I, 49, 153, 163, 182, 183; threatens friendship, I, 149. *See also* Friendship

Studium spirituali theoriae, I, 164

Stultitia,=worldly wisdom, I, 250

Style of letters, II, 29-44

Succurrendum, conversion *ad*, I, 160, 347, II, 134, 238

Suger, abt. of St. Denis, II, 6 n. 24, 27, 171, 188, 250, 297, 309, 312, 313 n. 14, 314, 315; Ep. 109 to, I, 271-272, II, 171; Ep. 165 by, I, 398-399, II, 209; Ep. 166 to, I, 399-400, II, 209; letters, I, 397, II, 15, 76; P.'s gratitude to, I, 272; visit to Cl., I, 272, II, 171

Sulpicius Severus, I, 288

Sunamites, I, 196

Susa, II, 234

Swicher, scribe, II, 109

Sword, allegorical, I, 176, 234, 281, 315, 324; of Christ's virtue, II, 282; of divine judgment, I, 334; of divine word, I, 130, 291, 406-407; episcopal, I, 25, 197; secular (imperial, royal), I, 25, 328, 331, 415, 446, (not to be used by monks) I, 406-407, 443; of schism, I, 196

Swords, two, doctrine of, I, 25, 406-407, 415, 446, II, 228-229

Sylvester II, pope (Gerbert), II, 235; letters, II, 5, 6, 7, 8 n. 32, 11 n. 48

Symmachus, II, 3 n. 8, 43

Tabernacle of the Lord, significance, I, 254

Tabitha, I, 167

Tablets, wax, II, 18

Taciturnitas, I, 31. *See also* Silence

Tancred, son of Roger II of Sicily, II, 207; liturgical commemoration, I, 394

Taranto, abp., *see* Philip

Tears: devout, I, 164, 167, 342; fruitful, I, 339; of hermit, daily, I, 39; useless, I, 341

Tegernsee (Ben.), MS. from, II, 63

Templars, I, 407-408; master, *see* Everard; besieged in Antioch, I, 397, 398; double war against spiritual and bodily foes, I, 407-408; novelty of their ideal, I, 408; P.'s admiration for, I, 407

Tezelin of Liège, Cl. monk, I, 229, II, 158

Theobald, ct. of Blois, II, 103

Theobald, abp. of Canterbury, II, 26, 253, 256 n. 26, 297
Theobald II, ct. of Champagne, I, 256, II, 163, 317
Theobald, messenger, I, 303, 317, II, 177, 347
Theobald, adc. of Paris, II, 106
Theobald, pr. of St.-Martin-des-Champs, bp. of Paris, II, 187, 307; Ep. 134 to, I, 338–339, II, 187, 188
Theobald, abt. of St. Columba, Sens, II, 194; Ep. 144 to, I, 353–360, II, 194–195; letter to P., I, 353–354; physical austerities, I, 359; pilgrimage to Jerusalem, I, 354, 358–360
Theobald, adc. of Sens, I, 222, 227, II, 154, 156; desire to visit P., I, 222
Theodard, pr. of La Charité, II, 103, 296, 297, 298, 341; Ep. 14 to, I, 21, II, 103; Ep. 30 to, I, 104–105, II, 121; Ep. 41 by, I, 136–137, II, 127; Ep. 42 to, I, 137–138, II, 127; Ep. 43 to, I, 138–140, II, 127; age and infirmity, I, 138–140; austerity, I, 139–140, II, 127; desire to resign, I, 138–139; gratitude to P., I, 136–137; P.'s affection for, I, 104, 137–138
Theodulf of Orléans, Bible of, II, 57–58
Theophilus, I, 171
Thérouanne: bp., *see* Milo; synod *ca.* 1139, II, 167
Thetford (Cl.), pr., *see* Stephen
Thiers, family of, II, 233 n. 3
Thizy, founded by Humbert III of Beaujeu, II, 166
Thomas of Mapleton, II, 72
Thomas of Northampton, P.'s notary, I, 141–142, 212, II, 128, 150, 264, 311, 348
Thomas, pr. of St. Victor, Paris, murder of, I, 24–25, II, 106
Thurstan, abp. of York, II, 133
Tiburtine hills, II, 318 n. 10
Timothy, I, 94, 434
Tiron (Ben.), P.'s visit, II, 222, 269. *See also* Peter of Gap
Tithes, I, 108–109, 110–112, 114–116, 117, 277, II, 172, 173; granted by Cl. to Cists., I, 108, 111, II, 123; lost by foundation of new monasteries, I, 108; owned by Cl., I, 56, 81–82, 108; pd. by Cl., I, 108
Tolls, owned by monks, I, 56, 83, 87
Toucy, family of, II, 189
Toulouse, I, 309; La Daurade (Cl.), II, 179
Tour d'Auvergne, La, family of, II, 233 n. 3
Tournai, St. Martin (Ben.), lost MS. from, II, 63
Tours, I, 266–267; abp., *see* Hugh of La Ferté; adc., *see* P.; St. Martin (Ben.-canons), II, 196; schools, II, 31

Town walls, built by hermits, I, 34
Translation of bishops, I, 265–266, 354, II, 168; change in laws concerning, I, 61, 89
Trasimund, papal notary, II, 33
Travel, I, 147; difficulties, I, 449; in Italy, I, 444, II, 227; speed, II, 28–29, 140, 143, 174–175
Trental, I, 153, 178, 400, 401, II, 132–133, 210, 239 n. 36. *See also* Liturgical commemoration, Prayer (intercessionary)
Trier, abp., *see* Altmannus
Trinity, denied by Moslems, II, 281–282
Trois-Fontaines (Cist.), II, 123, 227, 319 n. 18
Trojan War, I, 305
Trousers: use by Cls., I, 53–54, 64–65, 91, II, 117; use by high priest, I, 64
Troyes, I, 10, 256, 257, II, 24, 144, 162, 163, 203; bp., *see* Hato; chancellor, *see* Gebuin; adc., *see* Manasses, Odo; visct., *see* Milo of Bray; obit., II, 97; prebend offered to Cl., I, 6, 201, II, 98, 144; prebend provided by pope, I, 201, 203, 205, II, 143
Truth: immutable command of God, I, 89; of Virgin Mary, I, 237
Tuitio apostolica of monasteries, I, 7
Tunic, monastic, I, 63, 64, 282, 287; sent by P. to Pontius, I, 23–24
Turin, II, 234
Turks, I, 208, 219
Turtle dove, eaten by monks, I, 389
Tuscany, disturbed state, I, 331, II, 186

U (letter), use of, II, 85
Ugarit, II, 25
Ulger, bp. of Angers, II, 255
Ulric of Cluny, customs of, II, 115, 116–117, 118, 119
Ulric, bp. of Die, II, 286
Ulric, canon of Langres, II, 145, 147
Urban II, pope, I, 300, II, 300; consecrated bp. of Piacenza, I, 441; consecrated church of Cl., II, 124; lost privilege for Piolenc, I, 198, II, 141–142; privilege for Cl., II, 119

V (letter), use of, II, 85
Vainglory: danger to pilgrims, I, 359; odor, I, 204
Vallombrosa, color of clothing, II, 116
Vanitas, I, 276
Vegetables, eaten by monks, I, 54
Vendôme, the Trinity (Ben.), abt., *see* Geoffrey
Venice, II, 265; Holy Cross (Cl.), II, 227; P.'s visit, II, 223, 227
Verdun, II, 203; St. Paul (Ben.-Prem.), I, 144–145, 213, II, 130, 151; bp., *see* Albero
Vermandois, ct., *see* Ralph

Vert, Le, family of, II, 134–135
Vessels, ecclesiastical: anointing of, I, 354–355; bought by Jews, I, 329
Vézelay (Cl.), I, 193–194, 229, 256, II, 105, 158, 162, 194, 217, 218, 234, 244, 257, 266, 268, 269, 329; abt., *see* Alberic, Pontius, Rainald; charter for, II, 265; subject to pope, I, 193
Via romea (francesca, francigena), II, 114
Viaticum, I, 8, 169, 307
Vicar of Christ, *see* Patriarch of Jerusalem, Pope
Vicar of God, *see* Pope
Victor IV, antipope, II, 294
Vienna, Schottenstift (Ben.), MS. from, II, 63
Vienne: abp., II, 258 (*see also* Hugh, Stephen of Charolais, Stephen II); council in 1124, II, 258
Vigeois (Ben.), pr., *see* Geoffrey
Vigevano, II, 222
Vigils: of hermit, I, 40, 41; of monks, I, 116, 292, 367; of Raingard, I, 164; of Theobald of St. Columba, I, 359
Villefranche-sur-Saône, I, 261, II, 166
Villers (Cist.), MS. from, II, 70
Virgil, II, 12, 38, 39
Virginity, I, 428–434; of body and mind, I, 432, 433–434; rewards, I, 428–429. See also Chastity
Visions, I, 162, 163, 168–169. *See also* Dreams
Visitation, episcopal, defined by Gregory I, I, 80
Viterbo, II, 139
Viviers, I, 125; bp., *see* Peter of Lyons
Vizille (Cl.), I, 439, II, 224, 269
Voice, necessity of, to P., I, 381–382
Vulgrin, abp. of Bourges, attacked at Pontremoli, I, 51, II, 114
Vicarii, I, 73, II, 237

Waast, Le (Cl.), I, 265, II, 167
Walter, bp. of Chalon-sur-Saône, II, 225
Walter of Dervy (so-called), II, 11 n. 50
Walter, friend of Nicholas of Montiéramey, II, 321
Walter, pr. of Souvigny, II, 264
Warfare, spiritual: of hermits and monks, I, 16, 31, 32, 36, 37, 53, 91, 355, 408, 435; victory belongs to him who fights, not him who flees, I, 187
Wednesday, fasting on, I, 388
Whalley (Cist.), MS. from, II, 70, 72
White color: clothing, used at weddings, I, 289, (of Christ at Transfiguration) *ibid*; significance, (joy, glory) I, 57, 289, (monastic zeal) I, 288, 290
Wicardus, sacristan of Cl., II, 136, 339, 348

Wife, rights when husband enters religious order, I, 411–413
Wigo, dean of Cl., II, 348
William, abp. of Arles, II, 286
William VI, ct. of Auvergne, II, 213
William VII, ct. of Auvergne, II, 191–192, 213
William of Baffie, bp. of Clermont, II, 299 n. 1, 300
William IV, abt. of Brioude, II, 216
William II, provost of Brioude, II, 216
William, abp. of Canterbury, II, 255
William of Chamalières, bp. of Clermont, II, 300
William of Champeaux, bp. of Châlons-sur-Marne, I, 183
William, pr. of La Charité, II, 296, 297 n. 15
William, bp. of Chartres, II, 190
William of Cournon, II, 216
William I or II, abp. of Embrun, II, 102–103, 286; Ep. 12 to, I, 18, II, 102–103; attacked at Pontremoli, I, 51, II, 114
William I, k. of England, II, 103
William, bp. of Gap, II, 286
William I, patriarch of Jerusalem, II, 153
William of Jumièges, continuator of, I, 104
William, ct. of Mâcon, I, 443, II, 225, 226
William of Malmesbury, chron., II, 104, 256 n. 23, 298 n. 19
William, bp. of Le Mans, II, 296 n. 8
William, pr. of Cl., abt. of Moissac, II, 160, 348
William, ct. of Montpellier, II, 254 n. 10
William of Newburgh, II, 19, 53 n. 220
William II, bp. of Orange, II, 141; Ep. 67 to, I, 197–198, II, 141–142; controversy over Piolenc, I, 198; quarrels with monks, I, 197–198; skilled in divine and human law, I, 198
William, bp. of Périgeux, attacked at Pontremoli, I, 51, II, 114, 115
William, bp. of Poitiers, II, 336
William X, ct. of Poitou, duke of Aquitaine, II, 126, 299 n. 1, 336–339, 341; P.'s meeting with, I, 179; support of Anacletus II, I, 135, 179, II, 126, 137
William I, ct. of Ponthieu, II, 289–290
William of Sabran, bp. of Langres, II, 145
William, abt. of St. Père, Chartres, II, 19 n. 79
William, abt. of St. Thierry, Rheims, II, 274, 320 n. 21; revised own texts, II, 44 n. 182
William, bp. of Viviers, I, 348–349, II, 192; former Cl. monk, I, 349
William, unidentified "beloved son" of P., I, 233, II, 160
William, unidentified "brother and son" of Hugh of Rouen, I, 8, II, 100

Winchecombe, annals, II, 105
Winchester, II, 137, 138; bp., see Henry of Blois
Wine: allegory of, I, 200, 314, 427; allowed to monks, I, 65
Wine jars and vases, made by hermits, I, 39
Wisdom, see *Sapientia*
Women: leadership in war, I, 305; visiting Cl., I, 72. *See also* Preaching, Singing, Wife
Words, division of, II, 89–90
World: bad condition of, I, 385; growing old and nearing death, I, 97

Worms, II, 267
Writing, I, 48, 49; by monks, II, 18 n. 77, 20; by P., II, 20; hard work, I, 39; merit, I, 21. *See also* Letters

Year, beginning of, II, 94, 202, 238 n. 26, 323, 352
Yerres (Ben.), II, 114
York, abp., *see* Thurstan

Zacharias, I, 225
Zedekiah, I, 387
Ziba, servant of Mephibosheth, I, 351

MAP

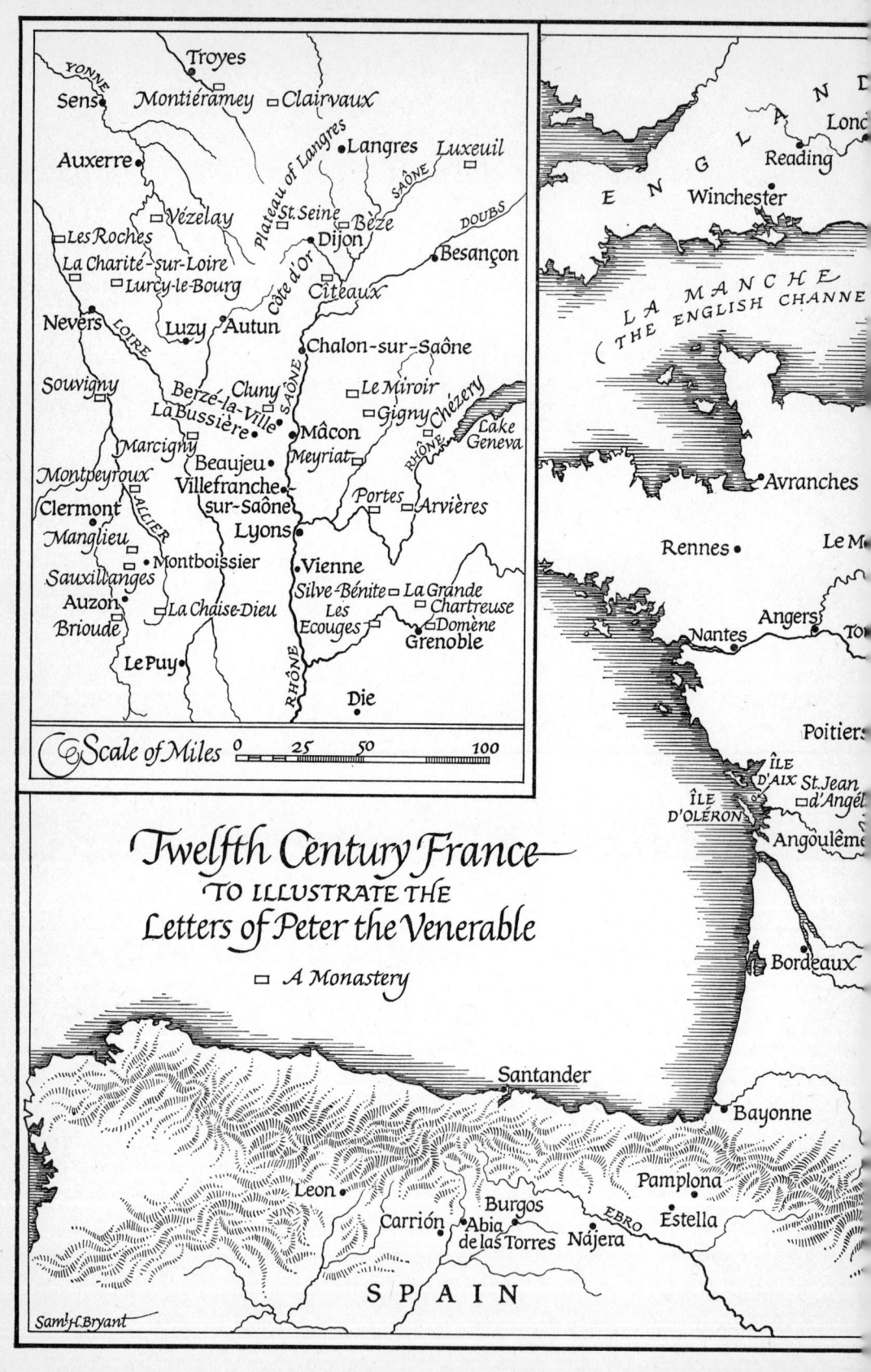

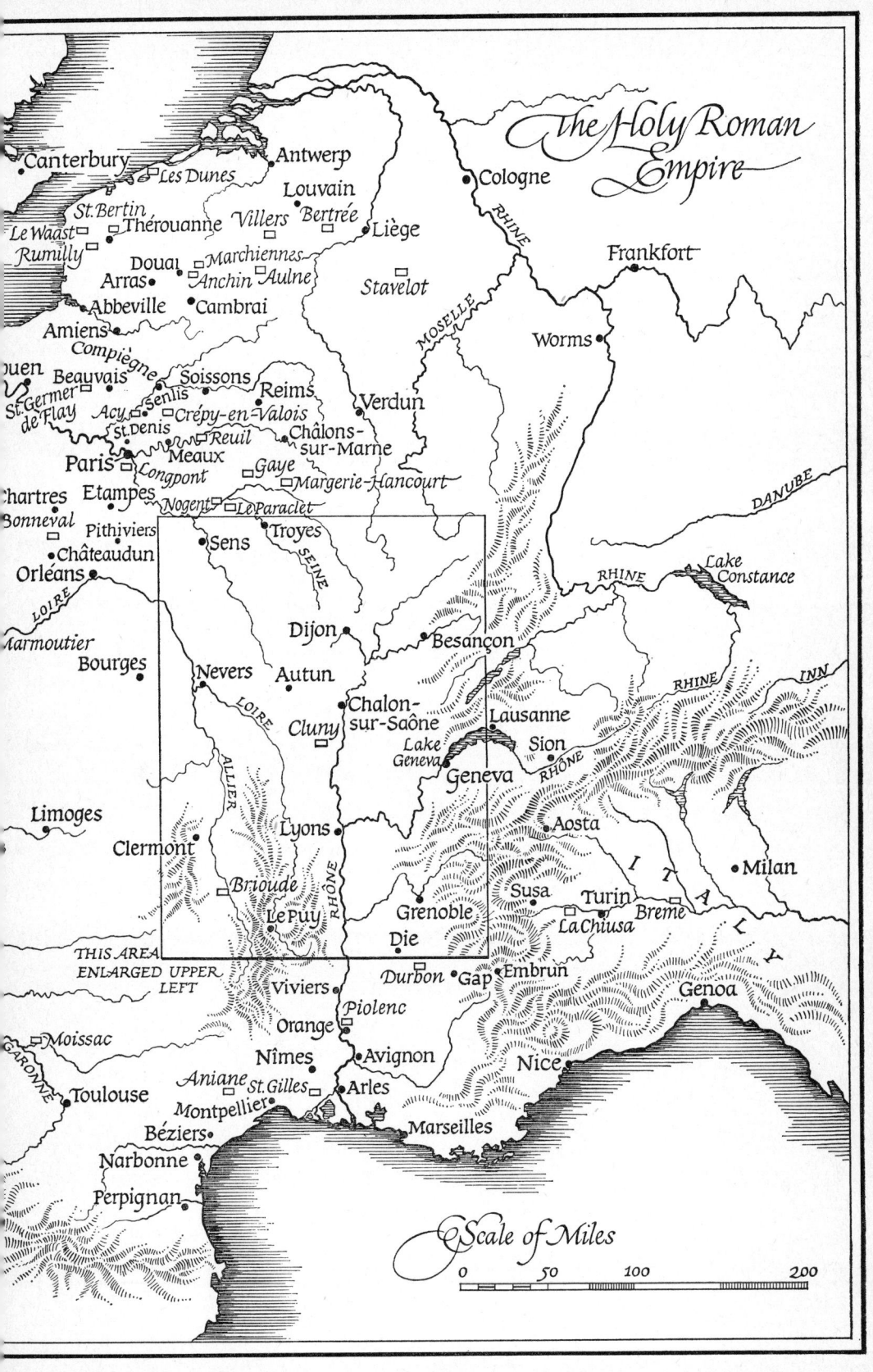